"You Ain't Heard Nothin' Yet"

BOOKS BY ANDREW SARRIS

The Films of Josef von Sternberg (1966)

Interviews with Film Directors (1967)

The Film (1968)

The American Cinema, Directors, and Directions, 1929–1968 (1969)

Film 68/69 (with Hollis Alpert) (1969)

Confessions of a Cultist: On the Cinema 1955–1969 (1970)

The Primal Screen: Essays on Film and Related Subjects (1972)

The John Ford Movie Mystery (1975)

Politics and Cinema (1978)

St. James Film Directors Encyclopedia (editor) (1997)

ANDREW SARRIS

"YOU AIN'T HEARD NOTHIN' YET"

The American Talking Film
History & Memory
1927–1949

NEW YORK ■ OXFORD
OXFORD UNIVERSITY PRESS ■ 1998

Oxford University Press

Oxford   New York

Athens   Auckland   Bangkok   Bogotá   Bombay
Buenos Aires   Calcutta   Cape Town   Dar es Salaam
Delhi   Florence   Hong Kong   Istanbul   Karachi
Kuala Lumpur   Madras   Madrid   Melbourne
Mexico City   Nairobi   Paris   Singapore
Taipei   Tokyo   Toronto   Warsaw

and associated companies in
Berlin   Ibadan

Copyright © 1998 by Andrew Sarris

Published by Oxford University Press
198 Madison Avenue, New York, New York 10016

Oxford is a registered trademark of Oxford University Press

Library of Congress Cataloging-in-Publication Data
Sarris, Andrew
"You ain't heard nothin' yet" : the American talking film,
history and memory, 1927–1949 / Andrew Sarris.
p.   cm.   Includes index.
ISBN 0-19-503883-5
1. Sound motion pictures—History.   I. Title.
PN1995.7.S27   1998   791.43'09'041—dc21   97-9476

"So Red the Rose, However You Spell It," by Ogden
Nash, copyright © 1935 by Ogden Nash, is reprinted
by permission of Curtis Brown, Ltd.

1 3 5 7 9 8 6 4 2

Printed in the United States of America
on acid-free paper

For Sheldon Meyer

ACKNOWLEDGMENTS

I am deeply indebted to Leona Capeless for the rigor and perceptiveness of her editing of the manuscript, to Joellyn M. Ausanka for her labors on the production of the book, to Tom Allen, Timothy Clinton, William K. Everson, and Stephen Gottlieb for their stimulating comments over the years of this enterprise.

I wish to thank the Rockefeller Foundation for enabling me to focus my thoughts on this book at the Bellagio Study Center, far from the madding crowd.

Last, but certainly not least, I am grateful to Molly Haskell for her ongoing inspiration in the art and the life.

CONTENTS

"You Ain't Heard Nothin' Yet"

Introduction

The first lesson one learns almost immediately after undertaking to write a comprehensive and critically weighed history of the American sound film is that one can never finish; one can only stop. After many years I have decided to stop, at least as far as the period between 1927 and 1949 is concerned. I could work until the next millennium sifting the endless trivia for clues to the tantalizing mysteries of the medium, but my marvelously patient editor has urged me to cease and desist, and I do so with a sense of relief.

Mine is more a macrocosmic than a microcosmic treatment in that I have chosen to focus on stylistic and thematic configurations rather than on minutely detailed descriptions. Having written regularly on film for more than forty years, and having taught film as an art and as one of the humanities for over thirty, I have been compelled to maintain an aesthetic lifeline between the past and the present. By contrast, archival specialists tend to develop so much of a rooting interest in their excavations that they discount the onset of the new, whereas journalist novelty-seekers keep trying to cut the umbilical cord that still links us to Lumière and Griffith. My own view of the talking picture from the twenties to the present is that it remains alive and well, but that it never seems to yield up all its meanings and beauties and associations the first time around. Ideally, film scholarship should have evolved as a cooperative enterprise by which each contribution could provide a foundation for its successor. Instead, recent decades of "discussion" have been characterized by an enormous amount of fiercely polemical writing that seems to have pulverized the subject beyond repair. The result is that every study has to start from scratch, despite the maddening repetitiousness of the process.

My own purpose, however, is not to exhume any ancient conflicts, but rather to chart some of the changing ways we have thought about film from period to period. What were once perishable memories are now preserved artifacts. With the spread of television, videotape, videocassette, and laser disc technology, the cinematic past is now a palpable presence in our cultural lives. Memories can be refreshed; judgments can be revaluated. Movies themselves can be shown to pass beyond the parameters of any methodology of the moment, be it sociology or semiotics, technology or stylistics, dramatic narrative or symbolic iconography. In this way a historical context can be reconstructed: this, in short, is the purpose of this book, and, I confess, its own controlling methodology.

Unfortunately, the problem of quantity alone seems virtually insurmountable with respect to the American sound film. There are so many movies, literally thousands and thousands of them, and it is very difficult to discuss a few without involving the rest. Literary historians, for example, have a much easier time in that relatively few trees from the forest of fiction are logged for the stately mansions of literature. Literary character types do not "cross over" from good books to bad books to the extent screen icons "cross over" from good movies to bad movies, a cultural phenomenon designated in the arcane methodology of the semiologists as "intertextual references." One thus does not have to become a print freak to function as a literary person.

Besides, the burden of cultural guilt falls more heavily on the casual reader than on the casual moviegoer. The reader who has not perused the "right" books according to the canonical tastes of his age must study literary history and criticism in order to repair the defect in his sensibility. By contrast, the moviegoer who has not seen the "right" movies according to the comparatively permissive and yet too often contentious Film Academy will argue up and down that the movies he has chanced to see are fully as relevant to the total subject as any others. The badgered film historian is thus obliged to fill in on all the possible movie encounters of his potential readers, and this can be a very tedious and soul-destroying process. Unfortunately, the most available alternative—cribbing a film history from faded news clippings and microfilm—is even worse.

Then, also, there are so many dream-like associations in the memories of millions of moviegoers, more than a few of whom insist on writing their own books on the subject. Star-gazing, for example, can be said to constitute one of the mass religions of our time. The Garbo and Sullavan cults have become as ritualized as their equivalents long ago for Isis and Osiris, except that the mass of star-worshippers have not formally accepted or authorized any high priests of criticism to mediate between the true believers and their deities. In this realm of abject reverence the illuminated icons demand incantations rather than insights. I, like most of my colleagues in the modest craft of movie-reviewing, cannot claim infallibility in these matters. We all have our blind spots and aesthetic afflictions, I suppose, and it is probably more advisable to acknowledge them frankly and openly than to let them fester in pseudo-objective phraseology about art and truth and beauty.

It is in this spirit of contrition that I relate an episode in the writing of my first book, *The Films of Josef von Sternberg*. Myron Gladstone, my very capable copy editor on that occasion, complained about my incessant repetition of proper names, suggesting instead "Marlene Dietrich" first time, "Miss," "Ms." or just plain "Dietrich" the second, and "she" or "her" the third. Stubbornly, I resisted my editor's very sound advice. Against even my own better judgment, I felt the compulsion to type out "Marlene Dietrich" in full again and again as if that were the only way to invoke her image. Once her full name perished in a pronoun, her face seemed to fade away as well into a figure of speech. Whereas my editor was concerned with my inefficient use of language as information, I was obsessed with my emphatic use of language as incantation. It was thought versus feeling, logic versus magic. But even monotony, I felt, was not too high a price to pay for the power of summoning Marlene Dietrich's glowing presence from the silver screen to the printed page.

At the time of my contretemps with my copy editor, I was reminded of parental scoldings in my childhood for referring to my mother as "she" in her presence. The mere use of the pronoun implied disrespect for the magical role of maternity expressed in the noun. Friends, acquaintances, and students have reported similar episodes in their own childhoods, and thus the noun-into-pronoun taboo must be a fairly universal phenomenon. It marks also another link between cinema and psychoanalysis, two dream-oriented flowerings that have co-existed and cross-pollinated from the very beginning.

The problem persists: How *does* one write about moving pictures with words that won't budge from their syntactical sequence? By taking the more efficient path of linguistic expression one tends to reduce the cinema to thematic synopses and bloodless categories. By taking the more expressive path one tends to supplant the cinema's sensibility with that of belles-lettres. I would hasten to add that there is absolutely nothing wrong with the practice of belles-lettres in the writing of film history as long as belles-lettres contents itself with commenting on cinema, and does not presume to impersonate it. The gap between movies and the words used to describe them must always be understood in any transaction between the writer and the reader. And it must be understood also that there can be no equivalent in even the most illuminating literary fireworks for the *son et lumière* that makes up the essential experience of the sound film.

Of course, there is and always has been a considerable literary component in the cinema. Too much, in fact, for most film scholars up through the 1950s. The novels and plays that were pillaged by studio story departments constituted an allegedly alien influence on what was purportedly a visual medium. The fact that most people went to the movies to see photoplays focused on stars rather than moving pictures shaped by images only confirmed the catchpenny vulgarity of the motion picture industry. Consequently, as long as the "purity" of the medium was at stake, it was relatively simple to dismiss most movies, and especially most Hollywood movies, as poisonously impure. Film histories could be written very easily in this snobbish atmosphere. One did not even have to go very often to the movies to qualify as an expert on the subject. A familiarity with a handful of silent film classics was sufficient preparation for scholarly scolding of the pernicious talkies, often sight unseen. Indeed, the American sound film was born in a state of original sin for having caused the death of the silent film with all the latter's poetic pantomime and metaphorical montage.

Perhaps the most literate summation of this general attitude was provided by Dwight MacDonald in 1942 in the course of a harsh critique of Sergei Eisenstein's *Film Sense* as a stylistic recantation on the stake of the Stalinist Inquisition:

> Was it only a dozen years ago that, with pious excitement, we went to "little" movie houses—the very term has disappeared—to see the new films from Russia? Is it so short a time since many of us were writing on the cinema as *the* great modern art form, the machine art whose technique was most in harmony with the dynamism of the machine age, the art that most powerfully affected such peculiarly modern areas as Freud's subconscious and Pavlov's reflexes, the only art that could sometimes bridge the gap between serious creation and mass taste, so that [*The*] *Birth of a*

Nation, Chaplin's comedies, *Potemkin*, and a few other films might be said to have been the only works of our time that have seemed both popular and great? Our enthusiasm was not misplaced, our theories were not unfounded. And yet the wonderful possibilities that lay before the cinema ten years ago have withered into the slick banality of Hollywood and the crude banality of post-1930 Soviet cinema. The potentialities, which really existed, which, for that matter, still exist and in even richer profusion, simply were not realized, and the cinema gave up its own idiom and technique to become once more what it was before Griffith: a mechanical device for recording stage plays. Like so much else in the past decade, it crept back into the womb, into the unconscious. It has been many years now since anywhere in the world, a film has been made which, aesthetically speaking, is cinema at all.

So much for the few thousand sound films made between 1929 and 1942, a period later hailed by many auteurist, genre, and otherwise revisionist film historians of the sixties, seventies, and right into the nineties as a Golden Age in its own right. The American sound film has reached its seventieth year, and it and its audiences are endowed with (perhaps even encumbered by) a more extensive historical consciousness than was ever before possible or feasible. The Theory of Progress which animated the socially conscious film histories of Lewis Jacobs, John Grierson, Siegfried Kracauer, Paul Rotha, Richard Griffith, Jay Leyda, Georges Sadoul, et al. has been supplanted by a vague, aimless nostalgia for the Good Old Days. With the past having become infinitely more promising than the future there is a tendency to suspend all judgments of old movies. The motives may range from the most awe-struck admiration to the campiest condescension, but the result is the same: to make the very subject of old movies the occasion for mindless "fun." I think that this attitude is both mistaken and short-sighted. The time has come for evaluation to walk side by side with elucidation, and not to loiter six paces behind. As a practicing polemicist on this issue for the past three decades, I am well aware of my own role in returning old Hollywood movies to the realm of serious study. But I never intended to foreclose the future behind a body of rigid dogma. We are all hostages to history, and we always shall be. Moreover, if we are to make any progress as film historians, we must learn to incorporate the opinions of the past into a valid context for the present. Methodology is no substitute for history. That I am widely regarded as a registered New York–based auteurist of the sixties, seventies, eighties, and nineties serves only to place my own writing in a historical context for future reference. I write without the slightest presumption that my own words shall be or should be the last words on the subject. *Pace* my Marxist-Progressive predecessors, I am merely one antithesis to your many theses, and I find now that I must explain your positions before I can fully expound my own.

This particular film history is motivated also by the conviction that film studies have become a legitimate part of the liberal arts curriculum. My conviction is not universally shared in academe, and so this book is addressed almost as much to the doubters as to the devotees. After more than forty years of published missionary work on the movies, I sense that I have reached the point of consolidation and summation with a subject that has been lurking luminously in the darkness for as long as I can remember. The American sound film is like an aged parent, whose own childhood I have researched in order to understand my cultural heredity. But I am always aware of the young people in my classes. And the eternal skepticism in their eyes makes me all the more eager to explain what has been so interesting and so edifying in the American cinema since the bawling, squawking birth of the talkies.

■   ■   ■   ■

On New Year's Eve, 1929, it was raining in New York, but the streets were still full. The theaters were packed as if there had never been a depression; the memories of 1929 and of the big slump were fading. People who had once preferred to stay home were coming out, filling the hotels and smart restaurants.

On Broadway, one could see Alfred Lunt and Lynn Fontanne in their newest drama, or *Bitter Sweet*, a play by the latest rage, Noel Coward. For those not able to afford the price of a theater seat, there were movies now, including Helen Morgan in *Applause*. With sound a commonplace now, and color, the simple two-color Technicolor that enlivened sequences of many musicals widely used, the movies were better than ever.

Hollywood in the Thirties, John Baxter

The two preceding paragraphs, which open John Baxter's study of thirties' talkies, reflect the irresistible temptation of many film historians to correlate sociological history with movie history. The bulk of Baxter's book is not sociologically oriented, but he feels obliged nonetheless to usher in the decade with references to "a depression" and "the big slump." The point of view expressed is that of fun-seeking New Yorkers on New Year's Eve, 1929, deluded by the false hope of a new decade to fill up the hotels, smart restaurants, theaters, and movie houses on Broadway's Gay White Way. A sprinkling of still legendary celebrities—Alfred Lunt and

Lynn Fontanne and Noël Coward on stage, and Helen Morgan on the screen—suggests that the glitter and frivolity of the carefree twenties may linger briefly into the thirties. Unfortunately, Baxter's sense of history is somewhat askew. An awareness of a great and irreversible economic depression did not overwhelm most people's minds with the stock market crash in October 1929. We have seen so many movies in which an entire era ends in the tumult on the floor of the New York Stock Exchange on Black Thursday, October 24, 1929, that we have come to believe in this fateful day as a kind of economic Pearl Harbor. Indeed, the thirties in America have often been defined as the period between the Crash and Pearl Harbor, despite the resultant encroachment on the twenties and forties. (For that matter the "movie" thirties can be said to extend technologically and stylistically from *The Jazz Singer* (1927) to *Citizen Kane* (1941), but there is no need in this particular study to stretch the point.)

The "Crash," however, was not an instant disaster like the explosion of the *Hindenberg* on May 6, 1937. After Black Thursday, October 24, 1929, there was a brief rally before Black Tuesday, October 29, 1929. The market then continued to fall until November 13, by which time $30,000,000,000 in capital values had been liquidated. Yet, as John Kenneth Galbraith has noted in *The Great Crash 1929*, the Depression that followed the Crash took a relatively long time to take full hold.

In January, February, and March of 1930 the stock market showed a substantial recovery. Then in April the recovery lost momentum, and in June there was another large drop. Thereafter, with few exceptions the market dropped week by week, month by month, and year by year through June of 1932. The position when it finally halted made the worst level during the crash seem memorable by contrast. On November 13, 1929, it may be recalled, the *Times* industrials closed at 224. On July 8, 1932, they were 58. This value was not much more than the net by which they dropped on the single day of October 28, 1929. Standard Oil of New Jersey, which the Rockefellers were believed to have pegged at 50 on November 13, 1929, dropped below 20 in April 1932. On July 8 it was 24. U.S. Steel on July 8 reached a low of 22. On September 3, 1929, it had sold as high as 262. General Motors was a bargain at 8 on July 8, down from 73 on September 3, 1929. Montgomery Ward was 4, down from 138. Tel and Tel was 72, and on September 3, 1929, it had sold at 304. Anaconda sold at 4 on July 8.

No one any longer suggested that business was sound, fundamental or otherwise. During the week of July 8, 1932, *Iron Age* announced that steel operations had reached 12 per cent of capacity. This was thought of its sort to be a record. Pig iron output was the lowest since 1896.

Galbraith makes only two references to movies in his account of the Crash, but both are provocative though peripheral. The first deals with the rickety financial structure of the film industry:

On August 17, the *Leviathan* and the *Ile de France* left port fully equipped for speculation on the high seas. Business on the *Ile* the opening day was described as brisk. One of the first transactions was by Irving Berlin, who sold 1000 shares of Paramount-Famous-Lasky at 72. (It was a shrewd move. The stock later went more or less to nothing and the company into bankruptcy.)

The economic misfortunes in the thirties of such studios as Fox, Paramount, RKO, and Universal were not the stuff of which popular scenarios were made. Nor could economic disaster be necessarily equated with aesthetic deficiencies. Many of the most interesting movies came off the most inefficient and most quixotic assembly lines. Nonetheless, Hollywood was part and parcel of the most speculative apparatus of the capitalistic system. Its moguls had much in common with the robber barons of oil, steel, railroads, automobiles, and pyramiding trusts generally. From its beginnings the film industry was plagued by patent wars, boycotts, double-entry bookkeeping, and endless litigation. Yet, remarkably few movies provided any insight into corporate power struggles over film or any other product. No genre could explain the Crash or the Depression that eventually rippled out from the financial wreckage on Wall Street.

In addition, a great many movies were set neither in the immediate present, nor in the United States. Josef von Sternberg's *Morocco* and Ernst Lubitsch's *Monte Carlo* were two of the most memorably innovative sound films of 1930, and two of the least appropriate models for sociological analysis. Lewis Milestone's *All Quiet on the Western Front* dealt in fraternal and pacifistic terms with a war of some two decades earlier recounted from the point of view of German soldiers in the trenches. Howard Hawks's *The Dawn Patrol* and Howard Hughes's *Hell's Angels* provided chivalric gloss for the aerial conflict above the trenches of the Great War of 1914–18. George Hill's *The Big House* and Mervyn LeRoy's *Little Caesar* were closer to the here and now in 1930, but both films dealt with romanticized criminal elements considered much too raffish to serve as "realistic" characters. King Vidor's *Billy the Kid* and Raoul Walsh's *The Big Trail*, two of the more ambitious westerns of the year, remained impervious to the troubles in the concrete canyons on Wall Street. One could go on and on through the entire roster of 1930 releases in a vain search for the cutting edge that snipped off the twenties from the thirties.

That movies for a time affected more people than any other art form led many influential Marxist critics to infer that Hollywood was grinding out frivolous entertainments as a deliberately counter-revolutionary service for the capitalistic system. On the other hand, a very large number of early talkies (as well as late silents) were grubbier and more sordid than one would expect "propaganda" movies to be. For every upper-class drawing room there was a lower-class bar-room. For every Ronald Colman there was a James Cagney. Indeed, the very persuasive Scottish documentarian and critic John Grierson explicitly warned Hollywood not to "Colmanize its Cagneys." Hollywood, at least on the surface, could be low-down even when it was not hard-boiled.

Galbraith's second reference to movies addresses itself with scathing irony to the frequently proposed mission of Hollywood during the Great Depression:

> The failure of the bankers did not leave the community entirely without constructive leadership. There was [New York's] Mayor James J. Walker. Appearing before a meeting of motion picture exhibitors on that Tuesday, he appealed to them to "show pictures which will reinstate courage and hope in the hearts of the people."

Mayor Walker was not to be alone in his exhortations. After the inauguration of President Franklin Delano Roosevelt in 1933, the advent soon after of the New Deal, and the subsequent passage of the ill-fated National Recovery Act with its NRA eagle emblazoned on the nation's screens, Hollywood was virtually mobilized to "fight" the Depression by accentuating the positive in whatever nook and cranny it could be found. This was as sure-fire a prescription for "escapism" as any. What is unclear is the extent to which movie escapism varied from 1929 to 1930. Had Mayor Walker and his contemporaries been depressed by movies before the Crash? Or, as is more likely, had the Crash itself transformed movies into potential morale-boosters?

In this context John Baxter's notion that movies were considered better than ever in 1929 seems bizarre. To be sure, the public was enthralled by sound for a time. Nonetheless, most film historians have considered 1929 the worst year artistically in the history of the American cinema.

What has occurred is a shift from one extreme to another. The standard film histories written before 1950 treat sound as a catastrophe from which the cinema never fully recovered. A book like Baxter's (published in 1968) absorbed the revisionism of the New Criticism while trying to deny it. Hence, according to Baxter:

> Among the first points to strike any researcher into the American cinema of the thirties is the inability of modern critical theory to cope with the bulk and nature of the material. There is no inflexible rule for allocating measures of blame and praise in films of the period, but the presence in Hollywood of hundreds of major film artists, most of whom contributed to many films other than those they directed, argues against the applicability of the *auteur* theory or any variation of it.

Having dissociated himself from the presumed spirit of auteurism, Baxter then crawls back to the practical application of *auteurism*: "But while films have been grouped throughout the book under directors, this system has been adopted as much for convenience as for any other reason."

Aye, there's the rub. How does a historian cope with the vast amount of material to research without some system of priorities. Also, Baxter seems oblivious to the fact that, if it were not for the revised perspectives of what he calls "modern critical theory," the Hollywood movies of the thirties would not be considered worthy of study and re-study at all. A revolution in taste has overthrown traditional condescension, but it is not sufficient simply to celebrate this revolution. We must track down the old movies to their own time, when they were taken much less seriously than they are today.

Still, film history can never be synchronized with so-called real history. In addition to the omissions, the distortions, and the over-simplifications, there is the inevitable factor of cultural lag. F. Scott Fitzgerald was particularly perceptive on this point in his essay, "Echoes of the Jazz Age," published in November 1931:

> Contrary to popular opinion, the movies of the Jazz Age had no effect upon its morals. The social attitude of the producers was timid, behind the times and banal—for example, no picture mirrored even faintly the younger generation until 1923, when magazines had already been started to celebrate it and it had long ceased to be news. There were a few feeble splutters and then Clara Bow in *Flaming Youth*: promptly the Hollywood hacks ran the theme into its cinematographic grave. Throughout the Jazz Age the movies got no further than Mrs. Jiggs, keeping up with its most blatant superficialities. This was no doubt due to the censorship as well as to innate conditions in the industry.

Fitzgerald continued his love-hate relationship with the movies to his death in 1940. Hollywood never ceased to disappoint him with its timidity and banality, and yet he was always attracted to the medium for its magical properties that he considered largely unfulfilled. Unlike Hollywood's puritanically leftist critics, who wanted to abolish the pleasure principle altogether, Fitzgerald preached a voluptuously hedonistic doctrine, but one more observant and more audacious than the censors would allow. In this respect, Fitzgerald was mercifully free of the moralistic cant spouted by so many of his colleagues. He was therefore taken less seriously than he should have been in the sanctimonious Hollywood of the thirties. One wonders what kind of movies he would have made if he had attained the power of a Mayer or a Warner. It is very possible that he would have eventually found himself at the head of a bankrupt studio. It is possible also that he might have had a shot at filming the Jazz Age in action just about the time sound came in, and not much later. The only period of film that came close to recording the roaring twenties ran from about 1927 through about 1932 or 1933. For that matter, the thirties dissolved into World War II before the darker corners of the Depression had been illuminated. And the ambiguities and absurdities of World War II did not begin to surface until the fifties and sixties. Hence, to demand instant topicality of the cinema is to reduce the medium to a news broadcast. One would never expect such haste from a supposedly serious and reflective art-form.

What fascinates me the most in Fitzgerald's observation is its substantiation of my own inability to find much trace on the screen of the supposedly optimistic "roaring twenties" that came crashing down on Black Tuesday, October 29, 1929, prompting the famous *Variety* headline of Wednesday, October 30: "Wall St. Lays an Egg." In the invaluable The American Film Institute Catalogue for feature films made between 1921 and 1930, there are fifty-some-odd references to "brokers," "stock brokers," and "the stock market" in movies of that decade. Yet, most of the synopses treat the stock market as an always precarious and often dishonest enterprise. People are being "ruined" on the screen all through the twenties, and some of the adapted literary properties date back to the Crash of 1893. The stereotype of the crooked, mustache-twirling Wall Street stock promoter pops up repeatedly in westerns and in a variety of honest, country-bumpkin melodramas. Indeed, D. W. Griffith had taken after the avaricious grain speculator in *A Corner in Wheat* as early as 1909. Of course, the melodramatic tendencies of movies attracted them to financial disasters as well as to every other kind, but there were also in American movies strong anti-urban and anti-speculative tendencies. Furthermore, Hollywood has always been comparatively vague and squeamish about the subject of money in the context of the "spiritual" values propounded on the screen.

Were the thirties, then, such an abrupt break from the twenties as we have imagined? If we are to think of the twenties as a giddy, carefree decade, we have to banish from our minds the infamous red-hunting Palmer Raids, which, in retrospect, made Joe McCarthy look like a parlor pink, or the convulsive Sacco-Vanzetti affair, which caused riots around the world. The enormous power of Protestant temperance groups and the Ku Klux Klan in this era somehow comes into conflict with the overly facile image of the flapper in the speakeasy as all-pervasive. Around the world, chaos and instability were the rule rather than the exception. Inflation demoralized Weimar Germany, and massive unemployment hobbled Britain years before Black Tuesday. (Even a 1982 valentine to the snobbery and sportsmanship of the twenties, namely the Oscar-winning *Chariots of Fire*, shows restless crowds of the troubled and unemployed in Britain.) Also, from the middle twenties the film-makers picked up from the poets and novelists the laments for all the slaughtered victims of a pointless world war.

It might be noted that even so perceptive an observer as Fitzgerald failed to detect the New Woman on the Hollywood screen because he was following the sociologist's habit of looking only at American actresses and contemporary "Americana" in Hollywood movies. One had to look for the New Woman not in Clara Bow or Joan Crawford, but in Greta Garbo, Pola Negri, Marlene Dietrich, and the Louise Brooks of such G. W. Pabst classics as *The Lost One* and *Pandora's Box*. The same mistake is made when sociologists confront the films of the thirties. It would never occur to them that Ernst Lubitsch's *Trouble in Paradise* (1932) (with a very pointedly egalitarian screenplay by Samson Raphaelson) had as much to say about the Depression as did King Vidor's *Our Daily Bread* (1933). Similarly, William Dieterle's *The Life of Emile Zola* is as much a rebuke to Hitler as it is a belated defense of Dreyfus.

If the twenties were not simply a succession of F. Scott Fitzgerald's wild parties, the thirties were not simply an album of Walker Evans's "poor folks" photographs. There were plenty of poor folks in the twenties, and plenty of wild parties in the thirties. There were few Hollywood films in the thirties as grim and pessimistic as Erich von Stroheim's *Greed* and King Vidor's *The Crowd* from the twenties. Actually, many of the changes between decades for movies had more to do with the coming of sound and the tightening of censorship than with worldwide economic convulsions. Because the motion picture industry weathered the Depression better than most other industries, a mixture of pride and guilt contributed to a lack of rhetorical urgency on the screen.

Most Hollywood movies were oriented toward a middle-class vision of life even in the thirties. The occasional bread line here, and the occasional chain gang there, were isolated occurrences in semi-religious light shows built around the rituals of family and courtship. But were the Walker Evans photographs any more "real" or "typical"? The issues of ideological Expressionism aside, the fact remains that though 24 percent of the work force was unemployed in the depths of the Depression, 76 percent was employed, and that a considerable portion of that 76 percent derived a certain satisfaction from the plight of the 24 percent. I write this from my own observations as a child of the dispossessed 24 percent. I would not argue that the middle-class smugness and self-satisfaction one finds too often in Hollywood movies of the thirties is admirable, but I *would* argue also that it is not necessarily a misrepresentation of the popular mood. It is for this reason that I find Hollywood movies, for all their flaws and puerilities, more truthful than the nobly angled portraits of the poor in collective poses reeking of the sanctimoniousness of "charity" drives. What I find more interesting in newsreel footage are the accidental revelations around the periphery of the ideologically imposed imagery. Willard Van Dyke's ill-advised diatribe against urban life and in favor of suburban sprawl in *The City* is undercut by the heart-stopping images of New Yorkers surging across Fifth Avenue and 42nd Street on a sunny day in the thirties. Every face, every article of clothing, conveys a precious message from the sweet, dead past. This is the ultimate thrill generated by the time machine for almost all old movies.

■   ■   ■   ■

FOR MOST of Hollywood's history as a center of movie-making, the studio system has often been blamed for the lack of individual creativity. The very word "studio" lost its traditional connotation of an artist's workplace, and suggested instead an enclosed factory and a ruthless assembly line. Occasionally, a director, a writer, a player, even a producer, might beat the "system," but the system itself was deemed too pernicious and too pervasive to be defied on any large scale. Hence, most movies were not merely inept, but completely mechanical and impersonal: this was the standard line of critics, scholars, and historians.

"When the movie industry was young," the late Hollywood director

George Stevens once recalled, "the filmmaker was its core and the man who handled the business details his partner. . . . When the filmmaker finally looked around, he found his partner's name on the door. Thus the filmmaker became the employee, and the man who had the time to attend to the business details became the head of the studio." There is in this archetypical anecdote the evocation of an era, when movie-making was more individual, less industrial. It is now impossible to prove that there was ever an era of artistic enlightenment inasmuch as most silent movies have disintegrated into dust. Nonetheless, D. W. Griffith remains to this day the ghost at all Hollywood banquets, though many of the idiosyncrasies of his personal vision made him eminently unfashionable even with the sternest critics of the corporate structures that eventually stifled his one-man enterprises. The exact date the cinema lost its soul to commerce is difficult to determine. Many film historians have testified to the existence of a Golden Age simply to create a context for the familiar rhetoric of decline and fall. The gold may have turned to brass before 1925 or 1920 or 1915, but certainly by 1929 the studio system had become stabilized to such an extent that critics hostile to the new talkies had a supply of contemptuous catch-phrases close at hand.

There were two particularly deplorable aspects of the studio system as far as its detractors were concerned: one, that it substituted committee approval for individual choice, and two, that the committee in question was capitalistically oriented, both in terms of making profits off screen and of promoting its ideology. Thus, there were two contrasting, if not conflicting, images of the artist against which Hollywood was counter-posed. One was that of the romantic, anarchic, alienated outcast in the ivory tower, accountable to no one, least of all the mass audience. The second was that of the responsible, concerned, constructive muse of the masses as those groundlings surged over the barricades to claim equality and justice. There is no need to debate these simplistic propositions at this late stage of revisionist film history. The only point to be made is that the studios were blamed for the faults of Hollywood movies for so long that when the virtues of these same movies were belatedly discovered by the auteurists in the fifties and sixties, a strong body of anti-auteurist opinion arose to champion the notion of studio as auteur. There arose a certain tension between the auteurist hypothesis that certain directorial auteurists overcame the limitations of the studio system, and the anti-auteurist hypothesis that the studio system itself was the source of much supposedly individual inspiration. The nature of the evidence—

i.e., the movies—shifted also from clues in solving a crime to signs in identifying a creation. It was no longer a question of who was to blame for Hollywood movies but rather, who was to get credit for them.

The principle of studio authorship has certain practical benefits for the opportunistic film historian. The property rights and physical possession of prints vested in the studios gives them powerful leverage with scholars, museums, and cinemathèques. Jean Renoir, for illustrious example, once told me that he did not own outright a single print of any of his films, not even for his personal use. Ergo, the many museum tributes to Zukor at Paramount, Zanuck at 20th Century-Fox, L. B. Mayer and Irving Thalberg (but not Samuel Goldwyn) at Metro-Goldwyn-Mayer, Uncle Carl Laemmle at Universal, Horrible Harry Cohn at Columbia, the worrisome Warner Brothers, David O. Selznick, and even ultra-nouveau Joe Levine. What is one Papal tribute more or less when the Sistine Ceiling is at stake?

Nonetheless, there is something more to the theory of the studio as auteur than there would be, say, to ludicrously marginal inquiries into the influence of publishers on novelists. Studios and their reigning producers, with or without portfolio, seem to have been something more than mere fiduciary agents, though something less than flowering artists. And at certain levels, movies did seem to bear the unmistakable imprint of a studio signature, be it in a neat hand or in a sloppy scrawl. As it happened, I grew up in the thirties and forties with a keen awareness of studio identities. By some quirk, I always lived closer to Loew's theaters, which showed Metro, Paramount, Columbia, and Universal releases, than to RKO theaters, which showed RKO, Warners, and Fox features, and I became aware very early in my moviegoing life of an imbalance in my screen diet. Studios *did* make a difference, but even now, with the benefit of much hindsight, the exact contribution of studios to the art of the cinema is difficult to determine. The separation of cause from coincidence must thus remain a very speculative venture. At the very least, however, the Hollywood studios can be said to have functioned for decades as a society within a society for American film-makers. That these studios were located on the Pacific coast rather than on the culturally more influential Atlantic coast has much to do with the tone, content, and reputation of Hollywood's output. Therefore, an adequately sociological study of the American cinema can hardly ignore the territorial imperatives of the monster-moguls ensconced in Southern California. Theirs was the power, if not necessarily the glory; the initiative, if not necessarily the inspiration; the bottom line of production, though not necessarily the higher spheres of creation. Fortunately, the studios were never a monolithic bloc of crass commercialism, but rather many raging torrents of conflicting tastes and aspirations. The official religion of the studios upheld collective craftsmanship over personal artistry, as did many of the practical requirements of the motion picture medium. At some point, however, craft lifted itself up into art, and an individual personality here and there found its own inimitable voice in the groupsing of studio film-making.

The quantitative challenge to any comprehensive study of the studio system is formidable indeed. Between 1929 and 1949 the major studios were credited with 6,848 features out of a total of 11,886 features released in America in that period. This would average out to be about 342 major studio movies each year out of a total of 594 American releases. The average number of foreign films imported to the United States each year in this period comes to about 150. We tend to assume that the great bulk of these movies, both domestic and imported, are of little serious interest, and our assumptions are probably correct, and yet we cannot be entirely sure that there are not still some archival treasures buried in the studio vaults. It would be simpler for film historians if most of the talkies had suffered the same fate that befell most of the silents. For the most part, however, the talkies have lived to tell their tales firsthand, and the critical sifting has not yet been concluded. It would be, therefore, premature to evaluate the studios on the basis of each year's ten-best, twenty-best, or even fifty-best and one hundred-best lists. Nor can we assume that all the films from so-called major studios qualified as major attractions, or that all the films from minor studios or independent producers were necessarily small-scale either commercially or aesthetically. The numbers and even the credits do not even begin to tell the whole story of the studio mystique.

It must be remembered first of all that most of the motion picture moguls entered the industry as theater owners. Thus, in many instances, exhibition was the tail that wagged the dog of production. The task of a studio was to turn out enough product to satisfy the needs of a theater. This meant not only feature-length films, but cartoons, short subjects, travelogues, and newsreels. Mickey Mouse and the other denizens of Disneyland generally worked under the aegis of RKO, Popeye was at Paramount, Bugs Bunny at Warners, Tom and Jerry at MGM, and, on a lower level, Mighty Mouse at 20th Century-Fox. Yet, now that we know more about the creative backgrounds of the various animators we can see that studio affiliations were marginal factors in the evolution of the style and content of the various cartoon figures. Similarly, the fact that there was a different trademark for each studio's newsreel operation as there was for each studio itself did not produce any discernible distinctions in the ideological treatment of the news. *The March of Time*, however, did project a more aggressive approach to news subjects, an approach associated with the Luce publications. Nonetheless, an infrastructure was set up in each studio to supply all the necessary ingredients for an evening at the movies. A composer here, a set designer there, could go a long way in imposing a particular motif on a studio. It is in the nature of sociological criticism to disregard these motifs as extraneous ornamentation, but it is out of this ornamentation that the stylistic nuances of Hollywood movies begin to emerge.

The growing popularity of double features and animated cartoons in the thirties caused the decline of the two-reel live-action comedies that survived most conspicuously and most creatively from the silents in the idiosyncratic works of Laurel and Hardy. Conversely, many "feature-length" films in the era of double features were barely an hour long. The whole subject of running time has more to do with the economics of movie-making than with its aesthetics. The average shot length, or A.S.L. as it is abbreviated in scholarly film journals, is another factor that may be more fiscal than formal. As much as André Bazin has written about the evolution of the long take and deep focus as a sign of stylistic maturity, the fact remains that the cheapest westerns tend to park the camera in front of a saloon set and let the leads and a horde of extras cavort within the frame of the lens (and, ultimately, of the screen) without any close-ups, change of angle, or cross-cutting. Thus, the average shot length of a poverty row production may compare favorably in duration with that of a well-rehearsed William Wyler superproduction like *The Best Years of Our Lives* (1946). Consequently, there is no statistical shortcut to the critical task of sifting through thousands of studio productions for the comparatively few films that transcend the studio-imposed limits of custom and commerce.

Nonetheless, the mythology of the omnipresent, if not omnipotent, mogul persists to this day, largely because the moguls themselves co-operated so avidly in even the ego-bashing publicity that proclaimed their power. In an era when assimilation was considered the better part of valor, the moguls made little effort to conceal their humble immigrant origins and lack of education. Their virtual illiteracy only added spice to their success stories, and their ostentatious Jewishness only confirmed the legend of their shrewdness. Of course, the myth of the mogul was

fabricated long before the Holocaust added a *frisson* of horror to even
the most casual caricature of allegedly Jewish acquisitiveness and *nou-
veaux-riches* affectations. Nonetheless, a post-Holocaust reader may be
somewhat startled to discover in the published Description of Characters
for Moss Hart and George S. Kaufman's *Once in a Lifetime*, a famous
1930 satire of Hollywood in the midst of the talkie trauma, the following
entry for Glogauer: "A good-natured, nervous, energetic little Jewish picture magnate. Aged 50."

The fact that Hart and Kaufman and many of their cohorts in the
Algonquin Circle were Jewish also does not eliminate a tinge of facile
anti-Semitism in the pose of cultural superiority toward the déclassé
dream merchants on the opposite coast. Not that these merchants laid
any great claims to intellectual aspirations. For one thing, they did not
want to alienate the uneducated, uncultivated multitudes that attended
movies. For another, they seemed to enjoy poking fun at themselves.
Carl Laemmle, the president of Universal Studios, signed his name to a
short foreword preceding the screen version of *Once in a Lifetime* to the
effect that people in Hollywood did not mind a good laugh at their own
expense. Laemmle himself never denied the story that he had forced
Erich von Stroheim to change the title of his epic of mountain-climbing
adultery from *The Pinnacle* to *Blind Husbands* because no one would
want to pay money to see a movie about a card game. Similarly, Adolph
Zukor was widely credited with changing the title of Cecil B. De Mille's
adaptation of James Barrie's *The Admirable Crichton* to *Male and Female*
because the paying customers might be misled into thinking they were
going to see a film about the navy! Samuel Goldwyn, the acknowledged
master of Malibu malapropism, employed an army of press agents led
by Lynn Farnol to coin classic gaffes of self-contradiction as "Include
me out" and "A verbal agreement isn't worth the paper it's written on."

The legend of the culturally moronic mogul became so pervasive in
the industry that when a college-educated producer popped up in the
front office, his intellectual pretensions were still good for a laugh, as in
the caricature of a Walter Wanger–like arriviste in Sam and Bella Spe-
wack's *Boy Meets Girl*, which, like *Once in a Lifetime*, went from stage
to screen with most of its anti-Hollywood satiric conceits intact. For a
long time this apparent ability to take a joke was not recognized as a
defense reaction against deep feelings of insecurity and self-hatred. The
contempt for movies within the movie industry itself has never been
properly chronicled. It is not surprising that many Hollywood magnates

ended up being prouder of the art collections on their walls than of the treasures in their film archives. Yet, their very benign neglect of their bread-and-butter occupation for the sake of the high-art snobberies in New York and Europe enabled many of their dedicated crafts employees to work creatively within the margins of dissent and irreverence.

1

The Hollywood Studios

THE STUDIO MYSTIQUE

The Myth of Metro

The pre-eminence of Metro-Goldwyn-Mayer among Hollywood studios from the twenties through the forties has been for so long a generally accepted bit of folk wisdom that it is difficult to dispute it. The Leo the Lion trademark, the Lion's Roar, *The Lion's Share* by Bosley Crowther, *The Last Tycoon* by F. Scott Fitzgerald, More Stars Than There Are in Heaven, Garbo Talks! Garbo Laughs! Gable's Back and Garson's Got Him!—indeed, the many clever publicity ploys of the genuinely witty Howard Dietz—have all combined to cast an aura of invincibility and infallibility around the studio and its output. With the bravos has come the inevitable backlash. As the quintessential Hollywood studio, MGM has been made to take the blame for most of Hollywood's alleged vices. It was always more a producer's studio than a writer's studio, and more a writer's studio than a director's studio, but, above all, it was the studio of the stars: Garbo, Gable, Gilbert, Shearer, Crawford, Garson, Tracy, Beery, Dressler, the Barrymores, Powell, Loy, Montgomery, Harlow, Rooney, Garland, Kelly, Taylor (both Robert and Elizabeth), et al. Metro was clearly the most popular (box-office grosses) and most prestigious (Oscars) of all the studios, and yet its standing among film scholars, historians, and cultists is quite shaky. Indeed, anti-Metro revisionist sentiment has become so strong that it is necessary to provide some perspective on the standards of comparison. First, MGM's movies were so successfully merchandised and so pervasively publicized and so widely distributed that they have become overly familiar. Consequently, there are few mysteries about MGM, and fewer occasions for archival discovery. Of Garbo's films there, only *The Divine Woman* seems to have vanished. Most of her other vehicles have been in general circulation for decades. For years the Marx Brothers were famous more for their MGM movies, particularly *A Night at the Opera* (1935) and *A Day at the Races* (1937), than for their earlier, more anarchic Paramount productions— *The Cocoanuts* (1929), *Animal Crackers* (1930), *Monkey Business* (1931), *Horse Feathers* (1932), and *Duck Soup* (1933). Spencer Tracy's MGM period is infinitely more celebrated than his Fox period, perhaps deservedly so, but Jeanette MacDonald's earlier, sexier Paramount reign in the witty, lilting musicals of Lubitsch and Mamoulian is generally overlooked and she's remembered for her later, stodgier stint at MGM in overstuffed operettas.

Of course, it is much harder to measure the claims of MGM's stars against those of their counterparts at other studios. Was Clark Gable more magnetic than Gary Cooper? Was Robert Taylor more the pretty boy than Tyrone Power? And how does one put Greta Garbo up against Katharine Hepburn and Marlene Dietrich and Bette Davis? That one stellar constellation grossed more money at the box office than another says nothing about the distinction between aging well and dating badly. Most histories of Hollywood seem to accept the commercial verdict of the time as binding for all time, but in the long run no ranking can be definitive. The commercial argument is particularly suspect in view of the hidden advantages of studio resources and block booking. Also, a film may be seen by a great many people without being fondly remembered. The fact remains that certain artistic choices at MGM can be traced to the middle-brow tastes of Louis B. Mayer and Irving J. Thalberg, and these choices had much to do with MGM's status in its heyday. Often it was a matter more of emphasis than of exclusivity. Every studio dabbled in roughly the same mix of genres and trends. Hits were copied and flops filed away and forgotten. Technological advances at one studio were absorbed by all the others. Stars and directors were lent and borrowed from studio to studio.

Nonetheless, MGM can be credited with having made the smoothest transition from silence to sound in the late twenties, even though Warners and Fox had served as technological trail-blazers in this transition. It can be argued that Paramount was more stylish in the twenties than MGM, and that Fox was artistically more ambitious. But with the virtually simultaneous shocks of sound and the Crash on Wall Street only MGM emerged with full solvency and prestige. With tighter organization and a higher level of craftsmanship for its lower-level productions, MGM averaged out better than the other studios. Thalberg's close supervision of writers enabled him to achieve a surface gloss for most of his productions. Through the thirties MGM became particularly adept at play adaptations, most notably with *The Guardsman* (1931), *Grand Hotel* (1932), *Dinner at Eight* (1933), *Reunion in Vienna* (1933), *When Ladies Meet* (1933) (1941) (twice), *The Barretts of Wimpole Street* (1934), *Night Must Fall* (1937), and *The Women* (1939). Among socially conscious film historians it is almost a reflex to dismiss these elegantly mounted productions as irrelevant to the class struggle. In addition, the purists of film have always been outraged by the many incestuous embraces shared by the cinema and the theater. Few cult classics emerged from adaptations of prominent plays. Thalberg's thirst for refinement and gentility found little favor among later film enthusiasts. With both Thalberg and Mayer notorious for meddling with the rushes in the cutting room, there was little possibility for those happy accidents out of which sleepers are born.

Still, it is easy to underestimate the virtues of polish and professionalism, particularly when MGM's relative wealth of writing talent enabled its producers to pan for *bons mots* amid the endless sludge of wisecracks. But much in the polishing of dialogue served only to illuminate the timidity of the content, particularly after 1934 when the censors began cracking down on the ribald and the risqué. But even in the early thirties, Thalberg and Mayer seemed to shrink away from the worlds of the gangster and the ghoul, the provinces respectively of Warners and Universal. From *The Big House* in 1930 to *The Asphalt Jungle* in 1950, MGM had shown itself periodically capable of venturing into the underworld, but the MGM image has remained one more of sweetness and light than of lurid shadow.

The Panache of Paramount

If indeed MGM were truly entitled to its status as Hollywood's most productive and most creative studio, which studio deserved the second position? Paramount? Warners? 20th Century-Fox? RKO? If MGM were not deemed worthy of its exalted reputation, then one of its aforementioned rivals would have to be considered for the top rung of the ladder. One must first balance the discernible assets and liabilities of those who would be clothed in the royal robes of Leo the Lion. Through the thirties and forties Paramount movies seemed at once more elegant and more anarchic than MGM movies. From Adolph Zukor's genteel tradition at Famous Players in the silent era to the madcap frenzies of the Marx Brothers, W. C. Fields, Mae West, and the "Road" company of Bob Hope and Bing Crosby, Paramount seemed to be governed by a high-low strategy with very little that was memorable in between.

From its formation in 1912 as the Famous Players Film Company, with Mary Pickford as its most prominent star, the company absorbed in succession Paramount Pictures Corporation, the Jesse L. Lasky Feature Play Company, and a dozen other production companies, until in 1927 the corporate name became Paramount Famous Lasky Corporation, and in 1930 Paramount Publix Corporation. It can be argued that Paramount was the pre-eminent studio in the silent era, with its star roster including (in addition to Mary Pickford) Wallace Reid, Gloria Swanson, Clara Bow, Mary Miles Minter, Adolphe Menjou, Rudolph Valentino, Douglas Fairbanks, John Barrymore, Mae Murray, Marguerite Clark, Pola Negri, Emil Jannings, Evelyn Brent, and Louise Brooks.

Paramount's affiliation with the famous UFA studio in Germany may have made it linguistically vulnerable during the difficult transition to talkies. Emil Jannings and Pola Negri returned to Germany, though Maurice Chevalier and Marlene Dietrich came the other way to restore the box-office balance. Unfortunately, Paramount seemed to lack strong executive producers to ride herd on its minor product with the result that the prestige productions of Ernst Lubitsch, Josef von Sternberg, Cecil B. De Mille, Mitchell Leisen, Leo McCarey, Billy Wilder, and Preston Sturges have put a gloss on the Paramount logo that the bulk of its productions never deserved.

Of the eleven hundred or so Paramount pictures made between 1929 and 1949, fewer than a hundred are the stuff of ten-best lists and Oscar nominations. But on a balance sheet the thousand forgotten Paramount films may or may not explain why Paramount Publix went bankrupt in 1933 to be reorganized as Paramount Pictures in 1935, and why movie pioneer Jesse L. Lasky and production chief B. P. Schulberg were deposed in such humiliating fashion as to become the stuff of Hollywood legend.

The overriding Paramount legend remains, however, a tradition of elegance owing almost as much to the set designs of Hans Dreier as the Europeanized sensibilities of Lubitsch, Sternberg, Wilder, Leisen, and Mamoulian, among other certified auteurs.

Warner Brothers

Warners is the only studio of which it can be said that it was a minor studio before sound, and a major studio after. Formed in 1923 by the brothers Harry, Albert, Sam, and Jack L. Warner, the company swallowed up Vitagraph and First National Pictures in 1925, and in 1926 joined with General Electric to promote a sound-film process patented as Vitaphone. By hitching this process to the charisma of Al Jolson in *The Jazz Singer* in 1927, Warners broke the logjam that had blocked the introduction of sound equipment (with its huge investment) to the nation's movie theaters. Warners took the plunge before its competitors— Garbo at Metro was still "silent" as late as 1929—and came up the winner.

What is generally overlooked, however, is that Warners was able to consolidate its position in the early talkies by a remarkable consistency in its gritty street entertainments. Movie for movie, Warners was the most reliable source of entertainment through the thirties and forties, even though it was clearly the most budget-conscious of them all. In the nineties, particularly, the razor-sharp cutting and frantic pacing look inspired to the point of absurdism. Not for Warners were the *longueurs* of MGM and the polish of Paramount. A Warners B picture seldom ran more than seventy minutes. MGM and Paramount production values padded their Bs to the eighty- and ninety-minute mark without adding anything of substance or originality.

Though the Warners mystique made a virtue of necessity, the tight-fistedness of the studio bosses inspired periodic rebellions by its biggest stars, most notably James Cagney and Bette Davis. Warners specialized at first in the gangster and prison genres, and later in the Great Man cycle. Still, most of the scenarios, especially after 1934, tended to be low-down without being hard-boiled. Underneath all the grime there was as much sentimental piety and conformist cant among the Brothers Warner as there was in L. B. Mayer. What we remember most fondly not only about Warners movies but about Hollywood movies in general are not the endings prescribed by the Hays Office and the mealy-mouthed moguls, but the beginnings and middles, during which all sorts of wickedly subversive mischief could be indulged. Yet from the world-weary showgirl incarnate in Joan Blondell to the delinquents represented by the Dead End Kids, Warners movies more than those from any other studio walked mostly on the shady side of the street.

20th Century-Fox

Though 20th Century-Fox came into existence as a corporate entity in 1935, the pre-hyphenated Fox studio dates back to William Fox's Fox Film Corporation of 1915. It was the studio of Tom Mix and F. W. Murnau, of Theda Bara and Janet Gaynor, of Raoul Walsh and Frank Borzage. For a brief moment in film history, Fox was poised to swallow up MGM, but the 1929 Crash intervened and Fox himself went bankrupt. Curiously, the Fox studio weathered the sound revolution with its Movietone process—actually a technological advance over the Warners Vitaphone—better than it weathered the Crash and the Depression that followed. Legend has it that Fox was saved from bankruptcy by the twinkling and golden curls of Shirley Temple much as Universal was supposed to have been saved by the golden throat of Deanna Durbin.

One might whimsically divide the history of Fox at 1935 into B. Z. (Before Zanuck), and A. Z. (After Zanuck). Darryl F. Zanuck, the former chief of production at Warners, served as vice-president in charge of production under Joseph M. Schenck, the president. Zanuck was one of the few gentiles (or *goys*) at that level of power in the film industry, and it hardly mattered except for a few marginal preferences such as not displaying an inordinate reverence for the Great Composers as did the Messrs. Mayer, Warner, Cohn, Laemmle, et al., while devoting a whole film to the works of John Philip Sousa. There were no trilling sopranos or tenors in Zanuck's time, only Alice Faye and Betty Grable and *Alexander's Ragtime Band*.

Fox movies both before and after the merger with Joseph M. Schenck and Darryl F. Zanuck's 20th Century are less well-known than those of other studios because of a court decision barring the block sale of pre-1948 Fox movies to television. Hence, the impression was created that most of these movies were of negligible interest despite such famous directors as John Ford, Frank Borzage, Frank Lloyd, Henry King, Otto Preminger, and Elia Kazan on the Fox roster.

20th Century-Fox was to be hailed by the cognoscenti as a directors' studio in the forties, but even as early as 1938, MGM contract director

Clarence Brown on "loan out" to Fox for *The Rains Came* (along with MGM star Myrna Loy in exchange for Tyrone Power as Norma Shearer's leading man in *Marie Antoinette*) averred that the studio facilities at Fox were technically superior to MGM's.

In addition to the court decision affecting pre-1948 Fox films, there were also various studio fires, making it even more difficult to evaluate the Fox output. The image of Fox through the thirties remained one of rusticity and Americana. The *Variety* headline of the mid-thirties: HIX NIX STIX PIX applied with particular force to Fox, whose biggest star had been Will Rogers before his death in an air crash in 1935. After 1935, Fox was saved not only by Miss Temple and her nemesis Jane Withers, but also by movies on such popular subjects as the Chicago Fire and the Dionne Quintuplets. The influence on Fox production schedules of American history–oriented producer Kenneth MacGowan should not go unmentioned.

RKO

RKO (less well known by its full name, Radio-Keith-Orpheum) is the closest thing we have had in Hollywood to a schizophrenic studio experiencing periodic nervous breakdowns. In its Dr. Jekyll interludes it was the studio of *King Kong, Citizen Kane,* Fred Astaire and Ginger Rogers, Katharine Hepburn in her feminist glory, Howard Hawks, George Cukor, Gregory La Cava, George Stevens on their happiest holidays from studio routine, Nicholas Ray, Fritz Lang, Jacques Tourneur, Edward Dmytryk, Sam Fuller, and Alfred Hitchcock and creative producer Pandro Berman all with dark masterpieces under the RKO radio-wave crackling logo. Then there was the Mr. Hyde spasms of Howard Hughes, Joseph P. Kennedy, and a long procession of ineffectual dreamers and bottom-line mediocrities.

Universal

Universal since its founding in 1912 had been more of a one-family studio than any other in Hollywood, as its global logo evolved over the years until in the mid-forties in a haze of glitz its airplane disappeared. Carl Laemmle and Carl Laemmle, Jr., added personal notes to their productions in the form of forewords and cast lists, and intermittently they attracted attention with stylist explosions like Lewis Milestone's *All Quiet on the Western Front* (1930), James Whale's *Frankenstein* (1931) and *Show Boat* (1936), Tod Browning's *Dracula* (1931) and *Freaks* (1932), and a succession of intelligent women's pictures with Irene Dunne, Margaret Sullavan, and Diana Wynyard that have only now been rediscovered in recent decades.

Deanna Durbin was Universal's brightest star and economic salvation through the Depression, though I must add very parenthetically that my own painful passage to puberty was aided in no small measure by Miss Durbin's projected successor, Gloria Jean, in the heartwarmingly egalitarian *The Under-Pup* (1939). Jascha Heifetz attempted in vain to repeat Leopold Stokowski's spectacular success in Miss Durbin's Depression era vehicle, *100 Men and a Girl* (1937), with his own debut in *They Shall Have Music* (1939), but even Joel McCrea and Andrea Leeds casting reverent glances couldn't transform Heifetz into a Jose Iturbi–like movie celebrity.

Columbia Pictures

Columbia Pictures was incorporated in 1924 out of the ashes of the C.B.C/Film Sales Company, founded in 1920 by the brothers Harry and Jack Cohn, and Joe Brandt, all of whom worked at one time for Carl Laemmle, founder of Universal Pictures. Through the thirties and forties, however, Columbia Pictures was regarded as the fiefdom of Harry Cohn, who was as much undervalued as a studio boss as the canonized Irving J. Thalberg was overvalued.

Columbia Pictures was never considered one of the major Hollywood studios, and most of its releases remain mysterious even to hard-core movie buffs. John Baxter dismisses Columbia in less than a sentence in *Hollywood in the Thirties*: "Columbia seldom managed to struggle out from under the control of 'King Cohn,' its inflexible, tasteless boss. . . ." The operative word in the preceding quotation is "seldom," inasmuch as it could have been said of each and every Hollywood studio that it "seldom" rose above routine.

Harry Cohn, the subject of at least one film *à clef*, *The Big Knife* (1955), always provided an easy target and scapegoat. Yet, his notoriety as a vulgarian, a womanizer, and a tantrum-throwing tyrant managed to obscure the fact that Columbia, very much like RKO, often offered talented performers an escape from the stereotyped personae imposed upon them by the larger studios. Clark Gable (MGM) and Claudette Colbert (Paramount) had their biggest success (and only Oscars) at Columbia in Frank Capra's *It Hapened One Night* (1934). Capra enjoyed more freedom under Cohn than did any MGM director under Mayer and Thalberg, and it was Capra who made James Stewart a star in a period when MGM had relegated him to second leads. MGM's Rosalind Russell and Robert Montgomery are remembered today largely for their "loan-out" appearances to Columbia for *His Girl Friday* (1940) and *Here Comes Mr. Jordan* (1941) respectively. Among the directors finding refuge at Columbia for pet projects were Howard Hawks, John Ford, Leo McCarey, Gregory La Cava, George Cukor, Orson Welles, George Stevens, Zoltan Korda, Dorothy Arzner, and the offbeat team of Ben Hecht, Charles MacArthur, and Lee Garmes.

Beyond the gleaming light held aloft by the torch-bearing Columbia Lady was a light-hearted, too often light-headed vision of life, which is to say that Columbia made many more mirthless comedies than it should have. The Columbia look tended to be sunny, the spirit frothy. Yet, any studio that allowed Leo McCarey to make *The Awful Truth* (1937), Howard Hawks *Only Angels Have Wings* (1939), Gregory La Cava *She Married Her Boss* (1935), Orson Welles *Lady from Shanghai* (1948), George Stevens *Talk of the Town* (1942), and John Ford *The Whole Town's Talking* (1935) was certainly doing something right.

2

Genres

THE MUSICAL

he Jazz Singer premiered at Warners' Strand in
New York City on October 23, 1927, a date en-
shrined in film history, with all the dread decisiveness of Waterloo, Sarajevo, and Pearl Harbor. On
this date the death knell of the "silent" movie was sounded, and the
"talkies" were born. It became a stock scene in movies on Hollywood
history (vide *Singin' in the Rain*) (1952): "Warners is trying a new experiment with Al Jolson in *The Jazz Singer*. It'll never catch on." Then,
a few days or a few weeks or a few months later, panic sweeps across
the prairies, a panic emblazoned in *Variety* headlines. Jolson and *The Jazz
Singer* are to the silent mimes in 1927 what Black Tuesday was to be to
the financiers of the Jazz Age in 1929.

For most film aestheticians, *The Jazz Singer* marked the beginning of
the end, rather than the end of the beginning. Well into the forties and
fifties, serious books and articles on the motion picture continued to
maintain that pure cinema was a thing of the past. It had died one night
in a theater where people were mesmerized by a Mammy singer. According to the film historians, however, it was not Jolson the singer who
shook the medium to its foundations, but Jolson the talker. One would
never suspect from all that has been written about *The Jazz Singer* that
this backstage musical was essentially a silent movie with several songs

interpolated on the soundtrack, and just a few lines of stage patter mixed in for good measure. *The Jazz Singer* is thus less a "talkie" than a "singie." Indeed, as its title would indicate, *The Jazz Singer* is a movie musical, the first of a genre that, more than any other, owed its existence to the coming of sound to the screen. Yet remarkably little has been written on this genre in serious film histories. Conversely, serious music people have tended to dismiss music in the movies. The uneasy marriage between cinema and music has thus been plagued by in-law problems from the beginning. And the beginning of which I speak long antedates *The Jazz Singer*. To understand why this is so it is necessary to put aside the myth of absolute silence in the cinema before "talkies."

How did this myth get started in the first place? Most people with even a smattering of film history, or first-hand recollections of the silent era, are aware that music, often very elaborate music, was played during screenings of silent movies. The prevailing image that has come down to us as period folklore is that of the resourceful piano player trotting out the same tried and true pieces as the shifting moods of the movie dictated. People who have studied the field more carefully have become aware that special scores were composed for large orchestras in the big-city engagements of silent movies. In recent years, with more and more silent classics appearing on television and cable in special revival houses, on video cassettes and laser discs, there has been a tendency to strike new prints with musical sound tracks. For example, Kurt Meisel's score for *Potemkin* is now inseparable from the film's images. This practice of post-synchronization has tended to obscure the fact that many famous "silents," from *Don Juan* in 1926 through *Sunrise* in 1927 to *City Lights* and *Tabu* in 1931, were formally integrated with their musical accompaniment at the time of production. Thus the issue of music in movies boils down to a distinction between an informal association in the movie house (a dead theatrical tradition) and a formal integration on the print itself (a vital union of two art forms).

For better or worse, television spectators are not visual purists. If a televiewer is confronted with absolute silence, this creature of visual radio expectations is likely to kick the set around until sound, or at least music, is restored. Young people particularly tend to fidget when their ears are not stimulated simultaneously with their eyes. This is nothing new or, I submit, immature or unnatural. If silent movies are to remain a living part of the film repertory, they must at least neutralize the clamoring of the contemporary ear for nourishment. This is to say that I prefer almost any musical accompaniment to no musical accompaniment. My only regret is that so many early silent slapstick farces have been need-lessly vulgarized by silly, gross, and unworthy sound effects.

Nonetheless, there remained until recently citadels of silence amid the towers of babble. The late Henri Langlois insisted that he would never tolerate musical accompaniments to the silent movies screened in his world-famous Paris Cinémathèque. "The images themselves provide their own music," he once told me. Still, it was at his Cinémathèque I saw a French-dubbed version of *Singin' in the Rain* (1952), an inauth-entic experience of grotesque proportions. Jonas Mekas has pursued a similarly puritanical policy on musical accompaniment to silent films at the Anthology Film Archives. At an Eastman House projection of Stro-heim's *The Merry Widow* (1925) many years ago I chanced to be sitting next to Herman G. Weinberg when he clamped his hands over his ears to protest the Franz Lehár score that had been added to the film. Wein-berg's was a very chic aesthetic attitude in some circles though I never fully understood why Lehár should have been barred from any version, however non-traditional, of *The Merry Widow*.

How then is the enormous impact of *The Jazz Singer* to be explained if one discards the notion of a totally mute cinema before October 23, 1927—a notion given credence post-sound by the stillness in which si-lent films were screened? The title offers a clue: "Jazz" suggests a raffish modernity in real or potential conflict with the old ways. There was certainly nothing new about melting-pot movies in 1927, and the conflict between the sacred and the profane was decidedly old hat, but a con-frontation on the sound track between "Kol Nidre" and "Toot Toot Toot-sie, Goodbye" added a new dimension to the expression of the theme. Many of the standard plots of subsequent musicals are present in *The Jazz Singer*: the backstage struggles and heartaches, the generational con-flicts over careers, the supplanting of classical music by some form of popular music, be it jazz, swing, boogie-woogie, or rock. The very sec-tarian Jewishness* of *The Jazz Singer* was not to be so common in sub-sequent movie musicals despite the many Jewish moguls in Hollywood. Nor were there to be many references, as there are in *The Jazz Singer*, to Jewish performers changing their names so as to "pass" among Gentile audiences.

---

*The 1927 program for *The Jazz Singer* at the Strand contains a glossary with the following entries: *Kibitzer*—a busybody. *Shiksa*—a Non-Jewess. *Cantor*—chanter of sacred hymns. *Kol Nidre*—sacred hymn chanted only on eve of Yum [*sic*] Kippur (Day of Atonement).

Curiously, the Samson Raphaelson Broadway show, which starred George Jessel, was more a play with incidental songs than a full-fledged stage musical. When Warners was unable to come to terms with Jessel, new songs were added to the movie to exploit Jolson's talents. The songs, in turn, enabled Jolson to transcend the melodramatic banalities of the plot with his vibrant projection of a performer in action. The songs, the music, comprised the poetic elements of his portrayal, and his few spoken words confirmed the prosaic realism of the performer. What electrified audiences was not the singing alone or the talking alone, but rather the dynamic contrast between song (lyrical flying) and speech (sensible walking). From the beginning, therefore, the magical formula of movie musicals was established in the medium's unique capacity to wed the realistic to the fantastic, the factual to the fanciful, the prosaic to the poetic.

Most of the movie musicals that followed hard upon the success of *The Jazz Singer* have somehow disappeared from the stream of film history. Even Jolson himself came to be regarded as the ultimately failed Messiah of the movie musical. Though *The Singing Fool* in 1928 was even more successful commercially than *The Jazz Singer*, it is seldom revived, and if it is remembered at all it is for the bathetic excesses of "Sonny Boy," a father-son ballad so fulsomely sentimental that it has been parodied on innumerable occasions by night-club, radio, and television performers. *Say It with Songs* (1929), *Mammy*, and *Big Boy* (both 1930) rounded out Jolson's first Warners period as a big star in decline. *Mammy*, at least, deserved better for its relatively deft integration of mistrelsy and melodrama. Lowell Sherman as Jolson's romantic rival was particularly valuable for providing a cooling urbanity to Jolson's sweaty boisterousness. It might be noted also that the Jolson musicals were clogged with gun play, police, and prisons. In *Big Boy*, however, the proto-*noir* was completely overshadowed by blackface as Jolson played a black jockey doubling as an old retainer for an aristocratic Southern family. At this stage of film history, blackface was on the way out not so much for its racist implications as for its affront to realism.

In any discussion of Jolson's "decline," however, it should be noted that he was already past forty when *The Jazz Singer* was released, and that his talent had fully ripened years before he faced his first movie camera. What has been overlooked also is that his intensity as a performer militated against prolonged modishness. His explosive force, once it had broken the sound barrier, proved excessive for the workaday tastes of the movie musical. He was the vibrant vaudevillian, the entertainer par excellence. Beneath the greasepaint and the blackface there seemed only more greasepaint and blackface. He was always "on," never relaxed. Yet it would be misleading to suppose that Jolson was supplanted by, say, Maurice Chevalier or Bing Crosby or by any other troubador of the medium. The genre itself seemed always to be on trial, and static singers most of all in this theatrically mobile art-form.

Jolson tried the Depression-oriented tramp routine in *Hallelujah! I'm a Bum* (1933), one of the most interestingly complex musicals of the thirties, and one, curiously, with a grown-up love story. Most knowledgeable reviewers chose to concentrate on the somewhat strained populist sentiments sung by Harry Langdon's vigorously Marxist trash collector. This sensitive pixie from silent pictures was transformed by Lewis Milestone's direction into a spirited prole, but Langdon's career, like Jolson's, was at a dead end, and no amount of experimentation with type-switching could save it. It is lamentable that the film's most melodious song (Richard Rodgers's "You Are Too Beautiful") is never sung, but serves instead as the background music for the love triangle of Jolson, Madge Evans, and Frank Morgan. Jolson, a kind of king of the hoboes, and Morgan, the socially prominent mayor of New York, are such good friends that their separate paths are fated to cross that of Madge Evans, who is indeed subtly beautiful enough to be pastoral waif in the park to one man, and elegant urban mistress to the other. Jolson's hobo-king gallantly and fatalistically returns the waif to the love-sick mayor, and then stands off to one side, smiling ruefully as he accepts the destiny of the troubador.

Jolson assumes the same downbeat posture at the end of his next movie, *Wonder Bar* (1934), a curiously chaotic night-club musical full of casual murders and cover-ups. *Go Into Your Dance* (1935) united Jolson with his wife, saccharine Ruby Keeler, who, along with dimpled Dick Powell, supplied the sweetness and light for the otherwise tough and cynical Warner Brothers musicals—*42nd Street* (1933), *Gold Diggers of 1933*, *Footlight Parade* (1933), and *Dames* (1934)—in which Busby Berkeley made his mark. But *Go Into Your Dance*, like *The Singing Kid* (1936) the next year, was not only Jolson on the downgrade, but Jolson dull and conventional besides. For Jolson the rest was mostly radio. He appeared in three Fox films in 1939—*Rose of Washington Square*, *Hollywood Cavalcade*, and *Swanee River*—which served to embalm him as a period performer. Then in 1946 and 1949 he supplied his voice to Larry Parks for *The Jolson Story* and *Jolson Sings Again*, and his career experienced a brief lift before his death in 1950. But there was never any great demand to revive his old movie musicals. Jolson carried his past around with him in his repertoire, but it remains ironic that the man who almost single-handedly rendered silent films obsolete should have become such an early casualty of the talkies. It is even more ironic that his trail-blazing movies of 1927 through 1930 are now deemed more archaic than the silent films they supplanted.

The traditional scenario for a historical outline of the movie musical tends to ignore the so-called formative years as much as possible. One may begin with Ernst Lubitsch's *Love Parade* and King Vidor's *Hallelujah!* as 1929 examples of creative cinema that was not immobilized by music. Each cut, each camera movement is treasured as a triumph over the cumbersome sound equipment. René Clair dominates the early thirties for historians focusing on the-cinema-as-rhythm-and-movement with *Sous les Toits de Paris* (1930), *Le Million* (1931), *A Nous la Liberté* (1931), and *Quatorze Juillet* (1933).

G. W. Pabst's version of the Brecht-Weill *The Threepenny Opera* was more highly regarded in the thirties than it is now. It is significant that Pabst chose to "make cinema" by cutting out many of the songs. In the late fifties the film was revived in New York, and many New Yorkers brought up on the Marc Blitzstein stage version of *The Threepenny Opera* (1931) lamented the lost songs. One wag dubbed Pabst's production "the worst movie I ever waited my whole life to see." That Brecht himself had repudiated Pabst's adaptation on ostensibly ideological grounds had little to do with the gut reaction of New York audiences. For this one work, the musical elements were considered even more crucial than the thematic elements. Of course, Brecht's penchant for fragmentation, alienation, and bare-faced didacticism had not yet been elevated to dogma in the thirties or even by the fifties. Pabst's moody, misty mise-en-scène, particularly the opening tracking shot of the harbor orchestrated to "Mack the Knife," was considered the essence of creative cinema, overcoming the constricting confines of the stage musical. Pabst, a realist of sorts in his fussy preoccupation with psychologically illuminating detail, was simply trying to make a coherent movie out of an episodic theater piece. The kind of structural stylization Brecht and Weill required (and probably demanded) would have been considered treason to the motion-picture medium at that time. Indeed, infidelity to the theater was seen as evidence of cinematic integrity.

Two early musicals often overlooked as examples of the genre are Josef von Sternberg's *The Blue Angel* (1930) and *Morocco* (1930). Yet their songs advance the feelings and actions of the characters more dramatically than do most songs in most musicals. Here the general feeling among film historians and categorizers happens to be that the dramatic action is too strong in its own right to be treated as a mere pretext for the music. By the same token, in the forties *Casablanca* (1943) and *To Have and Have Not* (1944) are never treated as musicals even though the rhythms of these films' action seem to flow out of the piano more than the moviola.

Yet Sternberg too received high marks from the cinéastes for not allowing the songs to paralyze the mise-en-scène. The late Richard Griffith, a traditional anti-talkie film historian, singled out Sternberg for commendation for the scene in *Morocco* in which Gary Cooper writes a note in lipstick on Marlene Dietrich's dressing-room mirror while Dietrich is singing off screen in the night club proper. This disjunction between what was seen and what was heard constituted for Griffith a revolutionary stratagem for the cinema of 1930. It was this kind of stylistically transcendent analysis that made it possible and even mandatory for reviewers not to mention just how effective the songs themselves happened to be. No song in *Morocco*, for example, is as memorably tuneful and psychologically illuminating as "Falling in Love Again" from *The Blue Angel*. That is why, though I prefer *Morocco* to *The Blue Angel* as a movie, I prefer *The Blue Angel* to *Morocco* as a musical.

Our traditional scenario for movie musicals now resumes with Rouben Mamoulian's innovative musical *objets d'art*: *Applause* (1930) and *Love Me Tonight* (1932). Mamoulian, an American Clair, was an innovative figure, like Clair, in the early sound era, who then, again like Clair, faded into an academic classicism when sound had become matter of fact. *Applause*, made in 1929 and released in 1930, was particularly audacious for its time in the strikingly oblique treatment of the relation between sound and image. But then again an excessive emphasis on technical innovation can distract the historian from mentioning the stirringly raunchy speech and costuming so characteristic of the period and the bumbling masochism of Helen Morgan's well-meaning but ill-fated burlesque queen, who dies almost unnoticed off in a corner as in the foreground the saga of her daughter's nobility and redemption unwinds. The songs here are less memorable than the low-life atmosphere that brings them into being.

Love Me Tonight has been seen as a rebuke to Lubitsch on the supposition that Lubitsch's achievements in the genre had been surpassed by Mamoulian. John Russell Taylor has put the matter as tactfully as possible in *The Hollywood Musical* (co-authored with Arthur Jackson):

And in all this confusion, there were only two people, in Hollywood at least, who showed any real sign of knowing what they wanted to do with the new monster medium. They were Ernst Lubitsch and Rouben Mamoulian. With Jeanette MacDonald or Maurice Chevalier, or both, Lubitsch created a new form of specifically screen musical in *The Love Parade* (1929), *Monte Carlo* (1930), *The Smiling Lieutenant* (1931), and *One Hour with You* (1932), and Mamoulian, with the same two stars, carried it a few steps further in *Love Me Tonight* (1932).

Since *One Hour with You* is itself enshrouded in directorial confusion, with George Cukor's unacknowledged contribution still very much a bone of contention among film historians, it may seem to the lay reader a matter of splitting hairs to debate the relative merits of Lubitsch and Mamoulian within a common studio tradition of a certain period. The studio in question was Paramount, and the period the early thirties. It was a time in which relatively relaxed censorship, Maurice Chevalier's "Continental" charm and the Lubitsch tradition of witty double-entendres gave rise to a modified operetta form in which the wink took precedence over the sigh. The last hurrah for this kind of musical was Ernst Lubitsch's production of Franz Lehár's *The Merry Widow* in 1934 with Maurice Chevalier and Jeanette MacDonald, but for MGM rather than Paramount. The switch in studios is significant in that it suggests Lubitsch's loss of influence at Paramount, and a decline in the box-office fortunes of Maurice Chevalier, who was well into his forties when he appeared in *The Merry Widow*. This was his twelfth Hollywood musical out of the fourteen he made in his prime, before he left Hollywood in 1937 to return to France, not to come back again until two decades later in Billy Wilder's *Love in the Afternoon* (1957). His name had become more than somewhat tarnished in France because of his alleged collaboration with the Germans during the Occupation (he figured very prominently in Marcel Ophüls's *The Sorrow and the Pity* (1970) in an ambiguous role). A critic for *Cahiers du Cinema* described Chevalier (on the occasion of his cameo appearance in *Pepe*) in 1960 as Mr. Anti-France. This suggests that the leftist young in France had few memories of Chevalier's contributions to the musicals of the early sound era. For that matter, most Americans of recent decades are more familiar with the genial self-deprecator of *Gigi* and innumerably ironic farewell appearances on the concert stage than with the great lover of the early screen musical.

Of course, Chevalier's secure place in the history of the early sound film can be attributed to his aforementioned four films with Lubitsch—*The Love Parade* (1929), *The Smiling Lieutenant* (1931), *One Hour with*

You (1932), *The Merry Widow* (1934)—and his one with Mamoulian—*Love Me Tonight* (1934). But the public had time to get their fill of Chevalier's personality in such lesser vehicles as *Innocents of Paris* (1929), *The Big Pond* (1930), *The Playboy of Paris* (1930), *A Bedtime Story* and *The Way to Love* (1933), *Folies Bergère* (1935), and *The Beloved Vagabond* (1937), not to mention his cameo appearances in *Paramount on Parade* (1930) and *Make Me a Star* (1932). These films are not complete losses—*Folies Bergère* is actually rather slick entertainment with its mistaken identity plot subsequently reused for Don Ameche (*That Night in Rio*, 1941) and Danny Kaye (*On the Riviera*, 1951). But Chevalier's beaming Gallic countenance lacked an appropriately ironic context when Lubitsch or Mamoulian were not on the premises, and American movie-goers in the hinterlands had never been entirely comfortable with Chevalier's sexual aggressiveness. Womanizing on a large scale did not come naturally to the American types made incarnate by Al Jolson, Bing Crosby, Fred Astaire, Dick Powell, and, to Nelson Eddy, Chevalier's successor as Jeanette MacDonald's operetta partner, least of all. Only James Cagney, with his gutter sensuality, came close to Chevalier's congenital Don Juanism in the musical genre, but Cagney had already established his credibility as a conqueror in his gangster classics. Through the thirties the musical, like most other genres, was abandoning upper-class fantasies of living it up for middle-class fantasies of settling down. Chevalier could play the street-wise Frenchman well enough, as he does in *Love Me Tonight* in a turtleneck sweater and jaunty cap. A Frenchman even of the working class, however, would be hard put to seem as sincere or as steadfast as an American, even one as elegantly attired as Astaire.

Chevalier's impending downfall in Hollywood gives *The Merry Widow* an added pathos lacking in *Love Me Tonight*, made only two years before. There is, of course, much more to Franz Lehár's old warhorse of an operetta than first meets the eyes and ears. Erich von Stroheim's savage satire of the Viennese aristocracy in his 1925 version only enhanced the aura of romanticism around the two lovers played by John Gilbert and Mae Murray, two flowers, as it were, blossoming on a dung heap. Lubitsch's touch is lighter, but ever so much more mournful, and "The Merry Widow Waltz" itself resonates with intimations of mortality. Alfred Hitchcock used the waltz to great effect in *Shadow of a Doubt* (1942), and Lubitsch himself reprised it for the poignant death scene in *Heaven Can Wait* (1943). It is not surprising that Ingmar Bergman once expressed a desire to film this operetta, no doubt as the ultimate Dance of Death.

Yet film historians still differ on whether Lubitsch's and Lehár's and Chevalier's *The Merry Widow* marked the end of a tradition, or its beginning. For years one of the most influential provider of impressions of Hollywood history was *A Pictorial History of the Movies* (1949) by Deems Taylor, Bryant Hale, and Marcelene Peterson. Their somewhat demeaning caption of a two-profile shot of MacDonald and Chevalier with Herman Bing in the middle background reads as follows:

> The couple eyeing each other in apparent consternation are Jeanette MacDonald and Maurice Chevalier as they appeared in Ernst Lubitsch's production of *The Merry Widow*, made by M-G-M in 1934. The picture was so expensive that only a box-office miracle could have made it profitable. The miracle did not occur.

This would seem to indicate that *The Merry Widow* was a flop. Curiously, there is no mention in *A Pictorial History* of any of the very popular movie operettas filmed subsequently with Jeanette MacDonald and Nelson Eddy for MGM. *Naughty Marietta* (1935), adapted from Victor Herbert's 1910 classic, deserves special mention in any book professing an interest in star and genre cycles. But it is quite clear that Taylor, Hale, and Peterson were not at all enchanted either by Jeanette MacDonald or the operetta genre.

By contrast, John Russell Taylor establishes a clear link between *The Merry Widow* and *Naughty Marietta*:

> Mainly on the strength of Lubitsch's name and reputation as a maker of hit films, MGM in 1934 agreed to have another go at the despised romantic operetta with a remake of the most famous of them all, Lehar's *The Merry Widow*, starring (on balance, most surprisingly) Jeanette MacDonald and Maurice Chevalier. To everyone's amazement, it was an enormous success. Nothing loth to follow it up, MGM then looked back among the old standbys for another possible vehicle for their leading lady, and came up with Victor Herbert's *Naughty Marietta* of 1910. This time they needed a real singer for a leading man (one could hardly imagine Chevalier tackling "Ah, sweet mystery of life" or "Tramp, tramp, tramp along the highway"), and to fill the place they picked a near unknown, Nelson Eddy. Again, unexpectedly, the die was cast: another institution had been created, and for the next five years, together or separately (but best when together) they worked their way through films of just about every classic stage operetta—*Rose Marie* (1935), *Maytime* (1937), *The Firefly* (1937), *Balalaika* (1939), *The New Moon* (1940), *Bitter Sweet* (1940), *The Chocolate Soldier* (1941)—not to mention an original score by Romberg for *The Girl of the Golden West* (1938).

According to Taylor, therefore, *The Merry Widow* was a big enough hit to give new life on the screen to a musical form already outdated on the stage. But is there indeed a link between *The Merry Widow* and *Naughty Marietta* or, rather, a break? Taylor establishes an elaborate genealogy for the operetta and the musical comedy, tracing the former to the Viennese operettas of Strauss and Lehár, and the latter to the "English light or comic opera of Gilbert and Sullivan." But in purely movie terms, it is the "operetta" *The Merry Widow* which seems truly "naughty" and the other operetta *Naughty Marietta*, which seems merely nice. W. S. Van Dyke's direction of *Marietta* is not without a certain breezy charm, but there is no Lubitschean strategy to deflect the literalness of the sentiment. Hence, time and again in *The Merry Widow* the point of view shifts from the romantic leads to peripheral characters who serve as ironic commentators. George Barbier as an unexpectedly tolerant monarch and Edward Everett Horton as a dithering diplomat hover around the frames of the action as surrogates for society. The very salty vernacular in the script of Samson Raphaelson and Ernest Vajda tends to balance the almost unbearably intense yearning of the Lehar score with a certain distance and perspective. But the biggest difference between the two productions is to be found in its leading men. Maurice Chevalier, the increasingly weary and resigned man of the world, is to be supplanted by Nelson Eddy, a callow, wooden, and single-minded suitor to the increasingly coy and saccharine Jeanette MacDonald. As with the Marx Brothers, the vinegar of Paramount is sweetened with the sugar of Metro.

■   ■   ■   ■

MODERN FILM AESTHETICIANS have tended to reduce the scope of Hollywood musicals in the thirties by focusing on the alleged opposition of Busby Berkeley and Fred Astaire. In this overly theoretical analysis, Berkeley's overhead angles and mass formations were contrasted with Astaire's eye-level intimacy and integral space. Whereas Berkeley organized hordes of hoofers into pulsating images of abstract movement, Astaire executed (most often with Ginger Rogers) an intricate choreography of a kinetic courtship. In some film histories Astaire has actually been credited with supplanting Berkeley stylistically in the evolution of the screen musical. This facile Berkeley-Astaire theory of film history oversimplifies an extraordinarily complex subject. It is true that for a time Berkeley and Astaire worked with virtual autonomy in the most collaborative of all genres. Also, their most celebrated effects have been anthologized apart from the total contexts of the films in which they appeared. Yet, it is impossible to talk of Busby Berkeley without talking also of the prolific song-writing team of Harry Warren and Al Dubin, and of the Warner Brothers Guys and Dolls Depression Stock Company. Similarly, the full flavor of Astaire required not only the radiant Rogers but also the polished floors and posh sets of RKO's Van Nest Polglaise, and the pulse-quickening melodies of Jerome Kern, George Gershwin, Irving Berlin, and Cole Porter. Of all the genres, the musical is the least susceptible to discussion in terms of directorial auteurs, largely because the music itself is so much in the foreground that even the most magical mise en scène must play second fiddle.

■   ■   ■   ■

THE SCREEN PERSONA of Fred Astaire is more enduringly charismatic than that of any other musical performer in the history of the medium. Yet, the now celebrated report on his Hollywood screen test in the early thirties gave little indication of things to come: "Can't act. Slightly bald. Can dance a little." As it happened, Astaire made his movie debut in *Dancing Lady* (1933), an MGM musical romance directed by Robert Z. Leonard. Astaire plays himself, so to speak, and is introduced to Joan Crawford by Clark Gable as Mr. Astaire, presumably in recognition of a Broadway stage career that went back to 1917 in tandem with Fred's sister Adele, who had just broken up their dancing partnership to marry Lord Charles Cavendish. As a result, though Fred Astaire was born Frederick Austerlitz on May 10, 1899, in Omaha, Nebraska, his brush with the British nobility if only as an in-law gave his stage and screen image that final touch of high society gloss that was not necessarily a handicap with Depression audiences seeking escape in the sepia-tinted rotogravure society sections of their Sunday newspapers.

Astaire's duet with Joan Crawford, possessed of minimal terpsichorean talent, and chaperoned besides by Clark Gable with his superior chemistry, did not provide Astaire with a reasonable replacement for Adele. That was to happen later that year in Thornton Freeland's *Flying Down to Rio* (1933), a haphazard musical romance in which the insipidly "straight" plot is handled by the two non-musical-type leads, Gene Raymond and Dolores Del Rio (complete with the obligatory other man played by a nobly self-sacrificing Latin lover nonentity, Raul Roulien). The comedy relief and show-stopping musical numbers are performed by the seemingly impromptu dance team of Fred Astaire and Ginger Rogers, thrown together for the first time, and then melded for the rest of the decade by an accident of compatability. Hard-boiled Hollywood producers of the period were later to marvel at the chemistry of the Astaire-Rogers union. Alone, Astaire was a skinny guy with a receding hairline and by Hollywood standards with about as much sex appeal as Neville Chamberlain. Miss Rogers had been typed as a shopworn blonde out of a chorus line by way of a hosiery counter, and with more sass than class. Together, however, these two non-stellar personalities ignited, especially when they went into their dance. Fred's seductive grace in motion together with Ginger's gracious compliance in response demolished all the puritanical defenses of the Production Code. The temporary release from censor-imposed inhibitions was only symbolic, of course, but it was then and is now exhilarating just the same.

It did not happen all at once, of course. *Flying Down to Rio* (1933), graced with a felicitous Vincent Youmans score ("Flying Down to Rio," "The Carioca," "Orchids in the Moonlight," "Music Makes Me"), kept Astaire and Rogers somewhat apart as romantic partners. "The Carioca," for example, with its mildly Busby Berkleyish choreography by Hermes Pan, established an Astaire-Rogers convention of "introducing a new dance craze" in a luxurious foreign setting: Rio for "The Carioca," Brighton for Con Conrad's "The Continental" in *The Gay Divorcée* (1934), and Venice for Irving Berlin's "The Piccolino" in *Top Hat* (1935).

The outrageously lyrical "Flying Down to Rio" aerial spectacle, featuring Ginger and the other fearless showgirls flying high over Rio, their shoes strapped to the wings, and their skimpy constumes buffeted by the simulated wind currents, was marked by a sublime silliness that continues to transcend the rest of the banal scenario. But the Fred and Ginger show at this stage of its evolution can hardly be described as intimate.

With *The Gay Divorcée* in 1934, the Astaire-Rogers formulas began to fall into place. Director Mark Sandrich, who was to direct five of the Astaire-Rogers musicals, Producer Pandro S. Berman, who would produce nine, and novelist, playwright, and screenwriter Dwight Taylor began structuring the dramatic framework of the Astaire-Rogers relationship with feature-length misunderstandings, prissy or pompous suitors as foils, the girl's virginal wisecracks as a way of fending off the boy's early advances and keeping the plot pot boiling. Edward Everett Horton, Eric Blore, and Erik Rhodes brought their fey farcical talents to bear on the otherwise predictable course of the romance. Astaire, Rhodes, and Blore had performed the same roles on the Broadway stage in the Cole Porter musical *Gay Divorce*, a title that was deemed too frivolous toward marriage by the movie censors.

Porter's "Night and Day" supplied the musical inspiration for the first of the famous Astaire-Rogers seduction song-and-dance numbers. The comic pathos of Erik Rhodes's professional co-respondent lent some spice to the proceedings, and the staging of "The Continental" reprises had more than a little of Busby Berkeley extravaganza about them. At this point the Astaire-Rogers mystique was still fresh and piquant for the general public. It would attain its popular zenith in 1935 with *Roberta* and *Top Hat*.

Roberta (1935) is less well-known than the other Astaire-Rogers collaborations because of the fact that MGM purchased the rights to this RKO property for its own 1952 re-make, *Lovely To Look At*, with Red Skelton, Kathryn Grayson, Howard Keel, Ann Miller, Marge and Gower Champion, and Zsa Zsa Gabor, and then per agreement proceeded to suppress the original. The same studio policy accounts for the unavailability for decades of the classic Universal 1936 production of *Show Boat* as the result of MGM's inferior 1951 re-make. In both instances, a superior work from a smaller, weaker, poorer studio was virtually obliterated by the same larger, stronger, richer studio.

Yet, when *Roberta* finally resurfaced, it was grossly underrated because of its comparatively cluttered "book." The strongest objections were directed at the parallel romances of Irene Dunne and Randolph Scott on the sentimental track as the main love interest, and of Ginger Rogers and Fred Astaire on the sardonic track almost as an afterthought. Based on the Alice Duer Miller novel *Gowns by Roberta* and a successful Jerome Kern–Otto Harbach Broadway stage musical, the movie deals with certain foibles and conventions that are difficult even to define more than half a century later. The fashion show as theatrical and cinematic spectacle, for example, had until very recently vanished from our cultural vocabulary. Nonetheless, audiences of the time were apparently mesmerized by lavish displays of elegant clothes most viewers could only dream of wearing. For sober-sided, socially conscious film historians, the popular appeal of this upper-class ostentation was incomprehensible.

Also, whereas Astaire and Rogers both sang and danced the glorious Kern score, Dunne only sang and Scott did neither. Hence, there was a stasis to the Dunne-Scott scenes that carried over and seemed to slow down the kinesis of the Astaire-Rogers numbers. "Seemed" is the operative word here because William A. Seiter's direction was unobtrusively graceful and fluid as was typical of this unappreciated stylist of the early sound period. Still, there were many oddities in the various performances, not the least of which was Rogers's peculiar imitation of Lyda Roberti, a heavily accented sexpot of both stage and screen, now almost completely forgotten except for her spirited Mae Westian repartee with W. C. Fields and Hugh Herbert in *Million Dollar Legs* (1932). Dunne contributed her share of the European motif by way of a White Russian rendition of the poignant "Smoke Gets in Your Eyes," complete with balalaika bells. For his part, Astaire ventured into the hitherto unexplored world of dance parodies by mimicking the mannerisms of workmen-like black tap dancers.

There are undeniable *longueurs* in the mandatory scenes of misunderstanding between Dunne and Scott. But all has to be forgiven when Astaire and Rogers emerge from their masks of badinage as the Benedick and Beatrice of the dance in the rousing "I Won't Dance."

When people talk about the high points of the Astaire-Rogers collaboration, the two musicals most frequently cited are *Top Hat* and *Swing Time*, even though *Top Hat* in 1935 represented the full flowering of the Astaire-Rogers mystique with the public, whereas *Swing Time* in 1936 reflected its decline. All musical sub-genres live on borrowed time in Hollywood inasmuch as a surface realism is one of the constants of the industry's illusionist contract with its audience. From my own vantage point as a collector and a connoisseur in the nineties, my favorite Astaire-Rogers movie would be a composite: the first half of *Top Hat*—with Irving Berlin's "Top Hat, White Tie and Tails," "Isn't This a Lovely Day To Be Caught in the Rain?," and "Cheek to Cheek"—and the second of *Swing Time*—with Jerome Kern's "The Way You Look Tonight," "A Fine Romance," and "Never Gonna Dance." This is to say that *Top Hat* starts enchantingly and ends conventionally, and *Swing Time* starts lethargically and ends ecstatically.

Between the peaks of *Top Hat* and *Swing Time* there was a comparatively mediocre Astaire-Rogers movie called *Follow the Fleet* (1936), an ill-fated attempt to reduce those sophisticates of cinematic song and dance to a gum-chewing, jitterbugging, and in all ways thoroughly common couple. The comparatively "straight" romance of Irene Dunne and Randolph Scott in *Roberta* is reduced in prominence in *Follow the Fleet* with the long-forgotten Harriet Hilliard and Randolph Scott, but the double-courtship formula unwisely creates the impression that Astaire and Rogers are still considered lightweight personalities in their non-musical moments. Even so, *Follow the Fleet* does enliven its soggy, not-so-fine romances with several lively variety numbers, including one wicked Astaire parody of MGM's tap-dancing star Eleanor Powell and

her penchant for being tossed head-over-heels between two rows of soldier or sailor chorus boys.

Curiously, the final number on the program is one of the more last-
ingly resonant of all the Astaire-Rogers flights of fancy: the ineffable
"Let's Face the Music and Dance," to the words and music of Irving
Berlin, and with an evocation of the elegance and glamour so lacking in
the rest of the movie, and yet also with a fatalistic recognition of hard
times. Along with Wini Shaw's and Busby Berkeley's mini-tragic rendition of the Dubin-Warren "Lullaby of Broadway" in *The Gold Diggers of
1935*, "Let's Face the Music and Dance" are the two transcendent hymns
to the Great Depression. The gallant grace of "Let's Face the Music" in
the midst of stormy seas has been reprised in the eighties in both Herbert
Ross's *Pennies from Heaven* and Federico Fellini's *Ginger and Fred*.

Not surprisingly, most people cannot identify the movie in which
"Let's Face the Music and Dance" appears, not only because *Follow the
Fleet* is so forgettable, but also because the song and dance has nothing
to do with the characters in the movie. It is simply a show within a show,
hence, a piece of vaudeville, detached from the narrative structure of
the movie, a vaudeville, moreover, with its own disorienting mise-en-
scène. The characters are suspended in the time of performance. Nothing moves, nothing changes. Fred and Ginger mark time as dramatic
characters as the movie within the movie transcends the feeble plot line
that precedes it.

Fortunately, *Swing Time* redeems the Astaire-Rogers team as an integrated musical-narrative conception. George Stevens introduces a new
comically ambitious but only partially effective style to the storytelling.
The tedious double-takes of Edward Everett Horton are replaced by the
cannier wackiness of Victor Moore, and Eric Blore's contributions are
kept to a minimum. Helen Broderick reprises her hard-edged female
chaperone role from *Top Hat*, but her teaming with Victor Moore produces sharper and more percussive slapstick than her sado-masochistic
games with the dithering Horton in *Top Hat*.

Top Hat and *Swing Time* both have their defenders and detractors
vis-à-vis the Astaire-Rogers oeuvre as a whole. Irving Berlin's score for
Top Hat is crisper; Jerome Kern's score for *Swing Time* is sweeter. The
characters in *Top Hat* are ritzier; the characters in *Swing Time* are row-
dier. *Top Hat* is redolent of escapist luxury; *Swing Time* is not entirely
a stranger to poverty and unemployment. Astaire's white tie and tails, for
example, are both professional costume and upper-class adornment in

Top Hat, whereas the same professional costume in *Swing Time* is merely a showbiz masquerade.

The difference also can be attributed in part to the differing directorial strategies of Mark Sandrich for *Top Hat* and George Stevens for *Swing Time*. Sandrich stated in interviews that he always attempted to balance the demands of the story-line with the inevitable disruptions caused by the musical numbers. Stevens, on the other hand, directed the silly plot of trivial misunderstandings with tongue in cheek. The gales of laughter on screen, if not off, in the final sequences of *Swing Time* irritated audiences and critics at the time and have been a bone of contention for genre historians since. One would think that Stevens would be forgiven his silliness for the sublimity of the mise-en-scène for "The Way You Look Tonight" with its alternating close-ups, with Astaire at the piano and in her dressing room Rogers, shampoo suds on her hair, listening to the song, wistful eyes fixed on the camera and the audience. There is nothing of comparable romantic intensity in all the Sandrich-Astaire-Rogers collaborations.

Still, Jean Domarchi, a film critic for *Cahiers du Cinema*, declared flatly in the early sixties that the embattled auteur-theory did not apply as strongly to Astaire-Rogers musicals as it did to other genres, and that there was little to distinguish Sandrich's approach from that of Stevens. Stevens, of course, had a much longer career in many genres than Sandrich, who died in 1945, still in his forties. His period of post-Astaire-Rogers assignments as both a producer and a director was limited mostly to vehicles for radio comedian Jack Benny (*Buck Benny Rides Again* (1940), *Love Thy Neighbor* (1940)) and for Paramount troubadour and number one box-office star Bing Crosby (*Holiday Inn*, *Here Come the Waves*). Among Sandrich's last efforts were two relics of World War II emotional hysteria, the female all-star *So Proudly We Hail* in 1943, and *I Love a Soldier* in 1944, the latter seeking in vain to recapture the pathos of the doomed pairing of Paulette Goddard and Sonny Tufts in *So Proudly We Hail*.

Nonetheless, *Swing Time*, for all its glories, marked the onset of the steady decline of the Astaire-Rogers mystique with American audiences. In 1937, Stevens directed Astaire with a new partner, an ingenue-ish Joan Fontaine, who couldn't really dance, and who had to leave all the heavy hoofing to the Burns and Allen comedy team. An exquisite score by George Gershwin accompanied a modern fairy tale by P. G. Wodehouse set in what the Gershwin song calls "A Foggy Day in London

Town." Astaire's delicate, indirect manner was ill-suited to the requirements of misty romance. Nearing forty, he did not sustain in the prose passages the ageless poetry of his dancing. Again, Stevens supplied an elegant visual style, but without the emotional impact of the Astaire-Rogers pairing in *Swing Time*. Also in 1937 Rogers was more successful than Astaire in that she projected a "straight" comedy-drama persona in Gregory La Cava's *Stage Door*, and embarked on a solo stellar career which culminated in a surprise Oscar in 1940 for her portrayal of Christopher Morley's working girl in Sam Wood's *Kitty Foyle*.

Mark Sandrich once more took the directorial helm, for *Shall We Dance*, and the signs of studio desperation were everywhere. The script was a shambles of high-brow pretense, fake accents, and tedious specialty acts, most notably by Harriet Hoctor and her acrobatic balletics. Back again were the excruciatingly pause-ridden comedy routines of Edward Everett Horton and Eric Blore. Jerome Cowan supplied an urbane presence as a cynical press agent, but the obtrusive plot cut into the running time of such extraordinary Gershwin melodies as "Let's Call the Whole Thing Off," "They Can't Take That Away from Me," and "They All Laughed." In his preoccupation with the evasions and misunderstandings of his tedious story-line, Sandrich accommodated the musical numbers as an apparent afterthought.

Still, misguided as it was, *Shall We Dance* was still a musical comedy. Mark Sandrich's *Carefree* in 1938 crossed the line to become a frantic screwball comedy with a few musical numbers. The uncharacteristically skimpy Irving Berlin score, with only one truly memorable song, "Change Partners," was subordinated to antics traceable to the newfangled Viennese fad, psychoanalysis. First, Astaire hypnotizes Rogers so that she will hate him, and then when he realizes that he loves her, he spends the rest of the movie trying to hypnotize her back into loving him, with the assistance of buddy Jack Carson, and over the strenuous resistance of Ralph Bellamy, already type cast after playing Cary Grant's patsy in Leo McCarey's *The Awful Truth* (1937). *Carefree* happens to be the first Astaire-Rogers movie I ever saw. I was only nine, and I recall that the resolution of romantic conflicts by manly fisticuffs was already familiar to me from other sexless courtship movies. I can still hear the audience laughing at the "cute" spectacle of Rogers sporting a "shiner" on her eye as she marched happily down the aisle with Astaire. How much jovial wife-beating such movies encouraged I dread to think.

The Astaire-Rogers swan song for the RKO-black-and-white thirties was, fittingly enough, *The Story of Vernon and Irene Castle* (1939), a pre–

World War I period piece of the famous dance team, ending with the death of Vernon Castle. The songs were period too—no Kern, no Gershwin, no Berlin, no Porter. It was as if the war clouds in Europe and the persistence of the Great Depression combined to produce a more somber mood in Hollywood movies. Ended too was the Sandrich-Stevens dialectic. Henry C. Potter directed here in his usually stodgy manner.

By playing once-famous people, Astaire and Rogers as the Castles lost forever their Fred and Ginger cachet. They would meet on the screen once more in 1949 at MGM in color with their knowing grins reflecting a Golden Age they had once shared on the RKO sound stages in the thirties. The movie was *The Barkleys of Broadway*, directed by Charles Walters, produced by Arthur Freed, written by Betty Comden and Adolph Green, and featuring the surly pianist-savant Oscar Levant. Now it was Ginger Rogers who was in the midst of a precipitous career decline, while box-office poison Fred Astaire had been resurrected by way of a new generation of dancing partners that would take him into his sixties with Barrie Chase at full tilt with the light fantastic, albeit, finally, on television. The ultra-professional musical tradition, as represented by Walters, Freed, Comden and Green, and Levant, would continue to embrace Astaire and turn its back on Rogers. As if to underline the pathos of their reversed positions, Astaire and Rogers reprised George and Ira Gershwin's "They Can't Take That Away from Me."

There is a sexist sub-text to the contrasting fates of Astaire and Rogers. After all, she was a dozen years younger than he, and yet, even in 1949, when she was not yet forty and he was past fifty, she was regarded as too "old" to be his partner. It can be argued that Astaire was such a genius in his craft that the camera forgave him for the loss of what little sex appeal he once had. It could be argued also that the camera cruelly discerned that Rogers lacked the cheekbones of the more enduring screen beauties; that and the dangerously artificial comedy style she had indulged in the forties, and a succession of disastrous roles.

Astaire did not let dust gather on his dancing shoes after *The Story of Vernon and Irene Castle*. He entered the MGM *Broadway Melody* cycle in 1940 with the formidable Eleanor Powell as his tap-dancing partner, and George Murphy as his hoofing chum. After having taken on Paulette Goddard as a dancing partner, and her then-husband Burgess Meredith as a non-dancing buddy that same year in *Second Chorus* (1940), Astaire had one last fling with true boy-girl terpsichorean romance with Rita Hayworth in *You'll Never Get Rich* (1941), and, more seductively, in *You Were Never Lovelier* (1942). Curiously, Hayworth was an accomplished dancer, but a dubbed singer (with the unbilled Nan Wynn doing the vocals). Originally an ethnic Latina named Margarita Carmen Cansino, Hayworth was transformed by Columbia into Rita Hayworth, All-American girl, and wartime G.I.s' pin-up. Enough Argentine nationality was encoded in her full lips and lissome body to make Astaire an understandably ardent suitor. The original story of *You Were Never Lovelier*, which was Argentinian in origin, celebrates the flowery Latin American rituals of courtship. Jerome Kern and Johnny Mercer supplied three beautiful ballads, "You Were Never Lovelier," "I'm Old-Fashioned," and "Dearly Beloved." By contrast, Cole Porter's score for *You'll Never Get Rich* was sub-par except for "So Near and Yet So Far." The rest was pseudo G.I. jive, in keeping with the brink-of-war atmosphere.

A newspaper poll in the 1940s asked readers which of Astaire's dancing partners they preferred. A surprising number selected Hayworth over Rogers, though not so surprising when one considers the collective amnesia of movie audiences, and the fact that in the forties Rita's star was rising as Ginger's was falling. Two years later Hayworth would soar to stardom opposite the other pre-eminent male dancer of the Hollywood musical, Gene Kelly.

Astaire dances, after a fashion, with Joan Leslie in *The Sky's the Limit* in 1943, but the highlight of the film was his vocal rendition of Harold Arlen's "One for My Baby," a torch song written especially for Astaire, later reprised with a foghorn delivery by sultry Ida Lupino in Jean Negelescu's *Road House* (1948). Then after two second-banana appearances with Bing Crosby in the enormously popular *Holiday Inn* (1942) and *Blue Skies* (1946) and two comparatively esoteric musical ventures with Vincente Minnelli and Lucille Bremer in *The Ziegfeld Follies* (1946)— featuring also an epochal dance duet with Gene Kelly—and *Yolanda and the Thief* (1945), Astaire announced his retirement, only to be pressed back into service when Gene Kelly was forced by an ankle injury to withdraw from the co-starring role with Judy Garland in Irving Berlin's and Charles Walters's *Easter Parade*, with the brash Ann Miller in whiz-bang dancing support. After the success of *Easter Parade*, Astaire's retirement was postponed for another decade and a half.

■ ■ ■ ■

IF ONE COULD reasonably stipulate that the three defining talents of Hollywood musicals in the thirties and forties were Fred Astaire, Busby Berkeley, and Arthur Freed, none of whom was primarily, if at all, a director, one would have to conclude that the movie musical fell outside the purview of directorial auteurism. Indeed, one might even see the studio as auteur: RKO (for Astaire), MGM (for Freed), and Warners (for Berkeley). This would presumably leave Paramount (at least after Lubitsch and Mamoulian), Fox, Universal, and Columbia out in the cold as far as musicals were concerned. Yet, Fox had come up with a *Sunny Side Up* (1929) and a *State Fair* (1945), Universal a *Show Boat* and *100 Men and a Girl* (both 1936), and Columbia with a *Cover Girl* (1944). Still, there was no theme, pattern, or ideology to these isolated delights to compare with the romantic individualism exemplified by Astaire, the Broadway sophistication nurtured by Freed, and the mass formation energy exemplified by Berkeley.

Nonetheless, the varying financial resources and theatrical outlets of the various studios had more than a little to do with the ebb and flow of the genre. There is no mystery why, for example the supposedly old-fashioned operettas of Jeanette MacDonald and Nelson Eddy for MGM outgrossed and outlasted the more urbane vehicles of Fred Astaire and Ginger Rogers for RKO. Then there were the uncertainties of shifting foreign markets in turbulent times. It is easy to understand why the war years were the most profitable for movie musicals with a distinctively Latin American beat, and that after the war the resistance of the restored European market to English-language musicals caused a loss of faith in the genre that more than any other had enabled American wartime audiences to escape the grim events overseas. Long before the war and its aftermath, however, the coming of sound, which gave birth to the movie musical, also reduced the universality of movies by presenting language barriers both in spoken dialogue and in sung lyrics.

■　　■　　■　　■

BUSBY BERKELEY WAS BORN William Berkeley Enos in Los Angeles on November 29, 1895, and died in 1976 in the midst of a revival of interest in "Busby Berkeley" musicals. His nickname came from Amy Busby, a turn-of-the-century theatrical luminary. His father was a stage director, and his mother an actress on stage and screen. When he was three, his family moved to New York, where he was in time to begin his career as a choreographer of Broadway musicals.

By the late twenties Berkeley was highly regarded in his field with twenty-one musicals to his credit, including *A Connecticut Yankee, Rainbow*, and *Sweet and Low*. Samuel Goldwyn brought him to Hollywood in 1930 to choreograph several movie musicals starring Eddie Cantor and the newly minted Goldwyn Girls. He also choreographed Mary Pickford's first and last musical, *Kiki* (1931). Seen today, Berkeley's early work in musicals is barely distinguishable from the stagebound and un-cinematic conventions of the All Talking! All Singing! All Dancing! stam-pede of 1929 and 1930, a brief period in which Broadway musicals and revues from the turn of the century through the twenties were tran-scribed with a stationary camera and fake stage scenery in the back-ground. The camera was parked front row center from the point of view of a theatergoer without opera glasses. Today these almost forgotten mu-sicals are esteemed primarily for their documentation of the live musical theater of the first three decades of the twentieth century.

In any event, before 1933 Busby Berkeley was not yet a name that conjured up a distinctive form of spectacle in Hollywood musicals. Al-though Berkeley's choreographic and directorial contributions were to span more than three decades, his lasting influence was exerted mainly through a series of Warners backstage musicals. At their best, Berkeley's transformations of chorus lines into moving abstractions possessed a giddy, vertiginous, disorienting charm. If his musical numbers were larger than life and the "legitimate" theater, it was because he found Hollywood studio sets could be less constricting than the Broadway boards. Berke-ley's vitality and ingenuity transcended the limitations of his scenarios, and he bequeathed to posterity an entertaining expression of an escap-ist era.

A choreographer from the crane, Berkeley scrawled a kind of sky-writing signature from the sound stages of *42nd Street* (1933) to the circus grounds of *Jumbo* (1962). As a moderately entertaining director, he held the fort for the musical between the end of the Astaire-Rogers cycle and the beginning of the Freed-Minnelli-Donen-Kelly-Garland pe-riod. Indeed, he was entitled to some of the credit for the spectacular evolution of Gene Kelly and Judy Garland into the titans of the MGM musical. If some of his socialized floral patterns have struck later com-mentators as quaint and naive, these massive valentines did have their time and place in the depth of the Depression when what they offered was very important. Berkeley deserves enduring respect as the Magical Méliès of the Movie Musical. French revisionist critics of the fifties and sixties did not go too far when likening the proletarian female energy of the Berkeley spectacles to the ideologically driven mass formations and cinematic coups of Leni Riefenstahl in *Triumph of the Will* (1934) and Sergei Eisenstein in *Alexander Nevsky* (1938).

My most poignant recollection of Berkeleyana is "The Lullaby of

Broadway" number, sung and acted by Wini Shaw in *Gold Diggers of 1935* (1935), when I was seven years old. For years and years I retained the image of a playgirl plunging to her death from a skyscraper ballroom, and then the lingering contemplation of an empty apartment with a hungry kitten waiting to be fed and outside somewhere a chorus singing "Good night, baby," as if perchance to die was but to dream of a lullaby as a requiem mass. *Gold Diggers of 1935* revisited in the 1990s turned out to be a long prologue, by turns cynical and fatuous, with a cast of reflex-action performers—Dick Powell, Adolphe Menjou, Gloria Stuart, Alice Brady, Glenda Farrell, and Frank McHugh—in a formulaic frenzy. I had almost begun to doubt my moviegoing memory when suddenly the playgirl plunged to her death and the traveling camera lingered over an empty apartment, and the lullaby engulfed the screen once more as it had once long ago in the darkest days of the Depression. The magic of Busby Berkeley had been movingly reconfirmed in a kind of Proustian miracle that is almost commonplace with remembered and recaptured movies.

The peculiar plot structure of *42nd Street*, a re-make of *On with the Show* (1929), threw all the famous, frequently excerpted Berkeley spectacle numbers to the end of the movie when the show is finally put on Broadway after many travails. The over-all mood is somber as an ailing producer played by Warner Baxter gambles on what may be his last chance to avoid bankruptcy. His expressions throughout range from rueful and cynical on the up side to angry and despondent on the down. His desperation achieves an absurd climax in his famous and often parodied (most notably in David Merrick's stage musical version of the film) exhortation to the nervous understudy played by Ruby Keeler, as "Sawyer," to go out there an understudy and come back a star. Why? Because everyone connected with the production needs a hit to survive in the Great Depression. The producer himself had been wiped out in the 1929 stock market crash. Everything is riding on the small shoulders and dancing feet of Ruby Keeler, the star-struck ingenue to end all star-struck ingenues. She is replacing an older star played by Bebe Daniels, who is philosophically resigned enough over her disabling ankle injury to give the newcomer some helpful dressing-room advice along with her blessing. After all, she is rejoining her first love (George Brent), a vaudeville partner who never made it to the big time as she had, and has always been willing to stay in the background so that her career could flourish. The scenes between Daniels and Brent are the only love scenes played with any degree of emotional seriousness. By contrast, Ruby Keeler and Dick Powell cavort as callow and dimpled innocents drawn together more by kittenish affection than grown-up desire.

Director Lloyd Bacon, scenarists Rian James, James Seymour, and Bradford Ropes have thus concocted more a drama with music than a musical drama. Mark Sandrich, the director of several Astaire-Rogers vehicles, prefered to space the musical numbers through the light plot so that there was a balance between plot and vaudeville. Bebe Daniels repeatedly performs the same song, "You're Getting To Be a Habit with Me," and the mournful melody serves also as background music for her dramatic scenes with George Brent. Their love triumphs in the end through a convenient misadventure, a star is born, and all should be well, except that the last shot of the film shows Baxter sitting on the steps of an outside staircase to the stage door ruefully savoring the comments of exiting first-nighters about how lucky he is to have great talent at his disposal.

This Warners street-wise fatalism runs through all the salty exchanges between chorus girls and the predatory males who seek to exploit their bodies as they "advance" their careers. This is pre-Code, post-Crash grittiness, and there is even a bit of the gangster genre on display when Baxter hires pool-room tough guys to scare off Brent from his show-threatening attentions to Daniels. In this characteristically low-down though soft-hearted environment, the gangsters and the show people share a common environment. One unintentional irony: Ginger Rogers plays a chorus girl supposedly perceptive enough and unselfish enough to refuse the star role because she can't "carry" the show, and then to recommend Ruby Keeler as the one chorus girl who can. And at the time no one laughed at Hollywood's myopia in appreciating new talent. A few years before Howard Hughes had turned down the then relatively obscure Clark Gable and James Cagney for the parts in *The Front Page* eventually played by Adolphe Menjou and Pat O'Brien.

■   ■   ■   ■

THE 1986 OBITUARIES for Vincente Minnelli were divided on the issue of his age—seventy-six according to Eric Pace in the *New York Times* versus eighty-three in Harry Haun's account in the *Daily News*. Ephraim Katz's *Film Encyclopedia* lists Minnelli's year of birth as 1910, as does my own entry for the director in *The American Cinema*. More recent sources, however, tend to agree on 1903 as the correct year, and there is a tendency to believe that people in general, and showbiz celebrities in particular, choose to err in these matters more on the side of youth than maturity.

As Oscar-winning director of some of the most famous Hollywood musicals of the forties and fifties, Minnelli himself would seem to have deserved the attention he received on the occasion of his demise. Nonetheless, there was just a touch of celebrity *frisson* to the name Minnelli attached to a onetime wife Judy Garland (1945–51) and their daughter Liza—shown in a tabloid funeral photograph by accompanied pop celebrity Michael Jackson. I mention this bit of trivia only to make the point that Minnelli's critical reputation itself may have suffered over the years because of the very glitter of his most impressive achievements.

Mea culpa, and all that. I, too, may have contributed to the underestimation of Minnelli as a force in film. For starters, Eric Pace's obituary in the *Times* quotes the last sentence of my entry on Minnelli in *The American Cinema*: "Minnelli believes more in beauty than in art." The late James Agee expressed a similar reservation when writing of Minnelli's *The Clock* in *The Nation* of April 29, 1945:

> By what I can see in the film, and have heard, Minnelli does not discriminate very clearly between the good in his work and the not so good or the downright bad, which in part he puts into it and which in part is forced on him. Much as I regret that, it may on the whole be just as well. If he knew better, he might be either much more of an artist or much less of one; in either case he would have a much harder time working in Hollywood. I suspect I may overrate the best of his films, but I also suspect that, twenty and fifty years from now, however embarrassing a lot of it is, it will be remembered.

We have finally passed the fifty-year mark to which Agee addressed himself, and Minnelli's best work is not merely remembered but treasured. And what is his best work? Instead of rattling off a list of titles, both musical and non-musical, I would prefer to reconsider a few sequences here and there that make it possible for me to entertain a more complex view of Minnelli than I have expressed in the past.

Minnelli was an MGM contract director for twenty-six years, and he was recognized as one of the prime contributors to the so-called Golden Age of the MGM musical. What is not generally realized as well was that MGM was a declining studio in 1940 when Producer Arthur Freed recruited Minnelli for his musical unit. Declining artistically, that is. Box-office grosses were soaring mainly because during wartime there was little else for people to spend their money on, but other studios were

making more interesting pictures in more interesting genres, and with
generally more interesting stars. MGM's only monopoly was the musical,
and it reigned supreme. Still, if you take Minnelli's musicals in this
period—*Cabin in the Sky, Meet Me in St. Louis, Yolanda and the Thief,*
and *The Pirate,* all in the forties—the faces that flash to mind are those
of Ethel Waters, Lena Horne, Judy Garland, Margaret O'Brien, Lucille
Bremer, Fred Astaire, Gene Kelly. But with L. B. Mayer's Graustarkian
taste in this area, the faces could just as well have been those of Jeanette
MacDonald, Nelson Eddy, Lauritz Melchoir, Kathryn Grayson, José
Iturbi, Esther Williams, and who knows who else in the semi-classical
vein.

At this point I must register disagreement with Agee's critique of
Minnelli's direction of the memorable scene in *Meet Me in St. Louis* in
which a tearful Margaret O'Brien runs down the stairs to destroy her
snowmen after Judy Garland's stirring rendition of "Have Yourself a
Merry Little Christmas." Agee complained that Minnelli didn't get close
enough to the action with his camera, that the snow didn't look real and
didn't come apart fast enough, etc. I recently screened *Meet Me in St.
Louis* for my class, and I found Minnelli's direction of the scene to be
just right, and the distance he maintains to be necessary to keep the
childhood hysteria in some sort of adult perspective, a thing seldom done
nowadays. But the key to the success of that scene, aside from O'Brien's
extraordinary talent, is Minnelli's seriousness and intensity in the staging
and the sustained camera movement.

If Minnelli could lend genuine emotion and conviction to the most
fantastical conceits, so could he lend color and gaiety to the grimmest
subjects. When I saw *Two Weeks in Another Town* in 1961 in Paris,
Minnelli was even then being dismissed in Hollywood as a has-been.
This fate was foreshadowed in his stylized self-portrait in *The Band
Wagon* (1953), his finest musical, as Fred Astaire sang "(I'll Go My Way)
By Myself" while an unheeding world passed him by and a sympathetic
mise-en-scène lyricized his loneliness. Even back in *Yolanda and the
Thief,* a work as under-rated as *The Pirate* is over-rated, Astaire danced
as a kind of Minnellian alter ego, a con-man maneuvering with his mise-
en-scène to swindle a susceptible heiress (Hollywood?).

Despondent self-deprecation came easily to Minnelli, who has been
quoted as saying in his autobiography *I Remember It Well*: "I work to
please myself. I'm still not sure if movies are an art form. And if they're
not, then let them inscribe on my tombstone what they could about any

craftsman who loves his job: 'Here lies Vincente Minnelli. He died of hard work.' "

That may be why there is a bittersweet aftertaste in what are supposed to be his most joyous successes, the Oscar-winning *An American in Paris* (1951) and *Gigi* (1958). I say "supposed to be" because as it happens I am not excessively fond of either work. Their purported charm strikes me as calculating in the extreme. I feel more genuine stylistic release in the concluding carnival sequence in *Some Came Running* (1959) and the unabashedly awkwardly staged telephone reconciliation in *The Bad and the Beautiful* (1952). In this context, Kirk Douglas and Fred Astaire served the somber/elfin functions for Minnelli that William Holden and Jack Lemmon performed for the tragic and comic sides of Billy Wilder.

When it comes to posterity, a director whose claim to fame is the musical genre is doubly handicapped, first because musicals are inescapably more collaborative than other genres, and second because most intellectuals do not take musicals seriously enough to talk about them intelligently.

Pace's aforementioned obituary of Minnelli quoted Judy Garland just before her marriage to Minnelli thusly, "Vincente is such a wonderful director, but he gets excited and stutters and doesn't finish his sentences—just says, 'Well, you know what I mean.' "

A more rounded view of Minnelli's modus operandi was provided by Agee in *Time* in May 1945:

> Much of the time, in his slow, expensive efforts at perfection, Minnelli drives writers, producers, actors, and technicians quietly out of their habit-hardened professional minds. But he does it so gently, and always for such excellent reasons, that they end up, as his producer Arthur Freed says, by "loving him." Says his cutter, George White, "He may drive you crazy but he gets what he's after. For a guy who has that much on the ball, I'll string along."

I met Minnelli only once, at a party in the late sixties, and we merely exchanged friendly pleasantries, but I could sense even on such a brief acquaintance the shyness, sensitivity, and steely elegance of the man. All movie directors are tyrants of of one kind or another. Some are all bluster and charge, but others dominate by reticence, vagueness, and often, outright withdrawal.

What must be emphasized finally about Minnelli was that his art was not merely decorative, any more than Sternberg's was. Something had to click for so many of Minnelli's pictures to generate compelling entertainment. The felicities of his style have been ignored for the sake of facile jokes about an obtrusively red couch here and a stereotyped Parisian "atmosphere" beret there. After all, his detractors quipped, hadn't Minnelli once been stage-show director of the Radio City Music Hall? (The "legitimate" Broadway musicals he directed were conveniently overlooked.)

Yet his stylistic signature was inscribed on all the small-talk party scenes that the director infused with volcanic energy and creative life, from the welcome New York bar-room clatter that enlivened an otherwise botched studio-bound adaptation of *Brigadoon* to Gil Lamb's acrobatic omni-presence in Judy Holliday's name-dropping extravaganza in *Bells Are Ringing*. Minnelli made his share of clinkers, too, but if I may be so bold, the best things he did, and they are many and varied, will be providing pleasure at least fifty years from now. At least.

■　■　■　■

GENE KELLY and Judy Garland appeared together for the first time in Busby Berkeley's *For Me and My Gal* (1942), a once and only union of three beacons of the Hollywood musical. Though Kelly and Garland co-starred only twice more—Vincente Minnelli's *The Pirate* (1948) and Charles Walter's *Summer Stock* (1950)—apart from separate cameo appearances in Minnelli's *Ziegfeld Follies* (1946) and Norman Taurog's *Words and Music* (1948), they represent the forties in much the way, though not the manner, Fred Astaire and Ginger Rogers represent the thirties. Whereas Kelly and Garland exuded wartime and postwar emotion and energy, Astaire and Rogers expressed Depression-era elegance and escapism. Kelly (1912–96) was ten years older than Garland (1922–69), but she burned out well before he and his métier faded. Both performers were working on borrowed time in 1942, but not for the same reasons.

In a sense, Gene Kelly was penalized vis-à-vis Fred Astaire because Kelly's presumed versatility as a dramatic actor never panned out with either the critics or the public. From his big Broadway break in the Rodgers and Hart *Pal Joey*, Kelly could and did play heels, something the more affable Astaire wouldn't be caught dead doing. Of course, there is a price to pay for showing one's darker side. Through the forties Kelly appeared in three non-musical roles in *Pilot No. 5* and *The Cross of Lorraine* (both 1943) and *Christmas Holiday* (1944). Aside from lending him dramatic credentials for his musicals, none of the three "straight" performances enhanced his reputation sufficiently to make him eligible for "serious" parts, which were assigned at MGM as a matter of course to Clark Gable, Spencer Tracy, Robert Taylor, Robert Walker, and even Van Johnson, a former Broadway chorus boy.

Robert Siodmak's *Christmas Holiday* (1944) was a haunting *film noir* with a grown-up Deanna Durbin as Kelly's co-star. Back in 1936 and through the thirties a teen-age Durbin had saved debt-ridden Universal with a series of semi-classical musicals, most notably Henry Koster's *Three Smart Girls* (1936) and *100 Men and a Girl* (1937). Universal later groomed Gloria Jean as Durbin's "successor" as soprano savior with Richard Wallace's *The Under-Pup* in 1939, but despite her charms Jean failed in the forties to repeat Durbin's success of the thirties.

Before Durbin's big breakthrough in 1936, she had appeared with Garland in *Every Sunday*, a famous double-audition short. Rumor has it that L. B. Mayer, in his heart of hearts, wanted Durbin but allowed his advisers to overrule him with Garland, after which Durbin was snapped up by Universal. The Durbin/Garland competition took many forms in Hollywood musicals of the thirties and forties, from the extremes of grand opera to hot jazz, from the concert stage to Tin Pan Alley, and sometimes in the same movie.

Ironically for Kelly, Durbin provided the only musical interludes in *Christmas Holiday* with her torchy soprano, while Kelly acted his non-musical heart out in a poignant but hardly star-making part of a weak mama's boy turned murderer. No matter. Kelly's dancing feet were already propelling him into orbit as the Astaire of the forties and fifties, first in marginally romantic roles in Roy Del Ruth's *Du Barry Was a Lady* (1943) and George Sidney's *Thousands Cheer* (1943). Both musicals were thinly disguised MGM variety shows for higher-billed Red Skelton and Lucille Ball in *Du Barry* (with Virginia O'Brien, Rags Ragland, and Zero Mostel in subordinate specialty parts) and for almost the entire MGM musical roster in *Thousands Cheer*—Mickey Rooney, Judy Garland, Red Skelton, Ann Sothern, Lucille Ball, Virginia O'Brien, and Lena Horne around an army-base courtship of Kathryn Grayson (on her way to becoming L. B. Mayer's reigning soprano after the fading Jeanette MacDonald). Kelly, as a scrappy army private, stopped the show with a dancing routine based on using a mop.

Kelly's star brightened perceptibly, as had previously been the case for MGM stars Clark Gable and James Stewart, on "loan-out" from MGM to Harry Cohn's Columbia Pictures for a co-starring musical role with Rita Hayworth in the lush and colorful *Cover Girl* (1944). As mentioned before, Hayworth had already danced with Fred Astaire in Sidney Lanfield's *You'll Never Get Rich* (1941) and more memorably in William A. Seiter's *You Were Never Lovelier* (1942). Hayworth had also attracted attention in secondary roles in Howard Hawks's *Only Angels Have Wings* (1939), Ben Hecht's and Lee Garmes's *Angels Over Broadway* (1940), and Rouben Mamoulian's *Blood and Sand* (1941). With *Cover Girl*, however, Hayworth became not only a major sex symbol on screen but America's premier pin-up of World War II.

For his part, Kelly found the best and most prestigious showcase of his movie career up to then for displaying the full range of his musical and behavioral talents from the sweet sentiment of his singing and dancing scenes with Hayworth to the rowdy hoofing duets with Phil Silvers. As had Astaire, Kelly projected in his solo numbers an incomparable virtuosity but also a chilling solitude. The celebrated and self-choreographed "Me and My Shadow" dual identity dance soliloquy also suggested a darker side to Kelly than was ever evident in the sunnier Astaire. On balance, Kelly's persona at best was more complex than Astaire's; at worst it was more pretentious.

George Sidney's *Anchors Aweigh* (1945) at Metro was Kelly's breakthrough film to full stardom. The full resources of the Arthur Freed unit at the studio were utilized to provide mid-forties audiences with the most varied musical menu a color film extravaganza had concocted up to that time. Kelly even danced with Jerry the Mouse, the co-star of the popular "Tom and Jerry" cartoon series at MGM. Tom the cat appeared in the live action/cartoon duet as King Jerry's obsequious butler. Audiences "got" the joke then as they were less likely to do in later decades when the MGM mystique had disintegrated with the decline and fall of the studio system.

Frank Sinatra, then an enormously popular crooner with screaming claques of bobby-soxers in tow, was billed above Kelly in a bizarre anti-type-casting role as a shy, virginal sailor tagging along after his shipboard buddy (Kelly) to discover the secret of making out with "dames." Sinatra, later a living legend as much for his womanizing as for his singing, is one of the allegedly outdated elements in the movie that accounts for its being less highly rated by later film historians. At the time, *Anchors Aweigh* was so much in tune with the *Zeitgeist* that Kelly was nominated for his only Oscar for acting as a result of his having "stolen" the film from Sinatra. Yet, *Anchors Aweigh* emerges in the 1990s as an accomplished assemblage of endearing and enduring musical interludes. Sinatra's singing of the Jule Styne–Sammy Cahn "I Fall in Love Too Easily" resonates with more mythic force in the nineties than it did in the forties, and Kelly's remarkable charm in talking, singing, and dancing with children was demonstrated for the first time.

Hollywood's wartime salute to the profitable Latin American market so obvious in the zooming careers of Carmen Miranda and Xavier Cugat in other musicals was expressed in *Anchors Aweigh* more subtly by the Hispanic slant of two of Kelly's dances, one with a little sad-eyed Mexican girl, and the other in a Zorro-like roof-leaping dance serenade to Senorita Grayson on a romantic balcony, a possibly athletic forerunner to George Sidney's *The Three Musketeers* in 1948, in which Kelly's D'Artagnan transformed the old Dumas chestnut into a tongue-in-cheek choreographed romp. Yet, with the end of World War II the clock was ticking for the Hollywood musical. The lost European and Asian markets were coming on line, and musicals did not "travel" as well as other Hollywood genres.

After performing a cameo duet in the plotless *Ziegfeld Follies* with his old idol Fred Astaire in 1946, Kelly suffered the first serious setback in his career in Gregory La Cava's *Living in a Big Way* (1947) with co-star Marie ("The Body") McDonald, one of the most soporifically bland blondes in Hollywood captivity ever. The movie is not as bad as its flop reputation suggests, and there is one strikingly generous Kelly gesture in a routine in which he befriends a group of little girls driven away by little boys from *their* games. Kelly improvises a series of dances incorporating all the games little girls like to play in another demonstration of his wonderful way with children.

Kelly rebounded quickly in 1948 with Vincente Minnelli's frolicsome *The Pirate*, a musical adaptation of a slyly sexy Lunt and Fontanne stage vehicle. That same year Kelly had been replaced by Astaire in Charles Walters's *Easter Parade* with Judy Garland and a bellwether Irving Berlin score. The reason: an ankle injury to Kelly. Kelly and Garland, like Astaire and Garland, were a bit like Kelly and Sinatra, and Astaire and Bing Crosby, as odd couple pairings of dancers who could sing a little, and singers who could dance a little, the basis of limited rapport between them.

Kelly found more of a dancing equal of the opposite sex in the blonde, pixie-ish Vera-Ellen in the all-star Rodgers-and Hart biopic extravaganza *Words and Music*. Kelly and Vera-Ellen performed Rodgers's pop ballet *Slaughter on Tenth Avenue* with a purity and sophistication that could pass muster with any ballet company in the world. Vera-Ellen had come to Hollywood after dancing in a revival of the Rodgers and Hart *A Con-*

necticut Yankee on the Broadway stage. She prompted the often churlish theater critic George Jean Nathan to remark in print that she could come dance on his typewriter anytime. She was an immediate specialty hit in two Danny Kaye vehicles for Samuel Goldwyn: H. Bruce Humberstone's *Wonder Man* (1945) and Norman Z. McLeod's *The Kid from Brooklyn* (1946), in both films playing second female lead to ex-Goldwyn Girl Virginia Mayo, but dancing up a storm nonetheless. That same year she was cast as the least of the three sisters in search of rich husbands, with June Haver and Vivian Blaine in *Three Little Girls in Blue* (1946). This much-made and re-made plot line served merely to spotlight Vera-Ellen's special talent. Her perky stage singing voice was considered too juvenile for Hollywood, and so her singing from the outset was dubbed, as was Rita Hayworth's.

Kelly's star was in the ascendant in 1949, as Frank Sinatra's was slowly declining, first in Busby Berkeley's comparatively conventional *Take Me Out to the Ballgame*, which Kelly co-wrote and co-choreographed. Sinatra was still top-billed, and swimming star Esther Williams was second-billed as the owner of the fabulous multi-ethnic double-play team of O'Brien (Kelly) to Ryan (Sinatra) to Goldberg (Jules Munshin). Yet third-billed Kelly was universally recognized as the prime mover and shaker of the MGM musical.

Kelly's status was officially established with *On the Town*, in which he shared directing duties with Stanley Donen and finally achieved top billing over Sinatra. Kelly, Sinatra, and Munshin now played three sailors who team up with Vera-Ellen, Betty Garrett, and Ann Miller in a brassy New Yorkish version of the Betty Comden/Adolph Green/Leonard Bernstein musical derived from Jerome Robbins's ballet *Fancy Free*. Unlike *Anchors Aweigh*, which took place in Los Angeles with a Hollywood studio as its backdrop, *On the Town* was all New York and was actually shot at its landmarks, with its main love interest centered on the contest search for a Miss Subways. In four years Kelly had departed from the warm sentiment of *Anchors Aweigh* to embrace the cool satire of *On the Town*, but the mass audience was less in tune with this new sophistication than were the delighted cognoscenti. For all its cleverness, *On the Town* marked the beginning of a commercial crisis in the genre despite the raves from the critics.

As seen from the vantage point of the nineties, *On the Town* teeters and totters between the hard-edged sassiness of Broadway and the soft-centered silliness of Hollywood. The ensemble dancing is more obtrusive and exhibitionist than it was in Berkeley's heyday with the *Gold Diggers* thirties musicals. Kelly himself embodied the cultural aspirations of movie dancing, an audacious approach that represented the integration of book, song, dance, and theme that had been established by *Oklahoma!* in the Broadway musical. It was far removed from the familiar Hollywood musical conventions still dominant in the Bing Crosby–Bob Hope–Dorothy Lamour–Betty Hutton hegemony at Paramount, and the bubbling blonde musicals of Alice Faye, Betty Grable, and June Haver at Fox.

High or low, however, the musical genre was running out of steam in the late forties as its icons aged, and there were no truly stellar replacements. There was one final burst of brilliance for the Freed unit in the fifties, and that's about all.

■ ■ ■ ■

JUDY GARLAND literally grew into stardom through her teens, which was also a time when studio pressures and the fallout from her traumatically stressed childhood combined to make her one of the earliest cautionary figures of Hollywood horror folklore. The slavish trade press of the period was so completely controlled by the major studio publicity departments that few scandals of substance abuse ever saw the light of day until long after the funeral orations were decorously delivered. With Garland, however, her victimized life found a context in the artfulness of her poignantly throbbing singing voice, particularly with her much repeated, universally enjoyed rendition of Harold Arlen's "Over the Rainbow" in the eternally revived and remembered *The Wizard of Oz* (1939).

The Wizard of Oz is the closest thing we have on film to an official national fairy tale. There is a catastrophe, a trip, and a razzle-dazzle affirmation of the obvious, all handled a bit heavily and stagily by the old hands of the MGM machine. But there is also a major upheaval in the musical numbers as the film launched Arthur Freed's musical unit at MGM, a catalytic force that was eminently trustworthy of the great score and lyrics by Harold Arlen and E. Y. Harburg. Pre-eminent in this coup were confident if self-conscious performances by Ray Bolger's Scarecrow, Bert Lahr's Cowardly Lion, and Jack Haley's Tin Man—as prestigious a trio of vaudevillians as was ever assembled for a matinee divertissement.

In the nineties it is still not generally known that *The Wizard of Oz* was a troubled production from the word go, and, more amazingly, a commercial failure in its theatrical release. Only endless replays of the classic on television have made it seem like a blockbuster. It was very much the same story with Frank Capra's 1946 flop *It's a Wonderful Life.*

During the production of *Oz*, Jack Haley had to replace Buddy Ebsen as the Tin Man because of a make-up mishap, and any number of MGM directors came and went on the project, with all agreeing to let Victor Fleming receive sole directorial credit. In a nineties television documentary it was revealed for the first time that George Cukor, no less, was responsible for the change of Garland's Dorothy dress and make-up from that of showbiz savvy nymphet to that of an innocent little farm girl from Kansas.

It is intriguing to note that in the year of *Gone With the Wind* (which served as a feeder source of exchanged directors like King Vidor and George Cukor and Technicolor consultants) *The Wizard of Oz* was not overwhelmingly embraced by the public. The film became an official classic thanks to television, which was never used to better effect as a medium to revive a special movie, especially since television better suits the film's strained stylization. TV made *Oz* a crucial pioneer movie in the shaping of an American film memory.

Ironically, the "Over the Rainbow" number was almost cut out of the movie because it "slowed down" the story, and it is this one song that to this day is the sort of national anthem of the world's gay population. Not that that process was begun as early as the thirties. For a time everything was coming up roses for Garland with both straight and gay audiences swimming together in the movie mainstream.

Garland was on "loan out" to Fox almost immediately after being signed by MGM. Her first feature was a pleasant college football musical with the self-defining title *Pigskin Parade* (1936). The amiably non-star casting teamed Garland with dour Stuart Erwin, raucous farceuse Patsy Kelly, Garland's eventual Tin Man, Jack Haley, never-to-make-it-big dancer Johnny Downs, and up-and-coming Betty Grable. Garland was not exactly the first among equals in this company, but only she and Grable were ever to see their names in lights.

Garland returned to MGM for two significant steps up. Roy Del Ruth's *Broadway Melody of 1938* (1937), in which she captured Hollywood's attention with her singing fan letter, "Dear Mr. Gable," to the wailing strains of "You Made Me Love You." Here again was the little girl with the disconcertingly huge voice transforming a teen-age crush into a cafe singer's grand passion. Then came the first of her nine appearances with Mickey Rooney, in Alfred E. Green's *Thoroughbreds Don't Cry* (1939), a routine racetrack programmer that provided little indication of the box-office heights the two co-leads would shortly scale both separately and together.

The diminutive Rooney, however, had less of a problem growing up on the screen in the cinematically and psychologically awkward years of adolescence than did the ballooning Garland, for whom diet pills were prescribed early on in her career. Yet she was still playing little girls at sixteen and seventeen in Edwin Marin's mediocre *Everybody Sing* (1938), George B. Seitz's *Love Finds Andy Hardy* (1938), and Edwin Marin's *Listen, Darling* (1938). Still, even in these marginal roles, a pattern was emerging in the treatment of Garland vis-à-vis more conventionally pretty girls, particularly in the hugely popular Andy Hardy series. In real life, one would think that Garland could do better than Rooney in terms of high-school dates. Yet, Rooney was the one whose eye was always straying from Garland's girl next door to such cuties as Lana Turner in *Love Finds Andy Hardy* and June Preisser in Busby Berkeley's *Babes in Arms* (1939) and *Strike Up the Band* (1940). Garland was eventually cast as the Girl in her major productions, but there was always the lingering suggestion that she was not the Guy's automatic first choice, even though she was nice and sincere and interesting, and, usually, was the possessor of an enormous musical talent. She was almost never cast with the most charismatic male leads available in her non-musicals, and even with Kelly and Astaire she was upstaged by an Ann Miller here and a bevy of beauties there.

Gradually Garland revealed a sophisticated comedy style that seemed to send up the hackneyed characters she was asked to play. This gift for irony began to surface in Norman Taurog's *Presenting Lily Mars* (1943), when she battled Broadway soprano star Martha Eggert for the affections of older man and mentor Van Heflin. At one juncture in the plot Garland performs a wicked parody of Eggert's diva musical mannerisms. Toward the end of her life, on her ill-fated television show, Garland offended many elderly admirers of Jeanette MacDonald by seeming to savage MacDonald's rendition of "San Francisco." At the solemn MGM studio, however, the opportunities for irreverent satire were few and far between.

Instead, Garland's wit and irony were as tightly regulated as her burgeoning body. Another brand of hyper-sophisticated chic in her persona was unveiled in Busby Berkeley's *Girl Crazy* (1943), with a glorious George Gershwin score. In forties terms this was one of the strangest musicals ever made in Hollywood. Ostensibly a vehicle for Mickey Rooney, the oddities begin with newcomer June Allyson's screeching a wild take-off of Betty Hutton, then a rising star at Paramount. Playboy Rooney is then trundled off by his parents to an all-male mining college in the West. There the president's daughter played by Garland presides over a

community of Broadway chorus boys playing mining students, but spend-
ing most of their time as a singing and dancing chorus for Garland's hip
and hot renditions of such Gershwin standards as "Embraceable You"
and "Bidin' My Time." At one point, Garland's white-jacketed dancing
partner is Charles Walters, who was to become one of MGM's most
proficient directors of musicals in the forties and fifties. Despite all of
Rooney's mugging as a girl-crazy lunatic, the dominant image is that of
Garland's ease and comfort with a screen full of young, handsome, worshipful males.

Garland's career reached its crest with Vincente Minnelli's *Meet Me
in St. Louis* (1944), in which all of Garland's many gifts coalesced for
the first time in a totally satisfying entertainment that deserved to become a more beloved classic than the much over-rated and over-
gimmicked *The Wizard of Oz*, but somehow didn't. Garland is both sweet
and sly, sincere and ironic, lyrical and lucid. She survives a series of
virtuoso scene-stealing maneuvers by the emotionally titanic tot Margaret
O'Brien. Garland manages to hold her own in the memorable cakewalk
"Under the Bamboo Tree" and the overpowering "Have Yourself a Merry
Little Christmas" that climaxes the family's decision to stay in St. Louis
and cancel the move to New York. Her renditions of the Ralph Blane–
Hugh Martin "The Trolley Song" and "The Boy Next Door" were heard
not only in the movie but were widely played on radios and on recordings
across the land. Like Crosby before her, like Sinatra at the same time,
and like Elvis Presley in the fifties and sixties, Garland was popular with
a public far beyond the movie theaters.

Minnelli's *The Clock* (1945) was Garland's last bid for a non-musical
triumph as a dramatic actress playing an everyday city innocent in a
romance with a soldier even less sophisticated than she. Robert Walker,
another figure of tragic Hollywood legend, was perfectly cast as her romantic partner. Yet Garland was only a half-dozen feature films away
from virtual screen oblivion after the release of *The Clock*. All were
musicals of one kind or another, and in all she sang beautifully even
when her psyche was being torn to shreds from the strains of illness,
four painful divorces, all sorts of addictions, and bitter life-long memories
of abuse.

So, the end seemed pre-ordained despite the many felicities of George
Sidney's *The Harvey Girls* (1946), Charles Walters's *Easter Parade* (1948),
Vincente Minnelli's *The Pirate* (1948), and Robert Z. Leonard's *In the
Good Old Summertime* (1949)—a failed attempt to recapture the charm
and feeling of Ernst Lubitsch's *The Shop Around the Corner* (1940) with

Garland and Van Johnson in the roles immortalized by Margaret Sullavan and James Stewart. Then followed Charles Walters's *Summer Stock* (1950), her last teaming with Gene Kelly, and *A Star Is Born* (1954), her heroic effort to win an Oscar as Vicky Lester to the Norman Maine of James Mason, one of Garland's longest and most loyal admirers, for both the woman and artist, on screen and off.

· · · ·

JAMES WHALE'S *SHOW BOAT* (1936), from a screenplay by Oscar Hammerstein II, based on his musical play and the novel by Edna Ferber, with Irene Dunne, Allan Jones, Paul Robeson, Helen Morgan, Hattie McDaniel, Charles Winninger, Helen Westley, and Victor Jory, was the second and by far the most accomplished screen version of the 1927 stage landmark. It remains to this day a feisty, rugged challenge to film musicals rather than the tamed mounting of a Broadway hit represented by the plush 1951 MGM Technicolor version. Whale was tackling musical forms with the same zest he applied to his famous horror films, and he is almost reckless in being as honest as the thirties screen allowed about miscegenation, the crux of the Ferber plot. This Universal production, therefore, gets off to a much crisper, driving start than the remake, and the narrative drive continues longer, until crashing on the anticlimax written into all of Ferber's novels as the sins of a weak male descend on the second and third generations.

Jerome Kern's fabulous, almost liturgical score for this prototypical American songfest (the operetta rebirthing into the musical comedy) also tends to lag when it is most needed by the plot. Nonetheless, there are true glories in this first sound adaptation of *Show Boat*, and foremost are the talent and feeling that Dunne invests in the unyielding innocence of Magnolia, the glorious bass of the immortal and electrifying Robeson, and the poignant luminosity of Morgan with such unforgettable torch songs as "Bill" and "Can't Help Lovin' Dat Man."

THE GANGSTER FILM

When the late Robert Warshow published what was to be an epochal essay, "The Gangster as Tragic Hero," in a 1948 *Partisan Review*, he referred explicitly to only two movies: *Little Caesar* (1930) and *Scarface*

(1932). Yet, we can trace the urban criminal on the screen from D. W. Griffith's *The Musketeers of Pig Alley* in 1912 to the present day. One of Buster Keaton's funniest short films—*The High Sign* (1920)—finds Buster struggling in the old slapstick tradition to survive in a Mafia-infested metropolis in which every fruit peddler is a potential "hit" man. But these virtually omnipresent "crooks" and criminals are not what Warshow had in mind when he wrote his essay. Instead, he dealt with a genre that consists of less than a dozen movies, beginning with *Underworld* in 1927 and ending with *Scarface* in 1932. The textbook titles in the standard film histories have not varied much over the years—*Little Caesar* (1930), *The Public Enemy* (1931), *Quick Millions* (1931), *City Streets* (1931). One might add *Dragnet* (1928), *The Racket* (1928), *The Alibi* (1929), *Broadway* (1929), *The Doorway to Hell* (1930), *Corsair* (1931), *The Secret Six* (1931), and *Blood Money* (1933)—but this list is already stretching the genre beyond its original conception of the gangster as subjective protagonist and romantic hero. The gangster as a type survives long after he has disappeared as a tragic hero. But he merely lurks in the background of urban life. In the murder mystery, for example, he is often a suspect, but no more so than the butler in the manor-house type of murder mystery. More often, he represents a lower order of being in contradistinction to the morally marginal hero who hovers between good and evil as he strives for money and power. Indeed, most urban melodramas are concerned with the hero's walking the fine line between legality and morality, between cutting corners and turning them irrevocably.

Crooks and criminals go back very far and down very deep in all cultures: Cain as a sinner rather than a criminal because killing violated God's law before there were any laws drawn up by men, The Thief of Bagdad, MacHeath in *The Beggar's Opera* and, later, in *The Threepenny Opera*, Fagin, Bill Sykes, Raskolnikov, Smerdiakov, the denizens of François Villon's Paris, the pirates, outlaws, highwaymen and cutthroats of song and story. There is also the Robin Hood legend with its indictment of a corrupt and unjust society. The movie gangster drew from time to time on all these prior cultural sources. *Scarface*, for example, was conceived as a conscious fusion of Al Capone and the Borgias. The Elizabethan and Jacobean revenge melodramas, and even Shakespeare's royal gangster sagas had bequeathed a bloody tradition to the movie-makers. When John Barrymore delivered the "Now is the winter of my discontent" soliloquy from *Richard III* in the Warner Brothers *Show of Shows*

(1929), he prefaced his rendition with the remark that Richard had been a more murderous miscreant than Al Capone.

The gangster movie was thus born full-blown, out of the union of mythology and sociology in literature and journalism. It is fitting that Ben Hecht should have been the scenarist for both Josef von Sternberg's *Underworld* (1927) and Howard Hawks's *Scarface* (1932), perhaps the beginning and the end of the notion of "the gangster as tragic hero." Hecht had been a journalist in Chicago before he was a novelist, dramatist, and scenarist. He and Charles MacArthur collaborated on *The Front Page* (1931), which, while not primarily concerned with gangsters, did suggest an atmosphere of corruption and venality in which lawlessness could flourish. A minor gangster character in *The Front Page* is kidded by reporters about his loan-shark activities. This was a very knowing touch, since gangster movies never dealt with loan-sharking as an activity of gangsters. Extortion, yes, but loan-sharking, no. Extortion as the taking of money from people involves a straight persecutor-victim relationship between the gangster and the honest citizen. By contrast, loan-sharking involves the complicity of the victim in his own victimization, and comes periously close to putting the gangster into the banking business. Similarly, the treatment of gambling in gangster movies was generally tolerant and sympathetic, particularly when the gambling hall was bathed in an aura of luxury and glamour. Again, gambling required the complicity of honest citizens and was therefore not as reprehensible as criminal activities in which the honest victim was absolutely guiltless.

Even in the treatment of bootlegging the emphasis was not on victimless crime, particularly in the omnipresent speakeasies, but on violence related either to the struggle for power between rival gangs or to armed robberies of presumably honest merchants. Both Little Caesar and Scarface are finally gunned down by police more as murderers than as gangsters. It would never do, either dramatically or morally, for movies to imitate reality by showing an Al Capone type sent to prison for tax evasion, as, indeed, Al Capone was in anti-climactic real life. Most crime reporters were well aware that Capone could not have flourished as he did if most of the Chicago police force and municipal government had not been on the take. Yet on the screen the over-all honesty of the police force was postulated as a civic verity. Little Caesar had his detective-avenger nemesis in the Lieutenant Tom Flaherty of Thomas Jackson, and Scarface in the grim-faced Guarino of C. Henry Gordon. The censors, even in the early thirties, set a limit to the degree of society's complicity in crime. Nonetheless, when the gangster reigned supreme in his own genre, the forces of law and order were reduced to a Greek chorus of Furies, howling over the hubris of hoods. The law always had the last laugh, but only after all the fun had been squeezed out of the subject for the audience.

From the moment that George Bancroft comes lurching out of a jewel store robbery in *Underworld* (1927), the criminal looms larger than life on the screen. Josef von Sternberg's crime trilogy with Bancroft—*Underworld, Dragnet* (1928), *Thunderbolt* (1929)—crossed the divide between silent pictures and sound pictures. Yet few film historians have taken Bancroft seriously as a prototype of the gangster hero. In Sternberg's stylized world, crime is a projection of sexual potency. The women—Evelyn Brent in *Underworld* and *Dragnet*, Fay Wray in *Thunderbolt*—are the ultimate prizes of criminal activity rather than mere fringe benefits, to which they are reduced in subsequent mobster sagas. As activators rather than accessories, Brent and Wray tend to feminize a brutish genre. Sternberg's underworld is a hellish cauldron of desire for dames smothered in feathers and furs. There will be dames and molls in post-Sternbergian gangster films, but they will never again seem so crucial to criminal existence. Also, Sternberg's slow tempo, dream-like decor, and romantic psychology tended to subvert the complicated intrigues of his scenarios. There was little or no feeling of a world above and beyond the underworld. One felt no laws or morals in Sternberg's world, only codes of honor. And as it turned out, Bancroft's blustering superman was a law unto himself, walking to the electric chair (in *Underworld* and *Thunderbolt*) with a majesty comparable to the descent into Hell of Molière's Don Juan.

Bancroft had been preceded in movie crime by Lon Chaney earlier in the twenties, but Chaney was more the crook than the criminal in that he was not blessed with Bancroft's bravado but afflicted instead with self-pity for his physical and spiritual deformities. It follows that, whereas Bancroft was a personality performer with buoyantly bulging cheeks and playfully popping eyes, Chaney was a make-up artist who delighted in his disguises. Bancroft was also more the gangster than Chaney in that the Sternbergian felon seemed to participate in some semblance of shadow government, whereas the Chaney wrongdoer was an eccentric free-lancer on the edge of certifiable lunacy.

If Edward G. Robinson's Little Caesar obliterated the public's memory of Bancroft and Chaney as underworld figures, it was because there was more fact and less fantasy in his very thinly veiled characterization of Al

Capone. W. R. Burnett's novel and Francis Faragoh's screenplay pick up Robinson's Cesare Enrico Bandello early in his career before he becomes that regal Rico—Little Caesar. The scenario thus unfolds as a depraved version of the American Success Story. The opening shots of Rico and his sidekick Joe Massara (Douglas Fairbanks, Jr.) staging a hold-up evoke laughter in later decades for the irrepressible villainy of the abrupt action. There is no time to interpret the influence of the environment on the criminal mind. The criminals are too busy shooting up the environment. But whereas Bancroft comes hurtling out at the beginning of *Underworld*, Robinson scurries in like a furtive rat. The audience hears the bang-bang inside, and laughs, but Rico himself is yet to emerge as a full-blown personality. Mervyn LeRoy's camera tends to stay at a middle distance as Rico does his meglomaniacal routines, thus giving the viewer a double perspective on the character. As big as Rico may think he is, he never floods the screen with the florid presence of Bancroft's Bull Weed in *Underworld*. Bancroft was of course a much larger man than Robinson, but there was no effort made to trick up Robinson's size as later was done with Humphrey Bogart and Alan Ladd in the forties, and there was no head-shot introspection attributed to this out-and-out punk.

Consequently, Robinson's portrayal of Little Caesar contains the seeds of its own parody. The oh-yeah tough-guy mannerisms are essentially comic rather than romantic. It was as if Robinson had *done* Capone once and for all. Henceforth, his roles tended to be more shaded, more civilized, more sympathetic, until 1948 in *Key Largo*, in which he lapses into self-parody as an updated Little Caesar. Most film historians have ranked Mervyn LeRoy's *Little Caesar* (1930) a poor third to Howard Hawks's *Scarface* (1932) and William Wellman's The *Public Enemy* (1931). This judgment is justified for the most part, but it might be said in defense of *Little Caesar* that it came out several months before *The Public Enemy*, and more than a year before *Scarface*. In the early years of sound, a few months made an enormous difference in the smoothness and slickness of the production values, particularly in the realm of sound. *Little Caesar* opened in New York near the end of 1930, and the sound of gunfire had already attained a more persuasively percussive timbre than in Sternberg's 1929 *Thunderbolt*, in which the boom-boom had a terribly tinny sound. Therefore 1931 and 1932 were years of rapid stylistic adaptation, contrary to the prevailing wisdom of some revered film histories that the sound film only came into its own in 1935 with *The Informer*. LeRoy himself displayed a considerable advance from the stultifyingly static camera set-ups and haphazardly neutral compositions of *Little Caesar* with the more dynamic devices of *Five Star Final* in 1931 and *I Am a Fugitive from a Chain Gang* in 1932.

The frog-faced Robinson was the least sexual of all the gangster leads, and, perhaps as a consequence, the plot of *Little Caesar* takes a peculiar turn when Rico proclaims that he is jealous of his pal's girlfriend (Glenda Farrell). The fact that the pal (Douglas Fairbanks, Jr.) is much more attractive than Rico gives the buddy-buddy romance an extra twist. One genre historian has suggested an outright homosexual attraction at work, but the plot is complicated even further by the banal determination of the pal to "go straight." When the showdown comes, Rico is unable to gun down his friend, and thus loses face with his mob. The viewer may interpret Rico's fatal restraint as the redeeming flaw of an evil man, or as the proof of his hitherto suppressed passion for his pal. Almost all is forgiven when Robinson asks aloud, "Mother of Mercy . . . is this the end of Rico?" James Cagney renders that line as an impromptu homage to Robinson in Billy Wilder's *One, Two, Three* (1961).

Whereas *Little Caesar* is locked into a series of tableaux, *The Public Enemy* roams more freely in time and space to provide an urban ambience for its gangster characters. We follow James Cagney's Tom Powers and Eddie Woods's Matt Doyle from delinquent childhood on pre-Prohibition city streets where beer buckets are prominently featured, to their bloody fates as gangsters of the Prohibition era. John Grierson and other socially conscious critics of the time hailed *The Public Enemy* for suggesting the evolution of criminals within a specific environment. Nonetheless, *The Public Enemy* has many of the same structural problems as *Little Caesar*, and at one point the camera takes the point of view of a rival gang as they lay in wait for the Cagney-Woods duo. Fortunately there are so many high points in Cagney's kinetic performance that the entire picture is carried along at a rollicking pace. The humor is richer, funnier, and more plentiful in *The Public Enemy* than in *Little Caesar*. Among the most memorable set pieces: Cagney pushing the grapefruit in Mae Clarke's kisser; Cagney and Woods getting a court order so that they can shoot a horse responsible for the fatal fall of their beloved boss (that the horse is shot off-screen only adds to the merriment); Cagney being seduced by an affectingly awkward Jean Harlow to the strains of "I Surrender Dear" on the radio; Cagney scooting around a corner with balletic grace to avoid a hail of machine-gun bullets.

The *longueurs* in *The Public Enemy* derive mainly from nagging family scenes in which an uptight brother (Donald Cook) and an upright mother (Beryl Mercer) provide a moralistic contrast to the depredations of the

Cagney character. Cagney developed very early in his career a mama's boy complex in his roles in the midst of all his womanizing. This complex was to resurface most spectacularly in *White Heat* in 1949. Yet, Cagney was the foremost gangster womanizer in this era, if one excepts Clark Gable's magnetic mobster in *A Free Soul* and *Night Nurse* (both 1931), both movies oriented to their female stars (Norma Shearer, Barbara Stanwyck). Gable's brief career as a gangster ended appropriately in the electric chair of *Manhattan Melodrama* (1934), not only the movie Dillinger saw the night he was shot down by the FBI but also the movie given prominence in *Gravity's Rainbow* by Thomas Pynchon, who described William Powell, the district attorney who sends best friend Gable to the hot seat, as a "chinless bastard." In his way, Pynchon may have registered a delayed reaction to the great change that took place in Hollywood in the mid-thirties. The execution of Gable as gangster may have served as a ritual murder of the entire genre.

Certainly the pressure was being felt by the time of *Scarface*, as evidenced by a clumsily inserted scene in which a pack of civic reformers preach directly to the camera in a clear breach of Howard Hawks's very rigorous consistency of narrative viewpoint. But the censors were up in arms over what they felt were incitements to crime in the glorification of gangsters on the screen. In their very useful reference work *The Great Gangster Pictures*, James Robert Parish and Michael R. Pitts seem to take the pious protestations of the good guys in gangster movies at face value. They also fail to make a distinction between the anarchic era, ending, more or less, with *Scarface* in 1932, and the authoritarian era, beginning, more or less, with *G-Men* in 1935.

But *Scarface* itself is nothing if not devious as it traces the rise and fall of Paul Muni's cross-scarred Tony Camonte, another Capone approximation. If we postulate *Little Caesar*, *The Public Enemy*, and *Scarface* as the great gangster trilogy of the early thirties, we find that the Muni character resembles the Robinson character in being introduced under an evil star without any environmental explanation or family connection. Camonte's first entrance is almost mystical, in the shadowy style of German Expressionism, as he comes upon his victim in a fatefully sustained camera movement by which the focus is fixed entirely on the fate of the victim. Yet, once the first murder is committed, Hawks shifts to a more lucid, more humorous treatment of the adventures of his gangster protagonist. The women (Karen Morley, Ann Dvorak) are far more subtly depicted than the women in *The Public Enemy*. Indeed, Karen Morley's sophisticated sensuality and eyes-gleaming perversity take

Scarface all the way back to the Sternbergian sirens of *Underworld* and *Thunderbolt*. Ann Dvorak's Cesca Camonte introduces more than an intimation of incest to the proceedings as she boldly confronts her brother's kinky possessiveness. The Robinson–Fairbanks, Jr. relationship in *Little Caesar* finds its parallel in the Muni-Raft relationship in *Scarface*. Indeed, Raft was in real life somewhat comparable to the Fairbanks character as a dancer with ties to the mob.

In *Scarface*, however, there is no hesitation in pulling the trigger on one's best friend. The violence has been ritualized into an imperative. For Hawks and his scenarists, character *is* violence. And when Camonte comically mispronounces "habeas corpus" as "hocus pocus" he not only encourages lynch law but encourages it against immigrant types who misuse the language as they break the law. *Scarface*, like all gangster movies, thus stirred up anti-urban and anti-immigrant bigotries, which was never taken sufficiently into account in Warshow's essay. To celebrate the sinful pleasures of the city was to stir up a storm of rural puritanism. In many ways *Scarface* proved to be the last straw. Yet *Scarface* was not so much innovative in and of itself, as it was a masterly summation of the entire genre. By 1932 the Chicago of *The Front Page* and *Little Caesar* had become a cliché. In *Scarface* the social context is thus stripped down to its most expressive elements. One no longer has to establish the premises of power-seeking; they are built into the genre. The need for exposition is gone. *Scarface* is consequently smoother, but still offensive to the law-abiding. An era ends, and the censors exploit the customary lethargy of movie distributors and make sure that it never returns either with new films of the gangster as hero, or with revivals of old.

In the process many gangster films are completely forgotten. Only in the sixties and seventies are they brought back into view. Among these a select few deserve to be revived and remembered for their own distinctive idiosyncrasies. Archie Mayo's *The Doorway to Hell* (1930) was released even before *Little Caesar*, but it never became part of movie mythology. Lew Ayres was the incarnation of mobster Louis Ricarno more in a sensitive baby-faced manner than in the brutal, swaggering style of Robinson, Cagney, and Muni. With Cagney playing Ricarno's sidekick, *The Doorway to Hell* would seem in retrospect to have been fatally miscast with the anguished Ayres as its lead. Nonetheless, the scene in which Ricarno returns to the tenements where he grew up is far more detailed psychologically and sociologically than any comparable scene in *The Public Enemy*. Adapted from a Rowland Brown short story,

A Handful of Clouds, by George Rosener, *The Doorway to Hell* may have been too disenchanting a descent into the underworld for the general public. The film seems to mourn the loss of innocence and trust without any compensation from the pleasures of criminal power. It may be Rowland Brown's influence on the project that makes it seem like a commentary on American life in general.

Brown is one of the mysterious figures of early talkies with a lingering reputation as the stormy-petrel Sam Peckinpah of his period. Kevin Brownlow has insisted that Brown had more flair for publicity than actual talent. Nonetheless, the films he did manage to direct—*Quick Millions* (1931), *Hell's Highway* (1932), and *Blood Money* (1932)—display a very original though erratic imagination. Documentary director John Grierson was profoundly impressed by *Quick Millions* as the kind of gangster movie in which crime served as a metaphor for capitalism, or, in the words of Louis Calhern's shyster lawyer in *The Asphalt Jungle* (1950), crime as merely the left hand of human endeavor.

That *Quick Millions* (1931) is not as well known as the three official classics of the genre can be attributed to several factors: the relative inaccessibility of early Fox films as opposed to early Warners films, the miscasting in retrospect of Spencer Tracy, like Lew Ayres, as a gangster lead, and Brown's curiously elliptical rendering of the action so that the movie turns out to be more pugnacious than violent. Brown clearly lacked Hawk's dynamic flair for story-telling and Wellman's eye for gritty detail, but *Quick Millions* is unique for its time in suggesting the natural affinity of racketeering and big business. There was also in Brown's vision of life a grown-up awareness of the nuances of the class struggle. "The society swells really have big weddings," one gangster tells another. "But we have big funerals." This last line of the film also serves as Tracy's requiem. He has been murdered by the mob for letting his letch for a high society dame (Marguerite Churchill) jeopardize gangland's delicate relationship with the establishment.

Hell's Highway (1932) was a far-fetched prison movie that seemed to have been influenced by the Russian cinema in the matter of defiant groupings of the convicts as if they were posing for revolutionary posters. But, again, Brown's narrative style seems remote and elliptical, as if he knows what everything means before he begins, and cannot be bothered to make his continuity seem plausible.

Blood Money (1933) is another matter entirely. George Bancroft is near the end of his tether as a character lead. Here he plays a bail-bondsman, dangling on the edge of criminality without ever losing his legal footing. The dames steal the show, however, with Judith Anderson's compliant, low-cut-gowned club hostess and Frances Dee's wild-eyed nymphomaniac giving Hollywood one last fling with grown-up sensuality before the age of Shirley Temple officially began.

Roland West's dilettantish contributions to the genre—*Alibi* (1929), *Bat Whispers* and *Corsair* (both 1931)—were richer in a menacing atmosphere of tricks and stratagems than in the psychology and sociology of gangsterdom. West's self-financed efforts were filmed at night, and reveal a leisurely cultivation of a pictorial style. Chester Morris, a much-neglected and under-rated performer from this period, was at the center of each of these films as either a hammy villain (*Alibi, Bat Whispers*) or a handsome hero (*Corsair*). The opening scene of *Corsair* is as overtly anti-capitalist as one could wish. Chester Morris plays a young stock-broker who, proclaiming his disgust at peddling worthless stock to unsuspecting little old ladies, decides to get into the relatively honest work of rum-running. A very complicated intrigue then ensues in which gravel-voiced, cigar-chomping deadpan Ned Sparks gives the performance of his life as a doomed double-agent.

Less impressive is *City Streets* (1931), Rouben Mamoulian's much over-rated *objet d'art*, in which Gary Cooper and Sylvia Sidney enact a turgid drama of frame-ups and escapes. Cooper, as a rural slowpoke type, is the most miscast gangster in the genre's entire history. The film has been hailed, however, as a textbook example of creative montage, composition, and symbolic expression in the early sound era. The narrative, unfortunately, functions in fits and starts, and the final denouement is so wildly improbable that it seems to belong in a musical. Still, the fact that the Cooper character becomes a gangster, and yet escapes unscathed, gives the film a heady quality of casual amorality, which will be tolerated by the censors for only a year or two more.

All in all, the period between 1927 and 1933 was marvelously uninhibited, and yet, oddly, unappreciated. It is in this period that Hollywood's ragingly raunchy unconscious was allowed to hang out in the name of a sordid realism. Most movies were mediocre, as always, but even in their mediocrity they breathed a demotic, demonic fire. It is entirely fitting that the period of *Little Caesar*, *The Public Enemy*, and *Scarface* was also the period of *Frankenstein* (1931), *Dracula* (1931), *Tarzan* (1932), *King Kong* (1933). Robinson, Cagney, Muni, each dies like a monster—Robinson a writhing reptile, Cagney a falling mummy, Muni a contorted creation of mad science.

For a time the id reigned supreme, and anarchic rebellion was everywhere.

The most powerful prison movie of all time remains George Hill's *The Big House* of 1930, a movie in which convicts Wallace Beery and Chester Morris wage such a powerful revolt that army tanks have to be called into the yard to quell the uprising. Never again would the censors allow such massive violence in the screen's penal system. What is curious is that the intellectuals never did rise to the defense of this defiant cinema until it was much too late. It would be decades after 1935 before Hollywood could recapture the lustful license it accepted as a matter of course in 1929.

In the interim, however, the gangster genre enjoyed a nostalgia-driven resurgence in the late thirties and early forties, largely under the aegis of Warner Brothers and the directorial exuberance of Raoul Walsh, particularly with the violent trinity of *The Roaring Twenties* (1939), *High Sierra* (1941), and *White Heat* (1949). During this period, James Cagney retained his dominant position atop screen gangsterdom, but Humphrey Bogart jumped past Edward G. Robinson and George Raft in the pecking order. The smooth-faced, glittery-eyed, Valentino-cloned Raft was the least convincing of the screen's mobsters, and yet also the most sinister in real life with his gang connections that eventually cost him a gambling license in England. Ironically, he refused to smoke or drink on the screen because he was afraid of offending his fans. Consequently, Raft turned down the roles in *The Maltese Falcon* (1941) and *High Sierra* that were to allow Bogart to eclipse him. Robinson, a more versatile and more talented actor than Raft, simply embraced a wider variety of roles, most of them closer to the marginalized evil of *noir* rather than the outright evil of organized crime.

The Roaring Twenties was suffused with a nostalgic glow for gangsters, speakeasies, and showgirls from a carefree period when the war clouds over Europe and Asia were the last things on anyone's mind. The screenplay, credited to Jerry Wald, Richard Macaulay, and Robert Rossen, was adapted from a story by Mark Hellinger, a journalist for the Hearst papers, who was to be to the forties what Ben Hecht had been to the thirties, an accredited chronicler of tabloid yarns for violent movie melodramas. In fact, a printed foreword to the film attesting to Hellinger's first-hand acquaintance with some of the characters in the movie is accompanied by Max Steiner's sweet-sounding chords of remembrance as if to mourn a raffish reality now sadly, and safely, past.

Cagney and Bogart continued their edgy good-bad-guy and bad-bad-guy camaraderie launched in Michael Curtiz's conformist gangster cocktail mixing religiosity and rascality and romance in *Angels with Dirty Faces* (1937), with Pat O'Brien supplying the unctuousness, the Dead End Kids the gutter deliverance, Ann Sheridan the hard-boiled romance, and Cagney and Bogart the contrasting shades of criminality. But the picture belongs to Cagney with his gift for pathos even as he with his caged physical energy is stretching his nerve endings to their limits. Who can forget the famous scene of Cagney's dying with balletic strenuousness on the church steps, and all for his unrequited love for incongruously nice girl (Priscilla Lane) and insufferably straight-arrow assistant D.A. (Jeffrey Lynn). Cagney is better served by the loving epitaph of blowsy saloon hostess Gladys George.

High Sierra (1941) took the nostalgia for gangsters in *The Roaring Twenties* one step farther by suggesting a decline and fall principle from old hoodlums like Humphrey Bogart's Roy Earle to the new generation of callow wrongdoers played by Arthur Kennedy, Alan Curtis, and Cornel Wilde. Adapted from W. R. Burnett's novel by John Huston and Burnett, *High Sierra* took the genre outdoors away from the urban environment and immigrant stock of the many Capone variations. Roy Earle was of rural American stock like Dillinger and Bonnie and Clyde. Indeed, in 1949 Raoul Walsh made *Colorado Territory*, which could be said to be a re-make of *High Sierra* as a western, with Joel McCrea in the Bogart role, and Virginia Mayo in the Ida Lupino role of loyal bad girl, and Dorothy Malone in the Joan Leslie role of ungrateful good girl. Lupino actually had top billing over Bogart in the studio's vain attempt to make her the new Bette Davis. With war raging on two continents, the sentimental treatment of an age-worn gangster striving for one last score did not offend the law-and-order types who were so vociferous in the thirties, certainly not with violence and lawlessness going global. The final shoot-out on a mountaintop was only a dress rehearsal for Walsh's supreme achievement in the genre in 1949 with *White Heat*, a Cagney vehicle with disturbing overtones and sub-texts.

White Heat (1949) begins with a brutal train robbery organized by a psychotic gang leader Cody Jarrett (Cagney) who adds a new postwar dimension to the gangster protagonist with the monstrous Ma Jarrett (Margaret Wycherly), who nurtures her son's most extreme homicidal delusions. By contrast, his floozy wife (Virginia Mayo) counts for little in his emotional calculations. Treachery and betrayal within the gang precede the intervention of a law-enforcement apparatus more sophisticated in its technology than any before it. The Treasury Department deploys a professional mob infiltrator (Edmond O'Brien) to gain Jarrett's trust so that the "fence" with overseas contacts to launder stolen American money can be identified and apprehended. For American audiences, the theme of the informer from the beginning created a conflict of sympathies. Cagney's projection of pathos gives the film an emotional charge that reaches its proper climax amid the *Gotterdammerung* finale atop a flaming chemical tower exploding right at the moment Cody Jarrett roars out his final message to his dead mother, "Top of the world, Ma." And thus the nuclear age was launched on the screen.

THE HORROR FILM

The Hollywood horror film might be designated as the misshapen offspring of German Expressionism and Gothic fiction. F. W. Murnau's (1888–1931) *Nosferatu* (1922) and Carl Theodor Dreyer's (1889–1968) *Vampyr* (1932) have been acknowledged as the genre's high-art classics. But in America, Tod Browning's (1882–1962) *Dracula* (1931) with Bela Lugosi (1882–1956) and James Whale's (1896–1957) *Frankenstein* (1931) with Boris Karloff (1887–1969) were the fountainheads of the Hollywood pop sound film prospering of the ghoulish and the horrific.

Browning was more morbid and less versatile than Whale, whose tastes were more elevated as evidenced by *Journey's End* (1930), *Waterloo Bridge* (1931), *The Kiss Before the Mirror* (1933), *One More River* (1934), *Show Boat* (1936), *The Road Back* (1937), and other non-horror projects. By contrast, Browning was best known before *Frankenstein* as the director who introduced Lon Chaney to macabre roles in the silent era with *The Unholy Three* (in 1925) followed by *The Road to Mandalay* (1926), *The Unknown* (1927), *London After Midnight* (1927), *The Big City* (1928), *West of Zanzibar* (1928), and *Where East Is East* (1929). In fact, Browning had already cast Chaney in the role of Dracula when Chaney's death forced him to substitute a Hungarian stage actor named Bela Lugosi, who had played the part on the Broadway stage.

It is typical of the time that both *Dracula* and *Frankenstein* were not adapted to the screen directly from the lavishly plotted and textured novels of Bram Stoker and Mary Wollstonecraft Shelley respectively, but from previous play adaptations by Hamilton Deane and John Balderston of *Dracula*, and by Peggy Webling of *Frankenstein*. In this way, the difficult task of "breaking down" the unruly complexities of novels was shared by the playwrights and screenwriters.

More than sixty years later, Francis Ford Coppola and Kenneth Branagh returned to the original texts of these two chillers with the self-consciously literary movie titles, *Bram Stoker's Dracula* (1992) and *Mary Shelley's Frankenstein* (1994), North Pole climax and all. Back in the thirties, however, screen fidelity to widely unread print originals was not high on Hollywood's list of cultural priorities. What audiences got instead were cautionary fables about the monstrous presumption of defying God by defeating death (*Dracula*) or creating life (*Frankenstein*).

Browning's direction of *Dracula* has been denigrated by later critics and historians for its allegedly static and stagey shortcomings. Mine may be a minority view, but I have always felt that the Browning style was appropriate for a mood piece, particularly one photographed by the incomparable Karl Freund. Even the comically deliberate line readings of Lugosi's Count Dracula, most notably the eternally imitated: "I don't drink . . . wine," contributed to the courtly atmosphere of what has always been in all its versions an erotic metaphor for a life-and-death love story.

Helen Chandler, one of the unjustly forgotten enchantresses of the early talkies era, had a plaintive pitch in her voice that would have made the virginal character she played irresistible to a tired old *roué* like the Count. Dwight Frye as Dracula's slavishly obsessed disciple, Renfield, and Edward Van Sloan as the cross-brandishing Professor Van Helsing instantly became inimitable archetypes in the vampire melodrama. The intensity of these performances gave this first American-made *Dracula* a gravity and conviction none of its many sequels and derivatives could match.

Browning had been a clown and a contortionist for a circus in his youth, but when he assembled all the sideshow performers in the world he could find for a 1932 circus melodrama fittingly entitled *Freaks*, he discovered that some realities were more horrifying to movie audiences than the wildest fictions. After a few preview screenings, the movie was cut and virtually shelved only to resurface in the 1960s as a midnight screening cult attraction. As much documentary as low-grade revenge fiction, *Freaks* stared unblinkingly and compassionately at a collection of midgets, dwarfs, pinheads, hermaphrodites, legless and armless creatures from the netherworld of existence.

Browning's career declined in the thirties along with the genre he helped popularize. MGM's tradition of gentility, which doomed *Freaks*, discouraged Browning further by imposing a trick make-believe ending on his otherwise creditable *Mark of the Vampire* (1935). After directing Lionel Barrymore in drag for *The Devil Doll*—an escape-from-Devil's-Island revenge fantasy in which an unjustly convicted protagonist punishes his evil enemies by reducing them to tiny dolls—Browning made two routine films before retiring from the screen. He remains a bizarre figure in the history of the one genre with which he will forever be identified. Stripped of his strangeness, he simply went through the motions of his "normal" projects.

One of the oddities of the Frankenstein craze in the thirties was the rapidity with which the public forgot that the name in the book and in the 1931 movie was that of the creator and not of his creation, which is to say that Colin Clive's Henry Frankenstein was the prototypical mad scientist responsible for bringing Boris Karloff's "The Monster" to life out of old brain and body parts. Karloff's persona was so persuasive, however, that the names Karloff and Frankenstein became interchangeable, much as William Powell's Nick Charles became inseparable from the book and movie title, *The Thin Man* (1934), which Dashiell Hammett and the screen adaptors of his novel had used as a headline sobriquet for a missing murder victim (played by Edward Ellis) mistakenly thought to be a missing murderer.

Frankenstein can also lay claim to one of the most grotesquely hilarious manifestation of bridal jitters in film history. Mae Clarke's Elizabeth, Henry Frankenstein's understandably nervous bride-to-be, is sitting alone in her bedroom fidgeting in her wedding finery when suddenly the Monster looms at a window in the background. Facing away from the window she does not see him as soon as the audience does, but when she turns . . . ! This single-shot composition encapsulates every maidenly fear of the monstrous phallus known to the symbolic imagination. Poor Mae Clarke had a tough year in 1931 between Boris Karloff's Monster appearing at her window on her wedding day, and James Cagney pushing a grapefruit in her face in William Wellman's *The Public Enemy*.

Another sub-text in *Frankenstein* was the demonization of doctors and scientists who went too far in their research and experiments into realms of the unknown better left to God's will. Curiously, this was the very attitude that was deplored in the noble genre of Great Men of Medicine and Science such as Pasteur (William Dieterle's *The Story of Louis Pasteur*—1936), Ehrlich (Dieterle's *Dr. Ehrlich's Magic Bullet*—1940), and W. F. G Morton (Preston Sturges's *The Great Moment*—1944). In each instance, the public was wrong, and the individual visionary right. The opposite is true in horror movies in which every form of sacrilege and perversion was practiced and eventually punished. The hubris of the genre embraced fantasy, science fiction, futurism, life after death, zombies, bestial fusions with humans, etc. In the end the morality of behavioral normality and religious conservatism would prevail.

A third sub-text to emerge from the flames of the Monster's immolation at the hands of a frenzied mob of villagers brandishing torches was the plight of the outcast in a hostile society. Grierson wrote in the thirties that the fire-bearing villagers in *Frankenstein* reminded him of a Southern lynch mob. Certainly, all the audience's sympathy was directed toward the Monster rather than to the torch-brandishing villagers, particularly after the studio edited out a sequence in which the otherwise lovable Monster casually flings a child deep into a lake to certain death. By contrast, the Monster's awed pleasure at the first music he hears is graphically expressed on Karloff's face, and thus endows the creature with an identifiable soul.

Whale's *Bride of Frankenstein* (1935) is one of the rare sequels to a hit movie that is artistically superior to the original. First, the very conception by Whale and his scenarists, John Balderston and William Hurlburt, of starting a Monster family was comically inspired enough, but the cream of the jest was the casting of the talented Elsa Lanchester as the mechanical bride. Her prolonged scream at her first sight of the intended groom evoked primal laughter with no need of sub-textual analysis. Colin Clive's Henry Frankenstein, now second-billed to Karloff's Monster, makes one last futile effort to redeem his disastrous experiment, this time with the beautiful and talented Valerie Hobson as his prospective bride, Elizabeth. Mary and Percy Shelley and Lord Byron were introduced in a framing episode to give the film an unusually literary provenance. Ernest Thesiger's fruity performance as Doctor Praetorious, to whom nothing human or inhuman was alien, contributed humor and a campy sang-froid to the proceedings, and Franz Waxman's musical score, a lyrical felicity lacking in the first *Frankenstein*, provided a romantic dimension to the fable.

With a few exceptions, *The Bride of Frankenstein* represented the last gasp of the horror film as a serious genre. The creeping disease of facetiousness crippled the genre even more distressingly than it had the gangster film. The dilution of creativity proceeded apace in both genres with anachronistic wise-cracking, farcical reactions, low-brow skepticism, and "darky" caricatures. Warners even promoted the miscegenation of genres with gangsters and ghouls, electric chairs, and haunted graveyards, and even Humphrey Bogart in Boris Karloff's Monster make-up.

On the plus side were the juicy opportunities provided to character actors for bravura characterizations. Fredric March in Rouben Mamoulian's *Dr. Jekyll and Mr. Hyde* (1932) and Spencer Tracy in Victor Fleming's *Dr. Jekyll and Mr. Hyde* (1941) repeated the sound-era characterization of the dual presence of the superego and the id in the same person, a phenomenon imagined long before its time in the story by Robert Louis Stevenson. John Barrymore had contributed his ultra-histrionic interpretation in the silent era.

The inimitable Charles Laughton chewed up the scenery a bit as still another mad doctor, on this occasion experimenting with animals of the jungle so as to transform them into half-human mutants. Adapted from an H. G. Wells story, Erle C. Kenton's *The Island of Lost Souls* (1933) supplies Laughton with a serviceable supporting cast including a benign Bela Lugosi, Richard Arlen, Stanley Fields, Kathleen Burke, and Leila Hyams. Laughton's mad Doctor Moreau receives his come-uppance in a gruesome manner that might be regarded as poetic justice.

Among the most interesting sequels to *Dracula* was Lambert Hillyer's *Dracula's Daughter* (1936), with an audaciously suggestive story and screenplay by Garrett Fort enabling Gloria Holden and Marguerite Churchill to enact a lesbian seduction under the ironically protective (from the censors) guise of vampirism. In 1990s street jargon, sucking blood was morally more acceptable than sucking skin, at least on the screen.

Rowland V. Lee's *Son of Frankenstein* (1939), from a screenplay by Willis Cooper, with Boris Karloff, Basil Rathbone, Bela Lugosi, and Lionel Atwill, is the most self-consciously literary of the cycle, and the most coherent structurally. As sequels go, it lacks the unexpected charm of the original and the unexpected perversity of *The Bride of Frankenstein* (1935), but it is, withal, sober, high-minded, stylish, and implacable—and the last true bright spot before the series went franchise soft. Karloff, perhaps sensing the end in his last appearance as Frankenstein's graveyard leavings, sustains a malevolent presence throughout as a stalker of the Baron's catacombs. He assured himself a gruesome farewell and one of the most striking images of the series when he ripped off a police chief's wooden arm and waved it about while standing astride an endangered child. Rathbone, particularly, added conviction to the moral dilemmas inherent in the familiar fable.

Edgar G. Ulmer's *The Black Cat* (1934) united Karloff and Lugosi in a very stately confrontation of non-monstrous characters in a crumbling post-World War I castle in the midst of a ruined European landscape. An interesting duel between two serious actors was as much a clash of rhetorical styles as a confrontation of evil (Karloff) by vengeful good (Lugosi) and a masterly Germanic mise-en-scène by the legendary Ulmer.

Merian C. Cooper and Ernest B. Schoesdack's *King Kong* (1933) is remembered today as much for the crudity and inconsistency of its animated rendering of *Kong* as in spite of it. The original uncut and uninhibited version which resurfaced in the seventies after decades of censor and studio fears that audiences would be repelled by the full lechery and bestiality of the rampaging primate put more bite (literally and figuratively) into an already lyrically ferocious new-world fable of Beauty and the Beast. Once Kong appears, Max Steiner's eerie score and Willis O'Brien's inspired special effects pack the screen with as much enchanted adventure as it can bear. The last twenty minutes, which grieve over Kong's downfall with a truly regal pathos, is nothing short of sublime. The rest is the most routine sort of B-picture filler though Fay Wray, Robert Armstrong, and Bruce Cabot endow the human component with the seriousness and urgency the subject demands. *King Kong* remains supreme in its genre as the happiest of happy accidents.

Indeed, the horror film, even at its most corrupted and compromised, managed to preserve through the thirties the visual mystique of German Expressionism, which was to be regenerated in the forties by Orson Welles with *Citizen Kane* (1941). The genre itself was so enfeebled by the end of the thirties that the stage was set for the arrival of its savior in the forties in a series of remarkable films at RKO produced by Val Lewton.

> The best fiction films of the year, *The Curse of the Cat People* and *Youth Runs Wild*, were made by Val Lewton and his associates. I esteem them so highly because for all their unevenness their achievements are so consistently alive, limber, poetic, humane, so eager toward the possibilities of the screen, and so resolutely against the grain of all we have learned to expect from the big studios.
>
> James Agee, *The Nation*, January 20, 1945

One may not necessarily agree with the legendary James Agee's notions of the best Hollywood "fiction films" of 1944, but one must still credit Agee (and his gifted contemporary Manny Farber) with rescuing the modestly financed Val Lewton-produced oeuvre from the flea-pit horror circuits of the forties. You almost had to be there to understand the full context of Agee's judgments. I happened to be passing from high school into college in that decade, and I had never heard of Agee or Farber and never realized that I had heard of Val Lewton. Even if I had, however, my own grotesquely genteel moviegoing tastes would have blinded me to what Agee and Farber were trying to say, and what Lewton was trying to show. Hence, the current resurrection of Lewton's classics on laser discs enables me to reconstruct an essential chapter in my sadly neglected moviegoing past.

Who *was* Val Lewton, and why is he remembered so fondly as a producer-auteur when so many more prominent and prestigious producers of his time have been almost completely forgotten? The answer, I think, lies partly in the very meagerness of his means providing a cautionary rebuke to Hollywood's fiscal extravagance coupled with its creative impoverishment. The Val Lewton movies generally wound up on the second half of double bills in neighborhood theaters after their "premieres" in specialized horror havens such as the Rialto in New York's Times Square, and the Hawaii on Hollywood Boulevard in Los Angeles. The catchpenny creepy titles—*Cat People* (1942), *I Walked with a Zombie* (1943), *The Leopard Man* (1943), *The Seventh Victim* (1943), *The Ghost Ship* (1943), *The Curse of the Cat People* (1944), *Isle of the Dead* (1945), *The Body Snatcher* (1945), *Bedlam* (1946)—were disreputable enough to keep most of the mainstream reviews in the mode of casual condescension. What a critical coup it must have seemed to perceptive iconoclasts such as Agee and Farber to declare that the bottom of the double bill was superior to the top, and that the dark or *noir* side of life Lewton explored was rendered more honestly and imaginatively than was the inspirationally sunny side of life in the euphoria of World War II mainstream movies.

But it was not simply the *noir* in Lewton movies that was championed, but also the principle of the B picture, in which less was often more. In this respect, Val Lewton was the Edgar G. Ulmer of producers as Ulmer was the Val Lewton of directors. Actually, Lewton was more a writer-producer than a transplanted accountant producer as was so often the case. In any event, from 1942 to 1946 Lewton inspired a cultish devotion that flourishes to this day.

In the history of movie genres, Lewton (1904–1951) arrived on the scene at a crucial moment for horror films. The glory days of Tod Browning's *Dracula* (1931) and James Whale's *Frankenstein* (1931) were long gone, and on the screen both vampires and man-made monsters had degenerated into figures of fun. When Richard Koerner hired Val Lewton to head a production unit in 1942, its mandate was rigidly defined: horror movies to cost no more than $150,000 and to run no more than seventy-five minutes. Lewton had previously worked for David O. Selznick over an eight-year period as story editor, in which capacity he had once advised Selznick to scrap his plans to film Margaret Mitchell's *Gone With the Wind*, and switch to Leo Tolstoy's *War and Peace* instead. Lewton's Russophile tastes came naturally to him inasmuch as he was born Vladimir Lewton in Yalta, on May 7, 1904. According to Joel E. Siegel's insightful and definitive biography, Lewton's mother, Nina Leventon, "was the daughter of Yacov Leventon, a Yalta chemist who, according to family history, served Tsar Alexander III and put up prescriptions for the tubercular Chekov."

Nina's younger sister Adelaide became the world-famous actress Alla Nazimova, and she brought Nina and her two children, Lucy and Vladimir, to America in 1909. Separated from his wastrel father when he was two, Lewton was brought up by his strong-willed mother and aunt. He became a voracious reader, and later a prolific but never distinguished writer. Nazimova provided him an entry into movies through various studio story departments and publicity departments. He wrote novels of every description, pornography included. A story once circulated that a producer asked a colleague if he should hire Lewton, and the colleague replied that Lewton had written "horrible" novels, and the producer misheard "horrible" as "horror" and hired him on the spot.

In my libidinous adolescence I once read a Val Lewton novel entitled *No Bed of Her Own* in a pocketbook with a racy cover. I was surprised to discover much later that this steamy saga of a homeless young woman going from man to man and bed to bed in the depths of the Depression had been translated into nine languages as a piece of social realism, and, furthermore, that it had been purchased by Hollywood as a vehicle for Carole Lombard and Clark Gable, retitled *No Man of Her Own* (1932), and scrubbed clean by the censors until it bore no resemblance to the original.

Still, Lewton found himself in 1942 with a curious hankering after the finer things even on poverty row. Universal had a virtual monopoly on vampires and monsters and mummies and werewolves and such. RKO was thus compelled to turn to wild animals and zombies, both more or less in the public domain. Lewton's first project became the instant classic *The Cat People* (1942), through a variety of low-budget coups with the writing, the direction, and the casting. Lewton recruited Dewitt Bodeen as a script writer and Jacques Tourneur as a director, but Simone Simon virtually fell into his lap after this French star, like her unhappy compatriot Danielle Darrieux, had failed to establish a viable Hollywood career. The feline beauty of Simone Simon lifted *Cat People* far above the usual level of B pictures. The original story had been set abroad, but it was Lewton's inspired decision to shift the locale to America that made Simon even more effectively exotic. Seen today, *Cat People* mixes the ordinary with the occult to create a subtler and more believable terror than would be possible in such hackneyed locales of the horror genre as Transylvania or foggy London Town. RKO executives were terrified by the first rushes of *Cat People*, with their measured pacing and matter-of-fact mildness. Yet after some initial restiveness, sneak preview audiences came alive with sudden bursts of terror, all the more exciting for arising out of a slowly suspenseful build-up.

Vincente Minnelli's *The Bad and the Beautiful*, from a screenplay by Charles Schnee, paid homage to both Val Lewton and his onetime employer David O. Selznick by making the Kirk Douglas producer character a composite of both Hollywood legends, with the script telling us that the imaginative producer of a quickie very much like *Cat People* would become big enough to both produce and direct *Gone With the Wind*, though in the Minnelli-Schnee version, unsuccessfully.

By making a virtue of necessity Lewton had shown in *Cat People* an ability to produce gripping sub-texts out of what started out as penny-dreadful material and publicity. He established a standard of empathy and sympathy with the twisted fantasies of the horror genre that has proven to be inimitable in subsequent decades.

Paul Schrader was fully justified in claiming in 1982 that his *Cat People* was less a re-make than an update of the 1942 cult classic directed by Tourneur and produced by Lewton. Significantly, however, the only two sequences copied from the original—the roaring bus lurching to a halt in the middle of a scary park, and a young woman jumping into a darkened indoor pool to escape a possibly feline pursuer—are botched in the later version. Worse still, Nastasia Kinski's Irena Gallier is not nearly as memorably mythological as that of the inimitably cat-like Simone Simon.

In the original *Cat People*, Kent Smith played the architect who marries the cat-like Irena (Simone Simon), and Jane Randolph played the uncomplicated other woman. Though Smith was an accomplished Shakespearean actor on the stage, the screen invested him with the aura of a B-picture leading man. The character he plays in *Cat People* is dull, conformist, humorless, unimaginative. Revival audiences in the fifties giggled at his unexpectedly overwrought love scene with Randolph. Still, in the forties, Smith and Randolph had served audiences as adequate *raisonneurs* to carry the plot past its more lurid speculations. At the center of the film was the sweetly menacing eroticism of Simone Simon as the mysterious cat person from Yugoslavia. It was wartime, remember, and one did not have to write much exposition for a presumed refugee.

It was also a time of heavy censorship and sanctimoniousness, a time on the screen when all sorts of forbidden impulses were beginning to surface, only to be submerged by a kind of common man, common-sense puritanism. Consequently, Simone Simon's Irena must die not so much for any consciously malevolent act, but rather for arousing in a dull society the dread demons of desire. Irena is not the only victim of the antisex furies of *Cat People*; a womanizing psychiatrist played by Tom Conway must be disposed of as well since he seeks to profit carnally from his insight into Irena's bestial-sexual nature. The Conway character is not a bad sort otherwise. Indeed, he and Irena project a civilized European sensibility completely lacking in the other characters. But in 1942 American audiences were unduly smug about the "normality" of their own society, and Irena and the psychiatrist were therefore unsettling representations of Old World decadence.

The Lewton-Tourneur collaboration continued through 1943 with *I Walked With a Zombie* and *The Leopard Man*, but the studio "promoted" Tourneur to bigger-budget pictures, and the harmony of the Lewton team began to show its first debilitating dissonances. Yet Robert Wise and Mark Robson moved into the directorial breach to provide Lewton with some of his finest work. My own favorite of all his works is the voodoo-driven variation on Charlotte Brontë's *Jane Eyre*, luridly titled *I Walked With a Zombie* (1943) and thus never receiving the recognition it deserved. Again a beautiful woman who never achieved stardom, Frances Dee in this instance, lifted *Zombie* far above its presumed level. Another remarkable achievement is the authentic flavor of the location shooting in the Caribbean. There is very little else quite like it in the movies of the forties. The only other Lewton movie in its class is *The Body Snatcher* (1945), in which Boris Karloff and Henry Daniell provided thoroughly rounded characterizations of a servant-master team of medically motivated grave robbers chained together by an eventually murderous fear and suspicion. There are stirring moments also in *The Curse of the Cat People* (1944), far ahead of its time in confronting the theme of the imaginary friends of childhood, and once more reveling in the now ghostly beauty of Simone Simon.

Through all the Val Lewton classics, however, is an unexpectedly cre-

ative sensibility at work on the fearful traumas of the dark and the unknown with an incongruous decency and humility toward the afflicted.
It is the light of love and humanity Lewton shed on the darkness of
horror that makes us remember and revive his work today.

THE SCREWBALL COMEDY

The so-called screwball comedy did not survive as a genre beyond that
indeterminate period in the thirties when the national economy supposedly encouraged certain patterns of eccentric behavior on the screen.
Film historians have never quite agreed on exactly what constituted a
screwball comedy or what movies qualified for the category. There has
been general agreement, however, that the period in question did not
begin much before 1934 or end much after 1938. One may begin with
Howard Hawks's *Twentieth Century* or Frank Capra's *It Happened One
Night* in 1934 and end with Hawks's *Bringing Up Baby* or Capra's *You
Can't Take It with You* in 1938. Gregory La Cava's *My Man Godfrey*
(1936), Leo McCarey's *The Awful Truth* (1937), and William Wellman's
Nothing Sacred (1937) would have to be added to the list as generally
acknowledged classics of screwballism. But within this very narrow range
of selection, we begin to encounter problems of definition. The one constant throughout the category is the teaming of a male star and a female
star as both love interest and comic center of the spectacle. There is
presumably no place in screwball comedy for Chaplin, W. C. Fields, Mae
West, the Marx Brothers, and Laurel and Hardy. Even so, can we then
demonstrate that this particular policy began in 1934 and ended in 1938?
I would hardly think so. Some nuance seems to have eluded us. Let us
therefore turn to some of the aforementioned film historians for possible
clues to the alleged uniqueness of screwball comedy.

Lewis Jacobs in *The Rise of the American Film* establishes a dialectic
between old-fashioned sentimentality and the new sophistication by ap-
plauding the supposed advanced tastes of movie audiences:

Cinderella, like Pollyanna, is distinctly out of style and even incredible.
Rich Man, Poor Girl (1938) was criticized as "trite"; films that show the
heroine stepping from gutter to penthouse (*Mannequin* (1937), *The Bride
Wore Red* (1937)) are no longer convincing. Remakes of such former do-

mestic triangles such as *Bluebeard's Eighth Wife* (1938) and *Angel* (1937), with the philandering and faithfulness on which they pivot, seem old-fashioned and dated—unreal. . . .

"Daffy" comedies became the fashion. Here the genteel tradition is "knocked for a loop": heroes and heroines are neither [sic] lady-like and [sic] gentlemanly. They hit each other, throw each other down, mock each other, play with each other. *It Happened One Night* (1934) was the first successful example of this school. *Twentieth Century* (1934); *My Man Godfrey* (1936); and *Theodora Goes Wild*; *Topper*; *True Confession*; *Live, Love and Learn*; and *The Awful Truth* (all 1937) similarly lampooned the dignified and accepted. These films were all sophisticated, mature, full of violence—hitting, falling, throwing, acrobatics—bright dialogue, slapstick action—all imbued with terrific energy. . . .

Emblematic of this new regard for the "wacky" are new hero and heroine types. Among the women Carole Lombard is the most outstanding in her "screwball" activity. Beautiful, frustrated, she asserts intense dissatisfaction with existing conventions and deep bewilderment in seeking justification of her desires. . . .

Among the men perhaps the most representative of the rebels are Fred MacMurray, Cary Grant, and Melvyn Douglas. These men are seekers of one sort or another; they point to maladjustments by pretending with child-like simplicity that they do not exist. They enter in conspiracies with themselves or comrades, telling long stories or building up long situations which are unconventional but which seem right. In *Holiday* Cary Grant turns cartwheels, with perfect English and restraint tells the heroine and the rich and dignified where to go, and dashes off and on the scene with a complete disdain of conventionality.

In his survey of the sociological implications of the screwball comedy, Lewis Jacobs mentioned the titles of twelve films and they all fall into the period between 1934 and 1938. Jacobs wrote the material quoted here almost contemporaneously with the movies he discussed—the chapter heading is "Contemporary Film Content"—and thus he was not viewing the thirties from the perspective of the forties and fifties. His attitude was benign, almost ebullient as he upheld the ideological virtues of rebelliousness and realism against what he considered to be old-fashioned convention.

Jacobs spread his blanket of rhetoric across too many films and genres, and, in the process, lost sight of whatever it was that was unique about the "screwball comedy." For several decades his was the most authoritative reference work on the American cinema, with the result that his formulations were paraphrased in many subsequent texts. At times he was inclined to depend on no more than the title of the film to convey its mood and meaning—his superficial description of Cary Grant's role and function in *Holiday*, for example, is misleading in the extreme. For one thing, the Grant character is at heart less of a rebel than the Katharine Hepburn character. It is his inner conflict between a life of conformity with one sister (Doris Nolan) and a life-long holiday with the other (Hepburn) that provides the dramatic suspense of the film. Besides, *Holiday* (1938) is based on a twenties play by Philip Barry, and it is difficult therefore to see why its content should be especially relevant to the political climate of the thirties even with its inserted reference to John L. Lewis. In fact, the over-all mood of *Holiday* is more reflective and regretful than that of most of the so-called screwball comedies. Grant's acrobatics are more pertinent to a special talent of the performer than to an ideological quirk of the character. And the film itself is almost totally insulated from the clamoring world outside, particularly with reference to a central character who wants to take off a few years from his work as a stockbroker for a "holiday" during which he can tour Europe in search of new ideas Out There. This is clearly more a dream of the twenties than the thirties. Certainly, with millions of people unemployed, how could this dilettantish dream of a holiday be granted any credence as a symptom of social consciousness?

One problem with a sociological interpretation of the cinema is that connections must be assumed between the screen and society even when seemingly no such connections exist. Because there was a Great Depression through the thirties, the movies of that period must reflect it even if they seem frivolous, escapist, and reactionary on the surface. Hence, Cary Grant's cartwheels (actually, somersaults) in *Holiday* must be transformed into revolutionary metaphors, even though his social attitude when he is standing upright is at best whimsically bourgeois. The entire genre, for that matter, is only fitfully concerned with the economic problems of the era. *Nothing Sacred* (1937), with its raucous send-up of the gullibility and sentimentality of the tabloid-transfixed public, could have been set in the twenties insofar as any explicit reference to bread lines and unemployment is concerned. Ben Hecht, the scenarist of *Nothing Sacred*, had collaborated with Charles MacArthur in the twenties on the play *The Front Page*, the prototype of scoop-chasing farces and melodramas through the thirties. The cynical reporter hero in *Nothing Sacred* (in the persona of Fredric March) appears also in *It Happened One Night* (in the persona of Clark Gable), and is a familiar figure on the screen through good times and bad. Indeed, the screwball antics of journalists in the movies are so commonplace that they are consigned to a genre of their own.

To continue with Jacob's own examples, *Twentieth Century* is a back-stage *Pygmalion* farce with sex and slapstick and much shouting and screaming, but with about as much "relevance" to the period as Pinero. *True Confession*, as a courtroom-scandal-with-the-complicity-of-the-tabloid-press comedy, is descended from Maurine Watkins's 1927 play *Chicago*, from which a movie was made that year, and which was remade in 1940 as a Ginger Rogers romp entitled *Roxie Hart*. *Bringing Up Baby* (1938) is a wild, frenzied, savage comedy, but it takes place mostly in an upper-class milieu where money is no object. This is even more true of *The Awful Truth* (1937), a marital sex comedy in which the two leads clearly belong to Society, and flaunt residences in both town and country. *Live, Love and Learn* (1937) was warmed-over Noël Coward-ish bohemian craziness that dates back to the beginning of the so-called Jazz Age. *Theodora Goes Wild* (1936) alternates its action between a well-scrubbed small town and the upper echelons of Manhattan publishing. *Topper* (1937) is a whimsical ghost story in upper-class surroundings where people party to all hours. *My Man Godfrey* (1936) at least begins with an atmospheric awareness of the Depression by focusing on a picturesque city dump where the "forgotten men" of the Depression cluster for survival. A bearded, ragged William Powell plays a forgotten man who is first recruited for a silly society scavenger hunt, and then hired as the butler for an eccentric family. His romantic entanglement with the young lady of the family suggests at first a reworking of Barrie's inter-class comedy, *The Admirable Crichton*, made into a movie by Cecil B. DeMille in 1920 under the title of *Male and Female*. But as Graham Greene noted at the time, *My Man Godfrey* even cheats on the initial titillation of class conflict by making Godfrey a Boston Brahmin down on his luck rather than an authentic representative of the masses. *Merrily We Live* (1938), a transparent imitation of *Godfrey*, is even less responsive to the presumably proletarian stirrings of the Depression.

Andrew Bergman's *We're in the Money: Depression America and Its Films* goes so far as to treat the screwball comedy as a reactionary trend, largely on a simplistic interpretation of the artistic decline of the Marx brothers between their Paramount peak as an anarchic force in *Duck Soup* and their domestication at MGM in *A Night at the Opera*:

> A new kind of comedy became popular in 1934, with the unexpected and gigantic success of Frank Capra's *It Happened One Night*. Labeled "screw-

ball" comedy, it stressed a breezy nuttiness that worked to pull things (marriages, social classes) together, rather than break them apart. It dominated film comedy for the rest of the decade. At another time, maybe the Grouchos could assume power, but for the time being they were relegated to more limited spheres. The public still loved the Marxes, so long as they knew their place. In *A Night at the Opera*, Groucho plays a jobless opera impresario; in *A Day at the Races*, a seedy horse doctor; in *Room Service*, a penniless Broadway producer.

Interestingly enough, the very title of Bergman's book is derived from a song Ginger Roger delivers ironically at the beginning of *Gold Diggers of 1933*. This is the movie that ends with Busby Berkeley's "Forgotten Man," perhaps the most famous of Hollywood's iconic impressions of the Great Depression. Movies from 1930 through 1933 tend to be rawer, grubbier, and franker than movies after 1934. Many of the characters—and not just those portrayed by Mae West and Jean Harlow—are bawdier and more mercenary. The big turning point in movies between 1933 and 1934 can be attributed less to the emergence of the New Deal than to the resurgence of the censors. Jacobs, Bergman, and the other sociological film critics tend to adopt a puritanical tone when writing about the content of movies. And yet an inordinately large proportion of movies made in America has dealt with issues arising during the periods of courtship and early marriage in the lives of extraordinarily photogenic men and women. This is particularly true of the screwball comedies, each of which is based scrupulously on male and female polarities. The thirties, more than any decade before or since, transformed the star system into the co-star system. And if millions of Americans managed to learn anything from movies it was how to meet "cute," kiss "good," and wisecrack their way through a date. Until Parker Tyler came along, however, the solemn pundits of the cinema continued to look past the steamy embraces in the foreground to the restless extras in the background. Tyler tended to condescend somewhat to movies from his vantage point of high art and a process he described as "sociopsychoanalysis." But he did understand the distinctions that had to be made between one star personality and another in "reading" Hollywood movies. Significantly, Tyler began writing about movies in the forties, a decade during which the cinema had become increasingly self-conscious and was no longer considered to be a mirror of reality. The movies of the thirties, by contrast, have remained inseparably linked to all the recorded off-screen events of their time.

In *The Movies*, a picture book by Richard Griffith and Arthur Mayer, there is a societal summation in prose of a four-page illustrated section called "Screwball Comedy":

> But both *The Thin Man* and *It Happened One Night* featured something new to the movies—the private fun a man and a woman could have in a private world of their own making. A new image of courtship and marriage began to appear, with man and wife no longer expecting ecstatic bliss, but treating the daily experience of living as a crazy adventure sufficient to itself. And if what went on in these private worlds was mostly nonsense, what sense could be found in the great world outside, where economic crisis and the threat of approaching war barred all the conventional roads to achievement and happiness? It is hard to describe today what these films meant to a depression-bred generation, and it is not surprising that the "screwball comedies," as they came to be called, usually ended in slapstick or violence. They mirrored a world of frustration.

The eleven films chosen for still illustration by Griffith and Mayer are: *It Happened One Night* (1934), *The Thin Man* (1934), *My Man Godfrey* (1936), *The Mad Miss Manton* (1938), *Hired Wife* (1940), *Nothing Sacred* (1937), *After the Thin Man* (1936), *Bringing Up Baby* (1938), *Friends of Mr. Sweeney* (1934), *You Can't Take It with You* (1938), and *Joy of Living* (1938).

Unfortunately, there is nothing in the material above about the screwball comedy that could not apply equally well to Noël Coward's *Private Lives*. But Griffith and Mayer at least acknowledge courtship and marriage as the dominant narrative elements, and their correlation of slapstick and violence with frustration is another step in the right direction. In the context of their argument it is fairly clear, however, that they attribute "frustration" in the screwball comedies to the "economic crisis" and "the threat of approaching war." But an analysis of the content of all the screwball comedies mentioned thus far reveals surprisingly little awareness in the characters of either an "economic crisis" or "a threat of approaching war." Even when we add the idiosyncratic examples of Griffith and Mayer to those of Jacobs and Bergman, we unearth only more evidence on screen of privilege and guiltless hedonism. Nick Charles in *The Thin Man* (1934) makes most of his income by "managing" wife Nora's sizable investments. Barbara Stanwyck in and as *The Mad Miss Manton* (1938) plays a spoiled society girl who meddles in police investigations of murders. *Joy of Living* (1938) is literally escapist as it demonstrates how a successful musical comedy star (Irene Dunne) with a family of leeches is lured away to a desert island by a charmingly aimless playboy (Douglas Fairbanks, Jr.). *Friends of Mr. Sweeney* (1934), a very genial and sophisticated muckraking and heavy-drinking bacchanal, is not technically eligible for the genre because the protagonist is played by the character actor Charlie Ruggles, while *Hired Wife* is too late (1940) and too gimmicky to qualify.

What then is the source of "frustration" in the screwball comedies? I would suggest that this frustration arises inevitably from a situation in which the censors have removed the sex from sex comedies. Here we have all these beautiful people with nothing to do. Let us invent some substitutes for sex. The aforementioned wisecracks multiply beyond measure, and when the audience tires of verbal sublimation, the performers do somersaults and pratfalls and funny faces. Cary Grant and Katharine Hepburn in *Bringing Up Baby* (1938) dig for a dinosaur bone on a Connecticut estate and pursue a pet leopard all the way into a small-town jail reminiscent of the Keystone Kops. Clark Gable and Claudette Colbert pass the time in *It Happened One Night* (1934) with cutesy debates on the arts of dunking, hitchhiking, and riding piggyback. Myrna Loy and William Powell get laughs in *The Thin Man* (1934) by pausing in front of every tree, post, and hydrant while their dog presumably does his business below the frame of the film. Carole Lombard and Fredric March haul off and sock each other in *Nothing Sacred* (1937). James Stewart and Jean Arthur turn a night club upside down in the name of non-conformity in *You Can't Take It with You* (1938). Irene Dunne and Cary Grant in *The Awful Truth* (1937) romp through a series of slapstick situations that would have given pause to Laurel and Hardy. From 1934 on it does not matter whether the couple is married or not: the act and the fact of sex are verboten. The nice naughtiness which characterized such early thirties comedies as *Laughter* (1930) and *Trouble in Paradise* (1932) and *The Guardsman* (1931) and *Reunion in Vienna* (1933) and *Design for Living* (1933) were supplanted by the subterfuges of screwballism. Even the seductive dance duets of Fred Astaire and Ginger Rogers may have been inspired at least partly by the need to discover a language of motion and gesture that would allow them to circumvent their sexual frustrations.

Jacobs was not aware of all the thematic and stylistic implications of his dismissal of *Angel* (1937) and *Bluebeard's Eighth Wife* (1938) as old-fashioned "philandering." Both films were produced by Ernst Lubitsch's unit at Paramount, and *Bluebeard's Eighth Wife*, which he directed, particularly seems to possess more of the properties of a screwball comedy than many of the movies on Jacob's list. Working with a relatively harsh and sardonic script by Charles Brackett and Billy Wilder, the usually suave Lubitsch has ventured into new realms of cruel, humiliating frustration in the battle of the sexes, a battle in which the much-married modern Bluebeard (Gary Cooper) is virtually driven insane by the shrewdly teasing tactics of his eighth wife (Claudette Colbert). *Angel* is much gentler and more delicate, but it insists as late as 1937 that adultery is still a reasonable option for a civilized woman.

Why should these two films be considered failures, and the screwball comedies be considered successful? Jacobs has not produced box-office figures, but he does quote the published remarks of exhibitors in such journals of hick opinion as the *Motion Picture Herald* and *Harrison's Reports*. It is curious that historians like Jacobs can at one and the same time condemn Hollywood for being too "commercial" and yet endorse movies ideologically simply because they are "popular." It seems that the studios can do no right, and audiences no wrong. Furthermore, the sociological film historian can transfer his own tastes to the people without acknowledging any personal bias.

But for every screwball comedy that we remember fondly today, there are at least ten that would make us grind our teeth over the witless shenanigans of unfunny *farceurs*. The grounds for our admiration are therefore more stylistic than ideological. Certain directors, certain writers, and, above all, certain comediennes suddenly materialized on the scene with a mastery of a self-contradictory genre, the sex comedy without sex. Ernst Lubitsch had been making sly, witty sex comedies in Hollywood since 1925, and he had developed an elliptical style of closed doors and deadpan reaction shots with which to wink at the subject. Still, this was not enough for American puritanism. In order to make his intrigues palatable to the provincials, he had to indulge in the fiction of "Continental" locales, most often Gay Paree. His players, like Sternberg's in romantic melodrama, became increasingly stylized until Marlene Dietrich in *Angel* evolved as a maze of masked ambiguities. Unfortunately, by 1937, the sex could only be hinted at in the most guarded tones. It was there, but in such a subdued state that audiences were no longer amused or titillated. Certain stars were on the rise, and certain stars were being denounced as box-office poison. Marlene Dietrich was considered box-office poison, but for a time so was Katharine Hepburn, and Joan Crawford. They all came back once they had altered some aspect of their image or switched genres. There was a trend away from exotic, upper-class, foreign types toward exuberant, middle-class, all-American types. Carole Lombard, Ginger Rogers, Jean Arthur, Irene Dunne, and

Myrna Loy were in the ascendant. This did not prevent Luise Rainer from winning two Academy Awards for tear-jerking performances in the most impeccably Continental manner. Nor did the supposed vogue for joyously non-philandering screwball comediennes between 1934 and 1938 prevent Bette Davis for winning two Oscars of her own for her two wicked temptresses in *Dangerous* (1935) and *Jezebel* (1938). The point is that one genre did not supplant another; the good movies simply eclipsed the bad ones.

There are a few constants for screwball comedy. First, children almost never exist, and babies absolutely never. The child-cult conventions of the thirties mandated "dramatic" treatment of child-custody problems. *The Awful Truth* goes so far as to exploit the absence of children in a divorce proceeding by waging a comical battle over custody of the dog. The "baby" in *Bringing Up Baby* is, of course, a leopard. *The Thin Man* notwithstanding, the great majority of screwball comedies save marriage for the final fade-out or even beyond. Screwball comedies are therefore generally comedies of courtship, and they may have been considered prescient for anticipating the quarrels that characterize most real marriages.

Howard Hawks once claimed that *Twentieth Century* (1934) was the first Hollywood comedy in which the romantic leads got their own laughs without the help of a pack of vaudevillians. This may not be entirely true since Walter Connolly and Roscoe Karns are on hand in *Twentieth Century* as they are in *It Happened One Night*, and middle-aged character buffoons were to be featured prominently in all thirties comedies, not just to make audiences laugh but to satisfy the audience's notion of common sense and mature wisdom. The last shot of *Nothing Sacred* is not of Carole Lombard and Fredric March embracing on the deck of an ocean liner, but of Charlie Winninger below in his stateroom, deep in his cups, hallucinating through his porthole that the "hotel lobby" was flooded. Nonetheless, Hawks was correct in his emphasis, and no other director went to such lengths to put his romantic leads through their paces. Yet, curiously, neither *Twentieth Century* nor *Bringing Up Baby* was overly successful with audiences in their own time, and these two films were clearly the maddest and most savage confrontations between the sexes. Frank Capra tended to complicate the screwball comedy, first with populist vaudeville (in *It Happened One Night*) and then gradually with populist melodrama in *Mr. Deeds Goes to Town, You Can't Take It with You,* and *Mr. Smith Goes to Washington,* until finally by the time of *Meet John Doe* in 1941 the melodrama had completely engulfed the comedy. Hawks, however, stuck with the primal man-woman struggle throughout his career, and his comedies remain the most audacious in examining the possibilities of role-reversal and sexual metaphor.

Leo McCarey's *The Awful Truth* is the most accomplished of all the screwball comedies in terms of the behavioral charm and breeziness of the humor, and Gregory La Cava's *My Man Godfrey* achieves a genuinely eccentric atmosphere with the least cruelty and violence. Nonetheless, it remains difficult to establish hard and fast boundaries for the genre. Why has no one hitherto mentioned *Three-Cornered Moon* (1933) with its whimsical treatment of a spoiled rich family goofily adjusting to the loss of its wealth in the Crash? The Paramount cycle of romantic farces with Carole Lombard and Claudette Colbert matched up in various combinations with Fred MacMurray, Robert Young, and Melvyn Douglas also made its contributions to the genre.

But if we are to isolate one factor above all others it would have to be the presence in Hollywood at one time of an incredible assortment of gifted comediennes with a variety of trick voices, insinuating mannerisms, and unearthly beauty. There was Irene Dunne, getting a little too close to forty, sometimes a bit too knowing, and her derisively drawling laugh too close to Lynn Fontanne's, but nonetheless with a prodigious warmth. There was Jean Arthur with her bewitchingly bewildered cadences and working-girl beauty—and why has no one mentioned Mitchell Leisen's *Easy Living* (1937) and *Remember the Night* (1940) from Preston Sturges scripts? There was Myrna Loy, of course, and Barbara Stanwyck, and a little later, Rosalind Russell. Ginger Rogers and Katharine Hepburn staged their famous confrontation in *Stage Door* (1937), Rogers the incarnation of the shop girl who rose to stardom, and Hepburn the rebellious rich girl who did not play by the rules. By contrast, the only actor indispensable to the genre was Cary Grant, whose strange mixture of shy, nervous detachment and clownish bravado fit into the underlying uncertainty of the sexual byplay in screwball comedy.

Grant was the first big star to escape bondage to a single-studio long-term contract though it has never been made clear which, if any, of his first twenty-six movies (before *The Awful Truth*) gave him the power to call his own shots. Mae West has tried to claim credit for "discovering" Grant for *She Done Him Wrong* (1933), but he had already made seven movies before the West come-on certified his stud status. The late George Cukor insisted that *Sylvia Scarlett* (1936) put Grant over with the moguls. Since the movie itself was such a commercial and critical dud at the time, and contributed mightily to making Katharine Hepburn "box-office poison," Cukor's assertion seems downright bizarre. Nor did Grant's involvement with Marlene Dietrich and Josef von Sternberg in *Blonde Venus* (1932) do much for his own image. Although he was listed in casts with such yesteryear icons as Carole Lombard, Sylvia Sidney, Tallulah Bankhead, Jean Harlow, Frances Farmer, and even Grace Moore, he was most effective in a light-fun way with Nancy Carroll in *Hot Saturday* (1932) and *The Woman Accused* (1933), and with Joan Bennett in *Big Brown Eyes* and *Wedding Present* (both 1936). *Topper* (1937), with Constance Bennett as his after-life consort, and with Roland Young as the eponymous survivor of this otherworldly farce-fantasy, helped establish a certain high society gloss for his persona, but was otherwise by far the least endearing and enduring of the "classic" screwball comedies.

Then came the one shot more than any other that provides the visual cue for the screwball era. It occurs early on in Leo McCarey's *The Awful Truth* when Grant is seen seated on the top of a luxurious sofa, his right elbow balanced casually on his right knee, which is bent over the sofa's arm-rest, while his left arm is extended to his left knee, which is bent over the seat-cushions. His shoes are thereby pressing rudely on the upscale upholstery as part of a posture of infantile irresponsibility. Off to his right stands Irene Dunne, as his wife, still swathed in ermine after a night out with her "music teacher," a perfectly type-cast snake-in-the-grass in evening clothes (Alexander D'Arcy). Two other couples are standing at either side of the frame, along with a seated but skeptical aunt (Cecil Cunningham) in the center, as witnesses to this early-morning-after marital misunderstanding.

The one conspicuously askew element is that of Grant, perched unconventionally in what would otherwise have been a traditional Coward-Maugham-Barry-Behrman drawing room tableau of suspected infidelity. The acrobatics of Archie Leach combined with the acquired sophistication of Cary Grant proved time and again thereafter that the rich need not be stuffy and stodgy in manner. The talkies had found at last a well-tailored romantic gentleman with the physical gifts of a baggy-pants comic. It was not just a matter of the pratfalls and somersaults Grant performed throughout his career, but innumerable bits of business that tilted this part of his body and that in some speedy flash of behavioral vaudeville.

On the distaff side, the one image, the one voice, the one kinetic force and exquisite surface that came to mind at the time in a flash of feeling was that of Carole Lombard. It can be argued that she started the genre off with *Twentieth Century* in 1934, and, in effect, ended it in 1939 when *Life* Magazine announced that the screwball comedy had gone out of style at the moment that Lombard began sobbing on the screen in *Made for Each Other* when she spotted an oxygen tank being wheeled into her baby's hospital room. In happier times, she could sidle up to a man in her clinging gown without seeming either a clinging vine or a voracious vamp. Lombard always gave something extra to her movie roles, so far transcending them with her luminous beauty that she stands outside them today as a figure of speech for all the sublime imagery that co-existed with the mundane, middle-class homilies of thirties movie scenarios.

THE WESTERN

The Western is perhaps the oldest and most durable of all the Hollywood movie genres; one can trace its ancestry back even before Edwin S. Porter's *The Great Train Robbery* in 1903, when the "Old West" was disappearing into the mists of frontier legend and pulp fiction. But it is not especially ironic that *The Great Train Robbery* was actually shot in New Jersey since movies had not yet moved west to the natural settings of the genre. Even when they did so later in the decade, the scenarios still originated in the fantasies of pulp writers in New York, Boston, and Philadelphia. In the westerns of the 1960s through the nineties, westerns became self-conscious and their heroes much more ambiguous.

But in the silent era, and even in the talkies of the thirties, westerns were as yet not far removed from the real-life characters on whom the legends were based. On the screen most of the action took place in the forty-year period between the end of the Civil War and the beginning of the twentieth century. The period of the French and Indian, the Revolutionary, and the other wars of the eighteenth and early nineteenth century had less appeal for film-makers than the more anarchic post–Civil War era. Horses became more important to the genre as time progressed. The sound of pounding hoofs became even more crucial to the visibility of westerns at the box office after the coming of sound to films.

William Everson, one of the more perceptive chroniclers of the genre, established a contrast between the harsh, serious, religiously redemptive early westerns of William S. Hart and the more flamboyant showmanship of Tom Mix. Yet *Riders of the Purple Sage* (1925), from Zane Grey's anti-Mormon parable, ended with Tom Mix's Lassiter and his new-found love, on the run from a posse, finding themselves as the result of a mountain slide the sole inhabitants of a New Eden, where they resolve to build a life together apart from the rest of civilization. The point is that the western is more varied in its narrative permutations and thematic variations than casual impressions of the genre would suggest. That Everson was born and raised in England is not extraordinary in that the love of the western had achieved universal appeal. Indeed, the cinematic influence of the western eventually spread across the Pacific as well, to Japan, China, and India.

The earliest sound westerns were constricted by the comparative immobility of the early talkies, with their cumbersome equipment. An early sound western like Raoul Walsh's *The Big Trail* (1930) continued the epic tradition of James Cruze's *The Covered Wagon* (1923) and John Ford's *The Iron Horse* (1924) of the silent era, while King Vidor's *Billy the Kid* (1930) continued the gunfighter sagas of Hart, Mix, and Harry Carey's Bronco Billy in the silents. In all instances, the sound film seemed less hospitable to the genre than the silent film had been. For a time, the western seemed to decline as the jazzier gangster film soared to new heights of popularity.

Given my first generation Greek-American background, in the movie houses of Brooklyn, Queens, and Manhattan I found myself less drawn to the wide open spaces of the western than to more congested urban and European genres. Charlie Chan and Philo Vance were more "fun" than George O'Brien and Hopalong Cassidy. My dreams were inspired more by spy pictures like Jacques Feyder's *Knight Without Armour* (1937) with Robert Donat and Marlene Dietrich; Gregory Ratoff's *Lancer Spy* (1937) with George Sanders and Dolores Del Rio; and Carol Reed's *Night Train* (1940) with Rex Harrison, Margaret Lockwood, and Paul Henreid, than by any mere horse opera. Hence, I still lack the childhood viewing memories to sort out the wide-range appeal of the western.

Only in retrospect have I been able to appreciate the deep sadness amounting to a tragic dimension in the less stereotyped ventures in the genre. Before John Ford's epochal *Stagecoach* in 1939, few 1930s westerns could have been memorable for me even had I seen them at the time. Of the ones I do remember being moved by, the two that stand out over all the rest are William Wellman's *Robin Hood of Eldorado* (1936) and Jack Conway's *Viva Villa!* (1934). Significantly, both end with the deaths of their Mexican bandit protagonists, Joaquin Murietta (War-

ner Baxter) and Pancho Villa (Wallace Beery). In both instances under-
dog Latinos lead their people in uprisings against overbearing Anglos in
the Wellman, and against tyrannical land-owning despots in the Conway.
This political aspect appealed to me in childhood possibly because I had
been imbued with an underdog bias due to my father's bitter, almost
paranoid ranting over modern Greece's poor treatment by the Allied Powers during Greece's ill-fated post–World War I defeat at the hands of
the Turks under Kemal Attaturk.

I asked William Wellman toward the end of his life about *Robin Hood
of Eldorado*. He told me that he had wanted Robert Taylor for the Murietta role because Baxter was too old for the part. Wellman was over-
ruled by the studio satraps because Baxter had won an Oscar in the first
Sound Film competition for his expert Mexican accent as the Cisco Kid
in the 1929 western *In Old Arizona*. Although Taylor had been an actor
of limited talent I could see Wellman's point in view of Taylor's memorably charismatic Billy the Kid in David Miller's 1941 Technicolor version.

Other pre-*Stagecoach* (1939) westerns of more than passing interest
in the thirties are Victor Fleming's *The Virginian* (1929) with Gary Cooper, Walter Huston, Richard Arlen, and Mary Brian; Edward L. Cahn's
Law and Order (1932), with Walter Huston, Harry Carey, Andy Devine,
and Walter Brennan, and its nihilistic script by a neophyte screenwriter
named John Huston; King Vidor's *Texas Rangers* (1936); and Cecil B.
De Mille's *Union Pacific* (1939). I happen to disagree with the perceptive
Charles Silver, whose *The Western* is one of the most cogently concise
and stylistically knowledgeable of all the writings on the genre. Indeed,
Silver's study is right up there in its insights with the Eversonian labors
of love. Whereas Silver expresses a preference for *Wells Fargo* (1937)
over *Union Pacific* (1939) in the American empire building sub-genre of
the western, I find De Mille's *Union Pacific*, like his *The Plainsman*, is
more foreground (character) than background (scenery), while Lloyd's
Wells Fargo is more background than foreground.

If I have not included Wesley Ruggles's *Cimarron* (1931), with Irene
Dunne and Richard Dix, among the notable thirties westerns, it is because, aside from the Oklahoma land rush sequence at the beginning of
the film, the bulk of the narrative is a turgid family saga in the most
tedious manner of Edna Ferber. Ironically, this very marginal western
was the only Oscar winner for the genre until Clint Eastwood's *Unfor-
given* (1992).

Hollywood seems to have taken to westerns in a big way after World

War II. It was as if the themes of power and conquest and empire-building had resonated from the fighting fronts in the world arena to the Hollywood back lots and nearby locations. Westerns were no longer predominantly B-picture serials, but A-picture adventures with big stars, big screens, and wild colors. The domains of these movies depicted not the pastoral landscapes of the silent era, but the sprawling ranges of the very late nineteenth century. Post-World War II westerns did not sanctify or even celebrate the frontier legends as earlier westerns had done. There was more questioning of the racist and sexist assumptions of the proto-typical literature on the subject. (There was even a silent western entitled *The Aryan*.) Still, by the end of the forties the questioning of past wrongs had not yet escalated to the outright revulsion which was evident during the civil rights and Vietnam traumas of the sixties, only to subside with the end of the massive American involvement in Vietnam.

The comparatively "classical" westerns of Ford and Hawks continued to co-exist with darker and more neurotic blood westerns (as opposed to the patty-cake pulp fisticuffs, singing cowboys, they-went-thataway plot lines of the juvenile westerns) such as the King Vidor–Niven Busch–David O. Selznick *Duel in the Sun* (1947), with Jennifer Jones, Gregory Peck, Joseph Cotten, Walter Huston, Charles Bickford, Lillian Gish, and Lionel Barrymore. In fact, *Duel in the Sun*, though unkindly greeted by most critics, launched the Freudian western with its orgasmic flames and overtly phallic gun duels. Then there were the social conscience anti-westerns, beginning with William Wellman's anti-lynch western *The Ox-Bow Incident* (1943), from a novel by Walter Van Tilburg Clark and a screenplay by Lamar Trotti. The noble savage western went back to the silent era with Thomas Ince's *The Indian Massacre* (1913), *Last of the Line* (1914), and George B. Seitz's *The Vanishing American* (1925) with Richard Dix playing an Indian; and, in the early sound era, Alan Crossland's *Massacre* (1934) with Richard Barthelmess as a college-educated Sioux, and Henry King's *Ramona* (1936) with Don Ameche as an outcast Indian. Delmer Dave's *Broken Arrow* (1950) and Anthony Mann's *Devil's Doorway* (1951) were more passionate and articulate in their advocacy of the Indian cause, but they were more the beginning of the new skepticism about the old screen legends than the continuation of what had gone before.

My own revisionist view toward the western genre is that if I had to choose between preserving every western before *Duel in the Sun*, and preserving every western after *Duel in the Sun*, I would reluctantly choose the latter course even though it meant losing John Ford's *Stage-

coach (1939) and *My Darling Clementine* (1946). To put it another way, the western is one genre that has become richer in feeling and more profound in form as it rode ever closer to utter extinction. Not that the western genre was ever entirely pure either formally or thematically. Many pulp westerns of the thirties and forties updated their plots to take in automobiles, movie studios, and even airplanes. By the end of the forties, the western was poised for a spectacular leap in creativity.

THE FILM NOIR

The *film noir* is very difficult to define or even categorize as a self-enclosed genre simply because it is largely a critical afterthought in film history. First there were many movies that were violent, morbid, pessimistic, obsessive, visually and literally dark, many of them relegated to the bottom half of double-bills. Gradually a few iconoclastic critics in various countries decided that a new genre had emerged from out of the murk of World War II and the postwar era, periods in which the *film blanc* of sunny optimism and constructive social consciousness had reigned supreme with the reviewing establishment and the American public.

Within the context of the American cinema, however, the *film noir* as it has later been defined or perceived does not seem to have become a full-fledged genre much before 1940. In the thirties there were Alfred Hitchcock and Fritz Lang, and the French lower-depths poetic realism of Jean Renoir and Marcel Carne and Jacques Prévert with its often tragic denouements in the gutters of great cities. But between the demise of the gangster movie (*Underworld, Scarface, Public Enemy*, etc.) and the two-pronged *noir* breakthrough of Orson Welles's *Citizen Kane* and John Huston's *The Maltese Falcon*, both in 1941, there had been a hiatus in which gangsters tended to be displaced by G-men. A lower-billed army of character actors took on gangster roles, while the onetime gangster stars were reformed and redeemed, often in comic variations on the crime genre. Edward G. Robinson, who had been immortalized as Little Caesar, actually parodied his own gangster persona in John Ford and Robert Riskin's *The Whole Town's Talking* (1935). Humphrey Bogart, a second-banana gangster type in the thirties, was often bumped off by his higher-billed colleagues in crime (now "responsibly" rehabilitated from their pre-Code roguishness) such as James Cagney in Michael Curtiz's *Angels with Dirty Faces* (1938) and Raoul Walsh's *The Roaring Twenties* (1939), and Edward G. Robinson in Anatole Litvak's *The Amazing Doctor Clitterhouse* (1938). There was a caste system in the casting of crime movies, and the conformist cream seemed to float to the top.

Indeed, the dominant genres in the thirties were so-called straight dramas and screwball comedies. The mise-en-scène tended to rotate more to sunlight than to darkness. When studio-generated night and fog were called for, as in John Ford's *The Informer* (1935) and Archie Mayo's *Winterset* (1936), the violence in both instances was "redeemed" by the poverty-era politics. For that matter, *Citizen Kane* itself was admired less for its classical *noir* features—its mystery, pessimism, the private eye in the ubiquitous persona of a Luce-like newsreel interrogator, its darkly Expressionistic style veering toward the gothic style of Alfred Hitchcock's *Rebecca* (1940)—than for its tendentiously political rhetoric and its satiric derision of great wealth. There was also too much of the grand manner in the promotion of *Kane* to qualify it for a genre that presumably had to be rescued from obscurity by sharp-eyed pop film historians. The main precursors of the new genre were mere flicks like Jacques Tourneur's *Out of the Past* (1947) and Joseph H. Lewis's *Gun Crazy* (1949) rather than big films like *Citizen Kane* (1941).

One must first be made aware of the prestige and popularity of so many inspirational productions in the 1940s. Most conspicuous and most topical, of course, were the patriotic war movies set on both sides of the Atlantic and the Pacific—*Wake Island* (1942), *In Which We Serve* (1942), *Sergeant York* (1941), *Yankee Doodle Dandy* (1942), *Mrs. Miniver* (1942), *Since You Went Away* (1944), *The Story of Dr. Wassell* (1944), *Thirty Seconds Over Tokyo* (1944), *Bataan* (1943), *So Proudly We Hail* (1943), *Cry Havoc* (1943). And then there were all the fatuously plotted escapist musicals and romances with sugary characterizations. When one adds up all these positive images of movie life for popular consumption, it is no wonder that the sinister, scruffy creatures of *film noir* provided a less inspirational atmosphere for more perceptive viewers.

Of course, those two veterans of the *film noir*, Alfred Hitchcock and Fritz Lang, who had been among the few specialists in the genre in the thirties, managed to transform even the war against fascism into demonstrations of their own thematic and stylistic idiosyncrasies, the former with *Saboteur* (1942), *Lifeboat* (1944), and *Notorious* (1946), and the latter with *Ministry of Fear* (1944), *Hangmen Also Die* (1943), and *Cloak and Dagger* (1946). Indeed, the most famous of all the wartime romances, Resistance sub-category—*Casablanca* (1943)—has many of the trappings and much of the mise-en-scène of *noir*.

For the most fastidious connoisseurs of *noir*, however, the war was too much of a "humanistic" distraction to accommodate the perversities of the genre. There can be no Noble Causes in quintessential *noir*, nor pure heroic characters. Life is lived in vintage *noir* within the margins of moral choice, and protagonists live on the edge and often plunge into the abyss. In a sense, therefore, the first stirrings of distinctively forties *noir* occurred in 1941 not with *Citizen Kane*, or even *The Maltese Falcon*, but in a curiously moody Betty Grable vehicle with the trashy title of *I Wake Up Screaming*. The previous credits of director Bruce Humberstone, scenarist Dwight Taylor, and Betty Grable's co-star Victor Mature do not prepare us for the obsessive force of this study of a man's unrequited passion for an unattainable woman. The ultimate auteur of *this* movie is Laird Cregar, a large, menacing actor with a softly insinuating voice and manner. He prowls around the edges of a routine pairing of the two stars with his unrevealed memories of Grable's slain sister, played with an uncannily and prophetically Pirandellian manner by the ill-fated-suicide-in-real-life Carole Landis. Cregar went on to establish a cult-ish *noir*-ish eminence in *This Gun for Hire*, in which he was taunted by a deadpan assassin played by Alan Ladd. Shortly before his death, Cregar consolidated his reputation in two closely related Jack-the-Ripper-type of psychological thrillers, *Hangover Square* (1945) and *The Lodger* (1944), both directed by John Brahm. Before his untimely death at twenty-eight he had been picked for the Waldo Lydecker role in Otto Preminger's *Laura*, which went to Clifton Webb instead.

In a period of extreme censorship with respect to the mildest suggestions of sexuality, the dark, violent, and presumably unreal worlds of *noir* offered escape valves for the arbitrarily repressed libido. Men and women could lust after each other without undue sentimentality or idealism. Laird Cregar, Clifton Webb, Elisha Cook, Jr., Sydney Greenstreet, and Vincent Price were the most eminent losers on the sexual battlefields of the *film noir*, driven to violent deeds by their defeats. But the "winners" were not much better off most of the time. All through the forties a new breed of male star emerged, less unambiguously moral than his stellar predecessors in the thirties: Robert Mitchum, Burt Lancaster, Kirk Douglas, Dana Andrews, Van Heflin, Edmond O'Brien, Richard Widmark.

Van Heflin was the first actor to win an Oscar for a gangster part, albeit in the supporting category, as the second-in-command to Robert

Taylor's glamourous mobster in the title role of *Johnny Eager* (1942). A prolonged crying scene, unusual for a movie male in 1943, was credited with focusing attention on Heflin's talent. He was seen as the successor to Spencer Tracy, who had made other people cry in 1937 as the stoically doomed Manuel in *Captains Courageous*, a performance that won him an Oscar.

Heflin went off to the war shortly thereafter, and when he came back, he was cast in one of the most memorable *noir* movies of the postwar period, Lewis Milestone's *The Strange Love of Martha Ivers* (1946) with Barbara Stanwyck, Kirk Douglas, and Lizabeth Scott. This violently Freudian stew of guilt, shame, murder, and redemption renewed talk of Heflin as the new Tracy, but subsequent casting trapped him in a series of bloodless romances. Only Fred Zinnemann's *Act of Violence* in 1948 came close to re-establishing Heflin's promise in *Ivers*, but the role was too ambiguous and guilt-ridden to make him a star.

As much as film historians have concentrated on certain directors and writers as the major auteurs, the role of actors, producers, cinematographers, and musical composers, particularly Miklos Rozsa in the forties, should not be overlooked. The success or failure of many *noir* films with reviewers, the public of the time, and subsequent revisionist re-reviewers, depended to a great extent on the aptness of the casting, as always, a key component of the screenwriting.

In this respect, the casting of John Huston's *The Maltese Falcon* (1941) is, among other things, a coup of eerie accuracy. How could Dashiell Hammett have anticipated back in the twenties when he wrote *The Maltese Falcon* that three brilliant character actors named Peter Lorre, Sydney Greenstreet, and Elisha Cook, Jr., would be available in the forties to fit uncannily into the colorful roles of Joel Cairo, Kasper Gutman, and Wilmer Cook respectively? Hammett's novel had been adapted twice before for Warners, the first time with Ricardo Cortez as Sam Spade, the top-billed Bebe Daniels as Brigid O'Shaughnessy, Dudley Digges as Kasper Gutman, and Dwight Frye as the "Gunsel" Witner. Digges and Frye are memorable screen presences from the early thirties, but they are no match for Greenstreet and Lorre, who became a *noir*-ish team in the forties as the "Fat Man" and the "Little Man" in *The Mask of Dimitrios* (1944), *Three Strangers* (1946), and *The Verdict* (1946), not to mention unconnected co-appearances in *Casablanca* (1943), *Background to Danger* (1943), *Passage to Marseille* (1944), and *The Conspirators* (1944). Greenstreet and Lorre, alone or in tandem, were nothing if not devious in their dealings with the rest of the world. Greenstreet's nearly 300-pound bulk and sonorously rumbling voice made him an overpoweringly authoritative screen presence, whereas Lorre's credulous bulging eyes enabled him to play the calculating *faux-naif* with the aid of the child-like timbre of his voice. Both actors tended to be apparitions of the night for a studio that specialized in dark Expressionism.

As well as providing John Huston with an opportunity to make his directorial debut after having made his mark as a screenwriter in the thirties, *The Maltese Falcon* catapulted Humphrey Bogart to star status. He made Sam Spade more of a *noir*-ish lone wolf private detective than had any of his thirties predecessors. The detective story, which went back to the last century with Edgar Allan Poe's C. Auguste Dupin and Conan Doyle's Sherlock Holmes, had become flabby from trivializing facetiousness and formulaic reiteration on the screen in the thirties. The private detectives of William Powell's Philo Vance and Nick Charles, Warner Oland's Charlie Chan, Walter Pidgeon's Nick Carter, Peter Lorre's Mr. Moto, Edward Arnold's Nero Wolfe, Warren William's Perry Mason, even Ricardo Cortez's Sam Spade, spent almost as much time on farcical digressions and alcoholic antics as on solving murders. Furthermore, thirties detectives worked in close, if often mocking collaboration with the police. Bogart's Spade drove a wedge between the forces of darkness and the forces of law and order by making the detective an anarchic and morally marginal hero, ultimately responsible to no one but himself.

■   ■   ■   ■

AFTER *THE MALTESE FALCON*, a new detective genre emerged—leaner, tougher, and darker than anything in the thirties. At lower levels of the movie industry the silliness continued with the debased Charlie Chans of Sidney Toler, the childishly cerebral Ellery Queen series, the precociously feminist Nancy Drew, Detective, Boston Blackie, the Saint, Mike Shayne, *inter alia*. In the realm of A-pictures, however, Raymond Chandler supplanted Dashiell Hammett as the major detective writer source in the forties. Chandler's gallery of detective heroes was made up of Dick Powell's Philip Marlowe in Edward Dmytryk's *Murder, My Sweet* (1944), Bogart's Marlowe in Howard Hawks's *The Big Sleep* (1946), Robert Montgomery's Marlowe in Montgomery's *The Lady in the Lake* (1946), and George Montgomery's Marlowe in John Brahm's *The Brasher Doubloon* (1947). More obliquely, his literary influence as a screenwriter pervaded Billy Wilder's *Double Indemnity* (1944) and George Marshall's *The Blue Dahlia* (1946). The Marlowe character has been reprised as late as the sixties and the seventies, with James Garner in Paul Bogart's *Marlowe* (1969) and Robert Mitchum in Dick Richard's *Farewell, My Lovely* (1975), but Chandler and Marlowe are locked forever into the fantasies of the forties about California and dangerous women.

The temptation to group all *noir*-ish movies of the forties into a few sociological formulas must be resisted at all costs. Too many cross-references abound. Directors, writers, players, cinematographers, composers, set designers, producers all swirled together into a variable mix of malaises. The world was simply a gloomier and more complicated place during and after the war than it had been before. A mentally disturbed war veteran figures prominently in the murderous plot of *The Blue Dahlia* (1946) and in the otherwise sentimental *I'll Be Seeing You* (1944) and *Love Letters* (1945), both directed by William Dieterle. The sanctified violence of the war thus contributed to the escalation of violence in civilian life.

The forties *noir* director most perceptibly influenced by World War II was John Huston, who directed only three feature films before joining the war effort as a realistic documentarian. After *The Maltese Falcon* was released in 1941, Huston was generally thought to be marking time on his Warners contract with *In This Our Life* and *Across the Pacific*, both released in 1942. From the point of view of Huston's biographers and film historians of the period, *In This Our Life* (1942), from Howard Koch's screenplay, based on Ellen Glasgow's novel, seemed an incongruously feminine interlude in an over-all career conspicuous for its displays of muscular virility.

Bette Davis as the man-stealing bad sister and Olivia De Havilland as the nobly suffering good sister effortlessly overshadow and outshine George Brent and Dennis Morgan, the well-groomed men in their lives. But there are more insights in this domestic melodrama than its obscurity might indicate. Aside from the personal involvement of Huston with De Havilland, and the stormy studio clashes with Davis over her uncompromisingly unsympathetic interpretation of her already villainous role, there are around the edges of the central drama Ernest Anderson's portrayal of a young, educated, sympathetic black male jailed in a miscarriage of justice; Charles Coburn's unexpectedly cowardly reaction to his character's terminal illness; Frank Craven's weak patriarch; and a cameo barroom appearance by Walter Huston with some of the cast of *The Maltese Falcon*. Hence, *In This Our Life* turns out in retrospect to have been more of a personal project for Huston than was evident at the time. The curious conceit of having the Davis and De Havilland female characters both christened with male names, Stanley and Roy respectively, is derived from the Ellen Glasgow novel set in thirties Richmond, Virginia, but it fits in almost too neatly with Huston's male-oriented ethos, which, like Ernest Hemingway's, possibly conceals a strong matriarchal influence in childhood. Thus, *In This Our Life* can be seen as emerging from the mists of film history as a *noir*-ish woman's picture directed with unaccustomed gusto by a man's director. Many of Huston's most expressive groupings and camera set-ups showed the influence of William Wyler's work in *Jezebel* (1938) and *The Letter* (1940).

Across the Pacific (1942), by contrast, was a muddled attempt to cash in on the Humphrey Bogart–Mary Astor chemistry in *The Maltese Falcon* with a plot that dwindles and self-destructs into the most hackneyed form of post–Pearl Harbor Jap-bashing. Sydney Greenstreet is on hand as the traitorous villain, but Peter Lorre and Elisha Cook, Jr., have been replaced as his equally evil companions by the topically more appropriate Keye Luke. Huston never resolved the ridiculous climax of the film in which Bogart is being held prisoner by a small army of Japanese as a sneak attack is about to be made on the Panama Canal. Vincent Sherman completed the patriotic movie in the midst of early wartime hysteria with a preposterous escape from and annihilation of the enemy by a Rambo-before-his-time Bogart. Still, much of the incidental badinage between Bogart and Astor, and between Bogart and Greenstreet, perpetuated the rapport established by these stylish performers in *The Maltese Falcon*. On one occasion, Bogart and Greenstreet compare the respective revolvers they keep concealed on their persons, and Bogart quips with mock priapic pride, "Mine is bigger than yours." For the most part, however, the *noir*-ish look of *Across the Pacific* merely camouflaged the red-white-and-blue banalities of a conventional pulp adventure.

Huston's next narrative film, *The Treasure of the Sierra Madre*, would not materialize on the screen until 1948, six turbulent years after *Across the Pacific*. In the meantime, he made three wartime documentaries— *Report from the Aleutians* (1942), *The Battle of San Pietro* (1944), and *Let There Be Light* (1945), the last a study of shell-shocked veterans that was suppressed by the War Department for many years after the war. Huston's run-ins with the House Un-American Activities Committee in the late forties added a political tinge to his *noir*-ish tendencies. His adaptation of B. Traven's *The Treasure of the Sierra Madre* demonstrated Huston's expanding world-view with its spectacular location shooting in Mexico. What in book form was a dream-like fable of greed in an expatriate's Mexico became on film a realistic adventure with cynicism and disillusion lurking at the end of the quest. In some ways, the movie was more nihilistic and despairing than the book. In others, the movie was more hopefully redemptive. The director's collaboration with his famous actor-father Walter Huston resulted in Oscars for both. James Agee hailed the postwar Huston as Hollywood's humanistic hero and likened *Treasure* to Erich von Stroheim's *Greed* as a study of the pernicious effect of gold on the fragile psyches of grasping humanity. Max Steiner's inspirational score tended to undercut some of the ironies of Huston's cautionary fable, and the touches of sentimentality added to the book's own terminal resignation only underscored the director's downbeat tendencies. Hailed for its "brutal realism" by many critics, *Treasure* was shunned by audiences for its forbiddingly bleak reputation. The ultimate value of the movie was somewhere in between the extreme verdicts. Huston's flair for physical action and colorful detail enabled him to utilize the bad acting of Mexican bandit chief Alfonso Bedoya in memorable confrontations with his Anglo antagonists played by Walter Huston, Humphrey Bogart, Tim Holt, and Bruce Bennett. No American movie before it had penetrated so prophetically into the colonial mind-set toward the Third World as did *Treasure*. A decade before *The Quiet American* and *The Ugly American*, Huston's grubby treasure-seekers were pillaging the Sierra Madre, and doing it entertainingly.

Where Huston was deficient was in the psychological development of the characters to the point of self-discovery. By postulating a cosmic indifference to their fate, Huston left them to indulge in spasms of hollow laughter. To the modest social edifice of *The Maltese Falcon* Huston had added a world-view gained from the war and the troubled peace that followed. In *Treasure* and his subsequent projects, *Key Largo* (1948) and *We Were Strangers* (1949), Huston was overloading the *noir* genre with social concerns and bloated One World rhetoric that force-fed the audience with special pleading. If Huston can be said to have originated the *film noir* in Hollywood with *The Maltese Falcon*, he can be said to have taken it close to its zenith in 1950 with *The Asphalt Jungle* before virtually abandoning it altogether.

■   ■   ■   ■

OTTO PREMINGER, one of the most accomplished *auteurs* of forties *noir*, was assigned initially to produce *Laura* (1944) with Rouben Mamoulian directing. The early rushes displeased Darryl F. Zanuck, or so the production story goes, and Preminger replaced Mamoulian. Also replaced was an "interpretative" painting of "Laura" by a more realistically illusionist rendering of Gene Tierney in the charismatic role of Laura. A tightly written script by Jay Dratler, Samuel Hoffenstein, and Betty Reinhardt, adapted from the novel by Vera Caspary, was acted out by an inspired ensemble.

The deadly males of the species—the stalwart phlegmatic detective played by Dana Andrews, the prissily sophisticated man about town played by Clifton Webb, and the shameless ne'er-do-well played by Vincent Price—gathered like moths around the flame of Gene Tierney's enigmatic beauty. Off to one side was Judith Anderson, a sexually hungry socialite with the piercing gaze of a Lady Macbeth, one of her famous theatrical triumphs. By keeping all his suspects in the same frame, as if they were scorpions in a bottle, Preminger achieved an ambiguity in the characterizations that slows down the rush of melodramatic excitement at the violent climax. Joseph La Shelle's Oscar-winning cinematography and the haunting pop melody of David Raksin's title tune give *Laura* a sheen and polish few pop entertainments of any age can match. Clifton Webb as the epicene columnist who loves Laura as a precious object d'art, and Vincent Price as the stud/gigolo, were just gaining attention in 1944 and were not yet the overfamiliar icons they later became. Similarly, Gene Tierney and Dana Andrews were glowing forties icons insufficiently appreciated in recent decades. Only Judith Anderson preserved her aura for the ages. Although *Laura* was clearly Preminger's most satisfying achievement in terms of sheer pleasure, it was also an albatross around his neck in that, like Orson Welles with *Citizen Kane*, Preminger was thought not to have lived up to the promise of *Laura*.

Otto Preminger (1906–86), the director American critics loved to hate, spent almost half a century in what the French describe as making cinema, thirty-five works to be precise, of which he produced twenty-one. Preminger acted out his patented bald-pate Prussian Nazi heavy in four other movies, most memorably in Billy Wilder's *Stalag 17* (1953). Unfortunately for his critical reputation, his real-life nasty-Nazi image was widely construed in real life as the key to his overbearing, publicity-seeking presence, excessive even by Hollywood's hyped-up standards.

Nonetheless, a small minority of cinéastes, including this reviewer, took Preminger more seriously as an artist and a stylist. We tended to divide his oeuvre into two major periods: (1) the 20th Century-Fox-studio-black-and-white-*film noir*, beginning with *Laura* (1944), ending explosively with *Angel Face* (1953); and (2) the big-project-wide-screen-public-occasion series, beginning with *The Moon Is Blue* (1953) and end-ing with *The Human Factor* (1980) at the close of his career.

Ultimately, in appraising Preminger's career, it is not a consistent theme we must look for but a consistent attitude. One critic has called it fairness, another the ambiguity of objectivity. I would prefer to stress the perversely objective camera viewpoint that keeps his characters in the same frame. Why did Preminger present his spectacles in this way? As he himself explained, he had come from the theater where he was accustomed to looking at drama as a spatial whole. Consequently, he intuitively resisted the mystique of montage. His movies are not cluttered with over-the-shoulder cross-cutting to equalize the close-ups allotted to co-stars, a practice derided by André Bazin as *"champs-contre-champs."* Without an inbred instinct for cutting, Preminger was not able to execute the movie gags for which Hollywood had developed an elaborate cine-matographic language. It followed almost logically that Preminger's sub-jects, more often than not, had a solemn, somber quality. His melodramas at Fox, particularly *Laura* (1944), *Fallen Angel* (1953), *Whirlpool* (1950), *Where the Sidewalk Ends* (1950), and his RKO loan-out, *Angel Face* (1953), are all moodily fluid studies in perverse psy-chology rather than crackling suspense movies. The characters clicked even when the action faltered. The reviewer in search of zippy melo-drama would have marked Preminger as a failure in most of these films, possibly all except *Laura* (1944).

Even Preminger's most ill-fated films bear the signs of an over-all conception and the marks of a personal attitude. If a *Centennial Summer* (1946) or a *Porgy and Bess* (1959) fails to come off, it is not because the director lacked a coherent style for these musicals, but, rather, because the various elements in the musicals (including the melodious scores of Jerome Kern and George Gershwin respectively) failed to connect with Preminger's conception. By contrast, *Carmen Jones* (1954) succeeds on its own questionable terms as the Preminger musical par excellence—drab, austere, unpleasant, and completely depoeticized.

Several times in his career Preminger moved into direct competition or comparison with other directors. *A Royal Scandal* (1945) and *The Fan* (1949) pointed up Preminger's relationship to Lubitsch, as did obviously *That Lady in Ermine* (1948), which Preminger finished after Lubitsch's death. It is not entirely fair to Preminger, however, to place him out of his time. As Lubitsch represented the unobtrusive cutting of the twenties and thirties, Preminger did the camera movement and long takes of the forties, fifties, and sixties. If Lubitsch summed up his time, Preminger was ahead of his in his Fox period. The Lubitsch virtues have disappeared from the cinema, and we are the poorer for it, but Preminger anticipated the conditions that would cause their disappearance. The grace and precision of Lubitsch's sensibility seem out of place in a world consecrated to the most grotesque explosion of the ego. Preminger's impassive gaze—accepting the good with the bad, the beautiful with the ugly, the sublime with the mediocre—is both more appropriate and merciful.

Preminger himself refused to compare *The Thirteenth Letter* (1951) with the 1943 Henri-Georges Clouzot French Occupation–era original *Le Corbeau (The Raven)*; but it might be noted that Preminger's version is less vicious and misanthropic than the original, and not merely because of the laundered Hollywood script. Preminger had no patience with the virus of suspicion, and he tended to give the show away rather than degrade his characters with the useless doubts of the whodunit.

This leaves us with a director who has made at least three fully articulated masterpieces of ambiguity and objectivity—*Laura* (1944), *Angel Face* (1953), and *Bunny Lake Is Missing* (1965)—a director who saw all problems and issues as a single-take two-shot, the stylistic expression of the eternal conflict not between right and wrong, but between the right-wrong on one side and the right-wrong on the other, a representation of the right-wrong in all of us as our share of the human condition. In the midst of the conflict stood Otto Preminger, right-wrong, good-bad, and probably sincere-cynical.

The sub-texts of *Laura* remain as enduringly tantalizing as its glittering surfaces. The point of view shifts repeatedly back and forth from Clifton Webb's wittily decadent Waldo Lydecker to Dana Andrew's morbidly hard-boiled detective Mark McPherson. One would expect that a murder mystery would have as its single point-of-view character the person entrusted to find the murder. Yet from the beginning Waldo weaves a spell by defining the world in which the murder took place. His is the only off-screen voice painting a portrait of the supposedly slain Laura as verbally luminous as her on-screen painting is visually. In a sense, McPherson falls in love with the Laura that Waldo has created for him, even though for the first half of the movie we are led to believe that Laura is dead. Waldo confronts McPherson with the taunt that the detective has fallen in love not with a ghost but with a corpse, as befits the gruesome taste of a vulgar detective.

When Laura herself materializes as in a dream, McPherson is forced to deal with a flesh-and-blood woman not as easily controlled as the supposedly dead Laura had been in his fantasy life. What is strange about the film is its leading the audience down the garden path of a ghostly romanticism only to shatter the illusion with a strong dose of logic and reality. It turns out that it was not Laura Hunt who was murdered, but a model named Diane Redfern whom Vincent Price's Shelby Carpenter had taken to Laura's apartment while she was away. We never see Redfern except for a fashion photograph, and since she was shot in the face with a double-barreled shotgun after she went to the door to answer a persistent ringing, the mistaken identification of Laura as the murder victim is easily accepted. All the bases are covered in this seemingly improbable scenario. Two shotguns, two clocks, two murder suspects, two possible victims add up to enough red herrings and false leads to sustain a mystery. But what makes *Laura* unusual is the social texture of a cosmopolitan society evoked by a handful of colorful, articulate characters in a handful of luxurious interiors lushly photographed by Joseph La Shelle. Indeed, the look of *Laura* is more brightly lit *film blanc* than darkly Expressionist *film noir*. There are a few shadows here and there, and a few exteriors, but the darkness is mostly indoors in the hearts and souls of the characters.

The movie ends not with the two charismatic lovers but with the dying words of Waldo Lydecker as he fails a second time to kill Laura, the love of his life, after McPherson and his fellow detectives intervene in the nick of time. The concluding metaphor is an ornate clock, given to Laura by Waldo, now shattered by his errant shotgun blast intended for her. By now we have become enamored of Waldo's scathingly snobbish critiques of the "earthy" relationship of ever so physically charismatic a couple as Laura and Mark. Hence, we grieve for the stilling of an amusing voice that concealed a murderous passion.

As for Mark and Laura, their later existence beyond the parameters prescribed by the movie projector would seem to be mediocre at best, disruptively contentious at worst. Having fallen in love with a romantically unattainable ideal, and then finding himself instead with a provincial Galatea deprived of her urbane Pygmalion, Mark might begin drinking the hard stuff even more heavily than he did in the film itself as a semi-alcoholic stereotype of the hard-boiled hero of the forties.

The success of *Laura* led to at least two less popular spin-offs, Otto Preminger's *Fallen Angel* (1945), from a screenplay by Harry Kleiner, adapted from a novel by Marty Holland, and Henry Hathaway's *The Dark Corner* (1946), from a screenplay by Jay Dratler and Bernard Schoenfeld, based on a story by Leo Rosten. The similarities to *Laura* are not so much in the casting inasmuch as only Dana Andrews appears in both *Laura* and *Fallen Angel*, and only Clifton Webb appears in both *Laura* and *The Dark Corner*, but in the basic motive for murder being the hopeless obsession of an older man with a young and beautiful woman. As we have noted previously, Laird Cregar began the process in Bruce Humberstone's *I Wake Up Screaming* (1941), and many other character actors followed in his footsteps.

Dana Andrews plays a more marginal, if less morbid character in *Fallen Angel* than he did as the detective in *Laura*. In the later movie he is almost on the wrong side of the law as a small-time confidence man out to swindle a young woman (Alice Faye) out of her fortune by first marrying her, and then absconding with her money in cahoots with a scheming waitress (Linda Darnell). When the waitress is murdered, he becomes one of the suspects along with another of the victim's lovers (Bruce Cabot) and the suspiciously watchful confidence man's sister-in-law (Anne Revere). Presiding over the investigation in the stifling small town in which the action takes place is a sadistic retired New York detective (Charles Bickford). The plot moves on two tracks in redeeming the initially cynical relationship between the Andrews and Faye characters as it solves the mystery of the murder in whodunit fashion. In an early shot we see Andrews, Bickford, and Cabot in the same frame being viewed by Preminger's and Joseph La Shelle's passively compassionate camera as three moths bewitched by the same fatal flame. The problem with the public was that the familiar virgin/whore dichotomy was less absorbing in *Fallen Angel* than the single female protagonist, played by Gene Tierney in *Laura*, combining the roles of temptress and redeemer in one character. Linda Darnell had not yet come into her own as a sexy comedienne as she was to do in Preston Sturges's *Unfaithfully Yours* (1948) and Joseph L. Mankiewicz's *A Letter to Three Wives* (1949).

For her part, Alice Faye was trying to salvage her fading career as Fox's torch-singer of the late thirties and early forties with an off-beat serious role. Neither Darnell nor Faye was able to evoke the erotic and romantic excitement endemic to the genre at the time. Dana Andrews was fading fast at Fox as Gregory Peck was rising meteorically as the new charismatic male star of the forties. Unfortunately, the chemistry was simply not there in the Andrews-Faye and Andrews-Darnell pairings. Yet Preminger fashioned a haunting *film noir* out of this small-scale melodrama of provincial frustration and twisted desire. Missing was the cosmopolitan elegance of *Laura* with its glossy view of Manhattan high life.

Fallen Angel (1945) returned *noir* to the West Coast wastelands of James M. Cain and Horace McCoy.

The Dark Corner (1946) was more conventional than *Fallen Angel* in that the moral alignments were never in question. Straight-arrow leading man Mark Stevens plays a beleaguered private detective caught up in a fiendish conspiracy to have a murder committed and have him framed for it. Loyal Gal Friday and sweetheart Lucille Ball plays it straight with the slightly goofy comic relief intonations that were later on television to make her fortune in *I Love Lucy.* Arrayed against them are Clifton Webb as a Waldo Lydecker-like art collector, Cathy Downs as his voluptuously faithless wife, Kurt Krueger as her doomed gigolo lover, and William Bendix as a private detective and particularly devious murderer whose own demise is as surprising as the murders committed by him. Here the emphasis is more on the intricacies of the villainies than on the obsessive force of sexual desire. Clifton Webb plays a character whose insane jealousy is revealed very slowly, almost teasingly, as the key to the convoluted murder plot. Cathy Downs as the faithless wife is relegated to a very minor role, and the result is a male-female buddy-bonding movie involving Mark Stevens and Lucille Ball. The most striking character presence is played by William Bendix, a gravel-voiced, Brooklyn-accented mug type, with deep emotional resonance. His bravura performances in Frank Tuttle's *The Glass Key* (1942) and Alfred Hitchcock's *Lifeboat* (1944) had established him as an explosive talent, and his best roles were in *noir* enterprises.

Henry Hathaway's career spanned five decades with innumerable routine projects in the realms of romance and adventure. He became associated in the mid-forties with Louis de Rochement's "semi-documentary" movement with such portentously publicized spy adventure films as *The House on 92nd Street* (1945) and *13 Rue Madeleine* (1947). The semi-documentary mystique eventually amounted to little more than extensive location shooting. The illusion of "newness" was aided in no small measure by the use of unfamiliar performers from the Broadway theater, particularly in Elia Kazan's *Boomerang* (1947).

■　■　■　■

FRITZ LANG (1890–1976) can be credited with virtually inventing the *film noir*, and with profoundly influencing such giants of the medium as Eisenstein, Hitchcock, and Buñuel. Such distinguished admirers as Claude Chabrol, Jean-Luc Godard, Luc Moullet, Mark Shivas, and Lotte Eisner have valiantly attempted to make a case for Lang's last and least

spasms of creativity, but in his style the warts have always co-existed
with the beauty marks. His movies have always appealed more to high-
brows, who are not put off by a pulp approach and silliness, than to
middlebrows, who demand at least a modicum of what passes for "realism."

Lang anticipated many of the horrors of our age. If Hitler had never
existed, the director would have had to invent him: Sooner or later,
Lang's masterful megalomaniac, Dr. Mabuse, would have degenerated
into *Der Fuehrer.* Lang repudiated Hitler and everything he represented,
but he seemed morbidly fascinated by the magnetic force of evil on the
screen. Never the sunny optimist prescribed by the aesthetics of social
realism, he prowled the dark corners of the soul, where destiny collided
with depravity.

Lang was, like Hitchcock, afflicted by the genre prejudices of critics
throughout his career. There were too many guns in Lang's movies. His
characters were never developed with any psychological precision, and
his world lacked the details of verisimilitude that were so important to
realist reviewers. Lang found himself unemployable by the mid-sixties,
when *film noir,* the genre he ennobled, became critically fashionable.

After he left Germany, Lang directed Ferenc Molnar's *Liliom* (1934),
one of his gentlest and loveliest films, starring Charles Boyer. *Liliom,*
with its extra-terrestrial emotions, falls into place only when one recalls
the lyrical intimations of mortality in *Spies* (1928), *You Only Live Once*
(1937), *The Big Heat* (1953), and *Moonfleet* (1955).

His first Hollywood feature, *Fury* (1936), immediately catapulted him
into critical favor. Norman Krasna's extremely agitated screenplay was
based on a widely reported, matter-of-fact lynching of two kidnapping
suspects in California in the early thirties. For once, the theme of the
film was considered "significant" enough to accommodate the full force
of Lang's Teutonically terrorizing style. The direction added a new dimension of dementia to mob violence against a working-class protagonist
(Spencer Tracy), who is caged like an animal on a false kidnapping
charge. Sylvia Sidney served as the rhetorical conscience of the film (as
she would in Lang's *You Only Live Once* (1937) and *You and Me* (1938)),
first against the lynchers, then against Tracy, her vengeful boyfriend who
has miraculously escaped the flames. The only unintimidated witness to
the lynching turns out to be some newsreel footage of the event. This
technological coup introduced a new theme—media manipulation—
which Lang would later explore in *While the City Sleeps* (1956) and *The
Thousand Eyes of Dr. Mabuse* (1960).

It was Lang's misfortune that his later Hollywood movies were measured against the presumed promise of *Fury* (1936). *You Only Live Once* (1937), for example, failed to consolidate Lang's standing in Hollywood, despite the film's tragic intensity and visual creativity. (In the sixties, this ironic love story would be perceived as the dark underside of *It Happened One Night* (1934), and the precursor of *They Live By Night* (1949), *Gun Crazy* (1949), *Bonnie and Clyde* (1967), and *Thieves Like Us* (1974).)

As the servant of an allegedly optimistic film industry, Lang was singularly successful in undercutting audience expectations of a moral balance regained. The prevailing image in his movies is a world ravaged and in flames. The hero is nearly burned to death in *Fury*, and mortally shot with his wife in *You Only Live Once*. In *Rancho Notorious* (1952), the hero's wife is raped and murdered—as is her child, in a direct evocation of the bouncing-ball murder of the innocents in *M* (1931). The wife (Jocelyn Brando) in *The Big Heat* (1953) is blown up when she presses the starter of the car, and her husband (Glenn Ford) must not only avenge her death but also assuage his guilt (he was the intended victim). But the most memorable violence in *The Big Heat* is the flinging of scalding hot coffee in Gloria Grahame's face by Lee Marvin, and later (in a vendetta worthy of Kriemhild), in his face by her. Lang's explosive mise-en-scène implies that the world must be destroyed before it can be purified.

Through the forties Fritz Lang's Germanic visual style found itself increasingly attuned to Hollywood's darkening moods. The war clouds of the late thirties had begun raining down real bombs and for a brief interlude the anti-fascist crusade had become patriotic duty. There was no shortage of writers, actors, and producers with a world-view similar to Lang's, and more than a few critics of the period singled him out for his distinctive artistry and accomplished craftsmanship.

Lang was cinematically Americanized, genre-wise, in 1940 with *The Return of Frank James*, the first of his trinity of revenge westerns—*Western Union* (1941) and *Rancho Notorious* (1952) following. At the time, Lang's graceful outdoors adventure was dismissed as a tame sequel to Henry King's fiercely populist and stridently self-righteous *Jesse James* (1939). Fortunately for Lang, Henry Fonda's relaxed cornpone timing, which stole every scene from Tyrone Power's furrow-browed Jesse James in the original, now had the opportunity to stretch out in the lead role of brother Frank, who, by the strictures of the censors, had to avenge Jesse's murder without actually killing anyone himself, a difficult task for any western less tongue-in-cheek than Lang's. On the distaff side Gene

Tierney was welcome as Fonda's low-key love interest, particularly after the laborious hysterics of Nancy Kelly in *Jesse James*.

Western Union was more familiar Lang territory in its story of a deadly sibling rivalry between good brother Randolph Scott and bad brother Barton MacLane. The twist in the Zane Grey novel adapted to the screen by Robert Carson is that after the bad brother gets the drop on the good brother and kills him, greenhorn Robert Young takes on the task of avenging the good brother more through the steadfastness of a virtuous man than through the skill of a gunfighter. Whatever the genre, Lang remained an implacable moralist.

Lang's next five films—*Man Hunt* (1941), *Hangmen Also Die* (1943), *The Woman in the Window* (1944), *Ministry of Fear* (1944), and *Scarlet Street* (1945)—kept him in Hollywood's mainstream through the end of the War. Lang's stylistic influence had helped spawn a new generation of Hollywood *noir* directors—Anthony Mann, Joseph H. Lewis, Robert Siodmak, Arthur Ripley, Jacques Tourneur, Anthony Mann, Joseph Losey, Jules Dassin, Andre De Toth, Robert Rossen, and Abraham Polonsky—who nonetheless stole much of Lang's thunder and lightning, with timelier variations of their own. Lang was already falling behind the *Zeitgeist* in 1946 with *Cloak and Dagger*, an espionage yarn concocted by Hollywood screenwriters Albert Maltz and Ring Lardner, Jr., who were later blacklisted. The movie concerns an American physics professor as an American agent spying in Germany, a role in which Gary Cooper, masquerading with a monocle, was woefully miscast. The *Secret Beyond the Door* (1948) descended into the miasma of an overheated Freudian lady-in-distress melodrama in which Lang regular Joan Bennett made her fourth and last appearance for the director opposite British theater great Michael Redgrave, who was not lucky enough to be given a role with the lucidity and panache of Laurence Olivier's Maxim de Winter in *Rebecca*.

Man Hunt (1941) is the Hollywood Lang film that comes closest to executing the geometric puzzle effect of his 1933 German classic *M*. Adapted from Geoffrey Household's ingenious thriller about a big-game hunter stalking Hitler in Bergtesgarten, first for fun, and then for real, Dudley Nichols's screenplay is as leanly constructed as Lang's inexorable editing and camera placement. Walter Pidgeon plays the hero with the subtly noble style that was not fully appreciated until he teamed up with Greer Garson. George Sanders projects an omnipotent malignity as the hero's deadly pursuer. Joan Bennett plays the doomed love interest in this the first of her four collaborations with Lang through the decade with the backing of studio boss husband Walter Wanger.

Hangmen Also Die (1943) was Lang's first contribution to the anti-Nazi resistance film genre that was at the height of fashion through the critical and popular success of *Casablanca* (1943) and *Watch on the Rhine* (1943). *Hangmen* was closer to the latter than the former in its ideological ferocity and lack of humor and irony. A makeshift cast headed by Brian Donlevy, Anna Lee, and Dennis O'Keefe with character support from Gene Lockhart and Walter Brennan provided discordant American accents as Czechs conspiring to frame a traitor in their midst, for the assassination of Heydrich. Singly or collectively, they were no histrionic match for the colorfully evil Gestapo chief played by Alexander Granach. The original story by Fritz Lang and Bertolt Brecht, and adapted by John Wexley, saved the best for last with the memorable death of the traitor on the steps of the cathedral.

Lang's three films in 1945—*Ministry of Fear, Woman in the Window*, and *Scarlet Street*—represent his last hurrah in Hollywood. In *Ministry of Fear* Ray Milland, in the pre-*Lost Weekend* phase of his career, made a charismatic protagonist in this very loose adaptation by Paramount producer and screenwriter Seton I. Miller of a Graham Greene novel. A mysteriously miscast Marjorie Reynolds as a foreign-accented refugee committee worker is overshadowed literally and figuratively by three splendid villains played by Carl Esmond, Dan Duryea, and Alan Napier. Lang's visual coups were awash with espionage paraphernalia as good triumphed over evil after a quintessentially Langian séance.

Woman in the Window and *Scarlet Street* can be considered as a continuous descent into adultery *cum* homicide with an infernal triangle consisting of Edward G. Robinson as an over-age Adam, Joan Bennett as a tarnished Eve, and Dan Duryea as a humorously reptilian opportunist. Adapted from a Nunnally Johnson screenplay about a married professor who runs afoul of a shady lady (Bennett) and a blackmailer (Duryea), *Woman in the Window* was better received than *Scarlet Street*. A comic dream-ending verged on the brink, but Robinson's comic gifts in *noir* situations saved the day. By contrast, *Scarlet Street* was much darker in its tone and pitiless in its moral judgments. Adapted by Dudley Nichols from a French play *La Chienne* by Georges de la Fouchardière, and filmed in 1932 by Jean Renoir, *Scarlet Street* was close also to *The Blue Angel* (1930) in depicting the downfall of a middle-aged bourgeois male through the machinations of a disreputable demi-mondaine, though Lang was colder and more sordid and more fatalistic than was the case of either the Renoir or the Sternberg.

■   ■   ■   ■

DOUBLE INDEMNITY (1944), adapted by Raymond Chandler and
Billy Wilder from the novel by James M. Cain, was ahead of its time as
an archetypal *film noir* with a morally marginal hero, and a sexually driven
Mickey Spillane-ish bang-bang climax that anticipated Spillane himself
by almost a decade. James Agee recoiled from its allegedly trashy sensibility by describing it as "masturbation fantasy triply distilled." Parker
Tyler was much closer to the mark in pinpointing the homoerotic overtones between Walter Neff (Fred MacMurray), the glib, sexually aggressive insurance salesman, and Barton Keyes (Edward G. Robinson), the
God-like claims adjuster and moral accountant.

Barbara Stanwyck's Phyllis Didrickson, stylized into a coldly calculating sluttishness with an unbecoming blonde wig and an overplayed insincerity, remains one of the most mysogynistic creations in the history
of the genre. Miklos Rozsa's score and the lyrical flashback narration
provided an overview worthy of Euripidean tragedy.

■   ■   ■   ■

THE LOST WEEKEND (1945) has stood the test of time more as an
Expressionist forties *film noir*, principally for such factors as the theramin
of Miklos Rozsa's score and the hallucinatory images of a swooping bat
and a bleeding mouse, rather than as a realistic treatment of the "problem" of alcoholism. Ray Milland switched type and stature in a harrowing
portrayal of physical and psychological disintegration. He was ably supported by Jane Wyman as an uncloyingly nice girl who stands by her
man, all filmed in the shadows of the old Third Avenue El. Doris Dowl-
ing did a neat turn as a flirtatious but ultimately pathetic bar girl, while
Howard Da Silva and Frank Faylen were on target as a no-nonsense
bartender and a fey male nurse respectively.

■   ■   ■   ■

JOSEPH H. LEWIS'S Gun Crazy (1949), a successor to Fritz Lang's
You Only Live Once (1937), developed an underground cult-following in
the late fifties and early sixties. It must be seen as a B-picture that sneaks
up on you through the dark mists enveloping doomed figures. The first
working title for the movie was *Deadly Is the Female*, and this title is
more appropriate as an indication of the moral imbalance between the
two lovers. The boy (John Dall) likes guns well enough, but it is the girl
(Peggy Cummins) who happens to be pathologically gun crazy. Lewis

has directed the movie in terms of the moral perspective of the forties, dealing with spiritual corruption as a constricting nightmare.

Dall and Cummins, as heretofore failed A-picture leads, are perfectly cast for their futile aspirations as seedy characters in this low-budget programmer. Indeed at first glance both Dall and Cummins seem much too elegant for this saga of low life, for which Dalton Trumbo is rumored to have written the original script. But as we look more closely at Dall we see traces of weakness and uncertainty, and as we look more closely at Cummins we sense a bottled-up hysteria that might be difficult for her to control if she ever let it loose. Lewis never gets too close to these characters, but maintains a contemplative distance so that the crazy feelings can be played out without engulfing the audience.

Back in 1949 society was regarded as neither wickedly conformist (*Bonnie and Clyde*, 1967) nor absent-mindedly absurdist (*Badlands*, 1973). Yet, the forces of law and order are hardly regarded as benign and accommodating. It is all over at the end for the boy (Dall) even though he has taken drastic steps to extricate himself from his *amour fou*. He took a wrong turning along the road, and that made all the difference. But there is not much fuss over his fate, only a lingering regret over all the waste of emotional energy in the false magic of gunfire.

■　　■　　■　　■

IN 1948 JAMES AGEE dismissed *Out of the Past* (1947) as a "conventional private-eye melodrama." But the plot convolutions alone make *Out of the Past* unconventional for any time. That Geoffrey Homes adapted the screenplay from his own novel does not help us very much, since the writer has remained obscure in the decades since. But the *film noir*, rediscovered in the sixties and seventies, is now one of the most fashionable genres for both stylistic and structuralist analysis. Jacques Tourneur's graceful, civilized direction of the intricacies of the intrigue of a pulpish plot enables the mythic configurations of the players to emerge more clearly. Robert Mitchum, under-rated in his own time, incarnates the stoical suffering of a hard-boiled cynic born to temptation. As the object of temptation, Jane Greer impressed even Agee as a "hot number." Kirk Douglas, in the early stages of his career, makes a likable villain, and Joseph Valentine, with his big-man dancer's grace, the villain's sympathetic henchman.

No one involved can help the world being what it is: a jungle overgrown with mercenary motivations. But movies are beginning to escape from the shadowy backlots of the early and middle forties. Hence, Agee praised Nicholas Musuraca's outdoor cinematography while deploring the unwholesome use of the outdoors, thus missing the irony of the film. For the Mitchum private-eye character the outdoors serves as a refuge from an impure past, but he can never escape his own guilt. This guilt comes hounding him in many forms until in the end death alone provides any hope of purification.

But if *Out of the Past* were to be measured merely by its pessimism it could not be considered seriously. What lifts it above most films in its genre is its transcendent lyricism as it describes a hard-boiled man's delusionary infatuation with a genuinely seductive temptress. Tourneur is said to have advised Greer in his halting English to keep her eyes wide open in the first half, and to narrow them in the second. Aside from the drop-dead beauty of Greer, the film is graced also by an above-average nice girl performance by Virginia Huston, and a chillingly cold and mercenary glamour girl appearance by Rhonda Fleming. Dickie Moore's deaf-mute gas station assistant to Mitchum frames the narrative with profoundly poetic lip-readings which define the archetypal power of the genre.

■　　■　　■　　■

ALTHOUGH *CRIME WITHOUT PASSION* (1934) and *The Scoundrel* (1935) precede the *noir* period, they are included here because I see them as forerunners. Ben Hecht and Charles MacArthur's *Crime Without Passion*, from their screenplay based on their story *Caballero of the Law*, with Claude Rains, Margo, Whitney Bourne, and Stanley Ridges, is a lurid gasp of independent film-making by a couple of ambitious ex-journalists who never became fully assimilated into the Hollywood factory. Hecht and MacArthur's idea of a Mosfilm production on the East River is a tale about a crooked Manhattan lawyer defeated by the women victims of his manufactured evidence. He is also stalked by the Three Furies, who vampirishly hover outside his skyscraper office. Slavko Vorkapich, in collaboration with cinematographer Lee Garmes, created the bravura Eisensteinian montages that provide the movie with a mythological underpinning as well as elaborate machinery that takes the wish-fulfillment revenge too far. Rains, in his dramatic debut, is mesmerizing in putting bite into the shyster melodramatics. *Crime Without Passion* is endlessly fascinating for film buffs, but in the long run was more quaint than influential in its end-run strategy of spoon-feeding the masses with cinematic razzmatazz.

Hecht and MacArthur's *The Scoundrel*, from their screenplay, with Noël Coward, Julie Haydon, Hope Williams, Alexander Woollcott, Lionel Stander, and Eduardo Ciannelli, was a New York-based movie that set out to beat Hollywood at its own game through an initially cynical but ultimately sentimental parable of an immoral publisher finding his comeuppance in the next world. Coward's cad was based upon the notoriously womanizing Horace Liveright (one of Carole Lombard's ex-lovers). Woollcott was taken aboard to give the film's Manhattan network of bitchy intellectuals the documentary ring of the Algonquin Circle. Gifted cinematographer Lee Garmes provided the technical expertise, and Haydon (the great love of George Jean Nathan's life) supplied the soulful love interest. On the other distaff end, the pert, bright, and heartlessly witty Hope Williams was more than a match for Coward in stylish bravado, and Stander and Ciannelli were wondrously nasty as bickering literati. The result, however, was too New Yorkish for the thirties viewer, despite generous dosages of Rachmaninoff's Second Piano Concerto for the sermonizing sequences.

■　■　■　■

JOHN GARFIELD (1913–52), the greatly talented alumnus of New York's Group Theatre, was a charismatic and tragic victim of the Hollywood Blacklist. Yet posthumously his star has not continued to shine as brightly as those of his macho male contemporaries. His screen career was *noir*-ish from the word go, from his failure-induced suicide in Michael Curtiz's *Four Daughters* (1938) to his ritualized death scene in John Berry's *He Ran All the Way* (1951), his cinematic swan song.

From the beginning he projected a street-wise social consciousness, in an age of movie assimilation, that made him a more poetically extroverted actor than the Method actors, notably Montgomery Clift, Marlon Brando, and James Dean, who followed him. Whereas they looked deep inside themselves for their demons, Garfield looked outside far and wide, at home and abroad, for the social injustices that afflicted humanity. His career began in the dark days of the Great Depression and the New Deal, and ended in an era of postwar disillusionment, the political persecution of "premature anti-fascists," and a still to this day vitriolic crossfire between Stalinists and Trotskyists, anti-Communists and anti-anti-Communists. Garfield, ill-educated and an easy target for cultural intimidation, found himself frequently patronized and exploited by ideologues.

Garfield played his only out-and-out gangster villain in Anatole Litvak's *Out of the Fog* (1941), derived from a pretentious Irwin Shaw stage allegory about the "little people" rising up against evil by way of a moody Popular Front screenplay by Robert Rossen (later the director of Garfield in *Body and Soul*, 1947), Jerry Wald, and Richard Macaulay. For the rest of his career he was tempted by evil, struggling against it, or consumed in its vortex. He seemed to be rehearsing his own downfall, even as he was developing and enriching his persona. Yet Tay Garnett's *The Postman Always Rings Twice* (1946) with Lana Turner should have made him a big star, but it didn't. Nor did he generate any chemistry with Geraldine Fitzgerald in Jean Negulesco's *Nobody Lives Forever* (1946). He was nominated for two Oscars—for Best Supporting Actor in *Four Daughters* (1938), and for Best Actor in *Body and Soul* (1947)—but, though he was respected as a performer, he was never adequately appreciated for his unique talent. The story is told of the producer circa 1950 who told an agent that he was looking for a John Garfield type, and the agent told him that he could get John Garfield himself, and the producer said he didn't want Garfield but a Garfield type.

One of his most memorable performances was given in Abraham Polonsky's *Force of Evil* (1948), a total flop at the box office, which proved to be the death knell of Garfield's dreams of becoming an independent producer. He is remembered today as a transitional figure between the hyperstoical male stars of the forties and the hypersensitive male Method stars of the fifties. In his heart he fought the good fight against the international bad guys in Richard Wallace's *The Fallen Sparrow* (1943) and John Huston's *We Were Strangers* (1949); he made a credible Hemingway hero in Michael Curtiz's *The Breaking Point* (1950); and he even played an honest-to-goodness explicitly Jewish character in Elia Kazan's tract on "tolerance," the Oscar-winning *Gentleman's Agreement* (1947).

Kazan and Fred Zinnemann provide only footnotes for *noir* in the forties with Kazan's "semi-documentary" *Boomerang* (1947) and Zinnemann's *Act of Violence* (1949) introducing fresh elements of sober realism to a traditionally hallucinatory and Expressionistic genre. But theirs was only a token involvement in *noir*. Their fashionable decade was to be the fifties, during which they both won Oscars, and both set the agenda for "significant" social comment on the screen. They were also closely identified with the screen personae of the Clift-Brando-Dean trinity of Method messianism.

THE WAR FILM

The war film generally presented itself from the silent era onward as a cautionary tale of pacifist morality while at the same time promoting profitably regressive behavior in the form of mass homicide. The war film traditionally exploited man's inhumanity to man while professing to deplore it. Among the violent genres, the war film was not a clear-cut Manichean morality tale like the western, or an illumination of the id like the gangster movie and the *film noir*. The war film usually made its polemical points by placing the blame for the violence on the unseen merchants of death in high places.

By the dawn of the talkies the American cinema had already provided restaged spectacles of the Spanish-American War and World War I. The Civil War (1861–65) antedated the invention of the motion picture, but it had been amply documented by the refined and improved daguerreotypes of Mathew Brady. D. W. Griffith's *The Birth of a Nation* (1915) spectacularly dramatized the theme of fratricidal conflict in the war film by having two blood brothers come face to face on opposing sides of the North-South battle.

Whereas a mutual respect was to characterize all subsequent reenactments of the Civil War, the first American treatments of World War I referred to the Germans as "Huns," a term of opprobrium never employed in World War II films. Indeed, the early disbelief during the Second World War in the reality of the Holocaust can be attributed at least partly to the exaggerated atrocity stories circulated by the Allies against the Germans in World War I.

But then after World War I had been demystified through the twenties and thirties, the Germans were seen as victims of a harsh and vindictive peace settlement. Whereas Griffith had cast Erich von Stroheim as a hateful, lustful Hun in *Hearts of the World* in 1918, he made the war-ravaged Germans his protagonists in the ironically titled *Isn't Life Wonderful* (1924). King Vidor's *The Big Parade* (1925) put John Gilbert's American doughboy into a shellhole with a dying German soldier. The action begins with an enraged Gilbert pursuing the German into the shellhole, and then seeing that his antagonist is wounded, giving him a cigarette instead of finishing the job. Those few moments of quiet rapport between two men sharing a humanity of which they had been deprived by their respective governments lingered for the entire period between the two World Wars when a passion for peace ruled the world, at least on its screens.

The scene is reprised from the German point of view in Lewis Milestone's *All Quiet on the Western Front* (1930), from a screenplay by Milestone, Maxwell Anderson, Del Andrews, and George Abbott, based on the world-famous novel by Erich Maria Remarque. In the Milestone version of the Vidor episode, a German soldier played by Lew Ayres bayonets a Frenchman played by Raymond Griffith, and then asks his victim for forgiveness.

All Quiet survives even today as an artifact of cinematic pacifism between the two wars, but most of its ideological pertinence is gone from our post-Holocaust world, especially Milestone's mesmerizing cross-tracking between charging ranks of infantrymen and the panning machine-gun mowing them down in their tracks. The excitement of these sequences may strike nineties peace partisans as somewhat self-defeating in that the orgasmic violence of war is celebrated as much as it is condemned.

The movie is still sad and downbeat, but then most war movies are sad and downbeat. Even when we do mourn the dead, the wounded, and the mutilated, we seem destined to be let down by the cease-fires and outbreaks of peace because they inevitably involve a loss of fraternal feeling and heroic stature. The worst horrors of history are usually transformed by war movies into the stuff of nostalgia; period helmets and uniforms are particularly evocative. *All Quiet* indulges even in beyond-the-grave visualizations before the last fade-out, in which images of dead soldiers ask the audience to realize the futility of war. The effect is dated because the nineties audience has seen death feigned by too many actors merely for the sake of sentimental theatrics. What the audience experiences is not so much pity for the victims of war as pathos for the end to camaraderie. The final irony of the film is too neatly turned out for any lingering moral uneasiness. The hero (Lew Ayres) reaches out for a butterfly. We see the hand crumple and die to the sound of a sniper's bullet—as neat a stroke of allegorical self-pity as has ever been served up to the softer side of our brutishness.

The emotional core of the film is embodied in the hard-bitten but soft-hearted Sergeant Katczinsky of Louis Wolheim, who died of cancer a year after the greatest success of his eleven-year acting career. "Kat," as he was nicknamed by his callow young recruits in the trenches, taught them in the middle of an artillery barrage to burrow into the earth of which he seemed such an integral part. His speech about the the world's leaders settling disputes by getting into the ring like prizefighters while the troops stood around cheering them on has always evoked cheers because of Wolheim's wondrous incarnation of the "common man," even though in his pre-acting life he had been a mathematics professor at Cornell University.

∎   ∎   ∎   ∎

CASABLANCA (1943), the most charismatic of all the Hollywood anti-Nazi resistance fantasies in the forties, has been seen so often by so many people around the world that virtually every frame poses a trivia question. Who plays the bartender "Sascha"? Leonid Kinsky. What does Claude Rains throw in the wastepaper basket? A bottle of Vichy water, a metaphor for his conversion from collaboration to resistance, and a metaphor moreover greatly admired by the eminent art historian Erwin J. Panofsky. Who can forget the rousing scene of the "Marseillaise" being sung in Rick's Cafe, though the idea was borrowed from Jean Renoir's *Grand Illusion* (1937), or of the police inspector's tension-releasing order "round up the usual suspects."

Most memorably of all, perhaps, is Dooley Wilson's rendition of "As Time Goes By." One can write volumes on Michael Curtiz's crisp direction in a distinctively Germanic Warners studio *noir* style; of the crafty screenplay by Julius J. Epstein, Philip G. Epstein, and Howard Koch, with their combined flair for thinly disguised exposition and interlocking climaxes; of an incredibly gifted acting ensemble from every corner of Europe: Paul Henreid, Peter Lorre, Conrad Veidt and Curt Bois from Germany; Sydney Greenstreet from England; Marcel Dalio and Madeleine LeBeau from France; S. Z. Zakall from Hungary; and, of course, Ingrid Bergman from Sweden. All in all, *Casablanca* remains an eternal treasure-trove of pleasure.

Ultimately, however, Humphrey Bogart's Rick shapes the redemptive spirit of *Casablanca* by beginning the film with some of the most cynical lines ever spoken by a movie hero, and ending it with a rhetorical flourish of self-sacrificial idealism that would have sounded like mush in the mouth of any other Hollywood male star or icon. From that moment on, the world's lovers have toasted each other with Bogart's wineglass-lifted tribute to Bergman, "Here's looking at you, kid," proving once again that the greatest love stories almost invariably end badly or sadly.

3

The Directors

D. W. GRIFFITH (1875–1948)

D. W. Griffith had long been a living monument when he died in relative obscurity July 23, 1948, in the Hollywood Knickerbocker Hotel. He had not directed a film since *The Struggle* in 1931, and his brave front had collapsed in the face of industry indifference. Had he lived, he would have celebrated his hundredth birthday on January 23, 1975. On that day, to commemorate the D. W. Griffith Centennial the Museum of Modern Art in New York City launched a massive retrospective of his works in a two-part cycle. Part One focused on one hundred of the five hundred films Griffith turned out between 1908 and 1913 at the Biograph Studios, located in that period at 11 East 14th Street on the island of Manhattan. Griffith's predilection for the realism of location shooting provided the historically and nostalgically minded with many glimpses of New York City as it looked before World War I. Part Two exhumed rather than revived the feature-length movies directed by Griffith from 1914 to 1931.

I had been "teaching" D. W. Griffith in my college courses for a number of years, sometimes by way of *The Birth of a Nation* (1915), more often by way of *Intolerance* (1916) and *True Heart Susie* (1919) (Jean-Luc Godard's favorite Griffith film). I had nothing but praise for the Museum's (and particularly Eileen Bowser's) diligence in preserving the precious heritage of Griffith's film achievements. We know more of Griffith's total oeuvre than that of all but a few of his contemporaries, most notably the preservation-minded Chaplin. Still, I am afraid that it is much easier to confirm Griffith's role as a "pioneer" in a certain period than to establish his credentials as a full-fledged artist for all time.

An inescapable problem in dealing with Griffith is his flagrant racism, not only in the still outrageous *The Birth of a Nation* (1915) but also in *Broken Blossoms* (1919), *Dream Street* (1921), *One Exciting Night* (1922), and *The Struggle* (1931). It can be argued that Griffith reflected the racism of his time more than he incited it. Indeed, Griffith presented *Intolerance* in 1916 as an alleged atonement for *The Birth of a Nation*. Unfortunately, the platitudinous generalities of *Intolerance* could never cancel out the dynamic images of *The Birth of a Nation*. The best that can be said for Griffith was that he was not fully conscious of all the issues involved in his treatment of Reconstruction after the Civil War.

The Birth of a Nation opened officially at the Liberty Theatre in New York on March 3, 1915, preaching peace at a time when much of the world was at war. President Woodrow Wilson, who honored the film with an unprecedented screening in the White House, is reported to have remarked, "It is like writing history with lightning." At that, Wilson's blurb came under the heading of Reciprocity, since Griffith's titles for *The Birth of a Nation* quote Woodrow Wilson the historian on more than one occasion for historical evidence of the evils of Reconstruction. Wilson, born a Southerner, like Griffith, was a liberal Democratic President in an era when most of the black vote, North and South, went to the Republicans virtually by default. Hence, there is no reason to believe that he felt unduly menaced by the race riots in Northern cities or the political protests from such lingering abolitionists as Jane Addams and President Charles E. Eliot of Harvard.

Unfortunately, the outcries against *The Birth of a Nation* served simply to drive racism underground without confronting the specific issues involved. By arguing that Griffith was being unfair to blacks, the white liberals succeeded in preventing any sequels to *The Birth of a Nation*, but they failed completely and perhaps deliberately to counter the impact of the film with a positive picture of the black on a scale comparable to Griffith's denial of black dignity. For decades thereafter, Southern theater owners exercised veto power over the slightest intimation of black-white miscegenation, and this veto power was never seriously challenged even by the proverbial swimming-pool-Stalinist Hollywood screenwriters of the thirties and forties. The left was always good for a few pickets to protest racial slurs in *Gone With the Wind* (1939) and *Song of the South* (1946), but there never seemed to be any countering scripts to restore sexual dignity to the black. Indeed, liberal tolerance was counterproductive to the extent that it blocked any consideration of race-sex taboos as being potentially harmful to the black race. *The Birth of a Nation* has failed to receive the detailed analysis it deserves because the liberal and left activist prefers to dismiss the entire film as a distortion, thereby evading the politically dangerous issues involved. If it isn't true, nice people will say, why discuss it at all? The answer is of course that a work of art need not be true for it to be deeply felt and fervently believed.

Marxist critics have been particularly handicapped in this particular controversy by their reluctance to open the Pandora's box of sexual mythology. To argue, however, as Griffith does, that no black man can ever aspire to any white woman goes beyond the bounds of political partisanship into racial taboo, and taboos must be broken, at least metaphorically, otherwise they poison the body politic. Certainly, out of all the interracial stories that have unfolded in the American experience, Griffith himself could have found some black-white version of *Broken Blossoms* (1919) had he been truly sincere in his professed desire to atone for *The Birth of a Nation*. But though there were many movies on the forbidden loves of whites and "Orientals," whites and "Indians," not to mention the intramural taboos among whites themselves, there were no movies until very recently to romanticize even one example of black-white intermingling from the millions that obviously have occurred.

The Birth of a Nation not only upholds the lily-white mythology of the Aryan Southland; it imputes to Thaddeus Stevens (alias Stoneman) sordid sexual motives to explain his vendetta against the defeated Confederacy dear Abe Lincoln wants to caress and forgive. Thus the ghost of Lincoln is allied with the formidable cultural presence of Griffith and Wilson in a blanket condemnation of black arrogance. Significantly, the uppity mulatto maid who seduces Stoneham merely by baring one of her shoulders is played by a white actress in black face. The effect of black face in white-oriented iconography is to emphasize the treacherous incongruity of darting white eyes and dagger-like white teeth. And the use of black face makes performers' blackness itself a state of being so inferior that even blacks themselves are incapable of interpreting and communicating its inescapable baseness. Hence, an American screen tradition is born in *The Birth of a Nation* to the effect that no authentic black man younger than Bill "Bojangles" Robinson will ever place his hand on the flesh of any white woman older than Shirley Temple. This taboo remained in force for so long that even as late as 1957 Joan Fontaine was deluged with poison-pen mail for merely holding hands with Harry Belafonte in *Island in the Sun*, and in the late sixties a TV functionary admitted snipping a bit of videotape on which singer Petula Clark was shown touching the presumably still untouchable Harry Belafonte.

Curiously, *The Birth of a Nation* has gained more ambiguity over the years than its professed bias would indicate. Mae Marsh, in particular, seems more than the conventional victim of black lust. Even by Griffith's outraged Victorian moral standards, Miss Marsh's fierce virgin over-reacts hysterically to every emotional challenge until finally she is doomed not so much by the relatively restrained black pursuer, who keeps insisting that he merely wants to talk to her, as by her own increasing inability to cope with all the demands made on her feelings. Mae Marsh and Lillian Gish were brilliantly directed by Griffith because he believed all of their Victorian-American affectations to be sublime manifestations of white womanhood, and he could not bear to see them buffeted about by the disorder represented by Reconstruction. By any standard, his small-town agrarian vision of the world was intellectually inadequate but there is no point suppressing *The Birth of a Nation*. It marks not only where we once were but where much of our racial hypocrisy still persists.

Nonetheless, the debt that all film-makers owe to D. W. Griffith defies calculation. Even before *The Birth of a Nation* he had managed to synthesize the dramatic and documentary elements of the modern feature film. By his artful use of the close-up in literally "closing in" on the narrative, he had intuitively formulated a dialectic between objective (long shot) and subjective (close-up) views of the same event. Also he had established on the screen a privileged area where the players could perform with more intimacy and subtlety than their gesticulating and emoting counterparts in the stage productions of that era.

Griffith devised a grammar of emotions through his expressive editing. Focal length became a function of feeling. Close-ups not only intensified an emotion, they shifted characters from the republic of prose to the kingdom of poetry. Griffith's privileged moments are still among the most beautiful in all cinema. They belong to him alone, since they are beyond mere technique: Griffith invented this "mere" technique and he also transcended it.

Griffith mastered most of the technical vocabulary very early in his career, and then proceeded to simplify his vocabulary for the sake of deeper psychological penetration of the dramatic issues that concerned him. His art had become so deceptively simple by the time of *Abraham Lincoln* (1930) that most critics assumed that he was in a state of stylistic decline. Only the historical "significance" of the subject earned him a marginal degree of respect. Yet today the rough-and-tumble directness and episodic structure of *Lincoln* looks amazingly appropriate for its slyly rambling subject and protagonist. Walter Huston's Lincoln is no mere wax work, but a living, breathing, chortling projection of Griffith himself in all his cantankerous individuality doing battle with an industry about to drive him from the screen forever. Through the last quarter-century of his existence on this earth he was generally written off in Hollywood as the very last of the Eminent Victorians. He was considered too solemn for the Jazz Age, and then too upright for the Depression. The false revival of his career at the onset of the sound era with *Lincoln* was to end with his swan song in the aptly titled *The Struggle*.

D. W. Griffith's last officially credited film is generally considered his least. *The Struggle* would titillate modern audiences with its opening anti-Prohibition titles written and lettered in the Victorian style of silent-movie captions. The opening sequences are visually dazzling and vocally distracting, which is to say that Griffith was better served by Joseph Ruttenberg's camera than by the scripting of Anita Loos and John Emerson. Griffith's "look" of unfettered urban realism from the stoop to the gutter reflected his ultimate alienation from the movie moguls of Hollywood. The sound, however, was awkward and grating. Griffith never really made the transition to the talkies, and he was not blessed here, as in *Abraham Lincoln*, with a Walter Huston to take up the slack. Hal Skelly was a maudlin stage performer—emotionally effective with Nancy Carroll in *The Dance of Life* (1929)—who looked and sounded too much like the archetypally fast-talking Lee Tracy to make a distinctive impression of his own, and Zita Johann was a stridently intense stage actress who was particularly irritating as Skelly's nagging wife.

On a conventional level *The Struggle* can be considered a complete failure, and yet the film is clearly the work of a giant even when the giant is thrashing about inarticulately. A plot synopsis cannot help but sound ridiculous. A young beer-drinking steel-worker starts drinking the heavier stuff when Prohibition ushers in speakeasies. He promises his sweetheart to stop drinking if she will become his wife. She accepts. He abstains. At least for a while. He lives blissfully with his wife, their sweet little girl, and his hearts-and-flowers younger sister. Two seemingly trivial incidents induce him to break his vow of temperance. On one occasion he tries to cheer up a fellow worker who has lost his job, and on another he cannot face up to a sober entrance to his sister's engagement party wearing the lavender necktie his wife has unaccountably insisted on.

Predictably, he disgraces himself at the party, breaks up his sister's engagement, offends a wealthy benefactor of the sister's fiancé, and in other ways causes consternation in the household. He sinks deeper and deeper, until his family is destitute and he is on skid row. The little girl takes to selling apples on the street, and heaven knows what her mother is doing. Then Griffith starts some fancy cross-cutting of parallel actions as daughter and mother in turn try to locate Skelly, and the action ends up with wild melodrama of mother and passerby breaking down the door of Skelly's room while he is close to murdering his little daughter in a fit of insanely drunken rage at being found. The coda is both abrupt and absurd, with Skelly kicking his habit, getting rich, and giving his blessing to his sister's marriage.

Like most montage directors, Griffith was not adept in endowing his narrative with the flow of inevitability. Griffith's great virtues are his force and lyrical intensity. Nonetheless he must be taken to task for both his inescapable sentimentality and his intransigent bigotry. *Intolerance* notwithstanding, Griffith never freed himself of the most rampant prejudices of his childhood. His greatest limitation is that he became urban without becoming cosmopolitan. Here in 1931, he caricatures not only a yas'm Negro maid but a Yiddish dialect insurance salesman of whom Skelly speaks contemptuously, an Italian dialect workman Skelly patronizes, and an Irish dialect workman Skelly mimics. When one recalls Lillian Gish addressing Richard Barthelmess as "chinkie" in *Broken Blossoms*, and Carol Dempster warning another Asian not to mess around with a white woman in *Dream Street*, it is hard not to believe that Griffith was responding to his deepest emotions in *The Birth of a Nation*.

Yet his inability to overcome, and, perhaps more to his credit, conceal his ingrown intolerance of non-Wasp America is perhaps the manifestation of a nature unable to escape a childhood trauma. There has never been a director anywhere who could have brought to *The Struggle* the intense feeling for family that Griffith gives us on the screen. There are so many staggering scenes that transcend the overheated plot, scenes that make one aware of volcanic emotions erupting beyond the bounds of coherent ideas. When Skelly's wife has had her baby, Griffith leaves Skelly awkwardly bent over her bedside for so long that the audience begins to cringe from the forlorn helplessness of the male before the mystery of life. Ingmar Bergman stages a similar scene in *Brink of Life* (1958) with more artistic distancing, but with less primal force.

Then there is the sequence which begins with Skelly's return to the empty apartment and looking across an inner courtyard to a neighbor's room in which Skelly's daughter is seen listening to a radio the neighbor's children are tuning. As an organ plays "Abide With Me" and a minister begins his sermon about the Resurrection, Skelly coils out of sight of the neighbor's window and contorts himself into a posture of abject guilt such as the screen has never shown before or since.

By not changing camera angles for "variety" in the studio mode of 1931, Griffith transforms his feeble characters into fearsome archetypes. Thus, far from representing a disgraceful exit, the failed greatness of *The Struggle* is worthy of the glorious opaqueness of Faulkner and the glorious banality of O'Neill, and assures Griffith's place with them as an American artist made inarticulate by the furies of a guilt-ridden past.

KING VIDOR (1894–1981)

The first media obituaries for King Vidor (1884–1982) identified him simply as the director of *The Champ* (1931), a film released a half-century before. Possibly, Franco Zefferelli's glossy 1979 re-make reminded people how good and gritty the original was. Later obituaries mentioned *The Big Parade* (1925), *The Crowd* (1928), and *Our Daily Bread* (1934). Even so, the media were stretching the resources of their research departments to get any kind of career fix on a moviemaker with fifty-six feature credits between 1918 and 1959. Fully half of his films fell within the silent era, and half within the talkie era. He received an honorary Oscar in 1979, but he never received a competitive one although nominated on five occasions. King Vidor's *The Citadel* did win the New York Film Critics Award in 1938, but Alfred Hitchcock was honored as Best Director that year for *The Lady Vanishes*.

In many ways *The Citadel* (1938) was Vidor's last hurrah for the taste-makers. The movies he made in the forties and fifties were either dismissed as routine or denounced as outrageous. In the latter category were such cult and camp classics as *Duel in the Sun* (1947), with Jennifer Jones and Gregory Peck performing their prairie *Liebestod* on a blood-splattered mountainside; *The Fountainhead* (1949), with Gary Cooper incarnating Ayn Rand's phallic fascist of an architect, and Patricia Neal seething as his tigerish mistress; *Beyond the Forest* (1949), with

Bette Davis etching the lament "What a dump" into Edward Albee's unconscious for Martha's tag line in *Who's Afraid of Virginia Woolf?* (1966); and *Ruby Gentry* (1952), with Jennifer Jones's provocative swamp hussy sensually illuminated by Charlton Heston's searching flashlight.

In my own estimation Vidor has risen over the decades from my early emphasis on the fragmentary nature of his achievements as a director for film clips with more great moments and fewer great films than any director of his rank. Yet for their time *The Crowd* (1928) and *Hallelujah* (1929) towered over all but a handful of Hollywood movies. In retrospect, Vidor's vitality seems ageless, and his emotionally volcanic images are especially appropriate for partings and reunions, and for the visual opposition of individuals to masses. Vidor's was an architectural cinema with none of Lang's determinism or Antonioni's alienation effects. It is no accident that the formalistic Japanese went wild over Vidor's films.

Many critics mesmerized by crypto-Marxist criteria fostered a feeling of regretful nostalgia for the supposed champion of the "common man" in *The Crowd* (1928) on one side of the Crash, and *Our Daily Bread* (1934) on the other. Indeed, realists Jean Renoir and Fred Zinnemann credited Vidor and Erich von Stroheim as among their earliest and most heroic models for a moviemaking career.

Yet when we relate Vidor to other directors, certain incongruities emerge in his own career. To begin with, he was hardly a firebrand like Stroheim, though for a time he was regarded as being as much a Zola-esque realist as the stormy director of *Greed* (1923). Vidor was stylistically indebted to Griffith, as everyone was and is, but for a native-born Texan Vidor was remarkably free of racial bigotry, particularly for his own comparatively unenlightened time. His vibrant sensuality had little affinity with Griffith's notorious susceptibility to the Victorian child-woman embodied most memorably in the virginal performances of the very young Lillian Gish and Mae Marsh.

I did not meet King Vidor until the last years of his life and, like most of his friends and acquaintances, was overwhelmed by his energy and lucidity. He seemed both physically and psychologically capable of taking over the directorial reins of a major production. Such was not to be the case, however, and his last imprint on the medium was his characterization of Walter Klein in James Toback's *Love & Money* (1982).

With Vidor's most persistent detractors it was often the problem of too much and not enough. The populist expectations aroused by such early Vidor breakthrough films as the aforementioned *The Big Parade* (1925), *The Crowd* (1928), and *Hallelujah* (1929) haunted his later efforts. By venturing into the ill-defined and sloganized realms of "realism" and "social consciousness," Vidor ran afoul of the peculiar puritanism of the left through the thirties and forties. One could not save mankind, it seemed, if one dabbled in fables of Adam and Eve. Worse still, Vidor projected the self-contradictory image of a rebel who was steadily employed, and he received little credit from the myth-makers for knowing when to bend without breaking.

Vidor's most ambitious defender in recent years has been Raymond Durgnat, a post-auteurist revisionist of prodigious cinematic erudition. For every auteurist paradox, Durgnat has devised a dozen anti-auteurist responses. Hence, Durgnat's book-length revaluations of Vidor in the July and August 1973 issues of *Film Comment* were used to beat the Hawks followers on the head. I was particularly struck by Durgnat's counterposing of Vidor's hot-blooded emotionalism in *The Champ* (1931) against Hawks's stylish stoicism and sang-froid. It is an opposition Durgnat employed before in upholding Wellman's *The Public Enemy* (1931) against Hawks's *Scarface* (1932).

Durgnat's critical sleight of hand is achieved by asserting, if not actually establishing, a parallel between Vidor's contradictions and America's. This is heady work for a British critic, and Durgnat often over-reaches himself culturally, most notably when he tries to relate the flashback structure of Vidor's *H. M. Pulham, Esq.* (1941) to *Citizen Kane's*. Durgnat does not seem to have been aware that the regretful flashback was such an organic part of J. P. Marquand's novelistic strategy in *Pulham*, and in the novels before and after, that the Marquand style was once easily parodied in *The New Yorker*. Not that *Pulham* is without feeling, despite the disastrous miscasting of Hedy Lamarr, as Pulham's lost love, and Vidor's sociological remoteness from the milieu. But, for that matter, Vidor was not all that close to the Hell's Kitchen denizens of Elmer Rice's *Street Scene* (1931) or the costumed mummies of *Solomon and Sheba* (1959). Yet time and again, Vidor's characters burst into life despite the absence of social context. And it is here that Durgnat is onto something in his revaluation.

Let us take the embarrassing matter of tearjerkers. It has never been that easy to make a good one. Vidor succeeded spectacularly on at least five occasions: *The Jack Knife Man* (1920), *The Big Parade* (1925), *Street Scene* and *The Champ* (1931), and, quintessentially perhaps, *Stella Dallas* (1937). The tears that Vidor elicits are honest, honorable tears and the weeper is not degraded. The pathos never degenerates into bathos. The rhetoric and the gestures are never false or exaggerated. The moral ambiguity of the scene is never vulgarized or coarsened. I have seen all of Vidor's talkies and about a third of his silents, and I never cease to be amazed by his felicities in film after film, often in less than congenial commissioned projects.

I am not sure that Vidor had a master plan or a recurring theme. Perhaps the driving paradox of his art is that he was a romanticist in a real world, and therefore sought out real trees under which to dream his wildest dreams. How else to explain the buoyant humor of *Show People* (1928), the unaffected eroticism of *Bird of Paradise* (1932), the heart-rending decency of *The Stranger's Return* (1933), and the curiously fastidious idealism of *The Citadel* (1938)? Vidor simply did not acknowledge the contradictions in his oeuvre. He waited for the climactic openings and moved in with a mysterious urgency and implacability. That is why his greatest emotional explosions can never be duplicated. The conviction that made it all possible has died with his generation of film-makers.

CHARLES CHAPLIN (1899–1977)

Charles Chaplin is arguably the single most important artist produced by the cinema, certainly its most extraordinary performer and probably still its most universal icon. Ironically, Chaplin's enormous popularity has never been used against him even by his severest detractors. Never a suggestion of compromise and commercialism, despite all the money that rolled in at the box office. Quite the contrary. There has been a greater tendency to criticize Chaplin for abandoning the simpler needs of his audiences in order to pursue his own idiosyncrasies and ideologies more faithfully and more explicitly, or, worse still, in order to cater to his high-brow admirers.

Though Chaplin was never as stylistically influential as Griffith, Eisenstein, or Murnau, he was fortunate to work in a genre that did not date irrevocably with the period in which it was first presented. Even his earliest and crudest one-reel appearances from his 1914 Mack Sennett period are today treasured as classics rather than tolerated as archaeological artifacts. And all through the thirties, forties, and fifties, when most of his feature films were shrewdly withheld from public view, his comedy shorts floated around in the public domain to help perpetuate his reputation. By contrast, D. W. Griffith was struggling without much success even in the twenties to overcome the stigma of outdated Victorian melodrama. And Murnau (reborn in the Expressionism and spatial unity of Welles) and Eisenstein (renewed in the razor-sharp montage of Resnais), though not exactly outdated, remain of concern to aesthetes rather than to the public at large.

Charles Spencer Chaplin was born, as far as we know, on April 16, 1889, in London. Though the date and place of birth have been fairly well established, there is no birth record of the name Charles Chaplin from that period. Theodore Huff, Chaplin's most reliable and meticulous biographer, has suggested that Chaplin may have adopted his father's name in childhood either before or after Charles Chaplin the elder died of alcoholism in St. Thomas's Hospital. Chaplin's father was descended from an Anglicized French-Jewish family, and his mother, Hannah (who performed under the stage name of Lily Harley), was reported to be of Spanish and Irish descent; having run away from home at sixteen, she was so completely cut off from her family circle that even her maiden name has remained unknown.

Alvah Bessie, a screenwriter blacklisted in the McCarthy era, has reported a conversation with Chaplin in the late forties in which the comedian explicitly denied being Jewish; though, he admitted, he had allowed the impression of his Jewishness to remain after *The Great Dictator* (1940) so as not to compromise his solidarity with the victims of Nazism. It is interesting in this respect that Chaplin's older half-brother, Sidney Chaplin, was the son of Hannah's former marriage to Sidney Hawkes, a Jewish bookmaker. But whereas Sidney Chaplin was later to be publicized as an ethnically Jewish comedian (much like Ernst Lubitsch in his early Berlin comedies), Charles Chaplin moved from the stoically English slapstick tradition of the Karno Company into the knockabout universality of the Sennett menagerie, where he evolved a stylized persona that was absorbed into every country's folklore.

The evolution of Charles Spencer Chaplin into the stylized creature known around the world as "Charlie," "Charlot," "Carlino," "Carlos," "Carlitos," had a beneficial side-effect for Chaplin's career, in that never having appeared "young" on the screen, he never seemed to age appreciably in the period of his ascendancy, which began in 1914 and ended in 1940 with *The Great Dictator*. A childhood traumatized by parental poverty, alcoholism, illness, and death had undoubtedly hastened his assumption of the role of an adult to the point of prodigious precocity. And, blessed with total mimetic recall, he was able to communicate emotionally with the troubled masses through all the convulsions of War,

Revolution, Inflation, Depression, and Disillusion that passed blindly across his pantomimic path. That he treated the symptoms of these convulsions instead of analyzing their causes seemed to bother him more than it did his admirers, but the gnawing intellectual insecurity of the artist may ultimately have expanded the informal dimensions of his films and enriched their emotional tone. Thus, it would seem that time is more on the side of his features than of his shorts, and that the most lasting image of Chaplin will be lyrical rather than exuberant, poignant rather than frenetic. And that the focus of his soul will shift from his floppy feet to his fierce eyes.

Chaplin, like most of the early stars, was lionized by the public long before the cultural chroniclers of the era could explain why. Although it was not until 1916 that articles on the phenomenon began to appear, the public had discovered the little fellow with the baggy pants, cane, and derby before they knew his name. Chaplin's costume was thrown together accidentally for a rush appearance in a children's car event at Venice, the Los Angeles beach resort. *Kid Auto Races at Venice* (1914), Chaplin's second film, was thus the birthplace of the Tramp. By his twelfth film (*Caught in a Cabaret*, 1914), Chaplin's name was spelled correctly in the public prints. On his thirteenth (*Caught in the Rain*, 1914), Chaplin took over the directorial reins, never to relinquish them. As Chaplin's star rose at Sennett's studio, Ford Sterling's (overstated body-oriented) fell. Max Linder, an earlier French pantomimist with a costume strikingly similar to the Tramp's, though with upper-class modifications, was soon to be completely eclipsed by Chaplin. Both Sterling and Linder attempted comebacks, Sterling with Sennett and Linder with Essanay, Chaplin's employer after Sennett and before Mutual. In each instance, Chaplin proved irreplaceable.

Although Chaplin's Keystone movies for Sennett had not yet marked a complete break between the music-hall performer for the Karno Company and the cinema's foremost clown, the Sennett flicks are fascinating today for all the tensions still evident between Chaplin's subtler inflections and the nihilistic physicality of the rest of the Keystone crashers. Within one year on the hectic Sennett schedule, Chaplin made thirty-five separate appearances in company with such comic colleagues and rivals as Mabel Normand, Hank Mann, Chester Conklin, Al St. John, Fatty Arbuckle, Ford Sterling, Edgar Kennedy, Minta Durfee, Mack Swain, Slim Summerville, Charley Chase, Marie Dressler, and even Mack Sennett himself. Chaplin is livelier but less coherent in this first year of his vocation than he will be in the years to come. He seems also more combative and misogynistic than he will seem later, but the roots of the later Monsieur Verdoux as well as of the Tramp have been firmly planted, and the cynic and the sentimentalist in him will be struggling for control well into the twenties.

From the outset Chaplin searched for a private space in which to perfect his characterization. He brawled with Sennett and director Henry Lehrman over the pacing and fragmentation of his screen image. He mistrusted montage at first to the full extent of his theatrical instincts, and it took him a long time to understand that theatrical mise-en-scène could be broken up into congruent shots on the moviola. At first, he could not believe that the movie audience would realize he was looking at a girl if he was not in fact looking at that same girl on the set. He had not yet learned that movie audiences had mastered the first rule of film grammar: to wit, that if shot A shows someone looking off into a distance, shot B represents what he is looking at seen from his point of view. But even when Chaplin became cinematically sophisticated, he never entirely abandoned his predilection for spatial integration.

For Chaplin the director, his other self on the screen was always the supreme object of contemplation, and the style that logically followed from this assumption represents the antithesis to Eisenstein's early formulations on montage. André Bazin brilliantly analyzed this fundamental opposition between montage and the one-scene sequence thus: "If burlesque triumphed before Griffith and montage, it is because most of the gags came out of a comedy of space, of the relation of man to objects and to the exterior world. Chaplin, in *The Circus*, is actually in the lion's cage, and both are enclosed in a single frame on the screen."

However, Bazin was not entirely historically accurate in lumping Chaplin and Sennett together against Griffith and montage. If anything, Chaplin and Griffith share many of the same Victorian tastes in the theater and in women; Edna Purviance is a sweetened, enervated version of such vigorous Griffith virgins as Lillian Gish and Mae Marsh. By contrast, Mack Sennett's wild slapstick was closer in spirit and apparent formlessness to the anarchic and surrealistic romps across time and space to come in the works of Keaton, Vertov, Clair, Buñuel, and Vigo. By the mid-twenties, however, Sennett's inability to develop coherent characterizations made him a has-been in the movie industry. Sennett's perpetual motion machine was ultimately no match for Chaplin's mythmaking, as the cinema moved irrevocably from a delight with movement and energy for their own sakes to absorption in a subtler form of romantic drama. What Chaplin perceived and what Sennett did not was that the cinema was inherently such a dynamic medium that unbridled kinesis created only chaos. Hence, a certain amount of stasis was necessary to set off the kinesis, and a certain amount of contemplation and reflection to motivate the action. Gradually, Chaplin perceived also that the cinema was such a hypnotic medium that an audience could lose itself in a character with whom it identified, and hence never notice that nothing was happening on the purely kinetic level.

Chaplin can be said to have enjoyed his greatest cultural and commercial pre-eminence from 1915 to 1925, a hectic decade in which he refined and enriched his tenacious Tramp creation to the point where it became the most endearing and most enduring myth ever propagated by the motion-picture medium. Theodore Huff evoked the plastic appurtenances of this myth:

> Chaplin's costume personifies shabby gentility—the fallen aristocrat at grips with poverty. The cane is a symbol of attempted dignity, the pert moustache a sign of vanity. Although Chaplin used the same costume (with a few exceptions) for almost his entire career, or for about 25 years, it is interesting to note a slight evolution. The trousers become less baggy, the coat a little neater, and the moustache a little trimmer through the years.

It is an anomaly of film history that, whereas most of the earliest "creative" people in the field came to be dominated by the "front-office" financiers, Chaplin actually consolidated his control over his career during the very years when the pioneers were being gobbled up by the producers. The meteoric rise of his salary, year by year, provides an index to his increasing independence. After the expiration of his Sennett contract, which ran through 1914 at $150 a week, Chaplin switched over to Essanay in 1915 for $1250 a week. From Essanay, he jumped over to Mutual for a contract guaranteeing him $670,000 a year, and within two years signed a million-dollar-plus contract with First National. At this time he was not yet thirty years old, and he was already one of the most famous men in the world.

With Chaplin one can make meaningful aesthetic distinctions between his Sennett Period (1914), his Essanay Period (1915), his Mutual Period (1916–17), his First National Period (1918–22), and his United Artists Period (1923–52). In the relatively anarchic Sennett one-reelers, Chaplin functioned as the most talented member of a troupe of madcap soloists, and he was often pushed out to the periphery of the action. In his one Sennett feature, the six-reel *Tillie's Punctured Romance* (1914),

Chaplin not only plays second fiddle to Marie Dressler's eponymous (and enormous) protagonist; he plays an unusually villainous variation of the Tramp as the city slicker, indeed almost a foreshadowing of Monsieur Verdoux. Torn (sometimes limb from limb) between Marie Dressler's Tillie and Mabel Normand's pert partner-in-crime, Chaplin's city slicker more than holds his own in terms of audience laughter without ever really being the focal point of attention.

The Essanay movies have often been lumped together and mingled indiscriminately with the Sennetts by the private promoters of this supposedly primitive era. Superfluous titles, sound and musical effects have been added and crucial footage subtracted, to give a misleadingly nonsensical impression of this crucial period in Chaplin's artistic evolution. Not that there are any of the Chaplin "classics" among the fifteen Essanays turned out in 1915 and 1916. Chaplin is still too close to the Sennett slapstick tradition, and he is still too busy experimenting with gags which he will later integrate more adeptly with character continuity. For example, the topsy-turvy tray-balancing routine in *Shanghaied* (1915) can be appreciated not only for its own sake but also as a dry run for a similar but seemingly more spontaneous exercise in equilibrium in *Modern Times* (1936). The real tip-off on the Essanays as transitional advances on the Sennetts is the emergence of Edna Purviance as the first of Chaplin's flowery heroines. For the first time, Chaplin had found his Victorian equivalent of what Lillian Gish and Mae Marsh signified to Griffith. After her debut in *A Night Out* (1915), Purviance appeared in no fewer than thirty-five movies, the only exception being *One A.M.* (1916), in which Chaplin did a stunning solo. Thus she became a myth in her own right as Chaplin's fantasy darling, and she began almost immediately to leaven the Sennett slapstick with a distinctively Chaplinesque sentimentality. Edna Purviance was not so much a comedienne as a leading lady, and (unlike the Sennett girls) less a professional challenge to Chaplin than an emotional correlative.

If there is indeed a line between "primitive" Chaplin and "classic" Chaplin, it can be drawn somewhere between the Essanay and Mutual films of 1916. Certainly, the Charlie of *One A.M., The Pawnshop, Behind the Screen, The Rink* (all 1916), and *Easy Street, The Cure, The Immigrant,* and *The Adventurer* (all 1917) had completely mastered the short form of cinematic farce. The sentimentality and the cruelty and the mimicry and the satire had been perfectly blended. Later, when Chaplin became more ambitious as an artist, his earlier efficiency as a comic craftsman would be remembered fondly, to his disadvantage.

Almost from the beginning of his career, Chaplin was confronted with conflicting pressures and subjected to contradictory advice. The commercial evolution of the film industry dictated feature-length films as opposed to the compact one-and two-reelers, but the more intellectual critics decried the injection of epic, romance, and sentiment into pure slapstick. At one and the same time Chaplin would be blamed for not changing with the times and for changing too much from his glorious past.

Unfortunately, the eight works made by Chaplin for First National Films between 1918 and 1922 were for many years among the least accessible. Hence, there was usually a break in the critical consciousness of Chaplin between the Mutuals of 1917 and *The Gold Rush* in 1925. But it is in *A Dog's Life* (1918), *Shoulder Arms* (1918), *Sunnyside* (1919), *A Day's Pleasure* (1919), *The Kid* (1921), *The Idle Class* (1921), *Pay Day* (1922), and *The Pilgrim* (1923) that one finds the first signs of the spiritual expansion of a craft into an art, of skittish farce into comic narrative. Having adapted the suggestive principles of pantomime to the literal spectacle of cinema, Chaplin felt free to experiment with various moods and themes. Epic Existential with Canine Correlative (*A Dog's Life*), Mock Heroic (*Shoulder Arms*), Pastoral Fantasy (*Sunnyside*), Middle-Class Satire (*A Day's Pleasure*), Dickensian Romance (*The Kid*), Dualism in Class Caricature (*The Idle Class*), Desperate Poetry of Lower-Class Survival (*Pay Day*), and Religious Hypocrisy (*The Pilgrim*). It is in this period also that Chaplin's players tend to be subtler and more nuanced in their characterization. And the sight gags had never before been as logical or inventive—or since.

One of the cinema's classic sight gags can be found in *The Idle Class*, a film in which Chaplin plays a dual role, alternately the familiar Tramp and a debonairly (though not villainously) alcoholic husband. The husband is reading a letter deposited dramatically on the cocktail table. The wife is leaving the poor wretch until he stops drinking. Cut to shot of husband from the rear. His shoulders begin to heave uncontrollably, and more and more. The audience's amusement is tinged with the suspicion of a switch. Obviously, this wastrel cannot really be sobbing. Not that Chaplin is a stranger to sentiment, but he would never turn his back on the audience for a tearful collapse when his eyes are so economically emotional. Also, Chaplin has conditioned us to the relative sang-froid of the character in question. Thus we all sense that there is going to be a reversal of the conventional expectations from this situation. But what is the switch exactly, and how is it to be rendered? We are almost afraid that even Chaplin will find himself hard put to meet our demands for a suitably ironic twist. Then Chaplin turns, his shoulders still heaving, his hands occupied furiously with a cocktail shaker, his exquisite face hilariously neutral between joy and sorrow. The audience roars with collective appreciation. Chaplin has not only topped our wildest fancies; he has done so with a beautifully logical double switch, thus by-passing the cynical denial of imagined grief with a spectacular demonstration of the character's obsession with drink. We laugh not merely at the inventiveness of the gag, but at its being deftly interwoven with the narrative. Chaplin's is a triumph of both conception and execution, of both director-scenarist and actor.

Contrary to the unified field theory of aesthetics, this gag could work only in the cinema, where the screen's hypnotic light field focuses our attention on the image of the shoulders heaving first with grief and then with cocktail-shaking. On the stage, the shoulder-heaving would have been subsumed under the decor of Victorian melodrama. On the printed page, the literary expression of the effect would have become an end in itself, and the problem of establishing a visual point of view for the reader would have been almost insurmountable. Also, the gag's suspenseful ambiguity was possible only in the silent cinema where the sound of either sobs or crushed ice was impossible. This may explain why the gag was never repeated with or without variations even by Chaplin.

The Idle Class is memorable also for that breath-taking moment when Chaplin both exposes and celebrates our traditional repressions by decorously lowering an errant kilt over a male knee in an amusing parody of modesty. In a similar vein of unearthly imitation, Chaplin assumes a wheedlingly maternal pose (in the trolley car scene in *The Kid*) which derives from a merciless mimicry of motherhood as a comic mode of behavior.

Chaplin's comic *coups* were not merely accidents of inspiration and improvisation. There were endless rehearsals for even the smallest bits of business, and there was an enormous amount of footage shot from every conceivable angle. Adolphe Menjou has testified that Chaplin subjected him on occasion to as many as fifty takes to secure a suitably subtle enactment of a scene for *A Woman of Paris* (1923), one of only two films which Chaplin directed without himself in a central role, *A Countess from Hong Kong* (1967) being the other, though Chaplin makes cameo appearances in both. *A Woman of Paris* has been a "lost" film for many years, and thus its reputation has tended to outdistance its actual merit. Critic Eric Bentley defended it on its own terms as unabashed

Victorian melodrama, but the conventional film historians have ventured more questionably into claims for the work's earth-shaking cynicism and irony, claims which a recent exhumation of the film has shown to be wildly exaggerated. *A Woman of Paris* displays instead a very studied pattern of directorial ellipsis and understatement in the service of a sentimentality made arid by the absence of Chaplin the actor from the heart of the drama.

It is instead with *The Gold Rush* in 1925 that Chaplin arrived at his highest plateau of public acceptance, and perhaps the final moment of unclouded adulation. After *The Gold Rush*, his personal image was tarnished by a combination of marital squabbles, divorce actions, sensational gossip, political controversy, and soured idolatry. More important, Chaplin seemed to stand still technically and stylistically in an age infected by the cult of modernism and the theory of progress. Motion picture art, especially, was heralded largely as a machine art, which involved infinite expectations of "improvement" as with any gadget created by almighty science. Audiences and critics resumed their love affair with Chaplin at screenings of *The Gold Rush*, but Charlie was no longer as pre-eminent a myth as he had once been. And even his admirers soon began to worry not only about how he would meet the rising challenges of Lloyd, Keaton, Langdon, but also about where he would fit in the exploding stylistic environment of *The Last Laugh* and *Potemkin*.

The nineties view of the comic situation in the twenties tends to be considerably more complex than earlier. That is to say that if today Chaplin seems considerably less old-fashioned than he once did, Keaton and Lloyd seem considerably more humanistic and less mechanical than they were once deemed to be in comparison with Chaplin. If anything, the startling rediscovery of Keaton has brought about an over-reaction against the relative over-familiarity (and hence alleged banality) of Chaplin. Nonetheless, though Chaplin owed a great debt to Linder, Chaplin, in turn, greatly influenced and generally anticipated every comedian of his time. Harold Lloyd, especially, was always the first to acknowledge that he had begun his career as one of the less blatant of the Chaplin imitators.

But if Chaplin survived the technological challenges he was unwilling to accept, it is because he cannily spaced out his work after *The Gold Rush*, thereby maintaining the demand by restricting the supply with *The Circus* (1928), *City Lights* (1931), *Modern Times* (1936), *The Great Dictator* (1940), *Monsieur Verdoux* (1947), *Limelight* (1952), and then in relative duress and durance vile, *A King in New York* (1957) and *A*

Countess from Hong Kong (1967). The tendency nowadays is to look at Chaplin's entire career as a single slab of personal achievement, and thus to flatten out the temporal perspective by which each of his films was viewed in its own time. Thus, the oeuvre looks more sublime and less strange than it ever did in segments. *The Circus*, for example, seems to have been inexplicably under-rated in its own time. But in 1928 the big thing in movies was not the ancient art of pantomime but the then current craze for sound in the bathetic vaudevilles of Al Jolson in *The Jazz Singer* and *The Singing Fool*. By the time *City Lights* came out in 1931, audiences had become nostalgic for the lost glories of the silent screen. By 1936 everyone had adapted so completely to the sound film that Chaplin's intransigently silent mimetics in *Modern Times* seemed willful, reactionary, and technologically cowardly.

By the time of *The Great Dictator* (1940), Chaplin had begun the painful process of dissociating himself from the myth of the Tramp. But even his devastating parody of Hitler was discounted by audiences and critics on the grounds that the old comedy conventions were inadequate for the sleek new tyrannies. Only when absurdist modes of expression became the rage in the sixties and seventies could *The Great Dictator* be appreciated for the psychologically complex vision it provided through its stylized spectacles. It was only when one realized that even Chaplin was mortal that it seemed logical for him to abandon the Tramp in 1940 when he was past fifty. Chaplin himself insisted that the Tramp could never be permitted to speak. "To talk," Chaplin reasoned, "he would have to step off his pedestal, the pedestal of the silent film."

Of all Chaplin's features, probably his most universally beloved is *City Lights*. What is most striking about *City Lights* in terms of Chaplin's over-all career is its apotheosis of the Tramp. All his other major films have some specific subject. *The Gold Rush* is concerned with Chaplin's view of success, money, luck, and fate; *The Circus* with the impingement of the comedian's emotional existence on his comic essence; *Modern Times* with machinery and modernity encroaching on the privileged do-mains of the individual; *The Great Dictator* with the lust for power lurk-ing in all of us; *Monsieur Verdoux* with the moral contradictions of capitalism and the hellish paradoxes of Don Juanism; *Limelight* with the wintry melancholy of old age; and *A King in New York*, generally his most misunderstood film, with America as a fantasy and a delusion, a marvelous world which he eventually revisited in triumph, but which he never reconquered.

By contrast, *City Lights* is not particularly about cities or about city life. Chaplin renders his metropolis in the scurrying grayness of the vertical figures which emphasize the black costume and sidelong gait of the Tramp as he turns corners to confront the adventures of the scenario. Chaplin's technique soundly emphasizes the spectacle of the Tramp turning the corner rather than the abstract motion of the turn itself. Marxist critics of the thirties were disconcerted by the Tramp's lack of class awareness, his allegedly Victorian sentimentality, and his gutter opportunism. Today the subject of *City Lights* is more clearly seen as the Tramp himself, precariously balanced between the domains of comedy and tragedy. Charlie is his own Don Quixote and his own Sancho Panza, a knight and a knave, a fool both damned and divine.

City Lights is a film of extremes. If the Tramp has never been more courtly than in the expression of his love for the blind flower girl, one has to go back to his Sennett days to find comparable coarseness in the humor. Audiences are reminded again and again that even while tears flow from the soul, urine still flows from the body. Chaplin's timing is so remarkably precise, however, that the white rose of his romanticism seems to flower in the base soil of his earthiness.

Another paradox in *City Lights* is the virtually equal weight given the themes of courtly love and male camaraderie. Indeed, one of the most interesting characters in the Chaplin canon is the rich man (Harry Myers) who embraces the Tramp during their nocturnal revels, but who invariably forgets their association by the dawn's ugly light after they have sobered up. Chaplin's fear of rejection is thus expressed in both the social and sexual spheres, in terms of both lowly class status and diminutive physique. Harry Myers happened to be a very gifted straight-man comedian in his own right, as demonstrated by his antics with Bea Lillie in the silent 1928 comedy *Enter Smiling*. There is in the Myers persona alongside Chaplin's a stylistic resemblance to Max Linder's early incarnation of the aristocrat as bon vivant. Linder was noted also for his drunk acts, and it is through drink that Charlie's tramp transcends his sorrows in *City Lights* and much, much later in *Limelight*.

Chaplin is the most satisfying of all comedians because he is the most harmonious. He carefully established his character within a dramatic context in each film, and then carefully leads up to that moment when the spectator must identify with the character completely, be he comic, tragic, or merely melancholy. As an example, audiences invariably laugh at the entrance of two *apache* dancers in the night club even before Charlie has seen them. This laughter of anticipation is based on the audience's confidence (and even pride) in the Tramp's chivalry. Indeed,

Charlie's chivalry is a mythic mandate of such proportions as to assure the viewer that the Tramp will intervene with beautiful grace and force to right an imagined wrong. No other comedian could so telegraph every pratfall and still make his audience laugh.

Modern Times was hailed or reviled in its time as the first Chaplin film to tackle a theme of social significance with any degree of ideological consistency. Its alleged topicality was always the least of its charms.

Chaplin, like René Clair before him in *A Nous la Liberté* (1931) and Jacques Tati after him in *Mon Oncle* (1958), hated machinery for reasons more aesthetic than ecological, the attitude more Luddite than Leninist. Still, the mechanical feeding sequence in *Modern Times* is probably the funniest episode in all of cinema. It is hardly surprising that the humor is derived not from the historical logic or technological plausibility of the feeder but from Charlie's reaction to his mechanical tormentor. Chaplin's factory may be half René Clair pseudo-modern and half Fritz Lang comic-strip totalitarian, but Chaplin himself is the supreme cinematic performer of all time.

Nonetheless, it is hard to believe today that an astute thirties critic like Meyer Levin could praise Chaplin for aligning the Tramp with the world's working stiffs. The feeling that emerges most clearly from Chaplin's characterization is a studied distaste for his comrades in industry. Nothing personal or anti-socialist, mind you. The Tramp just happens to hate work, and this hatred is consistent with the logic of his classical prototypes. His deepest instincts are more petit bourgeois than proletarian. He may chortle at the dove-like gyrations of a young middle-class married couple, but he ends up yearning for the most grotesque tokens of economic security—a cow to be milked at the front door, grapevines crawling around the cottage like Virginia creeper, and a resourceful street *gamine* as immaculate child bride: Paulette Goddard, here and in *The Great Dictator*, as the urban descendant of Mary Pickford's girl of the rural slums. For the sake of this regressively childlike and sexless ménage, the Tramp announces grandly that he will make the supreme sacrifice and go to work. He is clearly and congenitally one of the poetically unemployed, Mr. Micawber masquerading as Mother Courage.

At times, the Tramp's happiness is uncomfortably opportunistic. Unjustly imprisoned, he thwarts an attempted jail-break and is rewarded with a comfortable cell and other special privileges. The siren call of liberty holds no charm for him, and his fellow convicts, like his fellow workers, sink into the slough of anonymous grayness reserved for abject creatures of necessity. All in all, Chaplin's Tramp gets off quite a few stops before the Finland Station.

Despite the serious overtones in his work, there has always been a tendency on the part of Chaplin's critics to measure his art by the number of laughs per minute he provoked. By this standard, if by no other, *The Great Dictator* and *Monsieur Verdoux* represented Chaplin in decline, and *Limelight* and *A King in New York* were relative disasters. But having survived for so long, Chaplin seemed a study less in decline than in modal metamorphosis, and, if his audiences diminished in size, they gained in appreciation as they contemplated an artist who for more than half a century had used the screen as his personal diary. As he had outgrown Sennett, he had outlasted Hitler, and he had aged with extraordinary grace. He had even got around to recording his awareness (in *Limelight*) that he had lost his mass audience. He remains the supreme exemplification of the axiom that lives and not lenses stand at the center of cinematic creation.

BUSTER KEATON (1895–1966)

Buster Keaton enters film history in 1917 as Fatty Arbuckle's assistant in *The Butcher Boy* and exits his personal Pantheon in 1928 with *Steamboat Bill, Jr.*, arguably the richest product of his raging unconscious. *The Cameraman* (1928) and *Spite Marriage* (1929) are not without winningly comic passages, but the MGM lion is already beginning to claw Buster's screen persona in the editing room. The end is near, but the demystified Keaton is going to hang around Hollywood for more than thirty years, being put on display as one of the wax works in Billy Wilder's *Sunset Boulevard* (1950) and acting as second banana in Charles Chaplin's *Limelight* (1952).

Back in the early sixties, a cinéphile of my acquaintance proposed a tribute to Keaton at the San Francisco Film Festival. Keaton had never been honored officially in America, though the Paris Cinemathèque had given him a tumultuous *hommage*. Keaton, the legendary Stone Face, sobbed openly. In Hollywood to this day, after all, you're only as good as your last picture. The trouble was that Keaton's great movies had disappeared into the limbo of antiquity. In any event, my acquaintance failed to convince co-juror Shirley Temple Black that Keaton deserved any kudos at the San Francisco Film Festival. "He wasn't very good, *was* he?," Miss Temple asked semi-rhetorically. And that was that.

Lest the foregoing anecdote be regarded as a mere pretext for ridiculing Shirley Temple, a marvelously gritty talent who helped FDR get us through the Great Depression, let me hasten to the excellent woman's defense by adding that, when she was starting out as a child star in the early thirties, Keaton was floundering around as a pathetic, often drunken has-been, all too visible in the shrunken world of slapstick talkies. He was generally identified in his porkpie hat as one of a forgotten tribe of custard-pie hurlers. It was easy to suppose from this that Keaton had once been a frantically, fidgety low comedian on the run from the Keystone Kops, and we all knew what they were.

My own exposure to the classical splendor of Keaton came in three stages. Sometime in the fifties I saw *The General* (1927) at the Museum of Modern Art and was startled by its expensive production and epic flow. It was unlike anything I had ever seen involving a comedian. Like everyone else, I began trying to relate Keaton to a comic tradition, as James Agee had done in his 1949 *Life* magazine essay, "The Golden Age of Comedy." Then, in 1961, I spent a considerable amount of time in Paris at the Cinematheque, where I discovered a wild enthusiasm in critical circles for all of Keaton's silent works. A maverick group of critics at the 1955 Brussels World's Fair had already proclaimed *Sherlock Jr.* (1924) as the best film of all time. Around the British Film Institute there was and still is a strong tendency to elevate Keaton at Chaplin's expense.

After I saw more Keaton silents, I tried to improvise a contrast through which I could keep Chaplin and Keaton in the pantheon together. This attempt at reconciliation appeared in *The American Cinema*, which was published in 1968 but represented my position as of 1963.

> The difference between Keaton and Chaplin is the difference between poise and poetry, between the aristocrat and the tramp, between adaptability and dislocation, between the function of things and the meaning of things, between eccentricity and emotionality, between man as machine and man as angel, between the Girl as a convention and the Girl as an ideal, between the centripetal and the centrifugal tendencies of slapstick. Keaton is now generally acknowledged as the superior director and inventor of visual forms. There are those who would go further and claim Keaton as pure cinema as opposed to Chaplin's theatrical cinema. Keaton's cerebral tradition of comedy was continued by René Clair and Jacques Tati,

but Keaton the actor, like Chaplin the actor, has proved to be inimitable. Ultimately, Keaton and Chaplin complement each other down the line to that memorably ghostly moment in *Limelight* when they share the same tawdry dressing room as they prepare to face their lost audience.

The third stage of my enlightenment, however, shattered all my previous theories. It came in 1969 in the School of the Arts at Columbia University, where I taught a course in Buster Keaton. The late Tom Allen managed to secure all the Buster Keaton silents in 16-millimeter from the libraries that Raymond Rohauer was beginning to supply at that time. It was the most extraordinary learning and teaching experience of my life. The class was packed with knowledgeable enthusiasts, and I was not even one lesson plan ahead of my students. An entire career gradually came into focus, and the cinema would never seem the same again. I mention my own slow evolution into a Keatonian only to emphasize the point that people who have not been immersed in Keaton's burst of creativity between 1917 and 1927 have no conception of what he actually accomplished. You really must see everything to understand the choices he finally made, and you must eliminate any preconceptions you may have about what movie comedy is supposed to be. There was absolutely no one like Keaton, and there never will be. He was an American original. Yet, he brought nothing to the talkies to equal what he invented in the silents.

Keaton could be hilarious on occasion, but most of his work is not geared to a laugh meter. *The Frozen North* (1922) strikes me as his funniest film, with *Cops* (1922), *The High Sign* (1920), and *The Goat* (1921) not too far behind. Significantly, these are all short films. Even in these works, the virtuosity unveiled often transforms the wild laugh into an appreciative chuckle. All in all, Keaton is far from being the funniest comedian ever, yet he could generate the belly laugh when he so desired. *The Frozen North* is a case in point. It is primarily a savage parody of William S. Hart, but Keaton manufactured additional merriment by inverting the western genre so that the hero behaves like a villain and a cad.

If one thinks of comedy/ha-ha (as opposed to comedy/not tragedy) as the most important part of screen comedy, one must conclude that the funniest films are almost invariably destructive and subversive and, more often than we like to admit, ratty and mean-spirited. The eternal appeal of the ethnic joke attests to the criterion of cruelty in these matters. So much "humor" is based on feelings of contempt, superiority, and comparative sophistication and normality. Look at Groucho step all over Margaret Dumont. Look at the cretinously clumsy Clouseau of Peter Sellers demolish the civilized inspector of Herbert Lom. Almost always, some elaborate edifice is being undermined or destroyed.

Keaton's comedy, for the most part, does not deflate pomposity or overthrow the powers that be, at least not by conscious design. *Cops* became an underground classic in the late sixties because of the sheer number of "pigs" who were zapped and lampooned in the course of Buster's madcap adventures. But Keaton is no anarchic angel. Much of the havoc he wreaks is caused by his lofty indifference to convention. At his worst, he is heartless. More often, he's merely thoughtless. At his best, he is consumed by an obsessive logic that impels him into a physically and visually harmonious relationship with the world around him. His forte is construction rather than demolition. Keaton walking into the movie screen in *Sherlock Jr.* (1924), Keaton dangling confidently from the mast in *The Navigator* (1924), swinging from the falls in *Our Hospitality* (1923), fleeing from the hordes of would-be brides in a continuous shot in *Seven Chances* (1925), and, above all, riding the whirlwind, itself, to Oedipal reversal in *Steamboat Bill Jr.* (1928) by saving his father from drowning. If one assembles all these haunting images, and many more, the composite effect in one's mind is a spectacle at which one must gasp rather than guffaw.

Rudi Blesh reports in his biography of Keaton that in 1898, when Buster Keaton was three years old, a Kansas cyclone lifted him out of a second-story window and deposited him unharmed in the middle of an unpaved main street some four blocks away. His parents were touring vaudevillians in the same company with Harry Houdini. In *Steamboat Bill Jr.* Keaton seems to draw on intuitive insights into the cyclonic forces of nature, and the state of grace and adaptability necessary to survive them. In the end, he triumphs over adversity by a majestic submission to the forces of motion, the very forces that constitute the logic and magic of all movies.

HAROLD LLOYD (1893–1971)

Harold Lloyd may never be as beloved as the other great clowns of his time. Chaplin and Keaton seem to be enduringly fascinating to the in-

tellectuals; the comic masks of Laurel and Hardy remain instantly identifiable to revelers of all nations. Harry Langdon and Raymond Griffith
seem more interesting than Lloyd to the more esoteric researchers in
silent screen comedy. Fatty Arbuckle survives as a tragic victim of American puritanism run rampant. It is the old problem of persona. Lloyd has
either less of it or, at least, a less personable persona than his contemporaries. Lloyd has neither the tragic overtones of Chaplin nor the absurdist tendencies of Keaton. He is not patiently poetical like Langdon,
or suavely stoical like Griffith. Worst of all, Lloyd seems not to have
transcended his own time as the pushy go-getter of the Jazz Age. Critic
Walter Kerr has noted that Lloyd was not funny in and of himself, but
did funny things. Richard Schickel has championed the visual naturalism
of Lloyd's comedies against the stylized distortions of Chaplin's and Keaton's. Perhaps the time has come to look away from Lloyd's persona to
the actual movies he made. This may mean modifying some of the very
ambivalent assumptions I published about Lloyd in an obituary think-
piece for the *New York Times* in 1971.

> Even at his peak Harold Lloyd had neither Keaton's sublime serenity
> nor Chaplin's passionate poetry, but he was often funnier than either just
> the same. Lloyd was the man in the crowd, on the subway, in the elevator,
> at the office. He was the country boy who made good in the city less
> through inspiration than perspiration, and the skyscrapers from which he
> so often dangled expressed not only the upward mobility of his aspirations
> but also his morbid fear of falling back into the herd below. Ambition
> glinted in his glasses along with a wistful yearning for approval. Whereas
> Chaplin's balletic tramp struggled for survival and Keaton's saintly acrobat
> searched for the ecstasy of equilibrium, Lloyd's white-collar Everyman
> strained for success on the American Plan. It follows that though with
> Chaplin and Keaton we feel that we shall never see their like again, Lloyd's
> spiritual facsimile is an even-money bet to run up at the next convention
> of the Shriners, the Rotarians or the Elks.
>   Lloyd's golden age was almost exclusively in the silents. From
> *Grandma's Boy* to *Speedy*, Lloyd fulfilled the wildest success fantasies of
> the so-called jazz age. He was less effective in the sound era, and even
> the very special farcical gifts of Leo McCarey (*The Milky Way*) and Preston
> Sturges (*Mad Wednesday*) were unable to resurrect Lloyd as a comic fa-
> vorite. Audiences of the thirties were somewhat baffled and put off by this
> zany optimist with more energy than charm. Still Lloyd is hardly the only
> comedian who failed to cross the sound barrier. Keaton's fall was even
> more precipitous, and Langdon virtually disappeared. As Otis Ferguson
> remarked at the time, the comic tasks of the sound film were taken away

from the stylized clowns of the silent era and passed out to a passel of realistic bit players. Nonetheless, Lloyd's fall was only partly technological. His comic type simply became obsolete after the Crash. The aggressive values he embodied in the giddy twenties seemed downright irresponsible in the hungover thirties. Besides, a certain loss of resilience was inevitable in a comic persona exposed in over a hundred and thirty movies from the administration of Woodrow Wilson through that of Harry Truman. As it is, *The Freshman* seems as fresh and funny today as it must have seemed back in 1925 when college football knighthood was still in flower. And there is no better barometer of immortality than the earnest laughter of revival audiences. As we laugh, Lloyd lives.

In the more than a quarter of a century since Lloyd's death enough of his films have resurfaced to make it possible for me to revise my superficial analysis of his career as it seemed in 1971. It is very possible that we have done Lloyd a disservice by bracketing him with Chaplin and Keaton, when, actually, he belongs more in the mainstream of movie comedy. Also, it is possible to question his values without questioning his worth. And what are his values? Lloyd himself provides a partial answer in his 1928 autobiography, *An American Comedy*:

> There are two kinds of poor boys in America—the Tom Sawyers and the Huckleberry Finns, and Hollywood is full of examples of each who have reached the top in pictures. . . . It would be easy to make this more exciting by putting myself down as a Huck Finn, but it would not be true. I was a good example of a Tom Sawyer. . . . I might have been Master America most any year between 1893 and 1910. This is assuming that the average boy before the war was moderately poor, that his folks moved a good deal and that he worked for his spending money at any job that offered.

As a Tom Sawyer type Lloyd was temperamentally unsuited for tramp roles. Honest work haunts most of his roles, and there does not seem to be an anarchic or even rebellious bone in his body. Lloyd therefore did not qualify as a clown under the widely quoted rules promulgated by John Grierson: "Clowns are the world's incompetents. They are bound to the wheel of incompetence or they cease to be clowns."

Lloyd, like Keaton, was ultra-competent, and so much the worse for both in Grierson's view. "When comedy is merely a matter of artificial situations and expert gags, as in the case of Harold Lloyd and, to some extent, in the case of Buster Keaton, you laugh and are done with it.

They are clever fellows to work their way through such amusing scrapes, but they mean no more."

Certainly, no one can describe Lloyd as a "tragedian in disguise." In all his eighteen feature-length comedies there is a happy ending in terms of both the girl and success, which is to say that from 1921 to 1947 Lloyd was the soul of optimism on the screen. Keaton could be morbid on occasion, and Chaplin full of self-hatred, but Lloyd was always upbeat at the end even when he had to endure the most traumatic humiliations and perils to get there. Except for *A Sailor-Made Man* (1921), *Why Worry?* (1923), and *For Heaven's Sake* (1926), in which he played devil-may-care millionaires, Lloyd was the quintessential middle-class comic hero. I cannot recall one of his films in which he was hungry enough to steal food. He was thus denied the traditional means of gaining audience sympathy for the underdog. This is a trifling matter except as an explanation of his unpopularity with socially conscious critics. It is hard to believe but Getting the Girl was once interpreted as a convention that implied acceptance of the capitalist system.

What has never been adequately appreciated was Lloyd's avant-garde role in taking screen comedy from filler-length to feature-length. If scandal had not intervened, Fatty Arbuckle might have been the first illustrious feature-length comedian. As it happened, Lloyd jumped the gun on both Keaton and Chaplin with *A Sailor-Made Man* in 1921 and *Grandma's Boy* in 1922. These are important years in the gradual evolution of slapstick into new epic, narrative, and dramatic forms. For many nostalgic critics these were years of retrogression as pathos and pretentiousness supplanted the surrealist Sennett explosions, which enjoyed their greatest vogue between 1914 and 1918. Lloyd's reputation has thus been further deflated by the critical myth of a Golden Age of uproarious one- and two-reelers. Lloyd had less to lose than his contemporaries in this transition to longer movies. His shorts from 1915 on seem to have been relatively haphazard affairs until he dropped the Lonesome Luke character (imitative of Chaplin), and hit upon the character with the lensless eye glasses, thus entering the comic domain of Douglas Fairbanks, as Schickel suggested in his biography of Lloyd. Once Lloyd found his proper "persona" he was ready to embark on more elaborate comic adventures. Still, *A Sailor-Made Man*, for all its picaresque qualities, seems to be a short, flimsily premised film with much comic padding. Lloyd's playboy suitor of a society tease (Mildred Davis, later Mrs. Harold Lloyd) joins the navy in a ludicrously contrived ploy to follow her father's yacht into the troubled waters of a Turkish harem. To rescue his beloved the sailor must literally turn the harem upside down in a series of elegantly staged and resourcefully detailed chases. A great many of the gags involve ingenious concealments, and the harem pool provides Lloyd with what is to become familiar to Lloyd fans as both the ordeal and opportunity of immersion for a fugitive from superior powers. Most other comedians revel in gags that reveal them in moments of great danger. Only Lloyd understood the audience's intuitive identification with a character desperate enough to efface himself through concealment. And it is the instinctive desperation in Lloyd's reaction to danger that gives emotional force to his energy. Ultimately, the perpetual mobility of *A Sailor-Made Man* redeems it from its cardboard characterizations.

But if *A Sailor-Made Man* is little more than an elongated sketch for a comedy, *Grandma's Boy* is a fully articulated comic adventure extraordinary for its time. Unfortunately, many modern film historians come upon *Grandma's Boy* out of the context of its time and thus tend to compare it with the comedy classics of the middle and late twenties. This extra-historical approach is patently unfair to Lloyd's achievement in integrating gags with a character study. There is not much depth to the character study, to be sure, but there is a strange intensity to the characterization nonetheless. The boy with the lensless glasses has a very simple problem: he is a coward. But his grandma knows that it is only a matter of confidence. A confederate grandpa is invoked via flashback to demonstrate the miraculous potency of a magic charm. Fortified with this ancestral tradition, the boy vanquishes his erstwhile tormentor. When the boy realizes that the magic charm is spurious, he realizes that his grandma has dispensed instead her ancient wisdom on how to inspire the menfolk in the family. The film works dramatically, however, because grandma goes into action only when the boy has reached his darkest moment of fear and humiliation. As America was in transition in the twenties from a rural to an urban society, so Lloyd seemed to be in transition from a hick character to a go-getter. The rustic romances of Griffith and Ford and Charles Ray are more resigned and less restless than *Grandma's Boy*. There are still traces of Lonesome Luke in the terribly tight trousers in which the boy comes courting. Lonesome Luke's tight trousers were, of course, a derivation in reverse of Chaplin's baggy pants. The derivation is appropriate in that Lloyd's characters are conceived in a spirit of repression whereas Chaplin's Tramp is conceived in a spirit of release. Yet, it is this bottling up of anger and aspiration that enables Lloyd's characters to unwind with such furious force. Lloyd thus communicates more easily with general audiences than with critics and scholars, for it is the average moviegoer who is most receptive to fantasies of success and vindication. Lloyd's Tom Sawyer complex triumphs for perhaps the first time in *Grandma's Boy*, and it is left to the other comedians to pursue the inner triumphs of Huckleberry Finn.

Safety Last (1923) was one of Lloyd's most famous films, and its concluding set-piece—Lloyd's perilous "human fly" climb up the side of a department store—established for all time the spatial metaphor for an American's rise to the top in the midst of a fear of falling. As Lloyd became known as the comedian who would do anything for a laugh, the character he played became known as the Jazz-Age climber who would do anything to succeed. *Safety Last* begins with a celebrated visual gag by which the audience is made to believe that they are about to witness an execution. But one by one the telltale props—bars, priest, noose, tearful mother, and sweetheart—are demystified, and the boy with the dark-rimmed glasses leaves the country for the city, where he becomes a clerk in a department store. One of Lloyd's most effective scenes—a riot of voracious women shoppers at a bargain sale—rivals the brilliant misogyny of Keaton's *Seven Chances*. The humble clerk writes glowing letters to the girl back home about his great success in the city, and she decides to visit him before another woman grabs him and his money. The girl in this instance is a dreadful creature, and the boy has to perform prodigious feats to convince her that he is indeed as successful as she thinks he is. He has a much warmer relationship with his roommate, an unemployed human fly, who figures grotesquely in the denouement. Seizing an opportunity to improve his position at the store by coming up with a publicity stunt, the boy persuades his roommate to climb the side of the department store. But the friend has fallen afoul of a persistent policeman, and the boy himself must make the climb, always for just one more floor until he reaches the top, the girl, and success, though not necessarily in that order of preference. The entire film seems to have been constructed around the climb, and thus represents a structural regression from *Grandma's Boy*. There is a wildly lyrical moment when Lloyd is swinging crazily from a rope, a moment that Keaton might have extended in time for its feelings of freedom and exhilaration. Lloyd treats this moment as an interruption in the ultimate climb, and quickly returns to the business at hand. On the other hand, Lloyd gives us glimpses of an impervious city, and thus makes the spectacle more frighteningly real and more majestically social. The spectacular climax of *Safety Last* undoubtedly influenced Chaplin's cabin-teetering-on-the-cliff sequence in *The Gold Rush* (1925).

Safety Last was the last film Lloyd made with Mildred Davis as his leading lady. She had succeeded Bebe Daniels in 1919, and in 1923 she became Mrs. Harold Lloyd. Lloyd would make his next six films with Jobyna Ralston as his leading lady. Much has been written about the attitudes of Chaplin and Keaton to women in general and to their leading ladies in particular. In comparison with the messy private lives of Chaplin and Keaton, Lloyd's off-screen existence seemed cautious, prudent, and proper, as befitted a grown-up Tom Sawyer. With the exception of the Constance Cummings character in *Movie Crazy* (1932), the girls in Lloyd's comedies tended to have interchangeable roles. Passive, winsome, often more old-fashioned in looks and manner than the flappers around them, Lloyd's sweethearts remained mere objects of affection without much subjective spark of their own. They were neither shrines for sentiment as in Chaplin, nor partners in slapstick as in Keaton, but, rather, rewards for extraordinary feats of courage and daring.

Girl Shy (1924) turns away from the zany antics of *Why Worry?* (1923) to a subtle romanticism in which Lloyd explores more of the facets of courtship than he ever has before or ever will again. By now his collaboration with co-directors Fred Newmeyer and Sam Taylor have yielded a more modulated style with quiet camera ironies worthy almost of Lubitsch and Clair. As a shy young man who has written a dreamy textbook on making love to women, Lloyd must have tapped some of the sheltered impulses in his own awkward adjustments to the opposite sex. Lloyd was never to top his final chase heroics to avert the marriage of his beloved to a villainous would-be bigamist. Schickel has compared the ending to that in *The Graduate* (1967), and one can trace Lloyd's cross-cutting between wedding ceremony and hero's frantic rescue efforts all the way back to the suspense montage in D. W. Griffith's *The Birth of a Nation* and *Intolerance*. But the editing would not be nearly as exciting at the climax were it not the culmination of a very leisurely development of the feelings of the characters.

The Freshman (1925) represents Lloyd at the peak of his comic powers, but the film is also a resounding restatement of his dubious values of wordly success and social acceptance. When I used to screen *The Freshman* for the flower-child generation of students in the sixties, they would boo Lloyd's craven conformity. They simply could not imagine

identity of the Mr. Big of a Chinatown crime syndicate. There is more head-cracking violence in Lloyd's first talkie than in all his silent movies put together, and it is precisely in the realm of violence where Lloyd miscalculated most grievously. From the earliest Sennett days people could be hit over the head repeatedly without making the audience wince, but suddenly with sound the crunch of a blunt instrument on the human skull became a soberingly realistic catastrophe. Later in the talkies ways would be found to stylize the skull-cracking, but even then it was a comic ploy that had to be used very sparingly in the relatively realistic world of sound. But Lloyd had plunged into the mayhem and the chinoiserie as if he wanted to conquer talkies by conking as many Chinamen as it took to keep audiences laughing. Another of his devices that misfired was his startling blacking-out of the image when the lights were supposed to be out, and letting the sound carry the action. In a sense, he was inserting sequences of pure radio into a talkie. It was a completely original strategy, unique as far as I know to *Welcome Danger*, but it never caught on as a convention.

Worse still, the crook plot was barely on speaking terms with the love plot, and the action jumped from one location to another with little rhyme or reason. From the opening shot on a train, Lloyd puts his worst foot forward as a pushy, prissy know-it-all, the worst possible context for his speaking voice to be introduced to audiences. After the neighborly warmth of *Speedy* there is a terribly chilling effect in the relentless, unimaginative, tedious, one-man vigilante violence of *Welcome Danger*.

Lloyd might have been better advised to shelve *Welcome Danger* and enter talkies in 1930 with *Feet First*, a thrill picture that historians like Walter Kerr compare unfavorably with *Safety Last*, but which fits nonetheless into the tradition of Lloyd's silent comedies. Many of the dialogue sequences are still awkward and ill-paced, but Lloyd is beginning to get laughs through the sheer doggedness of his verbal personality. The social climbing is beginning to wear thin not so much because of the Depression, which has not yet taken hold on the screen, but because Lloyd himself seems to be aging as a go-getter starting at the very bottom as a shoe clerk. The problem with the skyscraper climax here is that it is more accidental and less aspirational than the one in *Safety Last*. Among the accidental elements that have not dated well is Willie Best's feckless "darky," who can be counted on to prolong the hero's ordeal at every opportunity to be of service. Sound presents a problem also in that the world below seems more intrusive, and thus the resulting realism makes

Lloyd's exploits seem more far-fetched. Nonetheless, *Feet First* marked an impressive rebound from *Welcome Danger*, but the trouble was that Lloyd's humor was still primarily visual rather than verbal at a time when the ears had it over the eyes.

Hence, by the time *Movie Crazy* hit the movie screens in 1932, Lloyd had lost most of his following. And irony of ironies, *Movie Crazy* succeeds on its own terms as a talking picture. For one thing, the love story (with Constance Cummings) is the most complicated and sophisticated in Lloyd's entire career. For another, Lloyd has fashioned an artful balance between the country bumpkin and city slicker elements in his personality. For a third, Lloyd has returned to home ground by contemplating the subject of his own career. Miss Cummings plays a down-to-earth movie star who is identified with the siren on the set, and when he meets her accidentally off screen he doesn't recognize her. The actress plays her double role with Lloyd to the hilt in order to test his sincerity. At first Lloyd betrays the real woman for the sake of the make-believe siren, but he finally redeems himself by thrashing her obnoxious co-star. The early sequences of grotesque cross-courtships are the wittiest and warmest since *Speedy*, and the climactic struggle in the studio-made flood is up to Lloyd's silent standards for sight gags. But the night-club sequence with the magician's coat spewing out rabbits, birds, handkerchiefs, and other illusionist paraphernalia lacks the motivational force of a similar scene in *The Freshman*. Also, Lloyd is here more the victimizer than the victim. Arthur Housman, a drunken type who preceded the immortal Jack Norton, takes up much of the footage with his patented character bits. Not that Housman posed much of a problem to Lloyd, but he was only one of a horde of humorous types who were beginning to infiltrate movies with bits and pieces of comic business, thus weakening the artistic autonomy of the classic clowns.

The Cat's Paw (1934) is one of Lloyd's strangest projects, but hardly a disaster on the scale of *Welcome Danger*. Lloyd and his collaborators were greatly influenced by the Capra films of this period. Indeed, the original story was by Clarence Budington Kelland, the author of *Mr. Deeds Goes to Town*. Lloyd returns to the chinoiserie so fashionable in the early thirties as he plays the son of a missionary in China, who applies Confucian guile to solve the problem of gangster politics in an American city. The lack of due process in the denouement endows *The Cat's Paw* with the fascist overtones of Cecil B. De Mille's *This Day and Age* (1933). Una Merkel provides a perky love interest, but the commercial problem with the film is that there are not enough laughs for a

Lloyd vehicle. What is enduringly interesting about the film is Lloyd's stubborn resistance to the temptation of satire. *The Cat's Paw* may thus be disconcerting to the Lloyd fan, but it is admirably faithful to its genre.

The Milky Way (1936) failed to save Lloyd's career in the talkies, but it was impressive enough to serve as a remake for Danny Kaye a decade later. As a consequence, the original version was suppressed for many years, and thus has never been adequately re-evaluated. Leo McCarey's direction is skillful enough and sympathetic enough to integrate Lloyd's performance with a wisecracking ensemble of Adolphe Menjou, Verree Teasdale, Lionel Stander, and George Barbier. The only improvement in the 1946 remake was Kaye's more balletic treatment of the bogus fight sequences. (One might also cite Vera-Ellen's dance numbers.) Otherwise, the remake is a startlingly literal remake of the original down to the tiniest bits of business. The biggest coup of *The Milky Way* is its flair with the exchanges between Lloyd's simpleton and Menjou's cynic. As Lloyd's milkman stumbles into the world championship, the lamb becomes a lion, the innocent degenerates into a celebrity. It is a transformation that Preston Sturges was to celebrate a decade later in *Mad Wednesday* (1947), originally *The Sin of Harold Diddlebock*. Sturges opened with actual footage of *The Freshman*, then provided a wry sequence of failure, aging, and disillusionment more in the Sturges mold, and concluded with a thrill sequence inspired partly by *Safety Last* and *Feet First*. But neither McCarey nor Sturges was able to resurrect the Lloydian tradition. For all its professed nostalgia, the moviegoing public had tired of the silent slapstick heritage. But Lloyd himself had done a more creditable job of adapting to sound than most film historians had ever realized. *Movie Crazy, The Milky Way,* and *Mad Wednesday* are much closer to the standards of the best silent Lloyds than had hitherto been supposed. Even Elliott Nugent's otherwise negligible *Professor Beware* (1938) contains graceful passages of physical movement in the midst of a turgid plot. Again, Lloyd was trying to adapt to a vagabond tradition in movies, though he himself was grievously miscast for the open road. After all, he remained to the end of his days a Tom Sawyer character in a culture infatuated with Huckleberry Finn. But his rapport with the medium and the audience was of such long duration, and his ingenuity in transcending his type was so inexhaustible, that a re-evaluation and almost certain upgrading of his total career would seem to be long overdue. And I say this as one of his erstwhile detractors.

JOHN FORD (1895–1973)

John Ford was suspected of being an artist long before movie directors became fashionable deities and obsessive objects of *la recherche des films perdus*. Until very recently the vast majority of Ford's films were not available for reappraisal. Excluding war documentaries, television serials, cameo, second-unit, acting, and otherwise curtailed assignments, there are some 125 titles in Ford's directorial filmography. Of these, sixty-six were released before 1930, and thirty before 1920. A 1969 press release of the American Film Institute suggests the dimensions of the research problem. Under an underlined all-caps scare headline: JOHN FORD'S FIRST FILM RESCUED BY AMERICAN FILM INSTITUTE; SEQUENCE TO BE SHOWN ON NBC, the release goes on to announce:

> The first feature film ever directed by the man generally considered to be America's foremost motion picture director has been "rescued" by the American Film Institute. John Ford directed *Straight Shooting*, starring Harry Carey with Hoot Gibson, in 1917 to begin a career that has grown in international renown over the last half century. The picture, long supposed lost, was tracked down by the American Film Institute which found the only known print in the Czech Film Archive.

As it happens, *Straight Shooting* (1917) gives us at most merely a tantalizing glimpse of Ford's artistic beginnings. But we can sense that the forceful images on the screen tend to transcend the feeble fictions behind them. Ford's framing of horsemen sliding down a sandy hill can be traced from *Straight Shooting* to *The Lost Patrol* (1934) to *The Searchers* (1956). Even as the narrative continues to move forward from background to foreground, Ford's imagery imprints itself on the visual memory of the viewer. Here we are at a time when the western was still relatively new even though the West was old, and the Old West virtually gone, and yet Ford is already casting a somber spell on the screen, his mise-en-scène already in mourning, his feelings of loss and displacement already fantasized through the genre. This elegiac element in his style helps explain why Ford was spotted as a stylist surprisingly early in his career. It is more than a matter of beautiful pictures. The silent screen was saturated with them. It is rather a matter of the dynamic counterpoint between the physical and emotional energy of his players and the reflective overview of his extraordinarily quiet camera.

Ford himself evolved out of a ruggedly physical tradition in film-making, both as a stunt man and as a pioneer in location shooting, and the flourish of fisticuffs was treated as a sign of manhood to the end of his career. But Ford's enactments of hand-to-hand combats were always less painful than percussive, less savage than ceremonial. I doubt whether all Ford's screened fistfights put together could equal the tissue-tearing brutalities inflicted in the circus combat between Ake Gronberg and Hasse Ekman in Ingmar Bergman's *Sawdust and Tinsel* (1953) or in the Mexican tavern tempest pitting Humphrey Bogart and Tim Holt against Barton MacLane in John Huston's *The Treasure of the Sierra Madre* (1948). With Bergman and Huston the inflicting of pain and humiliation takes precedence over the celebration of manhood, and the spectacle of suffering becomes the visual symptom if not indeed the vital center of the human condition. With Ford pugnacity is all, punishment nil.

On the first-hand evidence available, Ford's visual style seems to have become somewhat more Germanic and less Griffithian through the twenties. (For that matter, Griffith's did too.) But the issue seems somewhat more complicated today than it did just a few decades ago, when the total representation of Ford silents in the repertory of the Museum of Modern Art consisted of *The Iron Horse* (1924) and *Four Sons* (1928).

With the former film shot on location in Nevada, and the latter shot on a Fox set, it is not surprising that *The Iron Horse* should evoke Rubert Flaherty, and *Four Sons*, F. W. Murnau. After all, it would be just as hard to be Expressionistic out on the open range as to be naturalistic against painted backdrops. Still, *The Iron Horse* and *Four Sons* do happen to constitute in their obvious oppositions a visual duality in Ford's style that was to remain unresolved to the end of his career. Nonetheless, this counterpoint of day and night, sun and shadow, Manifest Destiny and Implacable Fate, would not be worth discussing in the context of two films as artistically undeveloped and as psychologically unexplored as *The Iron Horse* and *Four Sons* if Ford's career had not taken the strange turns it did after the coming of sound. One must remember that film techniques proliferated more rapidly in the twenties than in any decade before or since, and at the time of *Four Sons*, particularly, a misty German night was falling over the sunlit screen of D. W. Griffith. Indeed, Murnau's *Sunrise* (1927), the climactic masterpiece of studio Expressionism, had been shot at Fox the year before *Four Sons* (1928), and it would have been unusual for Ford *not* to have been influenced by the German master of camera mise-en-scène. Although as William Everson, a sort of film man for all seasons, has wryly remarked, Fox paid for its losses on *Sunrise* with the profits from its Tom Mix movies, there is no question that Murnau and his colleagues at UFA profoundly affected Hollywood thinking on what a film should look like.

For his part, Ford never became enamoured of Murnau's conspicuously expressive camera movements, which were later to be refined and extended by Max Ophüls and Kenji Mizoguchi. Indeed, Ford's camera remained relatively still throughout his career even in as supposedly mobile a genre as the western. French film historian Jean Mitry noted this paradox in Ford's style long before it was critically fashionable to isolate directorial figures of style, apart from their appropriateness to story content. And it was therefore Mitry who was able to deduce that even in Ford's supposedly epic westerns like *The Iron Horse* (1924) and *Stagecoach* (1939), the illusion of kinesis was created not through gratuitous camera gyrations, but through functional camera followings of the conveyance (locomotive, stagecoach) in each instance.

It is almost too chronologically appropriate that Ford's first film of the thirties—*Men Without Women* (1930)—marks his first collaboration with Dudley Nichols, a screenwriter with whom he was to be subsequently associated on *Born Reckless* (1930), *Seas Beneath* (1931), *Pilgrimage* (1933), *The Lost Patrol* (1934), *Judge Priest* (1934), *The Informer* (1935), *Steamboat 'Round the Bend* (1935), *Mary of Scotland* (1936), *The Plough and the Stars* (1936), *The Hurricane* (1937), *Stagecoach* (1939), *The Long Voyage Home* (1940), and *The Fugitive* (1947). The Ford-Nichols relationship, especially in the thirties, is therefore a crucial aspect of any assessment of Ford's developing reputation. In this respect, *Men Without Women* was more important at the time than it has seemed since.

Even the title of the movie signals the path Ford was to follow to his greater glory. Thus, *Men Without Women* implies Man without frivolous distractions or Hollywood conventions. Of course, a movie about fourteen men trapped in a submarine with an ever-dwindling supply of oxygen was hardly the stuff of an actress's dreams. Yet though Ford himself was no stranger to male-oriented scenarios, never before had a Ford film been endowed so elegantly with life-and-death suspense. The directorial turn of the screw here probably did more to enhance Ford's standing as a serious artist than all the grosses from *The Iron Horse* and *Four Sons*. It wasn't merely that *Men Without Women* made the ten-best lists of several critics and lingered in many moviegoers' memories; the unconventional nature of the achievement gave Ford an aura of individuality at a time when anonymity was the lot of most directors. And it helped smooth over Ford's hitherto bumpy transition to the talkies.

Dudley Nichols himself recalled that stormy era in a letter to Lindsay Anderson:

I landed in Hollywood in June, 1929. I had earlier finished ten years of journalism in New York (reporting, drama criticism, music criticism, columning, one year on a roving assignment in Europe) and had cut my journalistic ties to go on with fiction and other writing. . . . Winfield Sheehan, then executive head of Fox films, talked me into coming to Hollywood. Sound had arrived and writers were needed. I knew nothing about film and told him so. I had seen one film I remembered and liked, Ford's *The Iron Horse.* So I arrived rather tentatively and experimentally, intending to leave if I found it dissatisfying. Fortunately, Sheehan assigned me to work with Ford. I liked him. I am part Irish, and we got on. I told him I had not the slightest idea how to write a film script. I had been in the Navy during the war, overseas two years, and we decided on a submarine story. I told him I could write a play, not a script. In his humorous way he asked if I could write a play in fifty or sixty scenes. Sure. So I did. It was never a script. Then I went on the sets and watched him break it down into filmscript as he shot. I went to rushes, cutting rooms, etc., and began to grasp what it was all about. But I must say I was baffled for many months by the way Ford could see everything through a camera— and I could not. . . . Working with Ford closely I fell in love with the cinema.

Men Without Women is divided into two very unequal parts, the first—virtually a prologue—consisting of a nocturnal prowl in and out of Shanghai waterfront dives. The point of view tends to be collective rather than individualized, the vaudeville almost forebodingly half-hearted. There is a Man with a Past, and another man inquiring into that past, but the two actors involved (Kenneth MacKenna, Paul Page) look too much alike to establish much dramatic tension. (A talking print might have established idiosyncratic distinctions in their voices.) As if to counterbalance the impendingly claustrophobic stasis of the mise-en-scène inside the doomed sub, Ford made the Shanghai sequences more mobile than was his custom. As Nichols recalled the episode in question: "They believed long dolly shots could not be made with the sound camera. He did it—one long shot down a whole street, with men carrying microphones on fishpoles overhead."

Once aboard the sub, the barely introduced characters plunge to their dire destiny without much ado. The bulk of the film is taken up with the physical details of their ordeal. The beauty of Ford's direction is that he orchestrates a veritable symphony of fearful expressions without resorting to the showy cross-cutting of anguished angles. We see fear interacting from face to face within a fixed, communal frame. Stuart Erwin's luminously oafish radio operator is particularly memorable as a fixed point of tension in the midst of intermittent flurries of movement and feeling. On the surface of the ocean, the rescue ships poked through the Expressionistic mist of night and fog to plumb the Orphic depths. It is a mood of romantic despair which was to mark the Ford-Nichols collaboration through the thirties and into the forties.

■　■　■　■

AFTER A DECADE of comparative obscurity at Fox, Ford was borrowed by Samuel Goldwyn to direct *Arrowsmith* (1931), with a prestigious cast headed by Ronald Colman, Helen Hayes, Richard Bennett, and Myrna Loy, an even more prestigious script by Sidney Howard from the novel by Sinclair Lewis, and a score by Alfred Newman as an added guarantee of success. Ford made the most of his opportunity by demonstrating the ability to tell a wordy story in a sequence of crisp, forceful images. *Arrowsmith* was the kind of socially oriented property in which the players could be kept at a reasonable focal distance. Colman and Hayes did not engulf the screen with high-powered close-ups. The film was not really about their intimate insights so much as their expansive altruism. The ill-fated Leora of Helen Hayes is an especially poignant character because we see her so often in modest long shots as if she could never be more than a small part of her husband's obsessive concerns.

Arrowsmith remains basically a scriptwriter's movie with a theatrical climax in Ronald Colman's stirring integrity speech before the final fadeout. There were many such speeches in the idealistic thirties, notably Edward G. Robinson's in *Five Star Final* (1931), Walter Huston's in *Law and Order* (1932), John Barrymore's in *Topaz* (1933), Paul Muni's in *The Life of Emile Zola* (1937), Robert Donat's in *The Citadel* (1938), and, of course, to round out the moral aspirations of the decade, James Stewart's veritable flood of rhetoric in *Mr. Smith Goes to Washington* (1939). Ford did not entirely escape wordy scripts during the decade, but his style for the most part came to be defined by the implications of images rather than words. Hence, it was not the speech itself, however eloquently written or delivered, that revealed Ford's attitude, but the visual spin-off from the speech.

Air Mail (1932) marked Ford's return to his first studio, Universal, with a moody, fog-saturated saga of the early days of air-mail flying. It is the kind of good movie which in its time was dismissed because of genre prejudice. Unfortunately, *Air Mail* does not seem to have been available when the New Critics of *Cahiers du Cinema* and *Movie* were resurrecting Hollywood's action ethos of the thirties for highbrow auteur and genre revaluations in the fifties and sixties. Consequently, the misty aircraft movie genre tends to be identified almost exclusively with Howard Hawks because of *Dawn Patrol* (1930), *Ceiling Zero* (1936), and *Only Angels Have Wings* (1939), and actually deservedly so. *Air Mail* is not as fully or as finely articulated as Hawks's treatment of this romantic material. Curiously, *Air Mail* and *Ceiling Zero* share the same scenarist (Frank W. Wead) and virtually the same plot, and yet the two movies diverge decisively, mainly because of two contrasting directorial visions. Again, Ford's is the view from long shot, submerging the squabbling egos of the pilots in cameraman Karl Freund's luminous contemplation of the plane itself as the communal vehicle of all the hopes and fears of the characters. By contrast, Hawks's celebrated eye-level viewpoint concentrates on the aerial/Ariel aspirations of the fliers themselves, and reduces the planes to bird-like appendages of the presumptuous groundlings.

Ford returned to Fox in 1933 after a three-picture absence to make *Pilgrimage*, one of his biggest commercial successes up to that time. Again, as with *Four Sons* (1928), Ford capitalizes on the inherent sentimentality in the loss suffered by a mother, and again it is I. A. R. Wylie who provides the original story material (in this instance a story entitled *Gold Star Mother*). Philip Klein and Barry Connors were credited with the scenario, with dialogue attributed to Dudley Nichols. By any standard, *Pilgrimage* is a disconcerting project to associate with the Ford-Nichols integrity legend. First, the studio is all wrong. Ford and Nichols were later to make their reputations at RKO, whereas Fox always represented for Ford's critics the siren call of convention and compromise. Also, *Pilgrimage* looks back not merely to the maternal sentimentality of *Four Sons*, but to some of the worst excesses of the windswept melodramas of the silent era. The opening sequences are particularly overblown as Henrietta Crosman's jealous mother turns her son (a callow, wild-eyed Norman Foster, brother of Preston, and later nominal director of that Wellesian whirlwind *Journey into Fear*) over to the draft board to save him from the clutches of an especially angelic Heather Angel. The son is killed in the War To End All Wars, and his sweetheart bears his child, and cares for it in proud poverty, while the mother remains unforgiving and unrepentant as the wind howls through the trees on Fox's back-lot of rural America.

How will Henrietta Crosman's Hannah Jessop see the error of her ways? Simply by making a pilgrimage along with other Gold Star Mothers to her son's final resting place in France. There she will encounter another young man with another monstrous mother in exactly the same situation with which *Pilgrimage* began. By way of this mirror re-enactment, Hannah Jessop finds the wisdom to avert a second tragedy, and to reconcile herself to her responsibility for the first by acknowledging at long last her daughter-in-love and grandchild as her own flesh and blood.

So much for the scenario and its maudlin contrivances. The bulk of the film is another matter. Ford and Nichols do not merely transcend their material but skillfully subvert it by shifting the emphasis from the mechanics of the plot to the mood of an epic voyage of stoically Trojan women to the final resting places of their slain warrior sons. And, again, Ford's discreet camera distance and his behavioral doodling on the margins of the scenario create epic feelings without bombast or pretension. Especially memorable is Mrs. Hatfield (Lucille Laverne) with her corncob pipe, hillbilly high spirits, and womanly stoicism. But she too finally submerges herself in the ranks of one of John Ford's many unconventional armies.

■   ■   ■   ■

ALTHOUGH *PILGRIMAGE* was a great box-office success, especially at New York's Radio City Music Hall, John Ford's name had still not quite penetrated the critical consciousness, and it was not uncommon for Ford's films to be reviewed without even a mention of the director. This pattern of directorial anonymity became even more pronounced when Ford ventured into *Doctor Bull* (1933), the first of three projects he shared with Will Rogers, then the reigning star of the Fox studio and an authentic American legend in his own right. Born William Penn Adair Rogers on November 4, 1879, in the Indian Territory that was later to become Oklahoma, he died on August 15, 1935, in a plane crash which also took the life of the celebrated flier Wiley Post. Rogers, part Indian, had been a cowboy, a soldier in the Boer War, and a Wild West show performer before hitting Broadway with a lasso-twirling act interspersed with off-the-cuff comments on the state of the world. His talent as a roper has been preserved on the screen in three of his films—*The Ropin' Fool* (1922), *Ambassador Bill*, and *The Connecticut Yankee* (both 1931). Although he was appearing in movies from 1919 on, his greatest success came in the talking era. He was the middle-aged twangy-voiced star of twenty-one movies in little more than half a decade, and he helped keep Fox afloat until Shirley Temple could toddle to the rescue. In addition to his movies, the cracker-barrel persona of this quintessential American was purveyed in newspapers, lectures, and radio broadcasts.

Here then was a screen presence with an iconographical identity established long before Ford had made his mark, and yet Rogers's three films with Ford—*Doctor Bull* (1933), *Judge Priest* (1934), *Steamboat 'Round the Bend* (1935)—are strikingly different from his work with other directors. Ford, more than any of the others, surrounds the star with a social context in which he fits snugly despite Rogers's shot-prolonging off-beat improvisation. Indeed, Ford often sacrifices the personality of this adventurous ad lib performer to the balanced framing of evocative images of an old order dying slowly with its aging protagonist. By contrast, Frank Borzage's *They Had To See Paris* (1929) and *Young As You Feel* (1931) elicit the richest feelings from Rogers as a creature of the here and now. The Borzage films are especially interesting today because we are in the midst of rediscovering the behavioral beauties of the thirties, beauties that were too long obscured by a pedantic concern with abstract forms and social themes. Whereas Borzage brings out the pleasure-seeking side of the Rogers persona, Ford illuminates a devotion to duty. With Borzage, it is a matter of Rogers having a last fling. With Ford, it is a matter of Rogers making a last stand.

Not that Will Rogers wasn't in a decisive sense the major auteur of all his movies. The same man left the same tracks in film after film, but the better directors kept him from wandering off to the land of nodding self-indulgence, the ultimate task, after all, of any director. Still, it is interesting that Ford never tapped some of the more topical aspects of the Rogers persona to be found in such overtly political movies as *Ambassador Bill* (1931) and *The Country Chairman* (1935). Nor was the Ford-Rogers collaboration as deviously anti-city-slickerish as the James Cruze–Rogers collaboration on *Mr. Skitch* (1933) and *David Harum* (1934), nor as leisurely with its spinning of homespun wisdom as the Henry King–Rogers collaboration on *Lightnin'* (1930; a Ford project in the silent era) and *State Fair* (1933).

Rogers was not quite the biting satirist subsequent legends have made him out to be. His Middle-America populism was relatively mild even for its time. In Rogers, iconoclasm wrestles an often losing battle with philistinism, and, not infrequently, populism is smothered in the pieties of the plutocrat. The good-natured gibes at Jewish accents (though not in any of Ford's films) may seem more sinister after Hitler than they were meant to be before. Still, there is something undeniably refreshing about Rogers today. For one thing, he always acted his age. A man in his fifties, he never pretended to more potency than he felt, and yet he never hesitated to be generous with his dwindling assets. He was less a lampooner than a lamplighter of the virtues and vices of a kind of archetypal American. He was remarkably open to the world, open to learning and to travel. More than most movie stars, Rogers tended to record the times in which he lived, and most of his films were conceived and executed in the present tense. This makes it all the more remarkable that Ford was able to project Rogers so hauntingly into the past tense.

Of the three Ford-Rogers projects, *Doctor Bull* (1933) was the first in time and the least in impact. Adapted by Paul Green from an early novel (*The Last Adam*) by James Gould Cozzens, and with additional dialogue by Janet Storm, the script lacks the rich thematic texture of the Dudley Nichols–Lamar Trotti scripts for *Judge Priest* (1934) and *Steamboat 'Round the Bend* (1935). As a cranky Connecticut country doctor, Will Rogers spends most of the time outraging the community with the somewhat aimless antics of an aging rebel without a cause. There is a relaxed romance with a friendly widow (Vera Allen) and a dramatically redemptive epidemic and the familiar generational crisis of sweet young things stifled in their innocent love by stuffy old fools. Doctor Bull is afflicted also by the unfriendly competition of Ralph Morgan's mod Doctor Varney, a PR physician of test tubes and testimonials in the spirit of Jules Romains's *Doctor Knock*. But the movie is little more than the sum of its digressions, and the leisurely pacing seems more appropriate for turn-of-the-century Kentucky than for turn-off-the-turnpike Connecticut.

And yet Ford successfully imposes a distinctive sensibility on his meandering material by establishing the social coordinates of his milieu with an expressive panning shot which, in effect, circles the town square from sidewalk to steeple, and thereafter serves as the communal context for all the characters. To translate into spatial terms Doctor Bull's commitment in time to his merry widow, it is sufficient for Ford to show in very distant long shot the doctor's old roadster parked outside the widow's home on an autumnal carpet of fallen leaves. None the less, it seldom if ever occurs to anyone that Ford was by birth a New Englander, a Down-Easter to be more precise. Ford's odyssey, both physical and spiritual, took him west and south and, most often, backwards in time. And yet, east or west, Ford focused on what is most enduring rather than what is most ephemeral; he never left the small neighborly town lodged in his mind.

Between *Doctor Bull* (1933) and *Judge Priest* (1934), Ford made *The Lost Patrol* (1934) and *The World Moves On* (1934), and between *Judge Priest* and *Steamboat 'Round the Bend* (1935), he made *The Whole Town's Talking* (1935) and *The Informer* (1935). Hence, there has been a tendency for Ford's Will Rogers movies to be lost in the shuffle. *The Informer*, especially, so completely outshone every other Ford achievement in the critical consensus of its time that there has been a reaction ever since to downgrade the supposedly solitary pre-eminence of this instant classic. Unfortunately, neither were Ford's other films of the period particularly accessible for revival with the benefit of hindsight, so we recognize a much more diversified aesthetic than was commonly perceived at the time.

Judge Priest is especially interesting in this regard because of its unresolved conflict between what Ford had been and what he was to become. (Also, *Judge Priest* was less remade than reshaped some twenty years later into *The Sun Shines Bright* (1953), an expanded and deepened version of Ford's 1934 meditation on life and politics in a small Kentucky town still divided in 1890 by memories of the Civil War.) Will Rogers does not so much play Judge Priest as loosely inhabit him through a series of leisurely Irvin S. Cobb stories adding up ultimately to a form of anecdotage on the front porch of My Old Kentucky Home. The days bask in the lazy conviviality of small-town life a while or so back, but the nights are full of fear and foreboding and death as the yelping of bloodhounds is heard across the land. It is mostly mood, of course. The plot is too confused and congested to follow a clean line in any direction, and the slapdash melodramatics of the courtroom trial (complete with vindicating flashback memories of cavalry charges in the Civil War) go back beyond *The Birth of a Nation* (1915) to the contrived theatrics of plays like *The Copperhead*. As if to evoke the lingering influence of D. W. Griffith on Ford, it is the Little Colonel himself, Henry B. Walthall, who plays the key role of memory bank in the courtroom drama of *Judge Priest*.

But what is most memorable in *Judge Priest* is the scene in which the eponymous protagonist visits his wife's grave and talks to her as if he

were making a regular report on the life lingering just slightly beyond
her ken. Ford endows this one-sided conversation between the living and
the dead with more emotional resonance in such later Orphic enterprises
as *Young Mr. Lincoln* and *She Wore a Yellow Ribbon*. Here in 1934 Will
Rogers tosses off the scene with a reading that seems, for once, too
loosely improvised and too prosaic for the metaphysical rigor of the poetic
conceit. And Ford's camera treatment and cutting seem unduly tentative,
if not actually embarrassed. It was a decade in which people talked to
pictures, statues, headstones, and other mementoes. Death himself with
all his angelic agents floated across the nation's screens in a phospho-
rescent haze of consolation. But with Ford, the emotional emphasis was
not so much on the ultimate triumph and vindication of the dead as on
the spiritual submission of the living to memory, tradition, and even
habit.

If *Judge Priest* represented Ford in a state of transition in 1934, *Steamboat 'Round the Bend* represented Ford in a state of fruition in 1935, but
the film was completely lost amid the highbrow hoopla over *The Informer*,
released a few months earlier. Sadly, it was Rogers's swan song as a
performer, his death having preceded the release of this, his last film.
Sadly, for among many other reasons, because Ford and Rogers had
finally attained a marvelous rapport between their respective styles, thus
achieving a mature exuberance virtually unique in the American cinema.
Indeed, *Steamboat 'Round the Bend* is Ford's conveyance movie par excellence, even more than *Stagecoach* (1939) or *Wagonmaster* (1950). The
steamboat, after all, with all its gusto and energy and puffed-up egoism,
must still submit to that most richly symbolic of all American rivers of
life, the Mississippi, and both Ford and Rogers are alive equally to the
exhilarating promise of the steamboat and to the sobering relentlessness
of the river. Rogers is assisted ably by Anne Shirley, one of the more
talented of the self-mockingly innocent ingenues of the thirties; by Eugene Pallette, a roundly buoyant figure of a sheriff; and by Berton Churchill, a Ford regular as a villain but here more interestingly cast as a
religious fanatic with a hatred of hard liquor. If the word Americana had
not been squandered on so many trivial movies, it could be invoked this
once and this once only for the spectacle of the climatic steamboat race
in the course of which almost everything on board is sacrificed to the
flames of competition.

To backtrack a year or so from *Steamboat 'Round the Bend*, we must
turn to *The Lost Patrol* (1934) as another critical turning point in Ford's
career. This was the first time that Ford and Nichols were associated on

a project at RKO, and it marks the beginning of studio prominence in discussions of Ford's career. The influence of studio policies on Hollywood movies is more complex and less precisely measurable than most studio historians care to admit. After all, the same studio could and did sponsor John Barrymore and Rin Tin Tin, or Greta Garbo and Wallace Beery, or *Citizen Kane* and Hopalong Cassidy. Even in the thirties and forties, when studio esprit de corps was at least more conspicuous than at other times, one's impression of a studio is often considerably at variance with one's later research in depth.

Modern studio historians are not always too finicky about the once separate corporate strands (20th Century and Fox, Warners and First National), which for archival convenience have since been woven together. In Ford's case, it was actually during the shooting of *Steamboat 'Round the Bend* that the old-fashioned Fox studio founded by William Fox merged with 20th Century Pictures, the new-fangled company operated by Darryl F. Zanuck. For most of the thirties, Fox, with or without the Zanuck accretion, was Ford's home studio, his bread and butter base, the place where he could compromise to his heart's content, or so his legend went. By contrast, RKO was the studio of his conscience, of his artistic aspiration, of his moral commitment to his material. And the RKO part of the legend actually began with *The Lost Patrol*, a saga of a British cavalry patrol lost in the Mesopotamian desert, and being picked off at dramatic intervals by unseen Arabs until in the end only Victor McLaglen's Sergeant is left to tell the tale. But he remains mute when questioned by an officer in charge of a relief column, and just stares helplessly at the glistening swords marking the graves of his fallen comrades under the desert sun.

The irony implicit in men being killed by an unseen enemy gives the film a mystical quality. Here we have a fusion of the morbid pessimism of Dudley Nichols and the poetic mediation of John Ford's mise-en-scène. A large portion of the plot is concerned with the futile efforts of the men to catch even a fleeting glimpse of their enemy. As the frustrated victims stare into the void of the desert, they are grouped by Ford into a cluster of truth-seekers, into a parish of failed perceptions.

Just as with *Men Without Women* at the beginning of the sound era, *The Lost Patrol* and *The Informer* provided Ford with a directorial persona without which he could never have received any substantial critical recognition. Even so, one can see in *The Lost Patrol* those elements with which Ford is most congenial, and those with which he is most uncomfortable. The religious fanatic, for example, is regarded with little of the obsessive subjectivity one might anticipate as a matter of course from Tod Browning or Georges Franju. Ford had no patience with monsters or ideologues—they were too abstract and asocial for his taste. Ford's religion, like his patriotism, was essentially communal rather than intro- spectively individualistic. Action audiences laugh uproariously at the spectacle of Karloff climbing the sand dune to implant a cross on its crest. At least some of the laughter is generated by the detachment with which Ford's camera views this allegorical ascent. By contrast, Gypo Nolan's entrance into the church at the confessional climax of *The In- former* is treated with hulking subjectivity so that the audience itself can partake of emotional absolution through Gypo's confession.

Lindsay Anderson has criticized Ford's subjective treatment of the confessional scene in *The Informer* for muddling the moral issues and vulgarizing the character with excessive focal magnification. It is partly a question of the actors in the two roles: Ford has no feeling for Karloff's wormy persona. Victor McLaglen, on the other hand, is virtually a Ford creation. Indeed, his performance in *The Lost Patrol* is in some respects even more spectacular than his more famous one in *The Informer*. There are few moments in the cinema as exhilarating as the one in which McLaglen, now the last survivor of his platoon, explodes with convulsive laughter to the rhythm of his machine-gun as he mows down the handful of Arabs who have for so long made life hell for him and his men. It is a moment of orgasmic release through violence that even Sam Peckinpah has not approached in emotional intensity.

The Whole Town's Talking (1935) is one of the most likable and least likely works in Ford's oeuvre. Its subject (gangster parody) and script- writer (Robert Riskin) and studio (Columbia) mark it even in retrospect as a more logical assignment for Frank Capra. Ford handles the material somewhat more broadly than Capra might have done; that is, more as a tall story than as a folksy vignette. But it is interesting that Ford is fully sensitive to the spunky working-girl beauty and vitality of Jean Arthur a year before Capra made her one of the shining icons of the thirties in *Mr. Deeds Goes to Town* (1936). Of course, Ford doesn't go ga-ga over Arthur with any of Capra's lyrical close-ups. Ford keeps his distance so that the comic narrative can flow freely, whereas Capra delights in those privileged moments when characters are suspended in the hushed close- ups of their innermost feelings.

The Whole Town's Talking reflected a tendency around the mid- thirties to burlesque the *film noir*, the most extreme example being the incredibly slapdash, slapstick version of *The Maltese Falcon* released at

Warners under the title *Satan Met a Lady* (1936). As a character star of the thirties, Edward G. Robinson seemed especially eager to let the civilized side of his screen persona poke fun at its brutish side. In a forties poll of fan-magazine readers on the Warners gangster leads of the thirties and early forties, Jimmy Cagney was considered the toughest, Humphrey Bogart the meanest, George Raft the most sinister, and Edward G. Robinson the most lovable. Here Robinson was given a dual role through which his Walter Mitty side finally triumphed over his Little Caesar side. This Jekyll-Hyde form of cinematographic trickery was used quite often in the thirties and forties as a fairly elementary exercise in the art of acting out contrasting parts within the same visual frame.

The extraordinary critical acclaim accorded *The Informer* in its time can be understood at least partly as a form of aesthetic amnesia. It is hard to believe in the 1990s that there was ever a time in the 1930s when *The Informer* could be regarded as the first "creative" American sound film. Few reviewers in 1935 seemed to recall such early thirties sound classics as Sternberg's *The Blue Angel* and *Morocco* (both 1930), Ernest Lubitsch's *Trouble in Paradise* (1932), and Howard Hawks's *Scarface* (1932). What had been most completely forgotten was the tradition of German Expressionism which had peaked in 1927 with Murnau's sublime *Sunrise*. Hence, Ford's moving camera, ghostly shadows, tinkling symbols, and fog-shrouded studio backdrops stuck many reviewers in 1935 as spectacularly "cinematic" after years of talk, talk, talk on the sunny screens of theatrical adaptations. And six years later reviewers were to hail *Citizen Kane* for the same kind of gloom-and-doom innovations credited to *The Informer*, and again as if the German stylists of the twenties had never existed. Ironically, anti-Expressionist critics and scholars like Otis Ferguson, James Agee, and Richard Griffith were later to attack both *The Informer* and *Citizen Kane* for their alleged artiness and thematic superficiality.

The Informer did not become an instant classic simply for its formal style, however, but rather because its style was thought to be fused with a worthy theme. The fact that Gypo Nolan was a lower-class character with an empty belly was virtually sufficient in itself to make him a worthy Depression-era protagonist. Meyer Levin, a truly committed critic for *Esquire* in this period, made a special point of aligning himself with the grubby economic motivations for Gypo Nolan's Judas act in *The Informer* against the Gidean gratuitousness of the evil acts of Noël Coward's uppercrust publisher in *The Scoundrel*.

Still, *The Informer* remains one of the most disappointing of all official film classics in that its allegorical parallel with the Passion Play leads it away from pulsating drama into pious dogma. The biggest problem is with the character of Gypo Nolan, a pitiful giant doomed from the start to an endless night of need, shame, guilt, fear, and the most maudlin, drunken self-deception. With virtually the entire film devoted to his slow degradation and destruction, he remains helplessly muddled and inarticulate until Mother Church provides a false catharsis through Nolan's true confession to Una O'Connor's Mother Machreeish Mrs. McPhillip, not so much a real mother in mourning for her son as a ritualized figurine of forgiveness for her son's betrayer.

What makes *The Informer* particularly uncomfortable is Gypo's pathetic yearning to rejoin the ultra-Fordian community—the IRA—which has been mobilized to destroy him. By sentimentalizing Preston Foster's IRA leader in the movie into a moony patriot, Ford and Nichols sacrifice Liam O'Flaherty's ambivalent treatment of the revolutionary as a dedicated Communist, and hence as cold-bloodedly cerebral in his way as Gypo is hot-bloodedly visceral in his. O'Flaherty is also less misty-eyed toward the women in his story than Ford is to both Margot Grahame's Magdalene and to Heather Angel's Madonna.

Ford establishes a guilt-ridden distinction between the thirty pieces of silver (coins tinking symbolically on Steiner's soundtrack and shining with all the allegorical glow at the command of Joseph H. August's camera) and the twenty pounds (representing, in turn, conscience money to a blind man, dream money of a trip to America first-class, shame money to the dead man's family, love money to a whore, food and drink money for an orgy of fish-and-chips and a *Walpurgisnacht* of Irish dialect humor). If the thirty pieces of silver look forward to *The Fugitive*, the twenty pounds of currency negotiable in the things of this world look forward to the class yearnings of *The Grapes of Wrath* and *How Green Was My Valley*. All in all, *The Informer* never overcomes the handicap of its ignoble protagonist and its excessively pious sentimentality. But it is a film symptomatic of its time, and its stunning transformation of Margot Grahame to a Magdalene, simply by having her remove her shawl to reveal a perky hat, is one of the most privileged moments in all cinema, achieving with mise-en-scène what Vivien Leigh achieved with sheer beauty in *Waterloo Bridge* (1940) five years later.

Ford made three films in 1936—*The Prisoner of Shark Island* for 20th Century-Fox, and *Mary of Scotland* and *The Plough and the Stars* for RKO. And within this one year the Ford-Nichols-RKO mystique completely collapsed, and a new theory was born to provide a collective rationale for Ford's rising career. It was the 20th Century-Fox–Darryl F. Zanuck–Nunnally Johnson–Kenneth MacGowan–Lamarr Trotti–Phillip Dunne theory to take us from *The Prisoner of Shark Island* through *Young Mr. Lincoln, The Grapes of Wrath,* and *How Green Was My Valley.* Along the way there were all sorts of bumps and detours like *Wee Willie Winkie* (1938), *Four Men and a Prayer* (1938), *Submarine Patrol* (1938), *Drums Along the Mohawk* (1939), and *Tobacco Road* (1941), or so it seemed to informed observers at the time and after. It was as if John Ford's directorial soul were the arena for a titanic struggle between the romantic artifices of Dudley Nichols and the realist humanism of the Fox contingent. What was actually happening was that Ford's art was becoming richer and more complex as he played one aesthetic against another. He was not yet fully in command of his career, but he was discovering his true talents and affinities through productive experience rather than through effete predisposition. He was shifting the tasks from the pleasures, and, in the process, learning to tell all sorts of stories, the taller and fancier the better, with the utmost efficiency and dispatch. Hence, even his failures of this period help us to understand his later masterpieces.

The Prisoner of Shark Island (one of the most satisfying of Ford's thirties films) begins with a series of ceremonial vignettes culminating in the assassination of Abraham Lincoln—America's own Passion Play. The wax-works portrayal of Lincoln by Frank McGlynn, Sr., is in the traditional mold, but Ford does something special with this memorial figure who embodies both the homely and the heroic, the immediate and the immortal. In death Ford's Lincoln comes to rest in the slowly fading tapestry of legend, not with the sense of a personal destiny as in D. W. Griffith's and Walter Huston's Lincoln, but rather with the gentle implacability of submission to the needs of a nation.

The focus then shifts to the trials and tribulations of Dr. Samuel A. Mudd, a true-life victim of the miscarriage of justice that followed the Lincoln assassination. This is the year of *Fury* (1936) (inspired by a lynching in California), *Winterset* (1936) (inspired by the Sacco-Vanzetti case and its purported aftermath), and *Mr. Deeds Goes to Town* (1936). It is the year before *The Life of Emile Zola* (1937), with the Dreyfus case as its dramatic climax. Of course, audiences had to be assured in each instance that the victim was absolutely innocent of all the charges against him. It was, however, never argued too strenuously that all men must be presumed innocent until proven guilty, and that it was far better for a hundred guilty persons to escape punishment than for one innocent person to be punished unjustly. Quite the contrary. Many movies openly encouraged mob vengeance and vigilante tactics even as other movies sobbed over condemned innocents with whom audiences could lovingly identify. *The Prisoner of Shark Island* depends therefore on a dangerously sentimental plot premise when it suggests that people like us should not be locked up with people like them.

The condescending us-them (as opposed to the ennobling I-thou) dichotomy is nowhere more bothersome than in Mudd's imperious attitude to the cowardly black soldiers temporarily terrorized by the plague on Shark Island until Mudd's threats with a slave-owning Southern accent terrorize them even more. We are just a few steps removed here in 1936 from the general historical assumptions promulgated in 1915 by D. W. Griffith in *The Birth of a Nation*. Hence, aside from Father Abraham, the Northerners were a pestilential horde of Scalawags and Carpetbaggers visited upon the prostrate but still civilized Southland. The most disruptive act of all was the North's granting of guns and votes to the dear darkies, thus alienating them from their loving masters and mistresses, most notably Margaret Sullavan in the King Vidor–Stark Young *So Red the Rose* (1936) and Vivien Leigh in *Gone With the Wind* (1939). Still, the blacks are somewhat less degraded in *The Prisoner of Shark Island* (1936) and *So Red the Rose* than in most films of the time. If they are not yet irrevocably rebellious, they are at least poised on the brink of manly defiance. That they are not so much separatist as surly betokens the desperately limited options of the black in the cinema of the thirties, even under the most liberal auspices.

Nonetheless, Ford stages the violent confrontations in *The Prisoner of Shark Island* for everything they are worth. The black mutiny, especially, is photographed with a towering monumentality which somehow evokes both Eisenstein and Dumas, that is, both the phallic thrust of revolutionary history and the subjective vertigo of Gothic romance. Yet the most idiosyncratically Fordian images remain those of submission, redemption, and communion—Warner Baxter's Dr. Samuel A. Mudd vindicating himself not through escape or revenge, but through service to his sworn enemies; John Carradine's sadistic jailer demanding to be the first to sign Mudd's petition for a pardon; and, most memorably Fordian of all, the return home of Mudd and his black neighbor (Ernest Whitman) to their respective families, each with his separate reunion within the one communal frame of the family of mankind. That the black family of Buckland Montmorency "Buck" Tilford is conspicuously numerous next to the Mudd clan may be regarded as a racial cliché in the abstract, but not in the particularity of Ford's loving gaze.

■ ■ ■ ■

MARY OF SCOTLAND (1936) brought Ford into contact (and into an extra-marital affair as well) for the first and last time with Katharine Hepburn's radiantly brash beauty, Maxwell Anderson's pedestrian blank verse, and Fredric March's practiced hamminess in period roles. Most of all, it brought Ford face to face with his own deepest religious and ethnic prejudices: a woman named Mary, in history something of a Magdalene, but with the aid of Joseph August's camera filters, Ford's pure and sweet Madonna armed with her acceptance of herself as a woman against Elizabeth's monstrously repressed English Protestant spinster. I have triumphed over you as a woman, Mary declares on her way to the executioner's block. My son shall be king. Not I have loved, but my son shall be king. King of England or Crown Prince of Paradise, one madonna's pride is very much like another's. And with Katharine Hepburn cast as Mary and Florence Eldridge (Mrs. Fredric March) as Elizabeth, the dramatic one-sidedness of this historical pageant becomes oppressive.

For all its shortcomings, however, *Mary of Scotland* was at least a coherent film, whereas *The Plough and the Stars* that same year from the same studio emerged as ill-edited excerpts from at least two different movies. One of these movies involves the excruciating nagging of Barbara Stanwyck's Nora Clitheroe in her unsuccessful effort to keep Preston Foster's Jack Clitheroe from joining the Irish Rebellion in Easter Week, 1916. The second movie was adapted piecemeal by Dudley Nichols from Sean O'Casey's disenchanted bar-room drama of Irish character set against the ironic background of the Rebellion, and featured many of the original Abbey Players—Barry Fitzgerald, Dennis O'Dea, Eileen Crowe, Arthur Shields, and F. J. McCormick, the last-named especially memorable eleven years later in *Odd Man Out* (1947).

Wee Willie Winkie (1938) remains the most notorious assignment of John Ford's career in that as a supposed man's man he was called upon to direct the most exuberant of Hollywood childcult stars, Shirley Temple; and that as the supposed Irish patriot of *The Informer* and *The Plough and the Stars* he was compelled to perpetuate Hollywood's glorification of C. Aubrey Smith's British Empire, shifting from Liam O'Flaherty and Sean O'Casey to Rudyard Kipling. As the sweetest army brat in creation, Miss Temple seems in retrospect to have been too much the performing prodigy ever to generate genuine emotional responses. She always seemed much older than her years, supremely confident, aloof and self-sufficient. She lacked the emotional energy of Jackie Cooper and Margaret O'Brien and Roddy McDowall or the bratty virtuosity of Mitzi Green and Jane Withers and Jackie Searl, or the vulnerable precocious delicate beauty of Freddie Bartholomew, Dickie Moore, Bobby Breen, Gloria Jean, and Elizabeth Taylor. Still, she was the most popular child star in the history of motion pictures (if one excepts Mary Pickford's long career of counterfeit childhood), and as such she automatically provides sociological insights into mass tastes of the thirties, and especially the period's susceptibility to authoritarian goody-goodness.

Curiously, however, the movie is not unpleasing, with its zestful retelling of storybook romance from a child's wide-eyed point of view through a fringed curtain very much like a coarse camera filter. Victor McLaglen provides the blustering emotional coefficient to Miss Temple's pretty sang-froid, and Ford seized upon a rainy day to improvise the shooting of a stirring funeral, much as he later shot into a storm to capture the realistically climatic tension of an army patrol in *She Wore a Yellow Ribbon* (1949). Thus, Ford once again demonstrates his profound resemblance to Renoir in his willingness to tinker with the sacred scenario for visual truth.

■   ■   ■   ■

THE HURRICANE (1937) belongs at first glance to that interesting genre of natural disaster movies in which the thirties abounded, and for which James Basevi was justly honored for his special effects extraordinaire. The fires raging in *In Old Chicago* (1938), the typhoon in *Suez* (1938), the earthquake in *San Francisco* (1936), the swarms of locusts in *The Good Earth* (1937), and the hurricane here attest to a period passion for apocalyptic demons ex machina to resolve all the complications of the plot. Certainly, few plots have been more complicated than that of *The Hurricane*, adapted by Dudley Nichols and Oliver H. P. Garrett from the novel by Charles Nordhoff and James Norman Hall of *Mutiny on the Bounty* (1936) fame. Social significance, tribal tabu, allegorical archetype, and novelistic nuance are all crowded together on a placid South Seas Island where a French governor (Raymond Massey) observes the letter of the law in confining Terangi (Jon Hall) in prison. Terangi escapes again and again to rejoin his bride Marama, and each time (but the very last) he is recaptured and his sentence extended. On his last escape, Terangi kills his arch-tormentor among the prison guards (John Carradine), but is in effect pardoned for his crime against his oppressor by the native god of the volcano which destroys the island and most of its inhabitants.

Terangi and Marama (especially in the glossy pseudo-primitive incarnations of Jon Hall and Dorothy Lamour) possess none of the metaphysical stature of the passionate protagonists in F. W. Murnau's *Tabu* (1931). Terangi and Marama are merely the innocent victims of imperialist presumption and rigidity. The film's dramatic focus shifts therefore to the Europeans, and particularly to one of the most fascinatingly civilized of all movie couples—Raymond Massey's Governor De Laage and Mary Astor's Mrs. De Laage. *The Hurricane* is ultimately their story as they argue with exquisite delicacy and tact the conflicting claims of the law and the heart. (Curiously, Massey and Astor played a very similar couple at about the same time in the John Cromwell–David O. Selznick *The Prisoner of Zenda*, 1937.) C. Aubrey Smith's Father Paul and Thomas Mitchell's Dr. Kersaint provide the sacred and the secular resonance for the moral debate of the De Laages.

Unfortunately, the civilized subtlety of the Massey character seems to have been misremembered even in so accurate and authoritative a book as Peter Bogdanovich's *John Ford*, in which De Laage is described simply as "sadistic." Massey is closer to being a man for all seasons in that he insists that his principles govern his passions. Also, he finally redeems himself with a deliberated act of mercy, and such redemption and deliberation are hardly the marks of a sadist. Ultimately, however, the essential worthiness of the Massey character is reflected most luminously in the searching eyes of Mary Astor's complex creation of a wife, the most completely satisfying woman in all the predominantly masculine cinema of John Ford, and hence almost an intruder upon his vision of the world. The Vera Miles character in *The Man Who Shot Liberty Valance*, the Joanne Dru character in *Wagonmaster*, and the Maureen O'Hara character in *Wings of Eagles* are magnificent creations, but they tend more to emotional inscrutability characteristic of the forces of nature than to Mary Astor's single-track lucidity of mind and heart.

With *Stagecoach* (1939) Ford returned to a genre he had not dealt with in thirteen years and virtually re-invented it. Of this classic I wrote in the *New York Times* of May 12, 1968: "Dudley Nichols's script has received almost as much credit for *Stagecoach* as John Ford's direction, but the literary ghost hovering over the entire project is Guy De Maupassant."

None the less, the plot-line of *Stagecoach* is closer to such criss-crossing strangers-when-we-meet exercises as *Grand Hotel, Union Depot,* and *Transatlantic* than to the bitter social ironies of De Maupassant's *Boule de Suif.* As literary critic Leslie Fielder has observed, American folklore explicitly denies the feudal hangover of European class structures. For De Maupassant, the social chasm between Boule de Suif and her bourgeois traveling companions can never be bridged by sentimental plot devices. By contrast, Claire Trevor's Dallas is fully redeemed from her career as a Magdalene by her Madonna-like sweetness with the new-born babe of a respectable woman. And at the end of the film, the two men who have despised her most have had their come-uppance—John Carradine's gentleman gambler with an Apache bullet in his heart, and Berton Churchill's absconding banker by being publicly unmasked and hauled off to the hoosegow.

Thus, whereas De Maupassant's story evolves as a bitterly ironic investigation and indictment of bourgeois hypocrisy, *Stagecoach* emerges as a Christian-populist morality play with its heart on its sleeve. It might be noted in passing that the historical heavies in the De Maupassant story are Bismarck's victorious Germans, and so the tone is cynically defeatist in the Old World manner. Not so in the New World. *Stagecoach* is the first of the Seventh Cavalry celebrations of the extermination of the American Indian, and Ford does not spare the horses in pounding out a dance of racial triumph and exultation. It must be remembered that the audiences in 1939, particularly in the cities, were far from surfeited with the melodrama and mythology of the Indian savage on the warpath.

Thus *Stagecoach* was more the beginning than the summing up of a tradition, and when we think of the Seventh Cavalry riding to the rescue of white womanhood, we are thinking no further back than *Stagecoach*. In its own time Stagecoach was a stunning stylistic revelation. Why? First and foremost, it moved in the most obvious manner, and hence it was considered eminently cinematic. Today, it is surprising to discover how much of *Stagecoach* is conventionally theatrical (*Kane* ceilings and all) and Expressionistically shadowy, and how little of it actually opens up to the great outdoors of Monument Valley, Ford's private preserve for the next quarter of a century. *Stagecoach* was not actually the first movie shot in Monument Valley, but Ford made it seem that way.

With the benefit of almost sixty years of hindsight, it is now more apparent than ever before that *Stagecoach* could not have been made by anyone but Ford. What seemed once like a functional mechanism of entertainment now reverberates with an impressive array of Fordian themes and motifs—the redemption of the harlot (Claire Trevor), the rehabilitation of the drunkard (Thomas Mitchell), the revenge of the bereaved brother (John Wayne), the self-sacrifice of a self-condemned aristocrat (John Carradine), and the submergence of the group in the symbolic conveyance of a cause (the stagecoach itself). Above all, there is the sense of an assemblage of mythical archetypes outlined against the horizons of history.

Whereas *Stagecoach*, like *The Informer*, was overpublicized at the outset as a classic, *Young Mr. Lincoln*, like *Judge Priest* and *Steamboat 'Round the Bend*, took longer to become a legendary masterpiece in Ford's career. At the very least, *Young Mr. Lincoln* (1939) is the airiest Ford film up to this time, and the most relaxed in the deceptively casual and carefree manner so reminiscent of Renoir's *La Règle du Jeu* (1939). Ford's pacing had been leisurely enough in the past—*Just Pals* (1920) and the Will Rogers movies come immediately to mind for their slowpoke cinematics—but never before had he combined such slowness of narrative development with such intensity of emotional expression. The director was greatly aided by a promising young Fox contract player named Henry Fonda, with whose prairie populist features and shaggy dog vocalisms Ford was to be associated subsequently on *Drums Along the Mohawk* (1939), *The Grapes of Wrath* (1940), *My Darling Clementine* (1946), *The Fugitive* (1947), *Fort Apache* (1948), and finally *Mr. Roberts* (1955), the stormy production that caused a rupture in their relationship.

It is hard to believe that Fonda was once the third-ranking Fox leading man, behind Tyrone Power and Don Ameche, but such he was and such he might have remained had he and Ford not made film history together. Still, Fonda never achieved either the mythic magnitude of the personality movie stars like Cagney, Stewart, Grant, Wayne, Bogart, Cooper, and Gable or the critical cachet accorded to the likes of Arliss, Muni, Jose Ferrer, and other disguise artists for burying the personality in the part under a ton of make-up. Fonda's Young Lincoln was a case in point as an intermediate performance in 1939 between James Stewart's forceful projection of his own personality in *Mr. Smith Goes to Washington* (1939) and Robert Donat's uncanny incarnation of old age in *Goodbye, Mr. Chips* (1939), an illustrious example of seemingly aging from within.

Significantly, Stewart won the New York Film Critics Award that year, and Robert Donat the Oscar, but Fonda's performance fell by the wayside. Indeed, Raymond Massey was hailed the following year in the John Cromwell–Robert E. Sherwood *Abe Lincoln in Illinois* (1940) for so closely resembling the Great Emancipator visually, unlike Walter Huston's excessively idiosyncratic Lincoln for D. W. Griffith and Henry Fonda's for John Ford. As it was, Fonda's limited makeup (mostly around the nose) suggested Lincoln without subverting Fonda, so that over the years Fonda's performance has gained in stature as an actor's perceptive commentary on a legend.

The obsessive reincarnation of Lincoln in the American cinema through the thirties and early forties can be analyzed from many different perspectives. On the most edifying level, Lincoln exemplified, as few American national heroes have done, the egalitarian illusions of the American people, specifically the log cabin symbolism with which the Griffith film begins and ends. Lincoln's Gettysburg Address warms democratic hearts with its intimation of a commoner's brevity and simplicity prevailing in a public place over the rhetorical and metaphorical excesses of an elitist (Edward Everett). On the personal level, triumph commingles with tragedy. Lincoln preserved the Union and liberated the slaves, but at the cost of a Civil War. Death had claimed his first love, Ann Rutledge; and dissension clouded his subsequent marriage to Mary Todd. But somehow Lincoln's marital troubles made him all the more the quintessential American hero and martyr. Indeed, a radio series in the forties actually exploited the image of Lincoln as a hen-pecked husband in the Jiggs-and-Maggie tradition of the comic strip *Bringing Up Father*. *Young Mr. Lincoln* (1939) opened in that very pivotal period when a world economic depression was ending and a world war was beginning. Sacrifice and suffering were in the air, and it seemed fitting that the tragicomic muses of Frank Capra and Leo McCarey should be eclipsed by the more austerely tragic muse of John Ford.

Ford showed himself capable of symbolic ellipsis, particularly in his handling of Lincoln's shortlived romance with Ann Rutledge. Ford worked on the script with Lamarr Trotti, and thus managed to compress the romance into two lateral tracking shots, both from right to left, the first ending on a fence by the river in springtime, the second integrating the flow of an ice-strewn river with Lincoln's walk to the cemetery by the river, where he resumes his conversation with Ann Rutledge by asking her gravestone whether he should move on to Springfield or stay behind in Kentucky. He flips a coin, and the next lateral movement we see is from left to right into Springfield. Conversations with the dead go back to the *Oresteia* and beyond, but the low-key matter-of-factness with which Fonda and Ford handle this scene makes it comparable in its evocation of eternity to the greatest moments in Mizoguchi.

The dramatic core of *Young Mr. Lincoln* is a tumultuous trial in which two brothers are falsely accused of murder, and here Fonda's offbeat calm and delayed deadpan humor play to good effect against the assorted hysterics of Alice Brady's pioneer mother of the accused, Donald Meek's bumbling prosecutor, and Ward Bond's unmasked murderer. Alice Brady had passed from screwball society matrons earlier in the thirties to emotionally convincing pioneer matriarchs in Henry King's *In Old Chicago* (1938) and *Young Mr. Lincoln*. For his part, Donald Meek was so much a part of Ford's world as the little man with the perpetual quaver in his voice and the perpetual panic in his eyes that it seemed almost sadistic to send him up against Fonda's Lincoln in a Springfield courtroom, and especially the kind of boisterous courtroom Ford conducted out of his ill-concealed fondness for low humor and hammy theatrics.

After *Stagecoach* and *Young Mr. Lincoln*, Ford was entitled to a drop-off with *Drums Along the Mohawk* (1939), his first film in color and his only film to deal with the Revolutionary War period. The film is not without its stirring set pieces of ill-assorted settlers coalescing into a national army, and the James Fenimore Cooper horseless and foresty Indians are impressively cunning and menacing, but the film never recovers from Claudette Colbert's whining performance at the outset of her ordeal in the wilderness. Fonda's foot-race with two Indian pursuers and Edna May Oliver's patented grande dame heroics help make the movie entertaining enough, but the extensive detail of the Walter Edmonds novel and the woman's point of view embodied in top-billed Claudette Colbert and co-scenarist Sonya Levien (with Lamarr Trotti) were probably more than Ford felt he could handle conscientiously within one movie. *Drums Along the Mohawk*, like *How Green Was My Valley* (1941) and *Seven Women* (1966), was conceived more in matriarchal than in patriarchal terms. But as we shall see, Ford was more successful later in reconciling his patriarchal prejudices with uncongenial material than he is here in 1939 on the eve of his greatest critical triumph, *The Grapes of Wrath*, the film that was single-handedly to transform him from a storyteller of the screen to America's cinematic poet laureate.

Who is the actual (or even predominant) author of a film? This question had perplexed film scholars long before auteurism added a new dimension to the debate. Even when we stipulate multiple authorship in a collaborative art-form, we find that the problem has not been solved. Certainly, *The Grapes of Wrath* could not have become a motion picture if Darryl F. Zanuck or some other producer had not willed it into being by purchasing the rights to John Steinbeck's novel. The next-in-command after Zanuck was associate producer-scenarist Nunnally Johnson, who adapted the novel into a screenplay for John Ford to direct. Ford, in turn, worked very closely with Gregg Toland on the camera set-ups, but there was a great deal of second-unit work as well, and the final editing was very much a studio operation. But even if we could imagine a single ego which encompassed all the creative and productive functions represented by the names Steinbeck, Zanuck, Johnson, Ford, Toland, et al., we would still be confronted with the autonomous assertions of the players on the screen, not only on the stellar level of Henry Fonda's Tom Joad, on the archetypal level of Jane Darwell's Ma Joad, on the grizzled grandeur level of Charles Grapewin's Grampa Joad, on the messianic level of John Carradine's Casey, but also down to such cameo gems as Paul Guilfoyle's wry-mouthed born troublemaker or Grant Mitchell's benignly tut-tutting New Deal bureaucrat.

We would be confronted also with the vast area of affecting accident recorded by the camera for display on a canvas which extends in both space and time. Even the constituent viewer elements of the editorial "we" would provide a bewildering diversity of viewpoints and associations, and the passage of time would actually alter the "look," "sound," and "feel" of the film. When *The Grapes of Wrath* was screened for students at a Yale seminar I gave in 1970, the hostile reaction baffled me at first, but then I realized that what had seemed unusually courageous in 1940 seemed unduly contrived in 1970. And what had once seemed the last word in realism now seemed strangely stylized. Besides, times had changed to the extent that the original Okies of *The Grapes of Wrath* had become Ronald Reagan's staunchest supporters in California.

Of course, one can argue that few movies of any decade or any country can be said to be genuinely radical in opposition to the social substance upon which they feed. Eisenstein dutifully excluded Trotsky from the October Revolution in October, and one would search in vain for any signs of Hollywood pacifism between Pearl Harbor and Hiroshima. Even so, Ford's evolution as a conservative in the fifties and sixties has misled modern film historians into theorizing about a conservative conspiracy back in 1940 to subvert Steinbeck's scathing critique of American society by substituting New Dealish homilies. It all depends upon one's frame of reference. Compared with other Hollywood movies of 1940, *The Grapes of Wrath* seems anything but conservative; compared with the writings of Che Guevara and Eldridge Cleaver, it seems more like a hymn to honky capitalism and rugged individualism.

Back in 1940, however, the problem of adapting Steinbeck's novel to the screen must have been more one of poetics than politics. We are a long way from Theodore Dreiser's ideological commitment to Eisenstein over Sternberg for the film version of *An American Tragedy* (1931). Still, even Eisenstein, with all his clickety-clackety montage, never demonstrated how a long novel could be faithfully adapted into a short movie. As it is, *The Grapes of Wrath* runs for 129 minutes, not too long by the one-shot standard of *Gone With the Wind* but appreciably longer than the slightly under 91-minute average running time of Ford's twenty-six features in the thirties. Also, the evolving rationale of Hollywood screenwriting had become progressively less talkie-oriented all through the thirties. Ford, especially, had become a legend on the set for replacing preciously literary lines with eloquent silences. The trick was to find visual equivalents for wordy plots. Don't tell 'em, show 'em. Indeed, most critics had been brain-washed by highbrow aestheticians into believing that talk was the mortal enemy of cinema as an art-form. Hence, the process of reducing and simplifying a novel for the screen enjoyed critical approval.

Yet, only long after the event has it become possible to conclude that Ford's personal concerns were particularly inimical to Steinbeck's conception of his characters. Whereas Steinbeck depicted oppression by dehumanizing his characters into creatures of abject necessity, Ford evoked nostalgia by humanizing Steinbeck's economic insects into heroic champions of an agrarian order of family and community. But both Steinbeck and Ford share a kind of half-baked faith in the verities of rural existence, and a sentimental mistrust of machinery. Neither Steinbeck nor Ford would have fitted very comfortably in the Soviet scheme of things with its worship of industrialization. But the early forties were years of Popular Front sentimentality once the embarrassment of the Nazi-Soviet pact had been forgiven and forgotten, and in this ecumenical era it did not seem too far-fetched to link the rural evangelism in *The Grapes of Wrath* with world revolution. After all, more seemed to be at stake than a crass studio's desire to make money from a downbeat project. The minds and hearts of the movie-going masses were thought to be hanging in the balance. Why alienate these masses needlessly by reproducing Steinbeck's vision of existence as a dunghill of despair?

In hindsight, we might note that only a Luis Buñuel at his most outrageous would be capable of rendering all the gruesome horror of Steinbeck's saga on the relatively squeamish screen. But what would Buñuel have evoked with lurid fidelity to Steinbeck, tacticians of the time might have asked, beyond the nervous laughter of the sophisticates and the revulsion of the general public? By contrast, the strategy tacitly agreed upon by Zanuck, Johnson, and Ford enabled the audience to identify itself with the sufferings of the characters, partly by making these characters active rather than passive, partly by stressing their coherence as a family though not as a class, and partly by offering hope in the future through Jane Darwell's concluding we-the-people speech, in its own way almost as controversial as Charles Chaplin's world-peace speech in *The Great Dictator*. Still, it is worth remembering that Odetsian audiences in Manhattan balconies cheered wildly in the forties when Ma Joad dispensed her populist manifesto: "Rich fellas come up an' they die, an' their kids ain't no good, an' they die out. But we keep a-comin'. We're the people that live. Can't nobody wipe us out. Can't nobody lick us. We'll go on forever."

Resounding rhetoric aside, *The Grapes of Wrath* is graced with subtler virtues than its dated "message" would indicate. After being overrated in its time as a social testament, it is now under-rated both as a Hollywood movie (not glossily mythic enough) and as a Ford memento (not purely personal enough). What does stand up to every test of time, however, is Henry Fonda's gritty incarnation of Tom Joad, a volatile mixture of the prairie sincerity of *Young Mr. Lincoln* (1939) with the snarling paranoia of Fritz Lang's *You Only Live Once* (1937). Once more, Fonda was passed over for top acting honors by both the Academy and the New York Film Critics. Possibly, his was too unsettling a performance for easy audience identification. Fonda-Joad's physical and spiritual stature is not that of the little man as victim, but of the tall man as troublemaker. His explosive anger has a short fuse, and we have only his word for it that he is tough without being mean. Indeed, it is mainly his awkwardness in motion that suggests his vulnerability, but there is a tendency in the devious blankness of his expression to make him seem more sullen than he has any right or motivation to be. Consequently, his putatively proletarian hero becomes morosely menacing in that shadowy crossroads where social justice intersects with personal vengeance. Fonda's Joad is no Job, and as much as his mouth spouts slogans of equality, his hands are always reaching for a club or a rock or a wrench as an equalizer against the social forces massed against him. His is ultimately the one-man revolution of the ex-con with whom society can never be reconciled. By contrast, Jane Darwell's Ma Joad is the pacifier and unifier and high priestess of liberal reform at the altar of the sacred family.

Even within the Joad family, however, the significantly generational conflict between Charley Grapewin's Grampa Joad and Jane Darwell's Ma Joad is generally misunderstood and misinterpreted as the affectionate squabbling of quaintly rural types. But what is actually happening is nothing less than the transformation of the Joad family from a patriarchy rooted in the earth to a matriarchy uprooted on the road. It is no accident, even in the casting, that Charley Grapewin's Grampa dominates Zeffie Tilbury's Grandma Joad as completely as Jane Darwell's Ma Joad dominates Russell Simpson's Pa Joad. Once on the road, the men have a tendency to wander and finally run away altogether either via drink or via distance. The women of the family must then hold the fort and save the children as poverty and unemployment destroy the authority of the paterfamilias.

Ford's own feelings are so powerfully patriarchal that when Grampa dies, something in the movie seems to die with him. Hence the complaint of many critics that the first third of *The Grapes of Wrath* is superior to the final two-thirds. Parker Tyler noted astutely that even the surface of the screen seemed to change from lyrical dustiness to an antiseptic enamel finish. Ford's concern with the sacraments of the soil is expressed in the poetically sifting hands of John Qualen's maddened Muley and Grampa himself, and it is in this primal property gesture that we sense the conservative commitment of Ford's feelings to the dirt shrivelled by the wind into dust, but still drenched in all its dryness with the blood, sweat, and tears of generations. Later, in *They Were Expendable* (1945), Ford even redeems Russell Simpson (who is so diminished in *the Grapes of Wrath*) by making him Dad, chief of the shipyard, and a haunting hold-out who sits on his porch with his rifle poised on his lap, and his dog by his side, waiting, waiting, waiting for the invading Japanese. As doggedly loyal-to-the-land Dad, Russell Simpson restores the patriarchy which disappeared in *The Grapes of Wrath* somewhere on the road between Oklahoma and California.

■   ■   ■   ■

THE LONG VOYAGE HOME (1940) marked Ford's penultimate collaboration with Dudley Nichols, and the film is suitably moody, shadowy and romantically fatalistic for the occasion. The narrative is very slight, as befits an adaptation of four Eugene O'Neill one-act plays: *Bound East for Cardiff* (1916), *In the Zone* (1917), *The Long Voyage Home* (1917), and *The Moon of the Caribees* (1918). Peter Bogdanovich reports that the Ford-Nichols adaptation was O'Neill's favorite among the films made of his work, and the only one he continued to look at periodically. We are back in the familiar Ford-Nichols domain of *Men Without Women* (1930), a particularly poetic realm for film critics who seemed unduly impressed by the mere absence of Hollywood boy-meets-girl conventions. As it happens, *The Long Voyage Home* has dated worse than *The Grapes of Wrath.* Its collective saga of men at sea seems arbitrarily austere most of the time, and yet unexpectedly maudlin at its big moments. Ian Hunter's Smitty, an upper-class outcast, is cut from the same sentimentally redemptive cloth as Kenneth McKenna's Burke in *Men Without Women* (1930), Reginald Denny's George Brown in *The Lost Patrol* (1934), and John Carradine's Hatfield in *Stagecoach* (1939). But never before in a Ford film has this stock character seemed so obtrusive.

Part of the problem may be that *The Long Voyage Home* represents a conscious extension of the foggy Expressionism of the thirties into the programmed heroics of World War II. Producer Walter Wanger, Ford, and Nichols were all outspokenly anti-Hitler in this period, and thus *The Long Voyage Home* constituted a conscious tribute to Britain in its darkest hour against the Nazis, who here invade O'Neill's brooding seascapes with an air strike from out of nowhere. British critics C. A. Lejeune and Lindsay Anderson found Ford's flourish of the Union Jack on Smitty's coffin an unspeakably vulgar gesture, but Ford has always transformed flag-waving into a personal figure of style, be the flag the Union Jack, the Stars and Stripes (*The Battle of Midway* (1942), *They Were Expendable* (1945)), or that of the Irish Republic (*The Plough and the Stars*) (1936).

The redeeming twitches of idiosyncratic low-life are provided by a strong cast of character actors headed by the ubiquitous bulldog conscience of the era, Thomas Mitchell, and featuring John Wayne in one of the strangest parts of his career as the oafish Scandinavian innocent Ole Olsen, who is almost shanghaied by that oddest of all tavern wenches, Mildred Natwick's Freda. Actually, the most haunting passage of the film is the idyllic opening with its caressingly illuminated native women canoeing and carousing with the susceptible men of the S.S. *Glencairn.* By contrast, the end of the voyage on the fog-shrouded London docks marks the end of all the men's illusions of life on shore. In this respect, Ford and O'Neill are kindred spirits in that they share a tragic vision of life even though that vision is not as keenly articulated as that of the greatest tragedians of the past. It is a uniquely American–Irish-Catholic vision in which guilt, repression, and submission play a large part.

■   ■   ■   ■

TOBACCO ROAD struck a slightly sour note in the triumphant blast of trumpets for Ford through 1940 and 1941. The general impression at the time was that this project was not worthy of a director of Ford's stature. Whereas *The Grapes of Wrath* extolled the nobility of the deserving poor, *Tobacco Road* expoited the nuttiness of the undeserving poor. In this Fordian context, Charley Grapewin's white-trash Jeeter Lester was an especially embarrassing parody of his Grampa in *The Grapes of Wrath*. Erskine Caldwell's sub-Zolaesque novel of demented rural refuse in Georgia was not without a certain degree of social significance and erotic élan for its time, but on its way to the screen it stopped off in 1933 for a very profitable run on the Broadway stage in a hoked-up theatrical adaptation by Jack Kirkland.

Unfortunately, the Hollywood Production Code tolerated neither Caldwell's flair for bawdiness nor Kirkland's for boisterous outhouse humor, with the result that Ford and Nunnally Johnson had to perform prodigious feats of ellipsis to get the material on the screen at all. Gene Tierney's stylized barnyard crawl as the lustful Ellie May Lester typified the film's balletic sublimation of the novel's blatant sexuality. Moreover, William Tracy's excruciatingly strident Dude Lester suggested that Ford had devised loudness as a comic substitute for lewdness. Tracy's more controlled performances in Ernst Lubitsch's *The Shop Around the Corner* and Busby Berkeley's *Strike Up the Band* would seem to serve as a rebuke to Ford's broadness in *Tobacco Road*. On the other hand, Ford's extraordinarily sympathetic treatment of the elder Lesters (Grapewin, Elizabeth Patterson as Ada, his mate, and Zeffie Tilbury as the rebelliously disappearing Grandma Lester) transcends barnyard farce with bucolic fantasy. The parts may not cohere, but the somber mood is triumphantly Fordian. Shortly after World War II, the Tito regime in Yugoslavia decided to release *The Grapes of Wrath* and *Tobacco Road* throughout the country in order to demonstrate that the United States was no longer a land of great opportunity. Ironically, Yugoslav audiences were so enthralled by all the motor vehicles on the screen that this supposedly Marxist double feature was quickly withdrawn from distribution.

■   ■   ■   ■

HOW GREEN WAS MY VALLEY (1941) has suffered the dubious distinction of being remembered as the film that beat out *Citizen Kane* for an Academy Award. The Oscars have seldom served as a reliable index of cinematic quality, and least of all when an eccentric talent like that of Orson Welles was concerned. Nonetheless it can be argued that, apart from *Sunrise* in 1927–28, *How Green Was My Valley* was the most meritorious movie up to that time ever to win an Academy Award. Unfortunately, the film, which so closely expressed the emotional climate of its time, seems to have dated badly.

Curiously, Philip Dunne's screenplay (from Richard Llewellyn's novel) conspicuously failed to win an Oscar for 1941, that honor going to Herman J. Mankiewicz and Orson Welles for the screenplay for *Kane*. And yet of all Ford's films, *How Green Was My Valley* was one of the most strongly shaped by a novelistic screenplay.

Through most of his career Ford had employed narration even more sparingly than dialogue. In this context, the screenplay of *How Green Was My Valley* seems particularly inimical to Ford's patented brand of laconic lyricism. Still, there have probably been more tears shed over *How Green Was My Valley* than over any other Ford film. We cannot say that Ford himself earned all these tears with his own sensibility. The pathos of pastness embodied in the Dunne-Llewellyn narrative must take much of the credit. What Ford contributed above everything else was the tenacity of family feelings and the awesome irrevocability of archetypal experiences. I have never known anyone who could remain dry-eyed through Roddy McDowall's desperate search through the flooded mine-shaft for his trapped Dada (Donald Crisp). Here again was the misty realm of family epic to which Ford so often gravitated.

We must remember, however, that the archetypal characters and situations would not have seemed so moving to audiences and critics in 1941 were it not for an emotional correlation between memories of a Welsh mining family earlier in the century and the more immediate impressions of the Great Depression from which America was only now emerging. In this context, *How Green Was My Valley* served almost as a sequel to *The Grapes of Wrath*. There were the same conflicts between capital and labor, the same spectacles of social injustice, the same strains on the fabric of the family, and the same intimations of indomitability among the poeticized poor. There were differences as well. Thus whereas *The Grapes of Wrath* was filmed in the present imperative, *How Green Was My Valley* was filmed in the past indefinite. By the end of 1941 Americans could almost look back on the Depression as a saga now safely concluded. Within one year the cry for reform in *The Grapes of Wrath* could give way to the chant of remembrance in *How Green Was My Valley*. The colorful Welsh with their melodious chorales transcended their studio sets (the same sloping mining village used a year later for *The Moon Is Down*) to embody the glorious poor of all nations.

It was perhaps the last time that an American film could identify its own emotional concerns so intimately with those of the common run of humanity. Neo-realism was still only a gleam in the eye of a handful of Italian film-makers, and the Russian cinema had long since abandoned egalitarianism for statism, peasant for Tsar, the end of St. Petersburg for the defense of Stalingrad. The French cinema under the German Occupation was entering its Cocteau-Carné-Prévert period of stylish sleepwalking that would culminate in *Les Enfants du Paradis* (1945). England was only just hitting its stride with its wartime documentaries. Thus, Hollywood stood alone for a brief moment in history as the hope of the world, the champion of the common man and the defender of democratic values. Later in the forties Hollywood would be made to seem frivolous and irresponsible, but at the time of the release of *How Green Was My Valley* there was no industry inferiority complex to speak of. Nor was the dead hand of the past a demoralizing factor. Movies seemed truly better than ever, and even the New York film critics had been unusually sanguine about the future of the American cinema ever since *The Grapes of Wrath* had burst on the screen in early 1940. John Ford was named best director by both the Academy and the Film Critics for both 1940 and 1941, over such formidable competition as Chaplin, Welles, Wyler, Hitchcock, Lubitsch, Sturges, Hawks, Cukor, Lang, Huston, Stevens, Capra, *et al.* The awards to Ford were sincerely granted. People at the time genuinely believed that *How Green Was My Valley* was a better movie than *Citizen Kane*. It was warmer, more disciplined, less flamboyant, and less self-indulgent, in short, a repository of the classical virtues in contrast to the romantic vices of *Kane*.

Viewed purely as a socially-conscious mineshaft movie, *How Green Was My Valley* did not dig very deep for the kind of ideological ironies one finds in G. W. Pabst's *Kamaradschaft* (1931) (Franco-German fraternity) and Carol Reed's *The Stars Look Down* (1939) (Capital versus Labor). There is an air of religious resignation in Ford's treatment of the climactic disaster sequence as Sara Allgood's now widowed matriarch looks upwards at the heavens to acknowledge the ascension of her husband's soul from the muddy depths of the mine below her feet. By contrast, the trapped miners in *Kamaradschaft* and *The Stars Look Down* claw at the entombing walls to gain the light of life on this earth. There is no hereafter for Marxist miners; there is only the here and the now. But for Ford there is an unbroken chain of feelings between the living and the dead. Hence, the epilogue of *How Green Was My Valley* reunites a family fragmented by deaths and departures. Ford's ghosts are not the memory images imparted to Victor Sjostrom's old professor in Ingmar Bergman's *Wild Strawberries* (1957), but mystical incarnations of an unchanging world beyond the valley of death.

Ford is less successful in expressing visually and emotionally the film's matriarchal maxim: "If our father was the head of the house, our mother was its heart." Here it is Donald Crisp's father who prevails poetically over Sara Allgood's mother. Indeed, the emotional authority of the mother is fatally undermined when her youngest son Huw (the film's point-of-view narrator) chooses to leave home in order to live with and support his widowed sister-in-law (Anna Lee), for whom he feels a childhood longing of an extraordinary delicacy. Even so, the boy's attachments to his beloved sister-in-law, his sainted mother, and his beautiful sister (Maureen O'Hara) do not seem to be as deeply felt as the eloquent silences he shares with his father and brothers.

Curiously, the film's central plot, which concerns the ill-starred love between Walter Pidgeon's penniless, well-spoken minister, Mr. Gruffydd, and Maureen O'Hara's impetuous miner's daughter, Angharad Morgan, has always seemed peripheral to the saga of the Morgan family. The film marked Pidgeon's interesting middle period between his early emergence as an inoffensive musical comedy lead and his later embalming with Greer Garson in MGM's Great Couple series. Maureen O'Hara, a flaming red-haired Irish beauty, had hitherto been typed in roles of erotic masochism for such interestingly morbid romances as Alfred Hitchcock's *Jamaica Inn* (1939), William Dieterle's *The Hunchback of Notre Dame* (1939), and Dorothy Arzner's *Dance, Girl, Dance* (1940). It was only in the films of John Ford that Maureen O'Hara acquired any sort of dramatic dimension. Here, unfortunately, the Pidgeon-O'Hara love scenes (with Roddy McDowall's Huw as the go-between) become overly rhetorical because Ford is unable in this context and in this period to project the sexual hunger of the Maureen O'Hara–John Wayne fifties relationships in *The Quiet Man* (1952) and *Wings of Eagles* (1957). In 1941, sexual hunger was hardly a fitting subject for America's cinematic poet laureate and leading exemplar of social consciousness.

After *How Green Was My Valley* Ford went on active duty in the U.S. Navy as Chief of the Field Photographic Branch, a unit of the Office of Strategic Services (later glorified on the screen as the O.S.S.) with offices in Paris and London. Among the Hollywood hands Ford recruited for his documentary team were Gregg Toland, Garson Kanin, Budd Schulberg, Joseph Walker, Daniel Fuchs, Claude Dauphin, Robert Parrish, Jack Pennick, and Ray Kellog. Ford was away from commercial film production for more than three years, but this was considered appropriate for an artist in his quasi-official position. He even picked up an extra Oscar for *The Battle of Midway* (1942), America's first war documentary, and also a Purple Heart for wounds incurred in the engagement.

Of course, many other Hollywood directors went to war, among them Stevens, Wyler, Huston, and Capra. World War II was a war with something for everybody: fascism (against the treacherous Nipponese abroad and the helpless Nisei at home) for the American right, anti-fascism (in the European Theater) for the American left, and good old-fashioned patriotism for the American center. When Ford and Toland recorded the raising of the American flag on Midway in the midst of the Japanese attack, every American could cheer without any ideological reservations. The flag was not yet the divisive emblem it was to be during the Vietnam War. But Ford's allegiances never wavered. He is the only American film director who lent his artistic services to the Government through World War II, the Korean War, and the Vietnam War. The two later wars were as divisive as World War II was unifying. And even by the end of World War II, Ford's communal, patriotic attitude towards war was beginning to fall out of favor with the cultural establishment. Thus when Ford returned to Hollywood to film *They Were Expendable* in 1945, he was already out of synch with the prevailing *Zeitgeist*.

By any standard it was not a triumphal return. Not only was the war over by the time (late December 1945) *They Were Expendable* was ready for release; the film dealt with the very early misadventures of the war almost four years before. What could have seemed more perverse than Ford's celebration of gallant defeat in the aftermath of glorious victory? It was as if the director had become nostalgic for certain values he felt slipping away irretrievably in the forgetful postwar world. Indeed, there was something anachronistic back in 1945 in Ford's idealizations of unquestioning self-sacrifice, dogged devotion to duty, ingrained sense of responsibility, and transcendental faith in a nation's worthiness to accept the fearsome sacrifices of its expendable individuals.

Of course, American audiences had been completely saturated with war propaganda by the time *They Were Expendable* was released. Errol Flynn alone had won World War II many times over as romance, sometimes very graceful but more often merely glossy, prevailed over grim, grubby realism. The bloodiest of the documentary war films were not released to audiences until after the war. Even to this day, John Huston's

The Battle of San Pietro, for example, has been seen by very few people, and Huston's psychiatric study of shell-shock cases, *Let There Be Light*, by even fewer. Once the war was over, the war film tended to slide in social significance from a cause to a genre, from a statement of principles to a set of platitudes.

If *They Were Expendable* has stood the test of time as one of Ford's most evocative works, it is less as history than as mythology. Indeed, the entire film can now be viewed as an elegy to doomed individuals in a common cause. Ford had come out of the war with an image of man amid the rubble, humanity amid the Holocaust. We need not know if the cause be just or not. The fire and smoke, the death and destruction, the blood and tears, take us from Troy to Bataan and back in the never-ending epic of humankind. And Ford's camera again stands back at epic distance, for which he pays a price in the imprecision of his psychological delineation. Even his co-protagonists, Lt. John Brickley (Robert Montgomery) and Lt. Rusty Ryan (John Wayne), are conceived dramaturgically in conventional *What Price Glory* terms of bickering camaraderie. Fortunately Montgomery, with his refined edginess, and Wayne, with his raw energy, are never given time to develop trivial differences of outlook. Instead they are engulfed almost immediately (Pearl Harbor and its aftermath) by events beyond their control, and their histrionically diverse temperaments are harmonized with Ford's dominant theme of defeat and self-abnegation.

Montgomery, much the smoother actor of the two, settles into a paternally stabilizing relationship with Wayne's slightly unruly child warrior; Montgomery, a wary Odysseus, as it were, to Wayne's excitable Achilles. It follows with mythic logic that of the two the Wayne character is the more susceptible to injury. It follows also that it would be the Montgomery character who would seem to be burdened with some prior obligations, perhaps even by a Penelope of sorts, whereas the Wayne character would be footloose and fancy free enough to begin a love affair (with Donna Reed's Lt. Sandy Davis) at the very edge of eternity, a liaison severed with awesome abruptness by a broken telephone connection. Nonetheless, the shadowy images of Wayne and Reed as they ritualistically seek each other out are among the most intensely romantic images of love and death in the American cinema. Still, it seemed a little late in the day for a supposedly serious American director to be serenading the All-American Girl in Sternbergian patterns of light and shadow, courtesy of the classical lens of Joseph H. August.

By contrast, the earthier visions of Huston's *The Battle of San Pietro*

(1945) and Wellman's *The Story of G.I. Joe* (1945) did not envisage women explicitly, but put them in the longing, hungering faces of men at war. Huston and Wellman have always had a tendency in their manlier projects to treat women not in terms of Ford's chivalric idealism but as necessary evils in relieving male frustration; *vide* the strikingly similar bits of business with suggestive bar-room paintings in Wellman's *The Oxbow Incident* (1943) and *Yellow Sky* (1948), and the ostentatiously sluttish females at the fringes of just about every Huston movie. But only in wartime does male lust become ennobled as a significant symptom of the human condition. It is not that *San Pietro* and *The Story of G.I. Joe* were concerned primarily with this aspect of the war, but that they were taken more seriously than *They Were Expendable* largely because they eschewed the conventions of boy-girl romance. *San Pietro* seemed particularly impressive for not penetrating the awesome anonymity of the young American infantrymen marching up the mountain to certain death. As always, however, Huston tended to evade moral responsibility for the damning footage of this most botched-up of American campaigns. Indeed, General Mark Clark, the ill-famed American architect of the systematic annihilation of the American foot soldier, is actually introduced in the film as its narrator and raisonneur. Huston tried to have it both ways: War is Hell for the humanists; War is Noble for the patriots. Actually, Huston's sour, cynical, defeatist attitude towards human endeavor in *San Pietro* fell somewhere between the nihilism of his images and the nobility of their implications, somewhere between the mocking laughter of *The Treasure of the Sierra Madre* (1948) and the cold sweat of panic in *The Red Badge of Courage* (1951).

In the realm of fictional (as opposed to documentary) war films, *The Story of G.I. Joe* was regarded by most critics as decisively superior to *They Were Expendable*. For one thing, it was easier to isolate in one's memory the emotional high points in *The Story of G.I. Joe* than to reintegrate as an expressive whole the stylistic and spiritual fluidity of *They Were Expendable*.

Actually, *The Story of G.I. Joe* was more typical of Hollywood war films than *They Were Expendable*, in that the Wellman version of the war focused more on the individual whereas the Ford version focused more on the group. Whereas *The Story of G.I. Joe* was constructed very loosely of ill-connected character vignettes, *They Were Expendable* flowed gracefully on an epic stream of collective destiny which allowed little leeway for individual psyches. The ethos of the team is expressed in *Expendable* by Montgomery's superior officer in the baseball parlance of being called upon to lay down a sacrifice bunt rather than to hit a home run. By contrast, the G.I. Joes disdain the lofty rhetoric of duty and victory for the day-to-day exigencies of survival. It is interesting that both Ford and Hawks (*Air Force*) dealt with professional soldiers whereas Wellman and Milestone (*A Walk in the Sun*) (1947) dealt with citizen soldiers, indeed the thematic distinction between the nostalgic celebration in James Jones's *From Here to Eternity* and the cross-sectional dissection in Norman Mailer's *The Naked and the Dead*. It was the difference between the belief that the war had conserved the old values and the belief that the war had created new ones. It was the difference between going back and going forward. Ford was to go back.

Nothing is more symptomatic of Ford's falling out of step with the cultural establishment than his magnification of the MacArthur legend in *They Were Expendable*. As the General and his family are evacuated from Corregidor on PT boats, Ford begins with a newsreel-like objective long shot, and then holds the General's figure in the frame until he ends up looming in close-up on the foredeck, sunglasses, corn-cob pipe and all. A young sailor asks the General for an autograph, and the film cuts to a comically exasperated Ward Bond, throwing his arms and his eyes to the heavens, the martial music blaring all the while. This gag sequencing of shots tends to conceal an apotheosis of the General. The timing of the sequence is really too quick for a lingering laugh, and the young sailor's indiscretion is designed quite obviously to lend a human dimension to a solemnly superhuman occasion. Even before the war was over, however, Douglas MacArthur had acquired a controversial reputation for his glory-seeking personality. His personal courage was questioned with the epithet of "Dugout Doug," and he later became identified with the most reactionary elements of the Republican Party. Ford's artistic decision to treat MacArthur as though he were Lincoln was therefore out of sync with the critics and public. It was the superficially egalitarian Eisenhower who became the nation's unifying symbol as he went on to dismantle the New Deal and other populist initiatives. By contrast, the majestic MacArthur, for all his strategic acumen, dwindled finally to a failed De Gaulle. Still, Ford could not help admiring the General's patrician style of pride and resistance in the face of a humiliating defeat. But the war was over, and it had become somewhat tasteless to continue glorifying a General who was grandiose to begin with.

Another revealing aspect of *They Were Expendable* is Ford's paternalistic treatment of young men. The autograph incident is just one of the more telling examples of his association of youth with rash immaturity rather than idealistic rebellion. In the world of John Ford the young must learn from their elders, and the process is painfully and ridiculously slow. But by the same token, it is the sacred responsibility of the elders to look after the young and to teach them how to survive. It is not likely that Ford could ever have accommodated such modishly alienated actors of the fifties as Montgomery Clift, Marlon Brando, and James Dean. It would be all he could do to keep Jeffrey Hunter under control as the wildest of all his semi-juveniles.

■　■　■　■

FORD'S NEXT PROJECT after *They Were Expendable* was *My Darling Clementine* (1946), only his second western in twenty years; and it is significant that Ford's decline in critical esteem tended to coincide with his return to the Old West on a regular basis. In this respect, *My Darling Clementine* is the work more of a poet laureate than of a poet, a western for viewers with little interest in the genre. It is a western also in which the realistic touches outweigh the romantic flourishes, and in which the plot is merely a pretext to document the period. Consequently, the final confrontation of the Earps and Doc Holliday on one side, and the Clantons on the other, seems almost anticlimactic. Ford's leisurely narrative style is at odds with the malignant Manicheism of the revenge plot. Indeed, Walter Brennan's Old Man Clanton was the most evil character in the Ford oeuvre until Charles Kemper's Uncle Shiloh Clegg in *Wagonmaster* four years later. Both Old Man Clanton and Uncle Shiloh Clegg live just long enough to see all their grown-up sons gunned down by the avengers of law and order and morality. The respective avengers (Henry Fonda's Wyatt Earp and Ben Johnson's Travis Blue) try to refrain from using firearms, but they are finally roused to action by a senseless murder. In *My Darling Clementine*, it is the revenge murder of an Earp in return for the death of a Clanton which sets up the climactic Gunfight at the O.K. Corral, a historical occurrence previously celebrated on a B-picture budget and against a cheesecloth background in Allan Dwan's 1939 *Frontier Marshal*. By contrast, Ford's staging of the gunfight is three-dimensional, with wind and dust for realistic atmosphere. And it is the Ford movie which caused Wyatt Earp and Doc Holliday to turn up so frequently in westerns of the fifties through the nineties.

What proves most memorable, however, is not the confrontations and the gunfights. In fact, Ford virtually throws away a showdown between Earp and Holliday by shooting it (literally and figuratively) in long shot. Ford's westerns never depended excessively on the machismo match-ups of quick draws, but rather on the usually neglected intervals between the gun-shots, when men received haircuts, courted their sweethearts, and even partook of fragments of frontier culture. Alan Mowbray's Granville Thorndyke, a soused Shakespearian actor, pops up so prominently in *Clementine* that we are reminded once more of a certain degree of self-consciousness in Ford's depiction of his action characters. Ford's people very often seem aware that they are striking a pose for posterity, or having their existence on earth preserved for all time by way of a daguerreotype. But even as they preen themselves in all their pompous pastness, they scratch around for nagging necessities of survival. Their clothes itch and their stomachs growl, and time hangs heavy on their hands. Hence, Ford's penchant for directing away from the obligatory action climaxes towards the optional Waiting-for-God-knows-what interludes.

It follows that what Ford makes us remember most vividly about Henry Fonda's Wyatt Earp in *Clementine* is not Earp's skill with a gun, but his lack of skill on a dance floor. And not merely Earp's, but Fonda's as well. Ford had been taken with Fonda's jolting awkwardness in the square dance in *The Grapes of Wrath* (1940), and he resolved then and there to exploit the humanizing potential of Fonda's lurch-steps on every possible future occasion. But then of all the red-blooded Hollywood action directors, Ford was always the most enamoured of the dance as the most sacred of all social rituals. The sustained camera movement which follows Henry Fonda's Wyatt Earp round a corner to court his darling Clementine (Cathy Downs) and take her to a dance on the floor of an unfinished church tends to consecrate what is clearly the film's ceremonial high point.

What is odd about this visual convergence of the constricting forces of Civilization, Christianity, and Monogamy is how little regret Ford shows for the doomed anarchic spirit of the Wild West, epitomized in the Clantons and in Linda Darnell's tediously victimized and despised dance-hall girl. Ultimately, *My Darling Clementine* suffers grievously from an imbalance between the nice girl of Cathy Downs and the not-so-nice girl of Linda Darnell. For one thing, the iconographic content of the two actresses is out of all proportion to the dramatic content of their roles. The studio seems to have imposed Linda Darnell on Ford to the point of clogging his continuity with mystifying close-ups of Fox's rising star. Fortunately for Miss Darnell's career, she was only a couple of years away from more appreciative directors like Preston Sturges (*Unfaithfully Yours*, 1948) and Joseph L. Mankiewicz (*A Letter to Three Wives*, 1949).

Otherwise, Ford's unsympathetic treatment of her in *My Darling Clementine* is comparable to his grudging toleration of Barbara Stanwyck in *The Plough and the Stars*. Similarly, Ford seemed far less creative in embellishing the romantic role of Victor Mature's Doc Holliday than he was in inventing memorable bits of business for Henry Fonda's Wyatt Earp. All in all, *My Darling Clementine* seems divided against itself as Ford's personal concerns struggle against Fox's more conventional concepts. Ford, poet laureate and all, had not yet completely broken the studio mold, and in the year when American audiences and critics were mesmerized by *The Best Years of Our Lives* (1946), *Henry V* (1946), and *Open City* (1946), John Ford seemed at best to be very pleasantly marking time with a quaintly old-fashioned genre.

■　　■　　■　　■

AS IT HAPPENED, *The Fugitive* (1947) marked the last occasion on which the great majority of American critics made the slightest effort to confront Ford as a contemporary artist. After *The Fugitive*, Ford was widely regarded as a voice from the past, as an eccentric antique dealer with a good eye for vintage Americana. And Ford seemed to respond to this benign neglect by becoming surlier and more self-indulgent. *The Fugitive* (1947) seemed to have been designed to recapture the mystical, Expressionist aura of *The Informer* (1935). Unfortunately, Ford's monumental treatment of the material tended to be pious rather than religious. Whereas Graham Greene's saintly sinner (in the novel *The Power and the Glory*) was cursed with faith despite all his cowardice and lechery, the whisky priest of Ford, Nichols, and Fonda trudged through the film in a state of somnolent sanctimoniousness.

It was a year (1947) of noble martyrs and masochists—Verdoux, Ivan, Johnny McQueen in *Odd Man Out*, the children in *Shoeshine*, Aldo Fabrizi's persecuted patriarch in *To Live in Peace*, Maurice Chevalier's aging matinee idol in *Man About Town*, Sam Levene's crucified Jew on the cross of anti-Semitism in *Crossfire*, John Garfield's morally anguished boxer in Robert Rossen's *Body and Soul*, Victor Mature's suffering stool-pigeon in Henry Hathaway's *Kiss of Death*, and, most forebodingly of all, Alf Kjellin's traumatized student in Alf Sjöberg's *Hets* (*Frenzy* or *Torment*) with a script by Ingmar Bergman. It was a year in which pain and torture and paranoia had finally overwhelmed the *film noir*—Anthony Mann's *T-Men*, Jacques Tourneur's *Out of the Past*, Robert Rossen's *Johnny O'Clock*, Robert Wise's *Born To Kill*, Jules Dassin's *Brute Force*, Byron Haskin's *I Walk Alone*, Robert Montgomery's *Ride the Pink Horse*, Irving

Pichel's *They Won't Believe Me*, and Delmer Daves's *Dark Passage*. It was a year also in which Michael Powell and Emeric Pressburger were hailed for confronting the pathology of repression in the comely religious celibates of *Black Narcissus*. Against this background of spiritual and psychological disintegration, the glowingly pro-Catholic propaganda in *The Fugitive* seemed very naïve indeed. Even in 1947, it seemed unfair to stack the deck for the Catholic Church in any Latin American setting, however allegorical. What was paradoxical in the Greene novel became polemical in the Ford film, and what was dialectical became dogmatic. Worst of all, Mexico was neither Ireland nor the Old West, and despite the stylistic contributions of cinematographer Gabriel Figueroa and associate producer Emilio Fernandez, the Mexican characters in *The Fugitive* (1947) froze into a stone-faced stoicism more appropriate for a religious pageant than a psychological drama. (Ford was later to experience a similar failure with the Indian characters in his nobly intentioned *Cheyenne Autumn* (1964).)

Thus *The Fugitive* (1947) shares a certain gloominess and half-baked ambitiousness with the more fashionable films of the late forties; but the content simply isn't there. All the stock figures are seen so far from the outside that they become too prettily posed and expressively contorted: J. Carrol Naish's police informer crawling on the ground like a snake, Dolores Del Rio's Magdalene photographed with the shadowy serenity of a Madonna, Ward Bond's El Gringo outlaw posing before a WANTED poster in a low-angle shot more appropriate for a Station of the Cross, and Fonda's pursued priest, his back to an endless wall, his face moodily impassive and ox-like in its spiritual obstinacy. It is more in the spatial transitions between compositions than in the interplay of characters that one senses Ford's grand design of interlocking narratives. Even so, Ford generally promises more visually than he can deliver dramatically. Hence, the shot in which the outlaw and the priest pass each other on the road, and move in opposite directions to an ultimately shared destiny, is too portentous for the skimpily allegorical resolution of this shared destiny as that of a Jesus and a Good Thief in a two-bit gunfight with the evil authorities. And when Ford reaches the heart of Greene's novel in the final confrontation between the priest and the atheist revolutionary, there are no dramatic sparks from the encounter. Pedro Armendariz is too much the solemn heavy, and Fonda too much the sullen martyr, cut off by casting from the rhythmic truths of his supposed people. Even the eye-popping Ford-Figueroa chiaroscuro compositions falsify Greene's gray relativism with an inappropriately black-and-white Manicheism. All in all, Ford's achievement in *The Fugitive* is more painterly than poetic, more for the eye than for the mind or heart.

Fort Apache (1948) took Ford further and deeper into the Old West than he had ever before ventured, but in the process it removed him from the stream of supposedly serious film history. The films Ford made between 1948 and 1966 seemed out of time in their own time. It was not that he stood still or that his work was unvarying. Quite the contrary: the last two decades of his career were for his revisionist admirers at least his richest and most rewarding and most invigorating in that he became fully his own man. Indeed, the operative comparison is not with a Cecil B. De Mille or a Henry King, but rather with a Jean Renoir or a Carl Dreyer or a Kenji Mizoguchi. But to the critics of his time and even after, the late Ford appeared as a grizzled old prospector who lost his way in Monument Valley.

From *Fort Apache* on, Ford's films seemed to abandon Tradition of Quality for Cult of Personality. Ford seemed to let everything hang out, and especially his boozy, misty-eyed Irishness. His casting was more casual than ever, and casting had never been his strongest point. The same old faces kept popping up year after year, film after film, most often in western garb or military uniform. As Ford himself passed from his mid-fifties to his seventies, it became easier and easier for critics to write him off as an honored has-been. He would be remembered, the conventional wisdom asserted, for *The Grapes of Wrath* (1940) and *The Informer* (1935), and not much more. *Stagecoach* (1939), perhaps, and *My Darling Clementine* (1976) might survive as genre studies. Of his post-1948 output, only *The Quiet Man* (1952) had any apparent claim on posterity, but more as pleasant entertainment than as expressive art. For the rest, the establishment critics lowered their heads in embarrassment and regret for a faded talent.

Viewed together, *The Fugitive* and *Fort Apache* indicated a shift in Ford's sensibility from the shadowy world of Dudley Nichols to the sunlit world of Frank S. Nugent, from socially conscious allegory to crowd-pleasing adventure, and from the lies of art to the half-truths of legend. The very plot of *Fort Apache* suggested a conscious shift in the casting of the Ford hero from Henry Fonda, the star of Ford's Quality Period, to John Wayne, the star of the director's Personality Period. It was the first and last time Fonda and Wayne appeared together in a Ford film, Fonda as a Custer-like martinet of a colonel and Wayne as a wily Indian fighter. The iconographical tension alone makes *Fort Apache* one of Ford's most absorbing entertainments, but there is much more as well, and in some areas much too much. The casting of Shirley Temple as Philadelphia Thursday, the flirtatious daughter of Lt.-Col. Thursday (Henry Fonda), marked the reunion of Ford with his child star of *Wee Willie Winkie*. That Miss Temple's grown-up career had not flourished probably only strengthened Ford's resolve to employ her. But if Miss Temple's disastrously discordant performance could be chalked off to *auld lang syne*, John Agar's pretty-boy petulance as her young West Point suitor could only be explained as a misguided effort to exploit the real-life Temple-Agar marriage. As it was, the Temple-Agar sub-plot seemed so interminable that the extraordinary virtues of the main plot were almost completely submerged. The setpieces are among Ford's most memorable: the Grand March at the Enlisted Men's Ball; the women's farewell to the men going off to war; and the Apache massacre of the Seventh Cavalry.

Unfortunately, *Fort Apache* was released at a time when Hollywood was afflicted with realistic rigor mortis. Critics of the period lacked the language to describe and evaluate myth and romance. Problems and polemics were the order of the day, and *Fort Apache* seemed to have nothing new to say. The film's attitudes towards Indians, women, and military discipline seemed either conventional or conservative. Indeed, the final eulogy of John Wayne's Captain Kirby York for his fallen Custer-like commander, Henry Fonda's Colonel Thursday, tends to glorify command decisions to the point of incompetence and even insanity. Moreover, Ford seemed unduly sentimental in healing the old wounds incurred in the Civil War by proud soldiers on both sides. Hence, much of the tension between the Fonda and Wayne characters is generated by a series of Yankee-versus-Reb insult routines in which Fonda's officious nastiness is allowed to play against Wayne's submissive exasperation. But there is no corresponding ideological tension between the two officers. What unites them—the Seventh Cavalry rather than the Union—is much stronger than what divided them in the past largely through an accident of geography.

The American cinema has generally sentimentalized the Southern (or Trojan) position in the Civil War while reserving the right to be critical of the victorious Northern (or Greek) forces. For example, never was there a kind word for General Sherman, the master strategist of total war, and seldom an understanding word for John Brown, the ill-fated abolitionist who made the mistake of practicing his own emancipation of the slaves. The movie studios regarded the South as a distinct region with very deep and lingering emotions about the Civil War. By contrast, the North was credited with sufficient historical detachment to forgive and forget, and even to identify with the romantic plight of the defeated Southland. Ford's films did not always take the Southern point of view. Indeed, John Wayne himself played Sherman and Henry (Harry) Morgan played Grant in Ford's Civil War episode in MGM's Cinerama grab-bag demonstration, *How the West Was Won* (1962). *The Horse Soldiers* (1959) celebrated the feats of arms of a marauding Union cavalry unit far behind the Confederate lines in 1863, and Ford provided a sympathetic portrait of General Philip Sheridan by J. Carrol Naish in *Rio Grande* (1950), and of Grant as President by Edward G. Robinson in *Cheyenne Autumn* (1964).

Still, Ford preferred to accept history and even legend as it was written rather than revise it. Why are the Indians on the warpath from *Fort Apache* to *Cheyenne Autumn*? Not, according to Ford, because of American Imperialism or White Racism or Manifest Destiny, but because of the derelictions of the Indian Ring, "the most corrupt band of politicians in our nation's history"; graft and corruption on the local level rather than greed and conquest on the national level. For whatever reason, the Indian remains the Other in American history and mythology to the end of Ford's career. Even in the moderately revisionist *Cheyenne Autumn*, the Indians provide little more than an occasion for their conquerors to be merciful and belatedly virtuous. One of Ford's most tendentious films, *Cheyenne Autumn* comes to life only momentarily when the focus shifts from the nobly but opaquely suffering Indians to the wild frontier slapstick of Wyatt Earp (James Stewart) and Doc Holliday (Arthur Kennedy) as they debunk anti-Indian hysteria. One must, however, distinguish between reasons and excuses. Critics who claim to dislike Ford because of the implicit political positions of his westerns are generally not all that enthusiastic about the genre itself. Certainly, the aggressively anti-heroic westerns of the sixties and seventies did not provide a validly artistic alternative to Ford's vision of the region and the period. It is almost as if the ideology comes wrapped up in the genre so that the racism can never be dissociated from the romance.

Another excess of *Fort Apache* was its boisterous Irishness, particularly the boozy, brutish braggadocio of Victor McLaglen's Sergeant Mulcahy. McLaglen had long since won his spurs with Ford as a brawling giant, but as he grew older, his performances began to lose every semblance of substance and he degenerated into the most tedious of comedy reliefs. None the less, Ford stayed with McLaglen through *She Wore a Yellow Ribbon* (1949), *Rio Grande* (1950), and *The Quiet Man* (1952), and even managed to modulate his performances by suggesting the blubbering baby under the overgrown id. A standard Ford gambit with McLaglen was the taming of the giant by a little wisp of a woman after he had virtually demolished a tavern along with all its muscular male occupants. Thus was the Irish-Catholic Caliban calmed and conquered by the Madonna.

JOSEF VON STERNBERG (1894–1969)

Although Josef von Sternberg's directorial career spanned almost thirty years, he was a meaningful force in the cinema primarily between 1927 and 1935, an interval one might ironically designate as his Paramount Period. Even his work of this period was not seriously evaluated for decades after the mid-thirties when movies were supposed to crackle crisply to the proletarian point. Sternberg was then considered slow, decadent, and self-indulgent, while gloriously ambiguous Marlene Dietrich was judged too rich for the people's blood—it was a time for bread, not cake.

Even today, however, the art of Josef von Sternberg is too often subordinated to the mystique of Marlene Dietrich, with whom the director was associated in seven of his more familiar movies. Unfortunately, the Svengali-Trilby publicity that enshrouded *The Blue Angel* (1930), *Morocco* (1930), *Dishonored* (1931), *Shanghai Express* (1932), *Blonde Venus* (1932), *The Scarlet Empress* (1934), and *The Devil Is a Woman* (1935) obscured the more meaningful merits not only of these particular works but of Sternberg's career as a whole. In fact, the director's filtered feminine mystique neither originated nor disappeared with Marlene Dietrich, but indeed ecstatically embraced such other photogenic features as those of Georgia Hale, Evelyn Brent, Betty Compson, Olga Baclanova, Esther Ralston, Fay Wray, Sylvia Sidney, Frances Dee, Laraine Day, Gene Tierney, and Janet Leigh.

Josef von Sternberg was born in Vienna on May 29, 1894. His family emigrated to New York City when he was seven, and he attended public school there for three years, after which he and his parents went back to Vienna. They returned to the United States in 1908. His official film credits begin 1914 at the World Film Corporation studios in Fort Lee,

New Jersey, where he worked his way from film patcher and shipping clerk to chief assistant to William A. Brady, the head of the company. During World War I, Sternberg produced some training films and was later stationed in Washington, D.C., as a Signal Corps photographer. He returned to his old job briefly after the war, then set out on his own as cutter, editor, writer, and assistant director. In these capacities, he worked in the Fort Lee studios, hopped to England for a short stay, and finally went west to Hollywood, still a relatively young man.

In a sense, Sternberg entered the cinema through the camera rather than the cutting room and thus became a lyricist of light and shadow rather than a master of montage. He concentrated on the spatial integrity of his images rather than on their metaphorical juxtaposition. Sternberg's cinema, for better or worse, represented a distinctively Germanic camera viewpoint—from Murnau and Lang—in contrast to Eisenstein's fashionably Marxist montage. Rationales for composition and camera movement were rare in the thirties. Nevertheless, Aeneas Mackenzie in 1936 wrote both appreciatively and perceptively of Sternberg's style for *Life and Letters Today* in an article entitled "Leonardo of the Lenses":

> To understand what Sternberg is attempting to do, one must first appreciate that he imposes the limitations of the visual upon himself: he refuses to obtain any effect whatsoever save by means of pictorial composition. That is the fundamental distinction between von Sternberg and all other directors. Stage acting he declines, cinema in its conventional aspect he despises as mere mechanics, and dialogue he employs primarily for its value as integrated sound. The screen is his medium—not the camera. His purpose is to reveal the emotional significance of a subject by a series of magnificent canvases.
>
> Any such process in itself, of course, would be purely illustrative, and totally impractical because of its static nature. Nevertheless, a successful von Sternberg film is completely dynamic. The movement of a play on the stage (or or a stage play on the screen) is obtained by means of the literary principle of dynamic impulsion, the so-called *filmic motion* is induced by a regulation of the length and succession of its individual scenes, and the progression of the factory-made "movie" is procured by the introduction of entertaining irrelevancies; yet, all of these moments are denied to Sternberg by the very nature of what he is attempting to accomplish.
>
> In lieu of them he relies upon long and elaborate shots, each of which is developed internally—by camera movement and dramatic lighting—to a point where it detonates into shock, surprise, or startling beauty. And it is by means of this Ford-like internal combustion that a von Sternberg

film progresses in audience interest: before the effect of one emotional percussion has subsided, the next is under way. Consequently, the story does not move his picture; it is his picture which moves the story.

Mackenzie's was a voice with few echoes, and complaints about Sternberg's slowness continued in a decade which had no time for the studied and the deliberate. Worse still for Sternberg's reputation was his relative lack of interest in realist social themes. His ideological indifference was interpreted as an affront to popular critical standards of the period. In this polemical period, even Sternberg's "von" provided ammunition for a sharp-shooting anti-Hollywood sniper like John Grierson. "With *Shanghai Express*," Grierson growled, "Joe Sternberg has become the great Josef von Sternberg, having given up the struggle for good: a director so successful that even Adolph Zukor is pleased to hold his hand for a brief condescending moment."

Even in the nineties, however, critics and audiences may be reluctant to endorse Sternberg's story sense. Apart from "classical" assignments like *An American Tragedy* and *Crime and Punishment*, his plots seems far-fetched, his backgrounds bizarre, and his character motivations obscure, at least by conventional standards of storytelling. As in a dream, he has wandered through studio sets representing Imperial Russia (*The Last Command* (1928), *The Scarlet Empress* (1934)), China (*Shanghai Express* (1932), *The Shanghai Gesture* (1941)), North Africa (*Morocco* (1930)), Spain (*The Devil Is a Woman* (1935)), Austria (*The Case of Lena Smith, Dishonored* (1931)), France (*The Exquisite Sinner* (1926)), and Germany (*The Blue Angel* (1930)). Even his American locales focus primarily on the dregs or fringes of society, from the festive criminality of *Underworld* (1927), *The Drag Net* (1928), and *Thunderbolt* (1929) to the bawdy, brawling backwaters and back streets of *The Salvation Hunters* (1925), *The Docks of New York* (1929), and *Blonde Venus* (1932). Everyday life, as such, seldom appears in Sternberg's cinema. His characters generally make their first entrance at a moment in their lives when there is no tomorrow. Knowingly or unknowingly, they have reached the end or the bottom, but they will struggle a short time longer, about ninety minutes of screen time, to discover the truth about themselves and those they love. Although there is much violence and death in Sternberg's world, there is relatively little action. The various murders, duels, executions, suicides, and assaults serve merely as poetic punctuation for lives drifting to their destinations in reflective repose. Death in this context is less a conclusion than a termination. The paradox of violence without action is supplemented by the paradox of virtue without morality. There are no codes or systems in these dream worlds; the characters retain their civilized graces despite the most desperate struggles for psychic survival, and it is their poise under pressure, their style under stress, that grants them a measure of heroic stature and stoic calm.

Sternberg's films are poetic without being symbolic. We need not search for slumbering allegories of Man and God and Life, but rather for a continuous stream of emotional autobiography. Sternberg's exoticism is then less a pretense than a pretext for objectifying personal fantasies. His equivalent literary genre is not the novel, or the short story, or the theatrical spectacle but the closet drama, unplayable but for the meaningful grace of gesture and movement. There persists an erroneous impression that the art of a *Morocco* or a *Shanghai Express* consists of the magnifying of trivialities. Yet there is nothing trivial about the size of Sternberg's emotions, and nothing disproportionate in the means employed to express them. Also there is conscious humor in the director's awareness of his own absurdity though some spectators still imagine they are laughing *at* Sternberg when they are actually laughing *with* him. The colorful costumes, the dazzling décors, the marble-pillared palaces merely underscore by ironic contrast the painfully acquired wisdom of the all-too-human prisoners of grandiose illusions. The limitations of this aesthetic are self-evident. An insufficient grasp of one's time and place is hardly a positive virtue even for the most lyrical poet. It is only when we look around at the allegedly significant cinema of Sternberg's contemporaries that we recognize the relative stature of a director who chose to write with a camera in the first person long before Alexandre Astruc's "caméra-stylo" made such impious subjectivity fashionable and such personal poetry comprehensible.

Sternberg's career as a director of silent films extends from *The Salvation Hunters* in 1925 to *The Docks of New York* in 1928, a film that was previewed for critics, according to William K. Everson, an expert on the silent film, during the same week that *The Singing Fool* (1928) with Al Jolson was causing a frenzied clamor. (No print of the last silent Sternberg film, the 1929 *The Case of Lena Smith*, is known to exist. Also "lost" are *The Exquisite Sinner* (1925) for MGM, *The Sea Gull* (1926) for Chaplin—and reputedly destroyed by Chaplin—and *The Drag Net* (1928) for Paramount.)

The Salvation Hunters is not only the first film to bear Josef von Sternberg's name as director, but also his most explicitly personal work until the emotional recapitulation of *Anatahan* closed his career nearly thirty years later. Most film historians, particularly those in the English-speaking world, have discussed *The Salvation Hunters* as a depressing descent to the lower depths in the manner of Erich von Stroheim's *Greed*. The real drama of the film, however, is concerned not with the rise of the downtrodden but rather with the moving (emotion in motion) spectacle of a young woman waiting for a boy to grow into a man. The boy himself, a walking metaphor of faint-heartedness and futility, works on a barge bearing a mud-dredge which scoops out earth from the water only to have its efforts cyclically negated by the compensating collapse of the shore in the background.

Oddly enough, *The Salvation Hunters* (1925) is a modern film in a way that *Greed* (1925), *The Gold Rush* (1925), *The Last Laugh* (1924), and even *Potemkin* (1925) are not. What has always seemed oblique and obscure in Sternberg's art as compared with that of his contemporaries is the director's reluctance to reveal everything about his characters. On the purely visual level, this reluctance is expressed through veils and filters. On the dramatic plane, Sternberg has generally avoided the kind of direct confrontations in which characters spell out their motivations. Consequently, there is usually more to Sternberg's characters than meets the eye and, after the advent of the talkies, the ear.

Underworld (1927), famous for being the first gangster film, began Sternberg's Paramount association. Actually the movie is less a proto-gangster film than a pre-gangster film. In fact, Sternberg showed little interest in the purely gangsterish aspects of the genre, and his civilized characters consistently transcend the criminal codes of the genre films to come. Sternberg steers clear of the sociological implications of his material to concentrate on the themes that most obsess him and his heroes: love and faith and falsehood.

George Bancroft's "Bull" Weed is Sternberg's Byronic hero, preceding later gangsters more in the manner of poetic prophecy than of journalistic observation. Sternberg's hoodlums, like Cocteau's motorcyclists in *Orphée* (1949), partake of the manners and machinery of the modern world without ever escaping the dream world of their creator. The avenging forces of law and order are never related to society but rather to an implacable Fate which awaits every tragic hero.

Sternberg was never particularly fond of *Underworld* as an example of personal expression; perhaps the charges of commercialism leveled against it colored his judgment. Despite his expressed preference for *The Salvation Hunters* (1925) as reflecting his personality, it can be argued that there is more of his poetry in *Underworld*. Just from one aspect, no director in the history of the cinema can match Sternberg's preoccupation with the harmonies of hand signals. To light a cigarette, to grasp a coffee cup, to fondle furs is, for Sternberg, equivalent to baring one's soul.

Sternberg's first assignment after *Underworld* was to direct Emil Jannings, the eminent German star Paramount had imported to join Ernst Lubitsch and Pola Negri in Hollywood. The film Sternberg made with Jannings, *The Last Command* (1928), was generally considered the best of Jannings's brief American career. It is undoubtedly Sternberg's most Pirandellian film. The director laid claim to the plot despite the official credit assigned to Lajos Biro. Preston Sturges once called *The Last Command* just about the only perfect film he had ever seen, and both Sternberg and Jannings were amply honored at the time for their participation in the production.

The Last Command is the only time in his career that Sternberg confronted his own craft as a subject, his camera as an object. The story of a Czarist general reduced to the role of a Hollywood extra would seem to be a natural for both Sternberg and Jannings. Jannings, particularly, spent most of his career in sagas of decline and downfall, and he possessed the bulk, if not always the stature, for the most sordid tragedy. Here he savors every moment of authority granted to him by the texture of his fur-lined military overcoat and the aggressive angle of the cigarette holder clenched between his teeth. He is also sensually arrogant toward Evelyn Brent's Red Agent, and this we know by now constitutes the hubris of Sternbergian cinema. Jannings is humbled for his arrogance, not once but twice. Not only does the Revolution strip away the insignias of his rank, but he ends in Hollywood without a shred of his former power.

Sternberg's formal control of his material can be illustrated by a comparison of the angle at which Jannings reviews his troops at the beginning of the film with the angle at which William Powell as a Hollywood director reviews his extras at the end. Where Jannings moves laterally from left to right, Powell moves semi-vertically from right to left. The tempo is increased perceptibly for Powell's review, and this is as it should be for this musical aspect of cinema. Sternberg's technique thus exhibits a formal memory, and his "poetry," far from being vaguely disorganized in the currently pejorative sense of the "poetic," is actually a kind of visual versification.

Again Sternberg eschews the relentless expressiveness of some of his contemporaries, and it becomes difficult to decipher what *The Last Com-*

mand signifies in its characters. Brent's relationship with Jannings is as complex as anything in the modern cinema. She seems fascinated by his power, and yet, when he is completely helpless, she is not without pity and compassion. Brent, like all Sternbergian women, remains enigmatic beyond the demands of the plot. Her perverse nature operates beyond good and evil, beyond the convenient categories of virgins and vamps. What is unusual about Sternberg's direction of his players is that, unlike Murnau and Stroheim, he seeks to control performances not for the sake of simplicity but for the sake of ambiguity. For example, we assume from the plot that Powell chooses Jannings for the climactic charge mainly to humiliate a former adversary, but we are never entirely sure that Powell as the director is not motivated also by an inspiration of ideal casting. The personal, the political, the aesthetic are all intertwined influences for Sternberg. We are left then with no moral, no message, an only partially resolved melodrama of pride and punishment, a work of art rich in overtones but pitched at too many different keys of interpretation. As a stylistic exercise, *The Last Command* is almost too much of a good thing.

The Docks of New York (1929), released toward the end of the silent era, quickly vanished into undeserved oblivion. More than in any previous film, Sternberg has integrated spectacle with psychology, and his characters gain in clarity what they lose in complexity. Sternberg's direction of his players has never been more controlled as George Bancroft, Betty Compson, Olga Baclanova, and Gustav von Seyffertitz perform with force and subtlety as denizens of the lower depths. Sternberg's facility with the shifting moods of the film is equally remarkable. From the Hogarthian hullabaloo of a *Walpurgisnacht* in a dockside saloon to the glum remorse and resignation of the morning after in magistrate's court, Sternberg's camera finds the proper angle and distance. His final image of Compson in a crowded courtroom, in long-shot objectively anonymous but subjectively heroic, reveals a mastery of the expressive potentialities of the focal length of the lens.

Bancroft is once more Sternberg's Caliban, but Compson's fatalistic floozie is more prone to wearing her heart on her sleeve than most Sternbergian heroines. She is vulnerable, wistful, yet fully committed in the way Sylvia Sidney will be later in *An American Tragedy* (1931). The plot is something of a switch for Sternberg in that it is the man who deludes the woman, first with a mock wedding and then with a cynical honeymoon. The man satisfies his lust, but then surrenders to his conscience.

With *The Docks of New York* (1928), Sternberg takes his place with the directors of camera movement as opposed to the directors of montage. In one continuous flow across his decor, Sternberg shows Bancroft dragging his would-be bride past a universe of drunken revelers. The emphasis is on the movement itself rather than on its destination, or rather on the carnal passion expressed by the slow relentlessness of the movement. The language of Sternberg's camera movement here is not the language of dreams but the language of immediacy. Now, now, now, Bancroft seems to shout visually with each lumbering step, and the insinuating insistence of Sternberg's slow tempo augments the electrifying effect of the spectacle.

Sternberg's slow dissolves in *The Docks of New York* have been noted by some film historians as symptoms of stylistic self-indulgence when, actually, they serve the same function as Godard's jump cuts in *Breathless* (1960), and that is to indicate the meaninglessness of the time intervals between moral decisions. When time becomes a function of melodramatic action and reaction in the course of events leading up to Olga Baclanova's murdering an unfaithful mate, Sternberg's cutting is as crisp and clean as Fritz Lang's. Not until *Morocco* (1930) did Sternberg employ slow dissolves for symbolic linkage, and even then and after, he used them more sparingly than did George Stevens, the poet laureate of the slow dissolve after *A Place in the Sun* (1951).

At first glance, Sternberg seems like Visconti, a prettifier of poverty, except that Sternberg, unlike Visconti, never claimed to be realistic. His photography, full of light and shadow, is designed to give visual expression more to feelings than to facts. He is not concerned with social conditions on the docks of New York, or with the class consciousness of his characters. What interests him is the emotional force that impels a man to drag a woman across a crowded room to satisfy his desires, and that emotional force can be expressed in one manner and one manner alone: camera movement. Sternberg wants to drag us along with Miss Compson, and he succeeds, and then he shows us Miss Compson overcoming all this brute force, and we realize that we are back in the realm of Sternberg's feminine mystique. With *The Docks of New York*, Sternberg takes his place with D. W. Griffith and Frank Borzage as one of Hollywood's least condescending chroniclers of little people with big emotions. Sternberg stands alone, however, for his unique virtuousness untainted by sanctimoniousness.

Like *Underworld* before, *Thunderbolt* (1929) is less a gangster film than a gangster fantasy. Its speech is stylized, its noise of gunfire muted. *Thunderbolt* is generally overlooked when film historians evaluate Sternberg's contributions to the early sound film. Although 1929 is cited as the year of Lubitsch's *The Love Parade*, Vidor's *Hallelujah!*, and Mamoulian's *Applause*, Sternberg fails to come in for mention until *The Blue Angel* and *Morocco* launch him into sound and song in 1930. Nonetheless, *Thunderbolt* is, in retrospect, a startling experiment with the kind of asynchronous sound that Eisenstein and Pudovkin were issuing manifestos about at the time.

Sternberg is particularly resourceful in *Thunderbolt* in his use of sound and music for mood effects, and the very unreality of his style seems to justify the unusual density of his sound track. An indication of what really interests him is given in a scene that employs sound contrapuntally. When George Bancroft flees a police raid on a Harlem bar, the guns chatter offscreen but the camera remains focused on and hypnotized by Fay Wray clutching her furs as she sits alone at the table. For Sternberg, it is the woman who counts even during a crucial chase in what is supposed to be a gangster movie.

Throughout his career Sternberg refused to recognize that sound was exercising a naturalistic influence in the cinema. Audiences reacted to speech on the screen more for its prosaic immediacy than for its poetic imaginativeness. The ideal for dialogue was crisp currency rather than contrived cadences, and thus the player's tempo generally prevailed over the director's. (*The Public Enemy* (1931) is speeded up more by James Cagney than William Wellman, just as *City Streets* (1931) is slowed down more by Gary Cooper than Rouben Mamoulian.) Sternberg resisted the heresy of acting autonomy to the very end of his career, and that resistance is very likely one of the reasons his career came to be foreshortened.

The world that he created in *Thunderbolt* (1929) was a private one visually, as well as aurally. When the police question Fay Wray about her hoodlum lover they place her on a raised platform, where she sits in star-like splendor caressing her furs. Subsequent gangster movies fostered a far different impression of the third degree as imagination gave way to observation. Nor is Sternberg unduly concerned with plot likelihood. The frame-up of Richard Arlen on a murder charge is a ridiculously facile contrivance even for Sternberg, and it is obvious that his only interest is in the bar-shadowed spectacle of Arlen and Bancroft in opposite cells on Death Row, two doomed men thinking about the same girl. Once the preposterous machinery is accepted, the plot proceeds to its delirious denouement with force and conviction. Sternberg is not so much concerned with how or why people get where they are as he is with how they act and feel once they get there. There is a fatalistic spell in Sternberg's style, and at its best, the imagery transcends the improbability.

Wray's performance makes a curious contrast to her intense ingenue in Stroheim's *The Wedding March* (1928). Where Stroheim gave her an aura of innocence the better to set off the depravity of the world around her, Sternberg mixed the sugar and spice in more equal proportions. Thus, simultaneously rather than sequentially, the same girl is both a dazzling gangster's moll and a demure bank-teller's sweetheart. *King Kong* (1933) cultists notwithstanding, Wray was never one of the more overwhelming personalities of the American cinema, and her relative pliability makes her a meaningful manifestation of Sternberg's unified vision of Woman as both Magdalene and Madonna, a unity found also in Ophüls and Mizoguchi, but lacking in the divided vision of Ford and Visconti. (It is perhaps fitting that Dietrich's first name is a conscious fusion of Maria and Magdalene.) The family scenes of Wray, Arlen, and Arlen's mother, Eugenie Besserer, are played in a comfortable atmosphere of genial virtue, and although Sternberg disowned some of the film's shaggy-dog animal sentimentality, *Thunderbolt* gives him away once more as a virtuous man obsessed by the spectacle of vice.

The Blue Angel (1930) occupies a paradoxical if pre-eminent place in Sternberg's career. Emil Jannings reportedly requested Sternberg as the director to guide the silent star past the sound barrier, and Sternberg agreed despite a previous clash of temperaments in *The Last Command* (1928). The film was produced simultaneously in German and English language versions for the maximum benefit of the Paramount-UFA combine in world markets, and thus with this one excursion into Europe all the ambiguity of Sternberg's origins reappeared as the "von" in his name came into play once more. After *The Blue Angel* (1930), Sternberg would once again be treated as a European legend corrupted by Hollywood lucre.

The Blue Angel (1930) is undoubtedly the one Sternberg film the director's severest detractors will concede is beyond reproach and ridicule. It is worth noting, if only in passing, that Marlene Dietrich did not appear on American screens in *The Blue Angel* until after the release of *Morocco* (1930), actually her second stint with Sternberg.

Although *The Blue Angel* may have been admired in some quarters for the wrong reasons, the film stands up today as Sternberg's most efficient achievement both emotionally and expressively. There are no hidden corners, no nagging nuances, no puzzling paradoxes. For once

Sternberg is in complete rapport with his audience with a film that is at once his most brutal and least humorous. "In converting the novel into a film which would meet my standards of visual poetry," he recalled, "I introduced the figure of the clown as well as all the episodes and details that led the professor to be confined in a straitjacket."

The ultimately tragic irony of *The Blue Angel* is double-edged in a way Sternberg could not have anticipated when he undertook the project. The rise of Lola Lola and the fall of Professor Immanuel Rath in reel life is paralleled in real life by the rise of Dietrich and the fall of Jannings. When *The Blue Angel* was revived in the early fifties, the critical consensus upheld the public on Dietrich's directness over Jannings's detailedness. The tedious tics of elaborately Expressionistic acting had long since gone out of style, and there was still a tendency to underrate the Jannings performance. In the context of the screen's cuckolds, however, Jannings surpassed in tragic intensity even Raimu and Ake Groneberg. What he lacked in the style and stature of his Czarist general turned Hollywood extra in *The Last Command*, he more than made up for here with the nakedness of his passion.

Sternberg's sense of tragic dignity in the midst of tawdry downfall is best illustrated at that moment when Jannings hurls himself into a room to wreak vengeance on his wife and her strong-man lover. The camera remains at a discreet angle and distance from the doorway through which Dietrich escapes. The men with the straitjacket sweep past her, but we never actually see Jannings subdued by them, only Dietrich looking with ambiguous compassion at the spectacle of subjugation. Jannings has had his moment of masculine beauty on the stage by crowing like a maddened rooster at Dietrich's deception. In that soul-stirring moment Sternberg suggests through Jannings what it is to be a man, and Sternberg will not cheapen that moment by degrading a man who has been defeated.

The Blue Angel achieved its most electrifying effects through careful grading and construction. When Dietrich sings "Falling in Love Again" for the first time, the delivery is playful, flirtatious, and self-consciously seductive. The final rendition is harsher, colder, and remorseless. The difference in delivery is not related to the old stereotype of the seductress finally showing her true colors, but rather to a psychological development in Dietrich's Lola from mere sensual passivity to a more forceful fatalism about the nature of her desires. Lola's first instinct is to accept the Professor's paternal protection and her last is to affirm her natural instincts, not as coquettish expedients but as the very terms by which she expresses her existence. Thus, as the Professor has been defeated by Lola's beauty, Lola has been ennobled by the Professor's jealousy. It is in this complex interplay that *The Blue Angel* transcends the trivial genre of bourgeois male corrupted by bohemian female.

The sordid atmosphere with which Sternberg embellishes his drama emphasizes the grossness to be endured in grappling with desire. On one level of characterization, the Professor is a Lazarus resurrected from a dismal fastidiousness of death-like feelings by sniffing his way through Lola's life-drenched garments, objets d'art less of a symbolist than a fetishist. Fortunately, the niggling necessities of economics intervene between the drab decor and any of its frivolously sado-masochistic implications. It is not Lola who forces the Professor to peddle her gamey photos, but rather the financial realities of the situation. The shabbiness eventually engulfs the sensuality, but it is Lola's strength that she has lived with shabbiness long enough to know how to bend without breaking, and the Professor's tragic misfortune to bend first and still break afterward.

It is not specifically Germany or the German character with which Sternberg is concerned here, but rather the spectacle of a prudent, prudish man blocked off from all means of displaying his manhood except the most animalistic. Sternberg himself has explicitly removed *The Blue Angel* from the socially significant path Siegfried Kracauer traced in *From Caligari to Hitler*. Yet the fact that *The Blue Angel* is coincidentally Sternberg's only German-made film and his most violent work may suggest that he felt the conflict between order and nature would be more violent in a German setting than in any other. This supposition, however, does not justify the judgment that Sternberg's deliberately designed drabness reflects realistically observed details of a decadent society. The world of *The Blue Angel* (1930) is as much a dream world as the world of *The Salvation Hunters* (1925), but the illusion of reality is much stronger in *The Blue Angel* because the characters are less abstract. For the Professor there is only his life with Lola, and deprived of Lola there is nothing but death. There is no life for Lola and the Professor beyond the running time of *The Blue Angel*. There is no world beyond the outer limits of the set. Sternberg's profundity is consequently measured less by the breadth of his vision than by the perfection of his form and by the emotional force of his characters within that form.

How much more painfully poignant, too, is the scene in which Jannings helps Dietrich with her stockings than a similar Jannings maneuver with Lya da Putti in Du Pont's *Variety*, where Jannings as the dupe, pure and simple, is treated with amused contempt. By contrast, Dietrich's air of sensual complicity in *The Blue Angel* redeems the Jannings character from complete ridiculousness. There is in Sternberg a savoring of sensuality for its own sake that is both human and satisfying. The disassociation of Dietrich's sexuality from normal standards of dramatic psychology becomes more apparent in her later collaborations with Sternberg. In *The Blue Angel*, Dietrich is still somewhat submerged in her characterization and as yet not completely possessed by her personality. She straddles a chair as she will later straddle a horse in *The Scarlet Empress*, imperiously, magisterially, fully the measurer of men in the audience, but yet she is also an organic character who finds a certain kind of maturity in marriage. If "serious" criticism of the cinema were not as puritanical as it is, the experiences of Lola and the Professor would seem more pertinent to the hidden world of domestic sexuality than is now the case. The idea that all eroticism is hopelessly exotic has made Sternbergian cinema seem much stranger than it is.

In *Morocco* (1930) one is treated not to a heavy-breathing, Sardou-like safari across the desert sands, but instead to the paradox of characters unostentatiously impulsive, expressing the most delirious feelings with the most delicate gestures. Each bit of bric-a-brac, each shadowed shutter, each fluttering fabric moves the characters inexorably toward an emotional decision they would resist if they could. Yet if they surrender to disastrous, even faintly ridiculous impulses, they do so as undemandingly and as unobtrusively as possible. Here again a plot synopsis cannot possibly suggest the preciseness of Sternberg's sensibility. To say that a woman gives up everything for love is to oversimplify the civilized complexity of an intrigue triangulated by a cafe canary, a Foreign Legionnaire, and a mustachioed man of the world, a plot less written than wired for the star voltage generated by Marlene Dietrich, Gary Cooper, and Adolphe Menjou. On this latter level, *Morocco* is Sternberg's Hollywood film par excellence.

What Sternberg in *Morocco* and many of his more gifted Hollywood and UFA studio colleagues proved is that consistency of style is ultimately more convincing than documentary certification. Sternberg, in particular, creates conviction by motivating his milieu with light and shadow. In a world of illusions, his camera suggests, everything is possible and nothing is necessary. Poetry transcends plausibility when characters are too vividly depicted for common-sense criteria of behavior. Again Sternberg prepares the way for his delirious denouement with intimations of irrationality and perversity. When Dietrich materializes in top hat, white tie, and tails and is thereafter immortalized as the purveyor of pansexuality, the immediacy of impact makes Sternberg's audacity seem more gratuitous than it is. Aside from the lilting vertiginousness of vice involved in Marlene's mock seduction of a flustered female, Sternberg achieves all sorts of economies of expression in Marlene's meaningful masquerade. Her costume, for example, mocks Menjou's. Here is a representation of the European male as seen from the point of view of the woman he seeks to seduce with infinite patience, but yet the effect is not one of pure parody. Neither Sternberg nor Dietrich is completely sure of all the psychological twists. There is always chance, romance, and the inspiration of improvisation. Dietrich fondles the hair of the woman she is going to embarrass with a kiss, but she has none of the complacent confidence Garbo displays in a similar situation in *Queen Christina* (1933). Dietrich's impersonation is an adventure, an act of bravado that subtly alters her conception of herself as a woman, and what begins as self-expression ends as self-sacrifice, perhaps also the path of Sternberg as an artist.

When Dietrich asks Cooper if he wants to buy her apples, this obvious double entendre is rescued from crudity by the genuine awkwardness and uncertainty of the two players. Dietrich here is in the process of discovering herself, and the awakening of self-awareness visibly delights her. Never again will she be so defenselessly charming, so personally accessible to the audience at each instant of her performance. As for Cooper, it is difficult to believe that this natural American landmark ever planted a rose behind his ear or flourished a fan behind which he stole a discreet kiss from Dietrich. That Sternberg brings off such uncharacteristic affectations from Cooper is a mark of the director's fluency in the language of gesture.

In a limited sense, *Morocco* is a reversal of *The Blue Angel* in that a woman is humbled by a man. As in *The Blue Angel*, however, there is genuine interplay between male and female, but even more, there is a perverse interchange of masculine and feminine characteristics. If Gary Cooper's Tom Brown is Sternberg's most narcissistic hero, Dietrich is the supreme lover, male or female, and her final image of setting out into the desert sands, after discarding her spike heels, in search of her man is the most romantic gesture in Sternberg's visual vocabulary. The objection that a woman wearing high heels would not even start off into the desert is nonetheless meaningless. A dream does not require endurance, only the will to act.

Sternberg especially succeeds in reconciling style with feeling in the role of Menjou's La Bessière, part stoic, part sybarite, part satanist. Audiences sometimes laugh at him as a well-mannered masochist, particularly in the dinner scene of Dietrich's renunciation, but Sternberg has never been as close to any character as he is to this elegant expatriate who tries to maintain the decorum of his public posture as he watches the one great obsession of an otherwise ordered life disappear forever into the desert. In Menjou's pained politeness of expression is engraved the age-old tension between the Apollonian and Dionysian demands of art, between pride in restraint and passion in excess, between the formal protocol of self-control and the spontaneous eruptions of self-gratification. In the midst of his fears about Dietrich's decision, Menjou apologizes for not having listened to the babbling of a French general (played by Sternberg's old mentor, Emile Chautard). When Dietrich kisses him goodbye, Menjou clutches her wrist in one last spasmodic reflex of passion, but the other hand retains its poise at his side, the gestures of form and feeling thus conflicting to the very end of the drama. Had Sternberg been nothing more than a delirious decorator, his art would have long since faded into the limbo of fashion, but, like Menjou, Sternberg never loses his composure, and, consequently, he never sacrifices the contemplative aspect of his composition for easy effects of parody and pathos.

If Dietrich lives for love in *The Blue Angel*, and sacrifices for love in *Morocco*, she dies for love in *Dishonored* (1931). "The company decided to title the film *Dishonored*," Sternberg recalls in his autobiography, "disregarding my protest that the lady spy was not dishonored but killed by a firing squad." In its time, the spy genre to which *Dishonored* belongs was taken even less seriously than soap opera. Based on a Sternberg story called "X 27," the film suffers from its episodic structure. Victor McLaglen, a fugitive from the John Ford galaxy, was so far from being the ideal Sternbergian hero that Dietrich was unable to strike the sparks of her previous encounters with Hans Albers in *The Blue Angel* and Gary Cooper in *Morocco*. In Sternberg's conception of direction as total creation, the control of casting is essential to the expression of the director's idea, but such control has seldom been granted to any Hollywood director. In fact, the exigencies of production schedules everywhere in the world impose certain casting limitations on the most personal and most individual of directors, and Sternberg's predilection for reducing performers to mere details of the decor hardly endeared him to all the players he might have wanted to use at one time or another.

Despite or perhaps because of its thematic slightness, *Dishonored* is

Sternberg's funniest film. The grave deliberateness and delicate grace with which Dietrich plies her trade as a prostitute gives the show away from the very beginning. In no other film does Dietrich so self-consciously try on different roles for size and style. Her fantasy prostitute is no less committed than her fake peasant to the service of a love which transcends the trivial issues of politics. "Let me die," she asks, "in the uniform in which I served, not my country, but my countrymen." Let her die, Sternberg implies, for being faithful to her nature as a woman, for matters of sex rather than state. When an idealistic young officer refuses to participate in the execution, Sternberg quickly cuts away from the youth's foolish outburst of chivalric scruples to Dietrich's affirmative application of her last earthly makeup. This inspired injection of the cosmetic into the cosmic makes the audience laugh at the absurdity of female vanity, and there *is* humor in a situation balanced so precariously between gallantry and ghoulishness. It would have been a cheap joke for almost any other director, but for Sternberg it is closer to being an article of faith.

For Sternberg, sex is less the hard currency of politics than its shaping spirit. His political males strut about in their ridiculous costumes, genuflect before idiotic deities of war and country, conduct intrigues on a childish level of deception, and then pass judgment on the only life-giving force in their midst. Yet it is Dietrich who ultimately passes judgment on her judges by choosing to die as a woman without a cause in a picture without a moral. There may be also in the final spectacle of Dietrich's death more than a trace of directorial fantasy and wish fulfillment. To paraphrase Oscar Wilde and mangle his meter, each director kills the thing he loves, the coward does it with a fade, the brave man with a cut!

Sternberg's next film, *An American Tragedy* (1931), was in its time a contretemps of classic proportions. The internationally acclaimed Russian director Sergei Eisenstein had been invited by Paramount to transfer the Theodore Dreiser novel to the screen, but the treatment he prepared was rejected. Sternberg was asked to make the film instead, and Dreiser, who greatly admired Eisenstein's script, protested. After the film was completed, Dreiser sued Paramount to stop its exhibition but lost his case. Sternberg in his autobiography attests to having never seen the Eisenstein script. He also states, "I eliminated the sociological elements, which, in my opinion, were far from being responsible for the dramatic accident with which Dreiser had concerned himself."

Under this creative cloud, *An American Tragedy* has been reviewed less for the film it was than for the film it should have been. Where Eisenstein proposed a deterministic treatment of the subject to absolve Clyde of the crime committed under the pressures of a materialistic society, Sternberg preferred to consider Clyde guilty of an act conditioned by the sexual hypocrisy of his social class.

The one key scene in the film takes place in the factory where Phillips Holmes (Clyde) arranges the seduction of Sylvia Sidney (Roberta). He has forced her to capitulate by threatening never to see her again. She hands him a note when he passes by the assembly line where she is working. Holmes furtively opens the note in a secluded spot where his expression cannot be seen by the factory girls, and a smile of triumph flickers across his normally phlegmatic features. Since he is seen at an objective distance, he is irrevocably guilty at that very moment for his sexual presumption. Sternberg's sympathy for Sidney is expressed mainly through coolness to Holmes, and the modulated morality of the director's sensibility is reaffirmed. What must have moved Sternberg in *An American Tragedy* was the high price Clyde had to pay for self-knowledge. In this respect, at least, Sternberg removes Clyde from under Dreiser's sociological microscope and endows him with feelings with which Sternberg himself can identify. Sternberg seems oblivious to the claims and clamors of Progress and Dynamic Modernism. *An American Tragedy*, like most of his other films, remains focused on the dilemmas of desire which torment men and women eternally.

Sternberg's flair for impulsive fatalism found more play in *Shanghai Express* (1932) than elsewhere. A veritable *Grand Hotel* on rails, the steam-puffing vehicle from Peking to Shanghai conveys Anna May Wong and Warner Oland toward a fateful rendezvous with dishonor and death. But Marlene Dietrich and Clive Brook carry the heart of the drama, and a beating heart it is despite all the gloss of intrigue and illusion. That love can be unconditional is a hard truth for American audiences to accept at any time. Depression audiences found it especially difficult to appreciate Sternberg's Empire of Desire ruled by Dietrich. If, in fact, *Shanghai Express* was successful at all, it was because it was completely misunderstood as a mindless adventure.

This is the movie in which Dietrich tells Clive Brook: "It took more than one man to change my name to Shanghai Lily." Brook reacts to this news with a degree of stoic calm befitting a Noël Coward character of that era, and it becomes difficult for most audiences to take the Dietrich-Brook relationship very seriously from that moment on. Yet Brook's performance is deeply felt despite the stylization of Sternberg's direction of dialogue, and the last ten minutes of the film are as emotionally profound as anything Sternberg ever attempted. Brook's ritualistic delivery of dialogue, bursting out time and again two sentences in one breath, serves as a vocal mask for the pride and passion that seethe beneath the controlled surface.

It is remarkable that Sternberg managed to stylize performances as late into the talkies as he did. Standard aesthetic doctrine of the Anglo-Russian school stipulated that silent films were a director's medium and sound films were an actor's medium. The argument behind this doctrine was that silent directors, or at least some directors, could create performances in the cutting room à la Kuleshov-Mozhukin, but that dialogue created its own rhythms which were determined more by actors than by directors. The weakness of this argument in practice was that only the most obvious acting effects could be created through montage. Chaplin, the greatest screen actor, silent or sound, created his performances mainly through an integral frame with a bare minimum of intercut reaction shots. The subtler silent actors like Conrad Veidt, Richard Barthelmess, Adolphe Menjou, and Ronald Colman functioned best by underplaying the reactions their director's montage prescribed for them. Once the talkies had arrived, cross-cutting for its own sake became a foolish function of Hollywood star cinema. Sternberg's camera style generally eschewed pointless cutting within scenes, and thus anticipated a modern non-montage director like Michelangelo Antonioni.

The plot of *Blonde Venus*, another Sternberg film from 1932, exploits the sordid self-sacrifice which movies of this era prescribed for their female stars. Greta Garbo, Margaret Sullavan, Tallulah Bankhead, Bette Davis, Constance Bennett, Barbara Stanwyck, and Ginger Rogers paraded down Sin Street, usually more sinned against than sinning, but it was all for the sake of home and hearth. *Blonde Venus* could not have been produced after the censors clamped down in 1934, however, and thus quite accidentally a picaresque potboiler of its time acquired a distinctive pre-code flavor.

The picture starts off slowly with an idyllic courtship of Marlene Dietrich by Herbert Marshall, who rather abruptly burdens her with a son, the dimpled Dickie Moore, whom Marlene is called upon to mother solicitously. Dietrich clearly lacks Garbo's sweeter registers of innocence and maternal warmth. Garbo can gravitate between Freddie Bartholomew and Fredric March in *Anna Karenina* (1935) without sacrificing the emotional cohesion of her characterization, but Dietrich becomes unconvincing whenever she is called upon to express emotion directly. Dietrich's irrepressible irony and speculative humor make her a dubious *Hausfrau* indeed, and consequently *Blonde Venus* stumbles along until Dietrich begins dragging her child around Sternberg's Skid Row America from assignation to assignation. Sternberg's style muffles the sordidness here as it has muffled the violence in his gangster films. Dietrich's descent is more Orphic than odious, and her rise is completely redeeming.

Dietrich dominates the action throughout to a degree that reduces dramatic tension. A gangster, to whom Dietrich becomes a mistress, is played by a still callow Cary Grant, whose pairing with Dietrich is not particularly memorable. Yet it is doubtful that Grant and Dietrich would ever have been a satisfactory team. For all its smooth grace, Grant's style is essentially realistic. He is a real person, not next door necessarily, but somewhere. Dietrich is a fantasy figure from nowhere, and no actress can play properly with Grant without some sort of address. By the same token, Grant would only intrude on Dietrich's style of perpetual mystery with the demystifying lurch of his probing personality.

The Scarlet Empress, released in 1934, is Sternberg's most sumptuous exercise in style, a tapestry of tyranny so intricately woven and so luminously lit that audiences and critics of the time were stupefied. The big sleeper of 1934 was Frank Capra's *It Happened One Night*, which titillated Depression audiences with the democratic spectacle of a virile reporter knocking the nonsense out of a hoity-toity society dame. Audiences were thus hardly in the mood to be exhilarated by the ecstatic triumph of Marlene Dietrich's sensuality over the infantile cruelties of Old Russia.

Sternberg's conception of Catherine the Great is audacious in all aspects, and her mate is a pop-eyed Sam Jaffe, whose insanity never lacks for objective and visual correlatives. Jaffe's hi-jinks with a voyeur's brace and bit and a horde of pet Hessians struck some critics as antics more appropriate for Harpo Marx than Russian royalty, and this is more a compliment to Jaffe's performance than these critics realized. *The Scarlet Empress* shattered the decorum which was spreading over the American cinema like a shroud. Its very outrageousness was an index of the repressive reasonableness of most moviemaking of its time, and nothing is more outrageous than Sternberg's decision to be clear rather than coy about the sexual politics of Catherine the Great. But we see Catherine less through Marlene than Marlene through Catherine, and there can be no drama of self-awakening in a personality that provides all the answers before any questions are asked. The sweet curiosity of *Morocco* has now hardened into glacial guile. Romantic adventures have degenerated into erotic escapades; warm passion has frozen into calculating carnality.

Clarence Brown has acknowledged that the table-tracking orgy opening of *Anna Karenina* (1935) was inspired by Sternberg's banquet maneuvers in *The Scarlet Empress*, but a comparison of the two films reveals the difference between routine eclecticism and relentless expressiveness. For Sternberg a table was not merely a table, but a battlefield around which powerful personalities are arrayed, fully armed with metaphorical knives and forks. The continuous visual field provided by his crane enabled him to trace the course of the battle with the steady subtlety which would have been denied to him by mere cross-cutting. Dietrich and Jaffe are more evenly matched than one would expect, and Louise Dresser as the Czarina and John Lodge as the sardonic substitute for the impotent Jaffe fit with curious authoritativeness into the baroque background. Lodge, later governor of Connecticut and ambassador to Spain, never had much of a film career, but even his stiff handsomeness seems to fall into place in *The Scarlet Empress*, where stylish virility is sufficient stimulus for Marlene's mocking eyes.

What probably disturbed socially conscious critics of the thirties even more than Sternberg's ruthless eroticism was a detached view of power as an orgiastic experience. The murder of Jaffe is viewed as an ambiguous act, and Sternberg does not shrink from the pity even a grotesque tyrant evokes at the moment of his downfall. Jaffe dies as he has lived, loathing Dietrich with the last breath in his body. Dietrich's rapturous ride up the palace steps at the head of her Imperial Cavalry is the visual correlative of soaring sexual ecstasy, and land reform would seem to be the last thing on her mind when she finally turns to confront her subjects with the glittering eyes of now utterly unrestrained sensuality. The tyranny of a subhuman superego has been replaced by the tyranny of a superhuman libido. The dimensions of Sternberg's kingdom of the senses are deliriously defined for the first and last time, but Depression audiences could not have cared less.

The Devil Is a Woman (1935) was the last of the Sternberg-Dietrich sagas, and never before had Sternberg seemed as visible as he does here in the saturnine silhouette of Lionel Atwill, a darker side of Menjou's man of the world in *Morocco*. Atwill plays a morose victim of frustration and folly. There is something decidedly downbeat in Dietrich's being flanked by Atwill and Cesar Romero at this stage of her career, and the film's reputation for campiness can be attributed largely to this secondary casting. Atwill has been too frequently identified with the mad scientist (from Atwill to Zucco) repertory, while Romero has been considered a lightweight personality throughout his career, though it is hard to see how Joel McCrea, for whom Romero was a last-minute replacement, would have been much of an improvement. Yet if Atwill and Romero do not attain the high level of Brook, Bancroft, Jannings, Menjou, and Cooper, they are far from being inadequate for Sternberg's ironies. They play fools, but not foolishly. They are the last lovers Sternberg has postulated for Dietrich's screen incarnation, and their apparent absurdity only marks the death of desire.

The lack of overt sexual commitment on the part of Dietrich's "Concha" may be attributed to the intentional sadism of the Pierre Louys character or the intransigence of the Hays Office or both. Sternberg's original title, *Caprice Espagnol,* may have originally seemed more relevant to the final film than *The Devil Is a Woman,* but there is no gainsaying Dietrich's devilishness, particularly when she tells one of her admirers, "If you really loved me, you would have killed yourself."

Despite the sumptuousness of its surface, *The Devil Is a Woman* was Sternberg's coldest film. Its art is bone dry; its feelings parched in a desert of despair. Even the film's silliness around the edges is measured precisely, and nothing is sillier than the occasional stabs at social consciousness, starting with a tobacco factory right out of *Carmen.* More to the point, a motif of masks in the opening carnival sequence is carried through all of Dietrich's maddening deceptions, but Atwill persists in his passion because, under the implied intelligence and urbanity of his mask, he is motivated by his own lecherous designs, and the whole narration is revealed as dishonest in its didactic intention. Every acquisitively cluttered, riotously disordered frame in which Atwill appears with Dietrich contributes to the inner rage and frustration of his apparently impassive characterization. This is how, ideally, Sternberg directed his players: not by tampering with their faces to provide self-explanatory grimaces, but by creating a visual context in which the most unobtrusive acting effects become eloquently expressive. Sternberg's decor is then not the meaningless background of the drama, but its very subject, peering through nets, veils, screens, shutters, bars, cages, mists, flowers, and fabrics to tantalize the male with fantasies of the female. Yet far from exaggerating his effects, Sternberg has perhaps calculated too closely. Dietrich, particularly, has been polished to an inhuman perfection beyond the accidental beauties of impulse and instinct. Her beauty is now so uninflected by dramatic development that even her cruelties are trivial.

Sternberg did not know it at the time, but his sun was setting, and it was never really to rise again. There were momentary spasms in *Crime and Punishment, The Shanghai Gesture*, and even *Claudius*, but for the rest, the divorce between manner and meaning became complete in *The Devil Is a Woman* and incontestable until the final confessional of *Anatahan*. *Crime and Punishment* (1935) was a relatively impersonal assignment for the director. He inherited script, cast, and miscast with his two-picture Columbia contract, and he proceeded to demonstrate his efficiency and frugality as a studio director. Yet even under the most ideal conditions imaginable Sternberg would have been singularly miscast as a Dostoevskian director. For one thing, his dominant gestures are more physical than metaphysical; for another, he has no genuine grasp of evil and criminality as facts of life and facets of character. Instead Sternberg displays his own stylish bravado through the Napoleonic and Nietzschean poses of Peter Lorre's Raskolnikov. The director then counters this mock megalomania with Edward Arnold's Inspector Porfiry, a father figure too civilized to be bothered by youthful impetuosity and too mature not to care about its emotional consequences.

"God must have been very angry with me when I attempted to make *Claudius*," was Sternberg's summation of his difficulties in a notoriously ill-fated venture. A BBC documentary on the production confirms the clashes of temperament involved between Sternberg and Charles Laughton, but the two reels of footage shot for *Claudius* bear out Sternberg's prognosis: "That part of the film which was completed is on record as proof that in spite of his [Laughton's] antics it might have been a memorable film." It might indeed. *Claudius* contained all the thematic and stylistic potentialities for a genuinely great film. The theme of virtue finding its own reward before yielding to the folly of megalomania is one very close to Sternberg, and the filmed scene of Laughton groveling before Emlyn Williams's hysterical Caligula was directed with a profound compassion for Claudius and an incisive insight into the paradox that man must sink completely into the mud of his limitations before he can rise to his aspirations. When Merle Oberon was seriously injured in an automobile accident, the production was permanently shelved. All the participants agree, however, that Miss Oberon's accident was more a pretext than the reason for calling a halt. Oberon aside, of course, the big loser was Sternberg. *Claudius* turned out to be a lost chance to recoup all his former reputation.

After other aborted projects, Sternberg landed at MGM for *Sergeant Madden* (1939), a film of more sociological than aesthetic interest despite Sternberg's visually striking direction. His distinctive framing and filters give the movie a UFA look, and at times one can almost see the ghost of Jannings in Wallace Beery's unusually restrained performance. The plot was obnoxiously conformist in the mode of the police propaganda of the time and too unambiguous for Sternberg's subtlety to find expression. Beery's sanctimonious Sergeant Madden has two sons, one natural and one adopted, and naturally it is the natural son who goes bad after being framed as a "killer cop" by Marc Lawrence's engagingly evil gangster. Beery finally goes after his bad son himself, but the prodigal atones for his misdeeds and the trouble he has caused his father, brother, wife, and baby son by letting himself be shot by the law. The moral: society transcends family.

The Shanghai Gesture (1941), a marvelous joke on the *Zeitgeist* of the period, ushered Sternberg into the forties on a note of false promise. At a time when screen censorship was so rigid that films of the early thirties like *Arrowsmith* (1931) and *A Farewell to Arms* (1932) were re-issued only after extensive scissoring for salacity, *The Shanghai Gesture* had no ostensible subject except the decadence and depravity of a collection of people seemingly left behind by history and *The Shanghai Express*. Of course, all the depravity could not be spelled out exactly. "Mother" Goddam's joy house becomes "Mother" Gin Sling's gambling casino, and it now is too late for anyone to say, "It took more than one man to change my name to Shanghai Lily." Nor is it possible for characters to inhale opium as in the bygone days of Richard Barthelmess's *Broken Blossoms* (1919) and potent poppy seeds. Gene Tierney's name in *The Shanghai Gesture* is Poppy, but that is the only clue to her degradation the censors will permit. It is strange to remember that all narcotics were legal in America until 1924, and that the narcotics laws intersect film history at a point where a Victorian director like Griffith can be more explicit about the subject than a Baudelairean director like Sternberg.

Sternberg had been invited by Arnold Pressburger to bring John Colton's vintage stage shocker to the screen. Sternberg added the two crucial characters of Doctor Omar and Phyllis Brooks's Dixie Pomeroy to the denizens of his den of iniquity. Omar, "Doctor of Nothing," is an inspired comic creation, a languid sybarite full of fearfully transparent banalities, more impressive to the worldly sophisticates at the card tables than to a Brooklyn chorus girl like Dixie Pomeroy. The wonderful thing about Omar is that he knows how ridiculous he is, and yet he knows he has enough style to impose his personality in a setting so devoid of will and purpose. As Sternberg guided Victor Mature through his performance—the director reclining in a cot as part of his convalescence—was it possible that he recognized something of himself in Omar? Sternberg had always been kidded about his "von" and his alleged pants-pressing past in Brooklyn, and there was undoubtedly a conflict in his own personality between Austria and America, between pretense and pragmatism. The wonderful thing about Sternberg is that he can see the humor in the conflict and render it artistically. By the time of *The Shanghai Gesture* Sternberg is also far enough away from the conflict to see the humor of his own masquerade, and Omar is his comic testament, his fey Falstaff, as the voice in *Anatahan* is his unseen Lear.

Phyllis Brooks, one of those miraculously minor figures who define an era better than its major figures, is an obvious counterpoint to the exotically beautiful Gene Tierney, a buck-toothed beauty who made Broadway drama critics George Jean Nathan and Richard Watts lose their heads, but who was transformed by Sternberg into a vaguely Eurasian standard of sophistication for the forties. This is the first time that Sternberg's camera has witnessed the complete disintegration of a female mystique, and he may have added the comedy presences of Omar and Dixie as a means of cushioning the shock. What happens to a woman when she loses her style and mystery is not a pleasant thing to watch, especially for Sternberg. What Tierney's Poppy lacks here so crucially is not so much character as humor, intelligence, and an appreciation of the absurd. Passion makes her oblivious to parody, and she fails to notice Omar's ridiculously furtive gesture in concealing their kiss. To emphasize the ridiculousness, Sternberg shoots Mature's gesture from the far side so that Mature is framing rather than concealing the kiss as far as the movie audience is concerned. This apparently gratuitous gesture might be compared with Cooper's use of the fan to conceal his kissing Dietrich from the movie audience, a gesture Sternberg photographed from the near side so as to indicate that there was something genuine to conceal in the Dietrich-Cooper relationship. It follows with poetic logic that the ridiculousness of the Tierney-Mature relationship is revealed rather than concealed.

The rest of the plot is entrusted to Walter Huston and Ona Munson as old lovers confronting each other as total strangers, their enmity rising out of the ashes of an ancient love which we must take less on faith than fantasy. Yet real pastness is meaningless in a languorously stylized world in which all sense of time is negated by the metaphorical circle of the roulette wheel cybernetically descended from the dredge of *The Salvation Hunters*, the assembly line of *An American Tragedy*, and the banquet tables of *The Scarlet Empress*. Nevertheless, the civilized graces persist even in the midst of all this futility, and characters continue to consider their fates with the utmost seriousness.

Mother Gin Sling prepares for her last dinner by acquiring wax replicas of her guests. By arranging these replicas at the table, she creates the illusion of manipulating their destinies. Similarly, Sternberg's characters are generally only replicas of real people, but replicas endowed with real feelings, usually Sternberg's. Some of the minor characters like John Abbott's simpering escort for Gene Tierney may be overly caricatured. William Powell's revolutionary turned director in *The Last Command* (1928) and Ullrich Haupt's doomed cuckold in *Morocco* (1930) may be psychologically obscure. Yet, for the most part, Sternberg's characters derived their emotional resonance not from the specifications of the scenario but from a curious intensity of expression in the style of Sternberg's direction.

Certainly the vibrant feelings of *The Shanghai Gesture* cannot be attributed to John Colton's stage shocker, or even to Jules Furthman's flair for expressively epigrammatic dialogue. The weary grown-ups—Walter Huston, Ona Munson, Albert Basserman, Maria Ouspenskaya—look past their mature adolescence—Victor Mature and Phyllis Brooks—to their spoiled childhood incarnated in Gene Tierney, who makes her dramatic entrance at the last of Mother Gin Sling's dinners through the kind of meaningful memory filter that the remade Kim Novak enters for James Stewart's inspection in *Vertigo* (1958). Huston looks at his disheveled daughter as Sternberg himself might look at his own disordered life. From *The Salvation Hunters* (1925) to *Anatahan* (1953), Sternberg's recurring theme is self-awakening and we have been fortunate in having had directors like Sternberg and Renoir and Dreyer and Ford and Chaplin and Welles who could show us so expressively on film how an artist can record his entire life on a moving strip of celluloid.

What is most felicitous in *The Shanghai Gesture* and least appreciated in Sternberg's films generally is the sheer beauty and meaningful grace of physical gestures and movements—the way his players walk, the way they grasp objects and caress fabrics, the way they light cigarettes and exhale the smoke through their flared nostrils, and the way they eat and drink. In the realm of physical expressiveness, Sternberg is supreme.

Needless to say, this world of gesture and movement is not lacking in Freudian overtones, and subsequent analyses by such neo-Freudian critics as Lo Duca, Raymond Durgnat, and O. O. Green have helped clear away some cobwebs from the traditional critiques of Sternberg. Unfortunately, such analyses seem to operate as validly with the unconscious and the accidental as with the conscious and the intentional. If *The Shanghai Gesture* abounds with symbols and gestures of impotence, castration, onanism, and transvestism, so do *King Kong* (1933), *Tarzan the Ape Man* (1932), *Frankenstein* (1931), and *Freaks* (1932). Yet these latter films can hardly be said to represent the conscious art of *The Shanghai Gesture*, where all the gestures and movements of human bodies express the rapture of an artist's soul.

ALFRED HITCHCOCK (1899–1980)

Alfred Hitchcock was officially a British director through the thirties, but he became very prominent in the United States after *The Thirty-nine Steps* came out in 1935. *The Lady Vanishes* consolidated his American reputation in 1938, and Hollywood beckoned more forcefully thereafter. For many years Hitchcock was identified almost exclusively with the more obvious virtues of *The Thirty-nine Steps* and *The Lady Vanishes*: lightness, grace, guile, suspense, humor, movement. Americans attributed many of these virtues to the British gift for understatement. His films were considered a change-of-pace from the high-powered Hollywood models. This was the cross he had to bear through the forties and fifties, when he turned out high-powered Hollywood models of his own, beginning with the gothic romance of *Rebecca* (1940).

His reputation in England was somewhat more rounded through the thirties because critics and audiences there were more aware of the touches of realistic observation in his work. His was considered a relatively humble talent on the world scene, but authentically English-sparrow all the same. The French metaphysicians had not yet had at him, and there was as yet remarkably little formal and moral analysis of his work. He was considered both too minor and too pleasurable to have any depth. In England, however, he was known for a great many more films than had been released in the United States. *The Lodger* (1926) (with Ivor Novello falsely suspected to be Jack the Ripper) and *The Farmer's Wife* (1928) were well received in the silent era. Indeed, *The Farmer's Wife* reveals Hitchcock's flair for satiric pantomime much as Dreyer's *Master of the House* (1925) reveals the dour Dane's gift for warm, life-giving family comedy with a feminist slant.

It was with *Blackmail* in 1929, however, that Hitchcock was first widely acknowledged as a textbook director and innovator. While Eisenstein, Pudovkin, and Alexandrov were issuing manifestoes about the future of montage in the sound film, Hitchcock blithely demonstrated sound montage (and even psychological sound "close-ups" of key words). Still, Hitchcock's career in the early thirties was remarkably bumpy in an industry plagued by Hollywood-induced "quota-quickies," pathetic little British movies turned out solely to satisfy British protectionist laws based on the percentage of American and native films to be shown on British screens.

For his part, Hitchcock followed *Blackmail* the next year with a stage-bound rendering of Sean O'Casey's *Juno and the Paycock* (1930). The acting of the Abbey Players—Sara Allgood, Edward Chapman, Marie O'Neill, Sidney Morgan, *et al.*—was faithfully preserved on film, but the ending was sentimentalized simply by concluding with Juno in her grief rather than with the Paycock in his cups. It is possible that Hitchcock and Alma Reville, his wife and scenarist, decided that nothing could follow Juno's "Hail Mary, Mother of God" into the ears of movie audiences. It is possible also that O'Casey's bitter irony about the Irish people was more than the producers could bear. By and large, however, *Juno and the Paycock* falls between two stools in that there are even fewer drama buffs who know the movie than there are film buffs who know the play. Furthermore, the official critical line through the thirties was that play adaptations were automatically suspected of betraying the unique genius of the cinema. As canned theater goes, however, *Juno and the Paycock* is a reasonably entertaining transcription, and it was certainly not the last play Hitchcock would transfer to the screen. But it is the only Hitchcock movie of which one can say that there is absolutely nothing of Hitchcock in it.

As if swinging on a wild pendulum, from the stasis of *Juno and the Paycock* Hitchcock pulled out all the stylization stops in his next project, *Murder*, also of that relatively primitive year of 1930. In this curiously experimental mystery thriller, Hitchcock combined the morbid psychology of the German cinema with the associational montage of the Russians. Now that Hitchcock's career has ended, it is much easier to understand what he was getting at in the beginning with both *Murder* and *Blackmail*. In terms of the conventions of that period, the villains in both films are extraordinarily sympathetic, the heroines are extraordinarily vapid, and the heroes extraordinarily pompous and callous. Indeed, Hitchcock seemed to have gone out of his way to undermine the damsel-in-distress expectations of both plots by shifting sympathy to vividly life-like villains—the bumptious blackmailer in *Blackmail* and the tortured transvestite in *Murder*. The focus of the suspense shifts similarly from the ultimate fate of the ingenue to the ultimate fall (literal and figurative) of the man responsible for her plight. The girl in *Blackmail* is even guilty of murder (albeit in defense of her somewhat teasing honor), and thus the plot is left off-balance morally. By contrast, the girl in *Murder* seems almost masochistically inclined to suffer for a crime she has not committed. Her rescuer is a smug, upper-class dilettante with the time and resources to play God. But all the characters in *Murder* are distanced by a variety of stylized effects ranging from mental montage to a bogus play within a play. Hitchcock's cutting is jaggedly elliptical, his staging frenzied to the point of absurdism. Role-playing runs rampant as people of the theater continue their impersonations off-stage with fatal results. Claude Chabrol's conception of Hitchcock as one of the greatest inventors of forms in the history of the cinema makes more sense if one re-examines a relatively obscure early talkie like *Murder* in the light of later aesthetic theories. What was thus merely disquieting in 1929 and 1930 became stylistically psychoanalytical in the second-guess seventies and eighties—almost too much so. Both *Blackmail* and *Murder* were mere blueprints for the great Hitchcock films to follow. The forms were already taking shape, but the feelings had not yet matured.

A mark of Hitchcock's abstractness in *Murder* was his addiction to montage as a mental language. Hence, Herbert Marshall's amateur sleuth thinks of the hot meal he is missing at home in choosing to stay at a dingy hotel, and Hitchcock cuts to a spatially abstract shot of roast duckling purely as a mental expression of a gourmet's grief. This kind of abstract imagery had become increasingly rare in the talkies. One recalls Mamoulian's image of Miriam Hopkins's sexually provocative legs swinging in Fredric March's head as he affects the transition between Dr. Jekyll and Mr. Hyde. But this was mere German superimposition in the mental images of Freud rather than Russian dialectical montage in the materialist images of Marx. And even in the Russian school there was a sharp division between the psychological emphasis of the Kuleshov-Pudovkin school and the ideological emphasis of the Vertov-Eisenstein school. Hitchcock himself leaned more to the Germans than to the Russians, and more to Kuleshov-Pudovkin than to Vertov-Eisenstein. But as time went on, Hitchcock became less abstract in his imagery and less mental in his montage in favor of his intricate juxtaposition of objects and glances within a scene. Still, there are traces of this earlier predilection in such later Hitchcock films as the 1934 *The Man Who Knew*

Too Much (the shot of a train speeding into a station as the expression of Edna Best's shock over the kidnapping of her daughter) and the 1945 *Spellbound* (the much criticized shot of doors opening in Ingrid Bergman's head as she kisses Gregory Peck). The problem in both instances is that there is no level of reality for the train or the doors, and thus the images are less resonant than, say, the image of cars being lifted from a swamp superimposed on Tony Perkins's skull in *Psycho* (1960) as he utters the darkly ironic line: "I wouldn't hurt a fly."

Hitchcock's next four films did little to enhance his reputation. *The Skin Game* (1931) was a straightforward adaptation of John Galsworthy's didactic play, but class warfare was not exactly Hitchcock's cup of tea. Peter Bogdanovich has singled out the tense auction scene as the only "cinematic" interlude in the proscenium-like proceedings, but such occasions are usually showpieces anyway (*vide* Antonioni's scintillating stock-market-panic episodes in the otherwise languid *L'Eclisse* (1962)). *Rich and Strange* (1932) (released in America as *East of Shanghai*) was a picaresque comedy in which Hitchcock indulged certain surreal tendencies toward the tall story. The very loose, illogical plot gave Hitchcock room for his comic touches with Britons absurdly adrift on the waves. If *Rich and Strange* (1932) was charmingly unconventional in its devil-may-care disdain for genre expectations, *Number Seventeen* that same year was charmingly conventional in its tongue-in-cheek adherence to the crook melodrama complete with house-of-mystery (Number Seventeen itself) and the climactic chase (with miniature models of the train and car involved adding a visually quaint reminder of period illusionism).

In Hitchcock's own view he touched rock bottom in 1933 with *Waltzes from Vienna* (released in America as *Strauss's Great Waltz* in 1935). This particular Hitchcock film was out of circulation for many years after its release, and it didn't seem to "fit" Hitchcock in any particular way. Its genre was that of Lubitsch and Clair, not that of the supposed "Master of Suspense." Hitchcock also had particularly humiliating memories of a period in his career when the company for which he was working couldn't afford to buy the rights to the songs in the musical it had purchased. (Fortunately, Strauss's waltzes were in the public domain.) Still, *Waltzes from Vienna* is much more interesting than its reputation would indicate. The deadly father-son rivalry between Johann Strauss the elder (Edmund Gwenn) and Johann Strauss the younger (Esmond Knight) revealed a dramatic dimension seldom encountered in operettas set in the Vienna Woods. The musical numbers are edited expertly enough to bear comparison with the acknowledged masters in the field, but the morbid undertones are Hitchcock's alone. An invaluable film for the specialists in the meanings of Hitchcock's mise-en-scène; a relatively routine eye-opener for the skeptics.

The Hitchcock legend for legerdemain thus must wait until 1934 and *The Man Who Knew Too Much*, the first of Hitchcock's fully realized thrillers. The cast alone suggests an ascension to the major leagues of moviemaking. Leslie Banks, Peter Lorre, Edna Best, Pierre Fresnay, and the child actress Nova Pilbeam introduce a more Continental and less insular tone to Hitchcock's work. The sharp-eyed Londoner now seems to have an insight into world affairs. He is not to deal explicitly with the rise of fascism until well after the outbreak of World War II, but there is already an intimation in *The Man Who Knew Too Much* of a frightening new world of political fanaticism. Peter Lorre in transit from Fritz Lang's *M* to Josef von Sternberg's Raskolnikov embodies much of the charming contrast of a European sensibility in conflict with the stolid British passion for decorum. Hitchcock was inspired by Lorre's playful temperament to give him additional dabs of color both in *The Man Who Knew Too Much* (1934) and in *Secret Agent* (1936).

The bare bones of the plot do not begin to convey the psychological complexities of the characters. The daughter (Nova Pilbeam) of a British couple (Leslie Banks and Edna Best) traveling in Switzerland is kidnapped after the husband acquires some cryptic information on an assassination plot from a dying secret agent (Pierre Fresnay) of a foreign power. After many adventures, the plot is thwarted, and the daughter rescued. But not before a big shootout between the police and a band of terrorists led by Peter Lorre ends in the death of most of the terrorists and a few policemen. The action is deliberately disjointed as it hops from a Swiss chalet to a London tabernacle to the Albert Hall with just the slightest rhyme or reason. Especially rhyme. Hitchcock sets up emotional echoes with a frivolous skeet-shooting contest at the beginning of the movie and a life-and-death rematch of sorts at the end. Also, Pierre Fresnay is introduced to the audience with a fear-stricken expression on his face as he skis downhill, but the upshot of this expression is a minor collision on the course. Later he is dancing, a blissful smile on his face. A crack in the glass of the windowpane, a muffled bang on the soundtrack barely audible above the music, and Fresnay slowly slumps to the floor, his smile glazed into a death mask. His earlier fear on the ski trail had been premature but prophetic. Death generally finds Hitchcock's characters in the wrong mood and the wrong costume.

The *pièce de résistance* of the film is the now famous Albert Hall scene in which Edna Best sits enigmatically in the middle of a visualized moral dilemma, the life of her daughter weighing in the balance against the life of a foreign statesman, and the music playing on relentlessly to its preordained climax, with an assassin's shot to be muffled by this crash of cymbals. As the camera closes in on her inscrutable features, moral responsibility is transferred to the audience. But not entirely. Her feelings are complicated by regret and remorse. Her daughter has always been much closer to her father than to her. At the chalet the daughter dances with her father while her mother is dancing coquettishly with one of her admirers. (It is significant that in the 1956 remake of *The Man Who Knew Too Much* the daughter has been switched to a son who is much closer to his mother than to his father.) Indeed, in charting the transition of Hitchcock from Britain to America, one may note the pattern of fathers and daughters in Britain and that of mothers and sons in America. Thus, amid the genre conventions of guns and chases there lurks a lucidly realized world of family feelings.

The Thirty-nine Steps was so popular and so fashionable a film in its own time that there has been a tendency to underestimate it ever since. Part of the problem may be the curious resistance to Robert Donat as a Hitchcock hero. Donat's reputation did not travel well through the decades. Ill health prevented him from making enough movies to become a cult favorite, and his theatrical career never had the classical ring of Laurence Olivier's, Ralph Richardson's, John Gielgud's and Michael Redgrave's. He seemed too much the romantic leading man, though his Mr. Chips is as impressive a job of aging from within as Redgrave's old crock in *The Browning Version*. If anything, Donat's subtle charm was less lethargic than Leslie Howard's, and, as a Hitchcockian hero, he was considerably less indolent than John Gielgud in *The Secret Agent* (1936) and Michael Redgrave in *The Lady Vanishes* (1938). Donat's roles ranged across the anguished adulterer in *The Private Life of Henry VIII* (1933), the swashbuckler of *The Count of Monte Cristo* (1934), the sensitive idealist of *The Citadel* (1938), the turned worm in *Vacation from Marriage* (1945), the regenerated minister in *Lease of Life* (1954), and finally the dying Chinese mandarin in *The Inn of the Sixth Happiness* (1958), during which film Donat himself was dying. Even in Donat's supposedly stock roles, his touch was delicate, his humor quietly self-deprecating. Yet, his eyes could generate an electrifying intensity of feeling. For *The Thirty-nine Steps* Donat provided an indispensable blend of humor and urgency as he became the first of the quintessentially Hitchcockian heroes—the falsely accused innocent plunged into a nightmare of paranoia by being forced to flee from both the law and the lawless. Just when he thought he had found sanctuary in a crofter's cottage, he faced the peril of a murderously jealous husband (John Laurie), who has misunderstood the solicitude of his wife (Peggy Ashcroft) for a total stranger. Then the threat of betrayal, pursuit, escape, a Bible in a stolen overcoat blunting the deadly path of a bullet.

By the way the sequence was edited, Hitchcock enables us to see how the husband has misunderstood a gesture of kindness on his wife's part as a gesture of adulterous complicity. Our feelings of superiority toward the husband are complicated somewhat by our unconscious desire to maintain the deception so as to keep the hero from being turned over to the police. We are thus confronted with a situation when it is in our best interest not to have the truth told. What was unusual was that Hitchcock shifted the narrative point of view to a peripheral character, and an unsympathetic one at that.

If Donat was the first distinctively Hitchcockian hero, Madeleine Carroll was the first of the recognizably Hitchcockian blonde-bitch heroines. Critics and audiences of 1935 were regaled by the fact that Hitch had gone Frank Capra one better not only by sending a man and a woman on a bickering cross-country odyssey in the manner of Clark Cable and Claudette Colbert in *It Happened One Night* (1934), but by capping the jest in having Donat and Carroll handcuffed to each other. By 1935 critics and aesthetes were still concerned with the dangers the talkies posed for kinetic cinema. The "road" genre of that epoch therefore seemed to be one of the solutions to the problem of a stultifying stasis in the talk-ridden salon. Movies like *It Happened One Night* and *The Thirty-nine Steps* were thus seen as joyously liberated from the confines of canned theater as they took their action outdoors.

The Thirty-nine Steps, however, was not as sunny as *It Happened One Night*. There were too many corpses in closets, too much unresolved mystery, too much unassuaged guilt. Through the thirties and the forties, a 39 Steps Club met regularly to discuss the tantalizing ambiguities of the movie. James Thurber was one of the charter members. One of the issues up for repeated discussion was the exact motivation of Mr. Memory, the vaudeville performer, who ultimately was the key to the whole riddle of the spy ring's modus operandi. Why does Mr. Memory give the show away to Donat and the police? Is it his conditioned reflex as a performing memory expert or simply mental fatigue induced by his overloaded circuits? Hitchcock's music-hall coup at the end of *The Thirty-nine Steps* may have been influenced by the laughing clown intent on suicide ending of Fritz Lang's *Spione* (1928), just as Hitchcock's coup with the diving-to-his-death circus transvestite in *Murder* (1930) may owe something to E. A. Dupont's *Variety* and Josef von Sternberg's *The Blue Angel*. But the moral uneasiness at the end of all Hitchcock films is profoundly original. Unfortunately, a superficial view of *The Thirty-nine Steps* created a lasting impression of Hitchcock as all flair and flippancy with nothing more substantial underneath.

Yet, when Godfrey Tearle's villain departs on his last espionage mission, Hitchcock shows this unscrupulous man saying goodbye to his wife and daughter in a curiously tender and prolonged scene in terms of the traditions of the genre. The daughter, particularly, with her plain face and inhibiting spectacles, seems curiously dependent upon her doomed father. Indeed, this solemnly clinging girl bears a strong resemblance to Hitchcock's own daughter, Pat, whom we will encounter later in *Strangers on a Train* (1951) and *Psycho* (1960). *The Thirty-nine Steps* thus early on demonstrates in some detail Hitchcock's legerdemain in juggling our sympathies.

Hitchcock's next two films have created a great deal of confusion about their literary sources. *The Secret Agent* (1936) was based on Somerset Maugham's spy novel *Ashenden* whereas *Sabotage* (1937) was based on Joseph Conrad's novel of political terrorism *The Secret Agent*. Both films were relatively unsuccessful with the public because they lacked an acceptable protagonist. John Gielgud's Ashenden was a passive, reluctant hero who drifted through his role with no clear conviction. Madeleine Carroll is on hand not to doubt and bedevil Gielgud's Ashenden as she doubted and bedeviled Donat's Hannay in *The Thirty-nine Steps*, but rather to stiffen his spine with ruthless resolve, to turn a gentle, conscience-ridden man into an implacable murderer. Gielgud's Ashenden is made to seem even more unassuming and undecisive by being flanked by Robert Young's brash American lover-boy type (a surprise cover for a German agent) and Peter Lorre's amorous Mexican Lothario working with brutal dispatch on Ashenden's side. The whole point of the movie seems to be how richly and rewardingly it can be sidetracked from its original purpose. The plot is in perpetual motion to futility as Hitchcock emphasizes the confusion rather than the efficiency of World War I espionage operations. As the wrong man is being murdered on a mountaintop by Lorre, the victim's dog howls with pain and grief behind a locked door in the chalet. Gielgud and Carroll sit by helplessly, and Young transforms himself from Yank to Hun. The privileged moments are all incidental to the ultimate intrigue—a box of chocolates, a secret message on an assembly line, a dead man's head pressing an eerie note on a church organ, a convenient train wreck to sort out the active sinners from the not-so-innocent bystanders. Despite the relative fastidiousness of its two leads, *The Secret Agent* remains one of Hitchcock's most engaging films from his British period.

Of *Sabotage* (1936), by contrast, Claude Chabrol and Eric Rohmer have written that it is the favorite Hitchcock film for people who do not otherwise like Hitchcock. Whatever else it is, it is certainly Hitchcock's bleakest and most Germanic film. Its most extraordinarily suspenseful sequence involves a dim-witted delivery boy who is carrying a time bomb (embedded in a can of film) through the city of London. As various clocks tick away closer and closer to the time for which the explosion is set, the audience's normal, conventional expectation is to anticipate the release of a last-minute or last-second rescue. Instead, the bomb goes off in a crowded bus just as the doomed boy is petting an old lady's dog. Boom! The bus blows up. C. A. Lejeune, the very influential film critic of the *London Observer*, warned Hitchcock that he must never again do anything like that. And seemingly Hitchcock agreed with her. What is most interesting in Lejeune's dictum is that she never once considers the fact that Hitchcock is being faithful to Conrad in letting the explosion take place at the cost of the boy's life. By 1936 Hitchcock had become such a law unto himself that he was considered empowered to tamper with the most sacred plots in the interest of moviegoer sensibilities.

Curiously, *Sabotage* is less funny and less sardonic about the grubby world of political terrorists than is the Conrad novel. Hitchcock seems to have concentrated less on characters than on backgrounds—the aquarium where the saboteurs confer (a setting of predatory men against predatory fish which anticipated Orson Welles's staging of his scenes with Rita Hayworth in *Lady from Shanghai* against a full tank of killer sharks); the movie house in which Homolka and Sidney work in ironic counterpoint to their dismal "real" life, and the background screening of Walt Disney's *Who Killed Cock Robin?*, which plays such a prominent part in motivating the killing of Homolka.

Young and Innocent (1937) is one of Hitchcock's strangest and most entertaining thirties films. On the surface it is a murder melodrama in which an innocent man escapes from custody to find the real murderer to whom we have all been introduced at the beginning as a man with twitching eyes. The plot is comically contrived to fashion a fairy tale involving a young girl (Nova Pilbeam) who finds herself in conflict with her constable father (Percy Marmont) when she decides to assist the fugitive to escape. Derrick de Marney as the fugitive is not innocent in every sense. He has been something of a gigolo and an opportunist in the past, and he poses a genuine sexual threat to the young virgin who befriends him. Indeed, he is too callow and self-satisfied a character to win the sympathy of the audience to any great degree. He has none of the niceness of Donat in *The Thirty-nine Steps* or of Michael Redgrave in *The Lady Vanishes*. But if *Young and Innocent* is not as exciting as Hitchcock's more grown-up thrillers, it is more playful in its treatment of its sexual fantasies. Hitchcock is beginning to move closer to the gothic romances of *Jamaica Inn* and *Rebecca*, and there is a suggestion in the kittenish strength of Miss Pilbeam of the forthcoming performances of Maureen O'Hara and Joan Fontaine. Indeed, Pilbeam was the original choice to play the ingenue lead in *Rebecca*.

Young and Innocent contains one of the most spectacular sequences in all of Hitchcock. There is a crowded dance floor. Nova Pilbeam and a helpful hobo (Edward Rigby) are looking around the room anxiously to see if they can spot the murderer. The camera crane drifts (in those gloriously spatial days before the zoom) to close in on the band all in blackface, and then in on the drummer, all the way in to his twitching eyes! From that moment on, the point of view shifts back and forth between the girl and the murderer until the denouement. In the film Hitchcock also does wondrous things with a children's game of blindman's buff. Only the flimsy and underdeveloped surface plot remains a handicap to the movie as a whole.

The Lady Vanishes (1938) was the last great success from Hitchcock's British period. It was not the first of the "train" pictures. *Shanghai Express* (1932), *The China Express* (1929), *The Rome Express* (1932), and *The General Died at Dawn* (1935) all preceded it, not to mention Buster Keaton's *The General* (1927) and Abel Gance's *La Roue* (1923). What makes *The Lady Vanishes* relatively unique is Hitchcock's ability to convey the lurch and snap of the rails from the inside of the train. In other respects, however, *The Lady Vanishes* is one of Hitchcock's most superficial thrillers. Margaret Lockwood, a comely, straightforward actress, is caught in a prolonged paranoid situation in which no one will believe her story of an old woman's disappearance. The details of the plot are ingenious, but after a time the ingenuity becomes an end in itself so as to continue spinning the intrigue. Michael Redgrave has his comic moments as a whimsical gentleman to the rescue, but Paul Lukas plays a very standard villain for Hitchcock. Yet, what makes the movie superficial also made it commercially and critically successful. Frank Launder and Sidney Gilliatt provided Hitchcock with a light, playful, and still coherent screenplay. They later did a very similar job for Carol Reed in *Night Train*, a film which has the celebrated cricket enthusiasts Basil Radford and Naunton Wayne from *The Lady Vanishes*. Hitchcock's path diverges thereafter from that of Launder and Gilliatt (except for Gilliatt's contribution to *Jamaica Inn*), but they must be credited with some of the surface effectiveness of *The Lady Vanishes*.

On the other hand, Hitchcock must be credited with having given a Launder and Gilliatt script more depth than was ever likely to be achieved without his directorial style. For Hitchcock's direction is very much a function of screenwriting. He collaborated throughout his career with his wife, Alma Reville, on the continuity of his films. Another important screenwriting figure in his British period is Charles Bennett (*The Man Who Knew Too Much, The Thirty-nine Steps, The Secret Agent, Sabotage, Young and Innocent*, and later, *Foreign Correspondent*). A subsequent scenarist of importance for Hitchcock was Joan Harrison, who joined him for *Jamaica Inn* and stayed through *Rebecca, Foreign Correspondent, Suspicion*, and *Saboteur*. She later became a prominent producer specializing in *film noir*—and she probably shared Hitchcock's concern with the darker side of life. Hitchcock's influence on *film noir* is incalculable, but nonetheless he stands somewhat outside its most persistent conventions.

Jamaica Inn was a transitional film for Hitchcock between his British period and his American period. Daphne du Maurier's surface plot is curiously lacking in either suspense or surprise. A young girl (Maureen O'Hara) comes to live with her aunt and uncle and encounters a world of pirates and cutthroats. Her beauty attracts Sir Humphrey Pengaltan (Charles Laughton), the lascivious local magistrate, who is soon to be revealed as the brains behind a shipwrecking operation centered in Jamaica Inn. The eccentrically erotic relationship between Laughton and O'Hara, he sadistic, she submissive, gives the movie odd overtones which are never satisfactorily orchestrated within the skimpy plot. Hitchcock had a great deal of trouble with Laughton's time-consuming theatrical conceits, but Laughton is memorable nonetheless as the demented aristocrat living and loving beyond his means. Hence, the movie is affecting without being effective as the raging unconscious of its players is unchecked by any appreciable stylistic or thematic control.

Hitchcock came to Hollywood in 1939 to make *Rebecca* for David O. Selznick. The film won an Academy Award for the year 1940, but Hitchcock's reputation with cinéphiles never fully recovered. For years after, his British period would be fondly remembered at the expense of his Hollywood experience. Hitchcock himself contributed to this appraisal by seeming to agree in part with his detractors. In interviews Hitchcock has always seemed culturally hostile to the notion of women's pictures adapted from shopgirl novels for female audiences. In this respect, *Rebecca* was the ultimate women's picture. Its mousy heroine becomes the wife of one of England's richest and noblest and most neurotic lords, and the mistress of one of the realm's grandest estates, Manderley, which, along with Tara, attest to Selznick's taste for high romance.

The parallels between *Rebecca* and *Gone With the Wind* (including richly evocative scores) as Selznick superproductions extended to a "search" for the lead female role of the unnamed heroine who succeeded the late (and unseen) Rebecca as the second Mrs. Maxim de Winter. Ironically, Vivien Leigh, the eventually victorious Scarlett O'Hara, was one of the also-rans for the ingenue lead. Several of the tests surfaced in a seventies television documentary on Selznick's career, and Vivien Leigh's and Margaret Sullavan's and Joan Fontaine's were clearly the most compelling and most challenging. Both Hitchcock and Selznick preferred Fontaine, and one can see why. Margaret Sullavan was too assured, too confident, for the part of a socially intimidated bride hopelessly out of her depth. She would have had Judith Anderson's Mrs. Danvers doing windows in no time flat. Vivien Leigh was too overpoweringly beautiful to convince an audience that any husband of hers would waste time mooning over his first wife. Besides, the emotional electricity that crackled between Laurence Olivier and his then inamorata was too painfully evident to provide any psychological suspense to the on-screen relationship. By contrast, Fontaine's small, fearful eyes, her slightly affected manner, and her literally shrinking demeanor were not only perfect for the dramas and traumas of the second Mrs. de Winter, but set the standard for beleaguered Gothic heroines for the next two decades.

From the memorably dream-like narration that opens the film—"I dreamt last night that I returned to Manderley"—to the burning of the R emblazoned on the pillowcases inside the flaming ruins of Manderley, *Rebecca* unreels as an unprecedentedly fluid blend of romance and suspense, the privileged domains respectively of producer Selznick and director Hitchcock. Laurence Olivier's Maxim de Winter, an updating of his period Heathcliff and Darcy (in *Wuthering Heights* (1939) and *Pride and Prejudice* (1940)), marked the virtual end of his very short career as a broodingly mysterious matinee idol. Franz Waxman's hauntingly wistful score and George Barnes's dreamily focused cinematography contributed to the spell of an otherwise outrageous narrative that was hobbled besides by the censor's insistence that even Maxim de Winter couldn't get away with murdering his wife, and that therefore the murder in the Daphne du Maurier novel would have to be changed to an "accident" so as to get the newlyweds off the hook.

There was, nonetheless, more than enough lush suffering to go around. With every portentous incident seen through the eyes of the Joan Fontaine character, Hitchcock magnifies the menace of every social encounter in a comic-fantastic manner. Florence Bates's pushy American employer becomes a gorgon with a gargantuan appetite for chocolates and social contacts. George Sanders's Jack Favell emerges as the sneering cynic par excellence, and a hidden danger besides. Even benign presences like Gladys Cooper's family friend, Reginald Denny's family retainer, Sir C. Aubrey Smith's local inspector, and Leo G. Carroll's unassuming physician are the bearers of unpleasant news. The mood is always somber, threatening, murky, and yet the picture as a whole is exhilarating. The explanation for this apparent paradox is to be found in the clarity and lucidity of Hitchcock's narrative style of direction.

Hitchcock has complained that Selznick wanted the smoke billowing from Manderley at the end of *Rebecca* to be shaped in the form of an R. Nonetheless, Hitchcock returned to Selznick in 1945 and 1947 for *Spellbound* and *The Paradine Case*, two of his lesser works, but two of Selznick's last interesting productions.

For his next project after *Rebecca*, Hitchcock turned to a project that was considered more fittingly Hitchcockian, namely, *Foreign Correspondent* (1940). Hitchcock reportedly wanted Gary Cooper for the lead, but he was turned down and had to "settle" for Joel McCrea. This production-story anecdote has always been difficult to understand. It may be that Cooper was put off by the idea of still another newspaperman adventure, but, having starred in *The General Died at Dawn*, it is difficult to see how he could have felt superior to a political melodrama, however purple. In any event, the less-mannered McCrea was not at all a come-down from Cooper, and Laraine Day has been needlessly slandered by both Hitchcock and Truffaut. McCrea and Day were not the most critically fashionable couple on the screen, but they were charming nonetheless, and set off to advantage by the sophisticated support of a suavely continental cast, notably Herbert Marshall, George Sanders, Albert Basserman, Edmund

Gwenn, Eduardo Cianelli, and Martin Kosleck. Even as a change of mood and pace from the highly charged sequences of nail-biting suspense, the romantic couple more than served their purpose.

Viewed today as a grand shaggy-dog thriller about the adventures of a boyish American reporter on the fringe of Nazi intrigue, *Foreign Correspondent* (1940) was released in the year in which President Roosevelt promised "again and again and again" that he would never send American boys to fight in a foreign war. Surprisingly, producer Walter Wanger allowed a virulent anti-German slant on this project, but on the agitprop level. Hitchcock's ambiguous attitude toward the ruthless Nazi villains, played with stately dedication by Marshall and Gwenn, clouded the political issues. What was most memorable about the film was its picaresque spirit expressed in such vivid set pieces as the opening mock assassination in a rain-swept Amsterdam plaza, the terrorist torture of a diplomat (Basserman) in order to discover the secret clause in a treaty, and the swirling action fantasies played out around a windmill and on top of a cathedral. The set design and special effects of the legendary William Cameron Menzies evoked a sensibility as stark and fanciful as Hitchcock's, particularly in the climactic plane crash at sea, a brilliantly conceived and edited disaster coup that has never been surpassed.

Very loosely based on Vincent Sheean's *Personal History*, the witty screenplay employed the services of Hitchcock regulars Charles Bennett and Joan Harrison with additional dialogue by James Hilton and New Yorker writer Robert Benchley. Benchley also played the part of a clownishly cynical American reporter in London, and he presumably wrote his own dialogue, possibly to provide a Yankee counterpoint to the expert Oxonian cadences of the sardonic George Sanders's journalist-patriot on the track of traitors and spies. Almost as memorable as Mr. Memory in *The Thirty-nine Steps* is Edmund Gwenn's benignly avuncular assassin: a short, stocky cherub of cheerful malice; in some ways a mirror image of the director himself in his role as the scourge of his virile, handsome stars.

Mr. and Mrs. Smith (1941) was Hitchcock's first out-and-out American failure. Norman Krasna's script was graced with an interesting premise—a husband and wife have made an agreement not to leave each other's presence in the middle of an argument, and, as the picture begins, their argument has been raging for four days, and the husband is unable to get to the office. Finally he slams the door, as if he has left. There is a close-up of Carole Lombard's tousled blonde head popping up over the sofa, her eyes and lips tinged with sorrow and disappointment, and then we are shown Robert Montgomery, still in his pajamas, popping up on the other side of the room, and the couple kiss and make up. This is one high point in an otherwise tedious marital farce. Even so, Chabrol and Rohmer astutely criticized Hitchcock's lyrical close-up of Lombard as inappropriately introspective for the genre of screwball comedy, which requires a certain distance from the camera to allow the characters to perform physically.

There is, however, at least one sight gag in *Mr. and Mrs. Smith* worthy of inclusion in any anthology of screen humor. Montgomery finds himself at a night club on a blind double-date with two very vulgar females. His wife's unexpected entrance with her new beau places our hero in an embarrassing bind. He turns in the direction of a stunning blonde at an adjacent table, and unbeknownst to the blonde, lip-pantomimes an earnest conversation with her so as to impress his own wife. The blonde and her burly escort finally notice his strange behavior, and retribution is swift and violent. Hitchcock's choice of camera distance for the gag is here as inspired as his just mentioned close-up of Lombard was enchantingly incongruous.

Suspicion (1941) is Hitchcock bouncing back from misfired marital farce to more congenial marital paranoia. It was his first film with Cary Grant, and he had trouble making Grant out to be even a possible villain. Also, the film was criticized for altering the book's ending by having Grant innocent rather than guilty. The auteurist defenders of Hitchcock (notably Truffaut) have argued that the film works better with the revised ending. Whether one views the ending as compromise or inspiration, *Suspicion* is an unsettling experience. The early part of the film treats the courtship of Cary Grant and Joan Fontaine from an oddly satirical distance. Grant is seen from the outset as an improvident rascal with sexual arrogance, whereas Fontaine has evolved from the frightened maiden of *Rebecca* to a repressed spinster who wears glasses (a distinctively Hitchcockian "sign" of repression) when she reads. The mood is light and comic, and the treatment of Fontaine is sardonic except for a curious scene on a windswept studio-set hillside on which Grant tries to embrace a very frightened Fontaine. The scene is curiously ominous in its dream-like abstractness, as it sets the stage for the second part of the film with its angled, point-of-view style of paranoia. Suddenly Grant is looming in the foreground, emerging from doorways and stairwells, weaving his way in and out of intricate patterns of light and shadow. From an objective view of Grant the light comedian, we have shifted to a subjective view of Grant the heavy menace. All plot signs point to the logic of his planning to murder his wife for her insurance money, but

Fontaine remains curiously, almost masochistically passive. It is as if she doesn't really believe that he wants to murder her, but, rather, that she is seeking to dramatize or even melodramatize her role in his life. Ultimately, the plot is less crucial than the basic, universal situation of husband and wife at emotional cross-purposes in the midst of a complete breakdown in communication. In this context, the "happy" ending is relatively unconvincing, not because no murder takes place but, rather, because it is hard to believe that any reconciliation in the marriage can occur after such massive suspicion. Grant and Fontaine are superb nonetheless, as is Nigel Bruce, the erstwhile Doctor Watson, as Beaky, the family friend who dies under disturbingly suspicious circumstances.

Saboteur (1942) shifted Hitchcock from the marital paranoia of *Suspicion* to the political paranoia of sabotage. America was now in World War II, and explicitly anti-Nazi speeches became mandatory. The political landscape of *Saboteur* was peopled with oddly appealing traitors to America. The chase gambit was basic Hitchcock: our hero (Robert Cummings) is hunted by the police in the mistaken belief that he had set an aircraft plant afire. The only way he can clear his name is by finding the real saboteur. When he does finally trap him, it is at the top of the Statue of Liberty. The saboteur (with the pyromaniacal name "Fry," and played by Norman Lloyd) gains our sympathies by his desperate plight as he dangles from the torch of the Statue of Liberty, the hero holding his sleeve. Hitchcock's camera viewpoint is mainly downward to Fry's expression of anguished supplication, and when he falls to his death, the relieved reunion of the nominal hero and heroine (Pricilla Lane) loses any possibility of joyous celebration.

Saboteur, like *Foreign Correspondent*, is not quite as good as the sum of its set-pieces would indicate, and the romantic leads are clearly the most juvenile of Hitchcock's career. The villains take up some of the slack, particularly Alan Baxter as a soft-spoken American fascist with an off-screen little boy with beautiful long hair, and Otto Kruger as a diabolically elitist old-world spirit. Hitchcock wanted the beloved Harry Carey to play the Kruger role in the mold of the ruggedly individualistic American-Firsters of the period, but Carey's wife demurred for the sake of America's children.

Shadow of a Doubt (1943) was filmed largely on location in Santa Rosa, California. Hitchcock collaborated with Thornton Wilder on making the small-town background Americana as authentic as possible. Up to this point American critics had not been particularly aware of Hitchcock's penchant for unobtrusive realism in his British period. Hence,

Shadow of a Doubt seemed soft and sentimental even to so perceptive a Hitchcock admirer as James Agee. And for Bosley Crowther, the socially conscious critic of the *New York Times*, the film's remoteness from the issues of the war served as a decisive drawback.

Indeed, the plot did not seem too pressing by 1943 standards: a favorite uncle comes to town, and his favorite niece discovers his guilty secret, but she's the kind of nice girl who can't tell anyone because it would *kill* her mother. The uncle then decides that he must dispose of his niece, and the suspense arises from the niece's classically Hitchcockian and faintly comic dilemma of how to save her own life without hurting her mother's feelings. Various subplots involve: (1) the niece's romance with a detective, the one narrative element that slackens into sentimentality; (2) a running gag involving the niece's father and a middle-aged neighbor—who lives with his mother whom we never see, but who resonates as a Hitchcockian skeleton in the closet—as the two men debate the plausibility of various murder mysteries while a real murderer is loose among them; (3) a loving sibling rivalry between the niece and her younger sister.

Hitchcock projects these background relationships to put feelings of fear, guilt, suspicion, and paranoia in the foreground. François Truffaut has predicated a doubling pattern on the basis of uncle and niece both being named Charlie, on there being two sets of detectives (also in twos), two suspected "Merry Widow" murderers, one in the East and one in the West, two attempted murders, two scenes at the dinner table, two scenes outside the church. In addition, the first shot of Uncle Charlie shows him on a bed in a New York City rooming house, his head on the right side of the screen and his feet on the left; whereas our first glimpse of little Charlie shows her on her bed in Santa Rosa, her head on the left side of the screen and her feet on the right, as if a mirror image in malaise of her Uncle Charlie.

As the film progresses, the doppelganger, or double effect, takes on interestingly perverse overtones in the sexual tensions between uncle and niece. Teresa Wright, the all-American girl of that era after *The Little Foxes*, *Pride of the Yankees*, and *Mrs. Miniver*, was ideally cast as little Charlie, and Joseph Cotten puffed sinister smoke rings around his role of Uncle Charlie, exuding evil with every breath. Patricia Collinge as the slightly dotty mother and Hume Cronyn as the repressed next-door neighbor were particularly memorable as examples of the ultimate eccentricity of normality. Of all Hitchcock's films in the forties none is more successful in integrating the psychic furies of Hitchcock's style with the social features of the American landscape. It may be that the guilt and repression of the American family could not be faced in wartime. Also, little Charlie's behavior is not entirely plausible without a certain degree of voluptuous complicity in her fate. That a nice girl might be attracted to danger and evil is not a peculiarly Hitchcockian conceit.

Unfortunately, Hitchcock's reputation as the manipulative master of suspense prevented many critics from fully appreciating the ambiguity of his characterizations. Above all, Hitchcock was masterly in creating an eerie atmosphere out of everyday situations. The first intimations that there is something wrong with Uncle Charlie come not from little Charlie but from her little sister and brother. Hitchcock's ability to switch from the objective point of view to the subjective and back several times within a scene enabled him to show mental processes at work without excessively explanatory dialogue. At times, the audience becomes embarrassed—indeed, almost frightened—that the truth will out. Thus, we all become accomplices in the keeping of a guilty secret, the full dimensions of which remain tantalizingly obscure.

Among Hitchcock's films, *Lifeboat* (1944) is clearly the most didactically allegorical. As Hitchcock himself described the film to Truffaut:

> We wanted to show that at that moment there were two world forces confronting each other, the democracies and the Nazis, and while the democracies were disorganized, all of the Germans were clearly headed in the same direction. So here was a statement telling the democracies to put their differences aside temporarily and to gather their forces to concentrate on the common enemy, whose strength was precisely derived from a spirit of unity and of determination.

Nonetheless, Hitchcock was severely criticized by Bosley Crowther and others for showing the one Nazi character (Walter Slezak) as more than a match for his eight "democratic" antagonists (Tallulah Bankhead, John Hodiak, William Bendix, Mary Anderson, Henry Hull, Heather Angel, Hume Cronyn, and Canada Lee). It is difficult in the nineties to realize how sanctimonious people could be about the war in the 1940s. There was then no room for irony or self-criticism, and certainly no inkling of the revisionist, breast-beating self-denunciation of *Catch-22* and *Slaughterhouse-5* which was to inundate our culture in the fifties and sixties. But in the midst of all the pursed-lip piety about the war there emerged an anomalous disdain for the preachy contrivances of such war pictures. The disenchantment was gradual. From 1941 to 1943 the war was regarded as an edifying subject, worthy of awards, for example, *Wake Island* (1942), *In Which We Serve* (1942), *Mrs. Miniver* (1942), *Watch on the Rhine* (1943), and *Casablanca* (1943). By 1944, however, war propaganda was being discounted as dramatic entertainment. Significantly, the big picture of 1944 was *Going My Way*, and of 1945 *The Lost Weekend*, both prize-winning films virtually ignoring the war for the sake of "civilian" subjects. Even so, critics and audiences were not yet prepared for a subtle treatment of the Nazi evil.

Perhaps, *Lifeboat* would have aroused less controversy if it had seemed less overtly allegorical with its carefully calculated mix of rightists, leftists, and centrists. As it was, the shifting alignments in the lifeboat seemed to foreshadow postwar conflicts over ideology, if not the Cold War itself. Tallulah Bankhead's frivolous journalist and Henry Hull's fatuous industrialist actually form a temporary alliance with Walter Slezak's Nazi commandant to run the lifeboat in terms of the class structure in operation in the real world. But this elitist coup is forestalled by the proletarian rhetoric of John Hodiak's crewman, his fellow seamen (William Bendix, Hume Cronyn, and Canada Lee), and a nurse (Mary Anderson). The debates between Bankhead and Hodiak serve to intensify the sexual attraction between them, but from the beginning it is clear that Slezak is manipulating his adversaries through a shrewd knowledge of their vanities and weaknesses. He first flatters the journalist by pretending not to understand English in order to enhance her knowledge of German as a tool of translation. He then appeals to the industrialist's craving for order and certitude. The Nazi even "understands" the relationship between the journalist and the Communist crewman, and offers avuncular advice to the lady. All very strange and sophisticated for a Nazi in a 1944 Hollywood movie, but not nearly so strange for a Hitchcockian incarnation of evil as ambiguous and beguiling.

As it turns out, the Nazi's superiority is based on nothing more spiritual than his having concealed food tablets and water for his own use. When he is exposed the others turn on him like a pack of mad dogs, first beating him and then drowning him in a continuous action photographed from their rear. Only Canada Lee's religious black desists from the ritual murder, and he even tries, albeit unsuccessfully, to pull away Mary Anderson's gentle nurse from the killing. Even at a time when Lillian Hellman's antifascist hero had already murdered an opportunist in cold blood in *Watch on the Rhine*, and was sanctified for it, Hitchcock's more ambiguous treatment of the collective murder of a Nazi was regarded as disconcertingly anti-democratic. In allegorical terms, the War Effort had degenerated into the action of a lynch mob right out of *The Oxbow Incident* (1943).

Of course, *Lifeboat* arouses few ideological objections in the nineties. If anything, its Popular Front sentiments seem almost too "constructive" in a world that seems in retrospect to have been more absurdist than anyone had imagined. Agee complained about the excessive influence of John Steinbeck's script on Hitchcock's style. For his part, Hitchcock has tended to downgrade Steinbeck's contribution to the film. Certainly, Steinbeck's conception bears more than a passing resemblance to his allegorical creation in *The Moon Is Down*, but it is possible that Hitchcock may have added a few twists to the plot at the expense of some of the rhetoric in the theme.

Today the way of looking at *Lifeboat* is as a technical tour de force for Hitchcock. As Truffaut semi-rhetorically asks Hitchcock: "With *Lifeboat* we come to the type of picture that represents a challenge. Wasn't it pretty daring to undertake to shoot a whole film in a lifeboat?"

Hitchcock's answer is both revealing and devious at the same time:

> That's right, it was a challenge, but it was also because I wanted to prove a theory I had then. Analyzing the psychological pictures that were being turned out, it seemed to me that, visually, eighty per cent of the footage was shot in close-ups or semiclose shots. Most likely it wasn't a conscious thing with most of the directors, but rather an instinctive need to come closer to the action. In a sense this treatment was an anticipation of what was to become the television technique.

What Hitchcock reveals in his response to Truffaut is a deliberate strategy to emphasize the claustrophobic feeling aboard the lifeboat. Indeed, much of the humor of Tallulah Bankhead's performance arises from her aplomb in confronting the ridiculous lack of privacy in this situation. But why should *Lifeboat* be considered a technical tour de force at all? Even though Hitchcock had been so identified with chase stories and scenic stunts, the idea of shooting a movie in a lifeboat with nine survivors should not have seemed so unlikely for a master of montage. And indeed the interplay of different points of view keeps *Lifeboat* from ever being static as cinema or dull as dramatic narrative. Actually, Hitchcock is playing the trickster with the public when he complains about the constrictions of the lifeboat, for if *Lifeboat* is constricted it is because Hitchcock wanted it to be constricted. Had he wanted to extend the image of the lifeboat into a cosmic metaphor, he could have simply pulled back far enough on occasion to show the lifeboat bobbing on the waves as a vulnerable vessel of humanity. This metaphorical perspective pops up in such otherwise disparate sea films as John Huston's *The African Queen* (1951), Richard Lester's *Juggernaut* (1974), and Lina Wertmuller's *Swept Away* (1975). But not in *Lifeboat*. Of course, Hitchcock worked in a studio tank in the forties, and the relation of mise-en-scène to narrative was much tighter than it was to be in subsequent decades. Still, *Lifeboat* is striking for the intensity with which it expresses spatial constriction as a psychological conditioner. Indeed, the very unreality of Bankhead's jauntiness and Hodiak's swagger and the neat sociological niches of all the characters tend to create an ironic tension with the sheer terror of the story's premise. Shipwreck thus serves as a metaphor for war, and the survivors as representatives of a brawling, incorrigible mob of conflicting interests. For Hitchcock, *Lifeboat* seems to have provided an essentially comic vision of the war, and he was aided in his labors in no uncertain way by the relatively unfamiliar (to moviegoers) personality of Tallulah Bankhead. The rest of the cast was familiar, and producer Kenneth MacGowan's influence on the project level should not be underestimated.

Spellbound (1945) has always been dismissed as one of Hitchcock's lesser films, and one of his most overpoweringly lovey-dovey. When one adds up Ingrid Bergman, Gregory Peck, Sigmund Freud, Salvador Dali, Miklos Rozsa, Ben Hecht, and David O. Selznick, the total is bound to be deep purple. In 1945, Ingrid Bergman and Gregory Peck had skyrocketed to fame almost simultaneously, and the luminosity of their pairing tends to blot out the rest of Hitchcock's mise-en-scène. Hitchcock's greatest handicap is the laughably explicit process of Freudian analysis with which the "mystery" of the script is saddled. Through the forties the problems of characters were gradually deflected from society to the psyche as the Freudian and gothic genres criss-crossed. For that matter, *Rebecca* contained infinitely more interesting clinical material than *Spellbound*. Mrs. Danvers's relationship with the late Rebecca would have been sufficient for a whole case history in itself. But the gothic elements kept the Freudian elements at bay. In *Spellbound* the analytical attack on the plot is too literal for drama, and too contrived for diagnosis. The great stars are fixed in their firmaments: they must be contemplated whole, not carved up into convincing complexes. This is the iconographic problem faced by Hitchcock in *Spellbound*. The plot did not allow him sufficient scope for his irony, with the result that he had to gild the glossiness instead.

Peck presented a special problem in that he had to play a mentally afflicted character with the charisma of a self-reliant hero. Peck could never convey the insidious corruption of emotional exhibitionism, the slightest suggestion of which corruption would have made the character more interesting. Instead, Peck kept retreating into a sullen silence while Ingrid Bergman maintained a wordy vigil at the gate to his muddled memory. It was a movie with an inordinate amount of kissing, which suggests a certain lack of imagination in the relationship, down to the gag ending at the train station with the befuddled ticket-taker doing a double-take on a couple kissing before boarding the train *together*. It's-only-a-movie endings like this are among Hollywood's most annoying, and probably most avoidable, mannerisms.

The failure of Salvador Dali's contribution to the film is reflected in Hitchcock's comments on the subject:

> I was determined to break with the traditional way of handling dream sequences through a blurred and hazy screen. I asked Selznick if he could get Dali to work with us and he agreed, though I think he didn't really understand my reasons for wanting Dali. He probably thought I wanted his collaboration for publicity purposes. The real reason was that I wanted to convey the dreams with great visual sharpness and clarity, sharper than the film itself. My idea was to shoot the Dali scenes in the open air so that the whole thing, photographed in real sunshine, would be terribly sharp. I was very keen on that idea, but the producers were concerned with the expense. So we shot the dream in the studios.

Hitchcock was more successful in planting little hints of perversity among the minor characters, particularly the two Mom-oriented detectives, who seem particularly repressed. On the whole, however, *Spellbound* was too sentimentally conceived to allow Hitchcock's sense of strangeness full play. Michael Chekhov's cherubic analyst was only slightly less cuddly than S. Z. Zakall. Only in the sardonically debonair analyst played by Leo G. Carroll does the film achieve dramatic complexity and novelistic nuance. A rational man saddled with a fatal lapse of judgment, he ultimately turns a pistol upon himself, and, more important, upon the audience. This little "joke," which goes all the way back to Porter's *The Great Train Robbery* in 1903, may be interpreted by some as Hitchcock's revenge on a star-worshiping audience.

Notorious (1946) has always been considered one of Hitchcock's most effective entertainments. But in 1946, when *The Best Years of Our Lives* set the standard for significance, *Notorious* could hardly have been expected to acquire a serious critical reputation. Its plot was a curious blend of audacity and conventionality. A dissolute young woman, the daughter of a convicted Nazi agent, is induced by an American intelligence operative to use her contacts with her father's old Nazi crowd to assist her adopted country, the United States of America. Here the action shifts from Miami to Rio, mostly through process shots. Of course the audience does not need many clues to suspect a budding love between Ingrid Bergman as the woman spy and Cary Grant as the American agent. The billing would be sufficient even without the binary crosscutting of luminous close-ups, first Bergman, then Grant, then Bergman, then, perhaps, a torrential two-shot within the same frame, and then a swirling camera movement around the embracing couple to express the lyrical transport of the kiss. It is precisely at this moment of consummate bliss that the telephone rings, a jarring aural dissonance in the visual melody of love. We are made uneasy more quickly and more economically in a Hitchcock movie than in any one else's, which is to say that if the kissing sequence (which made 1946 Radio City Music Hall audiences gasp) were any less lyrical, the ring of the telephone would be far less disruptive.

Grant is called away from his rendezvous with Bergman to a meeting with his superiors. They tell him that a key Nazi (Claude Rains) has returned to Rio and that before the war he was infatuated with Bergman. Hence, he would be sufficiently susceptible to her charms to invite her to his mysterious house, where all sorts of Nazi demons congregate. Grant, stunned by the scandalous nature of his beloved's mission, is stung by the revelation that she once had a Nazi admirer (and who knows how many lovers). The beauty of Grant's performance is manifest in his facial expressions, which reflect a struggle between love and lack of trust a recurring theme in Hitchcock films. Yet the pivotal scenes in which the Grant-Bergman relationship is ruptured are reinforced by the metaphor of the champagne bottle, which Grant misplaces in true Freudian-phallic fashion. The reverse close-ups of the bottle itself left behind at intelligence headquarters, and of the knowing glance directed at the bottle by Grant's superior (Louis Calhern) is Hitchcock's cinematic way of showing us (as well as merely telling us) that love has flown.

With the entrance of Claude Rains as the Nazi fish before whom Ingrid Bergman is being dangled as bait, Notorious achieves its preordained triangular form. Rain's Alexander Sebastien is one of the most sympathetically tragic villains in all of cinema. Afflicted with a domineering mother (Leopoldine Konstantin) and menaced by a murderous

cohort (Ivan Triesault), Sebastien lives in a luxurious mansion which time
will transform from a lair to a tomb. But first he must be humiliated
right before our eyes in every way a man can be humiliated. Curiously,
we come to know more about him than we know about the ostensible
hero and heroine. Cary Grant's Devlin and Ingrid Bergman's Alicia Hub-
erman are relatively rootless creatures of instant romance. Indeed, they
are more like two powerful magnetic fields rather than bona fide characters. From a certain morbid point of view which Hitchcock encourages
at every turn, Devlin and Alicia exist primarily to torture Sebastien, first
with pangs of sexual jealousy, then with the shock of political betrayal,
and finally with virtual execution, always, of course, from his point of
view.

And what of the two lovers? They must torture not only their mutual
victim but each other. Some of their verbal exchanges are coarse and
unfeeling. "You're a rat, Devlin," Alicia declares. For his part, Devlin
treats Alicia as an incorrigibly wayward woman. Ben Hecht's very brittle
dialogue scrapes away at the idealized images of the two stars, but,
strangely, without dimming their luster. It is as if they were insulated
from the sordidness of the situation by their own majestic charisma.

Meanwhile, Alicia's intrigue succeeds beyond her wildest expectations: Sebastien asks her to marry him. Instead of being merely a guest
in the house of mystery, she will be its mistress. Devlin is dismayed by
this sensational turn of events, but he somehow lacks the will to claim
the young woman for himself. For her part, Alicia is convinced that
Devlin doesn't trust her, and thus masochistically she surrenders to the
arrangement. Devlin continues to serve as her outside contact and each
meeting is a ghastly charade of their former romance.

One evening Alicia and Devlin steal down to the wine cellar during
a gala party at Sebastien's mansion. There they accidentally drop a wine
bottle which spills out a mysterious substance known minerally as ura-
nium and cinematically as Hitchcock's McGuffin. A critic of this period
complained that two experienced agents should not be so clumsy as to
drop a wine bottle. This critic, like many of his contemporaries, assumed
that *Notorious* was primarily a spy yarn when, actually, the espionage
elements were merely incidental to the psychological conflicts. Again,
Hitchcock builds up the suspense by cutting between the major character and such metaphorical artifacts as the key to the wine cellar downstairs and the dwindling number of champagne bottles at the party
upstairs. The audience is torn between the excruciating fear of seeing
the lovers caught and the subconscious desire to witness the end of a

deceitful marriage. When Sebastien comes upon them in the cellar, Alicia and Devlin avert the immediate disaster of being discovered as spies by pretending to be lovers, a comic switch on all the old jokes about the excuses devised by adulterous couples in compromising situations. Then, after Alicia and Devlin have departed, Sebastien discovers that they are spies. From being the most ignorant member of the triangle, he becomes the most knowing. But now, to hide the disgrace of his having been duped from his ruthless cohorts, he must return his mother to a position of absolute authority in his life.

Together, Sebastien and his mother set out to poison Alicia slowly, almost imperceptibly. Alicia remains free to make contact with Devlin, but he interprets her "headaches" as a despairing resurgence of her alcoholism (evidenced in the first scene). Misunderstanding within misunderstandings. Then, magically, almost inexplicably, Devlin deduces that Alicia is in danger. He goes to the house and slips up to the bedroom where he and the very ill Alicia are reconciled. Clifford Odets walked out of the screenplay assignment with the complaint that only a pervert would make love to a dying woman. There is a perversity of sorts in the spectacle of Devlin leading the ailing Alicia to salvation, but it is consistent with their bitterly twisted relationship throughout the film. Sebastien and his mother are now caught between the irresistible force of Devlin's desire on the landing above, and the implacable discipline of the Nazi agents below. Suddenly, four people are descending the stairs to very individual destinies, Sebastien alternating between bravado and prudence, his mother preaching prudence with every step, Alicia delivered by an ecstatic helplessness in the arms of Devlin, and Devlin at last staking his life on his feelings. The succession of shots diminishes the distance between the fearful foursome and the arena of ultimate decision. But the audience's fear is diffused because of Sebastien's very palpable predicament. Significantly, the last image of the film is concerned not with Alicia and Devlin but with Sebastien's slowly mounting the steps outside his home toward his inevitable doom. Inevitable because Devlin has refused to let him enter the getaway car. It is an act of somewhat gratuitous revenge and it further clouds the ostensibly "happy ending." Thus, *Notorious*, far from being a simple spy story, turns out to be an incredibly intricate exercise in irony and ambiguity, and one of the outstanding testaments of Hitchcock's expressive complexity as an artist.

The Paradine Case (1947) represented a clear setback for Hitchcock's career. It also marked the end of Hitchcock's association with David O. Selznick. In his book-length interviews with Peter Bogdanovich and François Truffaut, Hitchcock has complained of the casting imposed upon him by Selznick. It is difficult to evaluate Hitchcock's complaints because they assume a degree of sexual sophistication in Hollywood movies that was not particularly apparent in the forties. Still, the director had visions of Greta Garbo coming out of retirement to play the beautiful, mysterious, notorious Mrs. Paradine on trial for the murder of her blind husband, with Laurence Olivier or Ronald Colman as the elegant English lawyer who falls in love with her while he is defending her, and Burt Lancaster or Robert Newton as the earthy D. H. Lawrence groom for whose love she has committed the murder. Instead, Alida Valli played Mrs. Paradine, Gregory Peck her attorney, and Louis Jourdan her lover. As it turned out, Valli was not electric enough, Peck not English enough, and Jourdan not earthy enough.

But the biggest problem may have been the plot, which was uncertainly derived from the Robert Hichens novel first by Hitchcock and his wife, Alma Reville, then by James Bridie, and finally by Selznick himself. In the book the attorney need only play a passive role in the defense of his client in order to get her acquitted of the murder charge, for which there is little hard evidence, but in his obsession with her decides to wage an active defense in order to restore her good name and inadvertently gets her convicted. With such fatal consequences, he is despised for his efforts by the woman he has come to love. In the movie the legal irony of the novelist is completely nullified. Peck tries to play detective by convicting Jourdan of the crime for which Valli is in the dock. Peck is finally repudiated by his own client, who confesses her guilt. Thoroughly rebuked, the attorney is then forgiven by his long suffering wife (Ann Todd), but at no point do any of the characters evoke any strong feelings in the audience.

Yet, Hitchcock produces some of his most elaborately expressive camera movements for this doomed enterprise. Even when the players are not vibrating with the appropriate emotions, Hitchcock's mis-en-scène produces its own meanings, particularly around a painting of Mrs. Paradine, a lecherous encounter between Ann Todd's discreet wife and Charles Laughton's hanging judge, and the various entrances and exits into the courtroom. Actually, it may not have been Seiznick's casting as much as the producer's overly expository writing that frustrated Hitchcock's intended moods of obsession and degradation.

Though *Rope* (1948) was not exactly Hitchcock on the rebound, it did provide him with his first opportunity to work with color, and, more spectacularly, to experiment with the enormous technical challenge of a "single-take" scenario. The script, adapted from Patrick Hamilton's play by Arthur Laurents and Hume Cronyn, very loosely evoked the Leopold-Loeb case. Two young homosexuals (John Dall, Farley Granger) with Nietzschean pretensions murder a classmate, stuff his body in a chest, and then hold a party around the chest. Among the guests are the victim's father (Sir Cedric Hardwicke) and the murderers' old college professor (James Stewart), who has supposedly inspired them to take life lightly. With most of the incidental action of the film swirling around the tell-tale chest, it is easy to see why Hitchcock was tempted to adopt a unified mise-en-scène for the story. The action takes place in a New York apartment (with a fake view of the New York skyline) in the evening between 7:30 and 9:15. There are no discernible cuts in the continuity, though the effect of the single-shot is achieved through artfully blocked-out transitions, usually on close-ups of the clothing of a character as he or she momentarily passes before the camera lens. Each roll of film runs ten minutes, which makes *Rope* a series of ten-minute takes without interruption or changed camera set-up.

As a movie, *Rope* suffers from the miscasting of James Stewart as the mock-Nietzschean mentor whose students take him too literally. The big problem with the picture, however, is that it has nowhere to go after its ghoulish premise is established except in the direction of hollow moralizing. The suspense is misplaced in that we do not care enough for the two murderers and their victim to have feelings about their fate one way or another. Nor is there any countervailing humor to be derived from the staging of a party at the scene of the crime. In this instance, at least, the two murderers are too proudly aware of their act to serve as victims of comic circumstances. Yet, they are too nervous and flustered to perform on the high wire of snobbish diabolism. They finally degenerate into case studies of fatuity and futility as the film ends in wearying anticlimax as little more than a stylistic stunt.

Nonetheless, *Rope* did inspire a great deal of discussion for its aesthetic legerdemain. Oddly, Hitchcock was subtly denigrated for his formal concerns in the hyper-realistic critical atmosphere of the late forties. It was as if the *what* were all important and the *how* merely incidental. Movies were supposed To Deal Honestly with Problems, and that was it. Hitchcock was considered too devious and ironical for such square dealing. Entertaining, yes; enlightening, no. Hence, he was placed in a special niche as the Master of Suspense, and forbidden to stray from the peril-filled path.

In terms of these expectations, *Under Capricorn* (1949) was a complete catastrophe. A costume picture with little suspense or surprise, with endless scenes of shame and humiliation, it caught both Ingrid Bergman and Alfred Hitchcock at the least fashionable juncture of their careers. For Bergman, the Rossellini affair had saddled her with all the disadvantages of a scandal and none of the advantages. *Under Capricorn* was sandwiched between her wooden *Joan of Arc* in 1948 and the esoterically convoluted *Stromboli* for Rossellini in 1950. Hitchcock had returned to England with Bergman in tow, but his initial feeling of triumph was quickly dissipated by the overwhelming feeling of turgidity connected with the project. In the United States *Under Capricorn* was seen by relatively few people, and quickly forgotten, but in France among cultish Hitchcockians it holds a high place for its deliriously dream-like mise-en-scène and its unrelenting sobriety. Indeed, its camera movements are more spectacular than those in *Rope*, and its moral relationships are subtly Hitchcockian in their genuine ambiguity. From *Rebecca* to *Under Capricorn*, Hitchcock had gone from the heights to the depths as far as the public and critical acclaim were concerned, but his style had become both sumptuous and supple as he enlarged on the morbid feelings of the forties.

Yet who could have foreseen in the winter of 1949 that Alfred Hitchcock was going to break out of the pack in the following decades on both theatrical screens and on television to be acknowledged as a master not only of suspense but of a whole range of cinematically expressed emotions. It is not that his work after 1950 dwarfed his work before, but rather that the critical climate shifted so dramatically that what had once seemed minor in his art became major. Hence, when the postwar footage he had shot on the Holocaust surfaced in the 1980s, it was treated seriously as a formative influence in the development of a profound sensibility. By the end of 1949, *Vertigo* (1958) and *Psycho* (1960) were still lurking in his unconscious, but the formal and thematic foundations had been laid down.

HOWARD HAWKS (1896–1977)

The belatedly exalted reputation of Howard Hawks reflected a critical revolution with respect to the American cinema. At the time of his death on December 27, 1977, Hawks had become such a respected figure in film scholarship that the Associated Press obituary described him as "the legendary movie director." It had not always been so. In the English-speaking world, particularly, Hawks carried little weight until the early sixties. His name was not to be found in the indexes of pre-sixties texts such as Grierson's *On Documentary* (which discusses many Hollywood directors), Lewis Jacobs's *The Rise of the American Film*, and Roger Manvell's *Penguin Film* series. Paul Rotha's *The Film Till Now* makes one brief reference to Hawks: "A very good all-rounder [who] stays in the mind with *The Crowd Roars, Scarface, Ball of Fire* and *The Big Sleep*."

By contrast, Hawks had been greatly admired in France at least since *Scarface* in 1932, and possibly from as early as *A Girl in Every Port* in 1928. But then it was easier to see *Scarface*, clearly a thirties masterpiece of the subjective gangster genre, in Paris than in New York through the thirties and forties. Many revival houses featured a double bill of William Wellman's *The Public Enemy* (1931) and Mervyn Leroy's *Little Caesar* (1930), but *Scarface* was always withheld from circulation by the estate of Howard Hughes. It would be interesting to know where and when Robert Warshow saw *Scarface*, to which he refers briefly in his famous 1947 *Partisan Review* essay "The Gangster as Tragic Hero," without, however, mentioning the name Howard Hawks.

The biggest problem in describing the cinema of Howard Hawks is its tendency to reveal its deepest feelings by way of the margins of the scenario. Hence, the plot and themes of his films are of less importance than the behavioral subtleties of his players as they go through their paces with infinite stylistic variations. Hawks was particularly resourceful in differentiating the members of an ensemble, whether in the airports of *Ceiling Zero* and *Only Angels Have Wings*, the ostentatious toothlessness of Walter Brennan in *Red River* and *Rio Bravo*, or the pairing of a garrulous villain with a laconic villain in *To Have and Have Not* and *The Big Sleep*.

The art of contrasts was fairly commonplace in Hollywood, but Hawks's ability to link his contrasts to dominant emotions in the dramatic situation created an unusual degree of psychological tension. And then to release some of that tension Hawks would devise an unexpected gesture or expression for comic relief. It is much like a man teetering along the edge of a cliff, but always lurching back to safety. If there be a basically Hawksian fable, it is that of the civilized being surviving the pitfalls of barbarism and brutishness. There is embarrassment, pain, and even death in the Hawksian universe, but never despair.

In this respect Hawks's refusal to direct the attempted-suicide plot of

Fourteen Hours because he disapproved of suicide plots takes on added significance. He suggested instead a plot in which a lover fakes a suicide leap from a hotel ledge after a husband has turned up unexpectedly at the hotel room door. An ideal plot, Hawks continued, for Cary Grant. Many years later, a French boulevard farce movie used the same situation, as did its Hollywood remake with Gene Wilder.

In the fifties Eugene Archer, a fellow film enthusiast, proposed a book on the six most significant American directors: John Ford, John Huston, Elia Kazan, George Stevens, William Wyler, and Fred Zinnemann. The book deal fell through, and subsequently Archer went to Paris on a Fulbright ostensibly to write about Henry James. Instead, he camped at the *Cinemathèque Francais*, and began reading *Cashiers du Cinema*. "Who the hell is Howard Hawks?" he wrote me plaintively. It was a question that was to be asked in print in the early sixties by Robert Fulford in Toronto and Raymond Durgnat in London. In the Paris of 1957 Archer had been shocked to discover that the *Cahiers* critics were unimpressed by Ford, Huston, Kazan, Stevens, Wyler, and Zinnemann, up against their sacred cows, Howard Hawks and Alfred Hitchcock. Archer and I thought we knew all about Hitchcock. He was supposed to be fun, but not entirely serious. But Hawks? Who was he? And why were the French taking him so seriously?

I had seen most of Hawks's films up to that time, mostly as revivals, but these were favorite film revivals, not Howard Hawks revivals, at least not until Dan Talbot's pioneering Hawks series in 1961. Curiously, the revival of Hawks in America proved to be less controversial than the revival of Hitchcock. Hawks, after all, had worked with William Faulkner. His Bogart-Bacall movies, *To Have and Have Not* and *The Big Sleep*, were enhanced by their respective associations with Ernest Hemingway and Raymond Chandler. He seemed more versatile than most of his Hollywood colleagues in tackling a wide variety of genres. Capra and McCarey, for example, never made westerns or gangster movies, and Ford and Hitchcock didn't make musicals. Hawks did them all.

This supposed versatility worked to Hawks's advantage in France, where genres were more appreciated. Also, Hawks profited from the post-Marxist orientation of *Cahiers* in the fifties and early sixties. Archer and I had never been Marxists at all, and so we slid rather easily into the casually apolitical routines of the *Cahier*-ists. In the process we elucidated Hawks without really evaluating him, thus, in a sense, placing him beyond criticism in a stylistic sanctuary rather shakily constructed by his French admirers.

In retrospect, the claims made for Hawks in the first flush of American auteurism seem more problematic than the claims made for Hitchcock. The French always sensed something in Hawks alien to their excessively cerebral sensibilities. He seemed clearly a man of action, a celebrator of stoic virility, an intuitive existentialist unburdened by roots and the other entanglements of family and history. The problem Archer and I had from the beginning, however, was that we could not correlate the mystical French formulations with any discernible figures of Hawksian style.

Hawks consciously shot most of his scenes at the eye level of a standing onlooker. Consequently, even his epic works were endowed with a human intimacy which the director did not disturb with pretentious crane shots. Hawks worked within a frame as much as possible, cutting only when a long take or an elaborate track might distract his audience from the issues in the foreground of the action. This was good, clean, direct, functional cinema, perhaps the most distinctively American cinema of all. It was certainly not the last word on the art of film-making, but its qualities were more unusual than most critics imagined. Even at the time of their release, however, the Hawks films were generally admired for their solid craftsmanship. The director worked with some of the most talented and creative cameramen in Hollywood: Gregg Toland, Lee Garmes, James Wong Howe, Tony Gaudio, Ernest Haller, Russell Harlan, and Sid Hickox. Hawks himself was never less than an old pro, but he was more as well. His technique served ultimately to express his personal Protagorean credo that man is the measure of all things.

Throughout his career Hawks adjusted to technological changes without blazing a trail for others to follow. He came late to the talking film, after Vidor, Lubitsch, Sternberg, and Mamoulian had explored its potential, extremely late to the color film, and despite an honorable effort in *Land of the Pharaohs* (1955), he did not seem to have been enchanted by the world of the wide screen. His technique was a function of his personality and the material he worked with. His scenarios, which invariably emphasized action within a short time span, did not lend themselves to decorative mannerisms. When confronted with epic subjects in *Red River* (1948) and *Land of the Pharaohs*, he split his story into two short segments of time a decade or so apart. He never used a flashback, and even in the thirties he seldom resorted to the degenerative montage of time lapses or so-called Slavko Vorkapich effects. His tracking, cutting, and framing through their impeccably logical service to the narrative in themselves never attracted much attention, and this may not be so much of a virtue as one might think. Critics who argue that technique should not call attention to itself are usually critics who do not wish to call attention to technique. If Hawks did not choose to use technique as a reflective commentary on action, it was because his personality expressed a pragmatic intelligence rather than a metaphysical profundity.

Aside from a few gibes at red-baiting in *His Girl Friday* (1940), Hawks never promoted any particular political agenda. The religious lunatic in *Twentieth Century* (1934), the revivalism in *Sergeant York* (1941), and the mordant piety after the brutal fact in *Red River* (1948) constitute what little there is of religion in the world of Howard Hawks. Except for *Sergeant York*, Hawks never dealt with the very poor as a class and, except for *Bringing Up Baby* (1938) never dealt with the very rich as a class. To the best of my memory there was never a divorce or a suicide as such in any of his films. *Dawn Patrol* (1930), *Today We Live* (1933), *Ceiling Zero* (1936), and *The Road to Glory* (1936) have quasi-suicidal climaxes in which characters accept fatal missions, but the moral arithmetic balances out in each instance because the martyr is a replacement in an obligatory situation. Still, it may be significant that these sacrificial episodes occurred in films of the thirties, an era in which the Hawksian virtues were most in tune with the times. A director of parts as well as a unified whole, Hawks stamped his distinctively bitter view of life on adventure, gangster, and private-eye melodramas, westerns, musicals, and screwball comedies, the kinds of things Americans do best and appreciate least.

■   ■   ■   ■

BORN IN GOSHEN, Indiana, in 1896, Hawks served with the American Army air force in France from 1917 to 1919. Upon his discharge as a first lieutenant, he worked in an aircraft factory (1920–23) and spent his vacations in Hollywood. He began his film career at Paramount, moving up from assistant film editor to scenarist. His first official writing credits are for the scenario of *Tiger Love* (1924) and the original story of *The Dressmaker of Paris* (1925). *The Road to Glory*, based on his original story and released in 1926, was his first directorial assignment and is apparently unrelated except by title to the film Hawks directed in 1936. Of the other seven films directed by Hawks, all, like his first, for the William Fox studio, have been seen since their release under archival auspices, and display much of the Hawksian "versatility" so evident in the sound era. The works in question are *Fig Leaves* (1926), *The Cradle Snatchers*, *Paid To Love*, and *Fazil* (all 1927), *A Girl in Every Port* and

The Air Circus (1928), and *Trent's Last Case* (1929). It might be noted that *A Girl in Every Port* strengthened Hawks's critical reputation in France retroactively largely because of the presence in the cast of Louise Brooks, an iridescent beauty of the twenties and ever after an icon. Here Brooks plays a circus high diver in a femme fatale role similar to Garbo's in *The Temptress* (1926), and her schemes, like Garbo's, to break up the beautiful friendship between two men come to naught. Victor McLaglen and Robert Armstrong play the buddy-buddies in the Brooks film. *The Air Circus*, listed by the *New York Times* as one of ten best films of 1928, was a part-talkie, and *Trent's Last Case*, adapted from a famous mystery novel by E. C. Bentley, was a "sound" film. Indeed, *A Girl in Every Port, Fazil*, and *Trent's Last Case* were all embellished with musical scores and synchronized sound effects as Hollywood and Hawks edged toward the Age of the Talkies.

The Dawn Patrol (1930) was Hawks's first all-talking film, and its history is typical of Hawks's luck in the matter of reputation and name recognition. The film was released at a time when the screen was saturated with imitations of Lewis Milestone and Erich Maria Remarque's *All Quiet on the Western Front* and James Whale and Robert Sheriff's *Journey's End*, not to mention such fondly remembered twenties classics as King Vidor's *The Big Parade* and William Wellman's Oscar-winning *Wings*. Consequently, the critics, though favorably disposed toward *The Dawn Patrol*, tended to dismiss it in the hope that the genre would sooner or later peter out. Nonetheless, the movie was well liked by the public and fondly remembered for years despite a glossier 1938 re-make starring Errol Flynn, David Niven, and Basil Rathbone, and directed by Edmund Goulding.

Hawks focuses here on the problem of moral responsibility in the crucible of action, a theme that will be amplified in later Hawks films. The exposition of *The Dawn Patrol* places Neil Hamilton in a command position on the front lines, where British planes of inferior quality, undermanned and outnumbered, are sent out each day with the foreknowledge that few will return. Richard Barthelmess, second in command, and Douglas Fairbanks, Jr., his closest friend, by their direct participation in the action are relieved of much of the moral burden. It is interesting to note that Hamilton and Barthelmess are further estranged by a previous off-screen argument over a woman. This conception of the female serving in an essentially masculine world as a source of friction, competition, and moral catharsis will be developed in later films when the uniquely Hawksian woman actually materializes on the screen.

When Hamilton is promoted to a higher chain of command, Barthelmess is compelled to assume the responsibility for sending men out to die, and finally ruptures his friendship with Fairbanks by sending the latter's younger wide-eyed brother on a fatal mission. To atone for his guilt, Barthelmess gets Fairbanks drunk and takes his place on the suicide flight. Fairbanks, as next in command, steps into the position of responsibility; the routine is resumed; the killing continues; the unnatural order is triumphant.

Hawks's treatment of the material is distinguished by his characteristic virtues: bare, clean, uncluttered technique, a stark story line entirely within the range of terse dialogue which states the situation and withdraws when the moral conflict becomes implicit in its action, and, most important, a pervasive atmosphere of hopelessness captured with economy and incisiveness.

The Criminal Code (1931) is perhaps the least known, least accessible, and least frequently revived Hawks talking picture. Based on a play by Martin Flavin, from which Seton I. Miller and Fred Niblo, Jr., wrote the screenplay, *The Criminal Code* takes Hawks on his only excursion into the popular thirties genre of the prison movie. The picture is dominated by the character-actor charisma of Walter Huston, who plays a cynical district attorney who boasts that he can successfully argue both sides of a case. When his political ambitions are stymied, he is appointed warden of a prison where many of the inmates owe their confinement to his prowess as a prosecuting attorney. The warden defuses an impending explosion of convict anger by boldly running the gauntlet unarmed and unguarded between two rows of angry revenge-seekers. This could be considered a Hawksian gambit were it not a staple of the genre.

Scarface (1932) is the bloodiest and most brutal of the gangster films that embellished the American cinema of the early thirties. Hawks and Ben Hecht patterned its Capone-ish characters after the Borgias. Paul Muni plays Tony, a killer with Napoleonic ambitions and a taste for silk shirts and sleek women, particularly wisecracking Karen Morley, who is the mistress of Osgood Perkins, Tony's superior until Tony has him murdered by George Raft, who is then murdered by Tony for what were actually honorable intentions toward Tony's sister, Ann Dvorak. Before Tony is dispatched, a new record is set for murders on the screen.

A lofty, neon-lit Cook's Tour sign, "The World Is Yours," plays a major symbolic role in the film, and when Tony and his henchmen attend the theater, they witness the first two acts of *Rain*, another drama of man's presumption in asserting his will over others; but before the third act of retribution, Tony and his entourage depart for more skulduggery. *Scarface*, with its titular connotation of mutilation, introduces a new motif into the films of Hawks, one which will evolve into a personal statement on the human condition in later films.

What is most remarkable about *Scarface* is its not having been recognized as one of the landmarks of the American sound film. As was the case with *Dawn Patrol*, *Scarface* marked the end instead of the beginning of a cycle, and lamentable genre-fatigue set in once more with a vengeance. However, the critics of the thirties were also unduly preoccupied with topical questions of social relevance, and the Hawksian personality could not meet the tests of social consciousness. For all its pessimism, *Dawn Patrol* does not expound the still-fashionable pacifism of *All Quiet on the Western Front*.

Despite a hypocritical foreword demanding public indignation for the entertaining spectacle which was to follow, and an obligatory scene in which a group of reformers stare at the audience and suggest a vague form of lynch law, *Scarface* is presented from the point of view of its gangster protagonist. His villainy is never traced back to slum or immigrant origins. He first materializes as a moving shadow slowly tracking towards a victim in a phone booth, and then and there one perceives that Hawks is working in the shadow of Murnau, taking the German master's fluid camera style beyond the sound barrier of the restrictive microphone.

Perhaps the most fascinating aspect of *Scarface* for modern audiences is the explicitly incestuous relationship between Tony and his sister. Hawks's matter-of-fact perverseness extends to the gangster moll, particularly in one memorable scene in which Karen Morley smiles with manic glee when she is told that Muni has murdered her erstwhile lover. George Raft's famous coin-tossing mannerism (and fatalism) is repeated by Thomas Mitchell in *Only Angels Have Wings*, and significantly both men are killed. The growing sophistication of dialogue acting in Hollywood can be measured by the distance Hawks has come from *Dawn Patrol* to *Scarface*. Barthelmess, Fairbanks, and Hamilton disconcert modern audiences with their deliberate intonations and pauses whereas the readings of Muni, Osgood Perkins, and even George Raft leave nothing to be desired. There were still a few reciters like Purnell Pratt and C. Henry Gordon to make the law sound even more awkward than it was, perhaps an unconscious inspiration provided by Tolstoy's *The Power of Darkness*.

In *The Crowd Roars* (1932), the action is even more gratuitous than in *Dawn Patrol*. The insane world of auto-racing is immediately evoked in a pre-credits sequence in which an accident on the speedway rouses the bestial roar of the crowd. Further documentation is provided in the opening scenes in which James Cagney makes a token effort to dissuade his kid brother from a career on the speedway. From then on, the characters forget about the hell they inhabit, accepting their abnormal existence on its own terms as the only one they know.

The plot is developed through Cagney's jealousy of his once-innocent brother who begins to acquire the same values of liquor and women which Cagney had made an indispensable part of his tightrope existence. When Eric Linden threatens to displace Cagney professionally, the break between the two brothers is complete. Their mutual friend, Frank McHugh, a married man with a child, attempts to keep their cars apart on the speedway and is killed for his efforts. As they cross the finish line, their cars crack up, but they continue their vocation by directing their ambulance to race another to the hospital. No excuses are made for the frenzied crowd. Even the women, Joan Blondell and Ann Dvorak, accept the rules of the game without flinching. The crucial racing scenes receive the bulk of Hawks's attention, but the dialogue scenes are pervaded with a bitter cynicism toward the world which has created this situation, reserving respect for the men who live up to its values.

Only superficially is *Tiger Shark* (1932) a triangle love story within an action frame. The plot seems simple enough. Edward G. Robinson falls in love with Zita Johann and marries her. He is overwhelmed by the idea of a woman's accepting him after he has lost an arm to the sharks in the California waters where he works as a tuna fisherman, again, as in all of Hawks, dangerously. For her part, the girl accepts Robinson because she finds herself in the classic *Anna Christie* situation, particularly after her father has been devoured by the sharks. Richard Arlen is Robinson's best friend, a relationship developed in the first scene, in which Robinson saves Arlen's life after they are shipwrecked. Arlen is young and virile and has always been more successful with women than Robinson. In no time at all, the girl is irresistibly drawn to Arlen and he to her. When Robinson discovers the intrigue, he tries to feed Arlen to the sharks, but suffers that fate himself when he is tripped up by a harpoon line.

The film is driven beyond its plot level by larger-than-life characters and the symbolism of the sharks. Robinson is presumptuously Ahab-like not only in delivering one enemy to the sharks at the beginning of the film and attempting to repeat the process with his rival at the end, but also in his obsession with killing as many sharks as he can. However, there is another, more Hawksian, aspect to the symbolism. At first glance, it would seem that Arlen has betrayed his friendship with Robinson by coveting his friend's wife, but ultimately it is Robinson who is unnatural in attempting to defeat the inexorable sexual attractions of nature. Here and elsewhere, Hawks remorselessly applies the law of nature to sex. The man who is flawed by age, mutilation, or unpleasing appearance to even the slightest degree inevitably loses the woman to his flawless rival. This may seem logical enough by any Hollywood standard in *Tiger Shark*, where Robinson is pitted against Arlen, but it is not nearly so obvious in later Hawks films where John Wayne is defeated by Montgomery Clift and Kirk Douglas is bested by Dewey Martin.

This uniquely cinematic idea is made explicit in *Tiger Shark*. Before his death, the girl's father tells Robinson that a man who has lost part of his body to the sharks can never hope to reach Heaven in such a state of incompleteness. When the elderly myth-dispenser dies later with both legs amputated by a shark, Robinson orders the shark killed and captured and then, acting with divine presumption, buries the shark at sea with the dead amputee, who can now enter Heaven intact. What is most interesting in *Tiger Shark* is that the standards of God are identical with the standards of Hawksian Woman, an inexorable force of nature which mercilessly rejects the physically imperfect.

Today We Live (1933) is the only MGM film Hawks ever directed to completion, and it marks Hawks's first screen-writing collaboration with William Faulkner. It was clearly intended as a star vehicle for Joan Crawford, but somehow a Hawksian mood of fatalistic male bonding overshadowed the love-making. The story concerns a trio of British comrades—Joan Crawford; Franchot Tone, her brother; Robert Young, her childhood sweetheart—and Gary Cooper, the rich American who comes to buy their ancestral home.

In spite of the nonsense that this conjures up (it must be admitted that the situation inspires some coy scenes between Crawford and Cooper), Hawks concentrates on the traditional codes and loyalties which are faced with imminent catastrophe. The action quickly shifts to war-torn France. In a fog-bound French port near the front lines, Tone and Young are torpedo boat pilots, Cooper a volunteer airman, and Crawford a valiant ambulance driver. When Young is blinded in a naval action, and learns that Crawford remains with him only out of pity and childhood loyalty when she really loves Cooper, he engages in a suicide mission (with Tone's stoical, pipe-chewing assistance as Young's eyes), forestalling Cooper's equally suicidal and equally sacrificial aerial mission to the same target.

Hawks started a second MGM film, *Viva Villa!* (1934), but the film was taken over and eventually signed by Jack Conway (who had directed a film from a Hawks scenario in 1923, *Quicksands*). The original plan of the film emphasized the male camaraderie between Wallace Beery and Lee Tracy, who was replaced by Stuart Erwin during the shooting of the film in Mexico. Motivated at first by a primitive sense of vengeful justice and his loyalty to Madero, Villa is gradually corrupted by the temptation of power coupled with an instinctual tendency towards brutality and sexual excess. Villa emerges finally as a gallant Hawksian figure, a man who has attempted an action beyond his intellectual capacities, but who has struggled honorably. One might note in passing that Hawks has criticized Kazan for sentimentally transforming Villa's equally brutal colleague, Zapata, into Marlon Brando's conception of an agrarian reformer.

Twentieth Century was one of the earliest screwball comedies and was performed with the frenetic pacing that typified his later efforts in the genre. Released in 1934 with a sophisticated Hecht-MacArthur script, *Twentieth Century* was a few years ahead of its time, and, as might be expected of a Hawks masterpiece, did not receive the popular and critical acclaim it deserved. Hawks can take the credit not only for John Barrymore's best bravura comedy performance, but also for the film that first established Carole Lombard as one of the finest comediennes of the thirties. Although this is a play adaptation, it enables Hawks to exploit two of his favorite devices for cinematic narrative: the odyssey and the enclosure, in this instance combined by the inner and outer aspects of a train—the Twentieth Century—speeding across the continent.

Hawksian comedy is even more bitter than Hawksian adventure as it confronts the disordered world of the twentieth century, and the title here is quite inspired as a key to Hawks's attitudes toward modern life. Exhausted by her frenzied theatrical experiences, the heroine tries to escape into a normal existence, but is thwarted by a series of farcical intrigues which would never have succeeded had she not been unconsciously drawn to the very insanity she sought to escape. However, unlike other comedy directors of the period such as Cukor, McCarey, and La Cava, Hawks never paused long enough to exploit the inherent pathos and emotional involvement of the situation. Without invoking the sentimentality of the theater except as a last resort, the director in *Twentieth Century* is simultaneously involved in the lunacy of the stage and yet determined to master it on his own terms. *Twentieth Century* is notable as the first comedy in which sexually attractive, sophisticated stars indulged in their own slapstick instead of delegating it to underlings.

Barbary Coast (1935) is a fog-drenched action picture which strikingly illuminates Hawks's sexual attitudes. Miriam Hopkins plays an impoverished Southern belle who comes to San Francisco to marry her fiancé, who has struck gold, and finds that he has been robbed and killed by hijackers. She sets out to make her fortune by joining Edward G. Robinson, the leader of the Barbary Coast underworld. Her capitulation to Robinson is prompted neither by emotion nor perversity, but by a healthy respect for jewelry. For Robinson, Hopkins is a cherished status symbol, and they get along famously until Joel McCrea, a victimized miner, is attracted to her. She falls in love with McCrea, but he is repulsed when he discovers her relations with Robinson. She nevertheless helps save McCrea from the vengeful crime czar, who is killed in the final action, leaving Hopkins and McCrea, together and penniless, to return to the mine.

Barbary Coast is foggy, dark, and very violent. Even after 1934, when the Hays Office clamped down on Hollywood's more lustful enterprises during the transition from Mae West to Shirley Temple, Hawks continued to treat sexual encounters frankly and intelligently. Men and women in Hawks's films go to bed together without any of the coy preliminaries or traumatic after-effects which mar so many Hollywood films even today. The Hopkins-Robinson-McCrea relationship here recalls *Tiger Shark* in that Robinson is doomed to failure more by his relative unattractiveness than by his defects of character. A reasonably sympathetic figure, he is moved to vengeance only when Hopkins betrays him. For his part, McCrea is horrified not by the abstract immorality of Hopkins's behavior but by the physically odious nature of her alliance.

Ceiling Zero (1936) is one of Hawks's best-remembered works, and with *Sergeant York* the Hawks film most highly regarded by the conventional critics of its time. Frank Wead, who wrote both the stage and screen versions of *Ceiling Zero*, was the hero of John Ford's *The Wings of Eagles*. James Cagney and Pat O'Brien were an overworked team at Warners, and some critics were dubious when they were announced for this project, but the team and the director turned out to be admirably suited to each other. Cagney, one of the great American actors, was hampered throughout most of his career by bad directors, while O'Brien was too often exploited for the hard-boiled sentimentality in his voice.

Here Hawks returns to his favorite subject, aviation, to dramatize the conflict between the pioneer spirit of the old carefree, ne'er-do-well pilots and the mechanized modern aircraft industry supervised by government bureaucracy. Hawks sympathizes completely with the old order as he tracks it to its doom. The director follows the well-made play in detail, but by merely dramatizing its aerial climaxes, he transforms the material into pure cinema.

The action takes place within two days and nights at Newark Airport, actually another of Hawks's enclosures, where fog and ice are nature's challenge to the human quest for the impossible. A meaningful shot of birds perched on the ground while planes crash in the air emphasizes man's unnatural presumption. The Cagney character is a man who lives according to the rules of an earlier era—war, pioneering, stunt flying, and danger for its own sake. When the times change, he cannot change with them. He has also succumbed to the temptation of heroism and is not above exploiting his own image to satisfy his irresponsible sex drives. O'Brien, Cagney's superior and erstwhile comrade-in-arms, accepts the more difficult and ultimately impossible task of reconciling the two ages of aviation. When Cagney fakes a heart ailment to duck a flying assignment so that he can seduce a hero-worshiping young girl, the pilot who takes his place is killed. Here again, Hawks destroys his comedy relief: one minute the familiarly hen-pecked Stuart Erwin, the next, a doomed figure of heroic proportions. Cagney performs his act of expiation by replacing the girl's fiancé on what amounts to a suicide mission. The scenes between Cagney and June Travis, culminating in her unabashed offer of her body as consolation for Cagney's guilt, are Hawksian in their tough directness. One of Hawks's most fully realized films, *Ceiling Zero* is directed at a breakneck pace which emphasizes its lean fibre and its concentration on the essentials of its theme.

The Road to Glory (1936) is a film which has been apparently neglected or perhaps unseen even by Hawks enthusiasts in France, and, needless to say, it has no reputation in America. It is as moodily fatalistic as anything Hawks has ever done. The plot concerns a doomed regiment whose members are aware of its glorious traditions. They are led by Warner Baxter, who enters an affair with June Lang so that he can have someone to whom he can leave his possessions when he is killed. Fredric March, Baxter's next in command, meets the girl during an air raid and tells her they must live for the moment. (The intensity with which Hawks transcends the most outrageously romantic clichés has to be seen to be believed.) Yet afterwards, he will not hear of her leaving Baxter, and when Baxter, discovering the intrigue, sends March out on one suicide patrol after another, March accepts the logic of the situation. Lionel Barrymore is Baxter's proud father, an enlisted man of the older generation to whom legends have acquired reality within his lifetime. Barrymore suddenly becomes a coward when he discovers that the glory he covets can be gained only by death. When Baxter becomes blinded from shell-fire, he responds to all the Hawksian imperatives—moral, sexual, and natural—by having Barrymore lead him on a fatal mission. The film ends with March assuming command and repeating Baxter's heroic invocation to death and glory for his troops in a pointless military situation which Hawks neither questions nor defends.

Come and Get It (1936) is one of those eternal mysteries. In the old days when William Wyler was considered one of the great American directors, the serious film historian tried to figure out what part of this Hawks-Wyler film Wyler had directed. Today it is more interesting to determine what Wyler did not direct. We know that Hawks started the film and Wyler finished it, that the beginning looks like Hawks and the end like Wyler. Certainly the conception of a power-mad lumber tycoon being defeated by life is Hawksian, but in this instance, the leading character, however heroic, has little chance against Edna Ferber's sprawling novel, which takes a far longer time span than Hawks has ever attempted. What seems alien to the project from a Hawksian viewpoint is the pathos of the unattained woman (Frances Farmer) sacrificed upon the altar of excessive ambition. This aspect of the plot seems to be more Wyler's speed, but the brawling sequences on the road to power do have a distinctively Hawksian flavor, and the tycoon character of Edward Arnold does have a certain extraneous interest as a symptom of the thirties.

Bringing Up Baby (1938) is undeniably the screwiest of the screwball comedies. Even Hawks has never equaled the rocketing pace of this demented farce in which Cary Grant and Katharine Hepburn made Barrymore and Lombard in *Twentieth Century* seem about as feverish as Victoria and Albert. This film passes beyond the customary lunacy of the period into a bestial *Walpurgisnacht* during which man, dog, and leopard pursue each other over the Connecticut countryside until the behavior patterns of men and animals become indistinguishable. Grant is a distinguished scientist who has labored for years to reconstruct a dinosaur. While seeking a donation for his museum, he collides literally and figuratively with a madcap heiress played by Miss Hepburn with a frantic style unlike that of any of her other performances.

Some critics have mistakenly defined Hepburn in terms of this isolated performance, but it is the Cukor and Stevens blend of brashness and emotional vulnerability which is most typical of her career in the thirties. Here she demolishes in minutes what it took the scientist she loves years to develop, and the film ends with Grant and Hepburn embracing over the ruins of the dinosaur. The film is so fast that it is impossible for the audience to stop even to enjoy it, much less to speculate on its interior meaning. The "Baby" of the title refers to a tame leopard which Hepburn forces Grant to share as a problem. The very quest to which Grant is dedicated involves the reconstruction of man's bestial origins which, Hawks suggests, are not too far from man's present state, particularly in the disorder of the modern world where the possibilities of regression seem infinite. The regression of man to a lower order will henceforth be one of the dominant motifs of Hawksian comedy.

Hawks, in *Only Angels Have Wings*, returns to his personal genre of the airplane. By 1939, the notion of air pioneering would have seemed somewhat out of date in America. Consequently, Hawks expatriated his characters to a Central American banana republic where aviation was still in its primitive, individualistic stages, and people were trying to maintain an airmail business against the hazards of the surrounding mountains and the foggy atmosphere. *Only Angels Have Wings* marks the end of an era, and it is one of Hawks's finest films. Once again the themes of responsibility and expiation are applied to men striving to perform the impossible for purely gratuitous reasons. The film also introduces the latter-day Hawks heroine, the tough, wisecracking chippy expertly played by Jean Arthur. Her exchanges with the laconic hero, Cary Grant, are repeated almost verbatim in *To Have and Have Not, Red River,* and *Rio Bravo.* Richard Barthelmess plays the aviator who must atone for his guilt in having caused the death of Thomas Mitchell's brother through cowardice. Grant's motives for giving him his chance are complicated by the fact that Barthelmess's wife, a pre-stardom Rita Hayworth, is Grant's own lost love. *Only Angels Have Wings* is the most romantic film of Hawks's career, and its pessimistic mood was the director's last gesture to the spirit of the thirties reflected in the doomed cinema of Renoir and Carné.

His Girl Friday (1940) is a loose remake of *The Front Page* with Hildy Parks transformed into Hildy Johnson, girl reporter, played by Rosalind Russell in her bright comedy period. The antagonistic male relationship of the original is deftly converted into sexual conflict. The film begins with the classic scene of Cary Grant ridiculing an unsuspecting Ralph Bellamy. Aside from permanently destroying Bellamy as a serious screen personality, this bit of hilarious sadism is consistent with Hawks's conception of Bellamy as the "square" outsider who attempts to rescue the heroine from the insane world of journalism, an attempt doomed to failure by the very structure of Hawksian comedy as the defeat of intelligence and dignity by the more discordant aspects of modern life.

It is mainly a matter of historical curiosity that Hawks directed the first ten days of *The Outlaw*, which Howard Hughes completed. Hawks once stated in an interview that he always searches for a comic angle on the grimmest material, and it is highly possible that Hawks is responsible for the zany conception of *The Outlaw* with its suggestive homoerotism in the strange relationship between Jack Buetel's Billy the Kid and Walter Huston's Doc Holliday. Of course, most critics were too distracted to get the joke, and sociologists cannot evade the fact that the bosom craze which swept America in the forties was caused more by the publicity for Jane Russell than by the atomic bomb.

Sergeant York is probably Hawks's greatest popular success due to its timing on the eve of Pearl Harbor by virtue of a government request to have the World War I hero glamorized. Yet, the film is completely Hawksian in its account of Alvin York's attempt to achieve the impossible in farming the hard, rocky soil of Tennessee, the temptations of liquor and violence, the sudden conversion to revivalist Christianity after a violent brush with lightning, and then the violation of all his moral convictions under the duress of the supreme disorder of war. Hawks parallels a prewar turkey shoot in which York gobbles at the turkeys to make them raise their heads and the same maneuver applied in the trenches to human targets. The ending finds York rewarded by the grateful people of Tennessee with a new house, but it is a sad ending for a man of conviction to be rewarded for his murders.

The public misunderstood the full implications of the film, and for once their conception of the hero seemed to coincide with Hawks's. Gary Cooper gave the best performance of his career in the title role, and secured the only Academy Award ever presented to a Hawks-directed player, if one excepts the fractional share of credit for Walter Brennan's supporting award in the Hawks-Wyler *Come and Get It* (1936).

Ball of Fire (1941) marks Hawks's only collaboration with the writing team of Brackett and Wilder, and is remarkably consistent with previously developed Hawksian conceptions. Once more a learned man concerned with the quest for knowledge is subjected to the inhuman excesses of the modern world. Gary Cooper is working with a group of professors on an encyclopedia. When he reaches "Slang" he enlists the services of a burlesque dancer (Barbara Stanwyck) who is fleeing the police. He is then forced out of his academic sanctuary in order to win the dancer from the gangster. The regression of intellectual man to the level of the caveman is accomplished here in the fast raucous style which is the Hawksian trademark.

Air Force (1943) makes a return to the odyssey of *Twentieth Century*, this time within the enclosure of a B-17. The inclusive title indicates the size of its aspirations, and the cross-sectional nomenclature (Winocki, Weinberg, etc.) confirmed the film's intentions, which though not entirely original were less hackneyed in 1943 than later. *Air Force*, one of the first World War II films, was easily the best until *They Were Expendable* (1945) and *The Story of G.I. Joe* (1945). Again the heroes of the film are confronted with an impossible task, the repair of a badly damaged bomber under the guns of the Japanese.

The film is marred by its propagandist ending, which displays the complete obliteration of a Japanese task force by a squadron of bombers. One of the assets of the film was the relatively unknown status of the male cast, which aside from John Garfield included Gig Young, Arthur Kennedy, John Ridgely, James Brown, and Charles Drake. Hawks's technique, confronted with epic material for the first time, reveals a new incisiveness in exploiting the calculated symbolism of a plane around which events swirl during its odyssey.

Howard Hawks produced *Corvette K-225* (1943) but assigned the direction to Richard Rosson. The film bears the Hawks imprint in its laconic account of the men sailing the convoys to England. The film is also notable for the presence of Ella Raines, a Hawks discovery and a distinctively Hawksian woman, visually as well as conceptually—gaunt, leggy, husky-voiced—a type later represented by Lauren Bacall, Joanne Dru, and Angie Dickinson.

To Have and Have Not (1944) and *The Big Sleep* (1946) represent Hawks in his Bogart-Bacall period, and here the two players create a personal myth derived from the Hawksian conception of sex—tough and direct, from the masculine point of view. *To Have and Have Not* was loosely adapted from what is considered Hemingway's weakest book; it retained what was best in the novel: the opening fishing trip and the fatalistic mood, switched from immigrant-smuggling Key West to Vichy-occupied Martinique, and concentrated on a Hemingwayesque love story between a cynically disengaged hero and a sultry tramp capable of sustaining sharp repartee. This time the impossible action is Bogart's attempt to retain his freedom and detachment, menaced by the war and the women who pursue him. He loses in both cases, but retains respect through his masculine independence. The emphasis is on the atmosphere and the wry wit rather than the action plot which Hawks does not treat too seriously.

In *The Big Sleep*, Hawks transcends the private-eye genre with his personal attitude towards apparently unmotivated violence as still another manifestation of the unnatural order with which man must cope. At first, Bogart treats his job with the professional casualness of a salesman who never heard of Arthur Miller, but he is soon corrupted by an obsession with the mysteries of a world in which evil is never adequately explained. (Hawks himself never figured out why one of the eight murders in the film had been committed. During the last stages of production, the director called Raymond Chandler, the author of the original novel, long-distance in New York, but the mystery writer was unable to provide an adequate solution.)

The Big Sleep is notable for its gallows humor and its sense of hopeless enclosure within an ominous cosmos. The sexual repartee achieved an extraordinary frankness for its time in a Bogart-Bacall scene written in racetrack parlance with Bacall observing that her performance down the home stretch depended on her jockey. However, gallantry is again the key to Bogart's renunciation of disengagement. Bogart unwittingly observes the murder by poison of a small-time hoodlum played by Elisha Cook, Jr., one of the marvelous supporting players with which Hollywood was blessed in its days of abundance. When Bogart discovers that Cook shielded an unworthy mistress even in the moment he faced certain death, the detective is transformed into an avenger. The most violent denouements never obscure the director's commitment to the decencies of human behavior. *The Big Sleep* demonstrates also that a director of Hawks's unusual intelligence can control the most lurid materials without descending to ludicrous sensationalism.

The Big Sleep is graced by one of the most memorable interrogation scenes in all cinema. Bogart is questioning Louis Jean Heydt, a petty gambler and blackmailer. While Heydt is telling one implausible lie after another, he keeps turning in his chair slowly to evade Bogart's eyes while the detective circles Heydt to maintain a meaningful eye contact. Hawks follows this reciprocal movement with a circular camera movement around his human reference points. The slowly circling camera can be one of the most portentous elements of cinematic expression. Dreyer employs this device in *Ordet* to deify his Christ-figure. Hitchcock's application of this maneuver in the carriage-house scene in *Vertigo* creates a Pirandellian ambiguity between past and present, illusion and reality.

There is, however, nothing mystical or vertiginous about Hawks. He circles Bogart and Heydt simply to emphasize a judgment of character. Almost every character in *The Big Sleep* lies to Bogart, including Lauren Bacall, but Heydt is uniquely treated because he lies badly and without style. Shortly after the interrogation, he is murdered quite pointlessly and forgotten immediately. Hawks and Bogart circle Heydt to express a contempt which is less moral than aesthetic. What is displayed here is a ruthless conception of human value. Even when a degree of sentimentality might be expected, the Hawksian position remains clear. In *Only Angels Have Wings* Grant sums up Noah Beery, Jr.'s, fatal crash with the comment that Beery just wasn't *good* enough. In the violent world of Howard Hawks, one has to be good to survive honorably or even to perish honorably, and, at least on this level, Hawksian heroes follow the canons of Sophoclean tragedy enunciated by Aristotle more closely than do Blanche du Bois, Willy Loman, and the tormented protagonists of Eugene O'Neill.

I Was a Male War Bride (1949) bitterly records the battle of the sexes in the modern world to the point of transvestism, Ann Sheridan in trousers and Cary Grant in a skirt; the corruption of European culture by Americanistic energy; and the dehumanization of man by modern bureaucracy to the extent that Grant is driven to the frenzy of an animal by his inability to find a place to sleep in accordance with the perforations of IBM mentalities. *Monkey Business* (1952) demolishes the poignant myths of childhood in its depiction of savagery and brutish self-indulgence, qualities amplified in the unforgettable image of George Winslow, the cigar-smoking toddler who is on the make for Marilyn Monroe in *Gentlemen Prefer Blondes*. *A Song Is Born* (1948) is a strident commentary on the modern world which fancies brassy jazz as its idiom and takes pride in the insane dislocation such a relationship implies. In *The Thing* (1951), the scientists are so obsessed with pure knowledge that they jeopardize human lives (and life?) to explore the fathomless mysteries of the universe. They even try to appease a monster which will devour them, warn an enemy which is their own enemy, sacrifice their obligation to their own survival in pursuit of an abstract, inhuman ideal of truth.

Red River (1948) was advertised at the time of its release as the spectacular successor to Cruze's *The Covered Wagon* (1923) and Ruggles's *Cimarron* (1931). *Life* magazine praised the film for being one of the rare westerns which indicated how cowboys made their living, but work of a hazardous nature has always been central to Hawksian cinema. What is most impressive about *Red River* is Hawks's concentration on character relationships amid the swirling dust of horses and cattle. Here the spectacle of a cattle drive is harnessed to the father-son relationship of John Wayne and Montgomery Clift. Wayne is obsessed with the ordeal of driving a herd of cattle from Texas to Missouri over obstacles raised by nature, wild Indians, and vengeful jayhawkers, a bitter legacy of the Civil War which has disrupted the cattle economy on which Wayne's wealth is based. (The jayhawkers never actually appear in *Red River* although their reported depredations are a decisive factor in shifting the route of the cattle drive. The jayhawkers finally arrive in Raoul Walsh's *The Tall Men* (1955), a loose remake of *Red River* produced by William Hawks, the original director's brother, and "supervised" by Darryl F. Zanuck, an indication of the outside interference which kept Walsh from rising to the level of Hawks.)

Clift breaks with Wayne over a moral issue influenced by tactical considerations. Wayne is about to hang two deserters from the cattle drive when Clift usurps his authority with the aid of his friends. This aid is necessary because Clift will not draw on Wayne, and Hawks will not inject a Freudian dose of parricide into an heroic genre. Here again Hawks is intelligent enough to provide Clift with an alternative policy which justifies the seizure of power. There have been rumors of a railroad extension west from Missouri to Abilene, Kansas. Clift accepts the risk of economic failure in Abilene to avert the possibility of bloodshed and defections in Missouri. Joanne Dru, another of Hawks's memorably tough women, intervenes to reconcile the two men, giving herself to Clift, offering herself to Wayne, and then firing on the two men to end the ritualistic violence of their reconciliation. Some American critics objected to the girl's decisive role in the action, but Joanne Dru's function in *Red River* is consistent with the Hawksian conception of women as men's accomplices in the most violent actions. By contrast, Ford's women usually wave goodbye to their men of action. The difference between Ford and Hawks is thus the difference between chivalry and gallantry.

ORSON WELLES (1915–1985)

In the first half of the twentieth century, a little boy could conceivably have *heard* Orson Welles long before he *heard of* him. The year was

1937, and over the ether came the cavernous, menacingly righteous growl: "WHO KNOWS WHAT EVIL LURKS IN THE HEARTS OF MEN? THE SHADOW KNOWS. HEH-HEH-HEH." A twenty-two-year-old prodigy, world wanderer, and eventually man for all media had assumed the radio role of the Shadow, alias Lamont Cranston, the man of mystery who could "cloud men's minds so that they cannot see him." (There is indeed in this description a foreshadowing of the magical tricks and Germanic Expressionism that were to go into the making of the film *Citizen Kane* in 1940.) Before *The Shadow*, the magnificently versatile Wellesian voice had been employed on the airwaves in the popular *March of Time* series for characterizations ranging from President Paul von Hindenburg of Germany to all five Dionne quintuplets. On into the forties, Welles was a regular presence on radio in a variety of formats even while he was engaged in stage and screen productions.

"Radio," Welles once remarked in an interview, "is a popular democratic machine for disseminating information and entertainment. . . ." He was not snobbish about popular entertainment per se. His radio shows ranged high and low—from *The Shadow* to Shakespeare—though he never treated the former lightly or the latter reverentially. In 1938, Welles signed a contract with CBS to create an hour-long, nationally broadcast dramatic show called *First Person Singular* which he would write, produce, direct, and perform. We must remember that radio in the thirties, like television today, was the dominant instrument of political control, and that Welles was deeply immersed in the ideological conflicts of his time. The most powerful politicians of that era—Roosevelt, Churchill, Hitler—had all mastered the art of communicating to their followers by radio, and Welles himself recognized the potential of radio to elevate the aesthetics of a larger public than could be reached by him on Broadway.

For Welles, radio and theater were conveniently adjacent activities in Manhattan. Many nights he would emerge from a stage door, his curtain-call costume and greasepaint still in place, enter an ambulance chartered for the occasion, and, with red lights flashing and sirens screaming, speed to a radio station for a West Coast rebroadcast (these being the antedeluvian days before taping). Obviously he thrived on being a human whirlwind even after *Time* magazine had hailed him as the "brightest moon that has risen over Broadway in years." "Welles should feel at home in the sky," *Time* raved on, "for the sky is the only limit to his ambition."

While his Broadway work was being heralded as putting "new fire into the art of the stage," Welles had demonstrated an equally high seriousness of purpose on radio even before his 1938 contract with CBS for the *Mercury Theatre on the Air*, with that subjectivist subtitle *First Person Singular*. In 1937 he played in radio adaptations of *Twelfth Night* and *Les Misérables*, and perhaps, most prestigiously of all, in Archibald Mac-Leish's *The Fall of the City*.

Most of the writings on Welles have tended, until very recently, to give comparatively short shrift to his radio persona by concentrating almost entirely on the outrageous publicity he received for his gimmicky adaptation of H. G. Wells's *The War of the Worlds*, the inspiration for the 1996 Sci-fi blockbuster, *Independence Day*. This *Mercury Theatre on the Air* broadcast about monstrous creatures from Mars invading Earth on the eve of Halloween 1938 capitalized on the period's crisis atmosphere full of headlines in the tabloids about imminent war in Europe. The show benefited also from a weak guest roster on the very popular Edgar Bergen and Charlie McCarthy program on a rival network in the same time slot. On Halloween itself, Welles found himself a worldwide celebrity. By calculation or by chance, he had demonstrated the manipulative power of the medium as it was never to be demonstrated again.

The Magic World of Orson Welles is an insightful analysis of all facets of Welles's artistic achievements, and author James Naremore is one of the very few scholars to place the radio work of the Mercury players in proper perspective.

> [One of Welles's] more important contributions had to do with the form of radio dramatics. This moribund art is usually regarded as an extension of playwriting, but Welles always thought of radio . . . as a narrative medium rather than a purely dramatic one. "There is nothing that seems more unsuited to the technique of the microphone," he said, "than to tune in on a play and hear the announcer say, 'the curtain is now rising on a presentation of—' this method of introducing the characters and setting seems hopelessly inadequate and clumsy." Welles wanted to eliminate the "impersonal" quality of such programs, which treated the listener like an eavesdropper.
>
> Welles's solution to the problem was simple and effective. With his magnificent voice, he could become the perfect storyteller. Explaining the techniques, he compared radio to oral narrative: "When a fellow leans back in his chair and begins: 'Now, this is how it happened'—the listener feels that the narrator is taking him into his confidence; he begins to take a personal interest in the outcome."

By making himself the center of the storytelling process, Welles established the impression of self-adulation that was to haunt his career to his dying day. For the most part, however, Welles was singularly generous to the other members of his cast and inspired loyalty from them above and beyond the call of professionalism.

Like Picasso, Welles was a dramatic painter of scenes in which he himself was often the gothic menace. It is not surprising then that he was attracted to such romantically brooding protagonists as Max de Winter in Daphne du Maurier's *Rebecca*—with Margaret Sullavan as his initially timid but ultimately dominant wife—and Mr. Rochester in Charlotte Brontë's *Jane Eyre*—opposite Madeleine Carroll in the title role. Both of these Campbell Playhouse broadcasts undoubtedly influenced the two movies that were adapted from the same novelistic material: Alfred Hitchcock's *Rebecca* with Laurence Olivier and then little known Joan Fontaine; and Robert Stevenson's *Jane Eyre*, with Welles repeating his Rochester opposite the screen's then-reigning gothic heroine, Joan Fontaine. *Rebecca*, particularly, popularized the tendency of screenplays of the forties to employ lyrical narration in order to create a mood. This was clearly a radio influence on cinema, an influence that has not been sufficiently appreciated in film histories. Welles was the most creative practitioner of this narrative method, but he was not entirely alone. Cecil B. De Mille, for example, lent his mellifluous voice to narration of the scene-setting openings of the *Lux Radio Theatre*, a weekly reprise of dramatized versions of current hit movies with an array of Hollywood stars.

Welles was much more than a mood-setting front man for his broadcasts, however, He often, though not always, played the main leads, and he wrote, produced, and directed a variety of stories ranging from *Sherlock Holmes* to *Treasure Island*. Of the last production, *The New York Times* review noted that Welles's voice was "more personal" than the standard radio announcer; "this . . . abetted by just enough sound effects of surf and shouts, screams and scheming, 'paints' the picture."

Not surprisingly, Welles took a personal interest in the much-satirized sound-effects subterfuges of radio technicians. (Welles himself had been practicing magic tricks since early childhood and had performed theatrically with them throughout his career.) Indeed, one of my fondest memories of Welles's gift (curse?) for self-parody is a skit he did with Fred Allen on *Les Misérables*, which Welles had performed on radio seriously a few years earlier. In the comically abbreviated version, the first act consists of Welles as Valjean clamoring through a verbose speech on justice and mercy, after which Allen as Javert is heard rapping on the door. Cutting into Allen's protests over how small his part is, Act Two continues with Welles orating on and on, after which Allen brings down the curtain with the sound of his police whistle. After more protests from Allen, Act Three takes place in a Paris sewer. Valjean concludes his final speech with the observation that he is tall enough to keep his head above the water, whereas his relentless pursuer is much shorter; Javert responds by gurgling as he drowns.

Welles's willingness to play the fool for a laugh was to work against him when the Hollywood herd turned against him. Just as his magic tricks allowed his detractors to claim that he was insincere and deceitful, his jokes about his multiple talents and credits on every project suggested to his enemies a fatal giddiness on his part. In a less self-destructive veim, he is redeemed by his deep feelings for the past. His father knew Booth Tarkington personally, and *The Magnificent Ambersons*—both on radio, in which he played George to Walter Huston's Eugene, and on the screen in his classic motion picture, which he narrates as Tim Holt plays George to Joseph Cotten's Eugene—serves as an allegory of Welles's own spoiled, tortured childhood in the Midwest.

This self-referential view of the past is also the theme of *Citizen Kane*, in which the ancient Oedipal conflict crystallizes in the revelatory symbolism of "Rosebud." Indeed, Welles's uncanny ability to play men and boys of all ages on radio, stage, and screen enabled him to play either side of the Oedipal seesaw at a moment's notice, whether as the callow youth in *Ah, Wilderness!* on the airwaves, as the ancient Shotover in Shaw's *Heartbreak House* in the theater, and, of course, as both the young and old Charles Foster Kane.

But there is much more that is endlessly fascinating about Welles's radio career than valuable clues to his inner life and artistic evolution. There are many luminaries of stage and screen to whom radio gave eternal vocal signature: Agnes Moorehead, Joseph Cotten, Ray Collins, George Coulouris, and Everett Sloane, from the *Mercury Theatre*; Gertrude Lawrence, Tallulah Bankhead, and Helen Hayes from Broadway; Margaret Sullavan, Burgess Meredith, and Fay Bainter from the stage and screen; Loretta Young, Lucille Ball, and Madeleine Carroll, from Hollywood; and Jack Benny and Fred Allen from radio itself.

Even when Welles tackled the familiar literary classics of the past, he tried to stir them into new life in the steaming cauldron of the present. This then was the substance of the Shadow: to educate, edify, and entertain the citizens of this republic with creative visions—most felicitously in sound—of our past, our present, and our future. Consequently, the radio heritage of Orson Welles tells us as much about America and the world from the mid-thirties to the mid-forties as it tells us about the man himself.

■   ■   ■   ■

CITIZEN KANE was first seen on the screen on May 1, 1941, at the Palace Theatre. The more prestigious and more profitable Radio City Music Hall had rejected the *Kane* booking presumably because of the unwelcome controversy surrounding the film's allegedly libelous treatment of William Randolph Hearst and his mistress Marion Davies. Although Orson Welles always insisted that Charles Foster Kane was a composite of several eccentric tycoons, Barbara Leaming's authorized biography of Welles contains the following startling passage: "Somehow, before making the movie, Orson had found out the secret name that Hearst used to refer to Marion Davies's genitalia: Rosebud." So much for all the arcane analysis of this most tantalizing of tinkling symbols in the cinema.

After more than half a century of relentless revaluation, however, the question still remains: Is *Citizen Kane* all that it is cracked up to be. If so, why? If not, why not? Believe it or not, many people on this planet have never seen *Citizen Kane*, and have little desire to do so. Of the few that have, fewer still have seen it more than once. We are not talking here about *Gone With the Wind* or *It's a Wonderful Life* or *The Wizard of Oz.* We are talking instead of a dark, shadowy slab of celluloid Jorge Luis Borges once described as that "centreless labyrinth" mentioned in Chesterton's *The Head of Caesar.* "It suffers," Borges wrote, "from grossness, pedantry, dullness. It is not intelligent, it is genial in the sombrest and most germanic sense of the word."

François Truffaut was much kinder to *Kane* though not without a certain ambivalence of his own: "It is a demonstration of the force of power and an attack on the force of power, it is a hymn to youth and a meditation on old age, an essay on the vanity of all material ambition and at the same time a poem on old age and the solitude of exceptional beings, genius or monster or monstrous genius."

Truffaut and his French colleagues on the staff of *Cahiers du Cinema* tended to meld the destinies of Charles Foster Kane with those of Orson Welles as the most explicit expression of *la politique des auteurs.* Most of the French revisionist critics were not able to see *Citizen Kane* until the end of the German Occupation in 1945. Hence, they saw the spectacular screen debut of Welles in the context of his precipitous decline and fall thereafter, at least in the eyes of the motion-picture industry. Welles himself turned up in Europe with the harried demeanor of a political exile. He was another Stroheim, another Chaplin, another Keaton, a genius to be ritualistically cherished in the generous French manner. *Kane* thus became inseparable from Welles and his ordeal at the hands of the American philistines.

Most film historians and cinéastes around the world continue to regard *Kane* as the artistic creation of Orson Welles. The only serious challenge to this commonly held assumption was mounted in 1970 by the feisty anti-auteurist Pauline Kael in a two-part article in *The New Yorker* on *Citizen Kane* ("Raising Kane"), ostensibly undertaken as a brief introduction to the published screenplay, but eventually expanded into a 50,000-word digression from *Kane* itself into a meandering expedition through the life and times and hates and love-hates of Ms. Kael. Hey, she shouted, what's all this incense burning at the altar of Orson Welles? Look over here at Herman J. Mankiewicz. He just wrote the damned picture. Predictably, Kael marshalled all the evidence she could to divorce the direction of *Kane* from its ultimate authorship. She was supported in her arguments by former associates of Welles, most notably, John Houseman. Counter arguments were published by Peter Bogdanovich, this reviewer, and several technical collaborators on the production itself. Kael's basic position was endorsed by Richard Corliss, who endeavored in the seventies to modify *la politique des auteurs* with *la politique des écrivains* as a way of calling attention to the shamefully unsung contributions of Hollywood's screenwriters to what the auteurist revisionists had rediscovered as a Golden Age.

Though Kael skewered Welles as he had seldom been skewered before, she was even more enthusiastic about *Kane* than the French had been. *"Citizen Kane,"* she declared, is perhaps the one American talking picture that seems as fresh now as the day it opened." The operative word here is "talking," the domain traditionally more of the screenwriter than the director. Of course, the tactical point of her hyperbole is to suggest that the later decline of Welles could be attributed to his loss of the story sense provided by Mankiewicz for *Kane*. In the end, however, Kael succeeded only in adding another layer of mythology to Welles as the man who "stole" *Citizen Kane* from Herman J. Mankiewicz. Earlier and later myths serve to entomb Welles as a burned-out prodigy, a wastrel, an unappreciated visionary, a trickster, a Renaissance Man for all media—cinema, theater, radio, television; an egomaniac, a compulsive storyteller right out of "The Ancient Mariner," a persecuted liberal and

New Dealer without portfolio, a failed newspaper columnist, a huckster, a public clown, a martyr to Hollywood philistinism, a raging sexist, a baroque mannerist, a man who scared a nation, a twentieth century incarnation of Sigmund Freud's Leonardo da Vinci, and an Oedipally crippled artist congenitally inhibited from finishing his projects. The problem was that Welles was all these things and more. No single tag line was adequate. His "genius," if it existed, was in recognizing his own complex personality, and in projecting it artistically.

In his memoirs, *Starting Out in the Thirties*, Alfred Kazin has written about Welles as a cultural hero for New York's left-leaning intelligentsia. Unfortunately, we must rely on aging memories and still photographs for clues to the Wellesian stage magic of a black-shirted, antifascist *Julius Caesar*, a Haitian voodoo *Macbeth* performed initially in the heart of Harlem, and a comparatively conventional agitprop production of Marc Blitzstein's *The Cradle Will Rock*. Welles was hardly an agitprop artist himself, but his political sympathies and associations might well have gotten him blacklisted as a "red" in the fifties—if the studio moguls had not virtually exiled him beforehand for allegedly being "in the red." In the coming attraction footage for *Kane* personally produced by Welles, it is clear that he was trying to sell ambiguity to the moviegoing public, and it wasn't buying. Nor were audiences entirely comfortable with his "cinematic" innovations liberally borrowed from his theatrical expressionism on behalf of the Faustian presumption of Kit Marlowe and the communal hurly-burly of Ben Jonson. Every bit of portentous lighting and shadowing in *Kane* was first manifested in the Wellesian theater of the late thirties. And what made *Kane* seem "fresh" in 1941 was its casting of theater and radio people—Joseph Cotten, Everett Sloane, George Coulouris, Dorothy Comingore, Ray Collins, Ruth Warrick, Agnes Moorehead, William Alland, Erskine Sanford, Paul Stewart, *et al.*—who had never before been seen on the screen. Welles himself was the biggest histrionic explosion on the movie scene, but to this day people differ on whether he was all that good and revelatory or all that bad and hammy purely as a performer.

Ultimately, no mere movie, certainly no single movie can sustain the enormous cultural burden imposed on *Citizen Kane*. Indeed, it can be argued that the endless dissection of *Kane* over half a century has not only demystified it, but also drained it of its last vestiges of *joie de vivre*. Not that *Kane* was all that much of a feel-good entertainment to begin with. The various conspiracy theories that seek to explain why it bombed at the box office rely too heavily on a right-wing publisher's wrath. It was no fault of Hearst's that *Kane* was a complete commercial flop in England where Hearst had as little influence as Lord Beaverbrook had in America.

Curiously, *Kane* can be enjoyed for many of the right reasons, and admired for many of the wrong ones. It is certainly worthy of revival and reconsideration, but it hardly stands alone even among the directorial efforts of Orson Welles. (I personally prefer *The Magnificent Ambersons*.) To believe that *Citizen Kane* is a great American film in a morass of mediocre Hollywood movies is to misunderstand the transparent movieness of *Kane* itself from its Xanadu castle out of *Snow White and the Seven Dwarfs* to its menagerie out of *King Kong* to its mirrored reflections out of old German doppelganger spectacles to its stylistic borrowing from John Ford and Fritz Lang to its Slavko Vorkapich newspaper headline montages and even to its supposedly revolutionary flashback structure profoundly derivative of the "narratage" of Preston Sturges in William K. Howard's Spencer-Tracy-starring-tycoon-saga in *Power and the Glory* (1933) and Dalton Trumbo's fetishistic-symbolic variant in Garson Kanin's *A Man To Remember* (1938). Yet, paradoxically enough, though *Citizen Kane* is not nearly as "original" as some of its critical encomiums would indicate, its large and lasting influence on subsequent cinema is felt to this very day in the works of Stanley Kubrick and the Coen brothers among many other cinéastes around the world.

I have argued for some time that if *Citizen Kane* had been released in the critical climate of the past three decades, the pundits of the medium would never have allowed the moguls to drive Welles out of the industry. But the three most perceptive American film critics in the early forties—James Agee, Manny Farber, and Otis Ferguson—were less than enchanted by *Citizen Kane*, and their resistance to *Kane* and Welles should not be discounted. Their reasoning still makes fascinating reading. One element of the anti-Welles argument is less fashionable in the nineties than it was in the forties, and that is the deep suspicion that Welles's razzle-dazzle with eccentric compositions, shock editing, and dizzying camera movements betokened a fatal lack of seriousnessness. He was considered too much the faker, the charlatan, and worst of all, the ivory-tower exhibitionist who in his oxymoronic way failed to address the problems of the "common people." Also though the words "communist" and "fascist" are bravely uttered by characters in *Kane* on a 1941 American screen, Welles alternates the two terms as epithets hurled at Kane more to confound his audience than to convert it. *Kane* itself has the look of a studio-enclosed production without any of the trappings of documentary realism. Much of it is in the past, making it a kind of costume picture. Only in its tone of derision toward great wealth does it escape the stigma of elitist snobbery.

On its most superficial if most entertaining level, *Kane* can be described as a mystery story with two eternally fashionable themes: the debasement of the private personality of the public figure through the scandal-seeking media, and the allegedly crushing weight on the soul of material possessions, which, in Hollywood, is known as having your cake and spitting it out, too. Taken together, these two themes enable the audience to feel both pity and moral superiority toward the bitter spectacle of great fame and wealth ending in futile nostalgia, loneliness, and death in a cartoonishly gothic castle left over from a Disney drawing board on the RKO backlot.

Charles Foster Kane (Orson Welles in old-age make-up to end all old-age make-up) dies with a close-up of his lips forming his last word: ROSEBUD. Who or what is Rosebud? One "clue" is a glass globe with a snow scene dropped by the dying man. Ultimately, it is merely a memory clue of free association forming a bond of sorts between the viewer and the protagonist. The "mystery," when it is finally and stirringly solved, will be revealed in such a perishable way that the viewer will always know and feel something about Charles Foster Kane that none of the people in his life could ever have suspected, at least not on the symbolic level at which Kane's entire life has been encapsulated.

The "detective" (William Alland) who seeks to solve the mystery is a reporter for a news service which produces *March of Time*-like newsreels. He is always photographed obliquely and obscurely as if he were a faceless surrogate for the audience, literally its private eye. The "suspects" are some of the persons and objects Kane encountered in his cluttered existence.

"Rosebud" is a pretext by which the past history of Charles Foster Kane is penetrated by the reporter-detective and the omniscient camera of Gregg Toland. Time is thrown back and brought forward in the four major movements of the film—the flashback recollections respectively of Kane's banker-guardian, Mr. Thatcher (George Colouris), his business manager, Bernstein (Everett Sloane, in a slightly raucous performance co-scenarist Herman J. Mankiewicz complained was too Jewish), his best friend Jed Leland (Joseph Cotten), and his second wife Susan Alexander (Dorothy Comingore in a shrill, misogynous caricature of Marion Davies). Each major flashback begins at a later point in time than its predecessor, but each flashback overlaps with at least one of the others so that the same event or period is seen from two or three points of view.

There is a fifth flashback—a newsreel of Kane's public career—which establishes the identity of Charles Foster Kane for the first time in the film. There is no establishing-shot transition between the opening scene of Kane dying in bleak grandeur, and the noisily startling appearance of the unframed newsreel. This is the first shock effect in *Kane,* and it derives from Welles's flamboyant showmanship in the theater and on radio. By isolating the newsreel from the main body of his film, Welles provides historical and biographical information, while at the same time dismissing it as a major factor in the overriding Freudian subtext of a rich little poor boy who never recovered from the loss of his mother.

The newsreel fades out; a sudden establishing shot picks up a darkened projection room. The first of the many disembodied voices in the film calls out from the darkness, and the shadow plot of *Kane* begins. A group of cynical newsmen discuss ways of pepping up the newsreel. The reporter is dispatched to find the secret of "Rosebud." The semi-colloquial dialogue is driven with line-stepping-on-line persistence from every direction. This mannered "spontaneity" of line-readings had been done before, but never so relentlessly. The same is true of Toland's celebrated deep focus.

The reporter begins his search and the major movements of *Citizen Kane* begin. Through a hard, wide-angle lens, the reporter enters a cavernous museum, a dingy night club, a solidly upholstered office in which Bernstein tells an ineffably touching story of a girl he once saw on the Staten Island ferry, a drab hospital ward in which Kane's best friend has become his most implacable foe, and, finally, the somber mansion of Charles Foster Kane, where he and Susan Alexander play out the joyless charade of their grotesque marriage.

The first Mrs. Kane is disposed of maritally in a series of artful flash-pans of the Kane breakfast table hailed by Milos Forman at a seventies AFI ceremony as his first youthful moviegoing experience in Czechoslovakia that demonstrated to him what a director did in movies.

The mystery of "Rosebud" is solved in an incendiary *coup de cinema.* Welles dismissed "Rosebud" in an interview with Dilys Powell of the *Sunday Times* (London): "It's a gimmick, really," said Welles, "and rather dollar-book Freud." Pauline Kael also disapproves of "Rosebud."

I disagree with both Miss Kael and Mr. Welles on "Rosebud"; with Miss Kael for the anti-genre prejudice her repudiation of "Rosebud" confirms and with Welles for—who knows—his canny instinct for self-preservation in repudiating "Rosebud" before it came out of screenwriter Herman J. Mankiewicz's ghostly past to haunt him.

When I interviewed director-screenwriter Joseph L. Mankiewicz in 1970 for *Show* magazine, I had no idea that he would reveal to me the origin of "Rosebud" as a bike that his brother Herman once lost as a child in Wilkes-Barre, Pennsylvania. But my feeling of discovery was based most of all on my abiding attachment to "Rosebud" as not only the missing piece of a jigsaw puzzle but also the beating heart of *Kane* as a movie. It is "Rosebud" that structures *Kane* as a private-eye investigation of a citizen in the public eye, and thus brings us much closer to *The Maltese Falcon* and *The Big Sleep* and the burning R's on the pillowcases of *Rebecca* not to mention the similar gates of Manderley and Xanadu.

The problem with defending "Rosebud" as a narrative device is that its very vividness makes it a running gag in our satirically oriented culture. How can we take "Rosebud" seriously, Miss Kael complains, after Snoopy in the comic strip "Peanuts" has called Lucy's sled "Rosebud"? The same way, I suppose, we can take "Potemkin" seriously after Woody Allen has sent a baby carriage rolling down the steps of a Latin-American palace in *Bananas*. Both Snoopy and Woody are paying homage to bits of film language transformed by the magical contexts of their medium into poetic metaphors. But where Eisenstein's baby carriage moves from prop to agitprop as it becomes an archetypal conveyance of revolutionary fervor, "Rosebud" reverberates with familial echoes as it passes through the snows of childhood (*les neiges d'antan*) into the fire, ashes, and smoke of death. Indeed, the burning of "Rosebud" in Xanadu's furnace represents the only instance in which the soul of Kane can be seen subjectively by the audience. It is as if his mind and memory were being cremated before our eyes and we were helpless to intervene and incompetent to judge. It is an image of transfiguration that transforms us through the flames into concerned witnesses of a life ending on a note of rueful regret.

I love to teach *Citizen Kane*. It is chockful of self-explanatory excerpts. Otherwise, I prefer to think of *Kane* as one of the many good movies turned out in Hollywood in the past eighty years. Even in 1941 there were several movies on the same level of excellence, and though there was something special about *Kane*, it was comprehensible in terms of a moviegoer's total experience. It was neither the beginning of anything, nor the end of anything, but simply a glorious middle. The moment someone tells me that *Kane* is the only good American film I immediately realize that that someone does not fully understand *Kane*.

■   ■   ■   ■

ORSON WELLES had long wanted to adapt Booth Tarkington's 1918 Pulitzer Prize–winning novel of changing manners and morals in the Middle West at the turn of the century and the coming of the automobile. In fact, Welles himself had acted the role of George Amberson in a radio dramatization of the Tarkington period piece. It was his second film at RKO after his epoch-making debut with *Citizen Kane*. As it turned out, *The Magnificent Ambersons* (1942) virtually finished Welles as a commercially viable artist in Hollywood. Re-cut and re-shot while he was scouting locations in Brazil for a film that was never finished, *Ambersons* was not even particularly appreciated by those who had hailed *Kane*. It was a complete disaster at the box office (like Jean Renoir's *La Règle du Jeu*), and even today it seems in retrospect to have been too depressing for audiences that needed cheering up during the grim aftermath of Pearl Harbor.

Its abiding unpopularity with the Hollywood mass audience is, however, a proof of its transcendent importance in the coming of age of America. Even in *Kane*, but especially in *Ambersons*, the young, brash Orson Welles had imparted to American movies a long overdue intimation of the mortal limits and disillusioning shortcomings of the American Dream. He dared to suggest that even Americans became old and embittered as the inexorable forces of family, capitalism and "progress" trampled them. In his twenties, Welles was the oldest man ever to make movies in Hollywood, and his direction of his players went beyond mere surface dramatics to metaphysical speculations. In this connection, Richard Bennett's death-scene speech about all life coming from the sun, and then returning to the sun at death, can be found word-for-word in the Tarkington novel, but Welles gave an appropriate visual accompaniment to this speech with a sun-like close-up of Bennett's face, and a slow sound fade-out to a silent blackness.

For some of us at least, *Ambersons* is to *Kane* what *The Marriage of Figaro* is to *Don Giovanni*, what *Anna Karenina* is to *War and Peace*, and what *Uncle Vanya* is to *The Cherry Orchard*. In other words, *Ambersons* is subtler and deeper than the more expansive and spectacular *Kane*. André Bazin suggested that Welles reversed the usual artistic order by creating his baroque work (*Kane*) first, and his classical work (*Ambersons*) second.

The cross-currents of history in transition and family fortunes in disarray are exquisitely acted by a magnificent ensemble. Except for the bastardized, chronologically shuffled ending, which was studio-imposed on the film, *Ambersons*, fragment by fragment, remains one of the most emotionally and intellectually articulate films ever made. Agnes Moorehead as Aunt Fanny, the poignantly frenzied spinster, takes top acting honors without shredding the delicately woven tapestry of family drama and trauma. Moorehead's tearful breakdown, when she is teased about her fruitless love for Eugene Morgan (Joseph Cotten) by her thoughtless nephew George Amberson (Tim Holt) and her careless cousin Jack Amberson (Ray Collins), was photographed in a single camera set-up by Stanley Cortez, and has stood the test of time as the quintessentially Wellesian flourish of stylistic objectivity and ambiguity. This supposedly "cold" treatment of explosively dramatic material was as responsible as anything else for Welles's failure to communicate with the mass moviegoing public.

In what little there was of a studio advertising campaign for *Ambersons*, the somber Wellesian meditation was misrepresented as a small-town family scandal sensation like the much more popular *King's Row* that same year, with its clinically insane and sadistic characters, and the sex-saturated *Peyton Place* (1957) that was to follow. In the case of *Ambersons*, audiences could not understand what all the fuss was about, with George Minafer Amberson storming about town protecting his widowed mother's "honor" because people were saying that she loved a man while she was still married to George's father, and now the interloper wanted to marry her. Tim Holt's lack of charm as he is played and directed made him seem the villain of the piece in blocking the more sympathetic Joseph Cotten and Dolores Costello characters from finding their long-delayed happiness. And when George is finally punished for his presumption, the audience is more depressed than vengefully exhilarated.

Where Welles may have miscalculated was in not realizing that a story in which vibrant characters grow old and sad and slowly die, one by one, is too depressing for audiences. He might have borrowed *Kane*'s and presumably Herman J. Mankiewicz's narrative strategy of interspersing the past with the present so that the characters would be seen as alternately young and old, hopeful and disillusioned, proudly triumphant and wretchedly defeated. As it is, the joyously familial ride on Eugene's new-fangled motor buggy that is destined to destroy the horse-and-buggy and the civilization built on it, is for a brief moment the occasion for a celebration of that doomed past in which everyone could sing "The Man

Who Broke the Bank at Monte Carlo" with uncomplicated gaiety, as Welles closed the scene with an iris fade-out reminiscent of D. W. Griffith and the doomed world *he* had once celebrated.

Ambersons is ultimately two films, one commercially misguided, the other artistically sublime. As in *Kane*, he transformed and transfigured someone else's story into a covert autobiography of his own. In *Ambersons*, he did not disguise his deepest feeling with satiric gibes at the possessors of great wealth and power. What shines through in *Ambersons*, more than a hundred snow-covered sleds named "Rosebud," is Welles's abiding love and respect for his wondrous characters in all their precious pastness.

When I watched Orson Welles's *The Lady from Shanghai* (1948) on television in the eighties, I kept trying to match the not-so-fat man on the screen with the very fat man of the television commercials. I'd never met Welles, and yet I felt I'd known him for most of my life. Many people have had a similar feeling all through his evolution from *enfant terrible* to media clown. The reactions to Welles over the years have run the gamut from adulation to ridicule.

Back in 1963 I paid tribute to his art in *The American Cinema*:

> Welles is still the youngest indisputably great American director. . . . Apart from *The Magnificent Ambersons*, in which his presence was exclusively vocal narration, every Welles film is designed around the massive presence of the artist as autobiographer. Call him Hearst or Falstaff, Macbeth or Othello, Quinlan or Arkadin, he is always at least partly himself, ironic, bombastic, pathetic, and, above all, presumptuous. The Wellesian cinema is the cinema of magic and marvels, and everything, and especially its prime protagonist, is larger than life. The dramatic conflict in a Welles film often arises from the dialectical collision between morality and megalomania, and Welles more often than not plays the megalomaniacal villain without stilling the calls of conscience. Curiously, Welles is far from being his own best actor. Actually, no actor-director in history has been as generous to his colleagues. Through less than a dozen films the roll call of distinguished performances is long indeed . . . with extraordinarily honorable mention to such limited performers as . . . Rita Hayworth (as the spectacularly mythic Lady from Shanghai shattered irrevocably in a hall of mirrors, a superb metaphor for the movie career of Orson Welles).

This time around I was struck even more than before by the wild romanticism and eerily prophetic self-revelation of the Welles characterization in *The Lady from Shanghai*: "Maybe if I live long enough I can forget her or maybe I'll die trying." Throughout the movie Welles keeps

describing himself as a fool, and so he was in a sense. I can remember
him from my childhood on town meetings of the air, debating on the
liberal Roosevelt side against fairly glib Republicans, coming out second
best, and, worse still, losing his temper and the audience. The occasional
"message" of his films was warmed-over Popular Front goulash with only
Marlovian bombast disguising banality. The rich were bad, to be sure,
but oh what entertaining follies they could stage.

Yet time has been kind to *The Lady from Shanghai* in a way that
vindicates Bazin's mystical view of the cinema as truth. I'm moved as
much now by the pathetic fate of the Rita Hayworth character, with her
zombie-like fatalism and her fear of dying, as by Welles's tragic awareness
of a flaw in his temperament that makes him flee in a giddy panic from
his own creations. There is in the treatment of Hayworth by Welles as
director some of the somnambulism of Sternberg with Dietrich, but none
of the sweetness.

Mark Shivas has established a Welles-Hitchcock contrast both thematically and technically, with the observation that Welles is concerned
with ordinary feelings of extraordinary people, and Hitchcock with the
extraordinary feelings of ordinary people. Whereas Welles flourished in
baroque settings, Hitchcock functioned in commonplace settings. To a
limited extent, at least, Wellesian cinema is as much the cinema of the
exhibitionist as Hitchcockian cinema is the cinema of the voyeur.

ERNST LUBITSCH (1892–1947)

Speaking of Frank Borzage and George Stevens, as we expect to do,
brings up the matter of the unsung motion picture director. We remember
a poll conducted by one of the theatre circuits not so long ago in which
the patrons were invited to name their favorite stars, pictures, stories, and
directors. John Public and his wife sprinted through the first three categories and bluffed or quit cold on the fourth. Adolph Zukor, of all people,
was voted the favorite director by some. Sam Goldwyn was another con-
tender. As we recall it, Ernst Lubitsch won it in a walk. His name seemed
to be easy to remember. Actually, it was no contest.
—Frank S. Nugent, *The* Sunday *New York Times,* June 12, 1938

Ernst Lubitsch enjoyed a curious immunity in the thirties in that his
reputation at the end of the decade was almost as high as it had been

at the beginning. Whereas by the forties, Josef von Sternberg, King Vidor, Frank Borzage, René Clair, Rouben Mamoulian, and Lewis Milestone had lost their early thirties pre-eminence, John Ford, Frank Capra, Leo McCarey, Alfred Hitchcock, Gregory La Cava, and William Wyler seemingly came out of nowhere in the middle thirties to shape the last half of that decade. Lubitsch had his ups and downs to be sure, but he never really passed out of fashion permanently. *Monte Carlo* (1930) ushered in the decade with an artful blend of sound montage and visual music in Jeanette MacDonald's rendition of "Beyond the Blue Horizon," and *Ninotchka* (1939) lowered the curtain on the thirties in a grand manner with Greta Garbo's exquisite evocation of an ideological iceberg melting in mirth.

Between these two epiphanies of his pastel palette, Lubitsch contributed distinctively personal sketches to two omnibus revues: *Paramount on Parade* (1930, the Chevalier Frenchie numbers) and *If I Had a Million* (1932, the famous Laughton raspberry). In addition, he directed seven other films outright: *The Smiling Lieutenant* (1931); *The Man I Killed*, originally *Broken Lullaby* (1932); *Trouble in Paradise* (1932); *Design for Living* (1933); *The Merry Widow* (1934); *Angel* (1937); and *Bluebeard's Eighth Wife* (1938). *One Hour with You* (1932) was directed by George Cukor from a Lubitsch plan, and signed by Lubitsch, thus providing an interesting mix of Lubitsch snap and Cukor stretch. Similarly, the Lubitsch-produced and Borzage-directed *Desire* offered an interesting stylistic conflict between the twinkle and the tear. All in all, a productive decade for a director who had survived the trip from Germany to America, the temper tantrums of Pola Negri and Mary Pickford, the transition from silence to sound, the rise in power (if fall in glory) from director to producer-director at Paramount, and the changing tastes of the fickle public. Still, Lubitsch never won a competitive Oscar or a New York Film Critics Award, a symptom perhaps of an ultimate lack of respect for the "mere" stylist and entertainer.

Herman Weinberg's very informative book *The Lubitsch Touch* is awash with noble quotations on the profundity of comedy, but the fact remains that comic talents are seldom given as much weight as tragic or even merely somber talents, and this is especially true in Hollywood. Consequently, the comic talents often overcompensate for their low estate by essaying completely humorless projects to prove their seriousness. (*Vide* Leo McCarey's discomfiture at getting an Oscar in 1937 for *The Awful Truth* rather than for *Make Way for Tomorrow*.) And so it was with Lubitsch in the thirties as he attempted to prove his serious worth (and even his pacifism) with *The Man I Killed* (1932). Of all his films in this decade, *The Man I Killed* emerges today as Lubitsch's least inspired and most calculated effort, all surface effect, all ritualistic piety toward a "noble" subject. *The Man I Killed* died at the box office, for the right reasons as much as for the wrong. Nonetheless, the critics held Lubitsch's hand during the wake, castigated the public for its inattentiveness at intolerable sermons and, with a sigh (and a subconscious sense of relief), returned the repentant jester to his more frivolous pursuits.

By contrast, strikingly unconventional comedies, more in the mellow manner of later Lubitsch, like *Design for Living* (1933), *The Merry Widow* (1934), and *Angel* (1937), have been dismissed by Weinberg and the other official film historians as failures without merit. *Design for Living* was invidiously compared in its casting (Gary Cooper, Miriam Hopkins, Fredric March) with the stage original (Alfred Lunt, Lynn Fontanne, Noël Coward), not to mention the sacrilege of Ben Hecht's brassily romantic screenplay presuming to improve on Coward's gilded cynicism. *The Merry Widow* lacked (at least in Weinberg's eyes) Stroheim's scathing documentation of imperial decadence in the 1925 version with John Gilbert and Mae Murray. Fortunately, Lubitsch also lacked Stroheim's snickering villainies and overstuffed ornamentation. As for *Angel*, it was simply misunderstood as failed bedroom farce à la Feydeau rather than as a rhyming exercise in Pirandellian role-playing. Far from being failures, *Design for Living, The Merry Widow*, and *Angel* mark an evolution of Lubitsch's style away from the sparkling balancing acts of *The Marriage Circle* (1925) and *Trouble in Paradise* (1932) to the somewhat heavier but richer concoctions of the forties—*The Shop Around the Corner* (1940), *To Be Or Not To Be* (1942), *Heaven Can Wait* (1943), and *Cluny Brown* (1946).

Of course, critics in the thirties could hardly have anticipated Lubitsch's last burst of stylistic development in the forties, but he might have been given more credit as an innovator in his own right, rather than being seen as a manipulative mimic of Charlie Chaplin and René Clair.

With René Clair particularly, it is difficult to believe how much superior to Lubitsch he was considered to be in the early thirties by critics who should have known better. Although Lubitsch long antedated Clair in the cinema, Clair was generally considered the source from which all cinematic wit and whimsy had sprung. Even Chaplin was condemned (by Otis Ferguson) for lifting Clair's assembly line in *A Nous La Liberte* for use in *Modern Times*. Part of Lubitsch's problem had to do with his power position at Paramount, which made him a spokesman for an unpopular industry. He was blamed for Sternberg's troubles at the studio. And he was criticized for stressing the need to please a mass audience. Look at Clair, the critics said. He doesn't care about audiences. He is concerned only with his own art. It was one thing for Frank S. Nugent (later John Ford's scenarist and son-in-law) to declare flatly that *The Informer* was infinitely superior to Max Ophüls's *Liebelei*—a turgid allegory is always superior in some aesthetics to a tender love story—but that Lubitsch's talent should be considered spiritually inferior to a more tinkly than tingly mechanical-doll talent such as René Clair's is almost beyond understanding. On any ultimate scale of values, Lubitsch's fatal sin seems to have been to have power in a situation in which highbrows computed glory in inverse proportion to power and even potency. As a result, Lubitsch has never been given credit for his undeniable influence on directors as disparate as Ophüls (*The Bartered Bride*) (1932), Hitchcock (*Strauss's Great Waltz*) (1933), Bergman (*Smiles of a Summer Night*) (1955), Renoir (*The Rules of the Game*) (1939), Mamoulian (*Love Me Tonight*) (1932), Chaplin (*The Countess from Hong Kong*) (1967), Hawks (*Paid To Love*) (1927), Sternberg (*The King Steps Out*) (1936), Milestone (*Paris in the Spring*) (1935), and more of Preston Sturges, Mitchell Leisen, Frank Tuttle, and Billy Wilder than we need mention at this time. Indeed, if "influence" were the sole criterion of greatness, Lubitsch's name would be near the top of the list with Griffith's and not too many others.

In another aspect, Lubitsch presents problems for the film historian over and above the usual one of sifting the coarse sands of a collaborative art form seeking the gold dust of an individual style. The writers alone would take a chapter: Samson Raphaelson (*The Smiling Lieutenant* (1931), *The Man I Killed* (1932), *One Hour with You* (1932), *Trouble in Paradise* (1932), *The Merry Widow* (1934), *Angel* (1937)) was especially conspicuous as a collaborator during the thirties. Other Lubitsch scribes worthy of mention (and perhaps even analysis) are Ernest Vajda (*The Love Parade* (1929), *Monte Carlo* (1930), *The Smiling Lieutenant* (1931), *The Man I Killed* (1932), *The Merry Widow* (1934)), Charles Brackett and Billy Wilder (*Bluebeard's Eighth Wife* (1938), *Ninotchka* (1939)), Ben Hecht (*Design for Living* (1933)), and Walter Reisch (*Ninotchka* (1939)). But these highly talented and idiosyncratic screenwriters were usually mere middlemen between bits and pieces of theater, fiction, and anecdotal conversations on one side and Lubitsch's storyboard implemented by an army of technicians (generally from Paramount) on the other.

The important thing to remember is that Lubitsch was as much a force as a beacon, a figure to be reckoned with. His influence at the Paramount studio is thus comparable to Zanuck's at Fox, Thalberg's at MGM, Laemmle's at Universal, and all the brothers Warner put together. Chaplin remained his own producer and his own creator throughout his career, but in the thirties Chaplin was too inimitably individualistic and technologically reactionary to exercise much influence on other directors. Capra had *carte blanche* at Columbia for a time, but he never meddled with the overall mediocrity of Harry Cohn's commercial factory. Alone among the distinguished directors of the decade, Lubitsch looked beyond his own creative concerns to the evolution of the public's taste.

The dividing line was 1934. The resurgence of censorship, the delayed realization that breadlines and Continental sophistication didn't mix and that a wink was no match for a wisecrack, and the pervasive humorlessness of both the left and the right resulted in hard times for such stylistically playful directors as Sternberg and Milestone and Mamoulian and Clair, and an end to many genres—most notably the subjective gangster film, the rhymed couplet musicals, and the upper-class soap operas (Goodbye, *East Lynne*, and Hello, *Stella Dallas*).

What makes Lubitsch's films of the period especially fascinating today is the evidence of strain between a director's sensibility within and a producer's sensitivity without. *The Smiling Lieutenant* (1931), for example, is gravely flawed by the contradiction between the director's exquisitely flavorsome treatment of Claudette Colbert's demi-mondaine and the puritanical resolution of the plot to allow Miriam Hopkins's prissy princess to come out on top for the sake of the presumably sacred marriage contract. Indeed, the Colbert character must even contribute to her own romantic downfall by advising her rival how to snare the smiling but straying Lieutenant (Maurice Chevalier) with a song about sexy underwear, as if lasting love were merely about consumer goods and textbook tactics. Still, Claudette Colbert's glowing performance in *The Smiling Lieutenant* is as much a testament to the winsome womanliness of her early thirties persona as her excruciatingly sadistic performance in *Bluebeard's Eighth Wife* (1938) is a reflection of the horrible torture inflicted on sex comedies when censorship reared its ugly head.

By 1938 American audiences had regained their emotional adolescence in their quest for seriousness and significance. It was as if Lubitsch had never come to these shores with his expansive smile, his cigar, and his gourmet tastes. And Lubitsch himself had to trim his sails after the colossal failure of *Angel* (1937), one of his most anachronistically civilized works, released as it was at a time when Harry Brandt had decreed that Marlene Dietrich, Greta Garbo, Katharine Hepburn, and Joan Crawford were all box-office poison.

Even in the early thirties, however, Lubitsch seemed aware of how limited was the leeway he had with an increasingly impatient audience. His four musicals follow a pattern of progressive stylization and self-consciousness as audience resistance to the integrated poetics of rhythmic mise-en-scène increases. *The Love Parade* (1929) is relatively carefree and unforced at a moment in film history when sound seems to be stifling movement. Artfully raised eyebrows and clever cutting between the royal couple and the watchful court made *The Love Parade* seem like the link between the visual mellifluousness of the silent cinema and the verbal-musical dynamics of the talkies. (Otherwise, *The Love Parade* was merely a one-song musical, with its one melodious tune—Victor Schertzinger's "Dream Lover"—popping up later in Billy Wilder's *The Major and the Minor* (1942) and Cecil B. DeMille's *The Greatest Show on Earth* (1952).

Monte Carlo (1930) came along at a time when the screen had been so saturated with musicals that producers, saddled with musical properties, were keeping the ridiculous plots and throwing out the redeeming songs. Jeanette MacDonald's acting had not improved appreciably since *The Love Parade*, and her new leading man (Jack Buchanan) lacked the charm and authority of Maurice Chevalier. But *Monte Carlo* succeeded nonetheless by virtue of Lubitsch's spectacular montage mounting of "Beyond the Blue Horizon" (MacDonald/train/countryside/peasants)—a sequence so spectacular that few viewers can remember much else about the movie, fortunately for MacDonald and Buchanan.

Lubitsch regained Chevalier for *The Smiling Lieutenant*, but he sensed that the operetta style of love duets was going out of fashion, and so Chevalier was flanked by two straight actress-personalities, Claudette Colbert and Miriam Hopkins. *The Smiling Lieutenant* thus stands almost halfway between the lilting lyricism of *The Love Parade* and the tempered ironies of *Trouble in Paradise*. In fact, Lubitsch was so busy with *Trouble in Paradise* that he delegated most of the directorial drudgery of *One Hour with You* (1932) to George Cukor (designated by Herman G. Weinberg in *The Lubitsch Touch* as the "dialogue director"). Without plunging into period memoirs over who did what and to whom, we can safely say that *One Hour With You* marks a discernible break stylistically with both previous and subsequent Lubitsch films. Cukor, like Preminger later, superimposed on a Lubitsch project an essentially theatrical mise-en-scène, lighter on the witty cut and heavier on the lyrically long take and sweeping camera movement.

Lubitsch's final fling with the musical (apart from his fatal misalliance with Betty Grable in *That Lady in Ermine* in 1947) reunited Maurice Chevalier and Jeanette MacDonald in that trusty warhorse of operettas, Franz Lehar's *The Merry Widow* (1934). There is one beautiful song in *The Merry Widow* that cannot be bluffed or faked or kidded by a music-hall style. It is "Delia," a showpiece number for a conservatory tenor, just as "The Angelus" is a showpiece number for a conservatory soprano—even the late Bobby Clark made himself scarce in stage revivals of Victory Herbert's *Sweethearts* when it came time for the soprano to sing "The Angelus." There are a few things in the world that are too beautiful to be burlesqued even by the most gifted clowns, and the most charming straw-hat rascals. Lubitsch knew that Chevalier couldn't sing "Delia" and yet the song was too good to be sacrificed. The solution? Maurice Chevalier's gawky country bumpkin orderly (Sterling Holloway) sings the song (dubbed of course by a straight tenor) with Chevalier standing behind him like a combination puppet-master/Cyrano, the sweetness tempered once more by the irony of a device breathtakingly ingenious in its audacious directness.

The evaluation of film musicals is sheer folly after a certain point. A song here, a dance there, performers at a peak or in a pique, can make all the difference. I know. And so I have no desire to argue with the persuasive defenders of Rouben Mamoulian's *Love Me Tonight* (1932) as the best of Lubitsch-like musicals. Nonetheless, I would not trade Lubitsch's daringly subdued and scintillatingly circular treatment of "The Merry Widow Waltz" as a prison-cell pas de deux for all the slow-motion and showy camera angles in *Love Me Tonight*. Lubitsch makes of *The Merry Widow* the last musical of a certain spirit and style to be made on this planet. And it is his intimation of a genre's mortality and the sad smile that goes with the intimation that makes Lubitsch ultimately inimitable and ineffable.

■   ■   ■   ■

BORN JANUARY 28, 1892, the son of a well-off tailor, Lubitsch made his acting debut with Max Reinhardt's Berlin theater company in 1911, and shortly thereafter began moonlighting in the film industry. From 1914 through 1919 he directed and acted in twenty-seven comedy shorts, in most of which he played a stock Jewish character of buffoonish aggressiveness. These films are not familiar today even to most movie buffs. Thanks to the invaluable Goethe Society, I have had an opportunity to see a few of these farces, and they made eerie viewing in light of Lubitsch's exalted reputation and the historical circumstances of the oncoming Holocaust, of which he—and everyone else during this comparatively innocent period—was so blissfully unaware. Lubitsch's own comedy persona has not ripened with age nor has it traveled well. His performances are broad, abrasive, and by today's standards, anti-Semitic. The Jew is shown to be cunning, grasping, shrewd, and lecherous as he lumbers through life with maniacal ambition. There is no Chaplin-esque little fellow here, and no Keaton-esque stoic, much less a Lloydian Everyman. What there is instead is an overbearing presumption in the eyes and an insinuating sensuality in the lips, combined with an absence of charm and grace.

Fortunately, Lubitsch stopped acting on the screen once he got into the whirl of feature film production. After his first full-length film *Als ich tot war* (1916), Lubitsch confined himself to very occasional gag or cameo appearances. With *The Oyster Princess* in 1919 he developed the first semblance of a witty comedy style based on suggestion, ellipsis, and visual incongruities. The charm and feeling that had been so conspicuously lacking in his acting was miraculously manifested in his directing. With *Madame Du Barry* (*Passion*), also in 1919, his fame as a "humanizer" and "debunker" of history spread throughout the world. He made, all in all, fourteen features in Germany before coming to America in 1922 to direct Mary Pickford in *Rosita* (1923), a commercial disappointment at the time but now something of an archival treasure. For the next quarter of a century he was associated with thirty films that helped revolutionize screen comedy both in America and abroad. There were a few solemn efforts along the way: most notably the legendary but lost czarist melodrama *The Patriot* (1928) and the wistfully pacifistic *The Man I Killed* (*Broken Lullaby*) (1932). For the most part, however, Lubitsch remained relatively light and lilting, which proved to be both his curse and his glory.

When I lectured on Lubitsch's *Heaven Can Wait* (1943) at the 1978 Los Angeles Film Festival, I was startled to find how much more moving and scintillating the film had become in the years since I had last seen it. For one thing, the preserved Technicolor print was heartbreakingly beautiful. For another, the timing of every shot, every gesture, every movement was so impeccably precise and economically expressive that an entire classical tradition unfolded before a stunned audience. Contemporary sloppiness of construction brought on by the blind worship of "energy" makes it almost too easy to appreciate Lubitsch's uncanny sense of the stylized limits of a civilized taste. Almost any old movie looks classical today; Lubitsch's best movies are nothing short of sublime.

Curiously, most people never really knew what Lubitsch himself looked liked when they read about the so-called Lubitsch touch. There was no widespread awareness of his big cigars and thick German accent. But many of his peers were aware of him as a broadly comical figure and an irrepressibly merry prankster. For his part, Lubitsch never ceased to be amazed that allegedly "serious" thinkers took comic genius so lightly. In the twenties he sputtered with rage when self-styled hobo-philosopher-journalist Jim Tully dismissed Chaplin's achievements as lacking social significance. In the thirties there were various accounts of an encounter between Hemingway and Lubitsch during a meeting in Hollywood on the Spanish Civil War, an encounter in which allegedly Ernest scolded Ernst for not being serious enough about Spain. (The unimportance of being Ernst?) In the forties *To Be or Not To Be* (1942) was condemned for its tastelessness in "making light" of the Nazi conquest of Poland by having a Gestapo chief (Sig Ruman) tell a Polish ham actor (Jack Benny) masquerading as a Gestapo agent: "What he [the Benny character] did to Shakespeare, we are now doing to Poland." One reviewer for the *Philadelphia Inquirer* even smeared Lubitsch as a "Berlin born" director who derived pleasure from the German bombing of Poland. No one at the time even vaguely understood the deep undercurrents of Jewish humor swirling about in the joke concocted by Lubitsch and his scenarist Edwin Justus Mayer. Bridging the abyss between humor and horror, a jovial man with twinkling eyes and a big cigar transcended the times in which he lived to become an artist for the ages. He had begun his career by making jokes. By the time he ended it he had traced the configurations of a vanishing civilization in which people played by the rules to the very edge of eternity. And the neatly clipped style that once seemed so sly and wicked now seems infinitely merciful and loving. Perhaps, what the high-brows have always resisted in Lubitsch is the presumption of genius in a fearlessly middle-class vision of the world.

Yet Lubitsch's lower middle-class origins were actually eulogized by Jean-Georges Auriol in an obituary first published in 1948 in *La Revue du Cinema*, and later translated and republished in 1967 in *Cahiers du Cinema*

> He [Lubitsch] was a great middle-class liberal, in fact, a self-made man— stout, nervous, jovial, although perhaps less stout than anything else. Born

into the lower middle class, he despised neither peasant nor working man nor the petty clerk that he had himself once been; he understood only that everyone should dress in his Sunday best to come to see his films before going off to dance at a family party or, as fortune decreed, in pairs.

The one Lubitsch movie, more than any other, to which Auriol's eloquent words apply is *The Shop Around The Corner* (1940). This ode to the modesty of middle-class yearnings came out at a moment in American history when people were turning away from the pathos and resignation of the Great Depression toward the dynamic challenges of a world at war and the economic recovery thereof. In this context *The Shop Around The Corner* is more the last film of the thirties than the first film of the forties. Adapted by Samson Raphaelson from Nikolaus Lazlo's Hungarian play, there is nowhere in the screenplay, or the acting, or the direction the slightest derision or condescension toward the properly attired clerks, male and female, in Mr. Matuschek's shop, an enclosed cosmos of a Cedric Gibbon-designed Budapest street and shop on the MGM lot. The two other sets, each used only once, are a restaurant and a hospital. But the action never seems stagebound. Unlike the artificial and arbitrary stasis of upper-class characters in parlor plays-into-films, the rigorously observed work-a-day restrictions on wage slaves, however genteel, make a virtue of necessity. Every morning except Sunday the "staff" gathers in front of the shop to await the royal entrance of Mr. Matuschek for the ritualistic unlocking of the portals. The plot soon thickens with intrigue which is to be resolved eventually both satisfactorily and sentimentally. The single villain (Joseph Schildkraut) of the piece is unmasked and discharged. The two pen-pals (Margaret Sullavan's Klara Novak and James Stewart's Alfred Kralik) are magically united after a massive misunderstanding.

Only the most exquisite delicacy and tact keep the plot from overheating into overblown whimsy. There is a sad wisdom at work here. When the avuncular go-between Pirovich (Felix Bressart) is privileged to monitor the progress of the romance, his benign smile of indulgence escapes smugness by suggesting instead a nostalgia for his own lost illusions. Similarly, when Kralik watches the ailing Klara perk up when she receives a letter from her admirer otherwise unknown to her, but known to us and to Kralik as Kralik himself, Kralik's gaze is made tender by the quiet happiness he derives from observing the innocent joy of his beloved. Though Kralik has written the letter in a comically manipulative fashion, he is not any less moved by Klara's response. The viewer is made to feel the deep respect Kralik expresses for Klara's vulnerability. The decency and generosity revealed here transcend the mechanics of the contrivance. And the stellar electricity generated by Sullavan and Stewart energizes even Lubitsch's elegant style to a new peak of emotion.

Ultimately, however, Lubitsch's reputation was trapped forever by the expectations raised by the socio-aesthetic perfection of *Trouble in Paradise* in 1932. This movie seemed to have everything: the grace and elegance of the twenties, the egalitarian conscience of the thirties, the visual wit of the silent cinema, and the verbal wit of the talkies. The triangle, formed by the jewel thieves of Herbert Marshall and Miriam Hopkins and the industrial heiress of Kay Francis, was toyed with in a tantalizing fashion, but then resolved with both class logic and fairminded sentiment. Also, the comedy relief routines of Charlie Ruggles and Edward Everett Horton were still fresh and sparkling. Never again was Lubitsch to experience such rapport with his audience and his medium. As his films became increasingly somber and reflective in the forties, he was regarded as increasingly out of touch with the tastes of the time. Twice in the decade, he attempted re-makes of previous successes in the silent era: *That Uncertain Feeling* (1941) from *Kiss Me Again* (1925), and *A Royal Scandal* (1945) from *Forbidden Paradise* (1924). In both re-makes, the severe censorship in force in the forties reduced sexual intrigue to sexual innuendo. *That Uncertain Feeling* also suffered from the glacial miscasting of Melvyn Douglas, Merle Oberon, and Burgess Meredith as the triangle. In the absence of dry wit, a desperate zaniness took possession of the film.

Ernst Lubitsch did not do most of the shooting on *A Royal Scandal*. He fell ill, and Otto Preminger completed and signed the picture with a mise-en-scène more theatrical in its long takes and integral space than we had come to associate with Lubitsch. Preminger, like Cukor (*One Hour With You*) and unlike Lubitsch, came to the cinema after sound, and therefore thought of image and sound simultaneously rather than discretely.

But if Lubitsch was unable to recapture the past in the forties he was far more successful when he moved on to relatively new terrain with *The Shop Around the Corner* (working-class whimsy), *To Be or Not To Be* (anti-Nazi farce), *Heaven Can Wait* (pathos of the bon vivant approaching death), and *Cluny Brown* (manners versus instincts in a topsy-turvy world). He was especially fortunate in the emotional warmth provided his heroines by such affecting actresses as Margaret Sullavan (*Shop*), Carole Lombard (*To Be*), Gene Tierney (*Heaven*), and Jennifer Jones (*Cluny*).

Ernst Lubitsch died of a heart attack on November 30, 1947. His next project was to have been *That Lady in Ermine* with Douglas Fairbanks, Jr., and Betty Grable. He lived only long enough to shoot eight days of this otherwise ill-fated film, which Otto Preminger completed and signed.

PRESTON STURGES (1898–1959)

To the end of his days Preston Sturges would describe himself as a writer rather than a director, and he would also have been the first to admit that the films he directed relied more on verbal wit than visual style. Still, all his screenwriting efforts in the thirties would now be of only the most esoteric concern if he had not made the decisive leap from the writer's cubicle to the director's chair with *The Great McGinty* in 1940, followed by *Christmas in July* in that same year, *The Lady Eve* and *Sullivan's Travels* (1941), *The Palm Beach Story* (1942), *The Miracle of Morgan's Creek*, *Hail the Conquering Hero*, and *The Great Moment* (all 1944), *Mad Wednesday* (1947), and, somewhat in decline, *Unfaithfully Yours* (1948), *The Beautiful Blonde from Bashful Bend* (1949), and *The French They Are a Funny Race* (1957). Although it is relatively common nowadays for writers to become directors, the switch was somewhat unusual in the craft-conditioned thirties when it was not unknown for producers to fire directors who had the temerity to tinker with the script. As it was, the successful accession of Sturges sparked a writer-director movement involving John Huston, Billy Wilder, Joseph L. Mankiewicz, Dudley Nichols, Clifford Odets, Nunnally Johnson, Robert Rossen, Samuel Fuller, Frank Tashlin, Richard Brooks, and Blake Edwards, among others.

But no Hollywood screenwriter-turned-director ever matched Sturges as the complete writer-director: nine of his twelve films are based on original screenplays, and even his three adaptations (*The Lady Eve*, *The Great Moment*, and *The French They Are a Funny Race*) bear the personal Sturges stamp of the free-wheeling flashback. By contrast, most of his aforementioned colleagues turned to other people's "properties" once they had switched their guild affiliation. Sturges threw in his script for

The Great McGinty (originally titled *Down Went McGinty*) for the privilege of directing it. Thus, unlike his colleagues, he took a cut in pay for
a rise in status. He proved his point and went on to become the brightest
comedy director of the forties. But he always remained something of a
loner, relatively speaking. Sturges told me on the occasion of an interview
before his death that he had never worked with another writer even
though his name had been coupled on credit sheets with writers as disparate as Edwin Justus Mayer and Clarence Budington Kelland. He began his movie career as a "dialoguer" (to use the terminology of the *Film
Daily Year Book*) on two Paramount films released in 1930 (*The Big Pond*
and *Fast and Loose*). He was hired presumably because of the success
of his Broadway comedies—*Strictly Dishonorable* and *Child of Manhattan*—but these two properties were assigned, by Universal and Columbia
respectively, to other screenwriters. It would have been considered incestuous for Sturges to serve as the dialoguer on his own plays. Such
was the absurd position of the screenwriter in the movie industry. All in
all, Sturges was connected in one way or another with the writing of
seventeen films through the thirties, ranging from the total responsibility
for an original screenplay for *The Power and the Glory* in 1933 to the
minutely marginal assignment of writing the lyrics to a song for *One
Rainy Afternoon* in 1936.

At first glance *The Big Pond* (1930) and *Fast and Loose* (1930) seem
logical prospects for Sturges in that they indulge the good-natured
whimsy to be found in his most successful plays—*Strictly Dishonorable*
and *Child of Manhattan*. *The Big Pond* presents Maurice Chevalier as
an impoverished French aristocrat in love with Claudette Colbert as the
daughter of an American gum magnate à la Wrigley played by George
Barbier, a pre–Edward Arnold big-business boomer. Chevalier makes his
fortune in America by hitting upon the idea of spiking chewing gum with
liquor, thus spoofing both Prohibition and American know-how with just
a soupçon of Chevalier's Gallic insouciance. Indeed, *The Big Pond* is so
completely a Chevalier vehicle that Miss Colbert is reduced to a somewhat petulant love interest, with none of the incandescent womanliness
Lubitsch was to allow her to project in *The Smiling Lieutenant* (1931).
By any standard, Hobart Henley's direction of *The Big Pond* clearly lacks
the lilt of Lubitsch, but there are little bits of satire at the factory that
might possibly be attributed to Sturges. Even the spiked chewing gum
might have been his brainchild, having invented a kiss-proof lipstick for
his mother's cosmetic firm. But four other writers on the project certainly
discourage any unduly creative speculation. Let us say that Sturges him-

self was in a style and a tradition with many other practitioners—Coward, Maugham, Barry, Behrman on the stage, Lubitsch, St. Clair, D'Arrast on the silent screen, and later Cukor and Leisen in the talkies. Many of the ingredients of the Sturges forties classics are here—the insane logic of the American success story (*Christmas in July*, *Miracle of Morgan's Creek*, *Mad Wednesday*), the modesty of heroes who dread the fate of being little fish in a big pond, and a suavely Europeanized view of America coupled with a brashly Americanized view of Europe so that the Jamesian dialectics of innocence and corruption are deflected from tragic irony to comic irony.

Fast and Loose (1930) combines the battle of the sexes with the struggle of the classes, and again the Sturges contribution is marginal if not minimal. Still, the rich-poor paradoxes of the plot bear more than a passing resemblance to the exquisitely elaborated conceits of *The Palm Beach Story* (1942). Otherwise, *Fast and Loose* is memorable less for Fred Newmeyer's labored direction than for the curious tension between Miriam Hopkins's screen debut as a rowdy society girl and Carole Lombard's relatively subdued sass as the poor chorus girl with a disconcertingly delicate beauty. Miss Hopkins overacts with an array of chin-jutting, eye-narrowing mannerisms. Miss Lombard hardly acts at all and yet steals every scene with a smoldering impassivity, the stuff legends are made of.

When *Strictly Dishonorable* finally materialized on the screen late in 1931, Preston Sturges wrote a letter to Carl Laemmle, president of Universal, congratulating him on the film's fidelity to the play. John M. Stahl was one of the more dramatically fluent directors of the thirties, and Gladys Lehman's screenplay was reasonably faithful to the Sturges original, but an especially big break for the film was the casting of Paul Lukas as the romantic opera singer and Lewis Stone as the tippling judge. Stone and Lukas both projected the civilized dignity of men of the world more with the zestful sweetness of a Sturges than with the world-weary cynicism one finds in the more vinegary Viennese comedies of Ernst Lubitsch and Billy Wilder. Sturges and Stahl were not so well served by Sidney Fox's determinedly diminutive ingenue complete with a poignantly innocent Southern drawl (a Valentine sampler projected more farcically the following year in *Once in a Lifetime* (1932) and more sentimentally in *The Mouthpiece* (1932), on both occasions eclipsed by wondrously woman-wise performances from Aline McMahon). George Meeker as the discarded roughneck boyfriend was one of the least prepossessing of Hollywood's gallery of losers and masochists in romantic intrigues—Ralph Bellamy, Robert Preston, Lee Bowman, John Howard, Jeffrey Lynn, Peter Lawford, Grady Sutton, Allyn Joslin, Donald Woods, Alan Marshall, Richard Carlson, David Niven (early) and Herbert Marshall (late)—all being somewhat more memorably rejectable than Meeker was.

The plot, as well as the mildly paradoxical title of *Strictly Dishonorable*, reflects the playwright's snug if not smug sophistication regarding the convenient confluence of materialism, mentality, and morality. Hence, though most American movies, particularly during the Depression, sought to console the masses with the notion that money did not bring happiness, Sturges quite casually suggested that the most provincial girl imaginable was more likely to find not merely sensual pleasure but even sacred respect from a philandering opera singer than from the dull boy back home. Later Sturges was to write a Shavian denunciation of poverty as a proposed life style in *Sullivan's Travels* (1941), making explicit what had always been implicit in his success-story-oriented Cinderella plots. Not that Sturges was a Pollyanna about the American capitalistic system, but the only way to beat it, he implied, was to hang loose, roll with the punches, dance around the ring, and wait for that one opening that can turn a life around from savage frustration to frenzied success. But even people who have long since stopped yearning for the winning-the-lottery type of success proposed by Sturges manage to find satisfaction by doing their own thing with as much style and brio as possible. Thus does Sturges overcome the boozy sentimentality of the speakeasy atmosphere in *Strictly Dishonorable* by carefully etching the autonomous individualities of extras, over-exploiting at times the prevailing ethnic caricatures of Italian restauranteurs and Irish cops, but at the same time supplying some warming idiosyncrasy to the stock characterizations. His forties stock company has not yet been assembled, and he is several years away from becoming the Brueghel of American comedy directors, but he is nonetheless on his way, influenced equally by a Broadway–West End–*Boulevards* tradition and the lost but still remembered art of silent slapstick.

The Power and the Glory took Sturges in an unexpectedly ambitious direction in 1933. Producer Jesse Lasky caused something of a furor by publicizing the film flamboyantly as a breakthrough in the art of "narratage." Not narration, mind you, some critics chortled, but narratage, and how fancy can you get, and all we have here is the good-old-fashioned flashback with a minor variation of having the narrator occasionally use his own voice to narrate what the characters are mouthing in the flash-

back. William K. Howard directed Spencer Tracy, Colleen Moore, Ralph
Morgan, and Helen Vinson through the intricacies of a surprisingly somber Sturges script. And, since it seems that Sturges was less than enchanted by Howard's direction, he may have resolved at this point that
he would eventually direct his scripts himself. Although the film was
neither critically nor commercially the success it set out to be with so
much serious effort from all concerned, it remains one of the more impressive films of the thirties, and not at all an entirely unworthy precursor
of *Citizen Kane* in the never-very-popular genre of grown-up pessimism
about the American Dream.

There is a tendency nowadays to underrate the contribution of William K. Howard to *The Power and the Glory*, one recent film historian
going so far as to view the film solely as an episode in the career of
noted cinematographer James Wong Howe. But it should be recorded
(though not amplified at this time) that Howard was a director more
serious and off-beat and original than most through a long career studded
with exceptions to commissioned routine, such as *White Gold* (1927),
The Valiant (1929), and *Back Door to Heaven* (1939). Nonetheless, *The
Power and the Glory* remains in retrospect more crucial to the career of
Sturges than to those of Howard, Howe, Tracy, Lasky, *et al*. The story
of a self-made businessman rising in public life as he falls in private life
bears some resemblance to the Orson Welles–Herman J. Mankiewicz
treatment of the Hearst-McCormick megalomania, but there are crucial
differences as well.

The Power and the Glory, unlike *Kane*, does not function implicitly or
explicitly as ideology. The Sturges sensibility is too ironic for the demands of dogma. True, the businessman protagonist causes the death of
some workers, but there is still something admirable (from Sturges's
point of view) in the character's courage and decisiveness. That the story
of his life is told after his death by a man he dominated and emasculated
(spiritually), a born Number Two man content to wait in the shadow of
Number One, gives *The Power and the Glory* an initially disturbing ambiguity which is never dispelled. Yet we believe the account of Number
Two as objective truth in a way we are never asked to believe the more
subjectively oriented recollections of characters in flashback movies such
as *Kane* and *All About Eve* and *Rashomon*.

Thoughout his screen-writing career, Sturges employed the flashback
not so much to express the selfish subjectivity of memory but to reor-
ganize, restructure, and resequence reality so that all its ironies, comic
and tragic, are more effectively expressed. Here in *The Power and the*

Glory, Sturges establishes very early that the businessman's son has grown up to be a wastrel, a sponger, a loafer, and an all-round spoiled brat. Part of the problem is that the boy is indulged by the mother, who feels somewhat neglected by her husband, whom she herself has driven to be a success. No one's fault really, just the way things are. Then, much further on in the movie, we proceed past late flashbacks to early flashbacks until we find ourselves inside the humble cabin where the protagonist's son has just been born. Spencer Tracy holds up the new-born babe proudly, and, as the music swells rousingly, declares his hopes and dreams for his son—hopes and dreams that we have long since learned are to be cruelly disappointed. And yet the scene is still played for all it's worth as if Sturges were trying to tell us that no matter how things end (and they always end badly), we must not deny our feeling of hope that they are going to end well. This is the affirmative, idealistic side of Sturges that came to the fore in *The Great Moment* (1944), when he began with the ignominious death and humiliations of Dr. Morton, and ended with the heroic decision of Dr. Morton to end pain at the cost of his own fortune.

Throughout *The Power and the Glory* there are exceptionally strenuous metaphors to express the abstract notions of rise and fall, superiority and inferiority, selfishness and self-sacrifice. On one occasion, Spencer Tracy and Colleen Moore keep ascending a hill higher and higher as Tracy tries to find the courage to propose. Earlier, the businessman as a child climbs a tree to ever more dizzying heights as a prophetic expression of heights that will be scaled in the business world. Sturges is often given to wildly visual conceits in his screenplays, many out of silent movies. One wonders if Sturges ever saw Harold Lloyd's *Kid Brother* back in the twenties, with its lyrical tree-climbing sequence. Since Sturges worked very knowledgeably with the Lloyd persona in *Mad Wednesday*, it is reasonable to assume some feedback.

Ultimately *The Power and the Glory* depresses audiences not merely for its pessimism, which it shares with *Kane*, but for its sordidness, in which it is unique. What finally destroys the protagonist in *The Power and the Glory* is the moral corruption of the milieu into which his wealth has propelled him. When he finds his own son making love to his second wife, he feels betrayed to the point of first questioning and then ending his own life. For Sturges himself—born and raised under still mysterious circumstances, in the circle of Mary Deste, Isadora Duncan, Gordon Craig, Isaac Singer—torn between European bohemianism and American materialism, between feminine fluttering and affectation on the one hand and masculine muscling and acquisitiveness on the other, the story that emerges in *The Power and the Glory* is too uncomfortably clinical for comfort. Still, Sturges treats it gingerly, tentatively, as if he were not yet sure what attitude to take to it. Oddly, he never returns to this sort of subject again, and never again comes close to an unguarded view of the frightful tensions he experienced in growing into manhood.

Sturges was associated with four other writers on the credits of *Thirty-Day Princess* (1934), a minor impersonation-Cinderella comedy too fragile and undistinguished for extended comment. Marion Gering directed with an appropriately anonymous style, and Sylvia Sidney made another feeble stab at being a comedienne mainly by winking excessively in the manner Rouben Mamoulian had found so expressive for his optical dissolves in *City Streets*. Miss Sidney was to remain the throbbingly proletarian princess of the thirties, and leave the gossamer comedy to others. Otherwise, the movie is interesting mainly for its cross-references to the evolution of Cary Grant and Edward Arnold from minor to major levels of casting.

Sturges's second play to be adapted to the screen—*Child of Manhattan*—was received with indifference. Nancy Carroll, a saucy early-thirties star, was slowly fading and John Boles continued to offend reviewers with his mannequin impassivity and light-opera hamminess. Most offended of all by Boles was temporary movie reviewer Graham Greene, who professed never to understand why lovely women on the screen succumbed to Boles's sensual arrogance. Again the plot emphasizes the niceness and consideration of all sorts of stock characters under the most sordid circumstances, the heroine actually launching the frothy farce with her illicit pregnancy, and then wishing to keep the playboy who has made the noble gesture from sacrificing his own life to her need, and he, on his part, not wishing to allow her to sacrifice her own happiness merely through a misguided notion of his own motives. We are light years away from the attitudes struck in *Way Down East* and *East Lynne*, but mere months away from a time when illicit pregnancy will no longer have the option of being taken lightly.

That Sturges reportedly collaborated with Maxwell Anderson and Leonard Praskins on Leo Tolstoy's *Resurrection* for Samuel Goldwyn and Rouben Mamoulian indicates only that Sturges was pegged as a relatively educated man on the Hollywood totem pole, and was therefore entrusted with arty foreign authors like Tolstoy, Ferenc Molnar (*The Good Fairy*), Marcel Pagnol (*Port of Seven Seas*), and François Villon via Justin Huntley McCarthy (*If I Were King*). Of these productions there is little to

note beyond their strained refinement. *We Live Again* (1934) caused a
slight ripple, less through Anna Sten's Slavic stupefaction and Fredric
March's laborious stylishness—which always made up in persistence
what it lacked in persuasiveness—than through some ideologically
pointed speeches about serfs, which, all things being considered, we
would be safer crediting to Maxwell Anderson than to Sturges.

The Good Fairy (1935) is notable mainly for William Wyler's graceful
direction of delicate comedy, the off-beat casting of Herbert Marshall as
the lawyer-lover, and the lovely, husky-voiced ingenue performance of
Margaret Sullavan, particularly in the movie's best and most Sturgean
scene in which she is a tearful usherette with a cast-from-home-and-
hearth-and-cradleside-tearjerker on the screen, the remorseless husband
uttering and re-uttering and fingerpointing his one word of dialogue:
"Go!" to great comic effect. Sturges later developed other movie-within-
movie routines for *Sullivan's Travels* (1941) and *The Miracle of Morgan's
Creek* (1944).

Sturges was not given official credit for *Imitation of Life* (1934) and
Next Time We Love (1936), two genuinely tasteful and above-average
sagas of self-sacrifice that deserve mention. Apart from Sturges's pres-
ently unknown contributions to their behavioral charms, both films deal
with the familiar Sturges subject of the American career on the rise.
Diamond Jim (1935) and *Hotel Haywire* (1937) are somewhat more pertinent to the personality of Preston Sturges than their meager reputations
would indicate. *Diamond Jim* takes Edward Arnold's big tycoon mannerisms into the climactically logical laughter of his hammily heroic-
ghoulish-gourmet self-destruction. *Hotel Haywire* represents the earliest
Sturges effort to work in pure farce, a genre then and later in which
Sturges tended to enclose his slapstick effects within the quotes of self-
conscious imitation. Sturges, like Welles, was a *nouvelle vague, hommage*-
addicted director before his time.

Which leaves us with two quintessentially Sturgean movies of the
thirties, *Easy Living* (1937) and *Remember the Night* (1940), both directed by Mitchell Leisen, a stylish middle-level figure at Paramount who
bridged the gap between Lubitsch and Sternberg at the beginning of the
thirties and Sturges and Wilder at the beginning of the forties. Which is
not to say that Frank Tuttle or Wesley Ruggles or Norman McLeod or
even Edward Sutherland (though it was a bit late for him) could not
have taken a stab at *Easy Living* and *Remember the Night*. There was a
self-operative tradition at Paramount within a reasonable margin of error,

but Leisen was something more than a studio artisan if something less than a full-fledged auteur. Curiously, *Easy Living* is the only film with which Sturges the writer was associated in the thirties that may be reasonably preferred to any of his own forties films. Not only is *Easy Living* funny and gracious and generous in the best Sturges tradition; it is also velvety smooth and comfortably movie-ish in a way no Sturges-directed film ever was. Always with Sturges's own work, directed and written in tandem, there crept in disturbing dissonances and ambiguities, unexplained tics and complexes, unresolved affinities and attractions.

There is none of this in *Easy Living*. The light likability of the milieu never crosses over into a more complex complicity. The brilliant bits of Luis Alberni as the frantically bluffing and blackmailing hotel impresario, William Demarest as the tough-guy gossip columnist, and Franklin Pangborn as the prissy-prune proprietor of the fashion salon, remain just cameos without coalescing into that Dickensian density of detail that Sturges will later fashion in his own films. There are memorable set pieces—the fur coat falling on the double-decker bus, the customers scrambling for food in an Automat gone beserkly ejaculatory, and the ticker tape always fouling up Edward Arnold's hands as if to answer the never-before-asked question of what happens to ticker tape day in and day out once it stops tickering—but the gags and the characters end in themselves coolly and completely without any carry-over or cross-over. There is a neatness and dispatch to the movie that marks it as a work more of expertly collaborative craftsmanship than of the most personal art. It's probably just a coincidence that Sturges was never again associated with Jean Arthur, who gives *Easy Living* much of its spunky-elegant resilience; but it is unlikely he would ever have veiled her with as much expertly mocking glamour as the eye-wise Leisen did in her brilliantly composed superluxury bedtime (rather than bedroom) scene in the hotel with Ray Milland. Leisen's homage to Sternberg-on-Dietrich is, like Arthur's ambivalent attitude toward her own working-girl beauty, satiric without being derisive, delighted in itself just this side of delirium.

Sturges's career as a scriptwriter, pure and simple, ends with *Remember the Night* (1940), a somber, low-key, delicately awakening light drama of love and redemption under the shadow of prison and all the guilt such a plot device implies. *Remember the Night* is a nice, sensitive, detailed, nuanced movie, and Leisen's direction is virtually faultless from a technical standpoint. But this wasn't enough for Sturges. He wanted something more, a richer tone perhaps, or a more complex mood, or a more personal style. Whatever the source of his discontent, it propelled him into one of the most brilliant and most bizarre bursts of creation in the history of the cinema.

■　　■　　■　　■

PRESTON STURGES ENJOYED his greatest vogue between 1940 and 1944 as the acknowledged successor to Ernst Lubitsch on the Paramount lot. *The Great McGinty* and *Christmas in July* (both 1940), *The Lady Eve* (1941), *Sullivan's Travels* and *The Palm Beach Story* (both 1942), and *The Miracle of Morgan's Creek, Hail the Conquering Hero,* and *The Great Moment* (all 1944) expressed a satirical, often savage vision of American life at a time when movies tended to be smothered in sanctimoniousness. Hence, even at the time of his greatest success, he was overshadowed somewhat by the emotions aroused by the war, and the stylistic revolution ushered in by *Citizen Kane*. He received an Academy Award for the script of *The Great McGinty*, and was nominated for *The Miracle of Morgan's Creek* and *Hail the Conquering Hero*, though again as a writer rather than a director. If anything, he was considered too much of a one-man band for the good of the studio system. The romantic aspiration of auteurism was not appreciated in Hollywood then, if indeed it is to this day. At that, Sturges was regarded as infinitely less subversive than Welles, and considerably more adaptable to the public's needs. By the same token, Welles's greater solemnity was taken as greater seriousness. And the young, particularly, prefer solemnity to hilarity in their cult heroes, which is why Stroheim and Welles have tended to fare better than Lubitsch and Sturges in the textbook histories of film.

What distinguished Sturges from his contemporaries was the frantic congestion of his comedies. The Brueghel of American comedy directors, Sturges created a world of peripheral professionals: politicians, gangsters, executives, bartenders, cabdrivers, secretaries, bookies, card sharps, movie producers, doctors, dentists, bodyguards, butlers, inventors, dilettantes, and derelicts. These were not the usual flotsam and jetsam of Hollywood cinema but self-expressive cameos of aggressive individualism. With his sensitive ear for dialect humor, Sturges managed to preserve all the lumpiness in the melting pot. In this context, Akim Tamiroff's quintessentially crooked political boss in *The Great McGinty* spoke for all of Sturges's genial rascals when he declared with ringing, heavily accented conviction: "America is a land of great opportunity." Unlike Capra and Riskin, with their Christian populist melodramas, Sturges never sentimentalized the "little people" of the earth. Hence his bit players never coalesced into a monolithic mob, but, rather, dispersed into a brawling aggregation of aggrieved babblers. In fact, Sturges was severely criticized in 1944 for toying with the emotional expectations of his audience by transforming an apparent lynch mob in *Hail the Conquering Hero* into a crowd of well-wishers. In a way, *Hail the Conquering Hero* and *The Miracle of Morgan's Creek* can be considered as sophisticated parodies respectively of *Mr. Smith Goes to Washington* (1939) and *Meet John Doe* (1941). Even in the casting of jug-eared Eddie Bracken as the persecuted innocent, Sturges seemed to caricature the Capraesque Christ-like agony of such icons of folksy idealism as James Stewart and Gary Cooper.

André Bazin perceived the significance of the transition from Capra to Sturges when the Sturges oeuvre surfaced in France after the war. Writing in 1949 of *The Miracle of Morgan's Creek* in *L'Ecran Français*, Bazin admonished his French readers:

> Make no mistake—this new American comedy is strictly the opposite of what we have seen in the past. Sturges is the anti-Capra. The author of *Mr. Deeds Goes to Town* (1936) made us laugh only to better instill our confidence in the social mythology that his comedies confirm. Sturges's streak of genius comes from having known how to protract American comedy by transforming humor into irony. What I fear is that in the same way he might herald the end of a genre that was, nonetheless, one of the greatest.

Sturges was criticized at his peak by James Agee and Manny Farber for an ambivalence in his work derived from a childhood conflict between a culturally demanding mother and an admired businessman stepfather. This unusually Freudian analysis of the director's work, unusual, that is, for its time, sought to explain the incongruity of Continental sophistication being challenged by American pragmatism. Sturges himself was seen as an uneasy mixture of savant and wise guy. On the one hand, his high literacy, rare among Hollywood screenwriters, enabled him to drop words like "ribaldry" and "vestal" into their proper contexts without a pretentious thud. On the other, he seemed to retreat into playful evasion whenever his deepest feelings were engaged. His movies therefore reflect a civilized skepticism about old conventions but lack the radical sensibility to create new ones. He could thus make jokes about the binary inevitability of boy-meets-girl scenarios, and then turn around to write the most lyrical love scenes of his era. Consequently, an appreciation of Hollywood movies for their own sake is necessary if one is to perceive the nuances of Sturges's talent. He made good movies, but not anti-movies, which is to say that he needed the system, much as the system needed him.

After 1944, when he left Paramount to form a short-lived partnership with Howard Hughes, Sturges's career suffered a precipitous decline. His three subsequent Hollywood films—*Mad Wednesday* (1947), *Unfaithfully Yours* (1948), and *The Beautiful Blonde from Bashful Bend* (1949)—were remote from the tastes of their time, and, during his long exile in the fifties, his one realized European project, the bilingual *Les Carnets de Major Thompson* (*The French They Are a Funny Race* (1955)), was a singularly lethargic letdown. He died of a heart attack at the Algonquin Hotel in New York in 1959, and he was never mourned or memorialized in the movie colony as he should have been.

Fortunately, the place of Preston Sturges in film history will remain secure as long as his movies continue to circulate widely. Seen in a series, the Sturges canon reveals a consistent stylistic pattern. Like most effective comedy directors, he depended more on the pacing of action and dialogue than on visual texture and composition. His canvas was flat, his sense of space shallow. Sturges employed long, uncut, "single-take" scenes to establish the premises of his elaborate scripts. In this he resembled the other directors who came to cinema after sound (Ophüls, Cukor, Mamoulian, Preminger). But when Sturges shifted to slapstick, he often cut to reactions before the action had been terminated. Indeed, his instinct for timing comedy montage made his films the funniest of their era in terms of audience laughter. He was capable of cinematic license with a talking horse or a portrait that changed expression. When he wanted to speed up the plot, he dispensed with dialogue altogether as he filled the screen with the hurtling bodies of silent farce. In *Mad Wednesday* (1947), he went so far as to begin with the last reel of Harold Lloyd's 1925 classic, *The Freshman*, after which he embellished Lloyd's vertiginous comedy effects with even wilder Sturges variations. Curiously, the very critics who lamented the Lost Golden Age of Silent Comedy failed to appreciate Sturges's rousing efforts at resurrection. Admittedly, some of the Sturges slapstick was clumsy and forced. There are a few too many slugging matches between Brian Donlevy and Akim Tamiroff in *The Great McGinty*, and a bit too much fruit-throwing in *Christmas in July* (both 1940). Eugene Palette throws too much of a tantrum at the breakfast table in *The Lady Eve* (1941), and Joel McCrea and Veronica Lake splash down once too often in the swimming pool in *Sullivan's Travels* (1942).

On the credit side of the comic ledger are the tumultuous tell-all honeymoon night of Barbara Stanwyck and Henry Fonda in *The Lady Eve* (complete with train steaming into tunnel), the Mack Sennett chase of a midget race car by a studio land yacht fully equipped with slapstick and cheesecake elements in the Swiftian (in more senses than one) *Sullivan's Travels*, the convulsions of the contest jury in *Christmas in July*, the morning-after confrontation of Eddie Bracken and William Demarest over a daughter's (Betty Hutton's) honor in *The Miracle of Morgan's Creek*, the election night frolic in *The Great McGinty*, and the instant masochism of Rudy Vallee's courtship of Claudette Colbert in *The Palm Beach Story*. In each instance, a piece of physical action is either set up or capped by a clever line of dialogue.

Still, the delicate mechanism of a Sturges scenario cannot be considered simply as a laugh machine. The dramatic structure is too intricate and convoluted, the mood invariably mixed. In the very midst of a loud guffaw one is surprised to find a lump in one's throat and tears in one's eyes. Unlike most film-makers of the seventies and eighties, Sturges could generally balance buddy-buddy camaraderie with man-woman comradeship. An exception is *The Great McGinty*, which is actually diluted by the school-marm reformism of Muriel Angelus when all Brian Donlevy (McGinty) and Akim Tamiroff (the Boss) really want to do is wallow in the trough of civic corruption. After *McGinty*, however, Sturges fashioned a gallery of tough, intelligent, and yet vulnerable females with Ellen Drew in *Christmas in July*, Barbara Stanwyck in *The Lady Eve*, Claudette Colbert and Mary Astor in *The Palm Beach Story*, Veronica Lake in *Sullivan's Travels*, Betty Hutton and Diana Lynn in *The Miracle of Morgan's Creek*, and Ella Raines in *Hail the Conquering Hero*. The distinctive sweetness of Sturges's films can be attributed to his deep emotional involvement with the roller-coaster rides to success and sexual fulfillment which he seemed to be satirizing. As a walking success story in his own right, Sturges never sneered at the people coming up on the wheel of fortune in his movie fables. Nor was there in his restless and unruly characters any of the radical chic litany of shared common values in the class struggle. People were always barging in where they weren't wanted in a Sturges movie, and, if they were booted out, well, they just brushed themselves off and went about their business, their pugnacity and self-esteem miraculously undiminished. Indeed, the sheer likability of his American characters marks Sturges as a throwback to the long ago and far away forties when Americans still liked themselves enormously.

Ultimately, Sturges can never be fully appreciated by non-English-speaking critics any more than Sacha Guitry can be fully appreciated by non-French-speaking critics. Sturges was by far the wittiest scriptwriter the English-speaking cinema has known, even though he tended to lapse into garrulousness. He loved to play with words and names for their own sake (e.g. Diddlebock, Kockenlocker, Woodrow Truesmith) with the result that his asides were usually more devastating than other writers' punch lines. In a Sturgean context it did not seem unusual for a gravel-voiced bus driver to use the word "paraphrase" nor for a hoodlum to invoke the ruinous symmetry of "Samson and Delilah, Sodom and Gommorah." A stereotyped performer like Eric Blore was virtually rediscovered savoring the line "I positively swill in his ale." Similarly, Edgar Kennedy was resurrected from two-reelers to play an inspired bartender reacting to a customer's asking for his first drink ever: "Sir, you rouse the artist in me." The Sturges stock company was particularly noted for the contrasting personalities of William Demarest, the rowdy roughneck, and Franklin Pangborn, the prissy prude.

Yet Sturges was capable also of great eloquence, as is evident in his passionate prologue to *The Great Moment* (1944), a piece of writing that is particularly admirable for its having been turned out in the midst of all the World War II propaganda:

> One of the most charming characteristics of Homo Sapiens—the wise guy on your left—is the consistency with which he has stoned, crucified, burned at the stake, and otherwise rid himself of those who consecrated their lives to his further comfort and well-being so that all his strength and cunning might be preserved for the creation of ever larger monuments, memorial shafts, triumphal arches, pyramids, and obelisks to the eternal glory of generals on horseback, tyrants, usurpers, dictators, politicans, and other heroes who led him usually from the rear, to dismemberment and death.

The Great Moment was, in other respects, the strangest of all Sturges's films in that its genre-juggling mixed The-Great-Man-of-Granite series, identified primarily with Paul Muni, and bits and pieces of discordant slapstick and cynicism. Joel McCrea's portrayal of Morton, the inventor of anesthesia, was far less reverent than Muni's of Pasteur, Zola, and Juarez; Edward G. Robinson's of Ehrlich, Spencer Tracy's of Edison, and Greer Garson's of Madame Curie. Indeed, if we track this genre from *The Story of Louis Pasteur* in 1936 to *Madame Curie* in 1944, we have registered also the approximate duration of the vogue for uplifting sagas about upstanding benefactors of mankind. Certain unfortunate conventions had been established in the depiction of these paragons. The profit motive, for example, was conspicuous by its absence. There was no humor, dark or otherwise. Worst of all, the exalted achiever seemed to be posing for posterity in virtually every frame of the film. It is not surprising that none of these much-admired and much-honored testimonials to high-minded altruism have aged well enough to be regarded as "classics."

By contrast, *The Great Moment* seems now to have been ahead of its time in casting shadows over the life of its hero. More a craftsman than an artist, McCrea's Morton was driven to his discovery by nothing more than a desire to "do neat work" on his dental patients. Unlike other heroes of the genre, however, Morton was not the only man seeking to end pain. He faced rivals and competitors, who in Sturges's ample and sophisticated view of the world, were not treated as vile and crass villains. Morton's downfall came about largely from a quixotic stubbornness that was reflected also in Sturges's own subsequent downfall, and in Joel McCrea's failure ever to attain the stellar heights. McCrea, more than any actor, certainly more than Eddie Bracken, served as Sturges's alter ego, much in the manner of Adolphe Menjou and Lionel Atwill for Josef von Sternberg, William Holden and Jack Lemmon for Billy Wilder, Gunnar Bjornstrand for Ingmar Bergman, Marcello Mastroianni for Federico Fellini, and Jean-Pierre Léaud for François Truffaut.

McCrea actually played Sturges himself in *Sullivan's Travels* from the professional vantage point of John L. Sullivan, the comedy director, the friend of Lubitsch, the quixotic hobo seeking "real life" away from Hollywood. McCrea in *The Palm Beach Story* was the virile if down-at-the-heels promoter of futuristic architectural schemes, but still Sturges on the rise. McCrea as Morton seems to be Sturges with a premonition of his own doom, but determined to go down with one last gallant and reckless gesture.

The traditional diagnosis for Sturges's decline and fall has been burnout, pure and simple, but it may be that his best comedies depended for their impact on a good-natured ribbing of the prevailing optimism reigning in Hollywood and America through the end of World War II. Once that optimism began to fade, Sturges had no suitable conventions to react against, and no hallowed plot-lines to twist ever so slightly. Everywhere there was a coarsening of comic traditions. Realism and neo-realism became the alibis for a vulgar frankness and an intense obviousness. The double-entendre went the way of the drawing room, and Sturges himself resorted to an ever more frantic style of farce, a style, moreover, that was out of date with the taste-makers.

Indeed, up through *Hail the Conquering Hero*, Sturges had managed to maintain an uneasy balance between the farcical and sentimental aspects of his art. The temperature on the screen was still warm at the final fade-out; the tried-and-true conventions, however underlined with irony, were still respected. With *The Sin of Harold Diddlebock/ Mad Wednesday* (1947), a chill began to set in with audiences. It was not *their* feelings Sturges was expressing so much as his own. By attempting to resurrect Harold Lloyd as a comic hero (with a newly discovered and since forgotten ingenue named Frances Ramsden), Sturges was counting on a nostalgic adventurousness of which the postwar, presumably forward-looking moviegoer was incapable. Success stories, however sardonic, had lost their point, and the spectacle of a lion let loose on Wall Street as an advertising ploy seemed more ho-hum than madcap.

With *Unfaithfully Yours* and *The Beautiful Blonde from Bashful Bend*, Sturges was betrayed even by his casting. Rex Harrison, an uncommonly cerebral actor, was hardly at home in the kind of sentimental farce called for in *Unfaithfully Yours*. He was cold and brittle in a way that McCrea never was as the jealous husband in *The Palm Beach Story*. Linda Darnell, a bit of surprise casting as the dutiful Desdemona, was closer to the mark, but somehow the farcical shenanigans of Harrison's fantasy revenges served more to get in the way of the relationship than enhance it. Rudy Vallee was on hand once more as the dim-witted foil to the protagonist, and Edgar Kennedy was again a mini-revelation as a mug with a passion for Mozart. But the eventual and inevitable reconciliation lacked the saving spark of inspiration that rescued previous "happy endings" from the curse of facetiousness. Despite all the fanfares from the concert hall in which Harrison's husband mimed Sir Thomas Beecham's conducting style, *Unfaithfully Yours* ended on a thin, tinny note with little emotional conviction. Even so, the worst was yet to come in *The Beautiful Blonde from Bashful Bend*, with Betty Grable, in a frantically unfunny vendetta with the ever callow Cesar Romero over an expanse of overcluttered studio set representing the Old West. The dialogue came hurtling out at a machine-gun clip as if to distract the audience from the total lack of charm in the characters and the proceedings. Sturges had transformed the most vulgar ingredients of movie entertainment into a spectacle at once excruciating and esoteric.

■   ■   ■   ■

IN BOTH his good and his bad films, Sturges displayed an unwavering predilection for notions and nostrums, for invention and inspiration. It is as if his characters were capable of being lit up from within by the cartoonist's device of the instantly ignited light-bulb in the hero's skull. Joel McCrea's movie director in *Sullivan's Travels* experiences and expresses such a flash of practical creativity at the stirring moment in the film when he proclaims himself to be his own murderer. Eddie Bracken's bogus Marine reacts in much the same excitable way in *Hail the Conquering Hero* when he thinks he has found a way out of his potentially humiliating predicament. Harold Lloyd's Harold Diddlebock takes a bit longer to come up with the advertising coup that will make him rich, but the important thing to remember about the Sturges characters is that they lived by their wits, and were confident ultimately of their own inner resources no matter how far down the social and economic ladder they may have found themselves at the outset. This is a vision of Americans in movies that had died even before Sturges did. That Sturges projected this vision more persuasively than any other American film-maker before or after can be attributed to both his expertise with well-timed bursts of oratory, and to his ironic twists on the expected homilies.

When you least expected it, Ellen Drew in *Christmas in July* would suddenly blossom forth in Shavian splendor in the midst of a Barrie whimsy to claim a chance for young men on the corporate chain-gang. Up to this point, the character she plays has been presented as a loving nitwit in the Hollywood Girlfriend tradition. Yet, Sturges does not falsify the character in the slightest. We come to believe that her words have welled up within her, and had to burst forth or she would die. Earlier in *Christmas in July* a philosophical office manager (Harry Hayden) has counseled patience, prudence, and resignation in the face of virtually inevitable defeat of one's highest aspirations. The Ellen Drew character refers to the office manager's rationalization of quiescence when she describes this same office manager as representative of the vast army of losers in the game of life, nay, not even losers, but people who never even had a chance to test their wings.

The actor who played the office manager in *Christmas in July* later played the perennial runner-up in a small town's mayoralty elections in *Hail the Conquering Hero*. Harry Hayden as the rueful also-ran was a Sturges creation, neatly etched and compassionately observed, a measure of Preston Sturges's sweet sophistication on all aspects of the American Dream.

BILLY WILDER (1906–)

People often ask if I have any regrets over my rankings of directors in *The American Cinema*. Actually, there have been shifts and slides, rises and falls, all along the line. Film history is always in the process of revision, and some of our earliest masters are still alive. *The American Cinema* was a very tentative probe designed mainly to establish the existence of a subject worthy of study. The rest is refinement and elaboration.

To go back to the question, however, at this time, I must concede that seemingly I have grossly under-rated Billy Wilder, perhaps more so than any other American director. His twilight resurgence in the seventies with such mellow masterpieces as *The Private Life of Sherlock Holmes* (1969), *Avanti!* (1972), and even the very flawed *The Front Page* (1974) made me rethink Wilder, but, mostly, I have been motivated by rueful memories of how somehow I managed to let people talk me out of my instinctive enthusiasm for his films. Whereas the moviegoer in me traipsed back again and again to see *The Major and the Minor* (1942), *Double Indemnity* (1944), *The Lost Weekend* (1945), *Sunset Boulevard* (1950), *Stalag 17* (1953), *Love in the Afternoon* (1959), *Some Like It Hot* (1959), and *The Apartment* (1960), the film critic in me was always heard clucking that Wilder was too clever and cynical for his own and everyone else's good. Somehow his clinkers always did double duty to discredit his classics. With other directors, the classics were credited to them, and the clinkers to the "system." But Wilder was thought of as the system personified with all its serpentine wiles and crass commercialism.

The year 1950 was very crucial in the evolution of my conflicting responses toward Wilder. I must have seen *Sunset Boulevard* about twenty-five times during its first run at the Radio City Music Hall. I was working then in a very menial position at David O. Selznick's New York office, and for the first time began meeting industry-wise film buffs. One such chap and I argued through most of the latter part of 1950 the relative merits of *Sunset Boulevard* and *All About Eve*. I stuck to *Sunset* through thick and thin, but I was defensive. I did not know how to counter arguments about Wilder's excessive morbidity, and about the facile pathology of the Norma Desmond character, played with unmodulated bravura by Gloria Swanson.

Perhaps the most damning bit of critical analysis of Wilder was put forth by François Truffaut in a *Cahiers* essay at about the same time of *Sabrina* (1954). The thrust of Truffaut's remarks was that while Wilder had a minor flair for comedy inherited from Lubitsch (also minor in Truffaut's *politique*), Wilder lacked the structural capability for more serious films (like *Double Indemnity* and *The Lost Weekend*). This was one of Truffaut's more cryptic essays, and though it would not in itself have been decisive, it helped drive the final nail in the coffin. For their part, the *Sight and Sound* and *Sequence* people had always doubted the depth of Wilder's commitment, and Agee himself had expressed strong reservations about both *Double Indemnity* and *The Lost Weekend*.

Certainly, there are flaws in almost all of Wilder's output but what is more important is the value we attach to Wilder's virtues. In *Double Indemnity*, for example, I was never able to perceive the motivational moment when Fred MacMurray's breezy insurance investigator and devil-may-care womanizer is transformed into a purposeful murderer. That is a weakness of characterization even in terms of the violent expectations of the genre, and yet it is also a reflection of Wilder's tendency to jump the gap between motivation and action by using very personal feelings of guilt and corruption. In *The Lost Weekend* there is a sketchy rendering of the psychological problems behind Ray Milland's alcoholism. The author Charles Jackson's intimations of homosexual conflicts in the film have been replaced by showy delusions of glassy-eyed grandeur. But in our concern with what Wilder was not about, we have neglected to explore the director's own feelings of perpetual insecurity. More important, we have always interpreted, or misinterpreted, the flamboyant glibness of Wilder's characters as proof of the director's insincerity. Hence, Wilder's brightness was too often seen as mere brashness. Now that dialogue in general is duller and more "sincere" than ever, Wilder's quick-wittedness seems more charming than ever.

If we trace the trajectory of Billy Wilder's directorial career in the forties, we find that he made a sparkling debut with *The Major and the Minor* in 1942, did his bit for the war effort and Erich von Stroheim with *Five Graves to Cairo* in 1943, fashioned a classic of the *film noir* with *Double Indemnity* in 1944, hit his peak of social significance and establishment eminence with *The Lost Weekend* in 1945, and then receded in a haze of respectability with an overly fluffy Franz Josef conceit out of the cuisine of Chez Ernst (*The Emperor Waltz*) (1948) and a cynical view of war-ravaged and Nazi-tainted Berlin (*A Foreign Affair*) in 1948.

Still, as the Paramount director par excellence he had outlasted Preston Sturges and outlived Ernst Lubitsch, and the very tasteful Mitchell Leisen, who had previously profited from scripts by Sturges and the Brackett and Wilder team, saw his career decline. By contrast, Wilder went on to a long and productive career, and was still employable, if only intermittently, in the seventies. But he never caught the brass ring of absolute auteurist pre-eminence. For too long he was linked with the very well-liked Charles Brackett, who, it was whispered in industry circles, exercised a restraining, civilizing influence on Billy Wilder's cynical, callous, morbid tendencies. Hence, when a Wilder movie seemed particularly heartless, Wilder got all the blame; and when a Wilder movie proved particularly compassionate, Wilder had to share the credit with Brackett.

Nonetheless, Wilder was always credited with a lively intelligence in revamping old narrative formulas. He was seen as particularly adept at switch-casting, notably in persuading Ginger Rogers to endure little-girl (not to mention Lolita) drag for *The Major and the Minor*, Fred MacMurray to abandon his likable persona for the part of a calculating murderer in *Double Indemnity*, and Ray Milland to make the switch from lounge lizard to lush in *The Lost Weekend*. In all instances, the players in question reportedly resisted playing against type at first, but eventually were to see their careers being given a new lease on life. Brackett and Wilder, who had been well publicized as a sterling script-writing team in the late thirties, by the mid-forties were being lionized as a film-making unit.

Wilder in one interview was adamant about his opposition to such Kris Kringle camera effects as shooting a scene from behind the fire in the fireplace, an impossible angle in terms of any personal point of view. Wilder may have been thinking of the showy shot of Jennifer Jones's being illuminated by the flames in *Love Letters*, which had been photographed somewhat in the old Germanic style by director William Dieterle and cinematographer Lee Garmes. The subtlety of the point Wilder was making was not fully perceived in that primitive period of stylistic analysis, but what he was suggesting was that photographic embellishment was no substitute for truly restructured narrative.

Even later, however, most of Wilder's critics failed to realize that his apparent cynicism was the only way he could make his raging romanticism palatable. The same problem had plagued Ernst Lubitsch before Wilder, and has plagued Richard Lester after Wilder. Cynicism and sophistication, relatively rare in movies at any time, are apt to be seized

upon as indicators of the full register of a director's personality. The
passion beneath the polish is thereby overlooked. In Wilder's case, the
seemingly facile reversals in his films obscured the deep sentiments of
his characters. For all its gimmicks, *The Major and the Minor* is one of
the most enchanting love stories ever told on the screen, and for all its
deadpan stoicism *Double Indemnity* strikes uncommonly sweet chords of
male camaraderie in its final confrontation between Fred MacMurray
and Edward G. Robinson.

Wilder managed to step on a few toes politically as well with such
films as *Five Graves to Cairo* (1943) and *A Foreign Affair* (1948), being
denounced for the former as anti-French by the influential French
Marxist film historian Georges Sadoul, and as irredeemably irresponsible
for the latter by just about every single solemn film critic. Sadoul was
particularly outraged by Anne Baxter's personification of France as a
soft-hearted whore at the beck and call of Nazi supermen played by Erich
von Stroheim and Peter Van Eyck. Sadoul's is a bizarre analysis, indeed,
but in a way it is symptomatic of Wilder's bad luck in getting penalized
for being more honest and more open about the realities of human sexuality than most of his Hollywood colleagues. Similarly, Marlene Dietrich's unrepentant Nazi siren in *A Foreign Affair* is a more daring
characterization than most that emerged after World War II. Indeed,
Wilder came closer to anticipating the bitter cross-purposes of the postwar world than his more idealistic One World-oriented contemporaries.
But with Lubitsch having been condemned for *To Be or Not To Be* in
1942, and Hitchcock for *Lifeboat* in 1943, for Wilder it almost could
have been an honor to be condemned for *A Foreign Affair* had it not been
for his needless brutalization of Jean Arthur—for which I attacked him in
The American Cinema and for which I have yet to forgive him.

Yet, am I blaming Wilder too much, and the devastating Dietrich too
little, for what happened to Miss Arthur in *A Foreign Affair*? After all,
Hitchcock once told me that Jane Wyman burst into tears when she saw
how she looked next to Dietrich in *Stage Fright*, and yet I never condemned Hitch for his cruelty. Why then condemn Wilder? I suppose
because of having been conditioned for many years to attribute the worst
motives to his movies, and even to suspect the ultimate source of their
undeniable charms, it is time at long last to come to terms with my most
primal moviegoing instincts. For me as a critic, Wilder has served in the
same manner Hitchcock has served so many of my colleagues: as a film-
maker one likes too much and too easily to respect properly.

■   ■   ■   ■

YES, BILLY WILDER BELONGS in the Pantheon of directors, at least in *my* Pantheon from which I so rudely barred him in *The American Cinema* in 1968. I have proffered my mea culpa to Mr. Wilder in person on two pleasant occasions—the first at the Carlton Hotel in Cannes in 1978 when he was presenting *Fedora* at the Festival to a very mixed reception, and the second in New York's Peninsula Hotel in April 1991 during his brief stay in town to participate in the Film Society of Lincoln Center's Audrey Hepburn tribute, and also to help kick off a massive Wilder retrospective at the Film Forum. Wilder was about to turn eighty-five on June 22, and I could hardly believe it. Time had not dimmed the mischievous twinkle in his eye, or dulled his razor-sharp wit.

My second meeting with Wilder began to take shape while I was having lunch with Wendy Keys, the knowledgeable organizer of the Hepburn event. I asked her if she had Wilder's Los Angeles number. She said yes, back in her office, and when she gave it to me later that day she warned me not to be surprised when Wilder himself answered the phone. So I called Wilder's number and, sure enough, a chirpy accented voice answered. He remembered me from Cannes, said he would be at the Peninsula Hotel, you know, the old Gotham, they've fixed it up real fancy. His tone was tinged with irony. Actually, he was being helpful inasmuch as my querulous "Peninsula Hotel?" indicated that I, a lifelong New Yorker, was not aware of the transformation of the homely Gotham into the ultra-chic Peninsula. I recalled the Cannes interview thirteen years earlier began with Wilder's observation that the Carlton had the best food in town, contrary to the received wisdom of the Michelin-mesmerized visitors. I recalled also that Wilder's father had had something to do with hotels in Vienna, and that the son's wanderings had deposited him in hotels from the Kempinski in Berlin, to a fleapit in Paris, to the ladies' room in the Château Marmont on Sunset Boulevard. Rich or poor, he had never been overawed by or unobservant of his surroundings. All his life he has had a sharp eye and a sharp tongue for the absurdities of the upper crust and the grotesqueries of the lower depths. His screenplays have been equally at home with the caviar and the cockroaches.

So how do you interview an old tabloid reporter who knows all the tricks of the trade? You don't. Or, at least, I don't. I am a terrible interviewer. (Manny Farber once described me as a semi-pro journalist, and I am not sure that he was paying me a compliment.) Paradoxically, I love

to read interviews, particularly the ones with all the personal questions
I can never ask. Anyway, by this time Wilder gives virtual carte blanche
to journalists to attribute to him almost any quotes they wish. I don't
use a tape recorder, so I cannot reproduce his colloquial speech rhythms,
but I can vouch for the fact that he is an expert raconteur, probably on
a par with his late Berliner compatriot and mentor, the legendary Ernst
Lubitsch.

Before the interview, I had boned up a bit on Billy Wilder by re-
reading *Billy Wilder* by Axel Madsen and *Journey Down Sunset Boulevard:
The Films of Billy Wilder* by Neil Sinyard and Adrian Turner. Sinyard
and Turner have taken me to task for my "belated" appreciation of Billy
Wilder—as well they might—though my turnabout was less a self-
revisionist reflex than a "return" (to invoke Norma Desmond's bristling
euphemism for "comeback") to an earlier enthusiasm.

After all, I was still in high school when I was reading about the
Brackett-and-Wilder miracle moviemaking team in the fan magazines.
This was the epoch of *Double Indemnity* (1944) and *The Lost Weekend*
(1945), each involving a casting coup in which Fred MacMurray and
Ray Milland were persuaded by the Brackett and Wilder boys to switch
type from glossy leading man to gritty semi-villain. This was hot stuff for
a high-school kid with the adolescent's yearning for intrigue and misdirection. But I had already lost my heart to Brackett and Wilder back in
1942, in the midst of all the romantic war fever, when Ginger Rogers
had been induced to play a twelve-year-old Lolita in *The Major and the
Minor*, though at a time when the horny frog of Humbert Humbert was
still buried deep in the forbidden unconscious of princely Major Kirby,
played by Ray Milland. Yet, miraculously, after fifty-six years *The Major
and the Minor* has lost none of its power to enchant. Indeed, I am
brought close to tears at the overpowering emotions unleashed by the
final embrace at the train station. How few worldly goods were needed
back then for us to feel warm and happy and fulfilled.

How then could I, ungrateful wretch, have deserted Billy Wilder in
the mid-fifties and my late twenties, when I was beginning to formu-
late (along with the late Eugene Archer) the *Cahiers du Cinema* aesthetic that was to culminate in Wilder's being demoted to the "Less
Than Meets the Eye" category in *The American Cinema?* Perhaps, I
mistrusted Wilder because I never had to work very hard to enjoy his
movies. (By contrast, my urban-ethnic political prejudices gave me a
devil of a time with John Ford.) Wilder's supposedly shrewd mixture of
cynicism and romanticism having seduced me at an early stage of my

aesthetic awareness, I came to suspect him of lacking high moral seriousness.

Wilder burst upon the cinema in 1929 with his collaboration on *Menschen am Sonntag/People on Sunday* with directors Robert Siodmak and Edgar G. Ulmer and cinematographers Fred Zinnemann and Eugen Schufftan. These key participants were eventually to arrive in Hollywood in flight from the Nazi terror. *People on Sunday* was set largely in a park in Wannsee, a Berlin suburb where, ironically, the Final Solution was later to be promulgated. Although Zinnemann was attuned to the documentary verisimilitude of the project, the bittersweet working-class romance already bore the stamp of Wilder's wry sensibility.

In the next four years Wilder was associated with the scripts of ten other minor German movies. As he described his "Weimar" period, he was merely a scriptwriter in the UFA factory with no access to the sets on which his stories were shot. Right after the Reichstag fire, he left Berlin for Paris, where he scratched out a day-to-day existence on the fringes of the film industry. His one credit during his brief stay in Paris was *Mauvaise Graine* (1933), a juvenile-delinquent, car-chase potboiler featuring a seventeen-year-old Danielle Darrieux. Wilder and director Alexander Esway collaborated on the script for this commercially marginal project, which Wilder has puckishly likened to Jean-Luc Godard's *Breathless*. Since the sixties, Wilder and many of his veteran colleagues have ridiculed *nouvelle vague* pretentiousness among American film-school graduates, particularly all the mumbo-jumbo about mise-en-scène and scriptless improvisation.

Wilder eventually found himself in Hollywood after an immigration-technicality-maneuvered side trip to Mexico, an experience that provided him with the atmosphere for the screenplay of *Hold Back the Dawn* (1941), which he and Charles Brackett would write for Mitchell Leisen.

Wilder's career took a giant step forward when in 1937 he was teamed by Paramount with Brackett (1892–1969), fourteen years Wilder's senior, a graduate of Williams College in 1915, a graduate of Harvard Law School in 1920, a novelist (*The Council of the Ungodly, Weekend, The Last Infirmity, American Colony,* and *Entirely Surrounded*), a magazine writer who sold stories to Hollywood from the early twenties on, a drama critic for *The New Yorker* from 1925 to 1929—in short, a practiced wordsmith with strong family connections in politics, finance, and high society. George Abbott recruited Brackett as a staff writer for Paramount in 1932 but, like Wilder, he garnered more credits than prestige with such flotsam and jetsam of the sound era as *Secrets of a Secretary* (1931),

Enter Madame, College Scandal, The Last Outpost, Without Regret (all 1935), *Woman Trap* (1936), *Rose of the Rancho, Piccadilly Jim, The Jungle Princess, Wild Money*, and *Live, Live and Learn* (all 1937).

Brackett and Wilder collaborated on thirteen films. Before long, as their joint writing careers flourished, Brackett was also serving as producer and Wilder as director. After their professional separation in 1950 following *Sunset Boulevard*, Wilder went on to become a producer but Brackett never became a director. Brackett and Wilder had parted company temporarily in 1944, Wilder to collaborate with Raymond Chandler on the lyrically implacable *noir* thriller *Double Indemnity* (adapted brilliantly from a below-par James M. Cain novel), whereas Brackett produced the kinder and gentler ghost classic *The Uninvited*, with Lewis Allen directing Gail Russell and a pre–*Lost Weekend* Ray Milland to a haunting score by Victor Young (a far cry from the doom-ridden score Miklos Rozsa supplied for *Double Indemnity*).

I ask Wilder about Brackett. He answers only obliquely with some zesty anecdotes about Brackett's WASP Establishment eccentricities, coupled with fond memories of the man's social kindnesses. And no wonder. Wilder has used conjugal terminology in past interviews to describe his longtime affiliations with Brackett and with I. A. L. Diamond, the Romanian-born, Columbia-educated graduate of Dennis Morgan–Jack Carson musicals who received his Ph.D. collaborating with Wilder on the screenplays for *Love in the Afternoon* (1957), *Some Like It Hot* (1959), and *The Apartment* (1960), among many others.

Wilder has been married to two different women and two different screenwriters. There have been many temporary liaisons, many casual affairs—but perhaps not all *that* many. Wilder may never have been as conventional as he might have been, but he has never been nearly as wicked as he seemed or, rather, as he allowed himself to seem. He has never posed as a moralist, but he has never been a hypocrite either. Still, how can you ask an eighty-five-year-old movie director in a hotel room to account for his life or his art? I ask instead about the missing footage of *The Private Life of Sherlock Holmes*, which, even as it stands, is one of the great films of the seventies. He tells me the footage exists but it has to be cleared through the Mirisch brothers. I then ask him about the filmed-but-deleted gas chamber finale of *Double Indemnity* in which the condemned Fred MacMurray's Walter Neff makes his final eye contact with Edward G. Robinson's compassionate Barton Keyes. Wilder tells me he didn't think the scene was necessary after the match-striking symbolism of the present ending, which, I might have added, the late

Parker Tyler perceptively described as one of the great love scenes in the history of the movies.

I was curious also about the original opening morgue scene in *Sunset Boulevard* with a group of corpses, each of whom has a story to tell about cause of death. Third in line is William Holden's Joe Gillis, who winds up telling the story of the film. Wilder tells me that preview audiences became hysterical when an identification tag was tied to a corpse's toe, and the mordant mood was shattered.

Wilder credits Erich von Stroheim with the suggestion of his character's sending Norma Desmond all the fan letters to foster her belief in a loyal audience out there waiting for her to go before the cameras again. But some of Stroheim's other suggestions were more bizarre. Wilder gets up to imitate an outrageously exaggerated limp Stroheim wanted added to his characterization. The movie would have had to stop dead in its tracks to watch Stroheim make his laborious way across the room. Even more questionable was Stroheim's desire to be shown lovingly washing Norma's lingerie. Wilder relates these episodes with affectionately admiring animation.

I had decided beforehand not to ask Wilder any questions about Marilyn Monroe or Humphrey Bogart, two of his least favorite stars. I was more interested in his negative feelings toward Mitchell Leisen, who directed the Brackett-and-Wilder screenplays *Midnight* (1939), *Arise My Love* (1940), and *Hold Back the Dawn* (1941). I had just revisited *Midnight* on cassette before my interview, and I cannot imagine a comedy script being directed more brilliantly, or the lines being read with more flair and precision by any cast other than Claudette Colbert, John Barrymore, Francis Lederer, Rex O'Malley, and, yes, Don Ameche. Yet when I mention the name Mitchell Leisen, Wilder is unguardedly contemptuous: "He was just a decorator like Minnelli. He never defended the script. He let the actors and the studio run all over him."

Again, I do not press the point. I suspect, however, that Wilder's main complaint about Leisen had more to do with the director's failure to control Charles Boyer in *Hold Back the Dawn*. Brackett and Wilder had written a scene in which Boyer talked bitterly to a cockroach climbing up a wall in the character's dingy Mexican hotel room. Boyer's character was based loosely on Wilder himself as an émigré in the thirties. Boyer considered it beneath his dignity as an actor to address a cockroach, and so Leisen had the scene cut from the script. I don't say anything to

Wilder at the time, but the more I think about it, the more I think Boyer and Leisen may have been right. In any event, Wilder was not one to forgive and forget. A year later, in *The Major and the Minor*, an unidentified little girl at a newsstand in Penn Station asks her mother to buy her a fan magazine with a cover story entitled: Why Charles Boyer Hates Women. This is an example of the Hollywood inside joke long before Jean-Luc Godard made a habit of it.

There was a time when I was struck above all by the gravity of Wilder's screen narratives. Stephen Gottlieb, a Freudian film scholar, had reminded me that Wilder was perhaps the most famous film director in the world to have lost his mother and other members of his family to the Holocaust, yet he never treated the subject explicitly in his films. On the contrary, he seemed to go out of his way to impart dignity and charm to such wartime or immediately postwar German characters as Erich von Stroheim's Rommel and Peter Van Eyck's lecherous subordinate in *Five Graves to Cairo*, Marlene Dietrich's defiantly undenazified Lorelei in *A Foreign Affair*, and Otto Preminger's camp commandant and Sig Rumann's camp guard in *Stalag 17*. One could never imagine Wilder's undertaking such earnestly well-meaning projects on the Holocaust as *The Diary of Anne Frank* and *Judgment at Nuremberg*. Partly, it is a matter of taste and genre. Wilder is a humorist and an ironist, not a polemicist and a propagandist. If there is a recurring theme in his most powerful films, it is that of wretched opportunists wistfully seeking redemption. Consequently, there are more profound reverberations of the Holocaust in the feelings of his regretful characters in *Double Indemnity*, *Sunset Boulevard*, *Ace in the Hole*, *Stalag 17*, *The Apartment*, *Kiss Me Stupid*, *Love in the Afternoon*, *The Private Life of Sherlock Holmes*, and even *Fedora*.

I would venture the hypothesis again that every film Wilder has ever written and directed represents an attempt to express the complexity of his feelings that have evolved over years of eager exile. The great dramatic moments in so many of his films could not have emerged if he had not had the courage to be profoundly honest with himself. It is this honesty, along with a prodigious craft, talent, and perseverance, that defines so much of his art.

But not all. There is the wit and the rigor as well. Hence his air of impatience and a low threshold of boredom. And above all, his horror at what he perceives as self-indulgence and style for its own sake in filmmaking. That is why he looks down on Leisen and Minnelli and their many admirers who believe that content can be transcended by form. Yet there is enough of Schnitzler and Ophüls in Wilder to have made him once consider casting Charles Laughton in *Irma La Douce* as what Madsen's biography describes as a "*La Ronde*-type master of ceremonies and commentator." But Laughton died and Lou Jacobi was cast instead in a role of reduced scope. Indeed, when I add up all the extra-base hits in Wilder's oeuvre as writer, director, and writer-director, he comes up with a batting average that would have made Ted Williams and Joe DiMaggio green with envy.

LEO McCAREY (1898–1969)

Leo McCarey graduated from the University of Southern California Law School, and had actually started practicing law before switching to movies as assistant director to Tod Browning on *The Virgin of Stamboul* (1920). His apprenticeship continued through the silent era, mostly in a supervisory capacity as director and gag writer for Charlie Chase and Laurel and Hardy shorts at the Hal Roach Studios. By 1929 McCarey was directing features combining sentiment and slapstick in an increasingly seamless fashion. Even when working with such frenetic clowns as Eddie Cantor (*The Kid from Spain*, 1932), the Marx Brothers (*Duck Soup*, 1933), W. C. Fields, George Burns and Gracie Allen (*Six of a Kind*, 1934), Mae West (*Belle of the Nineties*, 1934), and Harold Lloyd (*The Milky Way*, 1936), McCarey usually contributed an unexpectedly somber tone to the proceedings.

Ruggles of Red Gap (1935) established McCarey as a major director with a flair for off-beat humor and seriocomic situations. His vogue lasted barely a decade, but in that period he left his stylistic mark on the American sound film. Jean Renoir said of McCarey in this period: "Leo McCarey is one of the few directors who understand human beings." As it turns out, time has vindicated Renoir's cryptic judgment. In the late sixties McCarey was thought to represent a principle of improvisation in the pacing of his scenarios. Hailed for his relaxed digressions, McCarey was grouped with such other eminent veterans of silent screen comedies as Gregory La Cava, George Stevens, and Frank Capra.

For a long time, McCarey was overshadowed by Frank Capra because of the latter's "bigger" subjects packed with social significance. McCarey worked on a more intimate canvas, but his emotional colors proved to be richer and deeper than Capra's. Who can forget Charles Laughton reciting the Gettysburg Address in *Ruggles of Red Gap* or, even more enchantingly from that same film, Binnie Barnes teaching Roland Young to play the drums; or Victor Moore saying goodbye to Beulah Bondi in *Make Way for Tomorrow* (1937); Irene Dunne speaking to Maria Ouspenskaya in *Love Affair* (1939); Barry Fitzgerald embracing his mother in *Going My Way* (1944); Cary Grant and Irene Dunne reminiscing about their marriage in *The Awful Truth* (1937)?

McCarey, like Capra, was recognized in his own time. Both were Oscar winners more than once, Capra for *It Happened One Night* in 1934, *Mr. Deeds Goes to Town* in 1936, and *You Can't Take It With You* in 1938; McCarey for *The Awful Truth* in 1937 and *Going My Way* in 1944. There is on film a record of a thirties Oscar ceremony during which Capra and McCarey wrestled on stage for the statuette they both supposedly coveted. It was perhaps at that joyous moment that their joint pre-eminence was officially recognized, before the surge in prestige of John Ford, Preston Sturges, Orson Welles, and Billy Wilder.

Curiously, McCarey expressed disappointment at winning an Oscar for *The Awful Truth*, one of his most enduringly admired directorial achievements, because he preferred his work on *Make Way for Tomorrow*, a genuinely felt weepie on the plight of aging parents at the dawn of the nuclear family. In the critical climate of 1937 the "serious" work was always to be preferred to the "comic" work. It was a middle-brow reflex. Yet, though the high-brows tended toward an ironic view of Hollywood with an affectionate overvaluation of its most impious clowns, the intention of these culture heroes was more to disrupt dramatic narrative and emotional expression than to enhance it.

The early auteurist revisionists tended to downgrade *Make Way for Tomorrow* because it was saddled with a supposedly significant subject, whereas *The Awful Truth* was, comparatively, all froth and frivolity, a blank canvas on which the auteur-director could paint his personal portrait, and inscribe his stylistic signature. In the nineties, however, both *The Awful Truth* and *Make Way for Tomorrow* have emerged as two sides of the same creative coin. Hence, whereas the intermittent pathos of *The Awful Truth* enriches the volcanic laughter, the comic undertones of *Make Way for Tomorrow* rescue the sentiment from maudlin turgidity. In this respect, the casting is an indispensable element of the screenwriting. Victor Moore, a pudgy, puckish stage star of musical comedies, would seem at first glance to be an odd choice for the geriatric male lead in *Make Way for Tomorrow*. Beulah Bondi, by contrast, is ideally cast as his gallant wife, acting from deep inside her role to generate enormous feeling in such an unforgettable scene as the long-distance telephone conversation with her husband in the midst of her socially ambitious daughter-in-law's bridge party. As the initially amused guests lower their heads partly in shame and guilt, and partly in rueful recognition of the fate that awaits them all, it is a hard-boiled audience indeed of any era and of any age that can suppress its tears.

Yet, the pain would be unbearable if Victor Moore did not provide the relief of expertly comical self-awareness, and the ballast of a joke-telling temperament. As if anticipating André Bazin's praise of Vittorio De Sica's treatment of the pathos of old age in *Umberto D* (1952) for its violating the accustomed downward trajectory of aging with an interlude of sunny pleasure, McCarey and his scenarists insert a good-natured "reprieve" passage in *Make Way for Tomorrow* in the form of a magical tour of thirties New York City with all its glitter and heart.

■   ■   ■   ■

THE AWFUL TRUTH cannot be fully appreciated as a masterpiece of screwball comedy unless one has more than a nodding acquaintance with more than a few of Hollywood's failed farces of the thirties and forties. Indeed, the frenzied effort to make audiences laugh at all costs is responsible for more excruciatingly unwatchable movies than the attempt to make them cry. By 1937, particularly, moviemakers were forced to add hysteria to bedroom comedy scripts without the slightest suggestion of sex or even irreverence toward marriage. The instant and yet disconcerting success of *The Awful Truth* is reflected in the delightedly baffled and bemused tone of B. R. Crisler's review in the *New York Times* of November 5, 1937:

> The art of being Gallic, or bedroomish, in a nice way, is demonstrated with Celtic ingenuity (the principals are just interlocutorily divorced, not actually unwedded) and a technique which seems original, possibly because no one has dared to use it since the talkie revolution, in Leo McCarey's Columbia production *The Awful Truth*, at the Music Hall. To be frank, *The Awful Truth* is awfully unimportant, but it is also one of the more laughable screen comedies of 1937, a fairly good vintage year. Its comedy is almost purely physical—like that of the old Avery Hopwood stage farces—with only here and there a lone gag to interrupt the pure poetry of motion, yet its unapologetic return to the fundamentals of comedy seems, we repeat, original and daring.

Its obvious success with a modern audience is also rather disquieting. Just when it began to appear that an excellent case had finally been made out for spoken wit and adultness of viewpoint on the screen, the mercurial Mr. McCarey, who only a few months ago saddened us to the point of tears with his *Make Way for Tomorrow*, shocks us with comedy in which speech is subsidiary, and maturity exists only to be deflated into abject juvenility. Though the film has a certain structural unevenness—some of the scenes having a terrific comic impact, others being a shade self-conscious—the final result is a picture liberally strewn with authentic audience laughs which appear to be just as unashamedly abdominal as they were in the days of Fatty Arbuckle.

The notion that the talkies had made physical comedy, the staple of the silents, outmoded on the screen persisted well into the fifties. Hence, all through the thirties McCarey was treated as something of a gifted throwback. *Duck Soup* (1934), later heralded as the most uproarious expression of the manic Marx Brothers, was regarded at the time as one of their lesser and sillier efforts. Disconnected bits of comic vaudeville such as the fake mirror sequence (lifted but improved from Charlie Chaplin and Max Linder) and the pushcart duel between Harpo Marx and Edgar "slow burn" Kennedy were regarded as old-fashioned intrusions into the continuity. Today they are regarded as antic highlights of the period.

Similarly, *The Awful Truth* seems more profound in the nineties than it did in the more solemn, more genteel critical climate of the thirties. The essential childishness of adult behavior does not cause one to blush as markedly now as it did then. Of course, McCarey was blessed with a company of inspired farceurs in Cary Grant, Irene Dunne, Ralph Bellamy, Alexander D'Arcy, Cecil Cunningham, and Joyce Compton. Take the literally dog-eared sequence of the misplaced derby hat involving "Mr. Smith" (Asta, the mischievous terrier of *The Thin Man*), Grant as the soon-to-be ex-husband ducking into the next room to avoid Bellamy as the current suitor of Dunne, who is visibly concerned about the ruckus that will result when Grant discovers D'Arcy as the snake-in-the-grass type who is always hovering harmlessly around other men's wives. Cecil Cunningham, as Dunne's auntly chaperone, remains a comparatively detached observer of the mayhem that has been set into motion. And to make matters even more congested, Esther Dale, as Bellamy's protective mother from back home in Oklahoma, is on hand to add another reactive presence for the ticking time bomb of marital jealousy. Seven participants, both visually and aurally, are thus inextricably entangled in a situation of pure chaos. That everyone is perfectly and even broadly cast adds immeasurably to the merriment, but where McCarey's genius intervenes is in the faultless timing, pacing, and placement of a series of cascading gags culminating in the "unashamedly abdominal" laughter of which the *Times* reviewer wrote.

McCarey had learned everything there was to learn about building and detonating a gag from Charlie Chase, Stan Laurel and Oliver Hardy, but he added a layer of feeling and caring to his main characters that enriched the wildest humor. Dunne and Grant are meant for each other by the rules of the star system. McCarey could have left it at that and concentrated on thinking up more gags. Instead, he slowed the flow of physical movement with moments and even wrote scenes of sentimental recollection. By giving his leads hearts and souls, he can be almost cruel to such poor excuses for romantic competition as the provincially corny Ralph Bellamy character, the ridiculously foppish D'Arcy poseur, and the snooty, stuffy society belle played by Molly Lamont. Ultimately, the clarity of the comedy is enhanced by type-casting and even stereotype casting as long as McCarey, with his magical balancing act between the comic and the serious, is at the directorial helm.

■　　■　　■　　■

LOVE AFFAIR is a disconcerting "classic" of the thirties. The contrivances of its plot are unusually transparent and melodramatic. A playgirl (Irene Dunne) engaged to a wealthy man (Lee Bowman) meets an international playboy (Charles Boyer) on an ocean liner on its way to America, where a wealthy heiress is waiting to marry the playboy. Already, the spoiled upscale characters seem to belong to the late twenties more than to the late thirties. There is a somber interlude on an island on which Boyer's grandmother (Maria Ouspenskaya) takes a liking to Dunne and expresses the hope that she can save her grandson from a life that has been too "easy" for him. We then discover that Boyer has given up his painting for a more leisurely mode of existence, and Dunne has done the same with her career as a singer. At the end of the voyage they promise each other that they will meet in six months atop the Empire State Building after demonstrating that they can work for a living. But even with the hope of redemption and the regaining of self-respect, there is something socially unconscious in the story-line.

Although Delmer Daves and the redoubtable Donald Ogden Stewart are credited with the "screenplay," much of the dialogue and business was improvised in McCarey's slyly slapdash fashion, though with anyone but McCarey both Boyer and Dunne were very technical performers. The bubbling merriment of the early scenes on the liner can be attributed to this loose method of playing scenes, and to the sustained hovering of McCarey's and Rudolph Maté's behaviorally oriented camera with its middle distances and seemingly casual framing. After Dunne has delivered the mandatory song that she inserted contractually in every part she played after she became a star, the picture takes a sudden turn into melodrama when she is hit by a car as she is running across the street to keep her rendezvous with romance. Boyer waits vainly atop the Empire State as down below an ambulance siren becomes one of the cacophonous noises of the city.

The symbolic amplification of the Empire State Building, completed just seven years earlier, makes *Love Affair* one of the most memorable artifacts of Hollywood's long love affair with New York City. Still, the second half of the movie is full of inspirational passages that would normally make sophisticated critics and moviegoers cringe with embarrassment. Otis Ferguson of *The New Republic* praised *Love Affair* with a feeling of wonderment over this triumph of form over content: "Those excited over the mastery of form already achieved in pictures will like to follow this demonstration of the qualities of technique and imagination the film must always have and keep on recruiting to their service." Confronting the banalities of the movie head-on, Ferguson achieved an epiphany of critical prose with the following form-over-content peroration: "Clichés of situation and attitude are lifted almost beyond recognition by a morning freshness of eye for each small thing around."

Pare Lorenz, the celebrated critic-documentarian, focused on McCarey's economy of expression: "McCarey brought off one of the most difficult things you can attempt with film. He created a mood, rather than a story; he kept it alive by expert interpolations; he provided comedy when he needed comedy and poignancy when he needed substance; and he did it with the minimum of effort."

One might conclude that the supposed digressions in McCarey's style are really the heart of the matter. He searches in each preconceived situation for a burst of spontaneity from the performer that will inject new life into the character. "If you can paint, I can walk," the crippled Dunne character declares with a wild giggle as she ecstatically embraces the Boyer character at the emotional high point of *Love Affair*. As a responsible film historian, I cannot say that I am 100 percent sure of my theory that Boyer's temporarily baffled expression suggests that he wasn't expecting that particular line, with its double thrust of hope for the characters and gentle kidding of the unlikelihood in real life of the happy endings in movies. Still, a "reading" of that privileged moment in film history need not be divorced from directorial intentionality since even if McCarey had not meant such an interpretation to be made, his ambiguous shooting and framing left the scene "open" to posterity.

■ ■ ■ ■

AFTER IRENE DUNNE and Charles Boyer were enthroned in 1939 as the most poignant lovers of the decade in both McCarey's uplifting *Love Affair* and John Stahl's gallantly downbeat *When Tomorrow Comes*, McCarey's career, plagued by ill-health, began to grind to a halt. The critical and popular success of *Going My Way* and *The Bells of St. Mary's* in 1944 and 1945 was eventually demeaned by solemn clerics contemptuous of McCarey's blue-collar religiosity. The deceptive naturalness of Bing Crosby's laid-back performances obscured the indispensable launch pads McCarey provided Barry Fitzgerald in *Going My Way* and Ingrid Bergman in *The Bells of St. Mary's* for their histrionic flights of feeling.

Once Upon a Honeymoon (1942) was denounced as tasteless trash for mixing the wise-cracking romance of Cary Grant and Ginger Rogers with the buffoonish menace of the Nazis, much as Ernst Lubitsch's sublime *To Be or Not To Be* was similarly disparaged at the time even though it turned out to be the satiny swan song of Carole Lombard. *Good Sam*, with Gary Cooper and Ann Sheridan, was not appreciated in 1948 as a sardonic, anti-populist, anti-Capra take on the Good Samaritan legend. Although McCarey's career extended to the early sixties, he never again enjoyed the pre-eminence achieved by him in the thirties and forties. He died in 1969.

GEORGE CUKOR (1899–1983)

Patrick McGilligan's book is that rarity of rarities among Hollywood biographies: a full-bodied study of a man and his métier, equally insightful about the life and the art. *George Cukor: A Double Life* could not have been published while the film director was still alive because of its eye-opening description of an elegantly gay life flourishing amid an industry quaking in fear of the self-appointed media guardians of virtue, morality, conformity, and decency.

Mr. McGilligan has managed to pull Cukor posthumously out of the glass closet in which he had been permitted, by both the moguls and the mandarins of film, to conceal a part of himself from the tabloid columns and scandal sheets. That is to say that everyone in the "know" knew about Cukor's sexual orientation, but no one until very recently dared to attribute homosexuality to him directly. Instead, Cukor was demeaned with a wink as a "woman's director," a far cry from the womanizing he-men usually occupying Hollywood's directors' chairs.

That this thinly veiled condescension persisted even after Cukor's death in 1983 is indicated by a casual remark in Katharine Hepburn's best-selling autobiography, *Me*, to the effect that Cukor had not been "macho" enough to direct her and Spencer Tracy in *Woman of the Year* in 1942. It is a singularly unfortunate comment, the reader might think, to make about one's movie mentor, who, along with the producer David O. Selznick, virtually molded Ms. Hepburn in *A Bill of Divorcement* (1932) and who later directed her in nine of her most felicitous performances, among them *Adam's Rib* and *The Philadelphia Story*.

George Dewey Cukor was born in New York City on July 14, 1899, to a Hungarian-Jewish immigrant couple, Victor and Helen Cukor, living on East Fourth Street with their four-and-a-half-year-old daughter Elsie, George's only sibling. Mr. McGilligan explains the incongruity of Cukor's middle name with the densely textured detail typical of his tireless research: "From the hero of the Spanish-American War, Admiral George Dewey—not the progressive educator or the decimal systemator—Cukor received his patriotic christening. Cukor trotted out his unlikely and stolid middle name in letters and at festivities for the unfailing chuckle that it warranted."

Aside from the anecdotal perspective on assimilation that this passage provides, it reveals the shrewdly self-deprecating and ingratiating personality that Cukor richly employed in Hollywood. The family name was itself an Americanization of "Czukor," which in turn, Mr. McGilligan tells us, was an alleged Magyarization of "Chukor," even more dubiously the name of a hill in India settled by the sons of the biblical Joseph who journeyed to India three or four hundred years before the birth of Christ, at least according to a fanciful family tree prepared by Cukor's paternal grandfather. Cukor responded more strongly to the cosmopolitanism of his Hungarian heritage than to the religiosity of his Jewish faith. He and his immediate multilingual family disdained Yiddish, and though he told stories all his life about his parents coming over in steerage, he insisted that his upbringing had been comfortably middle class. Thread by thread, Mr. McGilligan undoes the web of the elaborate self-deceptions in which Cukor became ever more enthusiastically ensnared.

When his family moved to East 68th Street, Cukor became aware that his father, Victor, lived in the shadow of his richer brother, Morris, a prominent New York lawyer. Victor was the elder, but Morris was the family favorite and, like his nephew, George, "outgoing and full of mischievous charm, very funny, a gifted extemporaneous speaker and the life of any crowd." By contrast, Mr. McGilligan concludes, "compared to Morris, Cukor's father seemed colorless, the original two-dimensional man. At large gatherings, Victor seemed to shrink into himself."

Significantly, and perhaps a bit too schematically in Mr. McGilligan's telling, Cukor's mother filled the parental void caused by the shadowy father. "To his mother," the biographer muses,

> Cukor was more raptly devoted. She was terribly protective of him, and her sweet and gentle disposition gave Cukor one side of his personality. She composed and recited poetry, and was teased by her two sisters for being a highbrow. Most of the time, at family get-togethers, she was docile, but Cukor felt in her an unrequited aesthetic yearning. The film director often talked about his mother, and artist Don Bachardy remembered Cukor telling of the time his mother donned a costume at a family party and began to clown and entertain the guests. In an instant, she was transformed in the boy's eyes—in an instant, and for a lifetime in memory— into a magical and glamorous creature. "The family beauty" is how he always described his mother. Cukor's eyes always lit up when he spoke about her.

From early childhood through adolescence, Cukor was stage-struck and screen-struck. "At age twelve," Mr. McGilligan tells us, "he was smitten by the delectable Ina Claire, a vaudevillian who had made the leap to musical comedy and was beguiling audiences with her singing of 'Come to the Ball' in *The Quaker Girl*." Seventy-one years later the ninety-year-old Ina Claire would be one of the few show-business celebrities Cukor had known, directed and entertained throughout his illustrious half-century career to attend his funeral.

By the time of his death Cukor's career had become the virtually exclusive property of film cultists, revisionists, and auteurists in Paris, London, and New York, all sifting through the fifty-some films he had directed for clues to his thematic and stylistic obsessions. Mr. McGilligan is fully conversant with these frequently arcane speculations, and even adds some idiosyncratic comments of his own, underrating, for example, James Mason's haunting Norman Maine in *A Star Is Born* as much as he overestimates Judy Garland's hysterical Vicki Lester. The important thing, however, is that Mr. McGilligan does make distinctions and render useful value judgments, based on a detailed knowledge of all the intricacies and intrigues of film literature on his subject, notably Gavin Lambert's *On Cukor*, Carlos Clarens's *George Cukor*, Gary Carey's *Cukor and Company: The Films of George Cukor and His Collaborators*, and Gene Phillips's *George Cukor*.

George Cukor himself tended to be skeptical about critical incense burning on his behalf. Throughout his career he relied more on the kindness of studio potentates than the comments of cinematic pundits. The Zukors, the Thalbergs, the Mayers, the Selznicks, the Zanucks, and the Cohns were his true patrons, and even when they betrayed him, as did his childhood classmate David O. Selznick in a homophobic incident on the set of *Gone With the Wind*, Cukor remained loyal to the feudal system that had enabled his talents to flower.

The commonly told story of the *Gone With the Wind* episode is that Cukor was fired as director because Clark Gable suspected that his performance was being neglected for the sake of Vivien Leigh's and Olivia De Havilland's. This humiliating episode consolidated the canard of Cukor as a "woman's director," particularly since he was immediately reassigned to *The Women*, a film in which no male appears on the screen.

As a result, he never got credit for directing Leigh's two best scenes: Melanie's childbirth sequence, done in silhouette, and the shooting of the Yankee deserter at Tara. Under Victor Fleming's lackluster direction, Leigh's portrayal of Scarlett is spectacularly uneven, and her final parting from Rhett is bungled. In any case, *Gone With the Wind* is much more a woman's picture than a Civil War picture, and who has ever thought otherwise?

Mr. McGilligan's account of the Cukor departure is even more shocking than what was whispered at the time:

> The director was on the set . . . preparing a shot after a series of awkward moments with Gable. Selznick was there too, as always. Suddenly, Gable muttered audibly, "I can't do this . . . I can't do this scene. . . ."
>
> Everyone was dumbfounded. Because whatever else he was, Gable was an absolute professional. Somebody asked, "What's the matter with you today?" And suddenly, Gable exploded, "I can't go on with this picture! I won't be directed by a fairy! I have to work with a *real* man!"
>
> The atmosphere was deeper than silence. Footsteps echoed on the

soundstage. Cukor had walked off. He was beaten. This was a story Cukor told, on rare occasions behind closed doors, against himself.

The next day, Gable simply did not show up for work.

Cukor had hit career snags before, but nothing as traumatic as this. At Paramount he had become embroiled in a grubby credit-grabbing feud with Ernst Lubitsch over *One Hour with You* (1932). Two of the finest films of the 1930s by any current standard—*Dinner at Eight* (1933) and *Holiday* (1938)—were inexplicably under-rated by the critics. Far from looking like canned theater, as was said at the time, these two master-pieces of modulation vibrate with a distinctively cinematic sensibility. Similarly, *Little Women* (1933) and *David Copperfield* (1935), despite their fierce beauties of expression, were derogated by the period's cinema purists and social realists as contrived, overly genteel works, while out-and-out box-office bombs *Sylvia Scarlett* (1935) and *Zara* (1939) did not achieve until decades later the camp and cult following they eminently deserved.

In the 1930s and 40s, the rap on Cukor was that he was too much the company man, only as good as his casts and writers. He was never cultivated by the Algonquin Circle of George S. Kaufman, Robert Bench-ley, and Dorothy Parker, despite his theatrical roots, partly because of high-brow homophobia and partly because he clearly preferred the sybaritic delights of California to the ascetic rigors of New York. Yet what were once regarded as crippling defects in a film-maker now have come to be seen as shrewd stratagems to combine a productive career with a dangerous way of life. Cukor's amazing resilience and his total immersion in the world of illusion made him an impressive survivor. He seemed to remember every play and movie he had ever seen, and every-one in them from Isadora Duncan to D. W. Griffith. His career encom-passed some of Hollywood's most momentous legends and legendary moments. Cukor directed not only Garbo's greatest performance, in *Camille* (1937), but her disastrous swan song on the ski slopes, *Two-Faced Woman* (1941). That same year he directed the last, and perhaps least, Norma Shearer vehicle, *Her Cardboard Lover*, adapted from a play he had once directed in his salad days in Rochester when he was di-recting regional stage plays. And in 1962 he was the director of the abortive *Something's Got to Give*, the occasion of Marilyn Monroe's final crack-up before her suicide.

Curiously, Cukor reached new heights after the *Gone With the Wind* setback despite the decline and fall of the studio system. His collabo-

rations with Garson Kanin and Ruth Gordon led to a seven-movie cycle—from *A Double Life* (1947) to *It Should Happen to You* (1954)—
with more bite and realism than were to be found in his glossy prewar
films; he unearthed new layers of comic pathos with Judy Holliday, Jack
Lemmon, Aldo Ray, Katharine Hepburn, Spencer Tracy, and others.
Then, with the aid of a gifted color consultant, George Hoyningen-
Huene, he moved into the age of color and wide screen, crossing new
frontiers of colorful sensuality with Sophia Loren in *Heller in Pink Tights*
(1960), Claire Bloom, Jane Fonda, and Glynis Johns in *The Chapman
Report* (1962), and Jacqueline Bisset and Candice Bergen in *Rich and
Famous*, his last film, released in 1981.

And all the while he was living a double life of his own, and casting
his reflection in a broken mirror. As Mr. McGilligan describes the sub-
text of Cukor's existence:

> In the years after World War II, a Hollywood rivalry began to develop
> between Cukor's circle and another clique of homosexual men that gath-
> ered, also on Sundays, at the home of the celebrated composer and song-
> writer Cole Porter . . .
>
> An unspoken competition went on between these two world-class egos
> with their magnificent houses and friends in common, however, for each
> saw himself as the center of this unique homosexual universe. Behind
> their backs (no one would have dared say it to Cukor's face), some referred
> to them as the rival Queens of Hollywood. There was some competition,
> especially, over the handsome young soldiers and sailors who were abun-
> dant in postwar Hollywood, and jockeying, moreover, for the loyalty of
> those regulars who managed to divide attendance on Sundays between
> both houses.

Whereas most Hollywood party-givers had an A list and a B list, Cukor
specialized in an A list and a gay list. On the A list was everyone in
Hollywood who was anyone, from Garbo to Chaplin on down. The other
included such *litterateurs* as Somerset Maughman (with whom Cukor
once cruised for sailors in Nice) and Noël Coward. For the most part,
Cukor presided over two separate groups in two separate worlds for two
separate sectors of his psyche.

In the end, he gave more in sentimental devotion and thoughtfulness
than he ever received. Out of sheer admiration, he visited the sickbeds
of D. W. Griffith, John Ford, and even his arch-rival Cole Porter. In his
will he asked to be buried next to Frances Howard (Mrs. Samuel Goldwyn), whom he had known as a young actress in Rochester, and on whom

he had had a lifelong crush. He was a real man, and, like F. W. Murnau and Sergei Eisenstein, one of the covertly gay masters of the cinema.

WILLIAM WYLER (1902–1981)

Although William Wyler's credits extend officially from 1926 to 1970, his period of pre-eminence was between 1936 (*Dodsworth*) and 1946 (*The Best Years of Our Lives*). Orson Welles has called Wyler, not inaptly, the great producer among directors; that is to say, the masterly selector of shots, the compleat angler of the most gripping camera angles. André Bazin hailed Wyler for liberating the cinema from montage with his long takes and deep-focus compositions, and the battle cry for a time (for both Bazin and his colleague Roger Leenhardt) was "À *bas* Ford! *Vive Wyler!*" Earlier, John Grierson had praised Wyler for his high-minded sobriety. A more conventional view of Wyler around Hollywood was that of the punctilious perfectionist, the scourge of stars, particularly in the more affluent period in which he was nicknamed "Ninety-Take Wyler." As compensation for some of the victims of Wyler's painstaking devotion to detail are the Oscars resting on the mantel-pieces of Walter Brennan, Bette Davis, Audrey Hepburn, Olivia De Havilland, Greer Garson, Teresa Wright, Fay Bainter, Fredric March, Burl Ives, Charlton Heston, Barbra Streisand, and that agonizingly award-winning one-shot amputee, Harold Russell, who so traumatically tested the liberal conscience in *The Best Years of Our Lives*.

William Wyler was born in 1902 in Mulhouse, Alsace, then part of Germany. He received his education at Lausanne and the National Music Conservatory in Paris, where in 1920 he met "Uncle" Carl Laemmle, head of Universal Pictures, and accepted a movie job in New York. After moving up to publicity director in the distribution end of the industry, he went to Hollywood, where he worked his way from prop-boy to director of some fifty two-reel westerns in 1926 and 1927. "I made 'em in three days and for $2000." By 1928 he was promoted to five-reel Tom Mix vehicles and occasional "easterns." He gradually built a minor reputation at Universal with *Hell's Heroes* (1930), a film he took out of the studio vaults ten years later and re-edited to his own satisfaction; *A House Divided* (1932), a grim, Calvinistic picture patterned after Eugene O'Neill's *Desire Under the Elms*, with a memorable performance by Wal-

ter Huston writhing in Lon Chaney-ish contortions as a crippled patriarch; *Counsellor-at-Law* (1933), highlighted by one of John Barrymore's
best screen performances and one of the first cinematic intimations of
melting-pot politics and anti-Semitic snobbery; *The Good Fairy* (1935),
starring Margaret Sullavan, who quarrelled with Wyler during the shooting, married him when the picture was completed, and divorced him a
year or so later.

With *These Three* in 1936, Wyler began a long and profitable association with producer Sam Goldwyn and cinematographer Gregg Toland.
Critics became aware of a distinctive style in *Dodsworth* and *Come and
Get It* (1936), which Wyler finished after director Howard Hawks left
the project, *Dead End* (1937), *Wuthering Heights* (1939), *The Westerner*
(1940), and *The Little Foxes* (1941), in addition to such gilded Bette
Davis vehicles at Warners as *Jezebel* (1938) and *The Letter* (1940). In
close collaboration with Toland, who traumatized the industry in 1941
with his photography for Welles's *Citizen Kane*, Wyler developed an unusually deep focus for scenes, eschewing cuts and close-ups to keep
groups of characters within the frame for long periods without undue
"star" emphasis. This imposed a greater burden on actors to play a scene
through in one long take rather than in a series of intercut sequences.
Wyler explained his infrequent use of the close-up by citing films where
the cutting "didn't coincide with what I wanted to see. They'd hold on
to a close-up so long that I'd find myself trying to look around the corner
for the other characters."

During World War II Wyler served in the Army Air Force and went
on several bombing missions to obtain footage for his acclaimed war
documentary *The Memphis Belle* (1944). He also transcribed the exploits
of fighter planes in the film *Thunderbolt* (1945). After *The Best Years of
Our Lives* in 1946, however, Wyler's career followed an extremely eclectic pattern that went out of critical fashion.

Yet, even Wyler's directorial faults can be made to fit into the notion
of a personal style. Hence, his lack of a light touch makes him gravitate
most often to relatively serious subjects where the comedy, if any, can
be relegated to relief. But then again, his unobtrusively cool style seems
to soften the harsh contours of morbid romances like *Jezebel* and *Wuthering Heights*.

Although William Wyler belongs to that category of director who began in the silent era, he seems (even more than Ford and Hawks) to
have come into his own only at the dawn of the talkies. Hence, there is
no mention of Wyler in the conventional film histories before *Hell's He-*

roes in 1930. Basil Wright notes in his compendium of conventional wisdom, *The Long View*:

> In *Hell's Heroes*, a film of frank and frantic sentimentality by William Wyler, an effective *coup de cinéma* occurs when the sound of a church choir and congregation singing Christmas carols is suddenly switched off when the rough old villain staggers up the aisle carrying a baby he has brought across the desert at the cost of his own life. The audience is made to switch its identification from the church scene to the man himself at the point of death. It may sound a corny idea, but it was enormously effective.

Until 1936 Wyler worked exlusively at Universal, and many of his films from this period remain obscure to this day. Still, from 1928 on, Wyler never made more than two movies a year, which indicates that a certain care (or procrastination) went into his most routine projects. Thus, Wyler was never as prolific as such legendary first-take speedsters as William Wellman, Michael Curtiz, Mervyn LeRoy, and W. S. Van Dyke.

When Wyler left Universal for Sam Goldwyn in 1935, first to finish *Come and Get It* (1936) and then to do *Dodsworth* (1936) and *These Three* (1936), a distinctive Wyler look emerged on the screen. At first it was considered simply a Goldwyn look, and then, much later, a Toland look. Whatever it was, it was a look that lasted for ten years until it reached its apotheosis in *The Best Years of Our Lives* (1946). But it is unlikely that this look would have attracted much attention had it not been coupled for the most part with a serious, high-minded, liberal concern with various social issues. As a producer, Goldwyn could be credited with an itch for "significance," and he managed to recruit such writers as Lillian Hellman (*These Three*, *Dead End*, from the play by Sidney Kingsley, *The Little Foxes*), Sidney Howard (*Dodsworth*), Edna Ferber (*Come and Get It*), Robert Sherwood (*The Best Years of Our Lives*), and even Dorothy Parker for additional dialogue for *The Little Foxes*. What must be remembered is that the criticism of the sound film has seldom been able to appreciate stylistic achievements divorced from impressive "themes." Also, there was a carry-over effect when a director or producer changed pace with a divertissement after having done something "important." Thus, an aura persisted around such relatively frivolous Wyler enterprises as *The Letter* (1940), *The Westerner* (1940), *The Heiress* (1949), and *Roman Holiday* (1953) because of points previously scored with *The Little Foxes* (1941), *Mrs. Miniver* (1942), and *The Best Years of Our Lives* (1946).

Nonetheless, Wyler did achieve a special working relationship with Toland from their first encounter on the set of *These Three* (1936). As Wyler recalled this fateful and fruitful moment in film history (in *William Wyler* by Axel Madsen):

> I was in the habit of saying, "Put the camera here and shoot it with a forty millimeter," or "Move the camera this way, or Light it this way." Suddenly, Toland wanted to quit. I didn't understand why and he finally came to me to tell me he wasn't a man to be told every move. You just didn't tell Gregg what lens to use, you told him what mood you were after. When he photographed something, he wanted to go beyond lights and catch feelings. As we got to know each other, we evolved a smooth and beautiful relationship. We would discuss a picture from beginning to end, its overall "feel" and then the style of each sequence. Toland was an artist.
>
> The camera is a marvelous instrument. You have to use it with discipline. Any imaginative director who stages a scene or uses a set gets all kinds of ideas. That's great but you have to discipline yourself. Many cameramen's idea of a good scene is when all the actors hit their cut marks. Soundmen like it when everything is very clear. This is where Toland was different.
>
> His style of photography would vary just like my style of directing. In *Dead End*, we had a different style of photography than in *Wuthering Heights* or in *These Three*. Here, we are dealing with little girls' things. What was good was rather simple, attractive photography. In *Dead End*, we had flat, hard lights. We used open sun-arcs from behind the camera. We didn't try to make everybody look pretty. With Toland, I would rehearse and show him a scene. Then, we would decide together how to photograph it. I would have certain ideas and he would contribute to them and together we would determine what was best."

One might say that Wyler made a virtue of eclecticism even in his professional relationship with Toland, but it isn't as simple as that. If Wyler has been penalized by the auteurist critics, it is not because he lacked a personal style. Rather, it is because there is no thematic thread running from *Lazy Lightning* in 1926 to *The Liberation of L. B. Jones* in 1970. Wyler himself has never played the poetic personality game. More the captain of the team or the chairman of the board, he has nonetheless evolved into a recognizable stylist. From *The Letter* (1940) to *Funny Girl* (1968), Wyler's mise-en-scène for a triangular sofa and extended composition retains all its characteristic lines of force and tension. We can therefore deduce that from 1936 on, the very careful preparation of each Wyler project included stretching the screenplay to accommodate a scene in which two or more characters were suspended in the same frame of the film, but at a focal distance great enough to sustain a somber mood of conflict and alienation.

The danger, as always, is that the Wyler-Toland collaboration can be overstressed as an example of the paradigmatic fallacy: that tendency in film criticism to select only those sequences that illustrate a stylistic thesis. During Wyler's best period (1936–46) he was in close rapport with many talented people in the film industry, particularly such players as Walter Huston, Ruth Chatterton, and Mary Astor in *Dodsworth*, Bette Davis in her most prestigious films—*Jezebel*, *The Letter*, and *The Little Foxes*—Laurence Olivier in *Wuthering Heights*, and the talented all-star cast of *The Best Years of Our Lives*. He seemed in those years to be always on time, and no one noticed a certain coldness in his contemplative gaze, a certain fastidiousness in his manner—as if he could not bear to be too deeply involved with the feelings of his characters. Later, the coldness was unrelieved, and Wyler's career faltered during the death-throes of the studio system.

■   ■   ■   ■

THE BEST YEARS OF OUR LIVES was so over-rated in its time that there has been a tendency to under-rate it ever since. Actually, *Best Years* was honored not merely as the best film of the year but as one of the great films of all time. It happened to be *the* movie about the return and rehabilitation of "our boys" from the only officially Good and Necessary War in this century. The timing was perfect. Hollywood was still making war movies, and here at last was the first postwar movie with overwhelmingly redeeming social significance. Almost immediately after the somber opening credits, the relatively fortunate civilian audience was confronted with Harold Russell, a depressingly authentic naval veteran with two hooks for hands. Military mutilation had been shown on the screen before *Best Years*, most notably with John Gilbert's missing leg in King Vidor's *The Big Parade* in 1925, and with the late Ernst Lubitsch's camera view of a parade through the arch formed by an amputee and his crutch in *The Man I Killed* in 1932, but these were basically anti-war films, and the evidence of deformity was not dwelt upon for more than a scene or two, and, in Gilbert's case, we knew that he was not *really* an amputee, and in the Lubitsch film we never even saw the face of the man with one leg. Here in *Best Years*, one had to look at the hooks, and one had look at the other characters looking at the hooks, and it was all so hopelessly oppressive to any reasonably non-sadistic spectator that whenever the action cut to the upper-class banker's apartment where Fredric March kept making comical expressions over a cocktail, the audience roared not over the hung-over humor of the situation but from sheer relief over escaping moral responsibility for the man with the hooks. This is the mystique of March's prize-winning performance in *Best Years*: It represents the only sizable slice of comic relief in a work of humanitarian blackmail.

One of the movie's major problems is its uneasy mixture of realism and contrivance. The notion of three veterans returning home to three separate layers of society introduces a choice between class conflict and national reconciliation. The film chooses reconciliation with a liberal accent, the latter presumably Robert Sherwood's. The banker pontificates like a New Dealer, the glamorous soda-jerk (played intensely by Dana Andrews) is burdened by the innate decency of the common man, and the amputee wallows in self-pity. Meanwhile, smugness, bigotry, and incipient fascism parade in the persons of unpleasant-looking character actors.

Unfortunately, the soda-jerk protagonist (Dana Andrews) is the only one of the three veterans involved in any dramatic decisions, and he is so defeatist that only his good looks make it possible to believe that Teresa Wright's all-American banker's daughter could ever fall in love with him. The last speech of the film asks the audience to believe that Andrews and Wright are looking forward with joy to years of poverty and privation. This is admittedly a familiar Hollywood refrain for the very poor (in the script) and the very beautiful (on the screen), but it is grotesque in the context of the Wyler-Sherwood-Goldwyn realist mannerisms. The banker's daughter might fall in love with the soda-jerk because he is older and more virile and more experienced than the boys with whom she grew up in high school. Actually, this May-August attraction was a phenomenon more of the forties than of later decades when the generational gap widened because of the lack of public support of wars in Korea and Vietnam. Unfortunately, this subject is never adequately examined in *Best Years*, where the forensic tone of the script is too loud for the delicate nuancing of emotional intimacy. Everyone makes speeches about what life is all about, and every relationship is coldly externalized. Gregg Toland's penchant for deep-focus photography is occasionally effective within a dramatic context, particularly in one stunning composition within which March looks at Russell and Hoagy

Carmichael playing "Chopsticks" while the length of the bar away Andrews can be seen in a glass phone booth making a call to Teresa Wright. Otherwise, William Wyler's direction is precise, low-keyed, and carefully planned. The cameo performance of Steve Cochrane as a raffish profiteer and Gladys George as a dreary mother from the wrong side of the tracks have stood the test of time better than the picture as a whole. Perhaps, their earthiness, however stylized, seems refreshing as an antidote to the relentless sincerity of the film as a whole.

FRANK CAPRA (1897–1991)

Frank Capra came as close as any director in Hollywood's history to function in the public mind as a one-man studio in that he was for a decade the only "name" director under contract at Columbia Pictures. A Sicilian immigrant child of adversity growing up in Southern California, he lived the American Dream before he celebrated it on celluloid in a series of Depression-era populist comedy melodramas. Before garnering three directorial Oscars in the thirties (*It Happened One Night*, 1934; *Mr. Deeds Goes to Town*, 1936; and *You Can't Take It With You*, 1938), Capra had emerged from the training ground of Hal Roach's Our Gang kiddie comedies, and the clownish farces of Mack Sennett and Harry Langdon. Capra's three successful collaborations with Langdon and co-director Harry Edwards—*Tramp, Tramp, Tramp* (1926), *The Strong Man* (1926), and *Long Pants* (1927)—should have established Capra's reputation in the silent era. Unfortunately, for all concerned, Langdon resented the credit given Capra and Edwards, and dispensed with their writing and directing services to follow in the presumed path of Chaplin, Keaton, and Lloyd as a supposedly solitary auteur. The result was a series of personal and professional disasters that left Langdon penniless by 1931. Like Keaton, he subsisted on comic bit parts through the thirties and forties.

What Capra understood better than Langdon was the very volatile mix of humor and sentiment that constituted a viable comic movie. Langdon, the most child-like of the classic silent comedians, had a fatal weakness for lyrical self-indulgence. Except for a bright turn as a class-struggling street-cleaner in Lewis Milestone's *Hallelujah, I'm a Bum*, Langdon was like a fish out of water in the talkies. Even if Langdon had been more sophisticated about changing tastes and his own limitations, his predilection for soulful pantomime would have doomed him on the sound stages.

In terms of Capra's later oeuvre, however, his three classic films with Langdon are harbingers of the holy fools he would later fashion out of more virile icons such as Gary Cooper and James Stewart. In practical terms, however, Capra found himself virtually unemployable in Hollywood for a short period after his well-publicized bitter rupture with Langdon. A 1927 New York–based production, *For the Love of Mike*, starring Claudette Colbert, a newcomer from the stage, was such a flop that it returned Colbert to the stage, and Capra to Hollywood's poverty row until a contract from Harry Cohn changed his fortunes. In 1928 and 1929 Capra directed no fewer than ten potboilers of undeniable competence but indistinct style. These features ran the gamut of genres from adventure to domestic melodrama and suggested the pulpy range and productivity of a contract director at a minor-major studio of that period. More than an apprenticeship but less than a breakthrough, these almost completely forgotten films nonetheless acclimated Capra to a change from the stylized comedies of Langdon to more realistic modes of expression.

Some revisionist film historians trace Capra's richest period all the way back to *Ladies of Leisure* in 1930, and extending only up to *Broadway Bill* in 1934. With *Mr. Deeds Goes to Town*, in 1936, a newer, more overtly populist, more pretentiously "significant" Frank Capra emerges, a film-maker (producer as well as director) who preaches more than he entertains.

With *Meet John Doe* (1941), Frank Capra crossed the line between populist sentimentality and populist demagoguery. Capra's political films—*Meet John Doe, You Can't Take It with You, Mr. Smith Goes to Washington*—were innocuous and non-inflammatory by prevailing Marxist standards. Indeed, Gary Cooper embodied in John Doe a barefoot fascist, suspicious of all ideas and all doctrines, but believing in the the innate conformism of the common man. Capra's Shangri-La Hilton in *Lost Horizon* (1937) was an anti-intellectual paradise, a rest home for the troubled mind, with even the eternal problems of aging and dying miraculously banished from consideration.

Capra was nonetheless a genuine auteur, and there is no mistaking his point of view. The Kaufman and Hart *You Can't Take It with You* on Broadway related the story of an eccentric family which chose to live on the basis of its unconventional impulses. The Capra-Riskin version transformed the eccentric family into a mouthpiece for all the little people in the world, and perverted the play's stuffy businessman into a bloated shark of Wall Street (a thirties specialty of Edward Arnold) beyond even Eisenstein's power of caricature.

Capra's flair for improvisation was evident throughout his career. This flair made his fortune in It Happened One Night (1934), the sleeper of its year and the death knell of the more deliberately Expressionistic experiments of Sternberg (The Scarlet Empress), Lubitsch (The Merry Widow), and Milestone (Hallelujah, I'm a Bum). Capra's boisterous humor seemed in tune with the mood of Depression audiences, but there runs through most of his films a somber Christian parable of idealism betrayed and innocence humiliated. The obligatory scene in most Capra films is the confession of folly in the most public manner possible. Indeed, Spencer Tracy's hapless presidential candidate in State of the Union (1948) seemed particularly unstatesmanlike in his pathetic self-flogging speech to a national audience.

Since 1968 the amazing resurrection and virtual institutionalization of Capra's 1946 flop fantasy It's a Wonderful Life into a perennially admired Christmas classic has forced a reconsideration of Capra's populism and alleged Christ complex. For one thing, the swing to the right in national politics through the eighties and into the nineties has enhanced nostalgic appreciation of even the most demagogic forms of Capra's populism. Also, the rediscovery of the Capra talkies before It Happened One Night has given his career as a whole immeasurably more resonance, both stylistically and emotionally. The four tarnished-lady melodramas Capra made with Barbara Stanwyck—Ladies of Leisure (1930), The Miracle Woman (1931), Forbidden (1932), The Bitter Tea of General Yen (1933)—have been redeemed by feminist critics and pre-Code-tightening nostalgia from the opprobrium of the terms "soap opera" and "shopgirl romance." Capra has thereby been vindicated on many levels because certain tendencies in the thirties were undervalued at the time by the socially conscious critical establishment. The old distinction between "small" films and "big" films has been supplanted by an appreciation of spontaneity and intuition as means of pumping life into predetermined scenarios.

■   ■   ■   ■

IT'S A WONDERFUL LIFE opened at the Globe Theater in New York City on December 20, 1946, in the same week as the two other prestige productions of the season, The Best Years of Our Lives and The

Razor's Edge. All three films were suffused with varying degrees of post-war spirituality. *It's a Wonderful Life* seemed old-fashioned in the company of the ultra-topical returning-veterans theme of *Best Years*. *The Razor's Edge* came in a poor third with its period New Age mysticism from the bestseller novel by the misanthropic Somerset Maugham. Even so, it was less fanciful on the surface than the angel-afflicted *It's a Wonderful Life*.

Adapted by Frances Goodrich, Albert Hackett, and Frank Capra from Philip Van Doren Stern's Christmas story, *The Greatest Gift*, *It's a Wonderful Life* expanded the theme of a middle-aged man wishing he had never been born into his mediocre life—and then discovering through divine intervention that his existence had indeed made a difference—into a wildly melodramatic parable of near crucifixion and redemption in the patented mode of Capra's *Mr. Deeds Goes to Town*, *Mr. Smith Goes to Washington*, and *Meet John Doe*. Evil in the form of an avaricious banker played by Lionel Barrymore provided a more Manichaean motivation for the protagonist's suicide impulse than was to be found in the original story.

James Stewart's George Bailey (renamed from the book's George Pratt) was transformed into a populist crusader against Barrymore's Mr. Potter, an unapologetic exploiter of the poor. The Social Gospel preached by Capra was not entirely absent in *Best Years*, but it was cloaked with nice-guy liberal rhetoric on the fringes of the dramatic action. In nineties parlance, *Best Years* was cool on the subject of class differences whereas *Wonderful Life* was red-hot to the point of prewar New Deal common man battle-cries. The liberal banker played by Fredric March in *Best Years* was presented as heroic for giving one battle-tested veteran an unsecured loan for his farm, whereas the banker played by James Stewart in *Wonderful Life* fought tooth and nail with the richest banker in town to secure affordable housing for an entire community.

On the other hand, *Best Years* struck forties audiences as "adult" vis-à-vis *Wonderful Life* by dealing with the subject of extramarital romance albeit in a "tasteful" manner that left the censors' sleep undisturbed. Gloria Grahame did play a thinly disguised prostitute in *Wonderful Life*, but the assistance rendered her by George Bailey had more to do with the compassion of Jesus for Mary Magdalene than any contemporary transaction between a man and and a woman.

But as far as Stewart's George Bailey and Donna Reed's Mary Hatch Bailey were concerned, theirs was as close to an ideal marriage as could be found for a film destined to become an American *Christmas Carol*, though much bleaker and more despairing than the Dickens equivalent. Curiously, the censors never noticed that the villainous Mr. Potter gets away with robbery without being caught or punished in any way. Even more curiously, the critics of the time never adequately appreciated the force and fury of Stewart's acting and the pain and sorrow it so eloquently expressed. Stewart's angry, exasperated, anguished "proposal" to Reed is one of the most sublimely histrionic expressions of passion mingled with the painful knowledge that one's dreams of seeing the world outside one's small town were vanishing before one's eyes.

The last-minute happy ending never quite compensates for all the suffering that precedes it, and yet there is something unyieldingly idealistic in Stewart's persona that clears away any sour aftertaste from what in the final analysis is one of the most profoundly pessimistic tales of human existence ever to achieve a lasting popularity. Yet even in its darkest moments, *It's a Wonderful Life* achieves a mini-epiphany with a burly, surly patron sitting grimly at a bar near the despondent Bailey. When he hears the name "Bailey" mentioned, he hauls off and socks the already tortured protagonist seemingly without provocation until we learn that the assailant's wife is the schoolteacher whom the distraught Bailey has unfairly scolded on the telephone for letting his little girl go home alone in the snow and cold. The "heavy" in every sense of the word emerges as one of us as he movingly describes his wife's crying over the episode. In this one moment the humanism of *It's a Wonderful Life* cancels out all the cute, cloying embarrassments of the angel played by Henry Travers.

GEORGE STEVENS (1904–1975)

Katharine Hepburn has generally been credited with giving George Stevens his big break with *Alice Adams* (1935). Yet, it has never been quite clear what Miss Hepburn saw in his previous works—*Cohens and Kellys in Trouble* (1933), *Bachelor Bait* and *Kentucky Kernels* (both 1934)—that would move her to pick Stevens with such prescience. Her previous films do not suggest that she was starved for good direction. George Cukor had guided her rather spectacularly past the sentimental shoals of *Bill of Divorcement* (1932) and *Little Women* (1933). Lowell Sherman had helped her win an Oscar for *Morning Glory* in 1933, and even Dorothy

Arzner showed a certain flair in directing Hepburn in her one authentic camp classic, *Christopher Strong* (1933). Why then had she felt prompted to push a Laurel-and-Hardy and Wheeler-and-Woolsey program director into artistic prominence? Whatever the answer, Stevens turned out to be ideally suited for *Alice Adams*. Indeed, he emerged almost miraculously in the mid-thirties with a fully mature personal style. This style was a strange mix of Wyler's meticulousness and McCarey's sentimentality. Actually, *Alice Adams* is two distinct movies: the first in long-shot describes the petty snobberies of Booth Tarkington's Middle West, the second in close-up expresses Alice's (and Hepburn's) humiliation and redemption as the middle-class girl with hifalutin' social ambitions. Stevens moves gracefully from one plot to the other, often making the two plots intersect within a single shot. But critics of the period seemed to resent Hepburn's close-ups almost as if they were symptoms of her social self-indulgence. Meyer Levin of *Esquire* characteristically expressed greater sympathy for Alice's down-to-earth father and brother for their resistance to her program of putting on airs for the benefit of her upper-class boyfriend (Fred MacMurray).

The scene of social humiliation is peculiarly American in that it reflects the tensions created by social mobility, but no actress ever suffered more beautifully through this trauma than Katharine Hepburn in *Alice Adams*. So beautifully and with so much voluptuous masochism. And Stevens's enormous and sustained close-ups gave Hepburn's fine-boned beauty an expressive intensity such as audiences had never experienced before. It was almost too much of a good thing. Audiences would not long sit still for such camera adulation, any more than they had sat still indefinitely for Sternberg's lens-love-making with Marlene Dietrich in the early thirties.

After *Alice Adams*, the rest of the thirties was something of an anti-climax for Stevens. *Laddie* and *Nitwits* (1935) were in the program picture category, and *Annie Oakley* (1935) was, though pleasant, only moderately more presuming. Stevens was building up a reputation for Americana comparable to those established at Fox by John Ford and Henry King, and at MGM by Clarence Brown. Barbara Stanwyck as Annie was not a close-up-type creation, and she played best in middle-range rough-and-tumble. Stevens directed the sentiment and slapstick alike with a slow, steady beat so as to create an impression of concern for the outlandish characters with hearts of gold.

As an RKO contract director, Stevens virtually inherited Astaire and Rogers for *Swing Time* (1936). It can be and has been argued that *Swing*

Time is the best of the Astaire-Rogers musicals. Jean Domarchi of *Cahiers du Cinema* once argued the contrary by suggesting that it made very little difference whether Astaire was directed by George Stevens or Mark Sandrich, and that *la politique des auteurs* was relatively marginal in the realm of musicals. Stevens certainly cannot take credit for one of Jerome Kern's most enchanting scores ("The Way You Look Tonight," "A Fine Romance," etc.), Van Nest Polglaise's brightest Art Deco sets, and Astaire's most inventive choreography. Stevens should be given some credit for the relatively bearable comedy relief provided by Victor Moore and Helen Broderick, and the smooth transitions between the dramatic and musical interludes—between the prose and the poetry, as it were.

Stevens then proceeded to direct Katharine Hepburn, Franchot Tone, and Joan Fontaine in a very stagey version of J. M. Barrie's play *Quality Street*. Here Stevens is unusually and uncharacteristcally "distanced" from his characters and his material, and he is only intermittently graceful and lyrical. His next two pictures featured Astaire without Rogers (*Damsel in Distress*, 1937) and Rogers without Astaire (*Vivacious Lady*, 1938), George Burns and Gracie Allen taking up the dancing slack from the lead-footed Joan Fontaine in *Damsel*, and James Stewart picking up the screwball comedy love interest in *Lady*. Whereas *Damsel in Distress* is somewhat timidly romantic despite a tingling Gershwin score, *Vivacious Lady* is brightly erotic in its witty flirtation with double-entendres.

Stevens's last film of the thirties, *Gunga Din* (1939), became a great classic of children's matinees in the forties and fifties. The unrestrained hamming of Cary Grant, Victor McLaglen and Sam Jaffe as the eponymous *Gunga Din* provided a fitting counterpoint for the mock-operatic spectacle of Kipling's India in revolt. But as Otis Ferguson noted at the time, *Gunga Din* verged on self-parody as it exploited the adventure films of the mid-thirties (vide *Lives of a Bengal Lancer* (1935), *Viva Villa!* (1934), *Mutiny on the Bounty* (1935), *Captain Blood* (1933)) without retaining their seriousness of tone. Perhaps the world was coming too close to war to require the diversions of the adventure genre. For Stevens himself, *Gunga Din* was to be the last foray into period spectacle until the ill-fated *The Greatest Story Ever Told* in the mid-sixties.

■   ■   ■   ■

STEVENS DEVELOPED a more complex and more erotically challenging mix of comedy and sentiment through the forties after beginning the decade inauspiciously in 1940 with *Vigil in the Night*, a solemn saga of nobility and self-sacrifice in the medical profession. Adapted from an

A. J. Cronin novel that was less clearly focused than Cronin's *The Citadel, Vigil* wasted the talents of Carole Lombard and Anne Shirley on an insufficiently intriguing narrative.

Stevens bounced back the following year with *Penny Serenade* (1941), almost schizophrenically constructed as a light-hearted courtship comedy in the first half gaining in gravity and sexual hunger as it went along with the characters played by Cary Grant and Irene Dunne slowly pulling out all the stops as inevitably, inexorably married partners. Seldom in a Hollywood movie have the yin and yang of repression and release been so intensely illuminated. Then suddenly the emphasis shifts to Dunne's desire for a child in conflict with Grant's financial irresponsibility.

When the Tokyo earthquake causes the Dunne character to miscarry, the plot takes an irrevocably sentimental turn toward the emotional pressure to adopt, more on the wife's part than the husband's. What could have been a banal resolution of the problem was transfigured by a reversal in Grant's character from a man more in love with his wife than with the possibilities of a child to a fully emotionally committed father determined to keep his child from being taken away by the adoption agency. His tearful plea to the judge constituted one of the best pieces of dramatic acting Grant had produced up to that time. Dunne and Grant were aided in their eventful transition from lovers to parents by Beulah Bondi's sympathetic case worker and Edgar Buchanan's helpful family friend. The title of the film refers to its flashback framework with records of pop songs played through circular iris dissolves during the last moments of what seems like an irrevocably broken marriage. This device enables both suspense and surprise to come into play as narrative strategies.

In 1942 Stevens consolidated the success of *Penny Serenade* (1941) with two big-star comedy dramas with a rich mix of romance and social consciousness. *Woman of the Year* (1942) originated the long-running team of Tracy and Hepburn with a bittersweet feminist fable concocted by Ring Lardner, Jr., and Michael Kanin, from the real-life experiences of Sinclair Lewis and Dorothy Thompson. Joseph L. Mankiewicz was the urbane producer of the project, and Stevens provided the most erotic images of Hepburn up to that time as a deliciously conflicted career woman with both great gams (the introductory scene in the newspaper office) and an amorous proclivity for alcohol (the saloon sequence).

That same year *The Talk of the Town* (1942) utilized the stellar talents of Cary Grant, Jean Arthur, and Ronald Colman in a curious comedy drama involving a labor organizer (Grant) falsely accused of arson and

murder by corrupt corporate and government interests, a small-town secretary (Arthur) who shelters him, and a future Supreme Court Justice
(Colman) who chooses that moment to take occupancy of the house
Arthur is renting, and in which Grant is hiding. Stevens deftly balances
the madcap three-way romance shared by Grant, Arthur, and Colman
with a great deal of action melodrama over the life-and-death issues of
lynch law and municipal corruption. Arthur, the illustrious Capra icon
of the thirties, energizes the comedy and lightens the load of the good
government preaching to the audience. This was one of the more successful screen attempts in the forties to combine man-woman slightly
screwballish entertainment with serious-minded moral enlightment.

With *The More the Merrier* (1943) the comedy and the romance take
precedence over the comparatively trivial problem of a housing shortage
in wartime Washington. Actually, the housing shortage is reduced to a
plot contrivance to get Jean Arthur and Joel McCrea in the same apartment, which they share also with a benign businessman played with
charm and panache by the versatile character actor Charles Coburn. The
shortage of men in Washington offered many opportunities for female
office employees to hunt the random males in their midst with undis-
guised lust and licentiousness in their hearts and in their unnerving wolf
whistles.

Arthur at thirty-eight was nearing the end of an illustrious career as
a crack-voiced comedienne par excellence. McCrea was actually the
same age, but *Life* magazine singled out Arthur for managing to make
credible a spectacularly erotic petting scene on a Washington stoop on
which she responds to McCrea's skilfully seductive caresses and strategic
kisses with more knowingness and fervor than was to be found in any
other Hollywood movie that year. The resolution of the romance, however, is saddled with very contrived farcical devices of scandal and "lost
reputations," and the movie runs out of steam long before the final black-
out fade-out. Most of the notices and a Supporting Actor Oscar went to
Charles Coburn for his lovably avuncular match-making, and Stevens
was hailed for his comic flair at a time when audiences and critics were
beginning to tire of the more solemn war movies.

Stevens himself went off to war after *The More the Merrier*, made
a few wartime documentaries, and then returned with a mission to
make more "significant" films thereafter. His first postwar effort, *I Remember Mama* (1948), seemed modest enough in its immigrant saga
objectives, but one senses a new grandiosity in the Stevens style, more
elaboration in the editing, and more of a bravura flourish in the playing.

For better or worse, Stevens had now shifted irrevocably from a minor to a major key.

FRANK BORZAGE (1893–1962)

Frank Borzage was credited with the direction of eighty-two films between 1918 and 1959, about half of them released before sound. Records before 1918 are so fragmentary, however, that Borzage was possibly directing films as early as 1913. He was born in 1893 in Salt Lake City. He made his stage debut as an adolescent actor in 1906, and then somehow found his way into moving pictures. The *New York Times* first mentioned Borzage in 1920 as the director of *Humoresque*. Borzage appears in the *Times* index under two of that paper's uncorrected typographical mutations, the first as Frank Borzaga, and the second as Frank Borzange, the latter a Franco-angelic modification of the director's name for a Parisian hit, *La Femme au Corbeau*, the French release title for *The River* (1929), a sensitive late Hollywood silent which (like Josef von Sternberg's *Docks of New York* and Paul Fejos's *Lonesome*) passed almost unnoticed in America amid the hysteria of the all-talking, all-singing sensations of the hour.

Nonetheless, through the twenties and thirties, Frank Borzage films were making ten-best lists regularly and he won two Oscars for direction (*Seventh Heaven*, 1927, and *Bad Girl*, 1931). And yet Borzage remains an elusive figure in film history. His growing vogue as a directorial influence from the past is reflected in a special tribute to his career in the Spring 1973 issue of *Focus*, Chicago's film journal. Especially intriguing is the cryptic opening sentence of David Kehr's analysis of *Moonrise* (1948): "*Moonrise* is the last film Frank Borzage completed before the Blacklist forced him into a ten-year period of inactivity."

Borzage had never before been connected with the blacklist even though he had been associated with "prematurely anti-Nazi" projects in the late thirties (*Three Comrades*, 1938; *The Mortal Storm*, 1940). But his resurrection as a resonant director depends less on the ideological implications of his images than on the force of his feelings. And the new generations of the sixties, seventies, eighties, and nineties seem to have been attuned more to emotional intensity than intellectual irony. On that basis alone, *Lazybones* (1925), *Seventh Heaven*, *Street Angel* (1928),

Man's Castle (1933), *Little Man, What Now?* (1934), *No Greater Glory* (1934), *History Is Made at Night* (1937), *The Mortal Storm* (1940), and *Moonrise* (1949) reverberate with privileged moments of extraordinary intimacy and vulnerability. It is not simply a matter of the sentimental premises of the plots, but rather of the hauntingly sensitive figures of style to which one may at long last refer as Borzagian.

By any standards, Borzage was predominantly a director of the twenties and thirties, fading badly in the forties (except for *Moonrise*) and virtually disappearing in the fifties. Consequently, the new critics of *Cahiers du Cinema*, and later the London-based *Movie*, were too young to have experienced Borzage first-hand. Ironically, it is the Lindsay Anderson–Gavin Lambert–Penelope Houston–Karel Reisz generation of *Sequence* which must be credited with the earliest profound appreciation of *Moonrise*. Also, Henri Agel, an older French film historian with a Roman Catholic orientation, seems to have been moved by the Borzage of *The River* and *Man's Castle* to the point of hailing Nicholas Ray in the fifties as Borzage's spiritual successor. And Robert Sherwood once gave Borzage a kind of back-handed compliment by noting that as much as he despised tear-jerkers, he had to make an exception for Borzage's *Humoresque* (1920). But that had been a long time ago. At the time the *Cahiers de Cinema* and *Movie* iconoclasts were engaged in re-evaluating the American cinema, it seemed that some genres—westerns, *policiers*, musicals especially—were more fashionable than others. Violent flash, then as now, was in, and vibrant feeling was out. Thus Borzage simply did not qualify on the bang-bang level of pop aesthetics.

At the time of Borzage's death, a survey of the standard texts in service at the time indicated that in the stream of film history he had been almost completely submerged.

Lewis Jacobs uses the group approach to Borzage in *The Rise of the American Film* (1968):

> In the latter half of the period emerged a number of more significant directors who displayed unusual talents and achieved notable productions: King Vidor, Josef Von Sternberg, Lewis Milestone, Frank Borzage and William K. Howard. These men were now looming up as distinctive film-makers, but it was in the next period that they were to reach their prime.

The period to which Mr. Jacobs refers is 1919–29, and the next period is 1929–39. However, Borzage disappears until later in the book, where he is re-grouped.

Other contemporary directors, no less commercially proficient, and who occasionally also produce arresting pictures, are Mervyn LeRoy, Lewis Milestone, William Dieterle, Michael Curtiz, Rowland Brown, William Wyler, William Wellman, William K. Howard, W. S. Van Dyke, Gregory La Cava, Frank Borzage, George Cukor and Sidney Franklin.

Then Borzage and Clarence Brown are inexplicably paired as "the screen's leading romanticists." The last words on Borzage end with a damning interview:

Frank Borzage's best films, *Seventh Heaven* (1927), *Bad Girl* (1931), *A Farewell to Arms* (1932), *No Greater Glory* (1934) and *Little Man, What Now?* (1934) also displayed a sound knowledge of movie making and a flair for the poignant—which, in his later work, too often descended to bathos. These men have let their potentialities go unrealized. Borzage's statement in an interview in 1937 clearly sums up their artistic credo: "the trouble with most directors is that they take the whole thing too seriously . . . Making a motion picture consists merely of going on to a set, training a camera on competent players and letting them enact a good script."

Borzage's best films—*Lazybones, The River, They Had To See Paris* (1929), *Man's Castle, A Farewell to Arms* (1933), *History Is Made at Night* (1937), *Three Comrades, Little Man, What Now?*, and *Moonrise*—contain too many magical moments to suggest an accident theory for his career. The long dolly shot of the little girl in *Lazybones*, walking home from school and from one layer of consciousness to another, marks Borzage as a master of transcendent cinematic forms very early in his career. His apotheosis of Janet Gaynor in *Seventh Heaven* and *Street Angel* seems more impressive today than it did years ago when Borzage was completely overshadowed (literally and figuratively) by F. W. Murnau, who had molded Gaynor into a mousey *Hausfrau* in *Sunrise*. But it was always Borzage's bad luck to be treated as the minor element in his major works. Hence the charge that he betrayed Hemingway in *A Farewell to Arms* and blunted Lubitsch in *Desire* (1936). Even his contribution to *Three Comrades* (1937) was relatively obscured by the spectacular feud over the script between Joseph L. Mankiewicz and F. Scott Fitzgerald.

"There is about a man like Frank Borzage," Jim Tully wrote in the February 1927 *Vanity Fair*,

the mystery of propelling impulse. A labourer in a Utah coal mine at twelve years of age, he returned each night to his Italian father and mother who shared their squalid home with thirteen other children. To make the sit-

uation worse, they were all amateur musicians. Was it because he could
no longer stand the noise of fife and drum and fiddle, or was it something
burning in his soul that made him run away from home before he was
thirteen years old? What was the propelling impulse? Borzage is now, at
thirty-three, the youngest and one of the wealthiest directors in the world.
Little more than a vagabond until the early twenties, he now earns more
than a quarter of a million dollars a year. . . . Borzage asks no player to do
that which he cannot do himself. He plays each part before the members
of the cast . . . In true Italian fashion he has gathered the members of his
family about him. A brother is assistant director.

Tully's muscularly proletarian prose celebrated Borzage's intuitive gifts
garnered from the school of hard knocks, and it would seem that Borzage
came from the kind of background that spurred the emotional fantasies
of Charles Chaplin and Frank Capra. Borzage's full-bodied emotionalism
is saved from bathos by the director's heartfelt sincerity. But it was hard
for critics and film historians to describe Borzage's most successful
scenes without seeming to endorse a mindless sentimentality. The critical language had not been invented to describe the lyrical spell Borzage
cast over his audience with his conversations à deux. The wit and dynamism of montage were still uppermost in the minds of film aestheticians, and the stillness of the soul was not yet even a gleam in the eyes
of the New Critics.

Borzage's greatest gifts were lyrical rather than narrative, harmonic
rather than melodic, intimate rather than expansive. Hence we do not
think of great Borzage movies so much as great Borzage moments. These
moments usually culminate in an intense expression between two people—Helen Hayes and Gary Cooper in A Farewell to Arms (1932), Spencer Tracy and Loretta Young in Man's Castle (1933), Margaret Sullavan
and Douglass Montgomery in Little Man, What Now? (1934), Jean Arthur and Charles Boyer in History Is Made at Night (1937), Gail Russell
and Dane Clark in Moonrise (1949). But Borzage never needed dream
worlds for his suspension of disbelief. He plunged into the real world of
poverty and oppression, the world of Roosevelt and Hitler, the New Deal
and the New Order, to impart an aura to his characters, not merely
through soft-focus and a fluid camera but through a genuine concern
with the wondrous inner life of lovers in the midst of adversity. In this
respect, History Is Made at Night, with its fog-shrouded intimation of a
Titanic-like disaster at sea, is not only the most romantic title in the
history of the cinema but a profound expression of Borzage's commitment
to lyricism over realism.

Borzage's distinctive temperament on the set is exemplified by his extraordinary treatment of Janet Gaynor and Margaret Sullavan, actresses with screen personalities exalted by him, Gaynor as a Madonna of the Streets and Sullavan as a veritable mountain climber of emotional peaks. Many of Borzage's products, particularly toward the end of his career, were indisputably trivial in conception, but even in his lesser films, the behavioral beauties of his players shone through with a very warm glow. Like many film pioneers, Borzage ultimately discovered his emotional Eldorado in the human face, and thus proceeded to exalt the silent depths of even his most bedeviled characters.

JOHN STAHL (1886–1950)

Even the most systematic of the Hollywoodophiles at *Cahiers du Cinema* during its vintage years were unable to provide much of a dossier on John M. Stahl, a middle-range director of impressive sobriety and intensity throughout a career ranging from 1914 through 1947. For American auteurists, Stahl was a neglected figure whose career suddenly became illuminated (after his death in 1950) through an accident of film scholarship. Earlier, the French film historian Henri Agel had classified Stahl as a director with only one masterpiece: *Back Street* (1932). A subsequent recheck of Stahl's career for possible auteur analysis revealed a startling quality of consistency from 1932 on. For the most part, Stahl, like Sternberg and Douglas Sirk, was involved with outrageously improbable story material. Indeed, the parallel with Sirk is inescapable inasmuch as they worked in different decades on three of the same Universal projects—*Imitation of Life* (Stahl, 1934; Sirk, 1959); *Magnificent Obsession* (Stahl, 1935; Sirk, 1954), and *When Tomorrow Comes*, a 1939 Stahl production retitled *Interlude* for the 1957 Sirk version. The difference between Stahl and Sirk is very much the difference between the emotional social consciousness of the thirties and the stylistic self-consciousness of the fifties. Whereas Stahl's treatments are warmer, Sirk's are wittier. Stahl possessed the audacity of Sirk but not the dark humor. Whereas Stahl was capable of a straight, reverent treatment of *Keys of the Kingdom* (1944), Sirk transformed *The First Legion* (1950) into a devastating parody of the Jesuits.

It is interesting to note that Stahl in *The Eve of St. Mark* (1944) displayed a profound comprehension of the emotional implications of two-shots, as opposed to cross-cutting. At times Stahl's conception of contrasts was as forceful as Sirk's. In *The Immortal Sergeant* (1943), for example, Henry Fonda thirsts in the desert with a mental image of Maureen O'Hara emerging dripping wet from a swimming pool. It is this kind of audacious effect which resonates through time when more discreet images have receded. And who can forget in the same vein the lurid spectacle of Gene Tierney (with lips blood-red) on horseback as she spreads her father's ashes in *Leave Her to Heaven* (1945), or Margaret Sullavan's one last tryst with her forgetful lover on the second level of a duplex in *Back Street* (1941), or Irene Dunne's somber farewell dinner with a hopelessly married Charles Boyer in *When Tomorrow Comes* (1939), or Andrea Leeds with her *Letter of Introduction* (1938) to Adolphe Menjou? That many of these memorable moments pertain to what were once denigrated as women's pictures provides an additional explanation for Stahl's relative anonymity in the more solemn critical histories.

In his early years as a director, Stahl was known for his almost semidocumentary pictures, closely tied to the day's headlines, and for the filming of outstanding contemporary novels. He was known also very early in his career as a woman's director. Toward the end of his career he was identified mainly with a series of romantic dramas. He was under contract at 20th Century-Fox when he died. He became annoyed with his reputation for a "slow, measured tread" in the amount of time it took him to shoot a film. He insisted in a 1941 interview that he had never spent more than nine weeks in production. In a review of *Our Wife* (1941), a New York film critic claimed that, though Stahl was known as a "director of heavy, portentous dramas, full of meaning and serious thoughts," he had switched successfully on this occasion to light comedy. In retrospect, however, *Our Wife* seems relatively strained as a comedy, and, indeed, lacks the grace and charm of many of his "heavy, portentous dramas."

After ten years at Universal, Stahl decided to sign only one-film contracts in the manner of Frank Capra and Walter Wanger. Stahl made such a pact with Columbia, and another with United Artists, but cancelled the latter contract. He often cited the fact that he had brought in *When Tomorrow Comes* (1939) under budget. This kind of self-serving production story is often the last recourse of Hollywood directors accused justly or unjustly of extravagance, the very nebulous charge that served ultimately to wreck the careers of Griffith, Stroheim, and Welles. Stahl's obituary in the *New York Herald Tribune* noted that the late director's greatest successes had been *Magnificent Obsession* (1935), *Only Yesterday* (1933), and *Strictly Dishonorable* (1931).

A closer inspection of Stahl's career suggests an unusually complex pattern of plusses and minuses. On the debit side is Stahl's complicity with L. B. Mayer in adding a ludicrous "love interest" sequence to Ernst Lubitsch's tastefully elliptical *The Student Prince* with Ramon Novarro and Norma Shearer. It seems that the literal-minded Mr. Mayer felt that there was not enough boy-girl courtship in Lubitsch's relatively restrained treatment of the Sigmund Romberg operetta in its 1927 silent version. Stahl dutifully directed Novarro and Shearer *à deux* in a tableau of reclining romance set in a garishly glowing field of flowers. (Two years earlier Mayer had influenced King Vidor in the direction of a fleshier treatment of *La Bohème*.)

Stahl's intrusion into a Lubitsch project is all the more objectionable for its stylistic discordance. Ironically, the offending footage in *The Student Prince* (over-all one of Lubitsch's least interesting silents besides) is thus far the one trace of Stahl's career to have survived from the silent era. Until a few decades ago, the spirit of historical (and feminist) revisionism was not strong enough to encourage the resurrection of films with unpromisingly domestic and marital titles. Also, the implications of Stahl's "spelling out" sequence in *The Student Prince* tended to be especially incriminating during the long reign of Anglo-Russian montage theoreticians in most of the "serious" film histories written in English. In the context of montage and ellipsis, Lubitsch served as a heroic ironist in contrast to such supposedly soppy and soapy single-take sentimentalists (and despised woman's directors besides) as Frank Borzage, George Cukor, John Stahl, Edmund Goulding, Lowell Sherman, John Cromwell, William Seiter, *et al.*

Hence, Borzage's direction of the Lubitsch-produced project *Desire* (1936) was criticized for lacking the lilt and snap of Lubitsch. Or, more precisely, the film seemed to begin like Lubitsch (sardonic, twinkling) and end like Borzage (somber, tortured). Similarly, Cukor's direction of *One Hour with You* from a Lubitsch plan failed to sparkle with Monsieur Ernst's witty asides and reaction shots. Indeed, the only critically fashionable attitude a film-maker could take toward the bourgeoisie through the thirties was one of satiric derision. And the emotional problems of women were subsumed under the general heading of bourgeois self-indulgence. To make matters worse, the woman's film, like the western, was generally adapted from a culturally disreputable fictional genre, Fannie Hurst and Vicki Baum being the counterparts of Max Brand and

Zane Grey. Yet, if the movie western could claim a degree of aesthetic redemption through the majesty and grandeur of its natural landscapes, and through the kinetic energy of its heroic horsemen, the women's movie was no less deserving of admiration for the marvelously sculpted landscapes of an actress's face in luminously subjective close-up. Words alone cannot convey the grace and gallantry of Irene Dunne's performance in *Back Street* (1932), *Magnificent Obsession* (1935), and *When Tomorrow Comes* (1939), of Margaret Sullavan's in *Only Yesterday* (1933) and in Robert Stevenson's re-make of *Back Street* (1941), and of Claudette Colbert's resonant vulnerability in *Imitation of Life* (1934) as she reminded her grown-up daughter of the time long ago when the child-daughter had said with Proustian persistence, "quack-quack, I want a quack-quack, I want a quack-quack" . . . fade out. The emotional effect of the "quack-quack" is no accident; it is established by a lyrically lingering close-up of the rubber duck in the first scene of the movie.

As it happens, anti-montage aesthetics has enabled us to broaden our appreciation of the past more than to anticipate the future. By shifting the analytical emphasis from what was left off the screen to what was left on, Bazin made it possible for film scholars of the sixties and the seventies to re-evaluate many thirties, forties, and fifties films which had hitherto been denigrated for their lack of dynamism and dialectics. *Only Yesterday* is especially revelatory in this regard. What had seemed back in 1933 and through the thirties, forties, and fifties to have been a disappointingly superficial and sentimental adaptation of Frederick Lewis Allen's witty memoir of American fads and foibles in the twenties re-emerged in retrospective screenings as an astoundingly evocative film in the style and spirit of the early thirties. Scenes once pronounced dull and turgid now seemed poignant and vibrant. Particularly affecting is Margaret Sullavan's desperate decision at a New Year's Eve party to renew her relationship with an old lover—her first—who has completely forgotten her. The succession of self-questioning expressions in Sullavan's fiercely passionate eyes foreshadows a similar dilemma for Joan Fontaine in Max Ophüls's sublime *Letter from an Unknown Woman* (1948). But there are the remembered flaws also in *Only Yesterday* (1933): the smug, pompous preening of John Boles as the *homme fatal*, the mindless worship of childcult (a spiritual disease especially endemic in the thirties), the too-easy rhetoric of redemption, a foolishly written reunion scene between father and son on the occasion of the mother's death, and a certain sketchiness around the edges of the secondary characterizations.

By the same token, *Only Yesterday* seemed to improve with age through its behavioral beauties and incidental insights. For example, the comical informality of the courtship between Billie Burke and Reginald Denny seems to foreshadow the improvised duet on the bongo drums between Leila Hyams and Roland Young two years later in Leo Mc-Carey's classic *Ruggles of Red Gap* (1935). It was Stahl's misfortune also to have the Dunne-Boyer romance in *When Tomorrow Comes* (1939) eclipsed by McCarey's more inspiring and more inspirational treatment of the two stars in *Love Affair* (1939). Nonetheless, *Only Yesterday* seemed strikingly prophetic later with its brilliant vignette of Franklin Pangborn's slyly gay solicitude for his handsome young protégé and, above all, for the stirring portraits of New Women projected by Margaret Sullavan and Billie Burke.

Imitation of Life (1934), which seemed almost too painfully frank in its own time, now survives as a truer testament to the ineradicable racism of American life than most white Americans care to acknowledge. Again Stahl's extraordinary care and deliberation provide the key to his stylistic sincerity. That he had functioned on occasion in the Hollywood system as a producer and screenwriter indicates that he was far from being the lackey of L. B. Mayer that his unfortunate participation in the post-production tampering with *The Student Prince* would seem to indicate. Instead, Stahl, like many of his under-rated Hollywood colleagues, possessed virtues as an artist and as a craftsman which are in short supply in the overly syncopated and overly satiric seventies, eighties, and nineties. The emotional problems of women no longer seem as trivial and escapist as they once did, and the intensity of a director's gaze no longer seems static and anti-cinematic. Thus, Stahl's cinema eminently deserves continuing re-evaluation.

MAX OPHÜLS (1902–1957)

The productive career of Max Ophuls in Hollywood lasted about three years, during which period he turned out four films of stylistic distinction but of little relevance to the modish social consciousness of Hollywood in the late forties. *The Exile* (1947), *Letter from an Unknown Woman* (1948), *Caught* (1949), and *The Reckless Moment* (1949) were thus "lost" in their own time, and then rediscovered in the more scholarly sixties and seventies. Ophüls (labeled as Opuls in his Hollywood credits) came and went without many contemporary reviewers any the wiser. Hence, Agee ignored Ophüls's role entirely in his *Time* review of December 8, 1947:

> *The Exile* (Fairbanks; Universal) is one of those shy wildflowers which occasionally spring up almost unnoticed in the Hollywood hothouse. But because of its forced growth, half the freshness is off the bloom. The story is a pleasant little fraud. A trumped-up anecdote of King Charles II's gay undernourishment in continental garrets, it is designed chiefly to purvey the Tarzantics of Actor Douglas Fairbanks, Jr. But *The Exile* is also Young Doug's first fling as a producer, and he has concealed most of the fraud with both legitimate and handsome cinematic tricks. The script (which he is said to have written) has a charming, blank-verse hauteur that just possibly may be a bit asinine—but the direction saves the day by insisting on a witty, natural reading. Fairbanks has also inflicted an extreme lilt on the rhythm of the film—a lilt that would be annoying if were not necessary to keep the lame plot marching along.

Ten years later Richard Roud wrote in *Max Ophüls*: "Thanks to an old friend, Robert Siodmak, Ophüls was next engaged to direct *The Exile* (1947) for Douglas Fairbanks, Jr. Ophüls got on very well with Fairbanks from the beginning; and Fairbanks accorded him almost complete freedom to make the film he wanted." How to reconcile the contradiction? It depends to some extent on the point of view. As producer, scenarist, and star Fairbanks was obviously responsible for bringing *The Exile* into being. The content is all his, certainly, but what Agee described as "an extreme lilt on the rhythm of the film" can clearly be attributed to the Ophüls who fashioned this lilt in the early thirties for *The Bartered Bride* (1932) and *Liebelei* (1933). But Agee had no such fix on Ophüls (or rather Opuls) in the late forties. Film history was a much sketchier enterprise in that era than it was to become in the sixties and seventies. Nonetheless, Agee was sufficiently discerning to note the stylistic virtues of *The Exile* even though he lacked the research facilities to track down the source of the style.

The Exile is thus simultaneously an Ophüls film and a Fairbanks film, just as *Letter from an Unknown Woman* (1948) is an Ophüls film and a Fontaine film, and *Caught* and *The Reckless Moment* (1949) are Ophüls films and Mason films. Scenarist Howard Koch had much to do with originating *Letter from an Unknown Woman* as a movie project, and scenarist Arthur Laurents made a distinctive contribution to the scathingly anti-Howard Hughes image of the rich, psychotic villain played by Robert Ryan in *Caught*. Nor can it be doubted that Walter Wanger's involvement as a producer of *The Reckless Moment* had some connection with the major role played by his wife, Joan Bennett. Through this elaborate network of influences and accommodations the directorial career of Max Ophüls glided with more grace and conviction than anyone would have suspected back in the forties. Ophüls had been in Hollywood from the early forties as a political exile from Europe, but project after project had fallen through until the aptly titled *The Exile* came to the rescue. Curiously, Ophüls had experienced the frustrations of working for Howard Hughes on an ill-fated movie called *Vendetta* (1946). In fact, Ophüls had been "discovered" by Preston Sturges when the celebrated comic director screened a print of *Liebelei* (1932) one evening, but Sturges himself soon fell afoul of Hughes, and Ophüls went down with his sponsor.

Except for *The Exile*, the cinema of Ophüls tended to be woman-oriented cinema. From *Liebelei* in 1932 to *Lola Montès* in 1955, Ophüls expressed a lyrical concern with the fate of the female in the varied games of love. Hence, he seemed to have little to say about man. By confining himself to the boudoir rather than the assembly line Ophüls was deemed insufficiently realistic for serious analysis, or rather his films were deemed insufficiently realistic since Ophüls himself remained unknown. The auteurist revolution in the sixties and the feminist revolution in the seventies forced a reappraisal of the so-called woman's film.

Stylistic analysis was even more primitive in the late forties than thematic analysis. Still, it is hard to believe today that no one noticed Ophüls's extraordinary addiction to camera movement as a means of expression. James Mason, who appeared in Ophüls's last two American films, even wrote a poem on the subject:

> I think I know the reason why
> Producers tend to make him cry.
> Inevitably they demand
> Some stationary set-ups, and
> A shot that does not call for tracks
> Is agony for poor dear Max,
> Who, separated from his dolly,
> Is wrapped in deepest melancholy.
> Once when they took away his crane,
> I thought he'd never smile again . . .

Until the late fifties, Anglo-American montage theory was so dominant among aestheticians that a director was more likely to become notorious rather than famous for the use of camera movement. What was overlooked with Ophüls was that his supposedly showy style was deeply related to his two dominant themes: Ephemerality and Renunciation.

The Charles Stuart of Douglas Fairbanks, Jr. in *The Exile* renounces happiness with the Dutch milk-maid incarnated in the blonde beauty of twenty-three-year-old Tahiti-born actress Paule Croset. Joan Fontaine's Lisa Berndle sacrifices a lifetime and her life for an illusory romance with a thoughtlessly egotistical pianist played by Louis Jourdan in *Letter from an Unknown Woman*. The Leonora of Barbara Bel Geddes loses her baby and her popular magazine illusions in *Caught*. Joan Bennett's Lucia Harper, a dedicated housewife to the point of heroism, loses her complacency and peace of mind in *The Reckless Moment* as she tries to spare her family the pain of a lurid scandal. Here it is the male—James Mason's romantic blackmailer—who sacrifices his life for a woman locked in the trap of domesticity.

For his part, Ophüls passed through Hollywood almost unnoticed by the critics and film historians. (A recent uncritical celebration masquerading as a film history of Metro-Goldwyn-Mayer actually singled out *Caught* for censure.) Nonetheless, Ophüls was considerably ahead of his time in his strange mixture of irony and intensity. *Caught* and *The Reckless Moment* anticipate the stylish soap operas of Douglas Sirk in the late fifties, just as Sirk anticipates Rainer Werner Fassbinder's stylized spectacles in the late sixties and early seventies. Even in the seventies, however, the notion that significant films could have been adapted from such dubiously slick sources as Libbie Block's *Wild Calender* (*Caught*) and Elizabeth Sanxay Holding's *Ladies' Home Journal* story, *The Blank Wall* (*The Reckless Moment*), would not have gone down well with most critics. The two trends that have been working in favor of these two hitherto neglected films are auteurism (the discovery of the Ophülsian style) and feminism (the resurrected genre of the woman's movie). Hence, film history has been rewritten somewhat by various revisionists to include the Ophülsian oeuvre of the late forties in the aesthetic re-evaluation of that era. From this vantage point, Ophüls joined the darkening school of Orson Welles (*Lady from Shanghai*) (1948), Jean Renoir (*Woman on the Beach*) (1947), Jacques Tourneur (*Out of the Past*) (1947), Frank Borzage (*Moonrise*) (1949), Nicholas Ray (*They Live by Night*) (1949), André De Toth (*Pitfall*) (1948), Anthony Mann (*Side Street*) (1949), Abraham Polonsky (*Force of Evil*) (1948), Robert Rossen (*Body and Soul*)

(1947), and Joseph H. Lewis (*Gun Crazy*) (1949), among many others in the growingly pessimistic treatment of American life. Even in this company, however, Ophüls stands out for the spiritual nobility of his characters. However contrived the intrigues, the protagonists, male and female, seem to rise above their desperate state with almost miraculous courage and grace. But to appreciate the full stature of the characters it is necessary to perceive how they are ennobled by the rigor and restlessness of the director's style.

The single most precious legacy from Ophüls to the American cinema is *Letter from an Unknown Woman*, adapted by Howard Koch from Stefan Zweig's novel, and photographed by Franz Planer with a stylistic virtuosity that expressed both the opulence and the irony of the director's Viennese sensibility. The choice of Schubert as the leitmotif for a woman's love unrequited from childhood for a wastrel virtuoso is an inspired one. All the sweet sadness of the situation caresses the ear and the eye simultaneously. Ophüls and Koch made no concessions to popular taste, and somehow miraculously avoided studio pressure. There is nothing in the film that makes one say with exasperation, oh Hollywood!

Letter from an Unknown Woman is as fully suffused with tragic inexorability and lyrical feeling as the European classics of Ophüls—*Liebelei* (1933), *La Signore di Tutti* (1934), *La Ronde* (1950), *Le Plaisir* (1952), *Madame de . . .* (1953), and *Lola Montès* (1955). Without descending to foolish caricature or soppy sentimentality, Ophüls enters a woman's heart and a man's soul with breathtaking delicacy and steely precision. Everything counts and everything matters in this unadulterated gift from European culture to the Hollywood dream machine.

4

Actors and Actresses

GRETA GARBO (1905–1990)

What, when drunk, one sees in other women, one sees in
Garbo sober.

Kenneth Tynan

Maybe it is like the dreams you have when some one you
have seen in the cinema comes to your bed at night and is so
kind and lovely. He'd slept with them all that way when he
was asleep in bed. He could remember Garbo still, and Harlow. Yes, Harlow many times. Maybe it was like those dreams.
But he could still remember the time Garbo came to his bed
the night before the attack at Pozoblanco and she was wearing
a soft silky wool sweater when he put his arm around her and
when she leaned forward her hair swept forward and over his
face and she said why had he never told her that he loved her
when she had loved him all this time? She was not shy, nor
cold, nor distant. She was just lovely to hold and kind and
lovely and like the old days with Jack Gilbert and it was true
as though it happened and he loved her much more than
Harlow though Garbo was there only once while Harlow—

Ernest Hemingway, For Whom the Bell Tolls

GRETA GARBO REMAINS the most enduringly and endearingly mesmerizing after-image of the MGM star system. Garbo's art dissolves in her myth, and her myth seems to transcend even the cinema that first gave it form. The spine-tingling death scene in *Camille* (1937) transforms cinema into sculpture. The masthead close-up of *Queen Christina* (1933) flattens out the cameraman's perspective from the transparency of a screen to the opaqueness of a canvas. Without benefit of the perpetually avant-garde mannerism of stop-motion, Garbo stops the flow of images on the screen by enslaving the memory of the spectator. Her demoralizing beauty corrupts the optical habits of the wariest critic. After all, the art of cinema is concerned with montage and camera movements and spatial relationships and deep focus and the composition of images— but what are all these trappings of mise-en-scène to Garbo or Garbo to mise-en-scène? Let us say simply and finally that Garbo is and always has been her own mise-en-scène.

As myth or mise-en-scène, Garbo's inexhaustible visual force has swept away the petty differences between men and women, outdoors woodsmen and interior decorators, hard-boiled professionals and soft-headed dilettantes. What other goddess of the screen could claim equal devotion from Ernest Hemingway and Truman Capote? There is remarkably little pathos in her films, and virtually no trace of self-pity. What Garbo offers her worshippers is a vision of life without compromise, love without disenchantment, sexuality without sordidness.

Yet, Garbo's movies for the most part do not stand very close scrutiny as dramatic narratives. Of the twenty-five feature-length roles she undertook for MGM between her Hollywood debut in *The Torrent* in 1926 and her swan song in *Two-Faced Woman* in 1941, no more than three or four could be considered artistically compelling by even the most generous standards of popular entertainment. Working for the most puritanical studio in Hollywood, she was destined to play exquisite creatures doomed to death or disgrace. That the characters she played seemed to transcend their almost invariably unhappy fate is a tribute to her own cinematic self-sufficiency. It is not so much that the camera made love to her as that she made love to the audience through the camera. Furthermore, it was a love richly colored with irony, curiosity, and uncontrollably high spirits. In short, she seemed so much more sophisticated than the movies that enclosed her that she became their most perceptive critic. Her ongoing dialogue with the audience over the shoulders of the other performers created the impression of a continuous, comparatively unchanging persona. Nonetheless, Garbo herself was also an evolving cog in the history of the studio system.

She, like so many other artists, had been plucked by Hollywood from the European cinema. Garbo was only sixteen when she appeared in front of a movie camera for a commercial made for Paul U. Bergstrom's department store in Stockholm. She appeared the following year in another commercial and then in *Peter the Tramp*, a comedy written, directed, and produced by Erik A. Petschler. Her real name, Greta Gustafsson, was still her professional name as well. "Greta Garbo" did not appear on the screen until 1924, in Mauritz Stiller's *Gosta Berling's Saga* from the novel by Selma Lagerlof. Stiller, who, along with Victor Seastrom, led Sweden into a cinematic Golden Age in the middle period (1914–25) of the silent era, became Garbo's mentor, if not her Svengali. At MGM he was slated to occupy the same position vis-à-vis Garbo that Sternberg was later to occupy with Dietrich at Paramount. Mayer and Thalberg, however, were made of sterner stuff than the relatively permissive moguls at Paramount. One glance at the rushes of Stiller's grandiose and "Continental" conceptions persuaded Thalberg particularly that the studio would be ill-advised to persevere with another Stroheim in the making. Curiously, Garbo had portrayed innocent ingenues in her first two European features, the aforementioned *Gosta Berling's Saga* (1924), and G. W. Pabst's *The Joyless Street* (1925).

In both *The Torrent* (1926) and *The Temptress* (1926), however, Garbo erupted on the American screens in 1926 with all the sinfulness of the Old World inscribed on her beautiful features. Both films had been adapted from novels by Blasco-Ibanez, a Spanish author who had achieved world-class fame with *The Four Horsemen of the Apocalypse* (1922), the Hollywood adaptation of which five years before had launched Rudolph Valentino on his meteoric career as the Great Latin Lover. Fittingly enough, Garbo's first leading men in Hollywood, Ricardo Cortez in *The Torrent* and Antonio Moreno in *The Temptress*, were both regarded as Valentino imitators. The ill-fated original—dead in 1926 of a perforated ulcer—had slipped away from MGM's grasp after *Four Horsemen*, thus belying the myth of that studio's infallibility about talent. The circle was nevertheless complete: Garbo the Vamp teamed with the Valentino clones in heavy-breathing melodramas of lust and temptation set in the Wicked Old World. Garbo's expressive beauty eclipsed the mediocre uses to which it was put, and her own career-long scenario began. A simple girl from a lower-middle class family, she was frugal, private, and stubborn to the core. On the screen, however, she seemed to have burst into a modern world of neurotic, quixotic sexuality. In *Flesh and the Devil* (1927) she was forced to die in the ice so as not to jeopardize the beautiful friendship of John Gilbert and Lars Hanson, and yet all that anyone remembered from the film were her steamy love scenes with Gilbert. She was to be teamed twice more with Gilbert (her most publicized off-screen romance) in the silent era: in 1927 in *Anna Karenina* (with a dismally happy ending), and in 1929 in *A Woman of Affairs*, adapted from Michael Arlen's *The Green Hat*, which completed another circle of sorts if we recall that Arlen reputedly introduced Lady Brett to Ernest Hemingway.

Garbo all in all graced nine silent films—not counting a cameo appearance as herself in a tenth—before she was called upon with much trepidation to break the sound barrier. Ironically, her one silent performance directed by Victor Seastrom (*The Divine Woman*) in 1928 is the one Garbo feature that seems irrevocably lost. The rest of her pre-talkie work could be dismissed as moralistic melodrama very often clumsily contrived. Yet her career in the Hollywood of the twenties made a modicum of sense in the context of American attitudes in that supposedly roaring decade. World War I and its briefly idealistic aftermath had Europeanized large sectors of public taste. Indeed, the war itself had been responsible for shifting the center of film-making power from France to America, and MGM, along with all the other major studios, was fully aware of its imperial responsibilities. Throughout her career Garbo enjoyed great popularity and prestige abroad, and thus, even when she was considered too exotic for the more provincial communities in America, she was redeemed by her more cosmopolitan admirers around the world.

Movies before talkies were effortlessly universal in scope, and Hollywood movies in the twenties had become very comfortable with foreign locales and period costumes. Graustark and Ruritania, Gay Paree and Waltzing Vienna, Victorian England and Czarist Russia were as familiar on the Hollywood backlots as Main Street and Broadway. Though Garbo never actually played a monarch in the twenties, the characters she did impersonate were never situated too far from the lap of luxury. Consequently she was adorned in the most elegant gowns, made up for the most glittering social occasions, and endowed with all the camera magic at MGM's disposal. It is no accident that the cinematographer William Daniels loomed larger in her legend than most of her directors and scenarists.

By 1930 her beauty had become an end in itself, and her more discerning admirers could put together particularly felicitous shots here, and particularly felicitous scenes there, into a pastiche of cinematic perfection worthy of Garbo's unrelenting magnetism. One could begin with the stunningly wry reaction of Garbo's diva in *The Torrent* (1926) when she comes face to face with an old flame diminished into a flickering apparition of balding, middle-aged mediocrity incarnated with a commendably harsh realism by Ricardo Cortez. The dazzling love scenes with Antonio Moreno in *The Temptress* (1926), and with John Gilbert in *The Flesh and the Devil* (1927), could be anthologized for their generous sensuality.

Garbo has been credited by sharp-eyed film-historian Richard Corliss with extending the domain of desire in *Love* to motherhood:

> Anna had been able to live (before Vronsky) without a real husband, but she cannot exist now without her son. And in dramatizing this problem, *Love* [1927] suggests overtones Tolstoy may not have dreamed of. For Gilbert, however cuddly and cherubic, can never be a son to Garbo, but Philippe De Lacy, as Sergei, is almost treated as a lover.
>
> This may sound like acute critical fantasy, but anyone who has seen the film will have noticed the strangely erotic tension between Garbo and De Lacy. Garbo was, after all, only twenty-two when she played this mother of a ten-year-old boy. And De Lacy, who had already appeared in more films than Garbo, knew how to project a pre-Raphaelite sensuality that made him the perfect love object for a repressed and doting mother. This attraction may have been written between the frames, but if it escaped contemporary audiences, it is plain enough to modern ones.

Here then is the ultimate myth of Garbo in the silent era: an overflowing fountain of beauty capable of eroticizing everything and everyone around her. It thus became the function of her scenarios to sanitize her sexuality so as to titillate audiences without gravely offending them. Hence, the titles said one thing, and the images implied another. Morality was upheld for the masses even as the wildest fantasies were unleashed for the more discerning Garbo-watchers. From moment to moment, in even the quietest and most uneventful scenes, she cast her spell of contemplative passion, a spell beyond synopsizing. But would it outlast the screeching of the soundtrack? This was the fearful question confronting Garbo and MGM in 1930. As one of the last hold-outs—only Chaplin was more adamant—Garbo had already witnessed the disintegration of silent careers before the merciless microphone. John Gilbert, her co-star and erstwhile flame, became a cautionary legend in his own right with his high-pitched "I love you, I love you, I love you, I love you" in *His Glorious Night* (1929), a disaster parodied a generation later by Gene Kelly in Comden and Green's movie-within-a-movie sequence in *Singin' in the Rain* (1952).

Garbo was somewhat more fortunate in her first spoken lines from *Anna Christie* (1930): "Gimme a visky. Ginger ale on the side." As the waiter goes to fetch her drink, she turns her head to call after him, "And don' be stingy, ba-bee." Garbo, as we all know, had crossed the sound barrier in triumph. Her husky contralto voice seemed almost miraculously appropriate for what was now more widely perceived as the androgynous majesty of her beauty. Her voice was clearly more commanding than Gilbert's, and her continuing rise only emphasized his precipitous decline.

Yet more than voices were involved in the contrasting fortunes of Garbo and Gilbert. Thalberg and Mayer had played it safe, they thought, by casting Garbo in a venerable stage and screen property from the pen of Eugene O'Neill, but, more important, a tried and true vehicle, first for Pauline Lord on the stage, and then for Blanche Sweet in a 1923 film. And besides, Garbo was Swedish to begin with, and sentimental hookers were her specialty. Yet, how fitting that Garbo's first talkie, and her first film to be released after the Crash, should be set in the grubby barroom, dockside, and tugboat of a port city's lower depths. And that her first costume in the sound era should be so much shabbier than anything she ever wore in the silent era.

After *Anna Christie*, Garbo would spend much of the rest of her career—thirteen films in eleven years—in period costumes or chic contemporary outfits. But for that pivotal moment in film history represented by *Anna Christie*, Garbo sank low enough in social status to rise in public esteem. Garbo's Anna rose as well from the bedraggled bravado of her lurid entrance to the redemptive romance with Charles Bickford's brawling knight of the open road and the purifying sea. Now provocatively respectable in a warm sweater that may have inspired Hemingway's aforementioned tribute in *For Whom the Bell Tolls*, Garbo gave audiences a fair share of that sublime stillness that was supposed to have gone out with the onset of squawky talkies. Some critics of the period complained that Garbo came off second best in her boozy dialogue exchanges with practiced scene-stealer Marie Dressler, and it can be argued as well that Clarence Brown's direction was awkward and inappropriate next to Jacques Feyder's more impressionistic and fluid treatment in the simultaneously made-in-Metro German-language version, with Garbo's whore changed from early Stella Dallas to vintage Sternberg-Dietrich gleaming black satin. The Feyder version survives to this day as a stylistic oddity commemorating Hollywood's desperate effort to retain foreign markets in an age moving inexorably toward linguistic nationalism on the screen.

In America, however, the public perception of Garbo in her perky cloche hat and provocatively tattered blouse was that of a tough-minded dame down on her luck. *Anna Christie*, quite by accident, had reintegrated the torrential temptress of the twenties with the social reality of the thirties. The mythic spell of Garbo was thus not shattered by the mandatory realism of the early talkies. At a time when many foreign-born stars, better seen than heard, were being driven out of Hollywood careers with one-way tickets back to Europe, Garbo was being granted her citizenship papers on the soundtrack. Her resurgence was a particularly significant example of MGM's extraordinary luck in this difficult period, particularly vis-à-vis Paramount with its arty German UFA connections.

Garbo's actual performance in *Anna Christie* is more problematic in retrospect than it seemed at the time. The banal attitudinizing of the O'Neill dialogue is as much an affront to the contemporary ear as the studio-enclosed literalness of Clarence Brown's direction is to the contemporary eye. Also, only the most sophisticated film historians can make allowances for the static-stutter impression made by most early talkies. Still, the Feyder follow-up is much smoother than the Brown original. Garbo herself much preferred the German-spoken spin-off, and, indeed, Garbo's two contrasting Anna Christies offer a vivid expression of the gap she felt between her largely unfulfilled European aspirations, and her largely frustrating Hollywood experiences.

Garbo was nominated for Best Actress in 1930 for her portrayals in both *Anna Christie* and a more typical vehicle fittingly enough entitled *Romance*, in which, as an opera diva, Garbo taunted the supposedly traumatic soundtrack with a surprisingly expert Italian accent. Her "singing" voice, however, was dubbed by a trivia-question soprano named Diana Gaylen. Her moodily wooden leading man (Gavin Gordon) was, unfortunately, her weakest yet, and her over-spiritualized "motivation" weaker still. The plot, a creaky stage contrivance for Doris Keane, was one of the most turgid with which Garbo had ever been afflicted. Lewis Stone was on hand once more as her familiarly avuncular patron, but then Garbo pictures were never designed to launch co-starring "teams" of loving equals.

Nonetheless, things began looking up with respect to leading men in her two 1931 features: *Inspiration* and *Susan Lenox—Her Fall and Rise*.

Robert Montgomery in the former and Clark Gable in the latter were far from their stellar peaks, but they do make interesting iconography in retrospect. As was his wont, Clarence Brown short-changed Garbo visually in *Inspiration* at every opportunity all the way to a ridiculously silly last shot focused on Montgomery sleeping soundly in a chair while the unseen Garbo walks into the snowy street and out of his life forever. One would have wished instead for a glimpse of Garbo's face shrouded in the white mists. Ironically, Garbo always considered Brown to be her most devoted as well as her most frequent director, so much so, in fact, that she used the pseudonymous "Harriet Brown" when she wished to travel incognito.

Although *Inspiration* does provide a few behavioral graces in the delicate courtship of Montgomery's repressed junior diplomat and Garbo's world-weary demi-mondaine, there is, finally, a purplish pomposity in the awkward display of papier-mâché Parisian naughtiness amid Production Code no-nos. Garbo's tainted heroine resigns herself with an unreadable wistfulness as a sacrificial lamb on the altar of callow male careerism. Her performance is today merely of marginal interest as a tentative rehearsal for *Camille*.

By contrast, *Susan Lenox—Her Fall and Rise* is the closest thing in Garbo's oeuvre to an out-and-out fun movie, exhilarating even in its badness. Never again was Garbo to encounter a leading man like Clark Gable, who was already embarked on a flight to superstardom. Director Robert Z. Leonard, husband of the immortal Laurette Taylor, and an old warhorse of a silent director, handled the novelettish material extended to epic with the Expressionist éclat of the old "photoplays." The shadowy saga of a woman from birth in rural poverty to romantically redemptive maturity in cosmopolitan splendor bounces off salaciousness and squalor with zestful abandon. Even as Garbo is sinking so low as to dance in a bordello's chorus line, she projects a glamorous destiny. Garbo and Dietrich, the designated femmes fatales of MGM and Paramount respectively, were on the same career track as they confronted penny-dreadful visions of poverty-driven depravity. There was more complicity and humor in the Dietrich-Sternberg equivalents of *Susan Lenox*, but Garbo remained more popular than Dietrich by standing above the fray while playing (in the words of Molly Haskell) "the whore you could bring home to mother."

Garbo appeared in three movies in 1932—*Mata Hari, Grand Hotel, As You Desire Me*—and proceeded to astound Hollywood by blithely returning home to Sweden without renewing her contract with the studio. She did not make any scenes or throw tantrums. She simply vanished with all the exquisite economy of her acting persona. Her imperious silence on her motives constituted not so much a rebellion as an abdication. She could have claimed that she was being overworked inasmuch as she had played leads in eighteen films and a cameo in a nineteenth through the seven years of her first two contracts. After she returned from Sweden, she was to make but seven more movies over the last nine years of her career. The slower pace was not invariably more fruitful, but her three most memorable performances occur in this second phase of her reign at MGM.

Curiously her popularity did not soar with her prestige. As she made fewer and fewer fun-and-junk flicks like *Mata Hari* (1931), she became more and more a specialized taste. The ill-fated Dutch-born spy for Germany in World War I was executed by an Allied firing squad in 1917. (Mata Hari's real name happened to be Gertrude Margarete Zella McLeod.) Garbo's treatment of this lurid character ran the gamut of vice and virtue, raciness and repentance. She writhed and wriggled like a hootchy-kootchy dancer on a midway, and then expressed with a marvelous smile the most world-weary compassion toward her potential conquests. In even this role, her most fleshy, she projected a transcendent spirit of civilized amusement.

No other Garbo vehicle presents so great a disparity between the narrative's text and the star's sub-text. The result is often comically campy as when, as Kenneth Tynan has observed, Garbo manages to keep a straight tabula rasa face when Lewis Stone solemnly informs her that the British have developed a new weapon: The Tank. Another example is the dyspeptic vexation that passes across her face when Ramon Novarro presumes to cherish a candle-lit icon of his mother. Not a big challenge, perhaps, for a great actress, but it remains an amusing reminder of her earlier days as a treacherous charmer.

Grand Hotel (1932), based on the novel and play of Vicki Baum and directed by the amiably eclectic Edmund Goulding, was designed to exploit the MGM star roster. The refreshingly raw frankness of the early thirties is evident even in deluxe productions like this Oscar-winner. Under all the glitz and glitter is the grit and grime of Depression-era desperation. The urgent need for money drives the plot on its preordained tragicomic path. John Barrymore here and Charles Boyer five years later in *Conquest* (1937) were the only Garbo leading men who ever matched her in courtly savoir-faire.

Garbo acted her brief two-scene part as if it were a continuous dance. The effect of such a degree of stylized movement has struck some critics as unduly affected. Yet this is the one movie that seemed to represent for the public her innermost depths, much as they may have been, with the much misquoted tag-line: "I just want to be left alone." As the fading ballerina reborn in her great love for a redeemed jewel thief, Garbo seemed to float in a different sphere from her more prosaic co-stars—Joan Crawford, Wallace Beery, Lionel Barrymore, Lewis Stone. Indeed, Crawford's raw anguish seemed almost a demotic reproof to Garbo's aristocratic aloofness. The ages belonged to Garbo, but the times seemed closer to Crawford.

One would think that Garbo was moving upward as far as literary source material was concerned from Vicki Baum's catchpenny *Grand Hotel* (1932) to Luigi Pirandello's modernist dramatic lit *As You Desire Me* (1932). Actually, the opposite is true. *Grand Hotel* was at least an understandable Oscar-winner, whereas *As You Desire Me* was a complete botch, both as entertainment and as edification. Garbo does provide a striking parody of Dietrich at the outset with the aid of a platinum wig. Unfortunately the stodgy direction of George Fitzmaurice, the archaic villainies of Erich von Stroheim as the heroine's would-be Svengali, and the feeble theatrics of a still-aspiring Melvyn Douglas as her long-lost husband make a shambles of Pirandello's painfully playful ambiguities. Still, there are two or three Garbo line-readings that reveal a sensibility capable of more formidable cultural challenges. Can one ever forget the exquisitely precise timing and intonation of Garbo's response to a foppish admirer's request, "Get rid of these other fools." "Other?" Garbo replies with sweetly scathing wonder.

■　■　■　■

DURING AN IMPULSIVE VISIT to her homeland Garbo read a biography of Queen Christina, a seventeenth-century Swedish monarch with transvestite tendencies. The book had been recommended as desirable movie material by her friend and confidante, Salka Viertel, who had written a treatment with Margaret Levin. The finished screenplay, with dialogue by the prestigious American playwright S. N. Behrman, so impressed Garbo that she made it a condition of her new contract with MGM that she play Christina on the screen. A second condition was that henceforth she would not make more than two pictures a year, at $250,000 apiece. The studio assembly line for Garbo vehicles was thus dismantled by imperial decree from Sweden. Beginning with *Queen Christina* (1933) each new Garbo appearance on the screen was treated as a command performance.

The casting of John Gilbert as her ill-fated lover added to the enterprise a Pirandellian dimension that remains morbidly fascinating to this day. Whatever her motives, Garbo's generosity to Gilbert failed to arrest his decline at the studio and with the public. Even the billing, with Garbo above the title and Gilbert below, provided a cruel reminder of their reversed positions since their first appearance together on the screen in *The Flesh and the Devil* (1927) only a half-dozen years before.

To make matters worse, the studio cast as Gilbert's villainous rival an actor (Ian Keith) who resembled Gilbert in long shot, and who read his lines with slightly more competence. This disastrously misplaced doppelganger effect lends credence to the revisionist theory that L. B. Mayer was out to avenge himself on Gilbert for very personal reasons. For his part, director Rouben Mamoulian was so enraptured with Garbo that he made little effort to guide Gilbert's performance. Hence Gilbert's ludicrous double-take at his discovery that Garbo's Christina in male garb is not a young man could and should have been modulated by a director of Mamoulian's sensitivity. Instead, this noted stylist poured all his creative energy into the staging and lighting of Garbo's spectacular set-pieces—her deliciously androgynous flirtation with a barmaid, her fingertip remembrance trip around the furnishings of a loved-in bed-chamber, her renunciation scene, and, above all, her definitively enigmatic expression on her final close-up.

When asked in 1986 what he had told Garbo to think of when she was staring into the camera, Mamoulian replied:

> Ah, that is precisely the question she asked me: "What do I express in this last shot?" My answer was: "Nothing; absolutely nothing. You must make your mind and heart a complete blank. Make your face into a mask; do not even blink your eyes while the camera is on you." You see, with a tragic ending like this, no matter what feelings are portrayed by the actress, and these could range from hysterical sobs to a smile, some of the audience would disagree, find them wrong. This was one of those marvelous spots where a film could turn every spectator into a creator. If the face is blank, just like John Locke's *Tabula Rasa*, then every member of the audience will inevitably write in his own emotions. Thus, the "expression" would be true for every spectator because it is created by him. Incidentally, some of the scenes were shot to a metronome—to achieve a rhythmic

quality akin to a dance. You may recall the scene of Miss Garbo saying goodbye to her room at the inn—that was a graphic poem.

From the majestic peaks of *Queen Christina*, Garbo descended to the domestic plateau of *The Painted Veil* (1934) with perhaps her most plebeian role this side of Anna Christie. Despite its exotic title and white-man's-burden-in-the-Far-East theme, this adaptation of Somerset Maugham's novel, by John Meehan, Salka Viertel, and Edith Fitzgerald, directed by Richard Boleslavsky, a Russian émigré from Stanislavski's Moscow Arts Theatre, remains becalmed in the realm of the ordinary. For once, Garbo plays a down-to-earth phlegmatic woman very much like her "real" self. With no complexes or neurotic needs, she drifts into a dull marriage with an absent-minded scientist (Herbert Marshall) and, as she is neglected, drifts passively into an affair with an aggressive suitor (George Brent). Herbert Marshall, somewhat typed as the eternal husband, was described by the London critic C. L. Lejeune as a man who was always taking his coat off in the hall while his wife was concluding her big scene with the lover in the parlor. For his part, George Brent gradually dwindled from lover to husband in generally thankless leading man roles in Bette Davis vehicles.

For her part, Garbo seemed at ease with a part that called for an uncomplicated goodness and a spirit of self-sacrifice that stopped well short of disgrace and death. *The Painted Veil* verges on the ridiculous when Marshall fails to notice Garbo's presence as a nurse in a hospital full of cholera victims. How can any mere mortal not notice *that* face even in the most unlikely context? But the face itself is not without a trace of ironic self-mockery as it generously humbles itself for the sake of conventional morality and the period's unquestioning sexism.

Through the thirties there was an undercurrent of murmurings from theater people that Garbo for all her beauty was not as resourceful an actress as their own deities. *Anna Karenina* was Garbo's twenty-third film and a remake of *Love*, in which her Anna ends up happily with John Gilbert's Vronsky after her husband (Brandon Hurst) conveniently dies. It was not quite Tolstoy, but it was vintage MGM. Back in 1938, Mary Cass Canfield wrote a "Letter to Garbo" in *Theatre Arts Monthly* after the release of *Grand Hotel*, comparing her unfavorably with Eugenie Leontovich, who had played Grusinsaya with what was described as "Slavic" emotionalism. Garbo was clearly no Slav. And by the time of *Anna Karenina* she was compared by a later *Theatre Arts Monthly* critic unfavorably with stage-trained Basil Rathbone in his talkie version of Karenin. In *Theatre Arts Monthly* of course, the camera counted for little.

But it was no accident that Garbo's severest critics chose this occasion to descend on her en masse. Despite the impeccable screenwriting credentials of Clemence Dane, Salka Viertel, and S. N. Behrman, this treatment of Tolstoy's novel was at once superficial and turgid. Fredric March's Vronsky was more profile than passion, while Basil Rathbone's offended husband was effectively and appropriately supercilious. Clarence Brown's direction was eclectic to a fault, beginning with a pseudo-Sternbergian tracking shot across a long table of feasting and carousing Russian cavalrymen. This lustiness quickly gave way to the slowly paced gentility of MGM storytelling. Curiously, Garbo's supposedly favorite director once again missed all sorts of opportunities to let Garbo carry the otherwise ponderous spectacle on to a more lyrical plane. Instead, the director kept cutting to peripheral characters for needless reactions and banal exposition.

The first ballroom dance of Vronsky and Anna would have inspired Max Ophüls to follow the lovers round and round their enclosed cosmos, letting the rest of the world fly by. By contrast, Brown spends almost as much time on Reginald Owen's dancing with his harridan of a wife as on Garbo and March. Rumor had it that March, a notorious womanizer on the set, and Garbo, almost pathologically shy in her private life, did not hit it off in the love scenes, and the lack of chemistry shows on the screen.

There was also a smothering puritanism hovering over the production, particularly since a child (Freddie Bartholomew) was involved. Hence, the greater sympathy for the deceived husband than in the version made in the Roaring Twenties in the heyday of the New Woman. The thirties Anna thus had to pay for her infidelity not only to be faithful to Tolstoy but also to satisfy the strictures of the Hays Office. Garbo somehow transcended the transformation of a great novel into a tedious novelette by making the sum of her great moments add up to more than the dramatic whole. Among her scattered coups of exquisite expressiveness were remarkably maternal glances at her child, her delicate shadings of guilt and shame, and her sudden shift at the climax from reckless passion to suicidal fatalism. The New York Film Critics Circle, founded that very year to challenge the Hollywood Oscars, demonstrated their independence by honoring Garbo with the first of two acting awards, the equivalents of which she was never to receive from her "peers" in the Motion Picture Academy of Arts and Sciences.

Clarence Brown, the genially modest director of *Anna Karenina*, conceded in an interview given in Paris in 1961 that George Cukor had gotten more out of Garbo in *Camille* (1937) than he (Brown) ever could have. But, Brown added, Cukor did not really know much about making movies. The implication was that one had to choose between making good pictures or getting great performances. Whatever the merits of this dubious distinction, *Camille* is for Garbo's most discerning admirers her most accomplished portrayal. Indeed, her erstwhile theatrical detractors were compelled to admit that Garbo's might be the most incandescent Lady of the Camellias in any medium.

Charles Jackson's alcoholic Don Birnam is particularly eloquent on the matter in *The Lost Weekend*:

> On the mantel over the bar, tilted against the mirror, was a yellow card advertising the double-feature at the Select next door. Greta Garbo in *Camille*, and some other movie. It was like a summons, for God's sake. He had seen the picture three times during the week it opened on Broadway, a month or so ago. All of a sudden (but no, it was too early, it would have to wait) he had to see again that strange fabled face, hear the voice that sent shivers down his spine when it uttered even the inconsequential little sentence (the finger-tips suddenly raised to the mouth as if to cover the rueful smile): "It's my birthday." Or the rapid impatient way, half-defiant, half-regretful, it ran off the words about money: "And I've never been very particular where it came from, as you very well know." And oh the scene where the Baron was leaving for Russia—how she said "Goodbye . . . goodbye." ("Come with me!" The shake of the head and the smile, then; and the answer: "But Russia is so co-o-old—you wouldn't want me to get ill again, would you," not meaning this was the reason she couldn't go, not even pretending to mean it.) He knew the performance by heart, as one knows a loved piece of music: every inflexion, every stress and emphasis, every faultless phrase, every small revelation of satisfying but provocative beauty. There was a way to spend the afternoon!—the bartender slid the bottle across the counter and this time he poured the drink himself.

MGM's story department had outdone itself this time in recruiting Zoë Akins, Frances Marion, and James Hilton to pump screen life into that old stage chestnut, *La Dame aux Camélias* by Alexandre Dumas. Cukor's main contribution was not in getting something out of Garbo that wasn't there, but in allowing her to lighten her tone in pleasing contrast to the solemn melodramatics swirling around her. From her first smiling entrance in a carriage, Camille is every inch the playful courtesan whose heart is yet to be broken. Cukor's touch is not uniformly light with all the members of the ensemble. Laura Hope Crews and Leonore Ulrich as the most prominent other members of Marguerite Gautier's merrily mercenary demi-monde, are not, to say the least, notably restrained. Robert Taylor is inoffensively inexpressive as Armand, though his delicate male beauty suggests an adequately vulnerable innocence for a part that is difficult to cast with a good actor. Lionel Barrymore, unfortunately, defies direction with his ritualized scene-chewing. Only Henry Daniell as the sardonic Baron comes close to matching Garbo's supple bravura. And a very discreetly graceful portrayal of a covertly gay bon-vivant is provided by Rex O'Malley.

Cukor captured the essence of the collaborative process in working with Garbo in a 1964 interview with Richard Overstreet in *Film Culture*:

> It is hard to talk about Garbo, really, for she says everything when she appears on the screen. That is GARBO . . . and all you can say is just so much chit-chat. There she is on the screen. How she achieves these effects may or may not be interesting. She is what she is; and that is a very creative actress who *thinks* about things a great deal and has a very personal way of acting. You have to give her her head—let her do what she feels. If you remember in *Camille* when the father comes in to tell her to leave his son, she falls to the ground and puts her hand on the table. That's a very original thing to do. One must let her do these things and they happen marvelously.
>
> Also, do you remember in *Camille* when the man made her pick up her fan—he just stood there, the Baron de Varville. When she reached down she did the most unforgettable thing. Sweeping down, like a dancer . . . Isadora Duncan . . . she swept it up—the whole motion was done without bending her knees. She doesn't move like a ballerina acting—but like an actress acting. It is not dance but acting. This is an important point. She moves like an actress.

Garbo's incandescent Camille did not keep her off Harry Brandt's "Box-Office-Poison" list along with such other "flops" as Fred Astaire, Katharine Hepburn, Marlene Dietrich, and Joan Crawford. She was again nominated for an Academy Award after winning the New York Film Critics citation, but she lost the Oscar to Luise Rainer, who won her second in a row, this time in *The Good Earth* as a farmer's wife who barely speaks throughout the film. This comparative muteness was reckoned as an astounding tour de force after her hysterically chattering telephone scene in *The Great Ziegfeld* the year before. In an era of notorious studio block voting, MGM can be said to have let Garbo down once more, perhaps as a conditioned reflex to her unyielding aloofness.

Subsequent critical opinion, however, has reduced Luise Rainer to a footnote in Greta Garbo's voluminous chapter.

Greta Garbo's next vehicle, *Marie Walewska* (1937), kept her in costume—Empire period, to be exact—as the Polish mistress of Charles Boyer's Napoleon. Based on the novel *Pani Walewska* by Waclaw Gasiorowski and a dramatization of that novel by Helen Jerome, the screenplay was credited to that impeccable trio, Samuel Hoffenstein, Salka Viertel, and S. N. Behrman. Clarence Brown was on hand again for the last time in the director's chair for a Garbo film, and the eminent German Expressionist Karl Freund took over the camera from the customary William Daniels. Charles Boyer was admirably cast as Napoleon, so much so, in fact, that he was credited with "stealing" the picture though heaven knows there was not all that much to steal.

Brown's direction was as obtuse as ever in shifting the focus of the film from Garbo's charismatic capacity to transfigure even Napoleonic megalomania to the silly sloganeering of Napoleon's professed aim to forge a "United States of Europe," perhaps more for American audiences than for his alleged contemporaries. Hence, Brown and Freund are adept at staging a ball from a stately distance so as to invest the meeting of Napoleon and Marie with a certain social gravity, but what is lacking are the insightful scenes in which historical figures step out of their cardboard coverings to breathe life into the past. Only the irresistible iconography of Boyer's intense gaze of conquest toward a woman, even more than toward a continent, and Garbo's redemptive acquiescence provide this otherwise uninspired production with spasms of romantic and erotic excitement.

Ernst Lubitsch has been credited with jesting that Greta Garbo and Gary Cooper were the same person. To prove his unlikely thesis, he asked the rhetorical question, "Have you ever seen them together?" Certainly not on film. Garbo was eternally MGM, and Gary Cooper was strictly Paramount, and later Warners. Garbo had admired Lubitsch as far back as *The Love Parade* (1929), and may have had some influence on his being chosen to direct *Ninotchka* (1939).

Herman G. Weinberg (in *The Lubitsch Touch*) gave more weight to studio power in assigning Lubitsch to *Ninotchka*:

Five cinema "chess moves" followed next, manipulated by the studio overlords, in which Lubitsch was removed from the direction of *The Women*, based on the Claire Booth Luce play, and George Cukor was removed from the direction of *Gone With the Wind*. Lubitsch was then assigned to a picture with Garbo, while Cukor took over *The Women*, and Victor Fleming replaced Cukor on *Gone With the Wind*.

Whatever the genesis of *Ninotchka*, its fruition crowned Garbo once and for all not merely as, in the drunken words of Melvyn Douglas's Leon, "Ninotchka the Great . . . Duchess of the People! . . . Grand Duchess of the People:" but also the Queen of Tragedy *and*, at long last, Comedy. With *Ninotchka* "GARBO LAUGHS" supplanted "GARBO TALKS" as the watchwords of discerning moviegoers. From the moment she steps off a train in her commissar's costume, Garbo's exquisite gravity of expression and the metronomic doomsday delivery of her lines are as profoundly hilarious as anything in the history of talking pictures.

Garbo was assisted in her endeavors not only by Ernst Lubitsch but by a trio of rollicking bolshie clowns—Sig Rumann, Felix Bressart, and Alexander Granach; by a capable leading man and comic foil, Melvyn Douglas; by an exquisitely polished Czarist rival in Ina Claire's Duchess Swana; and by a razor-sharp script provided by Charles Brackett, Billy Wilder, and Walter Reisch, from a story by Melchior Lengyel. Reviewers of the time debated solemnly whether the movie was harder on the Communists or the Capitalists, but there was little disagreement on the quicksilver brilliance of Garbo's portrayal of an icy ideologue melted by bourgeois affability.

Garbo herself ranked Lubitsch over even Cukor as her greatest director. John Bainbridge (in his *Garbo*) describes Lubitsch's unusual modus operandi with Garbo on the set of *Ninotchka*:

> In working with Garbo he was a paragon of gallantry, thoughtfulness and charm. Arriving on the set in the morning, he called at Garbo's dressing room and formally paid his respects. Then he removed his coat and worked in shirt sleeves the rest of the day. At five o'clock, when work was over, Lubitsch again put on his coat and called at the star's dressing room, where he bade her a courtly good evening. This daily routine, as far as anyone could remember, was unprecedented on a Hollywood stage.

Near the end of her career as at the beginning, Garbo projected all the elemental choices involved in being or becoming a normal woman. The first flutterings of desire, the perennial fears of betrayal, the shame, the guilt, the joy of forbidden loves. Curiously, she shied away from the roles in which she could have gained in reputation what she lost in control. She was reluctant to play even the very mild and thoroughly enchanting drunk scene in *Ninotchka*. She was never cast as a madwoman, or a problem alcoholic, or an addict of any kind. The studio may have been as hesitant as Garbo in exploring more morbid subjects in which their star would have to forgo dignity and decorum.

Fortunately, *Ninotchka* demonstrated that Garbo had the talent and instincts to play the most demanding roles of Chekhov, Ibsen, Shaw, Pirandello, and any other tragicomic dramatist in the modern repertory. The instant shift in her great drunk scene from light farce to light pathos without missing a beat of conviction is a moment of rare sublimity in American talking pictures.

After *Ninotchka* there was *Two-Faced Woman* (1941), a career-ending disaster of such proportions as virtually to cancel out George Cukor's exemplary direction of *Camille*. MGM, disappointed in the grosses for *Ninotchka*, and alarmed by the war's elimination of the European market, decided to "Americanize" Garbo in an excruciatingly witless farce. Garbo retired, never to return. She was repelled as much by the disrespect shown her at the studio as by the bizarre moral condemnation of a movie in which a wife pretends to be her own sister so as to win back her husband, played by Melvyn Douglas mostly in his pajamas, from the other woman, played by type-cast Constance Bennett, a sultry adulteress from an earlier era. Roland Young and Ruth Gordon looked on quizzically as Garbo went through her paces, which included a brand-new rumba called the "chica-choca," undoubtedly for the Latin-American market growing ever more important since the decline and fall of Nazi-Occupied Europe.

Two-Faced Woman had its New York premiere on December 31, 1941, less than a month after Pearl Harbor. *Time* dismissed the movie as "an absurd vehicle for Greta Garbo," "a trick played on a beautiful, shy, profoundly feminine actress," and concluded: "Its embarrassing effect is not unlike seeing Sarah Bernhardt swatted with a bladder. It is almost as shocking as seeing your mother drunk."

Garbo didn't need the money or the aggravation. Her return was frequently rumored after the war, and Max Ophüls actually prepared a color screen test for Garbo in France for a production of Balzac's *La Duchesse de Langeais* with James Mason. Unfortunately, the money was not forthcoming from Producer Walter Wanger, ruined by the commercial failure of the Rossellini-scandal-tainted *Joan of Arc* of Ingrid Bergman. Richard Corliss has quoted Orson Welles's lurid claim: "I once wrote a scenario for Chaplin and Garbo, *The Loves of D'Annunzio and Duse* . . . two crazy monsters, degenerate hyper-romanticism . . . a ridiculous and theatrical passion . . . but neither would do it."

At thirty-six Garbo joined the screen's immortals. Time has not withered nor custom staled her inimitable cinemagic. All but one of her MGM films survive as her artistic legacy and as one of the greatest glories of the studio system. It is more than a matter of eyes and cheekbones strategically arrayed for the conquest of the camera, but it is certainly that at least.

JAMES CAGNEY (1899–1986)

James Cagney seemed to have been amply honored in his own lifetime: an American Film Institute Lifetime Award in 1973, an Oscar for *Yankee Doodle Dandy* in 1942, the New York Film Critics Award for *Angels with Dirty Faces* in 1938 and *Yankee Doodle Dandy*, instant popular and critical recognition for *The Public Enemy* in 1931, praise for his versatility as an acting hoofer in *Footlight Parade* in 1933, acclaim for ending an era of gangsterdom in 1939 with *The Roaring Twenties* and for starting another in 1949 with *White Heat*, prominent mention in all the standard film history texts, an apotheosis as the Depression's Everyman in a 1975 compilation film entitled *Brother, Can You Spare a Dime?*, and innumerable tributes to his talent from critics and colleagues. Indeed, it would not be too hyperbolic to describe Cagney as one of the axioms of the talking pictures. His street-wise stutter step, his jabbing and bobbing and weaving, his belt-hitching bravado, his rapid-fire chatter in a gutter dialect made him a prime target for night-club impersonators, but, more important, a principal justification of the early sound films in terms of kinesis (feared lost with the silents) and realism (enhanced by the psychological particularization of silent archetypes through speech).

Cagney was the man in motion in a medium of movement, and he made dialogue seem as dynamic a component of film art as montage. To the socially conscious critics of the thirties he was an accredited emissary from the masses. The eminent documentarian John Grierson once warned Hollywood of Colmanizing the Cagneys. Elia Kazan, who played a sympathetic gangster patron to Cagney's blinded fighter in *City for Conquest* (1940), has credited Cagney with influencing the evolution of later rebel types such as John Garfield, Marlon Brando, and James Dean.

The Cagney legend, nonetheless, did not flourish with all the film enthusiasts writing during the actor's twilight years. Thus one can detect an aggrieved tone in both Patrick McGilligan's *Cagney: The Actor as*

Auteur and Cagney's own *Cagney by Cagney*. McGilligan's book, much the more reflective and instructive of the two, seeks to elevate Cagney to a pantheon hitherto reserved by cultist critics for a small number of directors.

Unfortunately, Cagney himself tends to denigrate movie directors in a very actorish manner. The only directors he admires—George Kelly and John Cromwell from the stage—are directors who can step in and play all the parts. To Walsh, William Wellman, Michael Curtiz, and even Howard Hawks and John Ford, the disgruntled Cagney gives barely passing grades. Yet when Cagney himself took to direction, the over-all results were dismal. One can agree with McGilligan and Cagney that there may have been too much emphasis in recent years on the director at the expense of the actor and the writer, but we have come too far to deny the existence of directorial style altogether. I should add, however, that I have disagreed with many of my auteurist colleagues in France, England, and America by not ranking Walsh as high as Ford and Hawks. It has always struck me as too much of a coincidence that Walsh's resurgence in the late thirties came with his shift from Fox to Warners. Yet, McGilligan and Cagney are, if anything, harder on Warners than they are on Walsh. And here we come to the crux of the complaint: James Cagney, contrary to popular and critical impressions, was never permitted to become the consummate artist he was capable of being. So it is not a question simply of shifting credit from one person to another, but rather of mourning all the magnificent films that were never made. Cagney: poet, painter, philosopher, gentleman farmer, good citizen, faithful husband, and dutiful father. And how do we remember him most vividly? As the sociopathic gangster in *The Public Enemy* (1931) and the psychopathic gangster in *White Heat* (1949). The myth somehow is not the full measure of the man, and yet the full measure of the man has not found its own myth. Whenever Cagney escaped from the penny-pinching tyranny of Warners to his own personal projects (*Great Guy* (1936), *Johnny Come Lately* (1943), William Saroyan's *The Time of Your Life*) (1948)), his career hit the skids. The gentle whimsicality he sought in his own, now seldom-seen productions never made much of an impression on the public. Their Jimmy came to life for them only when he resolved the complexities of existence with a sock on the jaw or a bullet to the belly.

Both McGilligan and Cagney bemoan the fact that Cagney was not given more opportunity to sing and dance. Who can say? Today's film historians tend to treasure the Hollywood musical both because it is a largely vanished species, and because its conventions have been transformed into pre-Brechtian metaphors. But most people at the time did not think that musicals were worthy projects for grown-up actors and actresses. The vogue even for Astaire-Rogers lasted less than five years.

Still, it is not surprising that Cagney considered *Yankee Doodle Dandy* (1942) to be his crowning achievement. Yet, how badly its frenzied flag-waving and family sentimentality have dated. At about the same time Humphrey Bogart was appearing in *The Maltese Falcon* (1941) and *Casablanca* (1943). Hence, it was Bogart and not Cagney who became the prevailing mythic manifestation of the forties on college campuses in the sixties and the seventies. Cagney made three very fleeting and not very flattering references to Bogart in his book, one to note that the Dead End Kids literally took off Bogie's pants, another to indicate Bogart's weary cynicism at Warners, and a third to implant an image in our minds of Bogart as a compulsive nose-picker. Cagney went so far as to print a poem he wrote on the subject: "In this silly town of ours,/ one sees odd primps and poses/ But movie stars in fancy cars/ Shouldn't pick their noses." Cagney actually sent this poem to Bogart, and never got an answer.

What must have been particularly galling to Cagney was that a more limited actor like Bogart had gained the ascendancy in movie mythology. Cagney and Bogart started out at about the same time in Hollywood, but whereas Bogart's career petered out by the mid-thirties, Cagney's skyrocketed. Through the late thirties Bogart was a fourth banana to the Warners gangster triumvirate of Cagney, Edward G. Robinson, and George Raft. Then in the forties, the Bogart persona began to relate to women in a moody, romantic, fatalistic manner. His face wreathed in cigarette smoke, his voice clouded by whiskey, his eyes gazing indifferently at the angel of death, Bogart represented the sit-and-suffer forties as eloquently as Cagney had represented the get-up-and-go thirties. Also, Bogart died with a gallantry befitting his myth. There is no escaping his haunting presence. Cagney lived on to ruminate and to reminisce and, above all, to regret. In the process he seemed to have become somewhat alienated from his own myth. I hope that young people will catch up on Cagney and that college film societies pick up on the Cagney persona, particularly in the run of happy-hustler movies between *The Public Enemy* and *Angels with Dirty Faces* (1938). It does seem a bit late, however, to cry over the spilt milk of the studio system. The rough-and-tumble of Hollywood moviemaking may have been incapable of giving us more of

Cagney's sensitive soul, but a more genteel process of art-filming might have given us much less of his fighting heart.

My own feelings about Cagney as an actor are complicated by the marginally misogynous tendencies in many of his characters. On the screen he was much more often mother-oriented than father-oriented, and his sexual aggressiveness seemed to spring from an overly indulgent maternal sanction. Although I have never acquired any of his street smarts or mimetic genius, I still feel stirring deep inside of me some of the Cagney persona's excessive devotion to mother and family and country at the expense of a modishly cool cosmopolitanism to which all urban types like me once aspired. Cagney was a very warm actor, one of the few who could make you cry. I am thinking particularly of the moment when he realizes that he has been jilted by Rita Hayworth in *The Strawberry Blonde* (1941), and, even more, the moment he "recognizes" Ann Sheridan through the haze of blindness in *City for Conquest* (1940). My heart goes out to him in these scenes not merely because of his histrionic virtuosity, but because he has fully earned the emotions involved by playing straight and innocent with his characters. Never has he camped up his dopes and stiffs. He was always much too close to them in spirit to condescend to them. Hence, he came to incarnate the consummate urban provincial, and he never cheated on his characters by feigning a pseudo-worldliness. Cagney on the screen reflected what many of us were, not necessarily what we wanted to be. He was too realistic a type to fulfill all our fantasy requirements. We admired him, but few of us wished to emulate him.

I am indebted to McGilligan also for explaining the mystery of Cagney's bizarre crew cut in *Jimmy the Gent* (1934), an otherwise routine romance with Bette Davis. Cagney simply defied Warners through his coiffure, and got away with it. That he was more his own man than most contract stars of his era was all to his credit. And his presence alone made even the flimsiest flicks worth seeing. His Bottom in *A Midsummer Night's Dream* (1935) was an honorable failure, and his weird sadist in *Shake Hands with the Devil* (1959) was a completely unmotivated oddity in his career. For that matter, the unrelenting one-liners in *Boy Meets Girl* (1938) and *One Two Three* (1961) were more frenzied than funny. Indeed, I once felt that Cagney's career was unusually spotty for a performer of his magnitude. His leading ladies were seldom anything to write home about, and his directors were more often than not studio artisans rather than full-fledged artists. The same can be said of Garbo.

My current attitude is, therefore, so what? We take grace and beauty where we find them, and stop speculating about what might have been. Ultimately, the greatest stars melt down the boundaries between movies so that they can dazzle us with the one continuous movie in our minds.

From Cagney's screen debut in 1930 to his "comeback" in 1981, his sixty-two movies reflected his robust personality. These testaments to his talents have survived the ravages of time to serve as guarantors of his immortality, and for this we must be grateful.

EDWARD G. ROBINSON (1893–1973)

Edward G. Robinson was the most deserving movie star who never was even nominated for an Oscar. But before we indulge in some facile Oscar-bashing, let's try to think of all the "great" Robinson performances, the ones that stand above the rest. There's the 1930 *Little Caesar*, of course, and the fast-talking Keyes in *Double Indemnity* (1944). But what else in a career that spanned fifty years and had close to ninety movies? His frog-like features never came into fashion for screen love-making, but there were other qualities that made him both likable and popular.

In the late 1930s a fan magazine polled its readers on the four reigning Warners tough guys: James Cagney was voted the toughest, Humphrey Bogart the meanest, George Raft the most sinister, and Edward G. Robinson the most lovable. Yet Robinson, unlike his three rivals, almost never got the girl when he had any kind of virile competition. Quite often, he couldn't even hold onto his wife or live-in girlfriend once a handsome stranger appeared on the screen. He and Charles Laughton were the screen's most spectacular cuckolds in the great tradition of Emil Jannings in *Variety* (1926) and *The Blue Angel* (1930) and Raimu in *The Baker's Wife* (1940). Both Robinson and Laughton appeared in loose remakes of *They Knew What They Wanted* (1940), in which the Italian immigrant characters they played took back wives who had been impregnated by younger, better-looking men. Both gargoyles also played meek, henpecked husbands who were capable of murder when their adulterous desires were threatened.

But Robinson's career was very different from Laughton's, with fewer highs and fewer lows. Through the thirties and forties, particularly, Robinson chugged along with consistency through a wide variety of genres.

He could be very funny by playing off the celebrated malignancy of his screen persona with wit and self-mockery. John Ford's *The Whole Town's Talking* (1935), with a clever script by Robert Riskin, a Capra collaborator at Columbia, gave Robinson a delicious opportunity with a dual role to destroy the Little Caesar side of him and reveal the civilized charm of the real Edward G. Robinson who collected and appreciated great works of art.

But the beauty of Robinson's career is that you can't go wrong with *any* of his movies. He is always *there*, a dynamic presence for whom the contemporary buzz-word "energy" would seem a redundancy. From his childhood in Romania, to his young manhood on the Lower East Side, up to his first histrionic efforts with the Elizabethan Society at City College and the American Academy of Dramatic Arts, Robinson probably never even considered the option of lethargy.

He appeared on the screen with contrasting acting disciplines as diverse as those of Ralph Richardson, Orson Welles, and the intuitively laconic Steve McQueen, and he held his own in each instance without disrupting his normal rhythms. Still, if one has never seen Edward G. Robinson, one could walk in on any of his movies and get the full flavor of the man and his art. When Warners launched its Great Men series, Paul Muni hid his *Scarface* (1932) persona behind a musty beard in *The Story of Louis Pasteur* (1936), but Robinson somehow remained Robinson as the scourge of syphilis in *Dr. Ehrlich's Magic Bullet* (1940). Many people still hold that against him. When John Huston encouraged Robinson to return to his "Little Caesar" mannerisms of seventeen years before for *Key Largo* (1948), Robinson dutifully complied, but his heart didn't seem to be in it anymore. His impersonation of himself was, for once, lethargic, but there was so much else he had done, some of it curiously forgotten. One might try *Five Star Final* (1931) and *Scarlet Street* (1945) and *Flesh and Fantasy* (1943) just for starters.

Certainly, Robinson intersected with a great many great people in a now fabulous period of film history. But was Robinson great himself? There are many moments here and there where I think he is, but there are many other times when his steely steadiness can become unnerving. He often gives you more than you need, but is that necessarily overacting? Or does he keep his motor running for that fantastic sequence in *Two Weeks in Another Town* (1962) when he tells a suicidally inclined Claire Trevor not to take another overdose of sleeping pills because they'd just have to pump her stomach out again, and she knows how *sick* that makes him? Even Olivier could not read that line with any darker humor or more malignant luminosity. There is the word "malignant" again. Could that be a clue to why Robinson never won an Oscar nomination? It would not be the first time Hollywood confused the singer with the song.

HUMPHREY BOGART (1899–1957)

Is it possible that Bogie became a cliché? There has to be some disorientation about a career that pertains less to the nineties than to the sixties, when he was first rediscovered on the campuses, and less to the fifties, when he did his last work, than to the formative thirties and to the forties when he hit his peak. We have also come a long way since the *hommage à Bogie* of Jean-Luc Godard and Jean-Paul Belmondo in *Breathless*. That was 1960. The Bogart still in *Breathless* comes from his last picture, *The Harder They Fall* (1957), one seldom, if ever, revived on campuses. But the French worship a myth all the way to the bitter end. Hence, André Bazin's eloquent eulogy to Bogart as an actor followed throughout his career by the angel of death. The French critics were painfully aware through the fifties that Bogie was literally dying of cancer, whiskey, and cigarettes right before their eyes. This gallant process of endurance lent poignancy and stature to his famous *films noirs* of the forties.

By contrast, Woody Allen's *Play It Again, Sam* (1972) exploits a more cheerful image of Bogart as a cool womanizer made to order for Allen's adolescent fantasies of getting laid. From Woody Allen it is only a short step to the ironic television commercials in which the Bogart imitators poke fun at a familiar voice afflicted by a frozen upper lip. The time has come to liberate Bogart from his legend. In that way we may even recall how the legend got started in the first place.

Bogart started very slowly in the thirties, so slowly, in fact, that he had to go back to Broadway to recharge his movie career. His first nine roles led him into virtual oblivion in Hollywood, and it would take a real trivia expert to evaluate his work in *Up the River* and *A Devil with Women* (1930), *Body and Soul, Bad Sister, Women of All Nations*, and *A Holy Terror* (all 1931), *Love Affair* and *Three on a Match* (1932), and *Midnight* (1934). In this period he played both nice guys and bad guys, but he had not yet established himself as a tough guy. Today, of course, his image jumps out at you no matter what he is doing. In the mid-thirties, however, he drifted from studio to studio as a nondescript leading-man type. Since he was already past thirty when he made his first movie, he could not linger long in the juvenile range.

His big break came on the stage as the fugitive gangster Duke Mantee in Robert Sherwood's *The Petrified Forest*. Even so, it was only the intervention of the play's star, Leslie Howard, that enabled Bogart to return triumphantly to the screen in 1936 with a made-to-order tough-guy persona. (In gratitude, Bogart later named one of his children Leslie.) The second phase of his movie career then began as a struggle, mostly at Warners, to attain full-fledged stardom. Unfortunately, Warners was the one studio that was overloaded with tough guys to whom Bogart played a perennial second fiddle. Edward G. Robinson called the tune in *Bullets or Ballots* (1936), *Kid Galahad* (1937), *The Amazing Dr. Clitterhouse* (1938), and *Brother Orchid* (1940). And James Cagney called the tune in *Angels with Dirty Faces* (1938), *The Oklahoma Kid* and *The Roaring Twenties* (1939). Even George Raft was top dog in *Invisible Stripes* (1939) and *They Drive by Night* (1940).

More often than not, the supporting characters Bogart played were dead of gunshot wounds before the last reel. Bogart himself is said to have observed that his frequent death scenes kept his career alive into the forties. Robinson and Cagney were not averse to getting knocked off spectacularly either, but they had made their dead-end presence felt back in the early thirties (in *Little Caesar* and *The Public Enemy*) when Bogart was struggling to find an identity on screen. Discerning critics like Otis Ferguson had already begun to appreciate the subtle villainies of Bogart, who somehow never drifted into the Warners stock company of second-string mobsters. Bogart could be mean in *Bullets or Ballots* (1936) and *Kid Galahad* (1937), cowardly in *Angels with Dirty Faces* (1938) and *The Roaring Twenties* (1939), or cheerfully fatalistic in *Invisible Stripes* (1939). Yet, somehow there was always an undertone of irony in even his most conventional assignments. It is almost as if he were quietly amused at the low-life spectacle he was making of himself. Bogart, unlike Cagney, was never directly wired to the streets; he was more the loner, the aloof non-conformist.

My own most vivid early impression of Bogart came from his oily, pain-ridden, baby-faced gangster portrayal in *Dead End* (1938). I was only about nine at the time, but I found something so sneaky and malignant in Bogart's personality that I was not able to respond to him for years after. Hence, I missed most of his great forties performances, and, when a girl on whom I had a crush in high school declared her own crush for Bogart, I was frankly mystified. How could anyone love a man who had been so scarred by suffering that he became inordinately bitter and suspicious? I was brought up on the traditional view that the most beautiful people were those unmarked by life. Obviously, I had a lot to learn and unlearn. Still, I have put it to my students on more than one occasion that there would never have been a Bogart cult if he had made his last film in 1940; though his talent was impressive through the thirties, his type remained disquieting.

For one thing, he never got the girl in any way that counted mythically. In addition to *Bad Sister* in 1931, four thirties films featured both Bogart and Bette Davis: *The Petrified Forest* (1936), *Marked Woman* and *Kid Galahad* (1937), and *Dark Victory* (1939). Yet, they never really appeared opposite each other. Perhaps the chemistry would not have been there if they had. Their careers were to blossom separately in any event as they eventually became too big for each other. What they *did* have in common along with Cagney was a rebellious attitude toward Warners, certainly one of the least refined of all the studios, and one of the most raucous. One can make a case for both sides in the dispute. If Warners provided opportunities for Bogart's career in *The Amazing Dr. Clitterhouse*, and *Angels with Dirty Faces* (1938), *The Roaring Twenties* (1939), and *They Drive by Night* (1940), the studio also provided obstacles with such clinkers as *Men Are Such Fools* (1938), *The Oklahoma Kid*, and *The Return of Dr. X* (1939). Even his two films on loan-out to United Artists in this period split down the middle, with *Dead End* (1937) giving him a lift, and *Stand-In* (1937) proving to be a real dead end. Indeed, Bogart's role in *Stand-In* as a neurotic film director with a pet Pekinese always in his arms competes for camp honors with his western badman in *The Oklahoma Kid*, his imitation-Karloff ghoul in *The Return of Dr. X*, and his D. H. Lawrence, Irish-brogued horse-trainer in *Dark Victory*.

Then in 1941 Bogart vaulted into movie mythology with two great incarnations; one outdoors as Roy Earle in Raoul Walsh's *High Sierra* (1941), and one indoors in John Huston's *The Maltese Falcon* (1941). *High Sierra* gave Bogart more emotional depth and scope than he had ever been able to display before, and *The Maltese Falcon* provided him with a wit and an irony that had previously been more implied than expressed. Most important of all, Roy Earle and Sam Spade placed Bogart at the vital center of first-rate scenarios. No longer was he the peripheral punk, albeit with a touch of class. Nor was he the second-string lead. Suddenly he was the big noise, the brooding, sardonic protagonist.

When he talked, people listened. When he listened, people chose their words with care. And through all the violent action Bogart emerged as a curiously mature star. Now past forty, his face seemed to have weathered all his career non-happenings in the thirties. But from the audience's historical perspective it was a face that had survived the Great Depression with enough strength to meet the challenge of World War II.

High Sierra and *The Maltese Falcon* had made him a star; it remained for *Casablanca* (1943) to make him a legend. All three projects had started out as relatively routine projects, and all three ended up as classics. But for Bogart the role of Rick in *Casablanca* was the one indispensable catalyst in his career. Roy Earle, for all his vulnerability, was basically a hoodlum, and Sam Spade, for all his sophistication, was a jaded private eye. These characterizations, however romanticized, were still bounded by genre conventions from the thirties. Variants of Roy Earle had been done to death by Cagney, Robinson, and Muni, and *The Maltese Falcon* itself had been made into movies twice before. *Casablanca* launched Bogart into the forties, a period in which all his aggressions could be harnessed for the Allied cause.

And then there was the matter of sexual chemistry. Ida Lupino, the gang groupie in *High Sierra,* was clearly a diamond in the rough, but Roy Earle preferred to waste his emotional energy on Joan Leslie's dull, selfish waif with a Chaplinesque limp. As for Mary Astor's demi-mondaine in *The Maltese Falcon*, she was everything a grown-up man would desire, but Sam Spade invoked his code of honor to make her take the fall. In both films the women were too much on the shady side of the street ever to share a sunset with the man they loved. Lupino and Astor were classy dames, all right in their place, but not really the stuff that dreams are made on. Bogart had not yet met his here's-looking-at-you-kid sweetheart, who would break his heart, and change his type irrevocably from tough guy to great lover. *Casablanca* changed all that with a meeting made in Hollywood heaven: Humphrey Bogart and Ingrid Bergman, neither of whom had yet hit their stride, neither of whom ever took this ridiculously romantic melodrama seriously while they were making it. Indeed, much of the charm of *Casablanca* can be attributed to the intuitive grace of its throwaway performances.

Bogart had already joined the war effort in *Across the Pacific* (1942), John Huston's spin-off from *The Maltese Falcon. Casablanca* then completed the process of transforming cynicism into idealism as Rick stopped drowning his sorrows in drink long enough to join the Resistance. From 1942 through 1944 he kept up the struggle in *Action in the North At-*

lantic, Sahara, To Have and Have Not, and *Passage to Marseille*. Bogart became the thinking man's patriot: liberal, skeptical, sardonic, suspicious at first, but eventually heroic in the service of one unfashionable under-dog or another, black, Russian, refugee, colonial. The war had become Bogart's Petrified Forest, the hard edge from which he could not flinch on the screen.

Howard Hawks's *To Have and Have Not* (1945) introduced a some-what lighter note to the solemn proceedings by introducing Lauren Bacall with her growling sexual challenge to Bogart to whistle for her. Bogart and Bacall then perfected their mutual myth in Howard Hawks's *The Big Sleep* (1946), Delmer Daves's *Dark Passage* (1947), and John Hus-ton's *Key Largo* (1948). For a time Bacall rejuvenated Bogart as a ro-mantic lead. He was nearing fifty, a far more dangerous age for a star in that era than later. Huston had helped deglamourize and demystify him as a grizzled runt of a man in *The Treasure of Sierra Madre* and *The African Queen*, two showy performances for the actor, two costly reve-lations of the aging star in age-conscious Hollywood.

In the fifties, Bogart's most notable roles alternated between romantic despair (*In a Lonely Place*, 1950; *The Barefoot Contessa*, 1954) and scene-chewing villainy from his Duke Mantee days (*The Caine Mutiny*, 1954; *The Desperate Hours*, 1956). Yet, he could hold a good movie like *The Enforcer* (1951) together simply by playing a subdued straight man to a gallery of gangster grotesques. He even tried sixties camp at least a de-cade before its time in John Huston's and Truman Capote's *Beat the Devil* (1954). And he was making his share of bad movies all the way to the end. On balance, however, he managed to leave us a legacy of the spiritual ferment through which he and we lived.

If I had to choose one image by which to remember Bogart, it would be of that one mysterious moment in *The Big Sleep* (1946) when Bogart finds himself alone in a sinister room. The atmosphere drips with evil: the camera pauses at a contemplative distance. Bogart seems lost in thought as he looks for some invisible clue. But he is no merely deductive detective; he has staked his whole life on the solution to the mystery. He has thus brought to the screen his own very personal gravity. That is why he has proved to be irreplaceable in the decades since his death.

■   ■   ■   ■

HUMPHREY BOGART enjoyed one of his recurring resurrec-tions on big and small screens in 1997 with the New York release of an earlier version of Howard Hawks's 1946 classic mystery, *The Big*

Sleep. Bob Gitt, the preservation officer of the Film and Television Archive at the University of California at Los Angeles, a few years before had made this extraordinary archival find, containing eighteen minutes of hitherto unseen footage, and had provided a mini-documentary narrated by Mr. Gitt on the fascinating differences between the two versions.

Bogart may have been the most durable star personality ever to hit Hollywood. He belonged to many different people and to so many different generations that it would be presumptuous for one film historian even to attempt solving the mystery of Bogart's seemingly eternal charisma. All this lifelong Bogie-watcher can offer are some clues in the form of quirky notes.

My earliest childhood memory of Bogart dates back to the William Wyler–Sidney Kingsley–Lillian Hellman *Dead End* (1937), in which he played a gangster named Baby Face Martin who's undergone plastic surgery to escape the electric chair. He was not only bad, he was mean. Somehow I missed the later vehicles—*The Maltese Falcon* (1941), *High Sierra* (1941), and *Casablanca* (1942)—that transformed him in the forties into the matinee idol he had never been in the thirties.

Now that I have seen all but about a dozen of the eighty-one films in which he appeared, and read most of the literature on Bogart, Bacall, Hawks, Raymond Chandler, the Warners, and Hollywood history in general, I cannot think of another screen personality with so many highs and lows, and so much existential angst. Everything he was, managed to explode on the screen in one fable or another. The scar above his lip was a sign of painfully acquired maturity and richly earned cynicism.

For an action hero, he was a comparatively short man with a comparatively large head, which, also the case with Alan Ladd, enabled him to dominate his co-stars in two-shot close-ups. I happened to prefer the romantic Bogart of *The Big Sleep, In a Lonely Place* (1950), *Casablanca,* and *The Barefoot Contessa* (1954) to the realistic Bogart of *The Maltese Falcon, The Treasure of the Sierra Madre* (1948), and *The African Queen* (1951), which is to say I prefer Hawks to Huston, Chandler to Hammett, and redemption to derision.

I also much prefer the second version of *The Big Sleep* to the first, even though the whodunit aspects become cloudier. Not only is Ms. Bacall enhanced, but Martha Vickers is given an extra scene to display her sluttish wiles, and the now forgotten Peggy Knudsen is a marked improvement over the doll-faced Patricia Clarke in the small but crucial role of Mrs. Eddie Mars. In her tongue-in-cheek incarnation as the ul-

timate dame of a private eye's fantasy life, Dorothy Malone makes taking
off one's glasses and letting down one's hair one of the erotic epiphanies
of the American cinema instead of a hackneyed piece of business.

For people who had never seen *The Big Sleep*, which was, after all,
more than a half-century old, the archival discovery had all the great
scenes: Bogart's faithfully rendered Chandleresque conversation with
Charles Waldron's General Sternwood, every sequence with the ineffable
Elisha Cook, Jr., the confrontations with John Ridgely's Eddie Mars, the
gunplay with Bob Steele's vicious Canino, Bogie's gay masquerade in the
bogus bookshop with Sonia Darrin's Agnes, a hilariously hard-boiled moll
strictly out for a fast buck from whatever soft-headed sap she can en-
snare.

The big elisions from the first version involved Marlowe's close relations with a police buddy named Bernie (Regis Toomey) and a district
attorney named Wilde (Thomas Jackson). One effect of the cuts was to
make Bogart's Marlowe less the member of a law-abiding and law-
enforcing all-male community, and more an anarchic force on a chivalric
quest out to avenge the murders of two men he had come to admire.
Marlowe is more one of the boys in the first version, and more one for
the ladies in the second.

It's a pity that more of these miraculous discoveries of preserved studio
negatives have not materialized over the years to provide instruction on
the high level of craftsmanship in the process of re-editing and re-
shooting. Faced with orders from the front office to build up Bacall's
part, Hawks and his colleagues took great pains to avoid disrupting the
logic of the continuity, and not to jeopardize the over-all impact of the
narrative. *The Big Sleep* is socko in both versions, which provides another
reminder that all the agonizing about director's cuts and studio cuts has
to be kept in some perspective. A good film at the core cannot be entirely
ruined, and a bad film at the core cannot be entirely rescued.

As I read the background material on the two prints, it occurred to
me that the new version, the result of a great deal of work done in the
studio, might be considered anti-auteurist. Still, Hawks's assertion that
he wrote the racetrack-parlance dialogue for Bogart and Bacall in the
added restaurant scene remains unchallenged, confirming his claim that
he collaborated on the writing of every movie he directed. In fact, Sam
Goldwyn fired him from the set of *Come and Get It* (1936) when Hawks
admitted moonlighting as a writer on the script in addition to directing it.

Screenwriting, of course, involves more than dialogue. There is the storyboard level and the camera angle level as well. Also, *The Big Sleep* is now a certified success, and everyone wants to get credit. But what about the more numerous flops? Does the studio want credit for them, too? After all, the revisions in *The Big Sleep* were motivated by a desire to preserve Bacall's value to the studio after what was perceived as her "wooden" performance in Herman Shumlin's *Confidential Agent* (1945) opposite Charles Boyer. Could it be that it was Shumlin's direction that was wooden, despite the film's having been adapted from Graham Greene's novel by Robert Buckner with its antifascist message intact? But then New York's cognoscenti were shocked, shocked, that *Casablanca* won the Oscar for Best Picture of 1943 over the Shumlin-directed and Hammett-and-Hellman-written *Watch on the Rhine*.

One of Bogart's greatest charms is that he may have been the only actor in the world who could get away with lines like "Here's looking at you, kid," and, when he is holding the slain Ava Gardner's head on his lap in Joseph L. Mankiewicz's *The Barefoot Contessa*, "I can never remember the Spanish word for Cinderella," and the dialogue he recited as a tormented screenwriter to Gloria Grahame in Nicholas Ray's *In a Lonely Place* (1950), "I was born when I met you, I lived while you loved me, I died when you left me." The only comparable equivalent for anyone else is the Rhett Butler of Clark Gable telling the Scarlett O'Hara of Vivien Leigh, "I love you, Scarlett, I've always loved you." Only an actor so easily embarrassed by romanticism as Gable could bring so much emotional conviction to so simple a line. Similarly, only an actor with Bogart's terminal irreverence could break through banality to the other side of wild romanticism.

BETTE DAVIS (1909–1989)

Bette Davis acted in movies for nearly sixty years, ever since she made her Hollywood debut in *Bad Girl* (1931). There were many milestones along the way, most conspicuously her Academy Award–winning performances in *Dangerous* (1935) and *Jezebel* (1938), and her Oscar-nomination performances in *Dark Victory* (1939), *The Letter* (1940), and *All About Eve* (1950). Other notable portrayals are found in *The Private Lives of Elizabeth and Essex* (1939), *Deception* (1946), *Marked Woman* (1937), *The Corn Is Green* (1945), *Old Acquaintance* (1943), *The Petri-*

fied Forest (1936), *Of Human Bondage* (1934), *20,000 Years in Sing Sing* (1933), *The Sisters* (1938), *The Old Maid* (1939), *The Little Foxes* (1941), *Mr. Skeffington* (1944), *The Great Lie* (1941), and just about everything else she ever did, the point being that Miss Davis was never less than electric in anything she undertook.

It is impossible to sum up a career of this size, scope, and excellence with a few glib generalities, but we shall try. Most of the career stories told about her treat her as an ugly duckling who survived the coarse jests of Howard Hughes and Michael Curtiz on her lamentable lack of sex appeal. To overcome these taunts, the legend goes, she had to over-compensate for her lack of charm and glamour with hyperactive histrionics. In this context, the Davis caricature by night-club impersonators begins to take shape: the pop-eyes with the heavily mascaraed lashes, the highly bred crackling voice, the strutting, hip-heavy walk. The caricature becomes immortalized in Edward Albee's *Who's Afraid of Virginia Woolf?* when Uta Hagen mimics Bette Davis's Rosa Moline in King Vidor's *Beyond the Forest* (1949) with "What a dump," the three-word anthem of coarse arrivistes the world over. But there is something woefully incomplete about the caricature even when it is extended to encompass her bravura Margo Channing in Joseph L. Mankiewicz's *All About Eve* (1950), by far the best comedy vehicle with which she was ever blessedly endowed. All the emphasis is on her flamboyance, and it is significant that she won her two Oscars for this side of her talent, first as the Jeanne Eagels–type actress in *Dangerous*, and then for the impetuous pre-Scarlett Southern belle in *Jezebel*.

But there has been another and much subtler side of her mythic persona that has been neglected, the side on which the hysteria and the histrionics are bottled up beneath a repressive surface of calm and control. This is the side expressed with such eloquent understatement in *The Old Maid* (1939) and *The Letter* (1940) and *Now Voyager* (1942) and *Old Acquaintance* (1943) and *The Great Lie* (1941). The night club impersonators have fashioned the image of a high society tramp, a dame with delusions of grandeur, an uninhibited creature of unbridled impulses, a shopworn sadist putting on airs. Of course, the impersonators have no time to indicate the intelligence that gleams in her eyes even when they are glazed over with drink and debauchery. Nor do the impersonators come even close to suggesting the spiritual dimensions of the screen's ultimate spinster, the woman who freely chooses loneliness to compromise. And who but Bette Davis could have given history's greatest spinster, Elizabeth the Queen, that extra portion of majesty and poetry!

If I were to pick my favorite Bette Davis performance, it would have to be her Leslie Crosbie in William Wyler's *The Letter*, particularly her amazingly quiet, tense, sensitive scenes with James Stephenson's gently probing defense counsel, the scenes in which talk dribbles on and on until it is transmuted into the most ringing truth. There are also the sequences in which she does her needlework with such passionate devotion that we come to understand the many dimensions of quiet moments in the lives of all women.

This is not to say that her more outrageous roles are somehow lacking in substance and character. Whether she plays the vamp or the victim, a core of gallantry is to be found at the emotional center of her performance. Perhaps we somehow sense how much her own career has cost her. It has been said that she accepted subordinate roles in *Watch on the Rhine* (1943) and *The Man Who Came to Dinner* (1941) in order to make both the properties and their middle-aged stage leads (Paul Lukas and Monty Woolley) commercially feasible for the Brothers Warner. At times she was too eager to feign drabness in the name of "honest" acting. Still, one would never have prescribed frothy comedies for her. *The Bride Came C.O.D.* (1941) (opposite James Cagney) and *June Bride* (1948) (opposite Robert Montgomery) are more furious than funny. Even *All About Eve* (1950) requires the cutting edge of a career-ism run amok to make the comedy work. Dramaturgically there was never much margin for error in a Bette Davis film. There was little time for behavioral improvisation in the Leo McCarey manner. The moment Bette Davis appears on the screen there is an undercurrent of anxiety, her persona is projected not yearningly in the manner of the two Hepburns, but burningly in the manner of a woman who knows she has few options. Something has to Happen, and Quickly, for Bette Davis cannot sustain herself on complacency and self-satisfaction. She cannot play a waiting game; she must act for all she is worth, and she always did.

CARY GRANT (1904–1986)

There is little left to say in praise of Cary Grant after all the laudatory and somewhat repetitious tributes paid him at the time of his death in 1986. But perhaps I shall change the prescribed routine slightly by backing into my own tribute with a few footnotes.

1. Several obits referred to the "Oxford" accent Grant claimed to have

devised to conceal his lower-class Bristol origins. I am no 'enry 'iggins on the phonetic road from Bristol to Oxford, but I have known a few Oxonians, and none of them sounded remotely like Grant. For years, out of a mixture of carelessness and ignorance, I blithely assumed that Grant had impishly persisted tongue-in-cheek with a slight Cockney accent, and then Michael Caine came along, and I was rudely disabused of that assumption. When Jack Warner proposed to cast Cary Grant rather than the less "commercial" Rex Harrison for the movie version of *My Fair Lady*, Grant reportedly responded by saying that not only would he not play Henry Higgins on screen, but he would not even see the movie with anyone but Harrison in the role. He reportedly responded in similarly generous fashion when he was offered the Robert Preston part in the movie version of *The Music Man*. Curiously, his accent seemed too plebeian for the part in *My Fair Lady*, but yet too fancy for the Middle American milieu of *The Music Man*. From where then did his distinctive pronunciations come? A cheap acting school in London? Or merely from an inbred instinct to "pass" on both sides of the Atlantic without providing a specific address? Groundling Archie Leach of Bristol thus very slowly and very painfully transformed himself into Superstar Cary Grant, citizen of everywhere in general, and nowhere in particular. Still, when Grant starred with Ronald Colman in George Stevens's *Talk of the Town* (1942) it was Grant who sounded working-class American, and Colman who sounded Hollywood-British Raj.

2. Everyone seems to agree that Grant made more than token appearances in seventy-two films, not an inordinate number for an actor whose career spanned thirty-five years from *This is the Night* (1932), in which he lost his wife to the under-rated comic character actor Roland Young, to *Walk, Don't Run* (1966), in which he was considered too old to be in contention with the under-rated Jim Hutton for the affections of the under-rated Samantha Eggar. Actually, *Walk, Don't Run* was a remake of George Stevens's *The More the Merrier* (1943), with Grant in the Charles Coburn role of elderly godfather to the romance of Joel McCrea and Jean Arthur. And people wonder why the seemingly ageless Grant, who some wags had dubbed Dorian Grant, would choose to retire in a year when the opinion mongers were beginning to cater to the kiddie demographics!

3. Much Faustian nonsense has been written about the alleged "bargains" actors make with their careers. Even now Grant is being mildly derogated for not returning to the stage to play Hamlet and Lear, although his earliest catchpenny theatrical experience hardly constituted

an audition for the Old Vic. What people are really asking is why Grant wasn't Laurence Olivier. These same people blithely assume that the long memories they have of Olivier's charismatic turns in *Wuthering Heights* (1939) and *Rebecca* (1940) make it certain that he could have been as big a matinee idol as Cary Grant if he (Olivier) had been less pure of heart. We shall never know for sure, of course, but I strongly doubt it. In any event, an actor's career at even the highest levels is a very precarious mix of luck, timing, and talent, and very probably in that order. Cary Grant was in the right place at the right time in 1937, with a Depression-weary public in the mood for elegant escapism with just a touch of playful irreverence. He had the good fortune to find a remarkably gifted group of directors, most notable among them McCarey, Hawks, Hitchcock, and Cukor, who were able to give Grant enough time and space to fill the screen with an impressive range of idiosyncratic gestures and movements. From *The Awful Truth* in 1937 to *North by Northwest* in 1959, Grant induced in a whole generation of gently entranced moviegoers a perpetually induced smile of indulgent recognition and identification

4. When you come out of a bitterly envious and slanderous lower-middle-class milieu as I did, you receive from the local tavern-tabernacle two immutable articles of faith: (a) All Sporting Events Are Fixed, and (b) All Male Movie Stars Are Practicing Homosexuals. There have always been whispers about Grant's early relationship with his friend and co-tenant Randolph Scott, particularly in view of a highly publicized Hollywood costume party which Grant and Scott attended together in identical harlequin costumes. Grant's five marriages and one daughter? The tavern philosophers snicker at your pathetic innocence. Don't you know that all the most publicized Don Juans are merely trying to conceal their more shameful perversions? Unfortunately, the tavern know-it-alls are proven right just often enough to boast some shred of credibility.

With Grant the disparity between the public persona and the private personality was more difficult to define. There was a darker side to Grant even on the screen, most strikingly in the four films he made for Alfred Hitchcock—*Suspicion* (1941), *Notorious* (1946), *To Catch a Thief* (1955), and *North by Northwest* (1959). Grant, like Hitch, had a love-hate, attraction-repulsion relationship with women. Both men had very complex guilt feelings about their mothers, and both men were capable of displacing this guilt artistically with the blackest humor. Who can ever forget the morbidly hilarious crowded-elevator sequence in *North by Northwest*, the one in which Grant's mother (Jessie Royce Landis) laughs along with her son's would-be murderers much to the discomfiture of our terrified and unbelieving "hero"? It was this ineradicable feeling of emotional insecurity which enhanced his great dramatic moments on screen, as much as it probably accounted for his reportedly less-Cary-Grantish behavior off-screen. Without this darker side, the true greatness of Grant as an actor might be more difficult to demonstrate. It is what Ralph Richardson said of John Wayne: simply, that his face projected the mystery required of a great actor. Grant, like Wayne, invented a personality into which he grew until the Hollywood butterfly obliterated almost all vestiges of the Bristol lower-class caterpillar. Why should we now look to the dung-heap for the caterpillar's "real-life" essence instead of looking at all the flowers of artistry around which this colorful creature flew?

The NBC crew that came to record my reaction to Grant's death asked me if I had ever known the man. I said no very quickly. But having seen sixty-nine of his seventy-two movies, and having witnessed his marvelously gracious performances at several public occasions, can I be said to have "known" him less intimately than I would have if I had peppered him with journalistic queries at some marathon interview or other? Very probably, I "knew" much the best part of him, a part that I suspect he would have wanted me to know if he had had any inkling of how much I respected and admired all that he was, all that he had achieved, and all that he had overcome. Hence, instead of prying into the life of the allegedly "real life" Cary Grant (a.k.a. Archie Leach), I, for one, would prefer to salute the Jungian success story his life and career represent.

5. One final footnote. Grant's performance in Leo McCarey's *Once Upon a Honeymoon* (1942) is as much under-rated as his Ernie Mott in Clifford Odets's *None But the Lonely Heart* (1944) is over-rated. This foggy, pretentiously proletarian movie was dedicated to the Popular Front and middle-brow aesthetic principle that the poor never laugh.

MARGARET SULLAVAN (1911–1960)

Margaret Sullavan's performances became available in one medium or another during the seventies, and it become abundantly clear at least to me why she was such an instant success in John Stahl's *Only Yesterday* (1933), and why she remained a special attraction until the very end of her career. One may regret that she did not have more opportunities to display her deftness with comedy. Indeed, her humorous vehicles declined precipitiously from the William Wyler–Preston Sturges–Ferenc Molnar *The Good Fairy* in 1935 to William A. Seiter's *The Moon's Our Home* (despite some bright lines by Dorothy Parker and Alan Campbell) in 1936 and *Appointment for Love* in 1941. Ernst Lubitsch's *The Shop Around the Corner* (1940) (with Samson Raphaelson's brilliant adaptation of Nikolaus Laszlo's play) is, of course, a treasure trove of charm, but its wistful mood was second nature to Miss Sullavan. Most of her films were therefore located in the realm of sentiment, and sob-sister sentiment at that. This meant that in pre-feminist days her vehicles were denigrated even when her own performances were praised. Now that the so-called woman's picture has attained more cultural respectability, actresses like Margaret Sullavan can be treated with more seriousness.

Yet even by the critical standards of social significance many of her movies could not be dismissed as entirely escapist. Notable among these were *Little Man, What Now?* (1934) (unemployment), *Three Comrades* (1938) (postwar unrest), *The Mortal Storm* (1940) (Nazi tyranny), *And So Ends Our Night* (1941) (the refugee problem). Considering that Sullavan was never the darling of any major studio, gravitating from Universal (which went bankrupt in the mid-thirties) to Paramount to MGM to United Artists and then back to Universal and MGM and ending at Columbia, she managed to align herself with an above-average roster of directors. Frank Borzage (*Little Man, What Now?, Three Comrades, The Shining Hour* (1938), *The Mortal Storm* (1940)) provided heart to her career, Ernst Lubitsch (*The Shop Around the Corner*) wit, King Vidor (*So Red the Rose*, 1935) force, William Wyler (*The Good Fairy*, 1935) polish, and John Stahl (*Only Yesterday*, 1933) sincerity. These, the directors of no fewer than half of her vehicles, would be sufficient reason for Sullavan to be remembered affectionately and admiringly in film histories. Yet she has more than moments even with such middle-range directors as Robert Stevenson (*Black Street*, 1941), William A. Seiter (*The Moon's Our Home*, 1936, *Appointment for Love*, 1941), John Cromwell (*So Ends Our Night*, 1941), and Rudolph Maté (*No Sad Songs for Me*, 1950). She even glowed intermittently with such relatively weak directors as Edward H. Griffith (*Next Time We Love*, 1936), H. C. Potter (*The Shopworn Angel*, 1938), and Richard Thorpe (*Cry Havoc*, 1943).

To get some idea of Sullavan's original impact, one can turn to the string of bouquets penned by the usually cryptic and hard-headed Otis Ferguson. On *The Good Fairy*: "But Margaret Sullavan is, most of the time, entirely lovely, and if she isn't an actress I wouldn't know it; that is the way things are between Margaret Sullavan and me." On *The Shopworn Angel*: ". . . the girl was knowing and tired, pert with her small mouth, stem of a torso, and low, whispering voice, yet fresh with some wonder of dew still held in the inner leaves. . . ." On *The Shop Around the Corner* (1940): "Since Margaret Sullavan does something peculiarly basic to me—and I doubt if even the institution of marriage has ever scouted the male idea of some young-girl quality, rare and sweet—I would do well to get down to simple cases on the new picture she's in."

It is only because I happened to have seen Margaret Sullavan's poignantly bubbly performance in *The Voice of the Turtle* that I can bear witness to her stage magic. For many now alive and many more still unborn Sullavan's Broadway career must remain a subject of second-hand research. Maybe the floral doggerel entitled *So Red the Rose, However You Spell It* by Sullavan's contemporary, Ogden Nash, can impart some of the flavor of the stage phenomenon:

> Margaret Sullavan, Lovely Meg,
> Tell us the reason, pray,
> That you spell your name, O bewitching dame,
> Sullavan with an a.
> Do the Murphys fashion their tag with e,
> Or the Finnegans with a y?
> The way you spell could amaze John L.
> Margaret Sullavan, star alone,
> Spell it your own sweet way.
> The fairest of sights in twinkling lights
> Is Sullavan with an a.

Sullavan held her own with an impressive array of leading men, perhaps most congenially as well as most frequently with James Stewart (*Next Time We Love, The Shopworn Angel, The Mortal Storm, The Shop Around the Corner*), although her eye-to-eye rapport with Charles Boyer in *Back Street* and *Appointment for Love* runs a very close second to her passionate *pas de deux* with Stewart. Also very credible as consorts by any standard were Herbert Marshall (*The Good Fairy*) and Henry Fonda (*The Moon's Our Home*). On Maggie and Hank together Graham Greene rhapsodized: "It is to Miss Margaret Sullavan and Mr. Henry Fonda, as much as to anyone, that we owe the sense of something fresh and absurd and civilized, like a sixteenth-century epithalamion for a pair who will always be young and extravagant and at odds together in a Penshurst world."

Less fashionable but nonetheless felicitous were the softly forceful Douglass Montgomery in *Little Man, What Now?*, the lightly regarded but subtly resourceful Randolph Scott in *So Red the Rose*, the engagingly earnest Glenn Ford in *So Ends the Night*, and the deceptively quiet Wendell Corey in *No Sad Songs for Me*. Indeed, the only out-and-out clinkers among her co-stars were John Boles (*Only Yesterday*) and Robert Taylor (*Three Comrades*) during Taylor's long male ingenue apprenticeship at MGM. On Boles, Graham Greene was considerably less than rhapsodic: "I find Mr. Boles, his air of confident carnality, the lick of black shiny hair across the plump white waste of face, peculiarly unsympathetic."

For the attentive film scholar there is in Sullavan's sixteen vehicles a veritable universe of cross-references from the opening shots of Franklin Pangborn's knowingly fey man-about-town conducting his young male protégé to a fashionable party in *Only Yesterday* to Viveca Lindfors playing at the piano with a child actress named Natalie Wood at the fade-out of *No Sad Songs for Me*. In between are the comic counterpoint and feminist overtones of the blithely equal relationship of Billie Burke and Reginald Denny in *Only Yesterday*, the malignant self-absorption of Alan Mowbray's ham actor in *Little Man, What Now?*, Frank Morgan's fatuous and frustrated seducer in *The Good Fairy*, Walter Connolly's omnipresent patriarch in *So Red the Rose*, Ray Milland's sterling best friend in *Next Time We Love*, Charles Butterworth's inimitably demented upper-class suitor in *The Moon's Our Home*, Franchot Tone and Robert Young as the two most interesting of the *Three Comrades*, Walter Pidgeon's pre-Greer Garson man-of-affairs in *The Shopworn Angel*, Felix Bressart's shaggy, Mittel-European, middle-class warmth in *The Shop Around the Corner*, and, perhaps, a bit on the campy side, the desperate struggle between Miss Sullavan and Maria Ouspenskaya to be the one to impose her own fateful stare on the camera lens in *The Mortal Storm*. Also, let us not forget the very memorable and very hummable score by Frank Skinner for *Back Street*, and the interestingly intense contributions of Fredric March, Frances Dee, and Erich von Stroheim to *So Ends Our Night*.

Yet Sullavan has managed, at least in one's memory, to appropriate all the movies in which she appeared, and to impose upon them her own life-facing intuitions, tragic but not maudlin, playful but not frivolous, all too wise but quickly weary of the consequences of wisdom. In her fearful eyes one can see the end from the very beginning, but, wait, the lips and chin are moving whimsically and there is hope and humor for a very little while, though despair and death are never far from the surface of her smile. Ultimately, none of the disasters that befell Maggie in real life could have come as much of a surprise to her most appreciative admirers. Her fate was and still is writ large on the screen in the emotional iridescence of her face, voice, movements, and gestures. Perhaps too large. It is possible that audiences could eventually tire of the sheer magnitude of her gallantry and courage. Parker Tyler's perceptive but peevish comment in *Magic and Myth of the Movies* (1947) reflects a forties ennui with this high-voltage thirties actress: "The opposite of a sissy feminine voice is Margaret Sullavan's, so husky with 'human sympathy,' as I believe it is called, that I have sometimes imagined its quality the result of a sort of fatigue, as though the lady had been carrying around a man-sized load of sentiment for too long a time."

Whether as a Hercules of the heart or a Sisyphus of the soul, Margaret Sullavan remains to this day an heroic figure on the screen, but with wit and charm as well, the smile with the sob, as it were. My own favorite Sullavan anecdote is to be found not in *Haywire*, but in Bob Thomas's *King Cohn*:

> He [Harry Cohn] applied the same technique with Margaret Sullavan. At the end of a private conference he remarked to her, "Willie Wyler tells me you're great in the hay." Wyler had once been married to the actress.
>
> Miss Sullavan arose and replied scornfully, "You didn't hear that from Willie. He is too much of a gentleman to discuss such things with you."
>
> She turned on her heel and marched the length of Cohn's office. Before she went out the door, she added, "But I am."

The very sexist critics of the thirties did not believe that a slip of a girl like Sullavan (even via Stark Young's romantic recollection and King Vidor's dynamic direction) could quell a slave revolt on the plantation in *So Red the Rose* (1936). Otherwise intelligent people were still mesmerized by the masses in those days, and Sullavan's iron-willed Southern belle (in fact, as well as in fancy) seemed a much more exotic notion in 1936 than Vivien Leigh's Scarlett O'Hara was to seem in 1939 and through the forties. Even today many film critics find it difficult to describe a love scene between a man and a woman without lapsing into irony, but the more influential critics of the thirties and forties never even made the effort to convey to their readers the full emotional impact of close-ups of courtship. Hence, Margaret Sullavan's kingdom of feeling has never been fully charted, though her sixteen films have survived to enlighten and enchant sensitive cartographers the world over.

INGRID BERGMAN (1915–1982)

No one can begin to understand Ingrid Bergman's pre-eminence as a movie star without a full understanding of the emotional climate of the first half of the forties. Her key movies are *Intermezzo* (1939), *Casablanca* (1942), *For Whom the Bell Tolls* (1943), *Gaslight* (1944), *Saratoga Trunk*, *Spellbound*, and *The Bells of St. Mary's* (all 1945), and *Notorious* (1946). In the mid-forties, when her career was at its peak, three minor vehicles—*Adam Had Four Sons*, *Rage in Heaven*, and *Dr. Jekyll and Mr. Hyde* (all 1941)—were re-released to satisfy the insatiable cravings of her fans. "Vehicles" is perhaps not the right word for movies with male co-stars such as Leslie Howard (*Intermezzo*), Spencer Tracy (*Dr. Jekyll and Mr. Hyde*), Robert Montgomery (*Rage in Heaven*), Humphrey Bogart (*Casablanca*), Gary Cooper (*For Whom the Bell Tolls*, *Saratoga Trunk*), Gregory Peck (*Spellbound*), Bing Crosby (*The Bells of St. Mary's*), and Cary Grant (*Notorious*). Woody Allen and other ostentatious admirers of *Casablanca* tend to think of it exclusively in terms of Bogart's myth, though at the time it seemed to many of us that Bergman did more for Bogart than he did for her.

No one even now seems to want to remember how breathtakingly beloved Bergman was in her Hollywood heyday. Bergman herself tended to discourage the idolatry of nostalgia, or the worship of what she once projected at the expense of what she became. Her remarks, personally witnessed, at a 1980 screening of *Notorious* at the Museum of Modern Art seemed casually affectionate, but not unduly admiring. Apparently she could not bring herself to believe that the Hitchcock who once pulled her out of a crying jag with the consolation, "It's only a movie, Ingrid," might indeed have been the transcendent artist that his cultish champions describe in their lengthy disquisitions and that *Notorious* (1946) might indeed be a stirringly ambiguous masterpiece of love and betrayal and suspicion.

Ingrid Bergman indicated in other interviews that she was genuinely puzzled by the high regard of film enthusiasts for her Roberto Rossellini

flops. Yet she was remarkably perceptive about the great appeal of Rossellini's artistic aspirations in the challengingly visionary period after
World War II. And she was remarkably generous to affirm as she did
that their relationship did more lasting damage to his career than to hers.
Unfortunately, whatever one thinks of the cinematic virtues of the Ros-
sellini-Bergman collaborations—*Stromboli* (1949), *Europe 51* (1952),
Joan at the Stake (1954), *Journey to Italy* (1953), and *Fear* (1954)—it is
clear that Rossellini was less effective in enhancing Bergman than he
was in enhancing Anna Magnani, his earlier love, in *Open City* (1946)
and *The Miracle* (1948). Nor was the late Jean Renoir any more effective
with Bergman or with audiences in *Elena et Les Hommes* (1956), despite
Ingrid Bergman's gallant defense of the great French director. It remained for the comparatively tarnished Anatole Litvak to rescue her from
commercial and professional oblivion with *Anastasia* (1956), a competent
but uninspired romance that brought her back to America in triumph to
receive her second New York Film Critics Award (the first was for her
three 1945 films, *Spellbound, Saratoga Trunk*, and *The Bells of St.
Mary's*), and her second Oscar (the first was for *Gaslight* in 1944). Except
for a few sequences in Stanley Donen's *Indiscreet* (1958) with her very
loyal champion Cary Grant, and a few sequences in Ingmar Bergman's
Autumn Sonata (1978) with Liv Ullmann and her old acting classmate
Gunnar Bjornstrand, she never again really set the screen on fire as she
had in her younger days. For one thing, she spent much of her time and
emotional energy in the theater, on television, and in the very real life
she had been seeking since early childhood to escape through acting.

   Curiously, I had never thought of Bergman as Garbo's successor on
the screen, yet that is how it must have seemed to both Garbo and the
late L. B. Mayer when he borrowed Bergman from David O. Selznick
for *Rage in Heaven* (1941) and *Dr. Jekyll and Mr. Hyde* (1941) at a time
when Garbo was hinting at her retirement. When Garbo came along in
the twenties, she was immediately typed as the Continental siren who
lived only for love. As with Pola Negri and Marlene Dietrich, Garbo was
granted erotic options denied American actresses. By the time Bergman
came along in the late thirties and early forties, the censors and the
puritans were in complete control of Hollywood, and a great deal of
eroticism had to be sublimated in the increasingly neurotic nice girl.
Ingrid Bergman was not only more "moral" than her European predecessors, she was also more "natural" than her Hollywood sisters of American origin. Much has been made of the fact that the saintly image she
projected in Leo McCarey's *The Bells of St. Mary's* was the chief source

of her later problems with the public. An endless parade of dreary critics have dismissed *The Bells of St. Mary's* as only superficially religious. McCarey's genius, however, was not religious at all, but fundamentally emotional. Hence, what was overwhelming about Bergman in *The Bells of St. Mary's* was not her spiritual purity and dedication, but her over-whelmingly physical beauty in close-up at the altar. Her nun's habit only intensified the erotic frisson of her officially forbidden sexuality. We could all lie to ourselves about the nature of the attraction she exerted until that fateful moment when she jumped off her pedestal into a Si-cilian volcano.

Ingmar Bergman is quoted in Ingrid Bergman's autobiography (*Ingrid Bergman: My Story*, written with Alan Burgess) to very useful and illu-minating effect about the true impact of her screen presence in the Hollywood days:

> I saw all the pictures that Ingrid made in America. The only one I didn't see was the remake of *Intermezzo* with Leslie Howard. I was a young director in those days and we were all absorbed and fascinated by the American film and its techniques. We liked also the dark style of the French films, but we knew we had an immense amount to learn from the American way of making pictures. Of course, some of Ingrid's pictures in those early American years were not masterpieces, but I remember very clearly that whatever she did I was always fascinated by her face. In her face—the skin, the eyes, the mouth—especially the mouth—there was this very strong radiance and an enormous erotic attraction.
>
> It had nothing to do with her body, but in the relationship between her mouth, her skin, and her eyes. So I was always very attracted by her as an actress. One of the very first times I saw her in person she was already married to Lars Schmidt. She had been shopping in Stockholm, and we were sitting in the hotel suite when she came back—it was in the winter—and she came in loaded with packages and with a high coloring, and I had exactly the same feeling from the moment: a very strong erotic attraction and she was very beautiful.

Ultimately, Ingrid Bergman may have been punished by her public more for her prescience than for her presumption. She abandoned the comfortable cocoon of Hollywood's artifices just a few years before the film colony's confidence in these artifices began to crumble. She shat-tered the hypocrisy of American puritanism almost two decades before the children's revolt would shatter the complacency of American family life. She was prematurely mature, and naturally she had to be burned at the stake. Her surprisingly brief reign as the Swedish Empress of America's movie screens ended with a fall that would rival Marie Antoinette's in brutal abruptness. What was done to Ingrid Bergman in the press, the pulpit, and even on the floor of the United States Senate during the Rossellini affair amounted to ritual murder. Driven by neither greed nor lust, she stumbled into one of the century's biggest scandals while seeking only a broader and more realistic canvas for her artistry as an actress. If the cruel catcalls of the yahoos and the philistines were not so everlastingly disgusting, one could discern in her bizarre misadventures a comic irony of which even she was not completely aware.

I do not claim to be her avenger or vindicator. To their eternal credit, her more civilized friends and acquaintances, including the much maligned Howard Hughes, did so from the first through the last stages of her interminable ordeal. All I would like to do is to confess the deep love I felt for her on such occasions as when I watched the thirty-year-old Ingrid Bergman kiss the forty-one-year-old Cary Grant during *Notorious* on the gigantic screen of the Radio City Music Hall back in 1946. And I would like to confess even more that I now realize that what I thought was a purely spiritual love turns out to have been deliciously profane.

IRENE DUNNE (1898–1990)

Irene Dunne was denigrated by several influential critics and historians long after she had faded into oblivion. James Agee probably started the negative revisionism with his acid pans, which have been revered posthumously, but it must be remembered that Agee did not start reviewing until the forties, and Dunne's brightest period was in the thirties (and, not surprisingly, *her* middle and late thirties as well) with *Back Street* (1932), *Roberta* (1935), *Sweet Adeline* (1935), *Magnificent Obsession* (1935), *Show Boat* (1936), *Theodora Goes Wild* (1936), *The Awful Truth* (1937), *Joy of Living* (1938), *Love Affair* (1939), and *When Tomorrow Comes* (1939).

Even in the forties, however, she was more than intermittently lustrous in *Penny Serenade* (1941), *Unfinished Business* (1941), and *A Guy Named Joe* (1943). Some of her less accomplished performances were marred by a tongue-in-cheek teasing of her male co-stars, and she occasionally gave the impression of prim self-righteousness in the cut of her jaw. Yet one could also feel vulnerability and yearning in her eyes, which did not so much dance as shift uneasily from playfulness to passion. There was always a bit of the operetta heroine in her, but her squareness was also her strength. She had neither Lombard's breathtaking beauty nor Sullavan's heartbreaking pathos, but she projected a womanly dignity that made her erotically exciting in moderately repressed contexts. Indeed when she was caught innocently in her underwear in a police raid in *Together Again* (1944), the libidinous effect exceeded that of a dozen Gypsy Rose Lees, and the train compartment seduction scene with Preston Foster in *Unfinished Business* is amazingly audacious for a movie made in the age of the Production Code. As for those who still insist that she had no sense of humor, one might retort that her madcap society wife in *The Awful Truth* is one of the most uproarious creations of the comic cinema.

MYRNA LOY (1905–1993)

It has always been a mixed blessing for Myrna Loy to be regarded as one of the few level-headed grown-ups in the Hollywood community of neurotic children. Her gifts and persona had always eluded me, obsessed as I was by the cruel, mad, fatal beauty of Vivien Leigh, the inexhaustible reserves of gallant sentiment in Margaret Sullavan, the hopelessly undecipherable mysteries of Greta Garbo.

But Loy's upturned nose and lucidly crackling, no-nonsense cadences swept aside the careless languor of even the most sublime femmes fatales. Yet she was such a great beauty that a large part of her career was spent in roles barely above the level of hootchy-kootchy. Then came *The Thin Man* in 1934 and her image changed overnight. Like most successful movie legends, Loy and co-star William Powell carved out their own privileged position: the first on-screen Hollywood couple for whom matrimony did not signal the end of sex, romance, and adventure.

Yet, as Loy observes in her unusually illuminating autobiography, *Being and Becoming* (written with James Kotslibas-Davis), she appeared in roughly sixty films in the decade before *The Thin Man* was released. Add the sixty-some screen appearances after *The Thin Man*, and you get some idea of the dimensions of the old Hollywood work ethic. You also begin to appreciate the low-key intensity that enabled Loy to function in such a high-powered environment without using up her emotional juices.

Ironically, though audiences at the time of *The Thin Man* assumed that Loy and Powell were "obviously" husband and wife off-screen as well as on, they were never an item. Loy hovered around the edges of the celebrated Gable-Lombard-Powell-Harlow quadrille, but she fended off the advances of any number of leading men. She chose instead to marry a succession of self-confident executives (four), none in a position to promote her career.

Loy had always been unobtrusively independent, sometimes suspending her career for the sake of her political convictions. She was neither a flaming liberal like Hepburn, nor a seething studio rebel like Davis. With little noise or hoopla, she was her own woman, even as males both in the movies and in the audience yearned for her as a marital partner. Women of her generation tried to look like her through cosmetic surgery, much as a later generation emulated Jackie Kennedy.

Loy remained intellectually and socially curious all her life. She was brought up in an artistically stimulating atmosphere that might have encouraged her to follow in the footsteps of Isadora Duncan or Ruth St. Denis. Ironically, as she writes in her book, her unshapely legs were to be her only problem throughout her career. Fortunately, however, she became a star in the golden age of what the French called *le plan américain*, the mid-range shot that emphasized the body from the waist up.

In fact, I never gave a thought to Loy's legs when I was growing up. But that glorious face—glorious even in romantic trifles such as *Third Finger, Left Hand* (1940) with Melvyn Douglas, or a turgid melodrama like *The Rains Came* (1939). But even before *The Thin Man*, there was a joker in the deck. In both *Penthouse* and *The Prizefighter and the Lady*, both made in 1933, she displays a measured vulnerability, as she flowers into full stardom. She did not waste all those years in the Hollywood harem; instead, she learned to smolder in ever subtler ways. Loy was intelligent enough to understand the insecurities of her male co-stars and calibrated her approach accordingly. She was the ideal wife—the ideal chum, someone to trust. Much of her work has long been mistaken for artlessness, even complacency. The time has come to re-examine as much of her career as can be reclaimed from the vaults, to search for clues to the puzzle of how a great talent emerged from a morass of convention and contrivance.

NORMA SHEARER (1902–1983)

Norma Shearer died on June 12, 1983. Her obituary notices were remarkably tentative about her actual date of birth. Todd McCarthy in *Variety* of June 15, reported: "The Motion Picture Country House reported Shearer's age as 80, that her birth certificate listed her date of birth as August 15, 1902. On the other hand, some sources claim that she was born on August 10, 1900." Eric Pace, in the *New York Times* on June 14, cited other sources: "According to MGM records, the date of her birth was August 15, 1902, which would make her 80 years old. But Ben Crisler, the *Times* film critic, reported in 1936 that she was born in 1900, and by some subsequent accounts she was born as late as 1904."

As every woman knows, this is not a trivial issue, particularly in the star-lit world of Hollywood movies. Every year on her official dossier counted for Norma Shearer as she contemplated decline and fall in the early forties. A forty-year-old star might well refuse the lead role in *Mrs. Miniver* (1942) because she did not want to play the mother of a grown son. For a forty-two-year-old star, to do the same thing might be regarded as unduly squeamish. The part won an Oscar for Greer Garson, ironically the successor of Shearer in MGM's "Great Lady" tradition. Even more ironically, Greer Garson was eventually to marry her "son" (Richard Ney) in *Mrs. Miniver* and the publicity releases made it clear that she was only three years older than he was, though subsequent research suggests that the difference was closer to a decade. It was very important back then that the illusion of youth be preserved for the general public. Much as we would like to think that we are less coy and evasive about age today, we would just be kidding ourselves. The same old double standard prevails. A well-preserved (or even surgically reconstructed) male is praised for looking younger than his calendar age; a well-preserved female is ridiculed for her elaborate deceit. Actors can remain bankable after fifty, and even sixty; actresses have a hard time finding employment after forty. Indeed, what has changed most radically in the last thirty or forty years is the virtual extinction of the female of the species as star material.

Even in her own time, however, Norma Shearer was a very special case as the wife of the industry prodigy Irving J. Thalberg. Boudoir careerism was hardly unknown in Hollywood. William Randolph Hearst's notorious sponsorship of Marion Davies was crudely caricatured in *Cit-*

izen Kane, and only heaven knows how many unsanctified and unpub-
licized liaisons altered the casting constellations in the Hollywood
firmament. Many people, some like myself in retrospect, tended to resent
Shearer for the supposedly "special" treatment she received from the
studio. Could the Thalberg connection have been responsible for
Shearer's winning the Oscar in 1930 for *The Divorcee* over Garbo in
Anna Christie and *Romance*? I once even described Shearer in print as
cross-eyed but not without some sense of guilt. I felt somewhat vindicated by the following passage in the *Times* obit: "Gossips said that
skilled camera work hid a flaw in her beauty—which was that her eyes
were not perfectly aligned. Her eyes became a delicate subject in MGM
circles. A director who was so crass as to complain 'She is cross-eyed'
was punished by being sent to film a western on the Mojave Desert."

What surprises me somewhat is how little glory remains from all the
power once exuded by Shearer and Thalberg. MGM is far from being
regarded as the the most fashionable studio by movie buffs, and I have
never heard of a Norma Shearer festival anywhere. But it would be a
mistake to dismiss Shearer as a nonentity with gowns by Adrian. Thalberg's interest in her as a talent long preceded their romantic involvement. Like many stars of the early talkies, Shearer had had a longer and
more active career in silent movies than most thirties audiences ever
realized. Between 1920 and 1928 she had appeared in thirty-nine films,
whereas between 1929 and her retirement in 1942 she appeared in only
nineteen talkies. Even for a pampered star her output in the sound era
is strikingly meager. And yet this was part of her undeniable aura—that
she did not make movies lightly and frivolously, but with great care,
sincerity, and conviction. Thalberg must have seen something shining in
those unfocused eyes, something that dovetailed with his own aesthetic
credo that was to be so popular in movies throughout the thirties.

Sincerity: we can begin with that, but in an old-fashioned, lady-like
way. Ah, lady-like, that's getting closer. People sometimes ask me why we
don't have people like the Marx Brothers anymore, and I reply that we do
have people like the Marx Brothers, perhaps too many, but we don't have
anyone like Margaret Dumont anymore. We don't have dowagers or
stuffed shirts. Everyone, rich or poor, young or old, is a zany character with
a stand-up routine. There is no one for zaniness to play off against.

And so Norma Shearer represents something that is gone forever, and
no one is particularly interested in reviving it. Even if one were to develop
a taste for such dated sentiment, there would be more interesting people
to remember even on the second line of soulful icons—Ann Harding,

for example, or Shearer's more talented lookalike, Diana Wynyard. Actually, Shearer, even in her palmiest days, never intruded on the domains of such nonpareil goddesses as Garbo and Harlow. Her alleged ladies in waiting were instead such similar brunette types as Myrna Loy, Joan Crawford, and Rosalind Russell. It has never been clear how long this pecking order lasted, and what its practical consequences were. After *The Thin Man*, Loy's flair for domestic comedy and fun melodrama made her seem too buoyant and ebullient for the heavier Thalberg-Shearer undertakings. Crawford was more the Shearer type, and even imitated the original on occasion, but she would have been much better off if she had jumped to Warners a decade before *Mildred Pierce* (1945). As for Rosalind Russell, she was a gifted comedienne buried at MGM, until *The Women* (1939), in a succession of dreary leading-lady roles.

Only Shearer herself seemed truly wedded to the MGM mystique, that same mystique that made the Marx Brothers comedy relief in overproduced operettas, that removed all the traces of raffishness from the Spencer Tracy of the Fox era and all the feminism from the RKO Hepburn. This is the point that F. Scott Fitzgerald missed entirely in *The Last Tycoon*, a very thinly disguised fantasy of what Fitzgerald himself would have done and felt if he had come to earth as Thalberg. There was of course no place in that fantasy for Norma Shearer. Yet she was the visible sign of what Thalberg wanted in a woman and a movie. We may say with the benefit of archival hindsight that Norma Shearer was the antithesis of Louise Brooks. And yet which one of the two is likely to linger longer in the aesthetic memories of movie buffs?

So much has changed in the way we look at movies since Shearer reigned at MGM. The awe with which movie people regarded the stage is reflected in Shearer's slavish imitation of Lynn Fontanne. Yet Thalberg did not hesitate to give Alfred Lunt and Lynn Fontanne the full Shearer treatment at MGM for *The Guardsman* (1931), a strange kind of classic that enabled the Lunts to quit movies while still considered to be ahead. At about the same time Shearer and Robert Montgomery were aping Gertrude Lawrence and Noël Coward in *Private Lives* (1931), a strangely forgettable movie that languishes in that indeterminate limbo between the bubbly champagne of Lawrence-Coward and the stale beer of Elizabeth Taylor-Richard Burton.

Shearer and Clark Gable were even more leaden as screen replicas of Lunt and Fontanne in *Idiot's Delight* (1939), but by this time Shearer was a not so merry widow. Thalberg, her lord and protector, had died in 1936, and even before his death he had seen much of his autonomous power stripped away by the cabal around L. B. Mayer. She inherited a few million dollars (4.5 in the *Times* obit, 10 in *Variety*), but she was considered isolated and defenseless within the studio. Consequently, a legend has grown up around *Romeo and Juliet* (1936) as proof of Thalberg's worthy concern for her, and of *Marie Antoinette* (1938) as a demonstration of Mayer's malicious neglect. I wouldn't rank either movie with *Citizen Kane*, but I have always felt that *Marie Antoinette* was as much under-rated as *Romeo and Juliet* was over-rated. John Barrymore's Mercutio, for example, was overplayed, whereas his Louis XV gleams with a mordant wit and well-earned cynicism. For that matter, Robert Morley's pathetic Louis XVI is a singularly winning characterization. But the revelation for me is Shearer herself rising to emotional heights I never suspected. Was this not the role above all roles that she could relate to as she waited for the tumbrels on Sunset Boulevard to bear her to the guillotine reserved for discarded stars? And yet what hopes and joys there had been in the beginning when her prince had come courting from the vast kingdom of the lion.

It is not surprising that some of her best performances, notably in *The Women* (1939) and *Escape* (1940), were rendered after her supposed fall from studio grace and protection. In *The Women* she stood toe-to-toe with two of her most persnickety ladies in waiting, Joan Crawford, the shameless hussy herself, and Rosalind Russell, the hilariously catty farceuse with her claws unsheathed at last. Shearer stood her ground with a kind of half-baked nobility, defending family, decency, and honor against the pushy interlopers. Perhaps this is a clue to why she remained undaunted when facing rivals so much more gifted and luminous.

JEAN HARLOW (1911–1937)

Not the least strange of the paradoxes of Jean Harlow's career was that from a studio notorious for its gentility she emerged in the thirties as MGM's perpetually misunderstood and under-rated "dame" par excellence. Which is to say that Harlow on screen is surprisingly lucid in view of her lurid reputation offscreen.

First, there is the matter of the platinum, a home-made signal for semiotic analysis. According to Harry Haun in his perceptive tribute in the *Daily News* of Sunday, June 7, 1987, the fiftieth anniversary of Harlow's death: "In truth, the Blonde Bombshell was the accidental invention of an inept hairdresser. She emerged from the hair-dryer overcooked and white-hot platinum, making us forget there were blondes before her. It hardly mattered that this was a mistake; the look took and the rush was on. All across the country, drug stores had a hard time keeping stocked in peroxide."

One might add that Harlow's platinum hair turned out to be one of the glories of Hollywood chiaroscuro, a highlight of black-and-white film-making. The platinum, which at first looked freakish, ended up glowing as a nervy affirmation of playing the cards one is dealt, even by an incompetent hairdresser. And as with the orange hair of Cyndi Lauper and Molly Ringwald a half-century later, there was no ironic distance between the platinum and the performer. The important thing is that Harlow never became coy or self-conscious about the promise implied in the platinum. She kept her end of the bargain with an unflinching gaze.

Somehow she managed to rise from the untutored ranks of extras, which had always been a no-no in Hollywood. The conventional wisdom was that if you wanted to become a star you avoided at all costs becoming a face in the crowd. Yet there was the Blonde-Bombshell-to-be strutting her stuff in Laurel and Hardy custard-pie farces (most visibly in *Double Whoopee*) and in Ernst Lubitsch's *The Love Parade* and Charles Chaplin's *City Lights*. She reached a pinnacle of sorts by doing the Charleston and getting her name in the credits for the first time in *The Saturday Night Kid* (1929).

She returned to bit parts in Al Christie comedy shorts until she was discovered by an agent named Arthur Landau, who adroitly maneuvered her into the female lead in Howard Hughes's *Hell's Angels* (1930). This World War I aerial adventure had been started as a silent with Swedish-accented Greta Nissen, but once the movie crossed the sound barrier the xenophobic Hughes did not like what he heard in the sizzling sex scenes. Harlow could certainly sizzle well enough, though she was ludicrously miscast as an upper-class British hotsy-totsy coming on strong to a stalwart (Ben Lyon) of the British Royal Flying Corps with the ceremonially seductive invitation, "Pardon me while I slip into something more comfortable." Unfortunately, her inept line readings and unconvincing British accent made audiences laugh at rather than with her. Still, this was 1930, a time when movies had some guts where sex was concerned, and thus a raw talent could be discerned despite the handicap of inexperience.

Hughes signed Harlow to a contract with his Caddo Company at $250 a week, but he never employed her again in his own projects, choosing to parcel her out to other studios for seven movies in rapid succession, making a big profit in the process. Through 1931 and 1932 she appeared in George Hill's *The Secret Six* (MGM), in which she played a grim gun moll; *The Iron Man* (Universal), in which she played a grasping gold-digger to Lew Ayres's naive boxer and Robert Armstrong's "I-know-all-your-tricks, girlie" manager; *The Public Enemy* (Warners) as the snooty dame for whose high-flown advances Jimmy Cagney pushed a grapefruit into the whining face of the discarded Mae Clark; *Goldie* (Fox), in which Harlow failed to strike any sparks with Spencer Tracy; Frank Capra's *Platinum Blonde* (Columbia), in which she was stiff and stilted as the society girl competing with Loretta Young's down-to-earth newsgirl for the love of Robert Williams's whimsically virile reporter; *Three Wise Girls* (Columbia), still another exercise in the gold-digger genre; and *The Beast of the City* (MGM), a downbeat crime melodrama with Harlow as the standard gun moll.

Hughes finally sold her contract to L. B. Mayer for $60,000, and Harlow went on salary at $1250 a week. She had two pairs of guardian angels in her transition from a one-dimensional sexpot to a witty straight-shooter. Arthur Landau had guided her career expertly enough, but MGM was to provide her with Paul Bern, first as patron and protector in the court of Irving J. Thalberg and then as a sadistically impotent second husband, whose suicide was to haunt and humiliate Harlow for the rest of her short, unhappy life. The other pair of guardian angels were the screenwriters John Lee Mahin and Anita Loos. Mahin's contribution was his suggestion that Harlow and Gable co-star in *Red Dust*. Anita Loos—the creator, after all, of Lorelei Lee, the prototypical blonde whom gentlemen preferred—virtually created the wise-cracking Harlow persona in *The Red-Headed Woman* (1932) (for which Harlow tinted her platinum tresses) and *Hold Your Man* (1933), a low-down but soft-hearted mug-and-moll romance with Gable. Here, Harlow projected for the first time a winning combination of brassy humor and heart-stopping pathos.

Thus, by the end of 1932 Harlow had been successfully launched, and there were no major career missteps along the way. The fabled MGM production and publicity machines were purring for her at peak efficiency, much better, in fact, than for her tough-girl rival at the studio, Joan Crawford, who became box-office poison in parts Norma Shearer rejected; much quicker than for Myrna Loy, and much slicker than even for Greta Garbo. Harlow was especially fortunate in acquiring subtlety and complexity before the censors could crack down on her raw sexuality. In this respect, *The Red-Headed Woman* and *Bombshell* (1933) are cinematic treasures in their rich mixture of behavioral bawdiness characteristic of the early thirties with the verbal crackle characteristic of the middle and late thirties.

Yet Harlow herself was perturbed by the persistent image of herself as a truly shameless hussy. She was not all *that* promiscuous off the set, she argued, so why should she always play come hither and never go yonder in the movies? One might as well ask why in the eighties Congress snapped to attention when Oliver North's secretary, Fawn Hall, pointed her exquisite cheekbones upward at the television camera.

The fact is that even Harlow underestimated the amount of sympathy and admiration she generated for the characters she played during her MGM tenure. Even when the censors kept her from doing anything *really* naughty in *The Girl from Missouri* (1934) the audience was with her all the way in her poor-girl yearnings for all the best things in life that are never free. Hence, she could teeter on the edge of moral turpitude, and yet save her honor and get Prince Charming (Franchot Tone) besides.

Just a year earlier she was allowed to be less inhibited in letting it all hang out in a movie-ending clip that has been excerpted to death from George Cukor's *Dinner at Eight* (1934), adapted from the George S. Kaufman–Edna Ferber play by Frances Marion and Herman J. Mankiewicz. Harlow is going into dinner with Marie Dressler and announces that she has been reading a book. Dressler, never one to understate a reaction when she can drop an atom bomb instead, invariably gets a guffaw with her stop-dead-in-her-tracks double-take. Harlow continues with her recently acquired information that machines will soon replace everything, and Dressler responds with a lingeringly appraising glance at Harlow's silk-sheathed rear end, and assures the unflustered Platinum Blonde that she has nothing to worry about. Much sharper and more knowing is the scene in which Harlow stares with stoically rueful intentness at a sly maid blackmailing her out of some jewelry as the price of keeping quiet about an extramarital indiscretion.

In *Reckless* (1935), Harlow indulged in some Pirandellian doubling by re-enacting on screen her last great off-screen romance with a wistfully philosophical William Powell. *Reckless* has been generally under-rated because sordid plot elements seem to exploit the Paul Bern scandal and the Libby Holman case as well, yet Harlow seemed too generously good-natured to drive men to death and perdition. As an actress, she had outgrown her garish publicity.

In *Wife vs. Secretary* (1936), Harlow plays with uncommon sweetness the decent secretary who gets along with the boss's wife (Myrna Loy), but since the boss is Clark Gable the situation becomes so delicate that Harlow's gallantry and nobility burst forth as never before to soften the jagged edges of the triangle.

Harlow was disappointed when she was cast opposite Tracy again, instead of Powell (teamed again with Loy), in the lively screwball quadrille *The Libeled Lady* (1936). What everyone remembers (or should remember) from this movie is Harlow's climactic turnabout scene when she stops being the patsy and demands the requisite respect for her intelligence and sincerity despite all the outward appurtenances of a Platinum Bimbo. Then there is the look on Harlow's face as a pregnant convict in *Hold Your Man* (1933) when she sees that her scampish con man of a sweetheart (Gable) has returned to stand by her. It is a look of tearful joy that you just can't pick up in acting school. It is one of many primal moments that set Harlow apart from other "sex goddesses."

For the record, Jean Harlow, born Harlean Carpentier in Kansas City, Missouri, of middle-class parents March 3, 1911, died of uremic poisoning and the fanaticism of Mama Jean's Christian Science on June 6, 1937. The most prevalent gossip of the time was that Harlow had died of a bungled abortion. Her various biographers have rejected the abortion rumor and many others equally lurid. Injuries to the kidneys inflicted by her first husband, misguided maternal neglect, studied studio neglect all contributed to a medically untimely demise. MGM, a studio of jackals masquerading as lions, hushed up the circumstances of inadequate treatment to avoid offending the nation's Christian Scientists. The resulting damage to Miss Harlow's reputation hardly weighed in the balance. *Saratoga* (1937), her last and one of her least starring vehicles, employed stand-in Mary Dees for several scenes filmed after Harlow's death.

BARBARA STANWYCK (1907–1990)

Barbara Stanwyck, Hollywood's most dazzling dame, appeared in eighty-four theatrical movies, four television movies, one mini-series novelization, and a television series in a forty-eight-year-career ranging from 1927 to 1985. The numbers alone are staggering, and to certain modern sensibilities, damning. It is the work ethic run amok.

Stanwyck came from a unique age. Indeed, her biography reads like one of the plebeian sob stories they used to make into movies in the twenties and the thirties. Born Ruby Stevens in Brooklyn in 1907, and orphaned shortly thereafter, at thirteen she dropped out of school to work behind a department-store counter at fifteen, danced in a chorus line, at nineteen starred on Broadway in *The Noose*, and at twenty appeared in her first movie (the silent *Broadway Nights*). She married vaudeville headliner Frank Fay a year later and accompanied him to the west coast where their marriage (1928–35) fell apart in the fashion of *Burlesque* and *A Star Is Born* inasmuch as his star fell in the early thirties as hers lit up the heavens. Like *A Star Is Born*'s Norman Maine, he became a notorious drunk. Unlike Norman Maine, he made a spectacular Broadway comeback in the forties as the whimsically inebriated Elwood Dowd in *Harvey*, Mary Ellen Chase's comedy of a genial drunk with an imaginary six-foot-tall rabbit drinking companion. When asked at the time if she had seen Fay's stage triumph, Stanwyck replied ruefully that she had seen Frank Fay pull enough rabbits out of a hat, thank you. This real-life jolter of a kiss-off line was just what you might have expected of Stanwyck's hard-boiled screen persona.

Her marriage to Robert Taylor (1939–1952) had very little impact on either of their careers, and they appeared together only three times, twice before their marriage in *His Brother's Wife* (1936) and *This Is My Affair* (1937), and once after their divorce in *The Night Walker* (1965). With Stanwyck sizzling on the screen from the first reel to the last, eighty-four movies did not leave much time for a private life. Frank Capra once remarked that her first take was always her best, and that her retakes invariably went stale. Her earliest film that I have seen is *Mexicali Rose* (1930). It is a stinker by any standard, and Stanwyck does not have much of a part as a woman of easy virtue coming between a loving father (Sam Hardy) and his starry-eyed son (William Janney). Naturally, she has to die so that the kid's illusions can be preserved. But she never dogs it, and after a remarkably brief apprenticeship with three such journeymen directors such as Joseph C. Boyle (*Broadway Nights*, 1927), George Fitzmaurice (*The Locked Door*, 1929), and Erle C. Kenton (*Mexacali Rose*, 1929), she hit the directorial jackpot in 1930 with Frank Capra's *Ladies of Leisure*.

Capra was setting up his team at Columbia, Harry Cohn's minor-league bargain-basement studio that Capra single-handedly transformed into his own major-league base of operations. Joseph Walker's cinematography made Stanwyck an icon here in 1930 as six years later it made Jean Arthur an icon in *Mr. Deeds Goes to Town*. Scenarist Jo Swerling was also on hand for *Ladies of Leisure*, and was joined the next year on *Miracle Woman* (1931) by John Meehan and the ultimate Capra screenwriting-sidekick Robert Riskin. In *Ladies of Leisure* Stanwyck demonstrates the power to generate pathos from a low-down role. In *Miracle Woman* she displays the even more precious gift of playing tender, oblique love scenes with David Manners without crashing through the part with a street-wise raucousness. This is an interesting period for raw, sexy actresses on the screen, and it is instructive to compare Stanwyck and Joan Crawford in this era. Crawford is fascinatingly harsh, awkward, and vulnerable in *Rain* and *Grand Hotel* (both 1932), and she was not yet endowed with the ridiculously refined veneer that was to make her such a camp item later in the thirties. But she was not really a good actress. With much the same showgirl background as Stanwyck's, she is not wired very deep into her psyche. Crawford's acting and elocution lessons crackle on the soundtrack. Stanwyck's performance, by contrast, is all of a piece, and there are no short circuits of inexperience and inexpertness in the emotional electricity she generates.

If Capra and Stanwyck had made an accomplished movie like *The Miracle Woman* at a major studio like MGM they would have been immediately lionized. As it was, Capra had to wait for *It Happened One Night* (1934), and Stanwyck for King Vidor's *Stella Dallas* (1937), to achieve their big breakthroughs. In the meantime Stanwyck kept plugging away conscientiously at various studios for a wide variety of directors: Archie Mayo's *Illicit*, Lionel Barrymore's *Ten Cents a Dance*, and William A. Wellman's *Night Nurse* in 1931, with an almost comically villainous Clark Gable; Frank Capra's *Forbidden*, Nicholas Grinde's *Shopworn*, William A. Wellman's *So Big* and *The Purchase Price* (all 1932), and then finally in 1933 Capra's *The Bitter Tea of General Yen*, a very accomplished romance that played Radio City Music Hall.

Far from succumbing to gentility, Stanwyck winds up in prison in Howard Bretherton and William Keighley's *Ladies They Talk About*; as a manipulative gold digger in Alfred E. Green's *Baby Face* with such victims as George Brent, Henry Kolker, and John Wayne; in a soggy soap opera like Archie Mayo's *Gambling Lady* (all in 1933). Then in 1934 she appears in only one film, Archie Mayo's *A Lost Lady*, adapted by Gene

Markey and Kathryn Scola, from Willa Cather's novel. Having never seen this film, nor heard anything about it, I cannot help wondering if this did not represent some kind of failed turning point in Stanwyck's career, some futile stab at cultural respectability, the dame, as it were, laboring to become a lady of the industry.

Of the last seventeen films she made in the thirties, eleven can be written off as marginal potboilers: William Dieterle's *The Woman in Red* (1935); Sidney Lanfield's *Red Salute* (1935), an early sample of Hollywood red-baiting; George Marshall's *A Message to Garcia* (1936); Leigh Jason's *The Bride Walks Out* (1936); W. S. Van Dyke's *His Brother's Wife* (1936); Alfred Santell's *Interns Can't Take Money* (1937); William A. Seiter's *This Is My Affair* (1937); Santell's *Breakfast for Two* (1937); Lanfield's *Always Goodbye* (1938); and Jason's *The Mad Miss Manton* (1938), despite Stanwyck's first encounter on the screen with Henry Fonda. Of more interest to us in this period are such Stanwyck vehicles as George Steven's *Annie Oakley* (1935), John Cromwell's *Banjo on My Knee* (1936), John Ford's *The Plough and the Stars* (1937), though, unfortunately, not for Stanwyck; King Vidor's *Stella Dallas* (1937), the final sequence of which still brings on copious tears; Cecil B. De Mille's *Union Pacific* (1939); and Rouben Mamoulian's *Golden Boy* (1939).

With thirty-five movies in little more than a decade, Stanwyck had established a screen personality of force and authority, balanced precariously between *blanc* and *noir* subjects. Most of her big films—Mitchell Leisen's *Remember the Night* (1940), with a script by Preston Sturges; Sturges's *The Lady Eve* (1941); Capra's *Meet John Doe* (1941); Howard Hawks's *Ball of Fire* (1941), with a script by Charles Brackett and Billy Wilder; and Wilder's *Double Indemnity* (1944)—are still ahead, but Stanwyck's high voltage personality is running ever greater risks of irritating critics and audiences. There is enough modulation in the good films to enable her talent to project an engagingly wise and mature sassiness, but once the wit and the balance and the economy of expression are lost, her emotional engine tends to run out of control. Even her Oscar-nomination performance in Anatole Litvak's *Sorry, Wrong Number* (1948) is already too hysterical for comfort. "Wild Bill" Wellman could give Stanwyck her head in the early thirties, and the result was interesting and even exciting in terms of unfettered sexual energy. By the forties, the rough edges of Wellman's *The Great Man's Lady* (1942) and *Lady of Burlesque* (1943) seemed hopelessly anachronistic.

As Stanwyck passes into her forties and fifties, the world of *noir* and violence becomes her natural habitat, and as her price goes down she begins to cross the path of interesting cult directors: Robert Siodmak's *The File on Thelma Jordan* (1950). Anthony Mann's *The Furies* (1950), Fritz Lang's *Clash by Night* (1952), John Sturges's *Jeopardy* (1953), Douglas Sirk's *All I Desire* (1953), and *There's Always tomorrow* (1956), Gerd Oswald's *Crime of Passion*, and Samuel Fuller's *Forty Guns* (1957). She is now fifty, and the end of her career is near, but she never stops working until all her options have expired. The breathtakingly delicious moments in *The Lady Eve* and *Ball of Fire*, the overwhelmingly emotional moments in *The Miracle Woman, Stella Dallas*, and *Remember the Night*, the marvelously wistful moments in *Union Pacific* and *There's Always Tomorrow*, and the extraordinarily evil moments in *Double Indemnity* and *Crime of Passion* did not arise from Stanwyck's saving herself for the projects in which she believed, but rather from a lifetime of playing every scene to the hilt, and giving every role everything she had, down to her toes and back to the earliest yearnings of Ruby Stevens from Brooklyn.

If Barbara Stanwyck emerges in retrospect as a great movie actress, and I believe belatedly but fervently that she does, here is a kind of blue-collar greatness, rising from the streets with all the savvy and spiritual grandeur of her class.

Yet, for all her identification with just-this-side of sob-sister melodramas, Stanwyck can be credited with three of the brightest and wittiest comedy characterizations of the talkie era in Mitchell Leisen's *Remember the Night* (1940), Howard Hawks's *Ball of Fire* (1941), and Preston Sturges's *The Lady Eve* (1941). Significantly, Stanwyck in each instance initiated a relationship with a shy, repressed male who, after many setbacks, became totally and enthusiastically committed to a life with the invariably shady siren played by Stanwyck. Fred MacMurray in *Night*, Gary Cooper in *Fire*, and Henry Fonda in *Eve* were all deviously passive charmers with just enough male conceit to play a waiting game until a whirlwind named Stanwyck threw them for a loop. No other female star of her magnitude and pulchritude would have been expected to work so tirelessly to hook their mates. The Dunnes, the Lombards, the Arthurs, the Loys, the Russells, the Colberts, deflected male thrusts of desire with a repertoire of expert parrying maneuvers. But Stanwyck was the kind of dame who put all her cards on the table from the outset. Still, when the big hunks somehow stumbled past her emotional defenses, she became as lyrically starry-eyed as any of her sisters in enchantment. For censor-ridden and studio-driven Hollywood in the thirties and forties, lasting love was the only game in town, and no exception was made for Stanwyck.

CLAUDETTE COLBERT (1905–1986)

Claudette Colbert was at her best as the gilded lily of American romantic comedy. No rags-to-riches fables for her. Even when she played a modern Cinderella in Mitchell Leisen's scintillating *Midnight* (1939), from a witty screenplay by Charles Brackett and Billy Wilder, Miss Colbert's down-at-the-heels showgirl could hold her own in any society salon. She could exchange witticisms with on-screen aristocrats played smoothly by Mary Astor, John Barrymore, Francis Lederer, and that marvelously fey but forgotten gadfly Rex O'Malley.

In spite of or perhaps because of her innate refinement, Miss Colbert's career shone most brightly in the midst of the Great Depression. Characteristically, her one Oscar-winning role, opposite Clark Gable's *Front Page*-type newspaperman, cast her as a runaway heiress in Frank Capra's epochal *It Happened One Night* (1934). The Colbert-Gable sexual chemistry was reinforced by the period populist sentimentality, which obliged rich girl to marry poor boy only when it was proven that he wasn't after her money. The best things in life are free, and all that. Claudette Colbert transcended such nonsense with the twinkling sophistication of an essentially nice girl with above-average intelligence and knowingness.

She was also a dish, as Cecil B. De Mille amply demonstrated in such vulgar displays of flesh as *The Sign of the Cross* (1932) and *Cleopatra* (1934). Even in the gauziest garments De Mille could sneak by the censors, Miss Colbert could not suppress a sly amusement at the supposed effects of her voluptuous charms. Yet at the same time she could project a winsome womanliness in Ernst Lubitsch's *The Smiling Lieutenant* (1931), in which she stole this Maurice Chevalier vehicle from Miriam Hopkins. And she could evoke tears as well in *Torch Song* (1933) and John Stahl's *Imitation of Life* (1934).

Still, she was under-rated, not only because she seemed less vulnerable than her sobbier sisters in suffering, but also because she specialized in comedies rather than melodramas, at least in her younger years. Though she worked with some of the most accomplished directors in the business—Ernst Lubitsch, Preston Sturges, Gregory La Cava, and Mitchell Leisen most conspicuously—she was penalized by the more socially conscious film historians for failing to acknowledge that the thirties and forties were no time for comedy.

She did her bit for the war effort with *So Proudly We Hail* (1943) and *Since You Went Away* (1944), but in the latter film she crossed the forbidden barrier for female movie stars with sex appeal by playing the mother of a grown daughter (Jennifer Jones). In those days actresses in their thirties and forties were supposed to settle down and stop playing around as the love interest. Yet Miss Colbert was not even forty when she mothered Miss Jones in *Since You Went Away*. In the eighties, Jane Fonda could pass fifty and still be chased by men. Back then, however, she would have had to put up preserves for the winter.

Nonetheless, Claudette Colbert was lucky to be in the right place at the right time and in the right studio. Born Claudette Lily Chauchoin in Paris, she was brought to Manhattan at the age of six, and was educated at Washington Irving High School and the Art Students League, with the intention of becoming a fashion designer. How fitting therefore that she should have spent much of her career at the most soigné of all studios: Paramount. This dual citizen of Paris and New York found herself in the most Europeanized of studios at a time when tastes were more Eurocentric than they had been or were to be later.

The sex comedy, particularly, which reached its most exquisite fulfillment in Hollywood with Preston Sturges's *The Palm Beach Story* (1942), left us with an indelible image of Claudette Colbert at her most enchanting as she played off her musically inclined fool of an admirer (aptly Rudy Vallee) against her virile but stubborn husband (Joel McCrea). Add Mary Astor in a reprise of the duel in *Midnight* (1939), and you have all the ingredients for an extra-marital soufflé of incomparable buoyancy. If she had done nothing else, and she did a great deal more, Claudette Colbert would rank in magical insouciance with all but a handful of immortals. The one part that got away because Miss Colbert was indisposed is, of course, *All About Eve* (1950). Bette Davis was superb, although Claudette Colbert would have been superb, too, but in a different way. When asked how Miss Colbert could have functioned in the context of Miss Davis's take-off of Tallulah Bankhead, writer-director Joseph L. Mankiewicz replied graciously that, with Claudette, it would have been Ina Claire. Exactly. And anyway, Claudette Colbert had to pay *something* for the big break she got with *It Happened One Night* (1934).

W. C. FIELDS (1879–1946)

Back in 1968, in *The American Cinema*, I tried to sum up W. C. Fields
in terms of the following paradigm:

> The vogue for W. C. Fields is concerned more with the comedian's as-
> tringent personality than with any particular form of cinema. W. C. Fields
> is enjoyed as a critical reaction against the prevailing saccharinity of the
> American cinema, or at least that part of the American cinema that is
> sufficiently inane to justify the wildest Fieldsian frenzies against Man and
> Woman. A combined misanthrope and misogynist, Fields virtually demol-
> ished the mythology of the American family in the opening reels of his
> most successful screen incarnation, *The Bank Dick*. Fields was especially
> appealing when he was bullying little children who had it all too much
> their own way on the screen in the thirties and forties. Less successful
> was Fields's one appearance with Mae West in *My Little Chickadee*. West
> brought out all the wizened, infantile sexlessness of Fields, and the pairing
> was more funny/peculiar than funny/ha ha.
>
> The Fields enthusiasts have amassed a considerable literature on their
> unheroic hero. The standard line about Fields was that he had the grace
> of a juggler, but few of his sight gags bear comparison with the more
> distinctively Fieldsian throwaway delivery of comic lines. With a talent
> more verbal than visual, it is difficult to appreciate the success of W. C.
> Fields in the silent cinema, but the fact remains that he functioned with
> comic effectiveness for silent directors as disparate as D. W. Griffith (*Sally
> of the Sawdust*) and Gregory La Cava (*Running Wild, So's Your Old Man*).
> Some of his best comedy short talkies were directed by that very shadowy
> figure in film history, Arthur Ripley. My favorite Fields line occurs on a
> golf course (in *The Golf Specialist*) where, after he expresses the wish that
> his caddy lose a toenail, Fields hastily assures his female companion: "I
> was only fooling and pretending." The double disclaimer issues from
> Fields's lips with all the comic irony of Shakespeare's "Honest, honest
> Iago" from Othello's. All in all, Fields was a monstrous outgrowth of Amer-
> ican Puritanism, and not even Dickens could have imagined such devi-
> ously and intransigently petty malice in any human being.

Since 1968 the Fields cult has continued to grow into a well-organized
religion, but the rapport between Fields and films remains as dubious as
ever. To his admirers Fields functions in solitary splendor amid the mists
of faulty memory. So much so, in fact, that any prolonged exposure to
his films can be very disconcerting. As Wilfrid Sheed in 1974 stated the

problem in *the New York Review of Books*: "I have always felt that the idea of Fields is funnier than Fields himself; that even the face and voice he has taught us to remember are not quite the real ones. (I am always surprised when I attend a Fields movie by how wrong his imitators are, and by some troubling quality in his face that no cartoonist has captured.) There is something about Fields himself that leaves one staring vacantly after the laughter is over."

The truth of the matter is that Fields was much more of a prisoner of his family in *The Bank Dick* (1940) than most of the film's admirers care to admit. His gorgon of a mother-in-law won't let him smoke in his own room. His wife is a perpetual nag, and his children have picked up the quaint habit of throwing things at him. He is often tempted to retaliate, but never quite manages. What saves him finally from hen-pecked oblivion are a series of accidental triumphs over swindlers and bank-robbers. Fields is not truly a free soul in the style of Michel Simon's anti-bourgeois clochard in Jean Renoir's *Boudu Sauvé des Eaux* (1932). Fields is more the problem drinker and saloon Socrates who seeks freedom at the bottom of a bottle. He does not yearn for the open road: there is something inescapably urban, if not cosmopolitan, about him. He is everyone's impecunious uncle with valises full of worthless stocks. Hence, his inspired type-casting as Micawber in *David Copperfield* (1935). His bulbous nose and flushed features were merely the most conspicuous symptoms of a tendency to draw upon tomorrow in order to get through today.

Fields appeared in forty films between 1915 and 1945, eleven in the silent era (1915–28) and twenty-nine in the sound era (1930–45). Until quite recently, the silent films did not loom large in his legend. The non-verbal Fields seemed a contradiction in terms, since it is through his throwaway lines, and not through his movements and gestures, that he is most frequently imitated. What is most interesting about his silent films—at least after his vaudeville-type debut in *Pool Sharks* in 1915—is that they are more integrated as movies than most of his sound films. D. W. Griffith's *Sally of the Sawdust* (1925) and *That Royle Girl* (1926) were sentimental romances in which Fields assumed a sweetly paternal relationship to Griffith's spunky twenties-type ingenue, Carol Dempster. His two most effective films, silent or sound, were Gregory La Cava's *So's Your Old Man* (1926) and *Running Wild* (1927), two very carefully constructed farce comedies in which Fields tended to be less eccentric and misanthropic than he was to seem later when his voice could serve as an instrument of detached derision. Nonetheless, if his career had ended in the silent era, he would have been as marginally memorable as Will Rogers in *his* silent period.

Our impressions of Fields in the early sound era are derived disproportionately from a series of shorts he made between 1930 and 1933— *The Gold Specialist* (1930), *The Dentist* (1932), *The Barber Shop, The Fatal Glass of Beer,* and *The Pharmacist* (all 1933). In these orgies of wild, violent, illogical, disconnected slapstick, Fields established his hundred-proof comic persona against which all his other screen appearances would be considered sentimental dilutions. Besides, there had always been a feeling that short films were better suited than long films to the purposes of pure farce. This was a critical line that James Agee had applied to the earlier works of Chaplin and Keaton. Also, the very absence of logic in the Fields shorts encouraged critics to posit surrealist values in the works. Even in the shorts, however, the pacing was nothing short of exasperating, a quality prevalent in the early Laurel and Hardy talkies as well. With the coming of sound there was a tendency to let the spoken voice reverberate before cutting to the next action. But in the jumble of Fieldsian sadism represented in these shorts, the deliberateness of the pacing seems to add to the pain of the poor wretches whose fingers, toes, teeth, beards, and heads of hair fall into the path of Field's malevolent muse of mangle.

Overlooked in this period is the relatively sentimental patriarch Fields portrayed in William Dieterle's *Her Majesty Love* (1931) and *Poppy* (1936), not to mention the comfortable camaraderie he enjoyed with portly, matronly Alison Skipworth in *If I Had a Million* (1932) and *Tillie and Gus* (1933). Indeed, Otis Ferguson complained that Fields was being wasted in most of his Paramount features through the thirties. In retrospect, however, Fields may have been fortunate to have found himself in a studio as relatively anarchic as financially floundering Paramount. Although *Million Dollar Legs* (1932) and *International House* (1933), particularly the latter, tend to be more manic than mirthful, they give Fields more physical outlet than he will find later. His titanic arm-wrestling duels with fidgety Hugh Herbert in *Million Dollar Legs* are especially exhilarating displays of daffy muscularity in the context of the Olympic Games. Still, the most memorable performer in *Legs* is the ineffable Lyda Roberti, with her assertive flirting, and in *International House* Cab Calloway, with his legendary rendition of "Reefer Man." Fields was even less dominant in such grab-bag films as *Alice in Wonderland* and *The Big Broadcast of 1938.* And in *Her Majesty Love,* it is Leon Errol as the aging, defeated sensualist who provides most of the comedy and the pathos. Fields comes on very late in *Six of a Kind* and *Mrs. Wiggs of the Cabbage Patch* (both 1934), and yet he fits very felicitously into the patterns of the two films—in both instances as a catch-up raconteur who can sum up an entire life between two billiard shots or two cups of coffee. If his reputation often exceeded his roles, he never let his roles suffer in the process.

It was common knowledge in the thirties that Fields "wrote" most of his own lines. Whether this means that he improvised on the set or that he inserted much-muttered vaudeville patter into any appropriate juncture in the scenario, the end result was that he remained a remarkably consistent character-type from one appearance to the next. At the very least, he never appeared in a role which was unfaithful to his public persona. Hence, he could never have been cast as Uriah Heep in *David Copperfield* or as the malignant banker in *Mrs. Wiggs of the Cabbage Patch*. Indeed, it seems a bit strange even at this late date that Fields once poached on Groucho's terrain by persecuting Margaret Dumont in an excised episode from *Tales of Manhattan* (1942). But this is not to say that his performances were frozen into a fixed pattern of familiar mannerisms. His costume, for example, was extremely varied in its seedy ornateness, and was often aggressively archaic as well. He fidgeted about a great deal with canes and hats, but not always the same cane and the same hat. Certain oddly memorable bits of business were confined to a single movie. For example, his bizarre habit of blowing into his socks before he put them on is demonstrated again and again in the burglars-in-the-night routine in *The Man on the Flying Trapeze* (1935), but in no other Fields movie. Was this a bit of comic business or a touch of behavioral realism in the daily routine of a house-broken creature? We are never quite sure with Fields because he seems perpetually suspended between the fantasy of farce and the drudgery of domesticity.

As his own *auteur*, Fields responded to the perennial pressures on comedians to integrate their routines with a coherent story-line. But the Fields legend is composed almost entirely of his incidental asides as if he had spent his entire career commenting on his movies instead of playing in them. Thus in some ways his late Universal features seem more characteristic of Fields the commentator than his earlier Paramounts. *You Can't Cheat an Honest Man* (1939) represents the evolution of Fields as a popular comedian on radio (quintessentially the realm of the voice over the image) alongside his traditional nemesis, Edgar Bergen's Charlie McCarthy. In both *The Bank Dick* (1940) and *Never Give a Sucker an Even Break* (1941) there are episodes in which Fields is trying to sell a far-fetched scenario to a movie company. Perhaps there is a parallel here between the fictional frustrations of Fields at Universal with his earlier real-life rejection by Paramount. By the early forties, audiences had completely forgotten the so-called Golden Age of silent comedies and thus film-makers began quoting the slapstick classics with impunity. The process-shot car-chase had been a staple since the early talkies, but in *The Bank Dick* it was supplemented with a direct steal from Buster Keaton's *Sherlock, Jr.* with the bit of business about a speeding motorist passing a slew of synchronized ditch-diggers. A very famous still of this later period shows Fields delicately balancing a cherry (from an ice-cream soda) between two straws while his entire face puckers with delirious anticipation.

It suffices for the Fields legend that Fields should thus seem to parody Hollywood squeamishness about his own drinking proclivities to the extent of detouring him from his natural destination—the saloon—to that euphemism of "family entertainment"—the ice-cream parlor. As for maturing child actress Gloria Jean, Universal's delectable soprano Lolita of that period, there was never a question of Fields's tampering with *her* sentimental formulation. With Gloria Jean here as with Rochelle Hudson in *Poppy*, Fields played the patriarch marshmallow to a fare-thee-well.

By any standard, the transcendent reputation of *The Bank Dick* in Fields's career seems inflated (by me as well in *The American Cinema*). Ron Alexander's witty play about television, *Never Love an Albatross*, actually cites *The Bank Dick* as the funniest movie ever made. One wonders why. Hollywood talking comedy was at its peak in the decade 1934–44, and it is hard to believe that anyone exposed to Preston Sturges in that period could have been more satisfied by *The Bank Dick*. There is very little verbal wit beyond Fields's inquiry of a bartender as to the whereabouts of Mr. Michael Finn, preparing us for the forthcoming ordeal of a bothersome bank examiner played with gallant masochism by Franklin Pangborn. The family stuff with the three generations of female shrews is handled much more humorously in Noel Coward's one-act theater piece "Fumed Oak." And the melodrama with Grady Sutton's badgered suitor is rather strenuously mechanical. Worst of all, *The Bank Dick* doesn't really connect structurally as much as it reverberates mythically as an idea for a movie that never got made. By contrast, *It's a Gift* (1934) contains some of the most ambitious comic episodes in Fields's career, most notably the sequence with the malevolent blind man's wreaking havoc in Fields's grocery store. Even here, however, people gleefully misremember the ending of this episode by suggesting that Fields sends the Buñuelian blind wretch into heavy traffic in a futile attempt to dispose of him. Nothing of the kind. Fields thoughtfully sends the blind man across what starts out as an empty street and then suddenly fills up with dangerous traffic. The difference here between fact and legend is symptomatic of the Fields problem in film scholarship.

Another extraordinary episode sets up an entire apartment complex in long-shot beehive fashion so as to display the source and movement of every annoyance known to a would-be slumberer. Here Fields is victimized on such a massive scale as to make Laurel and Hardy look like princes of privilege, but we are not induced to laugh at his suffering as we do at theirs. The ambition is there, and the annoyance, but not the affect. Perhaps we sense that Fields is in some sinister way the architect of his own suffering for reasons that none of his movies dared to explore.

■   ■   ■   ■

ROD STEIGER'S INCARNATION of W. C. Fields in *W. C. Fields and Me* (1976) was about as good as one can expect in waxworks enterprises of this kind, which is not bad, not bad at all. Unlike the poor wretches impersonating Gable and Lombard, the substantially talented Mr. Steiger establishes a screen presence to which we can respond with some intelligent speculation. At the very least, he makes us wonder what the real W. C. Fields was like, what made him tick, and what made him endlessly fascinating to so many male intellectuals with no particular fondness for film. I have never known a woman who really liked Fields, and I have never known a man who could not resist taking a fling now and then at mimicking Field's flair with throwaway lines. Indeed, Fields always had so many amateur imitators that the professional imitators generally left him alone. I once saw Dustin Hoffman do a snatch of Fields in a Murray Schisgal stage farce, but for the rest, it has always been private auditions. That Fields seemed to be so easy to imitate may be a clue to his comic strategy: Supply the reaction and let the rest of the world supply the appropriate aggravation.

Robert Lewis Taylor, Fields's most admired biographer in his 1949 *W. C. Fields: His Follies and Fortunes*, makes extravagant claims for Fields: "By the time of his death, on Christmas Day, 1946, he was widely acknowledged to have become the greatest comic artist ever known." Taylor provides an interesting rationale for Fields's alleged pre-eminence: "He became a symbol of fun; the applied skill of Chaplin and other funny men delighted audiences, but lovers of comedy laughed at the mention of Fields's name."

Note the implied derogation of "applied skill" in the preceding passage. Taylor, a staff writer for *The New Yorker* in his time, exemplified the traditional *New Yorker*-ish condescension toward Hollywood movies. He seems not to have seen all the Fields movies and very few movies in general. And yet he praises Fields for projecting his own personality instead of creating a part or personality on the screen. Why then do anti-Hollywood people scold other movie stars for projecting their own personalities instead of playing Lear with a long beard? For Taylor and for many other Fields admirers, art seems to get lower grades than authenticity.

Another pro-Fields ploy recounted in the Taylor book and in the memoirs of his mistress Carlotta Monti (with Cy Rice), the latter book ostensibly the source reference for the Steiger movie, is the notion that Fields was always jealous of Chaplin's standing as Number One, the implication being that Fields was at least Number Two. I don't happen to believe that comedians can be ranked in this fashion. People who prefer Chaplin are likely to place Fields closer to twenty-two than to two, and people who prefer Fields probably don't like Chaplin at all. There is no way of telling in this instance because so much of Chaplin's art has been preserved on film, and so much of Fields's art from the stage has been lost. Chaplin happens to be an axis of the cinema, Fields merely a meteorite from another galaxy.

One can never resolve arguments about comedians. One can only explain one's own prejudices and predilections. Even the idea of Fields has never struck me as all that funny. Wilfrid Sheed very eloquently describes the poetic fantasy at the end and at the heart of *The Bank Dick*: "The family in *The Bank Dick* stand stiffly on the porch in their Sunday best: Egbert Souse, Fields's dream of himself, his masterpiece, escapes down the driveway to the Black Pussy Cafe and freedom."

Why then does not a tear trickle down my cheek as I smile at Egbert's exquisite deliverance from domesticity? Part of the problem may be that I have never known the joy of standing with the stags around a bar, drinking myself to a noisy oblivion. I was never seduced by the saloon culture. Not that I had anything better to do much of the time: I simply never fell into that particular pattern. Even the coffee-house syndrome of the sixties struck me as a waste of time. The forlorn consolation of conviviality, however mediocre, is consequently a Fieldsian message to which I cannot respond in my gut. I don't feel it, and I never will. As for the family on the porch in their Sunday best, they are very crude caricatures with just a touch of Stroheim's sarcasm in *Greed* (1923). If they were more real, Fields would seem less heroic to his champions. *The Bank Dick* harks back to silent movies with its overdrawn types for comic contrast, but Fields cheats with his verbal wit. We don't really "see" anyone else in the film because we listen only for Fields. Even Garbo with William Daniels on camera never had more of an edge on the rest of the company.

But though I can't respond deeply enough to Fields's fantasy life so as to love his comic vision of liberation—and love, not laughter is the key to appreciating comedians—I do find that the idea and the image of Fields are more complex than I had previously imagined. But now it is very difficult to sift the facts from the legends, and, as Sheed has suggested, it may not even be desirable to do. Even so, the Steiger movie (directed by Arthur Hill from a screenplay by Bob Merrill) seems to go out of its way to invent outright falsehoods as a way of goosing up the plot. The career chronology is all wrong. Fields is shown trying to get into movies around 1932 (via a still of *Shanghai Express* on the Paramount lot). Actually, he made his first screen appearance back in 1915, and appeared in several prominent pictures in the twenties. Nor did he arrive in Hollywood penniless but for the generosity of a midget friend. Actually, he had upward of $300,000 in his pockets.

Curiously, the Steiger movie drifts closer to Steiger than to Fields when lechery and machismo are introduced as leitmotifs. The "idea" of Fields does not sustain the notion that he ever went to bed with a woman, or even lusted after one. Indeed, the idea of Fields does not even acknowledge the existence of Carlotta Monti. As played by Valerie Perrine, the part of Carlotta seems even more a pointless distraction from the essentially sexless comic myth of W. C. Fields. Trying to play against her centerfold sensuality, Miss Perrine succeeds only in becoming a dull shrew with a heart of the most dubious gold.

Even the dentist comedy routine Fields allegedly did for the *Follies* is tricked up to make it appear that he was a Lenny Bruce ahead of his time. As it happened, Fields performed a version of this routine in a 1932 Sennett short called *The Dentist*. The censors banned it on the grounds that it was too suggestive of the sexual act. This sequence is reproduced in great detail in Richard J. Anobile's Fields picture book entitled *Godfrey Daniels* (Fields's movie euphemism for "Godamit"). The climax of the sequence with the lady patient's rolled-stockinged legs entwined around Fields's waist as he tried to work on her mouth—is positively pornographic, but only incidentally. Fields is actually frustrated because his patient's provocative gyrations are preventing him from getting at her mouth where he can inflict excruciating pain. Although it never came up in the casting, Fields always gave us the impression that he would get more pleasure from kicking a woman in the shins than from stroking her leg. More likely, he hated ugly women, and had given up on the pretty ones. In the Australian compilation film, *Brother, Can You Spare a Dime* (1975), there is a brief flash of Fields in an impromptu interview. "I feel like a June Bride," he exults. "What does a June Bride feel like?" he is asked. "I wonder," he replies with wizened wistfulness as he draws out these two words musingly so as to encompass a lifetime of yearning and regret. This gift of evoking instant identification and automatic autobiography with the most casual comment was invaluable to Fields. Most of his movies were thereby translated into personal newsreels with very indistinct backgrounds, and that is how his admirers tend to remember his movies and put them down in print. But if Fields is not seen as the center of the cinematic universe, his movies develop a bad case of the spaced-out longueurs.

Nowadays, people are so terrified of invoking Freud that they tend to overlook the most obvious clinical details. One can sense that Fields must have been a very unhappy man all his life. But until I had seen the Steiger movie and read up on the Fields literature I had not appreciated the full depths of his despair. It seems that Fields always loved to hear the sound of rain on the ceiling. It made him sleep more peacefully. His great regret was that it did not rain often enough in California. At the end of the Steiger movie, the dying comedian smiles as he hears the rain on the roof. It is actually Carlotta outside with a hose—*l'arroseuse maternelle*. The cinema suddenly discerns in a curious quirk an unmistakable longing to return to the wet sanctuary of the womb. It is on the screen that we most vividly witness the wish-fulfillment of a man who deeply desired never to have been born.

But, having been born, he saw no easy way out. Fields's comic method stressed the point that a prop could be bent, but never broken. Hence, the endless exasperation of his comic sequences deprived of the slapstick punctuation of custard pies and shattered crockery. No relief. No catharsis. Life went on in all its grim mediocrity and frustration. In this respect, *The Bank Dick* with its contrived optimism is less characteristic of the Fields style than the sado-masochistic middle-class agonies of *It's a Gift* and *The Man on the Flying Trapeze*. Significantly, few of Fields's movies made any appreciable amount of money in their own time. Now-adays everything from the thirties is quaint and nostalgic, but back then there was something in Fields that hurt too much to be laughed at. The trouble is that by being more than a comic actor, Fields was often much, much less. There are moments, as with Zasu Pitts in *Mrs. Wiggs of the Cabbage Patch*, when Fields seems actually to be acting in rapport with another human being. Most of the time, however, his virtuosity turns the screen into a shambles.

THE MARX BROTHERS

The Marx Brothers (Chico, 1886–1961; Harpo, 1888–1964; Groucho, 1890–1977) were a great many things: the only real-life sibling comedy team in movie history, the first clowns of the talkies to be spoken of in the same breath with Chaplin, Keaton, Lloyd, Langdon, Laurel and Hardy, *inter alia*, and fashionable figures of speech in an age when more bad jokes were told about the difference between Groucho Marx and Karl Marx than were told by Groucho himself. They were already middle-aged vaudeville and theater veterans when they made their screen debuts at the dawn of the sound era in 1929. They had drawn on their youth and comic energy in live but perishable entertainments for almost two decades before they finally cavorted in front of a camera at the old Par-amount Studio in Astoria. Consequently, one must be careful when talk-ing about a "decline" in their talents that one is not talking instead of the inevitable erosions of aging in the performing arts.

As the author of *The American Cinema* (1968) I failed to take these erosions into account in my measured evaluation of their oeuvre when I wrote that the Marx Brothers so completely dominated the slapstick scene in the early sound era that few moviegoers mourned the demise of pantomime. Except for Leo McCarey's relatively integrated *Duck Soup*, the Marx Brothers burrowed from within an invariably mediocre mise-en-scène to burst upon the audience with their distinctively anar-chic personalities. They were a welcome relief not only from the badness of their own movies but also from the badness of most of the movies around them. Except for Groucho's bad habit of doing double and triple takes after each bon mot to give his audience a chance to laugh, the Marx Brothers have worn reasonably well in the six decades since they burned themselves out somewhere between *A Night at the Opera* (1935) and *A Day at the Races* (1937). Their more intellectual admirers have compared them with everyone from the Brothers Karamazov to the Beatles. A case can be made for Groucho as Ivan, Harpo as Aloysha, and Chico as Dmitri. Groucho, the skeptic of the soundtrack, was often pitted against Harpo's Fool of silence. The highbrows laughed louder at Groucho, but they smiled more sweetly at Harpo. The Fool fell in more easily with the lingering aesthetic guilt over the demise of the silent film. For all practical purposes there were only three Marx Brothers. Zeppo and Gummo never counted, and Allan Jones was never anything more than one of Irving J. Thalberg's stray tenors. Groucho, however, was aided in no small measure by the exquisite dignity and self-abasement of Margaret Dumont, one of the greatest character comediennes in the history of the screen. Groucho's confrontations with Miss Dumont seem much more the heart of the Marxian matter today than the rather loose rapport among the three brothers themselves.

The limiting factor of the Marx Brothers is their failure to achieve the degree of production control managed by Chaplin throughout his career, and Keaton and Lloyd in the silent era. The Marx Brothers often had to sit by in compliant neutrality while the most inane plot conventions were being developed. *Monkey Business*, particularly, suffers from a studio-grafted gangster S. J. Perelman-punning intrigue in mock imitation of the gangster films of the time. It may seem trivial that Chaplin, Keaton, and Lloyd were always trying to get the girl, whereas the Marx Brothers were trying to get the girl for whatever straight man happened to be around at the time, but that is what made Chaplin, Keaton, and Lloyd major and the Marx Brothers minor.

Nonetheless, the best bits of the Marx Brothers were as funny as anything the sound film has produced. For starters, there is Groucho's land auction in *The Cocoanuts* (1929), Harpo's and Chico's bridge game in *Animal Crackers* (1930), Harpo's madness with the passports and the puppets in *Monkey Business* (1931), Harpo's and Groucho's bunny-nightcap confrontation in the imaginary mirror of *Duck Soup* (1933), and the stateroom scene in *A Night at the Opera* (1935). On the other side of the ledger were a profusion of piano and harp solos, bad puns from Groucho and Chico, and, toward the end, the desecrations of B-picture budgets and shooting schedules. As for the comparison between the Marx Brothers and the Beatles, the Marx Brothers, to borrow Priestley's phrase, tried to be mad in a sane world, whereas the Beatles tried to be sane in a mad world.

In the three decades since *The American Cinema* was published, the vogue for the Marx Brothers has appreciably diminished. Young people, particularly, do not "get" the humor of antic clowns pricking the pomposities of dowagers and stuffed shirts, themselves varieties of endangered species in the increasing informality at every stratum of society. Indeed, the Marx Brothers seem to exude an elitist elegance even in the midst of their madcap frolics. There is a tastefulness even in their wildest tantrums that excludes the gratuitous grossness that has engulfed screen comedy in the nineties. European to the core, they combined indefatigable melting pot energy with an authentically aristocratic force of expression. Far from being brutish despoilers, the Marx Brothers were supercivilized invaders of semi-civilized bastions. They were also quintessentially Jewish in demanding that one's subconscious impulses swirl to the surface of social behavior. In their early pictures, particularly, they seemed to purvey a more enlightened form of chic in their bizarre manifestations at otherwise mediocre festivities. Thus, they served ultimately as the salvation of the dull parties they destroyed. What audiences applauded most fervently was the visible and audible phenomenon of the Marx Brothers being the life rather than the death of every party they attended.

At their most inspired, the Marx Brothers not only memorialized their own personal history on the vaudeville stage from the turn of the century through the twenties; they also preserved for all time on film some sense of the loose, chaotic spirit of the early talkies, those strange hybrids suspended halfway between stage and screen. For a long time it was fashionable to deplore *The Cocoanuts* (1929) and even *Animal Crackers* (1930) for not conforming to purist theorems of the cinema. But with the lengthening perspectives of film history, the most archaic peculiarities of *The Cocoanuts* seem to catch the Marx Brothers off guard, as it were, at moments of uncharted reflex. Nor does the apparent misdirection of Robert Florey and Joseph Santley seem as crucial an issue as it once did. Joe Adamson's definitive study of the Marx Brothers (*Groucho, Harpo, Chico and Sometimes Zeppo*) suggests that some of the innovations in *The Cocoanuts* (mostly from George Folsey's overhead camerawork) anticipates the startling effects in Rouben Mamoulian's *Applause* (1929) and in the aerially balletic Busby Berkeley musicals. What Adamson cannot forgive in Florey's direction is his mishandling the Marx Brothers as funnymen.

■   ■   ■   ■

IN ANY EVENT, *The Cocoanuts* is the first, rawest, and crudest film by the Brothers Marx. It is celluloid at its most primitive, but it is historically fascinating and hilariously funny. Groucho has said of the two directors that Florey didn't understand English and Santley didn't understand Harpo. Scenarist George S. Kaufman and composer Irving Berlin watched their lines and songs (including "Always") completely disappear in the mayhem. Yet here were all the basic Marxian movie conventions being born, especially the verbal savaging that Groucho would inflict on Dumont as he invited her to "bull and cow" in the moonlight. Groucho—behind a seedy, vaguely establishment façade—bemusedly tolerates the anarchic Harpo in his debut here, in which he eats a telephone. Groucho is also infinitely patient with Chico's heroic stupidity, especially in the classic "Vy a duck?" routine.

Norman McLeod's *Monkey Business* (1931) is a Marxian merriment at the beginning of their peak Paramount period. Though Margaret Dumont was sorely missed, Groucho especially capitalized on the enhanced, elaborate verbal byplay supplied by the brilliant team led by S. J. Perelman, and the nonsense plot supplied some of Harpo's loveliest set-pieces and Chico's most felicitous team-work. Beginning with the rondelet on "Sweet Adeline" in adjoining herring barrels, the nonstop chase on an ocean liner is the Brothers' longest, most graceful movie passage. Other Marxian vehicles like *Duck Soup* and *A Night at the Opera* achieved greater highs, but none came near to stretching such a comic distance so smoothly and hilariously. When the liner finally berths, the movie almost collapses from exhaustion. But why quibble? The Brothers Marx are magnificent here, and the unjustly unsung Thelma Todd is no mean comic foil.

Leo McCarey's *Duck Soup* (1933) is the most zanily absurdist and the funniest of the Marx Brothers films. Not only is Groucho reunited with Margaret Dumont, whom he continues to torment without mercy, but he also takes delight in deflating her stuffed shirt suitor played with hilariously sputtering incomprehension by the Shakespearean actor Louis Calhern. As an ensemble act drawing upon the full weaponry of vaudeville humor, the Brothers unleash a comic anarchy that for once reduces kingdoms to shambles as they romp down corridors of palace power, through the halls of justice, and onto the final Armageddon of a crazy battlefield. *Duck Soup* is also the ultimate Groucho vehicle, a con man's fantasia, and he is able to change moods, scenes, and story-lines with surreal abandon. Much of the slapstick, including Harpo's inexorable destruction of Edgar Kennedy's vending cart, evokes the chain-reaction savagery of Laurel and Hardy, and the shock of a Sennett custard pie in the face.

But there are also inexplicable Dadaist insertions, like Harpo's diversion to a bathtub during a Paul Revere ride, and time for moments of grace, such as the Chaplin-esque classic mirror sequence with its mimetic split-second timing. At their best, the boys cornered all the big laughs of the Golden Age of silent comedy, and dressed them for the talkie era. And *Duck Soup* is their best. Sam Wood's *A Night at the Opera* (1935) was the most popular and is still the most fondly remembered of of all the Marx Brothers movies. It contains some of their most extended slapstick and a couple of Groucho's most extended riffs of verbal insanity. The trio was able to go back to their beginnings by teaming up again with Kaufman and Ryskind and, above all, by being allowed to fine tune the material by performing it as live vaudeville for a few weeks before shooting. Irving Thalberg at MGM was their new mentor and apparently approved of the shift toward Groucho's one-liners and Chico's malapropisms and away from Harpo's pantomimic surrealism. The musical love interest teaming Kitty Carlisle and Allan Jones was also more prominent than before. Indeed, my mother enjoyed the singers so much that she wondered aloud why those three crazy comedians were always breaking the mood. For people with more anarchic tastes there were such memorable scenes as the infamously hilarious stateroom sequence and the furious disruption of the Verdi opera itself.

SPENCER TRACY AND KATHARINE HEPBURN

Spencer Tracy (1900–1967)

Larry Swindell's remarkably knowledgeable biography of the late Spencer Tracy (*Spencer Tracy*) deserves the attention not only of the actor's admirers in particular but also of film scholars and historians in general. The author skillfully threads his way through a maze of Hollywood gossip, scandal, ego thrust, and power politics without losing sight of the myth and magic and even art of the movies. By contrast, Donald Deschner's book on the actor's career (*The Films of Spencer Tracy*) is strictly a paste-up of newspaper clippings and pall-bearing testimonials dedicated to the overfamiliar proposition that Spence was a nice guy who tended to underplay all his roles both on and off the screen, a far cry from the madcap Irish whirlwind Swindell describes in much breezier fashion.

Tracy, a child of the century (born Spencer Bonaventure Tracy in Milwaukee, Wisconsin, April 5, 1900), was well into his thirties before he became an Oscar-worthy adornment at MGM, and, occasionally, even a Box-Office Champion. Swindell's book is especially useful for its rediscovery of Tracy's young, lost years (for the myth-makers) between 1930 and 1936, when he was grinding out the kind of program pictures from which posthumous cults are conceived. Justice William O. Douglas (in the Deschner book) likens Tracy's "American" quality to that of Thoreau, Emerson, Frost, but this again is an image of the elder Tracy, in whose reformed features the indomitable granite jaw firmed up the sensual leprechaun lips and the guileful Irish eyes of the rascals he played in such undeservedly neglected early thirties movies as John Ford's *Up the River* (1930), Rowland Brown's *Quick Millions* (1931), Michael Curtiz's *20,000 Years in Sing Sing* (1933), William K. Howard's *The Power and the Glory* (1933), and Frank Borzage's *A Man's Castle* (1933), one of the very few films that managed to captured the emotional nuances of the Depression.

Tracy never really made it on his own as a star personality despite all the tributes heaped upon him by his peers. Laurence Olivier, for example, considered Tracy the premier actor on the screen. Even so, the studio did not consider Tracy sexy enough to compete with the Coopers and the Gables, or even with mere pretty-boys like Robert Taylor and Tyrone Power. He was not anarchic enough to fill the gangster slots of a Cagney or a Robinson, not earthy enough to swagger in character leads like a Laughton or a Beery. In his younger days he never successfully projected either the rural idealism of James Stewart and Henry Fonda or the urban non-conformism of Humphrey Bogart and John Garfield. At MGM he fell into the somewhat demeaning best-friend-who-never-gets-the-girl relationship to Clark Gable that Tracy's erstwhile New York roommate Pat O'Brien had fallen into at Warners with James Cagney.

Significantly, he won his first Oscar in a film (*Captains Courageous,* 1937) in which he had second billing to Freddie Bartholomew, and his second in a film (*Boys Town,* 1938) in which he played second fiddle to a diminutive virtuoso named Mickey Rooney. He played, albeit reluctantly, too many priests and too many men of dull distinction. Insult was added to indignity in 1943 when Tracy was forced to die in *A Guy Named Joe*, so that he could lose his sweetheart (Irene Dunne) to Van Johnson for the sake of teen-age audiences. Tracy's presence on screen as a ghost egging on Dunne and Johnson is as embarrassing today as his quiet contemplation of Irene Dunne serenading him by the fire with "I'll Get By" is enchanting.

Unfortunately, Tracy's habitual superiority to his material tended to limit the range of material offered to him. In later years, particularly, he tended to appear in sermons rather than movies. Still, there were the nine stylish Adam's-rib adventures in which he played a puckish Petruchio to Hepburn's luminous Kate, and those unforgettably vulnerable moments in *Captains Courageous*, *Bad Day at Black Rock* (1955), *The People Against O'Hara* (1951), and *The Last Hurrah* (1958), when Spencer Tracy gazed at the angel of death and showed the world through the art of acting what it means truly to be a man.

Katharine Hepburn (1907–)

The case for Katharine Hepburn begins with the stipulation that, among native American-born actresses, Lillian Gish (mostly in the silent era) and Hepburn (entirely in the sound era) have proven to be the most prodigious, the most durable, and the most dedicated of screen presences. They are both quintessential survivors. Yet, ironically enough, Gish had to outlive the stigma of being the last great Victorian tintype, whereas Hepburn has had to overcome all the ancient taboos against her eccentric brand of sassy feminism.

The crucial period for any significant revaluation of Hepburn's career is that between 1932 and 1938, beginning with her electrifying debut in *A Bill of Divorcement* and ending with her virtual banishment as "box-office poison" from Hollywood on the heels of her now classic performances in *Bringing Up Baby* and *Holiday*. Of the fifteen movies in which Hepburn appeared in the thirties all but one were made at RKO, whereas all but one of the eleven movies in which she appeared in the forties were made at MGM. Her career can thus be discussed in the thirties as her RKO period, and in the forties as her MGM period. Simply in terms of studio mystiques, RKO has always been as much under-rated as MGM has been over-rated. From another perspective entirely, however, though an inescapably obvious one, the thirties preceded the forties and Hepburn was younger, wilder, rawer, fresher, more vibrant, more vulnerable, and, most of all, more threatening. As the legend goes, she left Hollywood as much out of fashion as such other dispensers of "box office poison" as Greta Garbo, Marlene Dietrich, Fred Astaire, Joan Crawford, and Kay Francis.

Fortunately, Hepburn's career crisis was resolved spectacularly with her smash success on the stage in 1939 as Tracy Lord in *The Philadelphia Story*. More than forty years later, she was still a remarkably hot item in the motion-picture industry. And she did it all *her* way.

So much for the legend. Let's get on with the revisionism. I have never liked the movie version of *The Philadelphia Story*. I did not like it when I saw it originally as a twelve-year-old, and I have never liked it in revival. The characters are all too smugly exhibitionist as they prattle on about privacy and breeding. I had never seen the play performed before its disastrous reincarnation at Lincoln Center in 1981, but I had read Philip Barry's text, and aside from one ribald joke involving a pun on Wanamaker, and an additional member of the family, there did not seem to be much difference between the play and the screenplay. I could only fantasize about how Joseph Cotten had played the Cary Grant role in the original production, and how Van Heflin had played the James Stewart role, and how Shirley Booth had played the Ruth Hussey role, and how Katharine Hepburn had played the Katharine Hepburn role. But it was not until I actually saw Blythe Danner, almost invariably a luminous stage performer, groping desperately with the part of Tracy Lord that I perceived for the first time the real subject of *The Philadelphia Story*. The play was not about a spoiled mainline socialite *like* Katharine Hepburn. The play was about Katharine Hepburn herself, and what the American people thought about Katharine Hepburn in 1939, and what Katharine Hepburn realized that she had to do to keep her career going. *The Philadelphia Story* is quite simply the breaking, reining, and saddling of an unruly thoroughbred for the big races to come on Broadway and in Hollywood. It is Katharine Hepburn getting her comeuppance at long last, and accepting it like the good sport she was.

Indeed, the entire play consists of her being scolded incessantly for her shortcomings as a daughter and a wife. The fact that her wastrel playboy husband drank himself into a divorce was naturally her fault because she lacked wifely compassion. The fact that her father indulged in a scandalous affair with a chorus girl was also her fault because she lacked daughterly compassion. Though we never see the chorus girl on stage or screen, it does seem a bit unfair to write off her charms in such a fashion. But what nonsense! If you had been a better daughter, I would not have hurt your mother by committing adultery. Aren't you ashamed of yourself, Tracy Lord, alias Katharine Hepburn? How pathetic can patriarchal self-righteousness become before it degenerates into sheer idiocy? It is hard to believe that 1939 theater audiences and 1940 movie audiences accepted with straight faces this nonsensical guilt trip for Hepburn's Modern Woman. Indeed, were these audiences really any more advanced than those who fully expected Nora to return to her husband in the first productions of Ibsen's *A Doll's House?*

In a sense, therefore, *The Philadelphia Story* marks the beginning of Hepburn's domestication with her own consent and even collaboration. People were more comfortable with her in the forties. She had become a better actress, they said. Good old underacting Spencer Tracy had reportedly "cut her down to size," in the words of Joseph L. Mankiewicz, then producer of *Woman of the Year* (1942). Kate and Spencer, on screen and off, became a strangely reassuring couple. And there were dazzling moments in *Woman of the Year* and *Keeper of the Flame* (1942) when Hepburn is as beautiful and as sexually desirable as she has ever been. Sooner or later, however, each of her forties movies ends with her safely in the fold, just one of the herd. All the rebellion and hysteria and aggravating indecorousness of her RKO period have been drained out of her. She might still speak out for Henry Wallace, but she had finally been harmonized with the sexual politics of her time.

My earliest moviegoing memories of Kate are in *Mary of Scotland* (1936) and *Stage Door* (1937), and in the latter classic I was more taken with Ginger Rogers and Andrea Leeds than with Hepburn. It was not until I was older and began seeing her early films in revival that I began responding to something extraordinary in her talent. *Morning Glory* (1933), *Alice Adams* (1935), and *Holiday* (1938) remain the major revelations in the thirties, but there are flashes as well in *Little Women* (1933), *The Little Minister* (1934), *Sylvia Scarlett* (1936), and *A Woman Rebels* (1936). I even have a guilty affection for *Christopher Strong* and *Break of Hearts* (both 1933), two confused works that are virtually indefensible in the domains of dramatic narrative.

George Cukor, who was a quintessential survivor in his own right, tried to build up Hepburn's performance in *A Bill of Divorcement* at the expense of her Oscar-winning performance in Lowell Sherman's *Morning Glory*. Yet *Morning Glory* is an infinitely better movie by any standard, and Hepburn's performance is light years more advanced, with a self-mocking irony and delirious rapture that few actresses have ever attempted, much less achieved. It is as fantastically original a creation as Garbo's in *Camille* (1937), but, whereas Garbo strips away the conventions with a seductive humor, Hepburn explodes the conventions with a baroque hysteria. She is all the brashness of youth uncorrupted by the whorishly ingratiating tricks of the *grandes dames* of the theater. Take me as I am, rough edges and all, she seemed to say, and, naturally everyone said in response, learn to smooth out your rough edges. Make everyone love you even when you play a hateful part. That is not me, dear audience, that is the part. Look how awful the character I play happens to be.

Yet, Hepburn's rough edges generated an emotional electricity on the screen during her RKO period, but an electricity that has been appreciated only very recently for its transmission of deep feeling. From the beginning there were in Hepburn's voice and manner two distinctly annoying tendencies, the first a self-assured acknowledgment of her upper-class origins, and the second a Shavian independence of spirit. In some ways, she manifested radical chic before it was chic. She was a meddler in movies, but not ultimately a prima donna. Top billing, for example, never held any sacred importance for her, and she virtually sponsored many other people's careers. Yet she would fight tooth and nail over the direction of a scene. It was her intelligence and not her vanity for which she demanded tribute, and she did not bother disguising her assertiveness. Yet, though her performances were often demeaned by critics as abrasive and artificial, they have more guts in them than almost anything else of their time. In *Morning Glory* she documents every young girl's troubled dreams of becoming an actress. In *Alice Adams* she vibrates with every snub known to a girl straining to rise above her station. The nakedness of feeling in her thirties films enriched the cinema with an eroticism of the heart. The late André Bazin once wrote that Charlie Chaplin's cinema was the cinema of a free man. For a time, Katharine Hepburn's cinema was the cinema of a free woman.

Tracy and Hepburn

Woman of the Year was a fateful project for Spencer Tracy and Katharine Hepburn not only because it launched them on a turbulent extra-marital romance, but also because it foreshadowed the political tensions that were to traumatize Hollywood in the late forties and early fifties. In her 1985 authoritative biography of Katharine Hepburn (*A Remarkable*

Woman), Anne Edwards traces the genesis of the movie back to a sketchy treatment entitled *The Thing About Women* by writer-director Garson Kanin, who saw in the real-life experiences of world-famous journalist Dorothy Thompson and Nobel Prize–winning novelist Sinclair Lewis an ideal vehicle for Katharine Hepburn and Spencer Tracy. Thompson had been hailed in a 1939 *Time* cover story, even being paired with Eleanor Roosevelt as "undoubtedly the most influential woman in the U.S." Her expulsion from Germany in 1934 by Hitler was followed in 1935 by her being named Woman of the Year because (as Edwards quotes mystery writer Mary Roberts Rinehart introducing Thompson on that occasion), "she is the woman journalist at her best. She thinks and works like a man but remains very much a woman; and because she has made a success of her marriage with Sinclair Lewis, and that, I fancy, with that brilliant and talented person would be a career in itself for a woman."

As is so often the case with too-successful two-career marriages, Mr. and Mrs. Sinclair Lewis announced their filing for divorce two years after the Rinehart tribute to Thompson. This was the anti-feminist twist to the tale that fitted neatly with Hollywood's sexual politics at the moment in film history when it was required for Hepburn to be punished for her unwomanly presumption.

Kanin, one of Hepburn's personal friends, had given his treatment and added a Pirandellian touch by naming the Thompson character "Tess Harding," a sly meld of Tess Trueheart from the popular Dick Tracy comic strip and long-time Hepburn confidante and companion Laura Harding. But because of prior commitments to write and direct two war documentaries, Kanin turned over his treatment, actually little more than an outline, to his screenwriter brother Michael Kanin and Ring Lardner, Jr. In three weeks the two newly introduced scribes produced a 30,000-word novella told in the first person by the Tracy-Lewis character, and still entitled *The Thing About Women*. The script was then mailed to Garson Kanin, who trans-shipped it to Hepburn.

Thus began the legend of Hepburn's audacious maneuvers to get a major motion picture produced out of a script by two undervalued screenwriters whom she kept anonymous so as to jack up their price. Ring Lardner, Jr., particularly, was already considered a trouble-maker by the powers at MGM for his activities with the Screen Writers Guild. Lardner was later to be pilloried as one of the Hollywood Ten. But this was 1942, and the Soviet Union had been embraced even at MGM as a glorious ally.

Actually, the overt ideological content in *Woman of the Year* is innocuous enough. There are references to refugees, and some of these victims of Nazi aggression are even seen in the flesh, but Dorothy Thompson's bristling liberalism is suggested more by Hepburn's manner than by any inflammatory lines in the script. In their deliriously and deliciously photographed drunk scene, Tracy's Sam asks Hepburn's Tess what it was really like in the last days of the Spanish Republic. Such a query, common enough in the forties, would have earned the screenwriters a Congressional contempt citation in the fifties. In this moment of history, however, Spencer Tracy, the devoutly guilt-ridden Irish Catholic from Wisconsin, was in tune politically with Katharine Hepburn, the New England Protestant liberal, through their shared admiration for Franklin Delano Roosevelt.

Significantly, the strenuously deadpan treatment of Hepburn's agonizing attempt to make breakfast for a bemused Tracy concludes *Woman of the Year* on a reassuringly patriarchal note. This ponderously unfunny scene was not in the original Kanin–Lardner, Jr., script, but was added afterward, presumably to give more punch to the *Taming of the Shrew* motif. What up to then had been an emotionally developed comedy of character degenerates into a mechanical farce that relies on the recalcitrance of kitchen gadgets when handled by a feminist klutz.

It is not as if the anti-modern-woman message had not already been underlined by a parallel romance involving Hepburn's widowed father (Minor Watson) and her adopted mother and beloved feminist role model (Fay Bainter). Indeed, the "moral" of the movie could be encapsulated by the fame-and-public-self-fulfillment-are-no-substitute-for-the-private-joys-of-marriage speech Bainter delivers with a slight throb in her voice to the stubbornly skeptical Hepburn. Bainter not only articulates Hollywood's undisputed philosophy about the proper role for women; she also demonstrates the amazing ability of talented performers to deliver the most reactionary messages with grace and charm. Ultimately, *Woman of the Year* must be considered a progressive film but not for its final arguments, introducing Hepburn as a seductive alternative to Hollywood's dressed-up barefoot-in-the-kitchen ideal.

Woman of the Year served also as an extraordinarily prophetic expression of the discreet and devoted Tracy-Hepburn relationship that was to endure for more than a quarter of a century until his death in 1967. They remained an item without ever becoming a scandal. Scandal, after all, requires a drastic break from routine. Tracy and Hepburn had given short shrift to routine long before they met. Tracy had been tagged early on as a troublemaker, moody, contentious, chronically addicted to drink and wild, wild women. His affair with Loretta Young at the time of *A Man's Castle* (1933) was almost common knowledge. For her part, Hepburn aroused speculation simply by remaining single amid a bewildering array of a male and female associations. Her liaisons with John Ford and Howard Hughes now seem incongruous if not downright inconsistent with her professed feminist image of independence. But then Hepburn had always liked men. She simply chose not to be ordered about by them, and in Hollywood that constituted heresy.

To a certain extent, however, Hepburn can be said to have subordinated her own career to Tracy's medical and emotional needs. After *Woman of the Year*, both stars were approaching the great barrier reef of middle age, and their studio of choice, MGM, was gradually declining and failing as well. The Tracy-Hepburn mystique persisted, but very soon, despite brief flashes of brilliance in *Adam's Rib* (1949) and *Pat and Mike* (1951), for the general public the bloom was off the rose.

Adam's Rib belied its biblically sexist title when it surfaced in 1949 as an instant classic of feminist sass and savvy. Almost fifty years later time has not withered nor custom staled its bubbly sparkle. The triumphant reunion of Spencer Tracy and Katharine Hepburn, as married lawyers on opposite sides of the courtroom war between the sexes, occupied the comic foreground, while four extraordinarily talented newcomers to the screen filled in the background with incisively drawn farcical brushstrokes. Judy Holliday played the homicidally driven wife on trial for shooting up her spouse's love nest with said spouse and his sweetie still billing and cooing inside. Jean Hagen played the sweetie with some of the acerbic bitchiness she was later to lavish on Lina Lamont, her immortal satiric creation in *Singin' in the Rain* (1952). The rubbery-faced Tom Ewell was virtually type-cast as the wimpish husband, as was the feathery David Wayne as the campy heckler of the Tracy-Hepburn marriage, and Hepburn's songwriting "best friend" complete with a Cole Porter ballad ("Farewell, Amanda") for the occasion.

Director George Cukor and the screenwriting couple, Garson Kanin and Ruth Gordon, worked together to meld these expert soloists into a seamless ensemble. Cukor and Hepburn were particularly generous to Holliday in her one star-making nine-and-a-half-minute expository scene done without any of the prescribed cutaways to Kate. Still, Tracy and Hepburn remain the big show in their projection of a then-ahead-of-the-times modern couple, but one capable of responding to the clarion call of old-fashioned romance. On screen and off, Tracy and Hepburn held their contentiousness in check with the hallowed qualities of loyalty, devotion, respect, and an abiding affection. If Tracy and Hepburn put much of themselves into the bickering Bonners, Adam and Amanda, so probably did Kanin and Gordon with their own stresses and storms as a couple.

The opening sequence of the movie showing Holliday grimly following Ewell on his subway ride to Hagen's apartment is a deft job of imaginative location shooting in New York City for a big Hollywood movie. Cukor, his colleagues, and his cast all shared a New York sensibility that gives *Adam's Rib* an extra dollop of sophistication.

Once the movie settles in for a long, zany trial in the courtroom, the movie takes on a more familiar look. But with Tracy prosecuting Holliday for attempted murder, and Hepburn defending her, the scales are balanced in a completely original manner for 1949. What still remains passing strange about *Adam's Rib* is the corrosive acidity of Adam and Amanda's marital relationship, particularly in the memorable Turkish massage scene in which Adam in a meanly playful spirit whacks Amanda's towel-covered buttocks with a loud thwack. Amanda jumps to her feet in outrage at this deviously spiteful and sexist maneuver inasmuch as the Bonners were still engaged in an unresolved quarrel at the time. Despite Adam's protestations of injured innocence, he knows and we know that Amanda's instinct about body language is infallible. Hepburn's bristling outrage as a woman for all women over a violation of her dignity may not resound for all time as does Ibsen's Nora slamming the door of her Doll's House forever, but the uncomfortably uncompromising feminist fire blazes brightly in both situations.

For his part, Tracy never loses his manly stability even when he is lifted high over the courtroom by Hope Emerson, a hilariously deadpan Amazon actress. To win his point and his case, Tracy is prepared to shed fake, onion-induced tears, and even lapse into French (*vive la difference*) in response to Hepburn's last-ditch claim that there is almost no difference between the sexes. The movie's armed-truce ending is, however, not one of its strong points. Perhaps there is no easy way to close the Pandora's box of heterosexual hostility once it is opened as wide as it is in *Adam's Rib*. Cukor was no stranger to sexual role reversals in the movies, and that same year Cary Grant elicited loud laughter from audiences with his farcical drag routines in Howard Hawks's *I Was a Male War Bride*. Less funny was the trick special effects that turned Judy Holliday into a man and Tom Ewell into a woman as an illustration of one of defense attorney Hepburn's feminist debating points at the trial's climax in *Adam's Rib*. Something more deeply disturbing was going on than farcical transvestism. The year 1949 was dark and somber for Hollywood movies. The Cold War was about to heat up, McCarthyism and the black list were just around the corner in the next decade. The *film noir* was becoming more fashionable, and a cycle of black protest films— *Home of the Brave*, *Lost Boundaries*, *Pinky*, and *Intruder in the Dust*— raced each other to the screen in 1949. James Cagney returned to gangland and had the world blow up in his face in *White Heat* (1948), Fred Astaire and Ginger Rogers teamed up for the last time in *The Barkleys of Broadway* (1949), and Robert Rossen's *All The King's Men* (1949) won the Oscar for Best Picture with a withering portrait of political corruption in Huey Long's Louisiana. Movies seemed to be getting darker and more serious, and even the comedies such as Joseph L. Mankiewicz's *A Letter to Three Wives* (1949), the aforementioned *I Was a Male War Bride* (1949), and, above all, *Adam's Rib* had more bite and more bitterness than had their merry predecessors. All in all, *Adam's Rib* endures as a comedy that pointed the way to the mess in which men and women continue to find themselves today.

CLARK GABLE AND CAROLE LOMBARD

Clark Gable (1901–1960) and Carole Lombard (1908–1942) were for a remarkably brief period in the late thirties and early forties Hollywood's most glamorous married couple off screen, though they appeared in only one movie together, and that back in 1932 when both were married to other people: he to the Texas socialite Rhea Langham, and she to William Powell. The movie was *No Man of Her Own* (1932), a moderately charming romantic comedy directed by Wesley Ruggles for Paramount. Lombard played a straight-shooting blonde who wins gambler Gable on a nervy man-to-man bet risking the loss of her virtue. This otherwise negligible entertainment remains to this day prophetically emblematic of the frank, down-to-earth camaraderie that characterized their real-life relationship.

Yet, even at the time of her death, Lombard was denigrated by cranky liberal newscaster Elmer Davis for inspiring national mourning when it would have been more fitting for the country to mourn the army pilots who died with her in the same crash. When you add together the anti-movie star puritanism of the Left with the high-art snobbery of the literati, you have a powerful prescription for not taking Gable and Lombard seriously as the popular deities of their time. Yet, no American novelist of the past half-century has created a woman character one-tenth as fascinating as Carole Lombard, and character is the operative word here, for whereas Gable had a sparkling personality, Lombard had a sterling character.

It is something we sense in her brightest screen performances as the screwball with the touch of sadness, the breathtaking beautiful cheesecake flung about like a Mack Sennett slapstick prop, the madcap moralist for whom life and art became inseparable. Strangely, she didn't appear in nearly as many good movies as she should have. Out of fifty-seven screen performances, barely half a dozen constitute the stuff of her comic myth: *Twentieth Century* (1934), *Hands Across the Table* (1935), *My Man Godfrey* (1936), *Nothing Sacred* (1937), *True Confession* (1937), and her unforeseen farewell film, *To Be or Not To Be* (1942).

Yet, although she didn't come into her own until 1934, she was aware of her own and the screen's potentialities as early as 1930 when she failed to get the lead in *Laughter*, perhaps the very first of the screwball comedies. She yearned to work for Lubitsch in *The Smiling Lieutenant* (1931), *Trouble in Paradise* (1932), and *Design for Living* (1933), but the parts went to Miriam Hopkins. Her first husband, William Powell, kept her from working with Sternberg in *An American Tragedy* (1931), and she turned down an opportunity to appear opposite Noël Coward in *The Scoundrel* (1935) because the film's real-life subject, the celebrated publisher Horace Liveright, had been one of her lovers. She even shied away from *It Happened One Night* (1934) because she figured that Gable was on the prowl for her after her estrangement from Powell. A few years later she was to be heartbroken over not getting to do Scarlett to Gable's Rhett. But she was not just on the lookout for herself; she was always helping other people as well—John Bowers, the model for Norman Maine in *A Star Is Born*; John Gilbert, the most famous casualty of the talkies; Kay Francis, an erstwhile rival from the early Paramount days; up-and-coming contract players such as Fred MacMurray, Ray Milland, Anthony Quinn, Robert Stack, and one of her most illustrious benefactors turned has-been, John Barrymore. Her friendships and romances cover the whole spectrum of the Hollywood rainbow, but, once Gable entered the scene to stay, Lombard played it straight, and Gable didn't, and therein lie the bitter dregs of their legend as lovers.

Indeed, the best that can be said for Gable is that Lombard continued to love him despite his many infidelities. To the end of his life he was a compulsive womanizer even on the level of chambermaids and street-walkers. He was also a notorious miser with a narrow and suspicious view of life.

What was it then that made Gable one of the most likable men ever to work in pictures? It may have been a singular lack of narcissism in his temperament. Unlike most of his colleagues, he never exaggerated the modest dimensions of his talent. He was, if anything, too unde-manding of himself. Fortunately for the cheerful memory we have of him, his nonchalant attitude toward his craft was built into his mystique. There was never in the public image of Gable anything of the sissy actor. He seemed ever the reluctant thespian dragged back to the make-believe of the sound stages from such truly manly pursuits as fishing and hunting and shooting the bull with the boys. But he had never done any fishing and hunting before MGM had the idea of giving him an image of open-spaces sexuality. Although he was never as good a skeet-shooter (or ten-nis player) as the naturally athletic Lombard, he applied himself to his new pursuits with such diligence that his old self-doubting persona dis-appeared in the process.

On one occasion, he found himself in the same hunting party with William Faulkner. "What do you do for a living?" Gable asked. "I write." Faulkner replied. "What do *you* do for a living, Mr. Gable?" At first glance, a typical put-down of Hollywood barbarism, an ex post facto academic anecdote, a too-good-to-be-true touch of staircase wit. But the exchange is misleading in its imputation of smug malice to Gable. He was always so culturally insecure that even Marilyn Monroe on the set of *The Misfits* (1961) could make him feel like a lowbrow. His was the meteoric rise of a lower-middle-class American male to the highest strata of money and celebrity. On screen he was a sex god soaring far above mere material considerations. Off screen he was capable of brooding over the fact that in 1936 Gary Cooper had the same model Duesenberg he had. (For her part, Lombard had found Cooper incongruously effeminate off screen.)

Unlike Lombard, who managed her own career with Machiavellian guile, Gable virtually stumbled into stardom. Rejected by Warners be-cause of his big, floppy ears, he had the good fortune to make it at MGM in the few years before the censors would have smoothed over his raw brand of sexuality. Vintage Gable is the seethingly sinister Gable between 1931 and 1934. After *It Happened One Night* there is *Gone With the Wind* and not much else beyond the repetitious mannerisms of his masculinity. Ironically, he never wanted to do Rhett Butler, and he never made much effort to acquire a Southern accent for the part. Costume pictures made him feel uncomfortable, and he even tried to duck the role of Fletcher Christian in *Mutiny on the Bounty* (1935). A cautionary piece of industry wisdom grew up around his pedestrian performance as the Irish patriot Parnell who loved well but not wisely in John Stahl's otherwise under-rated production for MGM. As his one certified flop, *Parnell* (1937) became the perfect excuse to keep Gable thereafter at arm's length from any "serious" subject.

After *Gone With the Wind*, Lombard wanted to do *Woman of the Year* with Gable. When she learned that the property was controlled by Katharine Hepburn, she wanted Gable to do it with Hepburn, but Gable had no more desire to tangle with Hepburn than Brando did with Magnani a decade and a half later. Clark of the roving eye preferred to do *Honky Tonk* (1941) with the young and willing Lana Turner, one of the many blonde replicas of Lombard in his life before and after her death.

From the standpoint of a selfish cinéaste, it seems unfortunate that Lombard took World War II as seriously as she did, and that she virtually shamed Gable into becoming patriotic enough to volunteer her services at an Indiana war bond rally from which she was never to return. Yet if she hadn't cared deeply about Spain and Hitler and the Jews, she wouldn't have been able to communicate with Ernst Lubitsch and Sig Rumann on the set of *To Be or Not To Be* (1942).

How much longer Gable and Lombard would have stayed together is anybody's guess. Through the forties Lombard might have found a deeper register for her comic talents. George Stevens's *Vigil in the Night* and Garson Kanin's *They Knew What They Wanted* (both 1940) were well meaning but overly solemn dramatic vehicles, and Alfred Hitchcock was oddly miscast in directing her through through the extramarital mayhem of *Mr. and Mrs. Smith* (1941). Still, win or lose, she had kept her eyes peeled for the best directors and the most promising projects.

But Gable's time on top was coming to an end as the self-reliant hero gave way to the sensitive hero. The war had exposed the painful vulnerability of the male mystique, and the big crack-up of the star psyche had begun. Still, Gable and Lombard were something special. Even their flaws—the scar on her face, his false teeth—lifted them above mere creatures of flesh and blood. There was certainly more dissension between these deities than Michel Legrand's sweet violins for *Gable and Lombard* might indicate. There were also unsolved mysteries in their relationship. The only significant consolation for our ignorance about their lives can be found in their movies, and in one particularly, *No Man of Her Own*, the only film in which they fought and loved together.

VIVIEN LEIGH (1913–1967)

No still picture however luminous can do her ineffable beauty justice, for she lives in our minds and memories as a dynamic force rather than as a static presence. She *is* Scarlett O'Hara in *Gone With the Wind* (1939), the doomed dancer-prostitute in *Waterloo Bridge* (1940), Emma Hamilton in *That Hamilton Woman* (1941), and Blanche Du Bois in *A Streetcar Named Desire* (1951). Even in repose her flashing green eyes (at least in Technicolor) surge forward in search of her destiny. There is no complacency in her steady gaze, no narcissistic self-indulgence. She is still searching for her emotional soulmate even though she knows she risks madness and destruction in the quest. Indeed, this is ultimately a face that reflects a woman and an icon unafraid of going over the edge and into the abyss.

The sensuous and luxurious billowings in which she is loosely contained confirm that she plays for the highest stakes as she crashes through conventions and inhibitions. If we groundlings must dream of her, it is with a feeling of awe for the unattainable. She is waiting patiently for each of us to make our claim, but we know in advance that she is looking beyond us at a gallery of male gods who will bring her nothing but misery and unhappiness—Clark Gable's Rhett Butler, Laurence Olivier's Horatio Nelson, Marlon Brando's Stanley Kowalski. Come with us, we plead. We know how to appreciate you, and perhaps make you smile that kittenish smile that breaks our hearts because we know it can't last. Such dazzling perfection of expression is too fragile to survive the ravages of time and world-weariness.

But let's face it. There is just a hint of exquisite cruelty in your eyes. You could make us squirm and suffer with one withering glance of mock incomprehension. You have all your woman's weapons at your disposal, and you are prepared to surrender them all to the aforementioned gods of your heart, but you fend off us ordinary mortals forever, as much for own own good as for yours. This rejection leaves us free to worship your features with a devotion unmarred by self-interest. If, indeed, cinema is a new galaxy, you are one of its brightest stars. You are the dark lady of our sonnets, the princess of our passions, the deity of our desires.

The late François Truffaut, a man who loved women *à la folie*, once remarked that you could forgive Scarlett O'Hara all her cruelties and deceptions because of her beauty. But it is *your* beauty, Vivien Leigh, that we worship when we remember what you gave of yourself to give us Scarlett O'Hara, the suicidal ballerina on and off Waterloo Bridge, Emma Hamilton, and Blanche Du Bois. Perhaps you gave us too much for your own good, but thank you for the privilege of gazing at your image for the rest of our lives.

■   ■   ■   ■

GONE WITH THE WIND was such a phenomenon in its own time that its reputation has suffered ever since. Nonetheless, François Truffaut spoke for a generation of cinéphiles when he observed that what he had sought in Jeanne Moreau's Catherine in *Jules and Jim* was what he had found in Vivien Leigh's Scarlett O'Hara, a character beautiful enough to be forgiven all her cruelties and follies. Vivien Leigh belongs in the gallery of casting coups with Marlene Dietrich (Lola Lola), Wendy Hiller (Eliza Doolittle), Louise Brooks (Lulu), and Harriet Andersson (Monika). The logic and magic of the casting make it difficult to remember that the part of Scarlett was ever mentioned for Jean Arthur, Paulette Goddard, Frances Dee, Margaret Tallichet, Joan Crawford, Miriam Hopkins, Bette Davis, Tallulah Bankhead, Claudette Colbert, Susan Hayward, and Katharine Hepburn. Indeed, once Vivien Leigh had burst upon the horizon, her admirers regretted that she had not played Cathy to Olivier's Heathcliff in place of the cold-eyed Merle Oberon, that she had not played the grown-up Estella in *Great Expectations* (1946) (instead of Valerie Hobson, who little resembled the childhood Estella of cat-eyed Jean Simmons), that she had not played the lady in distress in Jacques Tourneur's interestingly atmospheric *Experiment Perilous* (1944), which suffered from the static, superficial prettiness of Hedy Lamarr.

Not that Miss Leigh was always adequate to every challenge even in *Gone With the Wind*. Her carrot-chomping heroics before the first intermission are not nearly as stirring as they once seemed, and her tears have never been the most convincing correlatives of emotion. The fact that her performance tapers off into tearfulness can be blamed entirely on Selznick's replacement of George Cukor by Victor Fleming. The one scene that has been completely credited to Cukor—Melanie's childbirth ministered to by Scarlett in shadowy silhouette—reverberates to this day with Scarlett's spine-tinglingly savage compassion for Melanie's ordeal. "Scream all you want, Melanie, there's no one to hear." Vivien Leigh reads this line with all the woman-to woman frenzy of a liberator before her time, and the scene builds steadily with both tact and force. By contrast, most of the other scenes tend to shoot their dramatic bolt too quickly and too obviously.

The distance we have come in the explicit expression of sexual behavior can be measured by the absence of audience laughter in the sixties and seventies when Scarlett O'Hara awakens with a delicious smile of carnal contentment on the morning after the night she was virtually raped by Rhett Butler somewhere in the dark at the top of the stairs where cinematic sex used to be consummated in the instant between a lustful fade-out and a pregnant fade-in. Whereas viewers of the forties and fifties would roar with laughter at Scarlett's audaciously honest reaction to a good lay, viewers in the sixties and seventies seemed somewhat disconcerted by the ellipsis between the approach to sex and its aftermath. The barebacked, kitchy-koo-under-the-sheets bedroom conversation has become such an obligatory scene in modern "adult" cinema that it has become increasingly difficult for moviegoers to realize that a sexual union could be effected without it. So much for the Lubitsch touch and the Sturges leer. Sex was thus no longer a laughing matter.

Over the years the look of *Gone With the Wind* dated badly. Not only have the original colors faded considerably (they tended to be monotonously garish even in their own time), the gnarled trees and stately mansions look very fake today—but they never did fool the more perceptive critics. Meyer Levin, the *Esquire* film critic of 1940, saw through all the Selznick-Menzies cardboard to the historical hollowness underneath. Otis Ferguson dismissed the whole concoction as "Clark of Seven Gables," a sly dig at this artifact of a woman-oriented romance. The big complaint about *Gone With the Wind* when it first came out was its subordination of social themes to personal plots. The camera lingered longer on the birth of a baby than on the birth of a nation, or so it seemed to the socially conscious critics of the thirties and forties, decades respectively of Depression and War. The most ambitious and most admired sequence in the film culminates in a receding and ascending crane shot of thousands of wounded Confederate soldiers in the railyards of Atlanta.

In the dismal overview of the eighties and nineties, Scarlett O'Hara no longer seems the silly Southern belle suddenly confronting the grim realities of life. It is no longer possible to feel morally superior to her giddiness and selfishness in the midst of human suffering. Indeed, it is now possible to identify completely with her irresponsibility and apparent irrelevance. In a curiously prophetic manner, she is turned off from the ugliness around her. She is alienated from the political processes of history, and she refuses to compromise with reality except where money is concerned. Scarlett O'Hara and Rhett Butler are modernists in a world of useless antiques. They seem ruthless at first glance, but they are the only characters in the film who understand the sacred importance of the three most irrevocable words in the English language: "I love you." Scarlett and Rhett act in accordance with their own emotions rather than the conventions of others.

Thus what once seemed like too little time spent on the issues of War and Reconstruction now seems like too much. We can certainly do without the one-liners about happy darkies, wicked carpetbaggers, white trash, and Southern slum clearance, night-rider style. The South of Margaret Mitchell remains a still-born fantasy in which blacks lack even the villainous dignity found in D. W. Griffith's *The Birth of a Nation* (1915). Selznick and his writers were too squeamish to allow black actor Blue Washington to put his hand on Vivien Leigh's body. Even in crime, the black man tended to the horse while his white confederate (none other than the legendary stuntman Yakima Canutt) tended to the attempted rape. The motivation behind this odd form of discrimination is probably as complex and ambivalent as the white liberal attitude toward the blacks beyond the hypocritical homilies of "tolerance."

Curiously, *Gone With the Wind* has become less offensive in the years since its original release when all bad faith on the racial issue was supposed to originate south of the Mason-Dixon line. Even though Butterfly McQueen is enough to make the most hardened bigot cringe, she too has been absorbed into the new sophistication about what things really are as opposed to what we would like to think they are. The shrill chirping of Miss McQueen, like that of her male counterpart Stepin Fetchit, resounds as the vocal heritage of castrated darkies in the Old Confederacy. Miss McQueen and Mr. Fetchit are all around us, like ghosts, both frightened and frightening, and the permanent suppression of *Gone With the Wind* and *The Birth of a Nation* can never exorcise them. There is more of the horror of history in one moment of minstrelsy with Butterfly McQueen than in all of the spectacle of the wounded in Atlanta.

5

Guilty Pleasures

THE B-PICTURE

L et us now praise the B-picture. But what is it exactly? Or, rather, what was it? In an age of inflation and instant insights, there is nothing on the screen to which we can point and say: This is a B-picture. A Z-movie, perhaps, but not a B-picture. There is too much ambition at one end, too little craftsmanship at the other, and the bottom has fallen out of the middle. Nor is there today in the nineties any genre lowly enough to be dismissed out of hand by the critical establishment. Kung-fu, porn (soft-core and hard-core), Damon and Pythias squad-car serenades, revisionist westerns, regressive Disneys, black-power fantasies, disaster and doomsday spectacles: all have their sociological and even stylistic rationales. The snobberies that afflicted supposedly serious film criticism in the 1930s, 1940s, and 1950s have been superseded in more recent decades by an open-mindedness that errs on the side of credulity. Another problem in finding a B-picture in the present is that the notion of the A-picture is more nebulous than ever, and you can't have B-pictures without A-pictures. Indeed, with the disappearance of the predetermined double feature in the seventies, it became hard even to remember the once familiar refrain: "I liked the second feature better than the main one." Nowadays a double feature is more likely to consist of two failed A-pictures, with the older one on the bottom of the bill.

Still, we are beginning to define the conditions that bred the B-picture even as we bemoan the absence of these conditions. The B-picture trudged out of Hollywood in the 1930s, 1940s, and 1950s. Silent movies tended to be major and minor rather than A or B, and comedy shorts and pulp westerns didn't really count at any time as Bs. From the point of view of the American moviegoer, the cheapest, tawdriest, silliest foreign-language film was still too exotic to qualify as a B-movie. The B-picture was thus almost by definition a product of the Hollywood studio system. The B-picture was usually in black and white, the feeling being that color was both too expensive and too immodest for a true B. Of course, color became so commonplace in the 1950s and 1960s that the black-and-white requirement went by the board. So much so, in fact, that the black and white used for *The Last Picture Show* (1971) seemed pretentiously archaic and A-picture-ish all the way.

There are at least two ways of looking fondly at any given B-picture. One is the way of the trivia hound, and the other is the way of the treasure hunter. Whereas the trivia hound loves all B-pictures simply because they are B-pictures, the treasure hunter loves only certain B-pictures because they have somehow overcome the onus of having started out as B-pictures. Thus, the trivia hound tends to be encyclopedic, and the treasure hunter tends to be selective. By necessity, the treasure hunter must share some of the zeal of the trivia hound, but the trivia hound need not recognize the aesthetic restrictions of the treasure hunter. I would tend to classify myself as a treasure hunter with a touch of the trivia hound. Hence, I cannot embrace all the B-ness of the B-pictures. Nor do I consider all genres equal.

Musicals and comedies, for example, seldom surmount the ritualized format of the Bs. Indeed, the big curse of the Bs as a class of movies is a dreary tendency toward facetiousness without wit or humor. Nothing is more depressing about a bad movie than its bad jokes or its failed musical numbers or its unimaginative slapstick. Thus, a disproportionate number of fondly remembered B-pictures fall into the general category of the *film noir*. Somehow even mediocrity can become majestic when it is coupled with death, which is to say that if only good movies can teach us how to live, even bad movies can teach us how to die.

But are we talking about really good movies, or merely good moments in bad movies? Even *King Kong* (1933) isn't much good until the last half hour; and it isn't great until the last ten minutes. Not that *King Kong* qualifies as a B-picture. *Son of Kong* (1933) qualifies, but not *Kong* itself. One might say that *King Kong* is the heroic night before, and *Son of Kong* the hung-over morning after. But I've always had a soft spot in my heart for the ratty fatalism of *Son of Kong*. In its depressing way, the last tramp-steamer two-shot of Robert Armstrong and Helen Mack on their way to no place in particular is every bit as poetically anti-climactic as Kong's last anguished expression atop the Empire State Building is poetically climactic.

Still, we can stipulate that the progression from an original to a sequel is often from A to B, not always, but almost always. *Dead End* (1937) is an A, but the Dead End Kids and East Side Kids series runs from B to Z. The Warner Oland Charlie Chans are either A or high B, the Sidney Toler Chans all B. *What a Life!* (1939) with Jackie Cooper as Henry Aldrich (and a Brackett and Wilder screenplay) is not only an A, but also one of the most sadistic studies of American adolescence in any medium. Andy Hardy was always A, and Blondie was always B, although both were fantastically profitable. *The Bride of Frankenstein* (1935) and *Son of Frankenstein* (1939), however, were every bit as ambitious as the original *Frankenstein* (1931). *The Curse of the Cat People* (1944) was even more literary, although less mythic than *The Cat People* (1942). Not so the sequels to *Tarzan, the Ape Man* (the 1931 version with Johnny Weissmuller and Maureen O'Sullivan) and *Planet of the Apes* (1968). There sequelitis was more interesting sociologically than stylistically.

If, as the late Robert Warshow suggested, the faces, bodies, and personalities of players constitute the linguistic tropes of the cinema, then Helen Chandler's mere presence in a Mayfair special entitled *Alimony Madness* (1933) is its own justification. Mayfair, Tiffany, Republic, Monogram, PRC, Eagle-Lion: these are corporate names with which to conjure any discussion of B-pictures. Almost everything they turned out was B or lower. Republic is a spectacular case in point. From 1941 to 1958, a Miss Vera Hruba Ralston, the wife and perennial protégée of Republic's president, Herbert Yates, made twenty-six indescribably inane pictures, all for Republic, a feat of conjugal devotion (on her husband's part) romantically credited with dispatching Republic into receivership. Paradoxically, Republic participated during this period in several very arty (though inexpensive) auteurist productions: John Ford's *Rio Grande* (1950), *The Quiet Man* (1952), *The Sun Shines Bright* (1954); Ben Hecht's *Spectre of the Rose* (1946); Fritz Lang's *House by the River* (1950); Nicholas Ray's *Johnny Guitar* (1954); and Orson Welles's *Macbeth* (1948), none of which fits into the campy category of Vera Hruba Ralston, and none of which qualifies as a B-picture.

Nor is the ideal B-picture simply a "sleeper" that catches on with audiences. *It Happened One Night* (1934), *Casbalanca* (1942), *Going My Way* (1944), *Sitting Pretty* (1948), *A Letter to Three Wives* (1949), and even *Easy Rider* (1969) were all authentic sleepers in their time, but either their casts were too prominent, or their aspirations were too fully articulated, or both. The late James Agee described *Double Indemnity* as "tellable trash," but that didn't make it a B-picture. In New York and other cosmopolitan centers in America, the run of the mill westerns tended to be so unfashionable that they seem to qualify as Bs in retrospect. Nonetheless it is difficult to consider an expansive spectacle on a wide screen and in color as a B-picture no matter how unfashionable it may be otherwise. Even a black-and-white, wide-screen western like Sam Fuller's *Forty Guns* (1957) seems somewhat too elaborate to be considered a B, despite Barbara Stanwyck's working at a lower salary, not to mention the mere presence of Barry Sullivan in the lead role. Sullivan was a born B-picture actor, and a damned good one, so good, in fact, that he usually lifts Bs in quality, if not in prestige. *The Gangster* (1947) is his greatest vehicle, and it is worth watching just for the pleasure of his understated authority setting up the histrionics of Akim Tamiroff and Joan Lorring. In A-pictures, Sullivan could never have been anything more than a leading man, and usually a secondary leading man. But in Bs, Barry Sullivan could be a tragic hero.

The last thing I want to do, however, is to restrict the range of the B-picture. Nor do I wish to dictate the conditions under which it can be discussed. It's much more fun, and perhaps more useful too, to throw out some recollections of a lifetime of moviegoing. One can never say that last word on this haunting subject. Not only are there too many memories to begin with, but also more and more are being reconstructed through revivals.

Black Angel (1946): Dan Duryea falls in love with June Vincent, who is obsessed with saving her unfaithful dullard of a husband from the electric chair. A very erotic movie for the 1940s. Peter Lorre and Freddie Steele are especially fascinating as underworld characters: Lorre lecherously and Steele sadistically, and the girl voluptuously masochistic in their midst. Roy William Neill directed—he also directed the best of the Sherlock Holmes adventures for Columbia, with Basil Rathbone and Nigel Bruce—and the plot is derived from a novel by Cornell Woolrich (the literary source of Hitchcock's *Rear Window*). But mainly, I think, it is Duryea, who takes the opportunity in a B-picture to pull a switch on the ratty villains he played in the As.

Detour (1945): Edgar G. Ulmer directed Tom Neal and Ann Savage in this most despairing and most claustrophobic of all B-pictures. *Detour* is not so much an example of a B that rises unexpectedly in class (like *Blondie's Blessed Event*, 1942, in the Blondie series) as of a poetic conceit from Poverty Row.

Rendezvous with Annie (1946): Allan Dwan's graceful direction in the old Triangle tradition redeems a one-joke comedy. Most memorable is the unstressed camaraderie of Eddie Albert's sharing a cake during the London blitz with Sir C. Aubrey Smith. In the same relaxed tradition is *Brewster's Millions* (1945), which Dwan also directed, and which looms as large in his later legend as his anti-McCarthy western *Silver Lode* (1954), with Dan Duryea as a villain.

When Strangers Marry (1944): Kim Hunter, Dean Jagger, and Robert Mitchum in a not-bad William Castle imitation of Alfred Hitchcock. The three leads give the film an A gloss, but the most memorable sound in the film is the rollicking, yet rasping laugh of a small, rotund, cherubic actor named Dick Elliott. His laugh is one of the most explosively distinctive expressions of mirth on the edge of malignancy in the entire history of the sound film, and yet I doubt that there are any more than a handful of moviegoers and trivia hounds who can put together name with the face, or even recall the face. No matter. He shall serve as my personal proxy for all the other unsung and unremembered favorites of other moviegoers. Dick Elliott has a small part in *Mr. Smith Goes to Washington* (1939), but I would never have noticed him if it hadn't been for his extraordinary eruptions in *Vogues of 1938* and *So This Is New York* (1948). In the latter film, Elliott heckles Dona Drake's hapless first-night performance as a maid in an atrocious play written by Bill Goodwin. Elliott's gusto in reading fairly ordinary insult lines transforms these lines into the roaring sounds of oceanic farce.

But it is in *Vogues of 1938* that Elliott's unique gift serves to fashion one of the most imaginative jokes in the history of the cinema. We first see Elliott at an out-of-town tryout box-office window. Twirling an outsize cigar, he asks for his usual house seats. The show's producer (Warner Baxter) asks the ticket-seller about the freeloader with the big cigar and is told that Elliott is notorious in New Haven for always guessing wrong on shows that later open on Broadway. If he likes a show, it is bound to be a flop. At the intermission, Baxter nervously follows Elliott into the lobby. At first, Elliott chuckles quietly to himself, but the bubbling merriment is beginning to spill over his face like lava from a live volcano, and the explosion is not long in coming. As the relatively grim members of the audience look on disapprovingly, Elliott begins to go into convulsions. The last damning peals of laughter occur off screen as Baxter goes to the telephone to make arrangements to close the show out of town. The sound of Elliott's laughter is one of the comic coups of the thirties, and an example of the many unrecorded glories of the movies from A to B.

LOUISE BROOKS (1906–1985)

Louise Brooks is known in educated film circles around the world primarily for her erotic élan in G. W. Pabst's *Pandora's Box* and *Diary of a Lost Girl*, both released originally in 1929, and both silent films with musical accompaniment. Many writers on film have rhapsodized on the beauty and sensuality of Miss Brooks. She and the late Kenneth Tynan published evidence of an incisive intelligence as well. Anyone who has ever met her, and I had that great privilege some years ago, has marveled at both the generosity and insightfulness of her comments on the wild and often brutal milieu of movie people in the twenty and thirties. Miss Brooks herself was never exactly treated with kid gloves by the moguls, particularly after she made it crystal clear that she intended to live by her own unique blend of hedonism and tough-mindedness. Louise was never "Our Miss Brooks," but strictly her own, and, as she has confessed herself, she tended to burn the candle at both ends at every opportunity, but, oh what a lovely flame she still makes on the screen!

It is hard to say what would have happened to her in the talkies of the thirties if she had played her career cards more shrewdly. Her voice was probably far from the disaster that her professional detractors of the period claimed. The period itself may have been a bigger problem. Between the Great Depression that replaced Good Times with Hard Times, and the toughening of the Production Code, the exuberant flapper embodied by Brooks became a vanishing social type.

Yet her books, her articles, and her interviews suggest a talent that might have been profitably diverted to movie journalism early on in the thirties. If a fifth-rate actress like Hedda Hopper could make her fortune in such an occupational switch, why not Brooks? Here again, Brooks might have been handicapped by a deficiency in cattiness and power-worship. I propose these speculations against the background of her visual eruption not only in *Pandora's Box* (1929) and *Diary of a Lost Girl*

(1929), but, previously, in such Hollywood films as Howard Hawks's *A Girl in Every Port* (1928) and William Wellman's *Beggars of Life* (1928). We must remember that the Brooks look had already manifested itself before Louise was summoned to Germany by the overtly Freudian Pabst. As one watches her glide gracefully and innocently past the over-burdened Expressionism of German acting and set design, one is re-minded of an Iowa farm girl named Jean Seberg floating calmly through the hyper-intellectualized Paris of Jean-Luc Godard's *Breathless* (1960). The Seberg boyish ingenue had already taken form in Otto Preminger's much reviled versions of Shaw's *Saint Joan* and Sagan's *Bonjour Tristesse*, two movies that look much more interesting today than they did at the time. If anything, Preminger's conception of Seberg was less conventional than Hawks's and even Wellman's of Brooks. In *A Girl in Every Port* (1928) Brooks plays the scheming temptress in what is essentially a buddy-buddy romance between Victor McLaglen and Robert Armstrong. The mischievousness of the Brooks character is not without its amusing touches, but Brooks under Hawks is a long way from the spunky Hawk-sian woman later to be incarnated by Jean Arthur in *Only Angels Have Wings* (1939), Rosalind Russell in *His Girl Friday* (1940), Lauren Bacall in *To Have and Have Not* (1944) and *The Big Sleep* (1946), Joanne Dru in *Red River* (1948), and Angie Dickinson in *Rio Bravo* (1959). The treacherous Eve of Brooks in *Port* is, if anything, closer to the schemingly enticing Joan Collins in *The Land of the Pharaohs* (1955).

Though Brooks is considerably more sympathetic in *Beggars of Life* (1928), here too she becomes somewhat submerged in the ultramacho rivalry between a nice-tough-guy protector played by Richard Arlen and a swaggering king of the hobos played by burpy, growly Wallace Beery. Brooks is strikingly androgynous in drag, but the startling implications of the images are stifled by the puritanical development of a self-consciously Whitman-esque plot. By suggesting everything and delivering nothing, Hollywood movies have traditionally tantalized intellectuals with the fantasy of filling in the libidinously blank spaces with outrages no censor would ever tolerate.

Enter G. W. Pabst with an unusually developed flair for Eros in the cinema even for a European. He is not so overt an iconoclast as Stroheim and Buñuel, nor as witty and as elegant a witness to sexual folly as Lubitsch, nor as strongly driven to grandiose designs of erotic domination as Lang. Pabst is more the urbane analyst, bemused by the desires de-picted in his films, occasionally even enchanted by them, but never hy-pocritical about his own complicity in the spectacle. What did he see in

Louise Brooks that led him to pick her over the then still widely unknown Marlene Dietrich for the lead in *Pandora's Box*? Not just another pretty face, to be sure, for there were a great many extraordinary beauties on the Hollywood screen at the time, and even a great many infinitely bigger stars. What Pabst had seen in Brooks was the energy and enthusiasm, and, yes, innocence of a New World blissfully unaware of the tired old rules and attitudes of the Old.

F. Scott Fitzgerald was to write a few years later that he had been looking in vain for the New Woman of the twenties on the screen. Pabst and Louise Brooks provided just about the only cinematic evidence that such a creature ever existed. Pabst achieved this effect by having Brooks either under-react or react inappropriately to the most melodramatic situations. Watch Brooks's expression as she exposes her ex-lover to a humiliating backstage scandal that ends his chance of an advantageous marriage to a "nice" girl. Brooks's face, still flushed with the exertions of passion, opens up with the fierce joyousness of triumph. She glows with healthy high spirits. It is much too original an affect for general audiences. Helen Hayes would have done the scene with more pain and embarrassment in her eyes, as if to reassure her loving audience that she wasn't really that cruel. (Don't get me wrong. Hayes had her moments on the screen, though the camera never really loved her.)

This is not to say, however, that Brooks was simply the beneficiary of a mindless cinégeneity. She was no mere creature of the camera, but a vibrant woman whose being was galvanized into aesthetic lightning by a master of the medium. He gave her a context in which she could wreak havoc with her good looks and yet emerge unsullied and spiritually redeemed. Her last moments with Jack the Ripper in *Pandora's Box* invoke a spiritual consecration on the altar of womanhood that is to find its subsequent expression in the sublime works of Sternberg, Ophüls, Mizoguchi, and, somewhat ironically, Fassbinder.

Pandora's Box and *Diary of a Lost Girl* are not great films in and of themselves, and they are certainly not feminist tracts on the order of Abram Room's amazingly un-Soviet *Bed and Sofa* (1926) from Russia at about the same time as *Pandora*. Pabst and Brooks are still ahead of their time commercially by not playing for cheap sympathy from the galleries. Despite all the talk of a sexual revolution, most people are still not comfortable with an authentic sex goddess who insists on ruling or ruining the lives of her adoring male subjects. It is amazing how close the right and left come on this issue as the ideologues on both sides gang up to defend their respective patriarchies. That is why Pabst himself had to run for cover to regain some of his lost critical standing by subsequently celebrating male camaraderie in such "humanist" works as *Westfront* (1918) and *Kamaradschaft* (1931).

Prix de Beauté (1930) was the last and least of Brooks's European vehicles, reportedly a shoestring venture caught awkwardly in the transition from the silents to sound. Directed by Augusto Genina, a very marginal figure in the cinema, with the collaboration of the illustrious René Clair, *Prix de Beauté* (1930) serves mainly as a pretext for the worshipful final glimpse of Miss Brooks's pleasure-loving beauty encased in its androgynous helmet of bobbed black hair.

MARY ASTOR (1906–1987)

As one gets older, one discovers that the beloved screen gods and goddesses of childhood and adolescence were never exactly angels. A vast variety of scandalmongers, not to mention embittered children of the movie deities, work overtime to disabuse us of our cherished illusions. We are urged to see our erstwhile idols not merely warts and all, but all warts.

Mary Astor, alas, did not have to wait for posterity to label her a slut. She was smeared in the thirties by an estranged husband, who released selected excerpts from her juicy diary in order to win exclusive custody of their daughter. For years one kept reading references to her steamy rendezvous with George S. Kaufman, of all people, in a New York hideaway. As with Ingrid Bergman and Roberto Rossellini, the beautiful Miss Astor was assailed as much for her aesthetic misjudgment as for her moral turpitude. How could she, the participant in a legendary love affair with John Barrymore, throw herself at a bespectacled egghead like Kaufman, and, besides, acclaim him for his sexual prowess beyond that of all the cover boys in tinsel town? This was simply not the stuff Hollywood dreams were made of.

But more because of than in spite of her being tarnished by the tabloids, Mary Astor always projected a larger-than-life womanly resonance in my fantasy life. As an ex-bookwormy nerd, who never dated a girl in high school, I could always console myself with the incontrovertible fact that at least one beautiful woman in the world had found ecstasy in the arms of a man with more brains than brawn, and more wit than wampum.

She appeared in more than a hundred films in a forty-two-year career, and most were routine, though she was extraordinarily likable in everything I have seen from *Red Dust* (1932) on. Still, she never became a real star, either before or after the scandal. In the silents she was an unmemorable ingenue in male adventures. From Lady in Distress she graduated to the Other Woman, in *Holiday* (1930) as the conformist sister of Ann Harding's free spirit (roles played respectively by Doris Nolan and Katharine Hepburn in George Cukor's 1938 re-make) and in *Red Dust* as the married woman who loses Clark Gable's Great White Hunter to Jean Harlow (roles repeated with an older if not wiser Gable by Grace Kelly and Ava Gardner in John Ford's 1954 re-make.)

Dodsworth (1936) was already in the can when the headlines broke, and Sam Goldwyn decided to stand by her if only to protect his investment. She was then thirty, a dangerous age for a screen beauty who had been toiling professionally since she was fourteen, and who was afflicted besides with money-sucking parents who were squandering most of her earnings. Astor had not yet been tapped for mother roles, but the actors with whom she was involved on the screen—Walter Huston as her married (to Ruth Chatterton) sweetheart in *Dodsworth*, Raymond Massey as her authority figure husband in *The Prisoner of Zenda* and in *The Hurricane* (1937), and John Barrymore as her patient spouse in *Midnight* (1939)—were older men with little sex appeal by the standards of that era. Barrymore, of course, had cut a more dashing figure a decade and a half earlier when Astor was his teenage mistress. By 1939 he was a drunken relic of the great Hamlet of another time and a pathetic reminder of Astor's own largely wasted career.

Then, as most of the obituaries would have it, came John Huston's *The Maltese Falcon* (1941), and with it Mary Astor was supposedly resurrected as a big star. It was not all that simple. Astor was at least the female lead, not having to play second fiddle to a Jean Harlow, a Madeleine Carroll, a Claudette Colbert, or even a Dorothy Lamour in *The Hurricane* (1937). The fact remains that Astor's Brigid O'Shaughnessy was sent down an elevator and up the river by Humphrey Bogart's Sam Spade, a transaction that did more for Bogart than for Astor as far as star-making audiences were concerned.

She did win an Oscar for *The Great Lie* (also 1941), and Astor has graciously credited her top-billed co-star, Bette Davis, for generously allowing Astor to "steal" the picture through what amounted to a creative collaboration of the two actresses to overcome the genially passive direction of Edmund Goulding. In addition to appearing in *The Great Lie* and *The Maltese Falcon* in 1941, Astor materialized in Huston's *Across the Pacific* (1942) (again with Bogart) and Preston Sturges's *The Palm Beach Story* (1942) (again as second fiddle to Colbert). Still, when you think about the interminable production schedules of recent decades, and the endless series of lunches to set up a project, what a year 1941 was for the work ethic in Hollywood.

The rest of the forties, fifties, and sixties could be summed up in the chapter heading, From Here to Maternity. Astor was the wholesome mother of Judy Garland and Margaret O'Brien in *Meet Me in St. Louis* (1944), of Elizabeth Taylor in *Cynthia* (1947), and of June Allyson, Margaret O'Brien, Elizabeth Taylor, and Janet Leigh in *Little Women* (1949), all of whom she loathed off screen. She played neurotically possessive mothers in *Desert Fury* (1947), *A Kiss Before Dying* (1946), and *Stranger in My Arms* (1949). Her only respite from matriarchal typecasting came with her fascinatingly shady barfly in Fred Zinnemann's *Act of Violence* (1949) and her guilt-ridden twilight lady in Robert Aldrich's *Hush . . . Hush, Sweet Charlotte* (1964), in which she was reunited with Bette Davis, and in which, also, she executed a lyrically lucid scene with Cecil Kellaway that is as good as anything she did in her entire oeuvre.

The soothing, compassionate, yet confident cadences of Astor's vocal presence may or may not be an example of Bazinian doubling. I would like to think that the occasional note of exasperation that crept into her portrayals was somehow related to the acquiring of wisdom. She was just this side of actresses like Evelyn Keyes and Paulette Goddard who seemed too intelligent, level-headed, and non-narcissistic ever to plunge into the murkier depths of make-believe. Timing is almost everything in acting careers, and Mary Astor kept perfect time for about five or six years when she was still young enough to suggest with ever so slightly ironic a smile the joys of sex, and yet old enough and experienced enough to perceive the trickery and deception involved in the chase.

As much as she may have inadvertently embarrassed her lovers with her rhapsodic entries in her diary, there was something in the frankness of her screen image that suggested to a vicarious sensualist like me a sexuality so generous and so merciful as to qualify for a sainthood of the sublimated flesh. I have loved many actresses, but I genuinely liked Mary Astor.

ANNE BAXTER (1923–1985)

The television obituaries for Anne Baxter ranged from the perfunctory to the downright peculiar. The clips from *All About Eve* made it seem that Bette Davis was being mourned more than Anne Baxter. And one particularly cretinous commentator had the effrontery to assert that the late Miss Baxter was best known for her role in *Hotel*, a conspicuously crummy television series. Her career certainly had its ups and downs, and long, long intervals of outs. Still, for all the very bad movies she made, there will always be a small corner of my heart that belongs to Anne. Ironically, the first two films I ever saw her in were directed by Jean Renoir (*Swamp Water*, 1941) and Orson Welles (*The Magnificent Ambersons*, 1942). Renoir was charmed by the then relatively unknown actress and writes of her in *My Life and My Films*:

> *Swamp Water* was my first encounter with American actors and actresses. It was the beginning of an idyll which caused me to recall my love-affair with French actors. I took a particular fancy, when the filming began, to Ann [sic] Baxter, whose acting and personality reminded me of Janie Marèse in *La Chienne*. There was no similarity between the two films but, in an entirely different role, she dominated the situation without wanting to do so. She tackled difficulties as they arose.

Baxter had a rougher time with Orson Welles in *The Magnificent Ambersons*, but she gives a glowing performance here in one of the great films of all time, and for that alone she should be fondly remembered. By contrast, her Oscar-winning impersonation of a maudlin, dissolute drunk in *The Razor's Edge* (1946) is 100-proof Hollywood hokum. Yet I happen to be one of the few people who sympathized with her Eve Harrington against Bette Davis's Margo Channing. After all, how *did* Margo get to the top in the first place? By working in her spare time with the poor and the homeless? Come on now.

As it happened, *All About Eve* (1950) came out at a time when I was turned on not only by Baxter's brand of cool, self-contained good looks, but also by girls in so-called real life who looked like Anne Baxter. Montgomery Clift hated her technical acting in *I Confess* (1953) and vowed never to appear again on the screen with a non-Method tactician. That didn't stop me from admiring her nice touches of behavioral enterprise in such trifling entertainments as *You're My Everything* (1949), *A Ticket to Tomahawk* (1950), and Fritz Lang's mesmerizingly trashy *The Blue Gardenia* (1953). She badly overacted in *Five Graves to Cairo* (1943), *Guest in the House* (1944), and *A Royal Scandal* (1945), but I liked her all the same for her quieter moments in even these setbacks. But Duse herself could not have survived the dialogue foisted on Baxter in her scenes with Charlton Heston's Moses in Cecil B. De Mille's *The Ten Commandments* (1956), and it was the height of bad taste for the TV people to dredge up all that cinematic sludge on the occasion of her death.

WANDA HENDRIX (1928–1981)

The death of Wanda Hendrix struck me with unusual force at the time because (a) she was only a few days older than I was, and (b) I had recently mentioned her as an object of my nymphet worship for a *Film Comment* series on the Guilty Pleasures of various critics and filmmakers. Wanda Hendrix—as a little slip of a girl capable of driving the strongest man to drink in *Miss Tatlock's Millions* (1948)—will always remain one of my fondest college memories. Her career never went very far, and most of the obituaries concentrated on her key roles: in *Confidential Agent* (1945), in which she was very dramatically and melodramatically involved with Charles Boyer and Katina Paxinou; *Ride the Pink Horse* (1947), in which she did a Hispanic adolescent to a poignant fare-thee-well, opposite Robert Montgomery's private eye; *Tatlock* (1948); and *Welcome Stranger* (1947), with Bing Crosby. That's just about it. But Wanda as Miss Tatlock remains a truly wondrous creature, and there will always be some sacredly sentimental delayed-adolescent part of me up there on the screen with her Miss Tatlock as she runs her fingers across John Lund's bare chest in a titillatingly pseudo-incestuous pre-*Lolita* frisson of the forbidden.

GASLIGHT

The mid-seventies revival of Thorold Dickinson's 1940 *Gaslight* threw light on one of the scandals of Anglo-American film relations. Most of us in America were already familiar with George Cukor's 1944 Hollywood version starring Charles Boyer, Ingrid Bergman, and Joseph Cotten, and featuring Dame May Whitty and Angela Lansbury. The original British production, however, with Anton Walbrook and Diana Wynyard, was withdrawn from distribution by MGM so as not to compete with its own re-make. Indeed, Metro's suppression was so complete that I was unable to see the British *Gaslight* even in the secret hideaways of film buffs.

A friend once told me that an MGM producer lecturing at UCLA had described the British *Gaslight* as a pathetic little movie in which the leads could not be understood by American audiences. My friend and I laughed at MGM's presumption that Anton Walbrook and Diana Wynyard spoke less intelligible English than Charles Boyer and Ingrid Bergman, hardly Hollywood's answer to Henry Higgins and Eliza Doolittle. By the mid-fifties, Anton Walbrook had made his mark not only in such British films as *The Invaders* (1941), *Colonel Blimp* (1943), *The Red Shoes* (1948), and Thorold Dickinson's *The Queen of Spades* (1949), but also in Max Ophüls's *La Ronde* (1950) and *Lola Montès* (1955), and Diana Wynyard had been rediscovered in such early thirties classics as *Rasputin and the Empress* (1933), *Reunion in Vienna* (1933), *Cavalcade* (1933), and *One More River* (1934). Hence, my mind was open on the relative merits of the two versions of *Gaslight*, smallness not necessarily being better, but not necessarily being worse either—which is to say that I was neither anti-Hollywood in the high-art manner nor anti-British in the *Cahiers* manner.

Actually, the issues raised by the two versions of *Gaslight* were not taken very seriously by the critics and historians when I first started scribbling about the cinema. Patrick Hamilton's *Gas Light* began its existence as a Victorian thriller in three acts on the stage on December 5, 1938, at the Richmond Theatre, London, with the following cast: Gwen Ffrangcon-Davies (Mrs. Manningham), Dennis Arundell (Mr. Manningham), Milton Rosmer (Rough), Beatrice Rowe (Elizabeth), and Elizabeth Inglis (Nancy). I must confess that none of these names mean anything to me in the way of iconographical vibrations. They are the names of performers and nothing more, but the five characters represented give us an indication of the economical drawing-room structure of the play.

The plot is almost boringly straightforward. Mr. Manningham is driving Mrs. Manningham mad so as to conceal a past murder and a past identity. A retired police inspector with a lingering curiosity about the old murder enters the house to rescue Mrs. Manningham and to trap her diabolical husband. It is in this same house that the husband murdered an old woman, whose missing jewels he now searches for in the attic above Mrs. Manningham's bedroom. Hence, the original title of the play: *Gas Light*, for the dimming effect on the gas light in the wife's bedroom whenever the husband is prowling about upstairs unbeknownst to her, a recurring phenomenon that helps convince her that she is going mad like her mother before her. At other times the husband helps these fancies along by playing a great variety of dirty tricks on her: hiding items which she then thinks she has lost or misplaced, making it appear that she pilfers his papers, and even staging an elaborate spectacle (for the benefit of the servants) in which she is exposed as a hider of paintings.

It all seems very one-sided: virtuous wife victimized by villainous husband. There is very little mystery or surprise to the play in the conventional sense, since the audience can smell a rat (indeed the right rat) very early in the proceedings. Yet there is considerable suspense because the audience can never be fully convinced that the wife will ever reach the end of her gullibility. Much of the time the situation verges on farce as the wife makes of herself an emotional doormat for her husband. Nonetheless, her almost incredible lack of perspicacity is essential to the structuring of the play, not only to elaborate her husband's villainy, but also to provide a justification for the inspector's lengthy exposition.

The play's big scene, a showpiece for any actress, finds the husband tied up by the inspector, alone in the room with his wife. He pleads, he wheedles, he cajoles, he seeks to assert his old mastery. The audience holds its breath when the wife picks up a knife, as if to cut his bonds or—no, the audience mustn't even think of such a grisly possibility so close to the final curtain. And the audience is not disappointed, but fully satisfied, as the wife achieves a conjugal catharsis by rejecting her husband's pleas for deliverance. "But how can a mad woman help her husband to escape? What a pity—If I were not mad, whatever you had done, I could have pitied and protected you! But because I am mad, I am rejoicing in my heart—without a shred of pity—without a shred of regret—watching you go with glory in my heart!"

When both the play and film came to America, the titles of both were changed to *Angel Street*, by which this property is now known and frequently revived in the American theater—in the early seventies for one, in a badly received revival with Dina Merrill in the lead. But in the early forties *Angel Street* enjoyed a three-year run on Broadway with the following opening-night cast: Judith Evelyn (Mrs. Manningham), Vincent Price (Mr. Manningham), Leo G. Carroll (Rough), Elizabeth Eustis

(Nancy), Florence Edney (Elizabeth). I never saw this production, but I can visualize its lady-in-distress dimensions with frail, fragile Judith Evelyn (later the trembling target in a similar piece of domestic stage gothic entitled *The Two Mrs. Carrolls*) being browbeaten by the towering Vincent Price.

Patrick Campbell's original conception depends for its plausibility on the fact that the play is set in Victorian England where husbands were notorious for tyrannizing their meek wives. The husbands on the stage were thus played by English types. In the movies, however, both husbands were exotically European, one might say even contemptibly Continental. Hence, the name Jack Manningham has been changed to Paul Mallen for Walbrook, and to Gregory Anton for Boyer. (Diana Wynyard's Mrs. Mallen has kept the name Bella from the play, but Ingrid Bergman's Mrs. Anton has had her first name changed to Paula.) More than mere trivia are involved in these alterations. *Angel Street* has been an extraordinarily popular play, and yet the names of its characters have never been sacrosanct. The reason, of course, is that the play does not deal with characters at all, but with archetypes. Husband, Wife, Detective *ex machina*, Faithful Housekeeper, Flirty Parlor Maid. Why then did both movies cast the role of the husband with a foreign actor? It might be suggested that England, already at war with Germany in 1940, may have been unconsciously conditioned for a Germanic villain like Walbrook. By contrast, Frank Pettingell's Rough barks like a British bulldog at Walbrook's decadent dachshund.

The casting of Boyer introduces a different dimension to *Gaslight* in the context of his image as the Great Lover. All his glowering grimaces assume their authority not so much through sexist tyranny as through sexual subjugation. The respective wives reflect the contrasting temperaments of the two husbands, Diana Wynyard's Bella seeking only a kind word, Ingrid Bergman's Paula yearning for a warm embrace. The sexual orientation of the Hollywood *Gaslight* is so pronounced that doughty Inspector Rough is transformed into Joseph Cotten's romantic rescuer Brian Cameron.

These changes from the original may have prompted the harsh dismissal of the Hollywood version by Ivan Butler in *Cinema in Britain*:

> With war and the menace of bombs and destruction shadowing everybody's mind, the best British film of the year was a Victorian thriller. The film has been the victim of a notorious piece of commercial vandalism, bought up and suppressed (legally) by a company intending to produce

another version. There could be a temptation to build up the reputation of Dickinson's version from sheer indignation at its treatment, but in fact, as those fortunate enough to have seen it on its original release will fondly remember, it is an excellent piece of period Grand Guignol in its own right. . . . The fine thriller is in every way superior to the travesty that replaced it.

A strong note of patriotism seems to have crept into Butler's critique of Cukor's *Gaslight*. It is reminiscent of British reactions to Errol Flynn's exploits in *Objective Burma*, and to Ben Hecht's pro-Zionist pronouncements in the tense, bloody (for the British) period before the partition of Palestine. Hollywood imperialism is a painful subject for British film historians—as I discovered some years ago when Roger Manvell prevented the publication of *The American Cinema* in England because I had presumed to lump together British films with American films. I plead guilty. When I was growing up I didn't make any distinctions between a British British spy picture like *Dark Journey* (1937) (with Conrad Veidt and Vivien Leigh) and a Hollywood British spy picture like *Lancer Spy* 1937 (with George Sanders and Dolores Del Rio). Indeed, there was a time when I preferred English movies to American movies, and I still think there are in the British cinema certain qualities—literacy, irony, wry understatement, salubrious cynicism—that most French critics can never fathom because of the language barrier.

Even so, I lean more to the view of Stephen Harvey at the Museum of Modern Art when he notes:

> Actually, though its virtues are undeniable, Dickinson's *Gaslight* lacks the resonance and detail of the Cukor version. Thirty minutes shorter than the American remake, the British *Gaslight* is both more compact and considerably more faithful to its original source, but it is also rather schematic in structure and academic in execution.

One must give some credit, I suppose, to an original for its originality. Thorold Dickinson's version of the play, from a screenplay by A. R. Rawlinson and Bridget Boland, did suggest an approach to the Cukor team, particularly to the sterling scriptwriting trinity of John Van Druten (*The Voice of the Turtle*), Walter Reisch (*Ninotchka*), and John L. Balderston (*Berkeley Square*). From the outset, the husband in the Dickinson is made less self-consciously histrionic than his counterpart on the stage: "You know, Bella, that must be a very superb sensation. To take apart and lose yourself entirely in the character of someone else. I flatter myself I could have made an actor." Walbrook never reads these lines, and neither does Boyer. The movie husbands become more intimate with the precious objects around them than with their own stylish imposture. But whereas Walbrook is content to convey calculating greed, Boyer is compulsively driven by his desire for the jewels—a desire which in his gleaming eyes reflects a sexual obsession stronger than any feeling for the warm, willing, whimpering creature of a wife tearfully waiting for him in the bedroom below the attic. Significantly, Boyer finds the fateful jewels through his own exertions, whereas the jewels are denied to Walbrook to the bitter end. In this the Dickinson version is more faithful to the play than the Cukor version.

But once it is conceded that the Hollywood version is structurally smoother and visually more opulent, we come back to the players and their directors, and the impact of their respective styles on the mythic meanings of the two works. On the whole, Thorold Dickinson keeps his distance from his characters so as to focus on the period decor. He thinks nothing of interrupting his film to present an affectionate portrait of a Victorian music-hall performance to which the husband has taken the saucy parlor maid. There are also little vignettes with lower-class touches in the vicinity of what started out on the stage as unfashionable Angel Street, and became progressively more elegant in its two screen adaptations.

Diana Wynyard's best scene as the wife is the one in which she mourns her lost looks in her mirror. The Richard Addinsell score accompanies her anguish with such intensity that the character never recovers sufficiently to provide a final catharsis. Somehow, no revenge against her husband can compensate for her lost happiness. She is ultimately inconsolable in that her suffering is more spiritual than substantial, more mental than physical. By contrast, Ingrid Bergman seems to be wasting away, body and soul, from a lack of love. A big, strapping woman seemingly miscast as a victim of this sort, she tears herself apart with ravaged expressions of uncommon vigor. This aspect of her art has been generally overlooked in the widespread emphasis on her sincere wholesomeness, but James Agee came eloquently close to describing the vital intensity of her disintegration in *For Whom the Bell Tolls* (1943): "Her final scene of farewell is shattering to watch. Not that it's perfect. But its sources and intention are so right, and so astonishingly out of key with the rest of the production. She seems really to have studied what a young woman might feel and look like in such a situation (not a moving picture)—half-nauseated and nine-tenths insane with grief, forced haste, and utter panic. Semi-achieved though it is, it is devastating and wonderful to see."

Bergman's convulsive breakdown in *Gaslight* (1944) and *Notorious* (1946) were still to come, and it was in this period that she played against the image of health and common sense with projections of the most nerve-wracking masochism this side of the asylum. Throughout her ordeal Cukor's camera stays so close to her that her feelings begin to transcend the petty intrigue in which she is involved. Escape and survival, which are sufficient for the lonely Wynyard wife, are completely inadequate for a woman of Bergman's potential vitality. Triumph and regeneration are prescribed for her as she finally soars over all her previous suffering. Fortunately, the balance in the Cukor *Gaslight* is so delicately maintained between Boyer and Bergman that the morbid attraction in their relationship transcends the feeble contrivances of the genre. (I am always uncomfortable with the clumsy device of having the husband tied up so that his wife can have her big scene. It reeks of greasepaint and high-school productions of *The Seven Keys to Baldpate*.)

Stephen Harvey suggests that it was this production of *Gaslight* that spawned such wife-in-distress successors as *Undercurrent* (1946), *Sudden Fear* (1952), *Caught* (1949), *Woman in Hiding* (1950), *Sleep My Love* (1948), *The Two Mrs. Carrolls* (1947), etc. Increasingly, however, the woman seemed to be acting out her fears in an emotional vacuum, and this form of the woman's picture finally expired in a death rattle of hammy hysteria. The sexual undertones of the Cukor-Bergman-Boyer *Gaslight* were replaced by shrilly sexless cries of fear and paranoia. Husbands served merely as abstracted agents of persecution. Of course, Max Ophüls's *Caught* (1949) and Douglas Sirk's *Sleep My Love* (1948) possess auteurist virtues which more than compensate for their genre vices, but they still lack the two-sided gaze of Cukor's *Gaslight* on husbands and wives.

Every genre contains within its conventions the seeds of its own destruction. Hence, elucidation without evaluation is as limiting in genre analysis as it is in auteur analysis. To trace narrative patterns without considering the stylistic rapport with the narrative is to make the drudgery of moviegoing superfluous. One might just as well stay home to peruse the printed synopses of unseen films. Even the nuances of casting can be crucial to the outcome on the screen. (All of Jacques Tourneur's eerie atmospherics cannot infuse Hedy Lamarr's wife in distress in *Experiment Perilous* (1944) with emotional conviction.) Therefore, we had to wait until both versions of *Gaslight* had manifested themselves on the screen before we could render our verdicts.

In the interim, however, many of our standards had changed. The

Hollywood star system now evokes more nostalgia than contempt. "Love interest" in and of itself does not connote shameful compromise with commercialism. The woman's picture has acquired more respect in the new perspective of the women's movement. Back in the forties we might have been swayed by the radio parodies of *Gaslight* (on the Jack Benny show, for example) into treating the whole genre as a joke. It would never have occurred to us to wonder why domestic gothic and the *film noir* happened to thrive during World War II and after, but not before. Even if we trace the beginnings of domestic gothic back to *Rebecca* (1940) and *Suspicion* (1941) rather than to *Gaslight* (1944), the parallel between war and woe seems too prolonged to be a coincidence. Escapism may be one factor. The revival of Germanic Expressionism after *Citizen Kane* (1941) may be another.

Still, it does seem that domestic gothic was very difficult to do with a straight face in the thirties. Through that supposedly turbulent decade every genre was eventually deflected into comedy, or worse, facetiousness. The monsters, the ghouls, the gangsters, the private eyes, even the cowboys strained harder and harder for self-parody. When the war came, outsized emotions came back in style as the most fanciful romance could not match the wild emotionalism of "real life." The self-reliant career woman still flourished in the sex comedies; but on another level, the constant fear of women for their husbands away at war generated a widespread feeling of helplessness not present before the war. It is not a simple case of cause and effect: the necessary production choices may not have been even fully conscious of the *Zeitgeist*. But somehow a responsive chord was struck, and a new genre suddenly flourished.

LOST HORIZON

Frank Capra's *Lost Horizon*, adapted by Robert Riskin from James Hilton's 1934 best-seller, was originally released to theaters in 1937. Its "restoration" in the 1980s has a comparatively complex history. In its time the film cost four million dollars, which in the 1990s would be the equivalent of forty-five million dollars. Columbia was a relatively small studio, and though Harry Cohn gave Capra virtually carte blanche as his ace director, the project itself seemed precarious from the outset. A disastrous sneak preview unnerved both Capra and Cohn, and the scissors came out. A basic problem in adapting the novel to the screen was its very slow buildup and extended exposition. Early preview audiences became restive as they waited for Hilton's protagonist, Conway, and his companions to unravel the mystery of Shangri-La, to which they had been mysteriously abducted in an airplane ostensibly rescuing Europeans from the turmoil of a Chinese revolution.

The first two reels have apparently been lost forever, but that was not the end of the cuts. When the film was revived in the forties, the United States was at war, and the pacifist sentiments of both the novel and the screenplay had to be toned down for purposes of morale. Hence, the restored footage brings the print almost back to its state in 1937 when it was released to the general public. I was nine years old at the time, and I never saw that version, but my father did, and that is a bit of a story in itself.

My father had been a successful real estate promoter until the Depression left him a penniless bankrupt, a Mister Micawber awaiting the apocalypse. Still, he went to the office every day, and an old friend named Skimmer would treat him to lunch and an occasional movie. But my father did not want to leave the impression that he spent all his precious time going to the movies. So he would come home in the evening to tell us about a movie "Skimmer" had seen. It would be all "Skimmer said this" and "Skimmer said that," but sometimes he would forget himself and start describing a scene so vividly that he would impersonate the actor and mimic the action. I can still remember the way he imitated Chaplin tightening bolts on the assembly line in *Modern Times* (1936). Working in a factory and not being one's own boss were horrible prospects for my father to face, and he successfully avoided conventional employment until the end of his life, which, I suppose, is why my life has taken many of the crazy turns it has. At the time, though, we never let on to my father that we saw through his guilty deception. Perhaps we sensed that his storytelling fulfilled him as a husband and father as much as it entertained us.

Anyway, my father was particularly fond of films with "ideas" or "morals" or "messages," if you will. And few films ever enthralled him as much as *Lost Horizon*. I think I must have heard Ronald Colman deliver some of the movie's inspirational dialogue, with his cultivated British accent, on the Lux Radio Theatre, presided over by the equally mellifluous Cecil B. De Mille. Between Colman's voice and my father's description, I had the impression of having seen the movie long before I actually did.

The next time I encountered Hilton I was a freshman in high school.

One night I read *Lost Horizon* and *Goodbye, Mr. Chips* at one sitting and was moved by the yearning sadness in both books. But by the time I caught up with the movie itself, in however bowdlerized a condition, I had completely outgrown the cast of mind that could find salvation in a sexless preserve of moderation and wisdom. Even reviewers of the period found Shangri-La hard to take as an ideal. The set design of the lamasery reminded some cynics of California post-office buildings in the Renaissance style. Still, President Roosevelt had given the term "Shangri-La" some sort of lasting legitimacy by naming a plane or a place—I can't remember which—after Hilton's Tibetan hideaway.

Now that I have both seen the partially restored movie and re-read the book that so stirred my adolescence, I find myself beset by conflicting impulses. On one hand I wish to applaud the prodigiously painstaking efforts the archivists have made on behalf of this and other works. But on the other I find myself entertaining the notion that just as an older generation was in error when it suggested that montage was everything and that every movie could be saved in the cutting room, our generation may be in error in overindulging its fetish for footage. There has always been something wrong with *Lost Horizon*, something irremediably boring, not merely for popcorn-popping preview audiences in Pomona or Pasadena, but even for a thirties nostalgia nut like me.

James Hilton, like many once fashionable authors, is not taken very seriously anymore. When I re-read him, I found his dialogue more stilted than I remembered, and his reticence about sexual matters downright anachronistic. In George Orwell's *Coming Up for Air* there is a donnish character who could fit snugly into the mold of Hilton's heroes. But Orwell's point about his academic recluse lost among his books and his classical learning is that he is essentially dead and irrelevant to the world as it is. Hilton's Conway makes no bones about the fact that Shangri-La reminds him very pleasantly of Oxford, where he once taught (Hilton himself was educated at Cambridge). Hilton was eighteen when World War I ended, and I don't know if he served in that conflict or not, but Conway was never the same after his tour of duty in the trenches.

Though Hilton, who happened to be working on the screenplay of *Camille* while *Lost Horizon* was being prepared, enthusiastically endorsed Robert Riskin's screenplay, there are significant differences in the characters and details that make up the same basic story.

1. India is the starting point of the book, China of the movie. Capra's flair for chinoiserie in *The Bitter Tea of General Yen* (1933) may have dictated the change.

2. Conway is a minor consular official in the book, a politically prominent diplomat in the movie. His impetuous second-in-command in the book is transformed into his brother (John Howard) in the movie. The adaptor's reason for the change here was to strengthen the motivation of Conway in leaving Shangri-La to protect a real brother rather than an old-school-tie classmate.

3. Conway has no love interest in the book and little interest in love. The movie Conway finds a new character (Jane Wyatt) who does not appear in the book. Presumably, American audiences would have demanded that he have someone in addition to something for which to return to Shangri-La. The "love" scenes between Colman and Wyatt are both too much and not enough. Tepid, one might say.

4. The American ex-swindler played by Thomas Mitchell is in the book, but Edward Everett Horton's dithering paleontologist was added strictly for comedy relief, and I am not holding my breath in anticipation of even more footage of Mitchell teasing Horton in between Colman's visits to Sam Jaffe's (as always unforgettable) High Lama, the two-hundred-plus-year-old founder of Shangri-La.

5. The one woman passenger in the hijacked airplane is a pushy missionary in the book and a vaguely tubercular blonde woman (Isabel Jewell) of doubtful virtue in the film. The missionary is no great loss to the movie, since her main novelistic function is to provide endless exposition by her brash, tactless inquisitiveness. Isabel Jewell, so memorably hysterical in Howard Hawks's *Ceiling Zero*, gives a routine role something extra.

6. Margo, as the centenarian who still has the looks of a young woman in the sheltered confines of Shangri-La, plays a much more active role in arranging the departure of Conway and his younger brother in the film. In the book the younger man makes all the arrangements with the porters. In the movie it is the Margo character who casts the most doubt on the wild stories told to Conway by the High Lama and his urbane subordinate Chang (H. B. Warner). Riskin's amplification of the Margo character is virtually a dramatic necessity, inasmuch as Hilton had not bothered to create a character out of a fragile piece of human porcelain. Without Margo to disrupt the dreadful decorum of the milieu, the movie would have been one long slumber party of the kind described in later decades as a "meditation." In the thirties, when Hollywood directors said "LIGHTS, CAMERA, ACTION!" their producers expected the emphasis to be on action.

7. The politics of Shangri-La express the point of view of what Jules

Feiffer has ridiculed as the "radical middle." Moderation in all things, including virtue, decides that if two men want the same woman, the one who wants her less politely defers to the one who wants her more. Money? Oh yes, there happens to be gold in the valley, and the outside world seems to value gold. Here in the lamasery we do not bother with such worldly details. The natives accept our enlightened, tyranny of good manners and good taste, but that, too, in moderation. Hilton is civilized enough to make his ideology of moderation more plausible by invoking as influences the relaxed humanism of Montaigne and the classical balance of Mozart.

Capra and Riskin had enough problems with Pomona preview audiences without bringing in Montaigne and Mozart. It is sufficient that some of the book's references to Chopin remain in the movie. Hilton himself was musical to the point that he once considered a career as a concert pianist. His seductive siren calls to the crisis-ridden readers of the thirties therefore consisted of creating a Utopia that was part research library, part concert hall, and part fountain of youth, the last component for the more credulous yokels among his readers.

In the nineties, more than ever, Shangri-La evokes a pleasant retirement community in Florida or California, with a restricted clientele limited to Oxbridge and Ivy League types. Both Hilton and Riskin refrain from promising life everlasting. And what's wrong with living a century and a half away from the hustle and bustle of making a living? A life without stress may be boring, but it probably delays a hardening of the arteries.

But to live a life away from the chaos and confusion of London and Paris and New York and all the other cosmopolitan centers of the world, even to avoid the threat of a nuclear holocaust (about which Hilton was uncannily prophetic in a passage written in 1933), is to embrace a genteel survivalism. The dark cloud that shall envelop the globe shall also enable, in the High Lama's vision, the meek and the moderate to inherit the earth. But first, a sanctuary must be established within the magic mountains to protect the artifacts of civilization from the savagery of the strong and the fanatical.

With Hitler and Stalin on the loose in Hilton's time, and innumerable ideologues with blood in their eyes in today's tabloid headlines, the appeal of escape, however sentimental, is not entirely foolish. As my father, with a hungry family to be fed at home (mostly through the ingenuity of my own Mother Courage), listened to the caressing cadences of Ronald Colman's resigned world-weariness, some of the stormy turbulence in his

own Depression-scarred heart must have been stilled if only for an hour
or two.

MY FOOLISH HEART

My Foolish Heart is the kind of movie that was culturally defenseless in
1949, when it opened officially for Oscar consideration, and in January
1950 when it opened in New York to something less than a blast of
trumpets from the immensely influential Bosley Crowther of *The New
York Times*: "Every so often there comes a picture which is obviously
designed to pull the plugs out of the tear glands and cause the ducts to
overflow. Such a picture is Samuel Goldwyn's latest romance, *My Foolish
Heart*, which had a quite aqueous opening at the Music Hall yesterday."

Crowther went on to synopsize the story without the slightest acknowledgment of the strikingly noirish look and mood of the film:

> Penned by the Epstein brothers, Julius and Philip, from a *New Yorker* yarn
> which bore the demoralizing title of "Uncle Wiggily in Connecticut," this
> picture describes in glistening detail the dewy raptures of a wartime ro-
> mance and the consequent despairs of the young lady when she finds
> herself with child and her unwed lover killed. It also dwells sadly at the
> terminals—which is to say, at the beginning and at the end—on the dreary
> state of this young lady seven years later, when she is married to another
> man.

An auteurist where producers were concerned, Crowther did concede
some saving graces to the Goldwyn endeavor:

> For it must be said that Mr. Goldwyn hasn't done an indifferent job, so
> far as putting together a production with style and devices is concerned.
> His picture is handsomely located in an assortment of New Yorkish sets,
> and the smooth tricks by which he strokes the tear glands are strictly and
> dutifully Grade A. His writers . . . have knocked out some pleasant dia-
> logue, and his director, Mark Robson, has put the whole thing into even,
> rhythmic gear. Also, it must be added that his music department was on
> the ball when it came to scoring a sound track that would inflate the
> sentimental moods.

The names of legendary cinematographer Lee Garmes and melodious
composer Victor Young do not appear in Crowther's tribute to the Gold-

wyn army of anonymous artisans laboring on the producer's assembly line. And the only member of the cast to meet with Crowther's approval is Robert Keith: "As the father of the girl in this dilemma, Mr. Keith handles a poignant role with humor and understanding. He is the most genuine thing in the film."

Since Keith appears in only three scenes in the movie, that leaves a great deal of footage for Crowther to condemn in a quaint style groping for the elusive hobgoblins of consistency and plausibility:

> But we're afraid that this picture's conception of the intelligence of a modern college girl is much too wistful and illusory for a hard-hearted realist. And the casting of Susan Hayward as this lady is a bit off the beam. Miss Hayward is a very brittle actress, and to see her fluttering at Dana Andrews' charm, freezing at his bold seductions, then yielding with highly accomplished grace, is not precisely conducive to the illusion of an innocent schoolgirl. It is hard to believe that her lady would be as sadly confused as she is here.
>
> And likewise, Mr. Andrews, for a fellow who has apparently been around and is so quick with clever sayings, seem a bit of a fathead for the beau. He is very attractive as a suitor, but we fear he is not quite consistent with the man he is meant to be. Lois Wheeler and Kent Smith are stolid in other conventional roles."

Even so, Crowther's unfavorable review is a rave next to A. Scott Berg's demeaning comments on the movie in his much-praised *Goldwyn: A Biography* (Alfred A. Knopf, New York, 1989). According to Berg, "Robert Sherwood could not help telling Goldwyn how 'phony' he found the picture, the victim of 'that long arm of coincidence.' John McCarten, *The New Yorker* reviewer, said *My Foolish Heart* 'was so full of soap opera cliches . . . it's hard to believe that it was wrung out of a short story . . . that appeared in this austere magazine a couple of years ago.' "

Berg went on to report that after the "bastardization" of "Uncle Wiggily," J. D. Salinger vowed never to sell any more of his writings to Hollywood, regardless of the financial sacrifice involved. Hence, *The Catcher in the Rye* remains unfilmed to this day.

What a burden for a mere movie to bear! Think of it: If the Epstein brothers had not persuaded Goldwyn to purchase a short story from which about ten lines of dialogue could be salvaged for the screen, a legendary author might have been saved from self-imposed exile. Not that it was unreasonable to change the title of a movie to anything but "Uncle Wiggily in Connecticut." Can't you just see it on the marquee?

Uncle Wiggily in Connecticut, not to be confused with *Christmas in Connecticut* (1945). Now there's a real "soap opera," full of irritations and
aggravations. Still, *My Foolish Heart* is incriminating enough in itself just
as a title to be dismissed sight unseen.

The title and a minimal plot synopsis lock *My Foolish Heart* into that
most despised of all genres, the woman's film—despised, that is, at least
B. F. (Before Feminism). A partial turning of the tide was signaled in
1974 by Molly Haskell with her deflation of John Grierson's bombastic
social consciousness in her seminal work *From Reverence to Rape: The
Treatment of Women in the Movies:*

> In his 1946 book *On Documentary,* the late John Grierson, the father of
> the "serious subject" critics, interrupted his anti-Hollywood and pro-social-
> realism diatribe to deplore Anthony Asquith's waste of time and talent on
> *Dance, Pretty Lady.* Grierson, admitting the film was "a delight to the eye,"
> nonetheless deplored its subject: "This is it, bless you. Claptrap about
> virginity. Why the entire sentiment that makes a plot like that possible
> went into discard with the good, prosperous, complacent Victoria. It was,
> relatively, an important matter then. But it is mere infant fodder now when
> you consider the new problems we carry in our bellies, and think of the
> new emphases we must in mercy to ourselves create out of our different
> world." Apparently the way to a socially conscious critic's heart is through
> his stomach. A woman's virginity (infant fodder, indeed!), and where and
> how she lost is, is at least as important as the high and mighty manly
> themes of the films Grierson approved of.

Nonetheless, my own defense and justification of *My Foolish Heart* is
motivated by neither feminist nor auteurist revisionism. I happened to
like *My Foolish Heart* from the very year of its release when I was in my
early twenties, and more than a decade away from the Paris of the Cinemathèque and *Cahiers du Cinema.* My late brother George, four years
younger, had seen the film first, and had reported to me its manifold
virtues, which I later confirmed for myself. What impressed us both the
most was Susan Hayward's blistering toughness in every crisis as if she
were a Brooklyn-born Scarlett O'Hara, a part for which she had once
auditioned. Neither of us was yet culturally brave enough to admit that
Victor Young's score really got to us, particularly in the car scene near
the end of the flashback when she decides to grab the life-preserver of
a loveless marriage. In this and every other big moment, Hayward displayed the distinctively American brand of gallows-humor spunk Murray

Kempton would admire a decade later in her death-house scenes in *I Want to Live* (1958). And as for Young's alleged schmaltziness as a movie music composer, if Mr. Young's scores for *The Uninvited* (1944), *Love Letters* (1944), and *My Foolish Heart* are schmaltz, then my musical taste is unabashedly schmaltzy.

The fact that I can never look at *My Foolish Heart* without thinking of my dear departed brother may raise the justifiable suspicion that I am engaged in a purely sentimental reappraisal. If that had been the case I would not have researched the subject so arduously. What motivated me instead is a startlingly new perspective on the film, one that struck me a few months ago when I was casually looking at it for auld lang syne.

Again, it is not particularly an auteurist perspective. I have nothing much more to say about Mark Robson than the nothing I said when I inadvertently left him completely out of *The American Cinema* two decades ago, despite his work for Welles and Lewton, and despite such undeniably respectable directorial efforts as *The Seventh Victim, Bedlam, Champion,* and *Home of the Brave*. Still, something quite stirring happened on the screen fifty years ago and Robson can be credited at the very least for letting it happen.

My new perspective took shape with the very first menacing shots of the film. A car on a highway. Pouring, pelting rain; ominous music. An unfamiliar woman (Lois Wheeler) turns anxiously from the wheel to look over her shoulder at a driveway. She backs up her car and enters the driveway in a semicircular trajectory as if she were approaching a mini-Manderley. Suspense. Mystery. Suddenly, a dark-haired woman (Susan Hayward) pops out of the garage right in the path of the moving car, and turns calmly with a defiantly inquisitive half-smile. Mary Jane—for that is the unknown character's name—stops in time, jumps out of the car, and exclaims, "Eloise, I might have hit you!" Eloise replies with edgy flippancy: "That's all right. I'm insured," with the "I'm" emphasized. She then suggests with mock exasperation that they get in out of the rain.

It is only in the last paragraph of the story that Salinger reveals that Eloise was originally brought up in or around Boise, Idaho, no more than a stone's-throw away from *The New Yorker's* proverbial old lady from Dubuque. The Epstein brothers constructed Eloise's Boise biography out of this one tantalizing reference to the suburban matron's provincial origins. Her father (the aforementioned Robert Keith) owns the biggest hardware store west of the Rockies. Her mother (the comically dithery Jessie Royce Landis, later to shine for Alfred Hitchcock in daffy mother

roles in *To Catch a Thief* (1955) and *North by Northwest*) (1959)) frets
and fusses and cries a lot. Salinger makes no reference to either of Eloise's parents, dead or alive.

A one-sentence reference in the Salinger story to a brown-and-yellow
dress bought in backward Boise is expanded by the Epsteins into a full-
fledged ballroom scene in a New York hotel in which Eloise, Mary Jane,
the snobbish Miriam, and the two men in Eloise's life, first-love Walt
(Dana Andrews) and eventual husband Lew (Kent Smith), all participate
in the first episode of the film's feature-length flashback. Walt is dressed
formally but is an outsider, and a lower-class one, to the fancy finishing-
school to which the others belong. He is, however, witty enough to "rescue" Eloise from her social humiliation with a very smooth putdown of
Miriam's dress in Miriam's red-faced presence.

Susan Hayward had turned thirty and Dana Andrews a very dissipated
forty when they performed these collegiate hi-jinx that so thoroughly
distressed a hard-headed realist such as Bosley Crowther. Admittedly, it
was a "stretch" for Miss Hayward to "act out" her impression of virginal
innocence by saying yes yes too quickly to date invitations, and for allowing eagerness to shine so nakedly on her face. The cinema has always
been unkinder than the theater to people acting younger or older than
their actual ages. And if the rest of *My Foolish Heart* had remained coyly
adolescent, it would be completely forgotten today.

The movie endures a bit more college-girl-waiting-by-the-telephone
atmosphere before Eloise and Walt manage to arrange a first date at a
little Italian restaurant in "the Village." Walt is transparently insincere as
he persuades the hesitant Eloise to venture into his bachelor lair. There
is music, an exploratory kiss, and a line consisting of Walt's attribution
of "aristocratic" qualities to Eloise's eyes and ears. The dialogue suddenly
sharpens for me and my brother, twenty-one and seventeen respectively,
in a difficult period when one tries to "make out" but doesn't want to be
completely swinish about it. Here the Epsteins' dialogue takes over where
Salinger's stories never venture. When Eloise asks Walt if he's used the
same line before, and he admits he has, she says, "I wish it wasn't just
a line. I wish you'd meant it. I wish you liked me just a little." When
Walt protests that he likes Eloise a lot, she says, "No not a lot, just a
little. Just enough to take me home and call me for another date."

Walt realizes that his game is up, and decides to cut his losses. With
him up to now, it has always been tonight or never, and he can accept
a nice girl's no with a certain degree of practiced resignation. When
Eloise suggests that there is no point in his taking her home, he responds

with a jocular coldness that he cannot argue with her logic. She leaves. He starts putting away the glasses. The camera is distant, but the seemingly gratuitous duration of the scene generates its own expectancy. The doorbell rings. Walt goes to the door and opens it in longshot. Eloise in the dark fur coat her daddy bought her in Boise, Idaho, stands defenseless, a figure in black for Lee Garmes's chiaroscuro composition. Like so many nice girls since, Eloise had capitulated. And in the movies of 1949, this is hardly a common occurrence. Walt, softened by his quarry's unexpected surrender, gallantly tells her that he is indeed taking her home, though, he adds ruefully, the "boys" in the proverbial locker room will never believe his forbearance. A would-be wolf has been emotionally snared by the passionate innocence of a nice girl.

This scene deviates from the wry sourness of Salinger and *The New Yorker* to the sad sweetness of Schnitzler and Zweig, Ophüls and Rohmer, but with an American accent. Susan Hayward's mix of toughness and vulnerability, so perplexing to Crowther, seemed to flower more in noir roles in *Deadline at Dawn* (1946), *They Won't Believe Me* (1947), *The Saxon Charm* (1948), and *House of Strangers* (1949) than in the inspirational and lugubrious characterizations which became her commercial stock-in-trade as one of the highest-paid woman stars in Hollywood in the fifties. A beautiful creature of the night, she endowed black satin with as strong an intimation of the forbidden as was possible in the censorship-hobbled forties.

In *My Foolish Heart*, however, she is endowed with a certain nobility undreamt of in Salinger's pessimistic philosophy. The notion that people can "improve" with age and experience is alien to Salinger's themes of adult corruption of childhood innocence. Early on in *Catcher in the Rye*, the quintessentially idealistic Holden Caulfield is told by his make-out artist prep school roommate that a girl the Lothario is dating says she knows Caulfield, and is waiting downstairs in the car to say hello to him. Holden says no, thanks, though he likes the girl, and has enjoyed a platonic friendship with her at her house in the company of her impossible parents. Having perceived with his exquisite teenage sensitivity how hopelessly mixed up this girl has become, the holy Holden just knows that his roommate is going to seduce her in the backseat of the car. He has seen this wretch "operate" before on helpless "nice girls." When the monstrous Romeo returns triumphantly to the room in the early morning, Holden hysterically assaults him, and thus establishes an irrevocable moral superiority for the campus hero of the fifties and sixties.

What Salinger's fictions can never apprehend is change and redemption in grownups. There is instead only disillusion and self-destruction as the dreams of childhood degenerate into nightmares of self-loathing. *My Foolish Heart*'s Walt, despite his wise-guy American idioms, is essentially a European conception of worldliness reformed by nostalgia for a lost innocence. He changes. Like the aging protagonist in William Faulkner's *Knight's Gambit*, he "improves."

Still, there are really only two great moments in the film: Eloise standing in the doorway, and Eloise in a car on a moonlit night numbly and yet instinctively maneuvering with stratagems worthy of Stendhal a man she does not love (Kent Smith) into marrying her, and thus getting her out of "trouble." Thus, *My Foolish Heart* is a dark and gloomy film that circumvents Salinger's sin of despair by ennobling a far from foolish heart. The Eloise of *My Foolish Heart* didn't want to "trap" Walt the way her father was trapped. Then when Walt is killed in a training accident after Pearl Harbor, she can't tell her father because he has developed heart trouble. Instead, she steals Lew from her best friend Mary Jane. The Epsteins don't really have an adequate ending for this situation, but they patch things up after a fashion by having Eloise keep her (and Walt's) daughter Ramona, and Lew go back to Mary Jane. All that is then left of Salinger's "Uncle Wiggily in Connecticut" is the sublime spectacle of a beautiful woman coming to terms with the void in her heart.

Back in 1949 my brother George and I had never even heard of J. D. Salinger. Years later my sophisticated acquaintances snickered at the notion of a movie entitled *My Foolish Heart* having been adapted from a Salinger story. I had become in the meantime only one of eleven people in North America to loathe the preppy presumption of *Catcher in the Rye*, but I plunged into "Uncle Wiggily in Connecticut" and Salinger's other writings. I'm not sorry I did. His "style" is admirable, but there is nonetheless a spiritual chasm not merely between his vision of life and mine, but also between his characters of shrunken possibilities and the dreamlike expansiveness of the movies. It was more than the cultural conflict between *The New Yorker* and Hollywood. It was also the intervention of such resolutely romantic icons of the forties as Susan Hayward and Dana Andrews who embodied the delirium of memory and desire for two susceptible young males, only one of whom would live long enough to revaluate the experience half a century later.

APPENDIX I
ACADEMY AWARDS:
NOMINATIONS AND
WINNERS,
1927–1949

1927–28

Picture

The Last Command, Paramount
The Racket, Caddo, UA
Seventh Heaven, Fox
The Way of All Flesh, Paramount
Wings, Paramount

Artistic Quality of Production

Chang, Paramount
The Crowd, MGM
Sunrise, Fox

Actor

Richard Barthelmess in *The Noose* (First National) and *The Patent Leather Kid* (First National)
Charles Chaplin in *The Circus* (Chaplin, UA)
*Emil Jannings in *The Last Command* (Paramount) and *The Way of All Flesh* (Paramount)

Actress

Louise Dresser in *A Ship Comes In* (Pathé–RKO Radio)
*Janet Gaynor in *Seventh Heaven* (Fox), *Street Angel* (Fox), and *Sunrise* (Fox)
Gloria Swanson in *Sadie Thompson* (Fox)

Director

*Frank Borzage for *Seventh Heaven* (Fox)
Herbert Brenon for *Sorrell and Son* (UA)
King Vidor for *The Crowd* (MGM)

Comedy Direction

Charles Chaplin for *The Circus* (Chaplin, UA)
*Lewis Milestone for *Two Arabian Knights* (UA)
Ted Wilde for *Speedy* (Paramount)

*Winners are marked with an asterisk.

1928–29

Picture

Alibi, Feature Productions, UA
*Broadway Melody, MGM
Hollywood Review, MGM
In Old Arizona, Fox
The Patriot, Paramount

Actor

George Bancroft in Thunderbolt
(Paramount)
*Warner Baxter in In Old Arizona
(Fox)
Chester Morris in Alibi (Feature
Productions, US)
Paul Muni in The Valiant (Fox)
Lewis Stone in The Patriot
(Paramount)

Actress

Ruth Chatterton in Madame X
(MGM)
Betty Compson in The Barker (First
National)
Jeanne Eagels in The Letter
(Paramount)
Bessie Love in Broadway Melody
(MGM)
*Mary Pickford in Coquette
(Pickford, UA)

Director

Lionel Barrymore for Madame X
(MGM)
Harry Beaumont for Broadway Melody
(MGM)
Irving Cummings for In Old Arizona
(Fox)
*Frank Lloyd for The Divine Lady
(First National), River (First
National), and Drag (First
National)
Ernst Lubitsch for The Patriot
(Paramount)

1929–30

Picture

*All Quiet on the Western Front,
Universal
The Big House, MGM
Disraeli, Warner Bros.
The Divorcée, MGM
The Love Parade, Paramount

Actor

*George Arliss in Disraeli (Warner
Bros.)
George Arliss in The Green Goddess
(Warner Bros.)
Wallace Beery in The Big House
(MGM)
Maurice Chevalier in The Big Pond
(Paramount)
Ronald Colman in Bulldog
Drummond (Goldwyn, UA)
Ronald Colman in Condemned
(Goldwyn, UA)
Lawrence Tibbett in The Rogue Song
(MGM)

Actress

Nancy Carroll in The Devil's Holiday
(Paramount)
Ruth Chatterton in Sarah and Son
(Paramount)
Greta Garbo in Anna Christie
(MGM)
Greta Garbo in Romance (MGM)
*Norma Shearer in The Divorcée
(MGM)
Norma Shearer in Their Own Desire
(MGM)
Gloria Swanson in The Trespasser
(Kennedy, UA)

Director

Clarence Brown for Anna Christie
(MGM)
Clarence Brown for Romance (MGM)
Robert Z. Leonard for The Divorcée
(MGM)

Ernst Lubitsch for *The Love Parade*
(Paramount)
*Lewis Milestone for *All Quiet on
the Western Front* (Universal)
King Vidor for *Hallelujah* (MGM)

1930–31

Picture

Cimarron, RKO Radio
East Lynne, Fox
The Front Page, Caddo, UA
Skippy, Paramount
Trader Horn, MGM

Actor

*Lionel Barrymore in *A Free Soul*
(MGM)
Jackie Cooper in *Skippy* (Paramount)
Richard Dix in *Cimarron* (RKO
Radio)
Fredric March in *The Royal Family of
Broadway* (Paramount)
Adolphe Menjou in *The Front Page*
(Caddo, UA)

Actress

Marlene Dietrich in *Morocco*
(Paramount)
*Marie Dressler in *Min and Bill*
(MGM)
Irene Dunne in *Cimarron* (RKO
Radio)
Ann Harding in *Holiday* (RKO Pathé)
Norma Shearer in *A Free Soul*
(MGM)

Director

Clarence Brown for *A Free Soul*
(MGM)
Lewis Milestone for *The Front Page*
(Caddo, UA)
Wesley Ruggles for *Cimarron* (RKO
Radio)

*Norman Taurog for *Skippy*
(Paramount)
Josef von Sternberg for *Morocco*
(Paramount)

1931–32

Picture

Arrowsmith, Goldwyn, UA
Bad Girl, Fox
The Champ, MGM
Five Star Final, First National
Grand Hotel, MGM
One Hour with You, Paramount
Shanghai Express, Paramount
The Smiling Lieutenant, Paramount

Actor**

*Wallace Beery in *The Champ*
(MGM)
Alfred Lunt in *The Guardsman*
(MGM)
*Fredric March in *Dr. Jekyll and Mr.
Hyde* (Paramount)

Actress

Marie Dressler in *Emma* (MGM)
Lynn Fontanne in *The Guardsman*
(MGM)
*Helen Hayes in *The Sin of Madelon
Claudet* (MGM)

Director

*Frank Borzage for *Bad Girl* (Fox)
King Vidor for *The Champ* (MGM)
Josef von Sternberg for *Shanghai
Express* (Paramount)

1932–33

Picture

Cavalcade, Fox
A Farewell to Arms, Paramount

**Note: Two winners this year

42nd Street, Warner Bros.
I Am a Fugitive from a Chain Gang,
  Warner Bros.
Lady for a Day, Columbia
Little Women, RKO Radio
The Private Life of Henry VIII,
  London Films, UA (British)
She Done Him Wrong, Paramount
Smilin' Through, MGM
State Fair, Fox

Actor

Leslie Howard in Berkeley Square
  (Fox)
*Charles Laughton in The Private
  Life of Henry VIII (London Films,
  UA–British)
Paul Muni in I Am a Fugitive from a
  Chain Gang (Warner Bros.)

Actress

*Katharine Hepburn in Morning
  Glory (RKO Radio)
May Robson in Lady for a Day
  (Columbia)
Diana Wynyard in Cavalcade (Fox)

Director

Frank Capra for Lady for a Day
  (Columbia)
George Cukor for Little Women
  (RKO Radio)
*Frank Lloyd for Cavalcade (Fox)

1934

Picture

The Barretts of Wimpole Street,
  MGM
Cleopatra, Paramount
Flirtation Walk, First National
The Gay Divorcée, RKO Radio
Here Comes the Navy, Warner Bros.
The House of Rothschild, 20th
  Century, UA
Imitation of Life, Universal

*It Happened One Night, Columbia
One Night of Love, Columbia
The Thin Man, MGM
Viva Villa!, MGM
The White Parade, Fox

Actor

*Clark Gable in It Happened One
  Night (Columbia)
Frank Morgan in Affairs of Cellini
  (20th Century, UA)
William Powell in The Thin Man
  (MGM)

Actress

*Claudette Colbert in It Happened
  One Night (Columbia)
Grace Moore in One Night of Love
  (Columbia)
Norma Shearer in The Barretts of
  Wimpole Street (MGM)

Director

*Frank Capra for It Happened One
  Night (Columbia)
Victor Schertzinger for One Night of
  Love (Columbia)
W. S. Van Dyke for The Thin Man
  (MGM)

1935

Picture

Alice Adams, RKO Radio
Broadway Melody of 1936, MGM
Captain Blood, Warner Bros.-
  Cosmopolitan
David Copperfield, MGM
The Informer, RKO Radio
Les Miserables, 20th Century, UA
Lives of a Bengal Lancer, Paramount
A Midsummer Night's Dream, Warner
  Bros.
*Mutiny on the Bounty, MGM
Naughty Marietta, MGM
Ruggles of Red Gap, Paramount
Top Hat, RKO Radio

Actor

Clark Gable in *Mutiny on the Bounty* (MGM)

Charles Laughton in *Mutiny on the Bounty* (MGM)

*Victor McLaglen in *The Informer* (RKO Radio)

Franchot Tone in *Mutiny on the Bounty* (MGM)

Actress

Elisabeth Bergner in *Escape Me Never* (Wilcox, UA–British)

Claudette Colbert in *Private Worlds* (Paramount)

*Bette Davis in *Dangerous* (Warner Bros.)

Katharine Hepburn in *Alice Adams* (RKO Radio)

Miriam Hopkins in *Becky Sharp* (Pioneer, RKO Radio)

Merle Oberon in *The Dark Angel* (Goldwyn, UA)

Director

*John Ford for *The Informer* (RKO Radio)

Henry Hathaway for *Lives of a Bengal Lancer* (Paramount)

Frank Lloyd for *Mutiny on the Bounty* (MGM)

1936

Picture

Anthony Adverse, Warner Bros.
Dodsworth, Goldwyn, UA
**The Great Ziegfeld*, MGM
Libeled Lady, MGM
Mr. Deeds Goes to Town, Columbia
Romeo and Juliet, MGM
San Francisco, MGM
The Story of Louis Pasteur, Warner Bros.
A Tale of Two Cities, MGM
Three Smart Girls, Universal

Actor

Gary Cooper in *Mr. Deeds Goes to Town* (Columbia)

Walter Huston in *Dodsworth* (Goldwyn, UA)

*Paul Muni in *The Story of Louis Pasteur* (Warner Bros.)

William Powell in *My Man Godfrey* (Universal)

Spencer Tracy in *San Francisco* (MGM)

Actress

Irene Dunne in *Theodora Goes Wild* (Columbia)

Gladys George in *Valiant Is the Word for Carrie* (Paramount)

Carole Lombard in *My Man Godfrey* (Universal)

*Luise Rainer in *The Great Ziegfeld* (MGM)

Norma Shearer in *Romeo and Juliet* (MGM)

Supporting Actor

Mischa Auer in *My Man Godfrey* (Universal)

*Walter Brennan in *Come and Get It* (Goldwyn, UA)

Stuart Erwin in *Pigskin Parade* (20th Century-Fox)

Basil Rathbone in *Romeo and Juliet* (MGM)

Akim Tamiroff in *The General Died at Dawn* (Paramount)

Supporting Actress

Beulah Bondi in *The Gorgeous Hussy* (MGM)

Alice Brady in *My Man Godfrey* (Universal)

Bonita Granville in *These Three* (Goldwyn, UA)

Maria Ouspenskaya in *Dodsworth* (Goldwyn, UA)

*Gale Sondergaard in *Anthony Adverse* (Warner Bros.)

Director

*Frank Capra for *Mr. Deeds Goes to Town* (Columbia)
Gregory La Cava for *My Man Godfrey* (Universal)
Robert Z. Leonard for *The Great Ziegfeld* (MGM)
W. S. Van Dyke for *San Francisco* (MGM)
William Wyler for *Dodsworth* (Goldwyn, UA)

1937

Picture

The Awful Truth, Columbia
Captains Courageous, MGM
Dead End, Goldwyn, UA
The Good Earth, MGM
In Old Chicago, 20th Century-Fox
*The Life of Emile Zola, Warner Bros.
Lost Horizon, Columbia
100 Men and a Girl, Universal
Stage Door, RKO Radio
A Star Is Born, Selznick International, UA

Actor

Charles Boyer in *Conquest* (MGM)
Fredric March in *A Star Is Born* (Selznick International, UA)
Robert Montgomery in *Night Must Fall* (MGM)
Paul Muni in *The Life of Emile Zola* (Warner Bros.)
*Spencer Tracy in *Captains Courageous* (MGM)

Actress

Irene Dunne in *The Awful Truth* (Columbia)
Greta Garbo in *Camille* (MGM)

Janet Gaynor in *A Star Is Born* (Selznick International, UA)
*Luise Rainer in *The Good Earth* (MGM)
Barbara Stanwyck in *Stella Dallas* (Goldwyn, UA)

Supporting Actor

Ralph Bellamy in *The Awful Truth* (Columbia)
Thomas Mitchell in *The Hurricane* (Goldwyn, UA)
*Joseph Schildkraut in *The Life of Emile Zola* (Warner Bros.)
H. B. Warner in *Lost Horizon* (Columbia)
Roland Young in *Topper* (Roach, MGM)

Supporting Actress

*Alice Brady in *In Old Chicago* (20th Century-Fox)
Andrea Leeds in *Stage Door* (RKO Radio)
Anne Shirley in *Stella Dallas* (Goldwyn, UA)
Claire Trevor in *Dead End* (Goldwyn, UA)
Dame May Whitty in *Night Must Fall* (MGM)

Director

William Dieterle for *The Life of Emile Zola* (Warner Bros.)
Sidney Franklin for *The Good Earth* (MGM)
Gregory La Cava for *Stage Door* (RKO Radio)
*Leo McCarey for *The Awful Truth* (Columbia)
William Wellman for *A Star Is Born* (Selznick International, UA)

1938

Picture

The Adventures of Robin Hood, Warner Bros.

Alexander's Ragtime Band, 20th
  Century-Fox
Boys Town, MGM
The Citadel, MGM (British)
Four Daughters, Warner Bros.-First
  National
Grand Illusion, R.A.O., World
  Pictures (French)
Jezebel, Warner Bros.
Pygmalion, MGM (British)
Test Pilot, MGM
*You Can't Take It with You,
  Columbia

Actor

Charles Boyer in *Algiers* (Wanger,
  UA)
James Cagney in *Angels with Dirty
  Faces* (Warner Bros.)
Robert Donat in *The Citadel* (MGM–
  British)
Leslie Howard in *Pygmalion* (MGM–
  British)
*Spencer Tracy in *Boys Town*
  (MGM)

Actress

Fay Bainter in *White Banners*
  (Warner Bros.)
*Bette Davis in *Jezebel* (Warner
  Bros.)
Wendy Hiller in *Pygmalion* (MGM-
  British)
Norma Shearer in *Marie Antoinette*
  (MGM)
Margaret Sullavan in *Three Comrades*
  (MGM)

Supporting Actor

*Walter Brennan in *Kentucky* (20th
  Century-Fox)
John Garfield in *Four Daughters*
  (Warner Bros.-First National)
Gene Lockhart in *Algiers* (Wanger,
  UA)
Robert Morley in *Marie Antoinette*
  (MGM)

Basil Rathbone in *If I Were King*
  (Paramount)

Supporting Actress

*Fay Bainter in *Jezebel* (Warner
  Bros.)
Beulah Bondi in *Of Human Hearts*
  (MGM)
Billie Burke in *Merrily We Live*
  (Roach, MGM)
Spring Byington in *You Can't Take It
  with You* (Columbia)
Miliza Korjus in *The Great Waltz*
  (MGM)

Director

*Frank Capra for *You Can't Take It
  with You* (Columbia)
Michael Curtiz for *Angels with Dirty
  Faces* (Warner Bros.)
Michael Curtiz for *Four Daughters*
  (Warner Bros.-First National)
Norman Taurog for *Boys Town*
  (MGM)
King Vidor for *The Citadel* (MGM–
  British)

1939

Picture

Dark Victory, Warner Bros.
*Gone With the Wind, Selznick,
  MGM
Goodbye, Mr. Chips, MGM (British)
Love Affair, RKO Radio
Mr. Smith Goes to Washington,
  Columbia
Ninotchka, MGM
Of Mice and Men, Roach, UA
Stagecoach, Wanger, UA
The Wizard of Oz, MGM
Wuthering Heights, Goldwyn, UA

Actor

*Robert Donat in *Goodbye, Mr. Chips*
  (MGM–British)

Clark Gable in *Gone With the Wind*
(Selznick, MGM)

Laurence Olivier in *Wuthering
Heights* (Goldwyn, UA)

Mickey Rooney in *Babes in Arms*
(MGM)

James Stewart in *Mr. Smith Goes to
Washington* (Columbia)

Actress

Bette Davis in *Dark Victory* (Warner
Bros.)

Irene Dunne in *Love Affair* (RKO
Radio)

Greta Garbo in *Ninotchka* (MGM)

Greer Garson in *Goodbye, Mr. Chips*
(MGM–British)

*Vivien Leigh in *Gone With the
Wind* (Selznick, MGM)

Supporting Actor

Brian Aherne in *Juarez* (Warner
Bros.)

Harry Carey in *Mr. Smith Goes to
Washington* (Columbia)

Brian Donlevy in *Beau Geste*
(Paramount)

*Thomas Mitchell in *Stagecoach*
(Wanger, UA)

Claude Rains in *Mr. Smith Goes to
Washington* (Columbia)

Supporting Actress

Olivia de Havilland in *Gone With the
Wind* (Selznick, MGM

Geraldine Fitzgerald in *Wuthering
Heights* (Goldwyn, UA)

*Hattie McDaniel in *Gone With the
Wind* (Selznick, MGM)

Edna May Oliver in *Drums Along the
Mohawk* (20th Century-Fox)

Maria Ouspenskaya in *Love Affair*
(RKO Radio)

Director

Frank Capra for *Mr. Smith Goes to
Washington* (Columbia)

*Victor Fleming for *Gone With the
Wind* (Selznick, MGM)

John Ford for *Stagecoach* (Wanger,
UA)

Sam Wood for *Goodbye, Mr. Chips*
(MGM–British)

William Wyler for *Wuthering Heights*
(Goldwyn, UA)

1940

Picture

All This, and Heaven Too, Warner
Bros.

Foreign Correspondent, Wanger, UA

The Grapes of Wrath, 20th Century-
Fox

The Great Dictator, Chaplin, UA

Kitty Foyle, RKO Radio

The Letter, Warner Bros.

The Long Voyage Home, Argosy-
Wanger, UA

Our Town, Lesser, UA

The Philadelphia Story, MGM

**Rebecca*, Selznick, UA

Actor

Charles Chaplin in *The Great
Dictator* (Chaplin, UA)

Henry Fonda in *The Grapes of Wrath*
(20th Century-Fox)

Raymond Massey in *Abe Lincoln in
Illinois* (RKO Radio)

Laurence Olivier in *Rebecca*
(Selznick, UA)

*James Stewart in *The Philadelphia
Story* (MGM)

Actress

Bette Davis in *The Letter* (Warner
Bros.)

Joan Fontaine in *Rebecca* (Selznick,
UA)

Katharine Hepburn in *The
Philadelphia Story* (MGM)

*Ginger Rogers in *Kitty Foyle* (RKO
Radio)

Martha Scott in *Our Town* (Lesser,
UA)

Supporting Actor

Albert Basserman in *Foreign Correspondent* (Wanger, UA)
*Walter Brennan in *The Westerner* (Goldwyn, UA)
William Gargan in *They Knew What They Wanted* (RKO Radio)
Jack Oakie in *The Great Dictator* (Chaplin, UA)
James Stephenson in *The Letter* (Warner Bros.)

Supporting Actress

Judith Anderson in *Rebecca* (Selznick, UA)
*Jane Darwell in *The Grapes of Wrath* (20th Century-Fox)
Ruth Hussey in *The Philadelphia Story* (MGM)
Barbara O'Neill in *All This, and Heaven Too* (Warner Bros.)
Marjorie Rambeau in *Primrose Path* (RKO Radio)

Director

George Cukor for *The Philadelphia Story* (MGM)
*John Ford for *The Grapes of Wrath* (20th Century-Fox)
Alfred Hitchcock for *Rebecca* (Selznick, UA)
Sam Wood for *Kitty Foyle* (RKO Radio)
William Wyler for *The Letter* (Warner Bros.)

1941

Picture

Blossoms in the Dust, MGM
Citizen Kane, Mercury, RKO Radio
Here Comes Mr. Jordan, Columbia
Hold Back the Dawn, Paramount
**How Green Was My Valley*, 20th Century-Fox
The Little Foxes, RKO Radio
The Maltese Falcon, Warner Bros.
One Foot in Heaven, Warner Bros.
Sergeant York, Warner Bros.
Suspicion, RKO Radio

Actor

*Gary Cooper in *Sergeant York* (Warner Bros.)
Cary Grant in *Penny Serenade* (Columbia)
Walter Huston in *All That Money Can Buy* (a.k.a. *The Devil and Daniel Webster*) (RKO Radio)
Robert Montgomery in *Here Comes Mr. Jordan* (Columbia)
Orson Welles in *Citizen Kane* (Mercury, RKO Radio)

Actress

Bette Davis in *The Little Foxes* (RKO Radio)
*Joan Fontaine in *Suspicion* (RKO Radio)
Greer Garson in *Blossoms in the Dust* (MGM)
Olivia de Havilland in *Hold Back the Dawn* (Paramount)
Barbara Stanwyck in *Ball of Fire* (Goldwyn, RKO Radio)

Supporting Actor

Walter Brennan in *Sergeant York* (Warner Bros.)
Charles Coburn in *The Devil and Miss Jones* (RKO Radio)
*Donald Crisp in *How Green Was My Valley* (20th Century-Fox)
James Gleason in *Here Comes Mr. Jordan* (Columbia)
Sydney Greenstreet in *The Maltese Falcon* (Warner Bros.)

Supporting Actress

Sara Allgood in *How Green Was My Valley* (20th Century-Fox)
*Mary Astor in *The Great Lie* (Warner Bros.)

Patricia Collinge in *The Little Foxes*
(RKO Radio)
Teresa Wright in *The Little Foxes*
(RKO Radio)
Margaret Wycherly in *Sergeant York*
(Warner Bros.)

Director

*John Ford for *How Green Was My
Valley* (20th Century-Fox)
Alexander Hall for *Here Comes Mr.
Jordan* (Columbia)
Howard Hawks for *Sergeant York*
(Warner Bros.)
Orson Welles for *Citizen Kane*
(Mercury, RKO Radio)
William Wyler for *The Little Foxes*
(RKO Radio)

1942

Picture

The Invaders, Ortus, Columbia
(British)
King's Row, Warner Bros.
The Magnificent Ambersons, Mercury,
RKO Radio
Mrs. Miniver, MGM
The Pied Piper, 20th Century-Fox
The Pride of the Yankees, Goldwyn,
RKO Radio
Random Harvest, MGM
The Talk of the Town, Columbia
Wake Island, Paramount
Yankee Doodle Dandy, Warner Bros.

Actor

*James Cagney in *Yankee Doodle
Dandy* (Warner Bros.)
Ronald Colman in *Random Harvest*
(MGM)
Gary Cooper in *The Pride of the
Yankees* (Goldwyn, RKO Radio)
Walter Pidgeon in *Mrs. Miniver*
(MGM)
Monty Woolley in *The Pied Piper*
(20th Century-Fox)

Actress

Bette Davis in *Now, Voyager* (Warner
Bros.)
*Greer Garson in *Mrs. Miniver*
(MGM)
Katharine Hepburn in *Woman of the
Year* (MGM)
Rosalind Russell in *My Sister Eileen*
(Columbia)
Teresa Wright in *The Pride of the
Yankees* (Goldwyn, RKO Radio)

Supporting Actor

William Bendix in *Wake Island*
(Paramount)
*Van Heflin in *Johnny Eager* (MGM)
Walter Huston in *Yankee Doodle
Dandy* (Warner Bros.)
Frank Morgan in *Tortilla Flat*
(MGM)
Henry Travers in *Mrs. Miniver*
(MGM)

Supporting Actress

Gladys Cooper in *Now, Voyager*
(Warner Bros.)
Agnes Moorehead in *The Magnificent
Ambersons* (Mercury, RKO Radio)
Susan Peters in *Random Harvest*
(MGM)
Dame May Whitty in *Mrs. Miniver*
(MGM)
*Teresa Wright in *Mrs. Miniver*
(MGM)

Director

Michael Curtiz for *Yankee Doodle
Dandy* (Warner Bros.)
John Farrow for *Wake Island*
(Paramount)
Mervyn LeRoy for *Random Harvest*
(MGM)
Sam Wood for *King's Row* (Warner
Bros.)
*William Wyler for *Mrs. Miniver*
(MGM)

1943

Picture

Casablanca, Warner Bros.
For Whom the Bell Tolls, Paramount
Heaven Can Wait, 20th Century-Fox
The Human Comedy, MGM
In Which We Serve, Two Cities, UA (British)
Madame Curie, MGM
The More the Merrier, Columbia
The Ox-Bow Incident, 20th Century-Fox
The Song of Bernadette, 20th Century-Fox
Watch on the Rhine, Warner Bros.

Actor

Humphrey Bogart in *Casablanca* (Warner Bros.)
Gary Cooper in *For Whom the Bell Tolls* (Paramount)
*Paul Lukas in *Watch on the Rhine* (Warner Bros.)
Walter Pidgeon in *Madame Curie* (MGM)
Mickey Rooney in *The Human Comedy* (MGM)

Actress

Jean Arthur in *The More the Merrier* (Columbia)
Ingrid Bergman in *For Whom the Bell Tolls* (Paramount)
Joan Fontaine in *The Constant Nymph* (Warner Bros)
Greer Garson in *Madame Curie* (MGM)
*Jennifer Jones in *The Song of Bernadette* (20th Century-Fox)

Supporting Actor

Charles Bickford in *The Song of Bernadette* (20th Century-Fox)
*Charles Coburn in *The More the Merrier* (Columbia)
J. Carrol Naish in *Sahara* (Columbia)

Claude Rains in *Casablanca* (Warner Bros.)
Akim Tamiroff in *For Whom the Bell Tolls* (Paramount)

Supporting Actress

Gladys Cooper in *The Song of Bernadette* (20th Century-Fox)
Paulette Goddard in *So Proudly We Hail* (Paramount)
*Katina Paxinou in *For Whom the Bell Tolls* (Paramount)
Anne Revere in *The Song of Bernadette* (20th Century-Fox)
Lucile Watson in *Watch on the Rhine* (Warner Bros.)

Director

Clarence Brown for *The Human Comedy* (MGM)
*Michael Curtiz for *Casablanca* (Warner Bros.)
Henry King for *The Song of Bernadette* (20th Century-Fox)
Ernst Lubitsch for *Heaven Can Wait* (20th Century-Fox)
George Stevens for *The More the Merrier* (Columbia)

1944

Picture

Double Indemnity, Paramount
Gaslight, MGM
Going My Way, Paramount
Since You Went Away, Selznick, UA
Wilson, 20th Century-Fox

Actor

Charles Boyer in *Gaslight* (MGM)
*Bing Crosby in *Going My Way* (Paramount)
Barry Fitzgerald in *Going My Way* (Paramount)
Cary Grant in *None But the Lonely Heart* (RKO Radio)
Alexander Knox in *Wilson* (20th Century-Fox)

Actress

*Ingrid Bergman in *Gaslight* (MGM)
Claudette Colbert in *Since You Went
  Away* (Selznick, UA)
Bette Davis in *Mr. Skeffington*
  (Warner Bros.)
Greer Garson in *Mrs. Parkington*
  (MGM)
Barbara Stanwyck in *Double
  Indemnity* (Paramount)

Supporting Actor

Hume Cronyn in *The Seventh Cross*
  (MGM)
*Barry Fitzgerald in *Going My Way*
  (Paramount)
Claude Rains in *Mr. Skeffington*
  (Warner Bros.)
Clifton Webb in *Laura* (20th Century-
  Fox)
Monty Woolley in *Since You Went
  Away* (Selznick, UA)

Supporting Actress

*Ethel Barrymore in *None But the
  Lonely Heart* (RKO Radio)
Jennifer Jones in *Since You Went
  Away* (Selznick, UA)
Angela Lansbury in *Gaslight* (MGM)
Aline MacMahon in *Dragon Seed*
  (MGM)
Agnes Moorehead in *Mrs. Parkington*
  (MGM)

Director

Alfred Hitchcock for *Lifeboat* (20th
  Century-Fox)
Henry King for *Wilson* (20th
  Century-Fox)
*Leo McCarey for *Going My Way*
  (Paramount)
Otto Preminger for *Laura* (20th
  Century-Fox)
Billy Wilder for *Double Indemnity*
  (Paramount)

1945

Picture

Anchors Aweigh, MGM
The Bells of St. Mary's, Rainbow,
  RKO Radio
The Lost Weekend, Paramount
Mildred Pierce, Warner Bros.
Spellbound, UA

Actor

Bing Crosby in *The Bells of St. Mary's*
  (Rainbow, RKO Radio)
Gene Kelly in *Anchors Aweigh*
  (MGM)
*Ray Milland in *The Lost Weekend*
  (Paramount)
Gregory Peck in *The Keys of the
  Kingdom* (20th Century-Fox)
Cornel Wilde in *A Song to Remember*
  (Columbia)

Actress

Ingrid Bergman in *The Bells of St.
  Mary's* (Rainbow, RKO Radio)
*Joan Crawford in *Mildred Pierce*
  (Warner Bros.)
Greer Garson in *The Valley of
  Decision* (MGM)
Jennifer Jones in *Love Letters* (Wallis,
  Paramount)
Gene Tierney in *Leave Her to Heaven*
  (20th Century-Fox)

Supporting Actor

Michael Chekhov in *Spellbound*
  (Selznick, UA)
John Dall in *The Corn Is Green*
  (Warner Bros)
*James Dunn in *A Tree Grows in
  Brooklyn* (20th Century-Fox)
Robert Mitchum in *The Story of G.I.
  Joe* (Cowan, UA)
J. Carrol Naish in *A Medal for Benny*
  (Paramount)

Supporting Actress

Eve Arden in *Mildred Pierce* (Warner Bros.)
Ann Blyth in *Mildred Pierce* (Warner Bros.)
Angela Lansbury in *The Picture of Dorian Gray* (MGM)
Joan Lorring in *The Corn Is Green* (Warner Bros)
*Anne Revere in *National Velvet* (MGM)

Director

Clarence Brown for *National Velvet* (MGM)
Alfred Hitchcock for *Spellbound* (Selznick, UA)
Leo McCarey for *The Bells of St. Mary's* (Rainbow, RKO Radio)
Jean Renoir for *The Southerner* (Loew–Hakim, UA)
*Billy Wilder for *The Lost Weekend* (Paramount)

1946

Picture

**The Best Years of Our Lives*, Goldwyn, RKO Radio
Henry V, Rank-Two Cities, UA (British)
It's a Wonderful Life, Liberty, RKO Radio
The Razor's Edge, 20th Century-Fox
The Yearling, MGM

Actor

*Fredric March in *The Best Years of Our Lives* (Goldwyn, RKO Radio)
Laurence Olivier in *Henry V* (Rank-Two Cities, UA–British)
Larry Parks in *The Jolson Story* (Columbia)
Gregory Peck in *The Yearling* (MGM)
James Stewart in *It's a Wonderful Life* (Liberty, RKO Radio)

Actress

*Olivia de Havilland in *To Each His Own* (Paramount)
Celia Johnson in *Brief Encounter* (Rank, U-I—British)
Jennifer Jones in *Duel in the Sun* (Selznick International)
Rosalind Russell in *Sister Kenney* (RKO Radio)
Jane Wyman in *The Yearling* (MGM)

Supporting Actor

Charles Coburn in *The Green Years* (MGM)
William Demarest in *The Jolson Story* (Columbia)
Claude Rains in *Notorious* (RKO Radio)
*Harold Russell in *The Best Years of Our Lives* (Goldwyn, RKO Radio)
Clifton Webb in *The Razor's Edge* (20th Century-Fox)

Supporting Actress

Ethel Barrymore in *The Spiral Staircase* (RKO Radio)
*Anne Baxter in *The Razor's Edge* (20th Century-Fox)
Lillian Gish in *Duel in the Sun* (Selznick International)
Flora Robson in *Saratoga Trunk* (Warner Bros.)
Gale Sondergaard in *Anna and the King of Siam* (20th Century-Fox)

Director

Clarence Brown for *The Yearling* (MGM)
Frank Capra for *It's a Wonderful Life* (Liberty, RKO Radio)
David Lean for *Brief Encounter* (Rank, U-I—British)
Robert Siodmak for *The Killers* (Hellinger, Universal)
*William Wyler for *The Best Years of Our Lives* (Goldwyn, RKO Radio)

1947

Picture

The Bishop's Wife, Goldwyn, RKO Radio
Crossfire, RKO Radio
*Gentleman's Agreement, 20th Century-Fox
Great Expectations, Rank-Cineguild, U-I (British)
Miracle on 34th Street, 20th Century-Fox

Actor

*Ronald Colman in *A Double Life* (Kanin, U-I)
John Garfield in *Body and Soul* (Enterprise, UA)
Gregory Peck in *Gentleman's Agreement* (20th Century-Fox)
William Powell in *Life with Father* (Warner Bros.)
Michael Redgrave in *Mourning Becomes Electra* (RKO Radio)

Actress

Joan Crawford in *Possessed* (Warner Bros.)
Susan Hayward in *Smash Up—The Story of a Woman* (Wanger, U-I)
Dorothy McGuire in *Gentleman's Agreement* (20th Century-Fox)
Rosalind Russell in *Mourning Becomes Electra* (RKO Radio)
*Loretta Young in *The Farmer's Daughter* (RKO Radio)

Supporting Actor

Charles Bickford in *The Farmer's Daughter* (RKO Radio)
Thomas Gomez in *Ride the Pink Horse* (U-I)
*Edmund Gwenn in *Miracle on 34th Street* (20th Century-Fox)
Robert Ryan in *Crossfire* (RKO Radio)
Richard Widmark in *Kiss of Death* (20th Century-Fox)

Supporting Actress

Ethel Barrymore in *The Paradine Case* (Selznick)
Gloria Grahame in *Crossfire* (RKO Radio)
*Celeste Holm in *Gentleman's Agreement* (20th Century-Fox)
Marjorie Main in *The Egg and I* (U-I)
Anne Revere in *Gentleman's Agreement* (20th Century-Fox)

Director

George Cukor for *A Double Life* (Kanin, U-I)
Edward Dmytryk for *Crossfire* (RKO Radio)
*Elia Kazan for *Gentleman's Agreement* (20th Century-Fox)
Henry Koster for *The Bishop's Wife* (Goldwyn, RKO Radio)
David Lean for *Great Expectations* (Rank-Cineguild, U-I—British)

1948

Picture

*Hamlet, Rank-Two Cities, U-I (British)
Johnny Belinda, Warner Bros.
The Red Shoes, Rank-Archers, Eagle–Lion (British)
The Snake Pit, 20th Century-Fox
The Treasure of the Sierra Madre, Warner Bros.

Actor

Lew Ayres in *Johnny Belinda* (Warner Bros.)
Montgomery Clift in *The Search* (Praesens Films, MGM—Swiss)
Dan Dailey in *When My Baby Smiles at Me* (20th Century-Fox)
*Laurence Olivier in *Hamlet* (Rank-Two Cities, U-I—British)
Clifton Webb in *Sitting Pretty* (20th Century-Fox)

Actress

Ingrid Bergman in *Joan of Arc* (Sierra
Pictures, RKO Radio)
Olivia de Havilland in *The Snake Pit*
(20th Century-Fox)
Irene Dunne in *I Remember Mama*
(RKO Radio)
Barbara Stanwyck in *Sorry, Wrong
Number* (Wallis, Paramount)
*Jane Wyman in *Johnny Belinda*
(Warner Bros.)

Supporting Actor

Charles Bickford in *Johnny Belinda*
(Warner Bros.)
José Ferrer in *Joan of Arc* (Sierra
Pictures, RKO Radio)
Oscar Homolka in *I Remember Mama*
(RKO Radio)
*Walter Huston in *The Treasure of
the Sierra Madre* (Warner Bros.)
Cecil Kellaway in *The Luck of the
Irish* (20th Century-Fox)

Supporting Actress

Barbara Bel Geddes in *I Remember
Mama* (RKO Radio)
Ellen Corby in *I Remember Mama*
(RKO Radio)
Agnes Moorehead in *Johnny Belinda*
(Warner Bros.)
Jean Simmons in *Hamlet* (Rank-Two
Cities, U-I—British)
*Claire Trevor in *Key Largo* (Warner
Bros.)

Director

*John Huston for *The Treasure of the
Sierra Madre* (Warner Bros.)
Anatole Litvak for *The Snake Pit*
(20th Century-Fox)
Jean Negulesco for *Johnny Belinda*
(Warner Bros.)
Laurence Olivier in *Hamlet* (Rank-
Two Cities, U-I—British)
Fred Zinnemann for *The Search*
(Praesens Films, MGM—Swiss)

1949

Picture

All the King's Men, Rossen,
Columbia
Battleground, MGM
The Heiress, Paramount
A Letter to Three Wives, 20th
Century-Fox
12 O'Clock High, 20th Century-Fox

Actor

*Broderick Crawford in *All the King's
Men* (Rossen, Columbia)
Kirk Douglas in *Champion* (Kramer,
UA)
Gregory Peck in *12 O'Clock High*
(20th Century-Fox)
Richard Todd in *The Hasty Heart*
(Warner Bros.)
John Wayne in *Sands of Iwo Jima*
(Republic)

Actress

Jeanne Crain in *Pinky* (20th Century-
Fox)
*Olivia de Havilland in *The Heiress*
(Paramount)
Susan Hayward in *My Foolish Heart*
(Goldwyn, RKO Radio)
Deborah Kerr in *Edward My Son*
(MGM)
Loretta Young in *Come to the Stable*
(20th Century-Fox)

Supporting Actor

John Ireland in *All the King's Men*
(Rossen, Columbia)
*Dean Jagger in *12 O'Clock High*
(20th Century-Fox)
Arthur Kennedy in *Champion*
(Kramer, UA)
Ralph Richardson in *The Heiress*
(Paramount)
James Whitmore in *Battleground*
(MGM)

Supporting Actress

Ethel Barrymore in *Pinky* (20th
Century-Fox)
Celeste Holm in *Come to the Stable*
(20th Century-Fox)
Elsa Lanchester in *Come to the
Stable* (20th Century-Fox)
*Mercedes McCambridge in *All the
King's Men* (Rossen, Columbia)
Ethel Waters in *Pinky* (20th Century-
Fox)

Director

*Joseph L. Mankiewicz for *A Letter
to Three Wives* (20th Century-Fox)
Carol Reed for *The Fallen Idol*
(London Films, SRO—British)
Robert Rossen for *All the King's Men*
(Rossen, Columbia)
William A. Wellman for *Battleground*
(MGM)
William Wyler for *The Heiress*
(Paramount)

APPENDIX II
NEW YORK FILM CRITICS
CIRCLE AWARDS,
1935–1949

Best Picture

1935　The Informer
1936　Mr. Deeds Goes to Town
1937　The Life of Emile Zola
1938　The Citadel
1939　Wuthering Heights
1940　The Grapes of Wrath
1941　Citizen Kane
1942　In Which We Serve
1943　Watch on the Rhine
1944　Going My Way
1945　The Lost Weekend
1946　The Best Years of Our Lives
1947　Gentleman's Agreement
1948　The Treasure of the Sierra
　　　　Madre
1949　All the King's Men

Best Actor

1935　Charles Laughton, Mutiny on
　　　　the Bounty and Ruggles of
　　　　Red Gap
1936　Walter Huston, Dodsworth
1937　Paul Muni, The Life of Emile
　　　　Zola
1938　James Cagney, Angels with
　　　　Dirty Faces
1939　James Stewart, Mr. Smith
　　　　Goes to Washington
1940　Charles Chaplin, The Great
　　　　Dictator
1941　Gary Cooper, Sergeant York
1942　James Cagney, Yankee Doodle
　　　　Dandy
1943　Paul Lukas, Watch on the
　　　　Rhine
1944　Barry Fitzgerald, Going My
　　　　Way
1945　Ray Milland, The Lost
　　　　Weekend
1946　Laurence Olivier, Henry V
1947　William Powell, Life with
　　　　Father and The Senator Was
　　　　Indiscreet
1948　Laurence Olivier, Hamlet
1949　Broderick Crawford, All the
　　　　King's Men

Best Actress

1935　Greta Garbo, Anna Karenina
1936　Luise Rainer, The Great
　　　　Ziegfeld

1937 Greta Garbo, *Camille*
1938 Margaret Sullavan, *Three Comrades*
1939 Vivien Leigh, *Gone With the Wind*
1940 Katharine Hepburn, *The Philadelphia Story*
1941 Joan Fontaine, *Suspicion*
1942 Agnes Moorehead, *The Magnificent Ambersons*
1943 Ida Lupino, *The Hard Way*
1944 Tallulah Bankhead, *Lifeboat*
1945 Ingrid Bergman, *Spellbound* and *The Bells of St. Mary's*
1946 Celia Johnson, *Brief Encounter*
1947 Deborah Kerr, *Black Narcissus* and *The Adventuress*
1948 Olivia de Havilland, *The Snake Pit*
1949 Olivia de Havilland, *The Heiress*

Best Direction

1935 John Ford, *The Informer*

1936 Rouben Mamoulian, *The Gay Desperado*
1937 Gregory La Cava, *Stage Door*
1938 Alfred Hitchcock, *The Lady Vanishes*
1939 John Ford, *Stagecoach*
1940 John Ford, *The Grapes of Wrath* and *The Long Voyage Home*
1941 John Ford, *How Green Was My Valley*
1942 John Farrow, *Wake Island*
1943 George Stevens, *The More the Merrier*
1944 Leo McCarey, *Going My Way*
1945 Billy Wilder, *The Lost Weekend*
1946 William Wyler, *The Best Years of Our Lives*
1947 Elia Kazan, *Gentleman's Agreement* and *Boomerang*
1948 John Huston, *The Treasure of the Sierra Madre*
1949 Carol Reed, *The Fallen Idol*

APPENDIX III
BEST DIRECTORS,
1927–1949

1927

F. W. Murnau, *Sunrise*
Josef von Sternberg, *Underworld*
King Vidor, *The Crowd, The Patsy*
Frank Borzage, *Seventh Heaven*
Ernst Lubitsch, *The Student Prince*
Buster Keaton, *College*
Alfred Hitchcock, *The Ring, Easy
  Virtue, Downhill*
Raoul Walsh, *The Loves of Carmen,
  The Monkey Talks*
John Ford, *Upstream*
Howard Hawks, *The Cradle
  Snatchers, Paid to Love*
Frank Capra, *Long Pants, For the
  Love of Mike*
Cecil B. De Mille, *The King of Kings*
Allan Dwan, *The Music Master; Joy
  Girl; East Side, West Side*

1928

Charles Chaplin, *The Circus*
Josef von Sternberg, *Docks of New
  York, The Last Command, The
  Drag Net*

Erich von Stroheim, *The Wedding
  March, Queen Kelly*
Howard Hawks, *A Girl in Every Port,
  The Air Circus, Fazil*
Ernst Lubitsch, *The Patriot*
King Vidor, *Show People*
Frank Borzage, *Street Angel*
Buster Keaton, *Steamboat Junior, The
  Cameraman*
F. W. Murnau, *The Four Devils*
D. W. Griffith, *The Battle of the
  Sexes, Drums of Love*
Alfred Hitchcock, *The Manxman,
  Champagne, The Farmer's Wife*
John Ford, *Four Sons, Mother
  Machree, Hangman's House,
  Napoleon's Barber, Riley the Cop*
Raoul Walsh, *Sadie Thompson; The
  Red Dance; Me, Gangster*
Allan Dwan, *French Dressing, Big
  Noise*
Cecil B. De Mille, *The Godless Girl*

1929

King Vidor, *Hallelujah*
Ernst Lubitsch, *The Love Parade,
  Eternal Love*

Chosen by Andrew Sarris, Spring 1963

Josef von Sternberg, *Thunderbolt, The Case of Lena Smith*

Alfred Hitchcock, *Blackmail, The Manxman*

Frank Borzage, *The River, Lucky Star, They Had To See Paris*

D. W. Griffith, *Lady of the Pavements*

Howard Hawks, *Trent's Last Case*

John Ford, *Strong Boy, The Black Watch, Salute*

Raoul Walsh, *The Cockeyed World, In Old Arizona* (with Irving Cummings)

Cecil B. De Mille, *Dynamite, The Godless Girl*

Rouben Mamoulian, *Applause*

Allan Dwan, *The Iron Mask, Tide of Empire, Frozen Justice, The Far Call, South Sea Rose*

Frank Capra, *The Younger Generation, Flight, The Donovan Affair*

Leo McCarey, *The Sophomore, Red Hot Rhythm*

Roland West, *Alibi*

Paul Leni, *The Last Warning*

Tay Garnett, *Flying Fools, Oh Yeah!*

Rex Ingram, *Three Passions*

OUTSIDE CONSENSUS CHOICES: *The Broadway Melody* (Harry Beaumont); *The Virginian* (Victor Fleming); *Disraeli* (Alfred E. Green)

Ernst Lubitsch, *Monte Carlo, Paramount on Parade* (with Edmund Golding, Rowland V. Lee, Victor Schertzinger, Dorothy Arzner, Otto Brower, Victor Heerman, Edwin Knopf, Lothar Mendes, Edward Sutherland, Frank Tuttle)

George Cukor, *The Royal Family of Broadway* (with Cyril Gardner), *Grumpy* (with Cyril Gardner), *Virtuous Sin* (with Louis Gasnier)

Raoul Walsh, *The Big Trail*

Cecil B. De Mille, *Madame Satan*

Lewis Milestone, *All Quiet on the Western Front*

Frank Capra, *Ladies of Leisure, Rain or Shine*

Leo McCarey, *Let's Go Native, Wild Company, Part Time Wife*

Tay Garnett, *Her Man, Officer O'Brien*

George Hill, *The Big House, Min and Bill*

John Stahl, *A Lady Surrenders*

Howard Hughes, *Hell's Angels*

Mervyn LeRoy, *Little Johnny Jones, Playing Around, Show Girl in Hollywood, Numbered Men, Broken Dishes, Top Speed, Little Caesar*

Harry D'Arrast, *Raffles, Laughter*

Allan Dwan, *What a Widow!*

Clarence Brown, *Anna Christie*

1930

Josef von Sternberg, *The Blue Angel, Morocco*

Howard Hawks, *The Dawn Patrol*

D. W. Griffith, *Abraham Lincoln*

F. W. Murnau, *City Girl (Our Daily Bread)*

John Ford, *Men Without Women, Born Reckless, Up the River*

Alfred Hitchcock, *Murder, The Farmer's Wife, Juno and the Paycock*

King Vidor, *Billy the Kid, Not So Dumb*

Frank Borzage, *Song o' My Heart, Liliom*

1931

Charles Chaplin, *City Lights*

F. W. Murnau, *Tabu* (with Robert Flaherty)

Josef von Sternberg, *Dishonored, An American Tragedy*

Howard Hawks, *The Criminal Code*

King Vidor, *Street Scene, The Champ*

D. W. Griffith, *The Struggle*

Ernst Lubitsch, *The Smiling Lieutenant*

Frank Borzage, *Bad Girl, Doctors' Wives, As Young As You Feel*

John Ford, *Arrowsmith, The Seas Beneath, The Brat*

Alfred Hitchcock, *The Skin Game*

George Cukor, *Tarnished Lady, Girls About Town*

Cecil B. De Mille, *The Squaw Man*

Raoul Walsh, *The Man Who Came Back, Women of All Nations, The Yellow Ticket*

Frank Capra, *Dirigible, The Miracle Woman, Platinum Blonde*

Leo McCarey, *Indiscreet*

John Stahl, *Seed, Strictly Dishonorable*

Rouben Mamoulian, *City Streets*

Lewis Milestone, *The Front Page*

Rowland Brown, *Quick Millions*

Roland West, *The Bat Whispers, Corsair*

Allan Dwan, *Man to Man, Chances, Wicked*

James Whale, *Waterloo Bridge, Frankenstein*

William Wellman, *The Public Enemy, Other Men's Women, Star Witness, Night Nurse, Safe in Hell*

Sidney Franklin, *The Guardsman, Private Lives*

OUTSIDE CONSENSUS CHOICES: *Cimarron* (Wesley Ruggles)

1932

Howard Hawks, *Scarface, The Crowd Roars, Tiger Shark*

Josef von Sternberg, *Shanghai Express, Blonde Venus*

Ernst Lubitsch, *Trouble in Paradise, One Hour With You, The Man I Killed, If I Had a Million* (with James Cruze, Norman Taurog, Stephen Roberts, Norman Z. McLeod, William Seiter, Bruce Humberstone)

Frank Borzage, *A Farewell to Arms, After Tomorrow, Young America*

George Cukor, *A Bill of Divorcement, What Price Hollywood, Rockabye*

John Ford, *Air Mail, Flesh*

Alfred Hitchcock, *East of Shanghai*

Erich von Stroheim, *Walking Down Broadway*

King Vidor, *Bird of Paradise, Cynara*

Cecil B. De Mille, *The Sign of the Cross*

Tay Garnett, *One Way Passage, Prestige, Okay America*

John Stahl, *Back Street*

Frank Capra, *American Madness, Forbidden*

Leo McCarey, *The Kid from Spain*

Raoul Walsh, *Wild Girl, Me and My Gal*

Edmund Goulding, *Grand Hotel, Blondie of the Follies*

Rouben Mamoulian, *Dr. Jekyll and Mr. Hyde, Love Me Tonight*

Mervyn LeRoy, *I Am a Fugitive from a Chain Gang, High Pressure, Heart of New York, Two Seconds, Big City Blues, Three on a Match*

Allan Dwan, *While Paris Sleeps*

Rowland Brown, *Hell's Highway*

W. S. Van Dyke, *Tarzan, the Ape Man*

Edward F. Cline, *Million Dollar Legs*

OUTSIDE CONSENSUS CHOICES: *Freaks* (Tod Browning); *Skippy* (Norman Taurog)

1933

George Cukor, *Dinner at Eight, Little Women, Our Betters*

Ernst Lubitsch, *Design for Living*

Frank Borzage, *A Man's Castle, Secrets*

John Ford, *Doctor Bull, Pilgrimage*

Sergei Eisenstein, *Thunder Over Mexico*

Howard Hawks, *Today We Live*

King Vidor, *The Stranger's Return*

Raoul Walsh, *The Bowery, Bad Boy, Sailor's Luck, Going Hollywood*

Frank Capra, *Lady for a Day, The Bitter Tea of General Yen*

Leo McCarey, *Duck Soup*

Cecil B. De Mille, *This Day and Age*

Rouben Mamoulian, *Queen Christina, The Song of Songs*

John Stahl, *Only Yesterday*

Mervyn LeRoy, *Gold Diggers of 1933, Hard to Handle*

Victor Fleming, *Bombshell*

Lowell Sherman, *She Done Him Wrong, Morning Glory*

Rowland V. Lee, *Zoo in Budapest*

Merriam C. Cooper and Ernest Schoedsack, *King Kong*

Alexander Korda, *The Private Life of Henry VIII*

Allan Dwan, *Counsel's Opinion, I Spy, Her First Affair*

Mitchell Leisen, *The Cradle Song*

Harry D'Arrast, *Topaze*

James Cruze, *I Cover the Waterfront*

William K. Howard, *The Power and the Glory*

Lloyd Bacon, *Forty-Second Street, The Picture Snatcher, Footlight Parade*

OUTSIDE CONSENSUS CHOICES: *Cavalcade, Berkeley Square* (Frank Lloyd); *Counsellor at Law* (William Wyler); *State Fair* (Henry King)

1934

Howard Hawks, *Twentieth Century, Viva Villa!* (with Jack Conroy)

Josef von Sternberg, *The Scarlet Empress*

Robert Flaherty, *Man of Aran*

John Ford, *The Lost Patrol, Judge Priest, The World Moves On*

Frank Borzage, *Little Man, What Now!; No Greater Glory; Flirtation Walk*

Ernst Lubitsch, *The Merry Widow*

King Vidor, *Our Daily Bread*

Frank Capra, *It Happened One Night, Broadway Bill*

Cecil B. De Mille, *Cleopatra, Four Frightened People*

John Stahl, *Imitation of Life*

Edgar G. Ulmer, *The Black Cat*

Leo McCarey, *Belle of the Nineties, Six of a Kind*

G. W. Pabst, *A Modern Hero*

James Cruze, *David Harum*

Victor Fleming, *Treasure Island*

Victor Schertzinger, *One Night of Love*

John Cromwell, *Of Human Bondage*

Henry Hathaway, *The Witching Hour*

Mark Sandrich, *The Gay Divorcée*

Mervyn LeRoy, *Sweet Adeline, Hi Nellie*

Allan Dwan, *The Morning After*

OUTSIDE CONSENSUS CHOICES: *The Thin Man* (W. S. Van Dyke); *The Barretts of Wimpole Street* (Sidney Franklin)

1935

Josef von Sternberg, *The Devil Is a Woman, Crime and Punishment*

John Ford, *Steamboat 'Round the Bend, The Whole Town's Talking, The Informer*

Alfred Hitchcock, *The Thirty-nine Steps, The Man Who Knew Too Much, Strauss' Great Waltz*

Howard Hawks, *Barbary Coast*

George Cukor, *Sylvia Scarlett, David Copperfield*

Frank Borzage, *Living on Velvet, Stranded, Shipmates Forever*

King Vidor, *So Red the Rose, The Wedding Night*

Leo McCarey, *Ruggles of Red Gap*

John Stahl, *Magnificent Obsession*

Cecil B. De Mille, *The Crusades*

Raoul Walsh, *Under Pressure, Baby Face Harrington, Every Night at Eight*

George Stevens, *Alice Adams, Laddie, The Nitwits*

Henry Hathaway, *Peter Ibbetson, Lives of a Bengal Lancer*

Ben Hecht and Charles MacArthur, *The Scoundrel, Once in a Blue Moon*

Mark Sandrich, *Top Hat, Follow the Fleet*

Gregory La Cava, *Private Worlds, She Married Her Boss*

Busby Berkeley, *Gold Diggers of 1935*

Victor Fleming, *Reckless*

Allan Dwan, *Black Sheep, Beauty's Daughter*

Wesley Ruggles, *The Gilded Lily*

OUTSIDE CONSENSUS CHOICES: *Mutiny on the Bounty* (Frank Lloyd); *Becky Sharp* (Rouben Mamoulian); *Black Fury* (Michael Curtiz)

1936

Charles Chaplin, *Modern Times*
Howard Hawks, *Ceiling Zero, The Road to Glory, Come and Get It* (with William Wyler)
Fritz Lang, *Fury*
Alfred Hitchcock, *Secret Agent*
John Ford, *The Prisoner of Shark Island, Mary of Scotland, The Plough and the Stars*
Frank Borzage, *Desire, Hearts Divided*
George Cukor, *Romeo and Juliet*
Josef von Sternberg, *The King Steps Out*
Cecil B. De Mille, *The Plainsman*
Frank Capra, *Mr. Deeds Goes to Town*
Leo McCarey, *The Milky Way*
King Vidor, *The Texas Rangers*
George Stevens, *Swing Time*
Raoul Walsh, *Klondike Annie, Big Brown Eyes, Spendthrifts*
Otto Preminger, *Under Your Spell*
Gregory La Cava, *My Man Godfrey*
René Clair, *The Ghost Goes West*
Alexander Korda, *Rembrandt*
Lewis Milestone, *The General Died at Dawn, Anything Goes*
Rouben Mamoulian, *The Gay Desperado*
Allan Dwan, *The Song and Dance Man, Human Cargo, High Tension, 15 Maiden Lane*
Henry Hathaway, *The Trail of the Lonesome Pine; Go West, Young Man*
William Wyler, *Dodsworth*
OUTSIDE CONSENSUS CHOICES: *The Great Ziegfeld, San Francisco* (W. S. Van Dyke); *These Three* (Wyler); *The Story of Louis Pasteur* (William Dieterle); *The Petrified Forest* (Archie Mayo)

Frank Borzage, *History Is Made at Night, Green Light, Mannequin, The Big City*
John Ford, *The Hurricane, Wee Willie Winkie*
Alfred Hitchcock, *Sabotage*
George Cukor, *Camille*
King Vidor, *Stella Dallas*
Leo McCarey, *The Awful Truth, Make Way for Tomorrow*
Frank Capra, *Lost Horizon*
Edgar G. Ulmer and Jacob Ben Ami, *Green Fields*
George Stevens, *Quality Street, A Damsel in Distress*
Raoul Walsh, *You're in the Army Now, When Thief Meets Thief, Artists and Models, Hitting a New High*
Gregory La Cava, *Stage Door*
John Stahl, *Parnell*
Otto Preminger, *Danger—Love at Work*
Tay Garnett, *Slave Ship, Stand In, Love Is News*
Allan Dwan, *Woman Wise, That I May Live, One Mile from Heaven, Heidi*
Mitchell Leisen, *Swing High, Swing Low; Easy Living*
John Cromwell, *The Prisoner of Zenda*
Richard Thorpe, *Night Must Fall*
William Wellman, *A Star Is Born, Nothing Sacred*
Wesley Ruggles, *I Met Him in Paris, True Confession*
Mervyn LeRoy, *They Won't Forget*
Mark Sandrich, *Shall We Dance*
Victor Fleming, *Captains Courageous*
OUTSIDE CONSENSUS CHOICES: *The Life of Emile Zola* (William Dieterle); *Dead End* (William Wyler); *Three Smart Girls, 100 Men and a Girl* (Henry Koster)

1937

Ernst Lubitsch, *Angel*
Fritz Lang, *You Only Live Once*

1938

George Cukor, *Holiday, Zaza*
Howard Hawks, *Bringing Up Baby*

Frank Borzage, *Three Comrades, The Shining Hour*
Alfred Hitchcock, *The Lady Vanishes, The Girl Was Young*
John Ford, *Submarine Patrol, Four Men and a Prayer*
Ernst Lubitsch, *Bluebeard's Eighth Wife*
Fritz Lang, *You and Me*
King Vidor, *The Citadel*
Frank Capra, *You Can't Take It with You*
Cecil B. De Mille, *The Buccaneer*
Raoul Walsh, *College Swing*
George Stevens, *Vivacious Lady*
John Stahl, *Letter of Introduction*
Edgar G. Ulmer, *The Singing Blacksmith*
Anthony Asquith and Leslie Howard, *Pygmalion*
Henry Hathaway, *Spawn of the North*
Michael Curtiz, *Angels with Dirty Faces, Four Daughters, The Adventures of Robin Hood* (with William Keighley)
Allan Dwan, *Rebecca of Sunnybrook Farm, Josette, Suez*
Garson Kanin, *A Man to Remember, Next Time I Marry*
Mark Sandrich, *Carefree*
Richard Wallace, *The Young in Heart*
OUTSIDE CONSENSUS CHOICES: *Jezebel* (William Wyler); *Boys Town* (Norman Taurog); *Alexander's Ragtime Band* (Henry King); *The Great Waltz* (Julien Duvivier)

1939

John Ford, *Stagecoach, Young Mr. Lincoln, Drums Along the Mohawk*
Howard Hawks, *Only Angels Have Wings*
Ernst Lubitsch, *Ninotchka*
George Cukor, *The Women*
Alfred Hitchcock, *Jamaica Inn*
Leo McCarey, *Mr. Smith Goes to Washington*
Josef von Sternberg, *Sergeant Madden*
Raoul Walsh, *The Roaring Twenties, St. Louis Blues*

King Vidor, *Northwest Passage*
Cecil B. De Mille, *Union Pacific*
George Stevens, *Gunga Din*
Victor Fleming, *Gone With the Wind, The Wizard of Oz*
John Stahl, *When Tomorrow Comes*
Garson Kanin, *Bachelor Mother, The Great Man Votes*
Gregory La Cava, *Fifth Avenue Girl*
Edmund Goulding, *Dark Victory, The Old Maid, We Are Not Alone*
George Marshall, *Destry Rides Again, You Can't Cheat an Honest Man*
Victor Schertzinger, *The Mikado*
William K. Howard, *Back Door to Heaven*
Allan Dwan, *The Three Musketeers, The Gorilla, Frontier Marshall*
Zoltan Korda, *Four Feathers*
Roy Kellino, *I Met a Murderer*
Busby Berkeley, *Babes in Arms*
OUTSIDE CONSENSUS CHOICES: *Wuthering Heights* (William Wyler); *Goodbye, Mr. Chips* (Sam Wood); *Juarez* (William Dieterle); *Confessions of a Nazi Spy* (Anatole Litvak)

1940

Charles Chaplin, *The Great Dictator*
Alfred Hitchcock, *Rebecca, Foreign Correspondent*
John Ford, *The Grapes of Wrath, The Long Voyage Home*
Howard Hawks, *His Girl Friday*
George Cukor, *The Philadelphia Story, Susan and God*
Frank Borzage, *The Mortal Storm, Strange Cargo, Flight Command*
Cecil B. De Mille, *Northwest Mounted Police*
Ernst Lubitsch, *The Shop Around the Corner*
Fritz Lang, *The Return of Frank James*
Preston Sturges, *The Great McGinty, Christmas in July*
King Vidor, *Comrade X*
Raoul Walsh, *They Drive by Night, The Dark Command*

George Stevens, *Seven Sinners,*
  Slightly Honorable
Mervyn LeRoy, *Waterloo Bridge,*
  Escape
Mitchell Leisen, *Remember the Night;*
  Arise, My Love
Lewis Milestone, *The Night of Nights*
Gregory La Cava, *The Primrose Path*
Busby Berkeley, *Strike Up the Band*
Edward F. Cline, *My Little*
  Chickadee, The Villain Still
  Pursued Her, The Bank Dick
Allan Dwan, *Sailor's Lady, The Young*
  People, Trail of the Vigilantes
William Wyler, *The Letter*
Richard Thorpe, *The Earl of Chicago*
OUTSIDE CONSENSUS CHOICES: *Our*
  Town (Sam Wood); *City for*
  Conquest (Anatole Litvak); *Pride*
  and Prejudice (Robert Z. Leonard);
  The Stars Look Down (Carol Reed);
  Of Mice and Men (Lewis
  Milestone)

1941

Orson Welles, *Citizen Kane*
Howard Hawks, *Sergeant York, Ball*
  of Fire
Alfred Hitchcock, *Suspicion, Mr. and*
  Mrs. Smith
Josef von Sternberg, *The Shanghai*
  Gesture
Jean Renoir, *Swamp Water*
John Ford, *How Green Was My*
  Valley, Tobacco Road
George Cukor, *A Woman's Face, Two-*
  Faced Woman
Raoul Walsh, *High Sierra, The*
  Strawberry Blonde, They Died with
  Their Boots On, Manpower
Fritz Lang, *Western Union, Man*
  Hunt
King Vidor, *H. M. Pulham, Esq.*
Preston Sturges, *The Lady Eve*
Ernst Lubitsch, *That Uncertain*
  Feeling
Frank Borzage, *The Vanishing*
  Virginian, Smilin' Through
George Stevens, *Penny Serenade*

Frank Capra, *Meet John Doe*
John Huston, *The Maltese Falcon*
René Clair, *The Flame of New*
  Orleans
Gregory La Cava, *Unfinished Business*
Mitchell Leisen, *I Wanted Wings,*
  Hold Back the Dawn
Edmund Goulding, *The Great Lie*
William Wyler, *The Little Foxes*
Alexander Hall, *Here Comes Mr.*
  Jordan
Allan Dwan, *Look Who's Laughing,*
  Rise and Shine
William Dieterle, *All That Money*
  Can Buy
Robert Stevenson, *Back Street*
OUTSIDE CONSENSUS CHOICES:
  Tom, Dick and Harry (Garson
  Kanin)

1942

Orson Welles, *The Magnificent*
  Ambersons, Journey into Fear (with
  Norman Foster)
Alfred Hitchcock, *Saboteur*
Preston Sturges, *Sullivan's Travels,*
  The Palm Beach Story
Cecil B. De Mille, *Reap the Wild*
  Wind
Ernst Lubitsch, *To Be or Not To Be*
George Cukor, *Her Cardboard Lover*
Michael Curtiz, *Casablanca, Yankee*
  Doodle Dandy
Frank Borzage, *Seven Sweethearts*
Raoul Walsh, *Desperate Journey,*
  Gentleman Jim
Leo McCarey, *Once Upon a*
  Honeymoon
George Stevens, *Woman of the Year,*
  Talk of the Town
Billy Wilder, *The Major and the*
  Minor
David Lean and Noel Coward, *In*
  Which We Serve
Edgar G. Ulmer, *Tomorrow We Live*
Arthur Ripley, *Prisoner of Japan*
Albert Lewin, *The Moon and*
  Sixpence
Mervyn LeRoy, *Random Harvest,*
  Johnny Eager

Henry Hathaway, *China Girl, Ten Gentlemen from West Point*
René Clair, *I Married a Witch*
Allan Dwan, *Friendly Enemies, Here We Go Again*
Jacques Tourneur, *Cat People*
OUTSIDE CONSENSUS CHOICES: *Mrs. Miniver* (William Wyler); *Wake Island* (John Farrow); *Roxie Hart* (William Wellman); *King's Row, Pride of the Yankees* (Sam Wood); *The Invaders, One of Our Aircraft Is Missing* (Michael Powell and Emeric Pressburger)

1943

Alfred Hitchcock, *Shadow of a Doubt*
Howard Hawks, *The Air Force*
Jean Renoir, *This Land Is Mine*
Fritz Lang, *Hangmen Also Die*
Ernst Lubitsch, *Heaven Can Wait*
George Cukor, *Keeper of the Flame*
Frank Borzage, *Stage Door Canteen, His Butler's Sister*
Douglas Sirk, *Hitler's Madman*
Vincente Minnelli, *Cabin in the Sky, I Dood It*
John Stahl, *Holy Matrimony, The Immortal Sergeant*
George Stevens, *The More the Merrier*
Raoul Walsh, *Background to Danger, Northern Pursuit*
Otto Preminger, *Margin for Error*
Billy Wilder, *Five Graves to Cairo*
Edgar G. Ulmer, *My Son, the Hero; Girls in Chains; Isle of Forgotten Sins; Jive Junction*
Edmund Goulding, *Claudia, The Constant Nymph*
H. C. Potter, *Mr. Lucky*
Jacques Tourneur, *I Walked With a Zombie, The Leopard Man*
Victor Fleming, *A Guy Named Joe*
Mark Sandrich, *So Proudly We Hail*
Allan Dwan, *Around the World*
OUTSIDE CONSENSUS CHOICES: *Watch on the Rhine* (Herman Shumlin); *The Human Comedy* (Clarence Brown); *The Ox-Bow Incident* (William Wellman)

1944

Otto Preminger, *Laura; In the Meantime, Darling*
Alfred Hitchcock, *Lifeboat*
George Cukor, *Gaslight, Winged Victory*
Howard Hawks, *To Have and Have Not*
Preston Sturges, *The Miracle of Morgan's Creek, Hail the Conquering Hero, The Great Moment*
Douglas Sirk, *Summer Storm*
Frank Borzage, *Till We Meet Again*
King Vidor, *An American Romance*
Vincente Minnelli, *Meet Me in St. Louis*
Robert Siodmak, *Christmas Holiday, Phantom Lady, Cobra Woman*
Leo McCarey, *Going My Way*
Cecil B. De Mille, *The Story of Dr. Wassell*
Frank Capra, *Arsenic and Old Lace*
Billy Wilder, *Double Indemnity*
Edgar G. Ulmer, *Bluebeard*
Raoul Walsh, *Uncertain Glory*
John Stahl, *The Keys of the Kingdom, The Eve of St. Mark*
Arthur Ripley, *Voice in the Wind*
John Cromwell, *Since You Went Away*
Budd Boetticher, *One Mysterious Night, The Missing Juror*
René Clair, *It Happened Tomorrow*
Mitchell Leisen, *Lady in the Dark*
Charles Vidor, *Cover Girl*
Allan Dwan, *Abroad With Two Yanks, Up in Mabel's Room*
Robert Wise, *Curse of the Cat People*
Joseph H. Lewis, *Minstrel Man*
OUTSIDE CONSENSUS CHOICES: *Wilson, The Song of Bernadette* (Henry King); *None But the Lonely Heart* (Clifford Odets); *The Seventh Cross* (Fred Zinnemann); *Murder, My Sweet* (Edward Dmytryk); *Destination Tokyo*

(Delmer Daves); *The Purple Heart* (Lewis Milestone)

1945

Jean Renoir, *The Southerner*
John Ford, *They Were Expendable*
Alfred Hitchcock, *Spellbound*
Fritz Lang, *The Woman in the Window, Ministry of Fear, Scarlet Street*
Otto Preminger, *Fallen Angel, A Royal Scandal*
Frank Borzage, *The Spanish Main*
Vincente Minnelli, *The Clock, Yolanda and the Thief*
John Stahl, *Leave Her to Heaven*
Robert Siodmak, *Uncle Harry, The Suspect*
Raoul Walsh, *Salty O'Rourke, Objective Burma, The Horn Blows at Midnight*
Leo McCarey, *The Bells of St. Mary's*
Billy Wilder, *The Lost Weekend*
Allan Dwan, *Brewster's Millions, Getting Gertie's Garter*
René Clair, *And Then There Were None*
Edgar G. Ulmer, *Detour, Strange Illusion, Club Havana*
Joseph H. Lewis, *My Name Is Julia Ross, The Falcon in San Antonio*
Gustav Machaty, *Jealousy*
Robert Wise, *The Body Snatcher*
Elia Kazan, *A Tree Grows in Brooklyn*
Michael Curtiz, *Mildred Pierce*
David Lean, *Blithe Spirit*
Michael Powell and Emeric Pressburger, *The Life and Death of Colonel Blimp*
Albert Lewin, *The Picture of Dorian Gray*
OUTSIDE CONSENSUS CHOICES: *The Story of G.I. Joe* (William Wellman)

1946

Alfred Hitchcock, *Notorious*
John Ford, *My Darling Clementine*

Jean Renoir, *Diary of a Chambermaid*
Howard Hawks, *The Big Sleep*
Orson Welles, *The Stranger*
Douglas Sirk, *A Scandal in Paris*
Frank Borzage, *I've Always Loved You, The Magnificent Doll*
Ernst Lubitsch, *Cluny Brown*
Fritz Lang, *Cloak and Dagger*
Robert Siodmak, *The Killers, The Spiral Staircase, The Dark Mirror*
Otto Preminger, *Centennial Summer*
Vincente Minnelli, *Ziegfeld Follies, Undercurrent*
David Lean, *Brief Encounter*
Raoul Walsh, *The Man I Love*
Frank Capra, *It's a Wonderful Life*
Arthur Ripley, *The Chase*
Allan Dwan, *Rendezvous with Annie, Calendar Girl*
Charles Vidor, *Gilda*
Edmund Goulding, *The Razor's Edge*
Joseph H. Lewis, *So Dark the Night*
Don Siegel, *The Verdict*
Laurence Olivier, *Henry V*
Michael Powell and Emeric Pressburger, *Stairway to Heaven*
Edgar G. Ulmer, *The Wife of Monte Cristo, Her Sister's Secret*
Jean Negulesco, *Three Strangers, Nobody Lives Forever, Humoresque*
Joseph L. Mankiewicz, *Dragonwyck, Somewhere in the Night*
OUTSIDE CONSENSUS CHOICES: *The Best Years of Our Lives* (William Wyler); *A Walk in the Sun* (Lewis Milestone)

1947

Charles Chaplin, *Monsieur Verdoux*
Max Ophüls, *The Exile*
King Vidor, *Duel in the Sun*
Jean Renoir, *Woman on the Beach*
Douglas Sirk, *Lured*
Frank Borzage, *That's My Man*
Raoul Walsh, *Pursued, Cheyenne*
John Ford, *The Fugitive*
Cecil B. De Mille, *Unconquered*
Otto Preminger, *Daisy Kenyon, Forever Amber*

Leo McCarey, *Good Sam*
John Stahl, *The Foxes of Harrow, The Walls of Jericho*
Carol Reed, *Odd Man Out*
David Lean, *Great Expectations, This Happy Breed*
Michael Powell and Emeric Pressburger, *Black Narcissus, I Know Where I'm Going*
Jacques Tourneur, *Out of the Past*
Robert Wise, *Born to Kill*
Charles Walters, *Good News*
Edgar G. Ulmer, *Carnegie Hall, Dangerous Illusion*
Anthony Mann, *T-Men*
Allan Dwan, *Northwest Outpost*
Joseph Losey, *The Boy with Green Hair*
Joseph L. Mankiewicz, *The Ghost and Mrs. Muir*
Robert Montgomery, *Ride the Pink Horse*
Edmund Goulding, *Nightmare Alley*
Henry Hathaway, *Kiss of Death*
Robert Rossen, *Body and Soul*
Zoltan Korda, *The Macomber Affair, A Woman's Vengeance*
OUTSIDE CONSENSUS CHOICES: *Gentleman's Agreement, Boomerang!* (Elia Kazan); *Crossfire* (Edward Dmytryk); *Miracle on 34th Street* (George Seaton); *Dark Passage, The Red House* (Delmer Daves)

Frank Capra, *State of the Union*
Fritz Lang, *The Secret Beyond the Door*
King Vidor, *On Our Merry Way*
Abraham Polonsky, *Force of Evil*
Raoul Walsh, *Silver River, One Sunday Afternoon, Fighter Squadron*
Laurence Olivier, *Hamlet*
Michael Powell and Emeric Pressburger, *The Red Shoes*
Edgar G. Ulmer, *Ruthless*
Allan Dwan, *The Inside Story, Angel in Exile*
Preston Sturges, *Unfaithfully Yours*
Charles Walters, *Easter Parade*
Rouben Mamoulian, *Summer Holiday*
Billy Wilder, *A Foreign Affair, The Emperor Waltz*
Robert Siodmak, *Cry of the City*
Anthony Mann, *Raw Deal*
Budd Boetticher, *Assigned to Danger, Beyond Locked Doors*
Joseph H. Lewis, *The Return of October*
Jean Negulesco, *Johnny Belinda, Road House*
Michael Gordon, *Another Part of the Forest*
OUTSIDE CONSENSUS CHOICES: *The Treasure of the Sierra Madre, Key Largo* (John Huston); *The Snake Pit; Sorry, Wrong Number* (Anatole Litvak); *The Search* (Fred Zinneman)

1948

Max Ophüls, *Letter from an Unknown Woman*
Orson Welles, *The Lady from Shanghai*
Howard Hawks, *Red River, A Song Is Born*
John Ford, *Fort Apache*
Frank Borzage, *Moonrise*
Robert Flaherty, *Louisiana Story*
Alfred Hitchcock, *Rope, The Paradine Case*
George Cukor, *A Double Life*
Douglas Sirk, *Sleep, My Love*
Vincente Minnelli, *The Pirate*
George Stevens, *I Remember Mama*

1949

John Ford, *She Wore a Yellow Ribbon, Three Godfathers*
Alfred Hitchcock, *Under Capricorn*
Max Ophüls, *Caught, The Reckless Moment*
Howard Hawks, *I Was a Male War Bride*
Nicholas Ray, *They Live by Night, Knock on Any Door, A Woman's Secret*
King Vidor, *The Fountainhead, Beyond the Forest*
George Cukor, *Adam's Rib; Edward, My Son*

Douglas Sirk, *Shockproof, Slightly French*

Raoul Walsh, *White Heat, Colorado Territory*

Otto Preminger, *Whirlpool, The Fan*

Stanley Donen and Gene Kelly, *On the Town*

Samuel Fuller, *I Shot Jesse James*

Allan Dwan, *Sands of Iwo Jima*

Cecil B. De Mille, *Samson and Delilah*

Joseph H. Lewis, *Gun Crazy, Undercover Man*

Vincente Minnelli, *Madame Bovary*

Carol Reed, *The Fallen Idol*

Joseph L. Mankiewicz, *A Letter to Three Wives, House of Strangers*

Syron Haskin, *Too Late for Tears*

Edgar G. Ulmer, *The Pirates of Capri*

Robert Wise, *The Set-Up*

Don Siegel, *The Big Steal, Night Unto Night*

Preston Sturges, *The Beautiful Blonde from Bashful Bend*

OUTSIDE CONSENSUS CHOICES: *The Heiress* (William Wyler); *All the King's Men* (Robert Rossen); *Intruder in the Dust* (Clarence Brown); *Champion, Home of the Brave* (Mark Robson); *Battleground* (William Wellman)

APPENDIX IV
BEST PERFORMANCES,
1929-1949

1929

Greta Garbo, *The Kiss* (Silent)
Helen Morgan, *Applause*
Bessie Love, *Broadway Melody*
Ruth Chatterton, *Madame X,*
   Laughing Lady
Ann Harding, *Paris Bound,*
   Condemned

Maurice Chevalier, *The Love Parade*
Ronald Colman, *Bulldog Drummond,*
   Condemned
George Bancroft, *Thunderbolt*
Chester Morris, *Alibi*
Richard Barthelmess, *Weary River*

Margaret Dumont, *The Cocoanuts*
Sara Allgood, *Blackmail*
Irene Rich, *They Had To See Paris*
Lillian Roth, *The Love Parade*
Joan Peers, *Applause*

Louis Wolheim, *Condemned*
Dudley Digges, *Condemned*
Richard Arlen, *The Virginian,*
   Thunderbolt

Chosen by Andrew Sarris, Fall 1965;
grouped in the categories of actress, actor,
supporting actress, supporting actor, special
citations

Lewis Stone, *Madame X, Wild*
   Orchids
Cyril Ritchard, *Blackmail*

The Marx Brothers, *The Cocoanuts*
   (Special)
Fay Wray, *Thunderbolt* (Ingenue)

1930

Greta Garbo, *Anna Christie, Romance*
Marlene Dietrich, *Morocco, The Blue*
   Angel
Marie Dressler, *Min and Bill*
Sara Allgood, *Juno and the Paycock*
Ina Claire, *The Royal Family of*
   Broadway

Walter Huston, *Abraham Lincoln*
Ronald Colman, *Raffles, The Devil to*
   Pay
Richard Barthelmess, *The Dawn*
   Patrol
Chester Morris, *The Big House*
Colin Clive, *Journey's End*

Marie Dressler, *Anna Christie*
Henrietta Crosman, *The Royal Family of Broadway*
Marjorie Rambeau, *Min and Bill*
Margaret Dumont, *Animal Crackers*
Zasu Pitts, *Monte Carlo*

Louis Wolheim, *All Quiet on the Western Front*
Adolphe Menjou, *Morocco*
Raymond Griffith, *All Quiet on the Western Front*
Glenn Anders, *Laughter*
Ian Keith, *Abraham Lincoln*

Helen Chandler, *Outward Bound* (Ingenue)
Nancy Carroll, *Laughter* (Ingenue)
Helen Twelvetrees, *Her Man* (Ingenue)
Mary Brian, *The Royal Family of Broadway* (Ingenue)
Jean Harlow, *Hell's Angels* (Demi-Ingenue)

1931

Marlene Dietrich, *Dishonored*
Greta Garbo, *Susan Lennox, Her Fall and Rise; Inspiration*
Sylvia Sidney, *An American Tragedy, Street Scene, City Streets*
Helen Hayes, *Arrowsmith, The Sin of Madelon Claudet*
Lynn Fontanne, *The Guardsman*

Charles Chaplin, *City Lights*
James Cagney, *Public Enemy*
Ronald Colman, *Arrowsmith*
Wallace Beery, *The Champ*
Alfred Lunt, *The Guardsman*

Aline MacMahon, *Five Star Final*
Irene Rich, *The Champ*
Frances Starr, *Five Star Final*
Beulah Bondi, *Street Scene*
Zasu Pitts, *The Guardsman*

Adolphe Menjou, *The Front Page*
Gustav Von Seyffertitz, *Dishonored*

Roland Young, *The Guardsman*
Richard Bennett, *Arrowsmith*
Ed Brophy, *The Champ*

Jackie Cooper, *The Champ* (Special)
Virginia Cherrill, *City Lights* (Ingenue)
Frances Dee, *An American Tragedy*

1932

Greta Garbo, *Grand Hotel, As You Desire Me, Mata Hari*
Marlene Dietrich, *Shanghai Express, Blonde Venus*
Katharine Hepburn, *A Bill of Divorcement*
Irene Dunne, *Back Street*
Helen Hayes, *A Farewell to Arms*

Paul Muni, *Scarface, I Am a Fugitive from a Chain Gang*
John Barrymore, *A Bill of Divorcement, Grand Hotel*
Maurice Chevalier, *One Hour with You, Love Me Tonight*
Clive Brook, *Shanghai Express*
James Cagney, *The Crowd Roars*

Aline MacMahon, *One Way Passage, Once in a Lifetime*
Anna May Wong, *Shanghai Express*
Karen Morley, *Scarface*
Ann Dvorak, *Scarface*
Genevieve Tobin, *One Hour with You*

Roland Young, *One Hour with You*
Charles Ruggles, *One Hour with You, Love Me Tonight*
Osgood Perkins, *Scarface*
Warner Oland, *Shanghai Express*
Vince Barnett, *Scarface*

Maureen O'Sullivan, *Tarzan, the Ape Man* (Ingenue)
Elissa Landi, *The Sign of the Cross* (Ingenue)

1933

Greta Garbo, *Queen Christina*
Katharine Hepburn, *Little Women,*
Morning Glory
Jean Harlow, *Dinner at Eight*
Marie Dressler, *Dinner at Eight*
Mae West, *She Done Him Wrong,*
I'm No Angel

Charles Laughton, *The Private Life of*
Henry VIII
Lee Tracy, *Bombshell, Dinner at*
Eight
Wallace Beery, *Dinner at Eight*
Spencer Tracy, *A Man's Castle*
James Cagney, *Hard to Handle*

Elsa Lanchester, *The Private Life of*
Henry VIII
Aline MacMahon, *Gold Diggers of*
1933
Margaret Dumont, *Duck Soup*
Mary Boland, *Three-Cornered Moon*
Ruth Donnelly, *Hard to Handle*

C. Aubrey Smith, *Morning Glory*
Adolphe Menjou, *Morning Glory*
Walter Connolly, *The Bitter Tea of*
General Yen, Lady for a Day
Edward Everett Horton, *Design for*
Living
Frank Morgan, *Bombshell*

Jean Parker, *Little Women, Lady for a*
Day (Ingenue)
Madge Evans, *Dinner at Eight,*
Beauty for Sale (Ingenue)

1934

Marlene Dietrich, *The Scarlet Empress*
Bette Davis, *Of Human Bondage*
Greta Garbo, *The Painted Veil*
Carole Lombard, *Twentieth Century*
Claudette Colbert, *It Happened One*
Night, Imitation of Life, Cleopatra

Victor McLaglen, *The Lost Patrol*
John Barrymore, *Twentieth Century*
Clark Gable, *It Happened One Night*
Maurice Chevalier, *The Merry Widow*
Will Rogers, *Judge Priest*

Louise Dresser, *The Scarlet Empress*
Maureen O'Sullivan, *The Thin Man*
Flora Robson, *Catherine the Great*
Elizabeth Allen, *Men in White*
Lucile Watson, *What Every Woman*
Knows

Sam Jaffe, *The Scarlet Empress*
Walter Connolly, *It Happened One*
Night, Twentieth Century
Adolphe Menjou, *Little Miss Marker*
Roscoe Karns, *Twentieth Century, It*
Happened One Night
Boris Karloff, *The Lost Patrol*

1935

Katharine Hepburn, *Alice Adams*
Greta Garbo, *Anna Karenina*
Bette Davis, *Dangerous*
Madeleine Carroll, *The Thirty-nine*
Steps
Miriam Hopkins, *Barbary Coast,*
Becky Sharp

Ronald Colman, *A Tale of Two Cities*
Robert Donat, *The Thirty-nine Steps*
Charles Laughton, *Ruggles of Red*
Gap
Victor McLaglen, *The Informer*
Edward G. Robinson, *The Whole*
Town's Talking, Barbary Coast

Mary Boland, *Ruggles of Red Gap*
Margot Grahame, *The Informer*
Hope Williams, *The Scoundrel*
Julie Haydon, *The Scoundrel*
Peggy Ashcroft, *The Thirty-nine Steps*

Peter Lorre, *The Man Who Knew Too*
Much
Roland Young, *Ruggles of Red Gap,*
David Copperfield

Wallace Ford, *The Informer, The Whole Town's Talking*
J. M. Kerrigan, *The Informer*
Donald Meek, *The Whole Town's Talking, The Informer*

Fred Astaire, *Top Hat* (Special)
Ida Lupino, *Peter Ibbetson* (Ingenue)
Anne Shirley, *Steamboat 'Round the Bend* (Ingenue)
Alexander Woollcott, *The Scoundrel* (Evocation)

1935

Carole Lombard, *My Man Godfrey*
Ruth Chatterton, *Dodsworth*
Jean Arthur, *Mr. Deeds Goes to Town, The Plainsman*
Sylvia Sidney, *Fury*
Madeleine Carroll, *The General Died at Dawn, Secret Agent*

Charles Chaplin, *Modern Times*
Walter Huston, *Dodsworth*
Charles Laughton, *Rembrandt*
Gary Cooper, *Mr. Deeds Goes to Town, The Plainsman, The General Died at Dawn, Desire*
Robert Donat, *The Ghost Goes West*

Mary Astor, *Dodsworth*
Elsa Lanchester, *Rembrandt*
Maria Ouspenskaya, *Dodsworth*
Alice Brady, *My Man Godfrey*
Ruth Donnelly, *Mr. Deeds Goes to Town*

Peter Lorre, *Secret Agent*
Akim Tamiroff, *The General Died at Dawn*
Eugene Pallette, *My Man Godfrey, The Ghost Goes West*
Charles Bickford, *The Plainsman*
John Carradine, *The Prisoner of Shark Island*

Paulette Goddard, *Modern Times* (Ingenue)
June Travis, *Ceiling Zero* (Ingenue)

1937

Greta Garbo, *Camille*
Irene Dunne, *The Awful Truth*
Sylvia Sidney, *You Only Live Once, The Woman Alone (Sabotage), Dead End*
Jean Arthur, *Easy Living, History Is Made at Night*
Carole Lombard, *True Confession, Nothing Sacred*

Robert Montgomery, *Night Must Fall*
Ronald Colman, *Lost Horizon, Prisoner of Zenda*
Henry Fonda, *You Only Live Once*
Cary Grant, *The Awful Truth*
Charles Boyer, *History Is Made at Night, Conquest*

Mary Astor, *The Hurricane, Prisoner of Zenda*
Fay Bainter, *Make Way for Tomorrow*
Marjorie Main, *Dead End*
Cecil Cunningham, *The Awful Truth*
Laura Hope Crews, *Angel*

Thomas Mitchell, *The Hurricane, Lost Horizon, Make Way for Tomorrow*
Oscar Homolka, *The Woman Alone (Sabotage)*
C. Aubrey Smith, *The Hurricane*
H. B. Warner, *Lost Horizon*
Barton MacLane, *You Only Live Once*

Andrea Leeds, *Stage Door* (Ingenue)
Janet Gaynor, *A Star Is Born* (Re-Ingenue)
Victor Moore and Beulah Bondi, *Make Way for Tomorrow* (Social Security)

1938

Katharine Hepburn, *Holiday, Bringing Up Baby*
Wendy Hiller, *Pygmalion*
Margaret Sullavan, *Three Comrades*

Bette Davis, *Jezebel, The Sisters*
Jean Arthur, *You Can't Take It with You*

Cary Grant, *Bringing Up Baby, Holiday*
Leslie Howard, *Pygmalion*
James Cagney, *Angels with Dirty Faces*
Robert Donat, *The Citadel*
John Garfield, *Four Daughters*

Fay Bainter, *Jezebel*
Jean Dixon, *Holiday*
Spring Byington, *You Can't Take It with You*
Elizabeth Patterson, *Sing You Sinners*
Dame May Whitty, *The Lady Vanishes*

Lew Ayres, *Holiday*
Wilfred Lawson, *Pygmalion*
Charles Ruggles, *Bringing Up Baby*
Basil Radford, *The Lady Vanishes*
Naunton Wayne, *The Lady Vanishes*

Frances Farmer, *Ride a Crooked Mile* (Ingenue)
Priscilla Lane, *Four Daughters* (Ingenue)

1939

Greta Garbo, *Ninotchka*
Vivien Leigh, *Gone With the Wind*
Jean Arthur, *Mr. Smith Goes to Washington, Only Angels Have Wings*
Bette Davis, *Dark Victory, The Old Maid, Juarez, The Private Lives of Elizabeth and Essex*
Irene Dunne, *Love Affair*

Henry Fonda, *Young Mr. Lincoln*
James Stewart, *Mr. Smith Goes to Washington*
Laurence Olivier, *Wuthering Heights*
Cary Grant, *Only Angels Have Wings*
Charles Boyer, *Love Affair*

Ina Claire, *Ninotchka*
Claire Trevor, *Stagecoach*
Geraldine Fitzgerald, *Wuthering Heights, Dark Victory*
Gladys George, *The Roaring Twenties*
Maria Ouspenskaya, *Love Affair*

Thomas Mitchell, *Only Angels Have Wings, Stagecoach, Mr. Smith Goes to Washington, Gone With the Wind*
Richard Barthelmess, *Only Angels Have Wings*
Harry Carey, *Mr. Smith Goes to Washington*
Edward Arnold, *Mr. Smith Goes to Washington*
Charles Coburn, *Bachelor Mother*

June Duprez, *Four Feathers* (Ingenue)
Jane Bryan, *The Old Maid* (Ingenue)
Betty Field, *What a Life!* (Ingenue)
Judy Garland, *Babes in Arms* (Nymphet)

1940

Katharine Hepburn, *The Philadelphia Story*
Vivien Leigh, *Waterloo Bridge*
Joan Fontaine, *Rebecca*
Bette Davis, *The Letter*
Margaret Sullavan, *The Shop Around the Corner, The Mortal Storm*

Charles Chaplin, *The Great Dictator*
Henry Fonda, *The Grapes of Wrath*
Cary Grant, *His Girl Friday, The Philadelphia Story*
James Stewart, *The Shop Around the Corner, The Philadelphia Story*
Robert Montgomery, *The Earl of Chicago*

Jane Darwell, *The Grapes of Wrath*
Judith Anderson, *Rebecca*
Betty Field, *Of Mice and Men*
Florence Bates, *Rebecca*
Mildred Natwick, *The Long Voyage Home*

Conrad Veidt, *Escape*
James Stephenson, *The Letter*
Akim Tamiroff, *The Great McGinty*
Albert Basserman, *Foreign Correspondent*
Thomas Mitchell, *The Long Voyage Home*

W. C. Fields, *The Bank Dick* (Special)
Ellen Drew, *Christmas in July* (Ingenue)

1941

Mary Astor, *The Maltese Falcon, The Great Lie*
Joan Fontaine, *Suspicion*
Bette Davis, *The Little Foxes*
Greta Garbo, *Two-Faced Woman*
Ida Lupino, *High Sierra, Ladies in Retirement*

Humphrey Bogart, *High Sierra, The Maltese Falcon*
Robert Montgomery, *Here Comes Mr. Jordan*
Cary Grant, *Penny Serenade, Suspicion*
Gary Cooper, *Sergeant York*
Orson Welles, *Citizen Kane*

Patricia Collinge, *The Little Foxes*
Agnes Moorehead, *Citizen Kane*
Sara Allgood, *How Green Was My Valley*
Anna Lee, *How Green Was My Valley*
Margaret Wycherly, *Sergeant York*

Conrad Veidt, *A Woman's Face*
Walter Huston, *All That Money Can Buy, Swamp Water, The Shanghai Gesture*
Sydney Greenstreet, *The Maltese Falcon*
Peter Lorre, *The Maltese Falcon*
Elisha Cook, *The Maltese Falcon*

Dorothy Comingore, *Citizen Kane* (Marion Davies Award)

Maureen O'Hara, *How Green Was My Valley* (Ingenue)
Anne Baxter, *Swamp Water* (Ingenue)
Gene Tierney, *The Shanghai Gesture* (Ingenue)
Teresa Wright, *The Little Foxes* (Ingenue)

1942

Ingrid Bergman, *Casablanca*
Carole Lombard, *To Be or Not To Be*
Anne Baxter, *The Magnificent Ambersons*
Katharine Hepburn, *Woman of the Year*
Dolores Costello, *The Magnificent Ambersons*

Joseph Cotten, *The Magnificent Ambersons*
Ronald Colman, *Random Harvest*
Humphrey Bogart, *Casablanca*
Eric Portman, *The Invaders*
Spencer Tracy, *Woman of the Year*

Agnes Moorehead, *The Magnificent Ambersons*
Mary Astor, *The Palm Beach Story*
Betty Field, *King's Row*
Gladys Cooper, *Now Voyager*
Florence Bates, *The Moon and Sixpence*

Claude Rains, *Casablanca, Now Voyager, King's Row*
Richard Bennett, *The Magnificent Ambersons*
Ray Collins, *The Magnificent Ambersons*
Van Heflin, *Johnny Eager*
Sydney Greenstreet, *Casablanca, Across the Pacific*

Nancy Coleman, *King's Row* (Ingenue)
Veronica Lake, *Sullivan's Travels, This Gun for Hire* (Ingenue)
Diana Lynn, *The Major and the Minor* (Nymphet)

Ginger Rogers, *The Major and the Minor* (Pseudo-Nymphet)

1943

Dorothy McGuire, *Claudia*
Irene Dunne, *A Guy Named Joe*
Teresa Wright, *Shadow of a Doubt*
Gene Tierney, *Heaven Can Wait*
Ida Lupino, *The Hard Way*

Joseph Cotten, *Shadow of a Doubt*
Cary Grant, *Mr. Lucky*
Henry Fonda, *The Ox-Bow Incident, The Immortal Sergeant*
John Garfield, *The Fallen Sparrow*
Spencer Tracy, *A Guy Named Joe, Keeper of the Flame*

Patricia Collinge, *Shadow of a Doubt*
Ina Claire, *Claudia*
Florence Bates, *Heaven Can Wait*
Marjorie Main, *Heaven Can Wait*
Audrey Christie, *Keeper of the Flame*

Alexander Granach, *Hangmen Also Die*
Peter Van Eyck, *Five Graves to Cairo, The Moon Is Down*
Erich Von Stroheim, *Five Graves to Cairo*
Charles Bickford, *Mr. Lucky*
Ward Bond, *A Guy Named Joe*

Laraine Day, *Mr. Lucky* (Ingenue)
Simone Simon, *Cat People* (Masked Perversity)

1944

Gene Tierney, *Laura*
Jennifer Jones, *Since You Went Away, The Song of Bernadette*
Ingrid Bergman, *Gaslight*
Tallulah Bankhead, *Lifeboat*
Barbara Stanwyck, *Double Indemnity*

Clifton Webb, *Laura*
Charles Boyer, *Gaslight*

Humphrey Bogart, *To Have and Have Not*
Joseph Cotten, *Since You Went Away*
Dana Andrews, *Laura*

Judith Anderson, *Laura*
Ethel Barrymore, *None But the Lonely Heart*
June Duprez, *None But the Lonely Heart*
Angela Lansbury, *Gaslight*
Anne Revere, *National Velvet*

Edward G. Robinson, *Double Indemnity*
Elisha Cook, *Phantom Lady, Dark Waters*
William Demarest, *Miracle of Morgan's Creek, Hail the Conquering Hero, The Great Moment*
Walter Brennan, *To Have and Have Not*
Freddie Steele, *Hail the Conquering Hero*

Ella Raines, *Hail the Conquering Hero, Phantom Lady* (Ingenue)
Lauren Bacall, *To Have and Have Not* (Demi-Ingenue)
Gail Russell, *The Uninvited* (Ingenue)
Jane Ball, *Winged Victory* (Ingenue)
Sigrid Gurie, *Voice in the Wind* (Ingenue)
Danny Kaye, *Up in Arms* (Special)

1945

Ingrid Bergman, *Spellbound, The Bells of St. Mary's, Saratoga Trunk*
Dorothy McGuire, *The Enchanted Cottage, A Tree Grows in Brooklyn*
Jennifer Jones, *Love Letters*
Joan Crawford, *Mildred Pierce*
Ella Raines, *The Suspect*

Robert Montgomery, *They Were Expendable*
James Mason, *The Seventh Veil*
Robert Mitchum, *The Story of G.I. Joe*

Robert Walker, *The Clock*
Gregory Peck, *Spellbound*

Margaret Rutherford, *Blithe Spirit*
Angela Lansbury, *The Picture of
Dorian Gray*
Geraldine Fitzgerald, *Uncle Harry*
Florence Bates, *Saratoga Trunk*
Mildred Natwick, *The Enchanted
Cottage, Yolanda and the Thief*

Charles Bickford, *Fallen Angel*
Dan Duryea, *Woman in the Window,
Scarlet Street*
Herbert Lom, *The Seventh Veil*
James Dunn, *A Tree Grows in
Brooklyn*
Freddie Steele, *The Story of G.I. Joe*

Deborah Kerr, *Colonel Blimp, Love
on the Dole, Vacation from
Marriage* (Ingenue)
Donna Reed, *They Were Expendable*
(Ingenue)
Ava Gardner, *Whistle Stop* (Ingenue)
Jeanne Crain, *Leave Her to Heaven*
(Ingenue)

1946

Celia Johnson, *Brief Encounter*
Ingrid Bergman, *Notorious*
Dorothy McGuire, *The Spiral
Staircase, Till the End of Time*
Anne Baxter, *The Razor's Edge*
Vivien Leigh, *Caesar and Cleopatra*

Laurence Olivier, *Henry V*
Michael Redgrave, *Dead of Night*
Cary Grant, *Notorious*
Henry Fonda, *My Darling Clementine*
Trevor Howard, *Brief Encounter*

Ethel Barrymore, *The Spiral Staircase*
Renee Asherson, *Henry V*
Judith Anderson, *Diary of a
Chambermaid*
Leopoldine Konstantin, *Notorious*
Joan Lorring, *Three Strangers*

Claude Rains, *Notorious, Deception,
Caesar and Cleopatra*
Steve Cochran, *The Chase, The Best
Years of Our Lives*
Walter Brennan, *My Darling
Clementine*
Elisha Cook, *The Big Sleep*
Peter Lorre, *Three Strangers, The
Verdict, The Chase*

Dorothy Malone, *The Big Sleep*
(Ingenue)
Rita Hayworth, *Gilda* (Vive les
Gants!)

1947

Jennifer Jones, *Duel in the Sun*
Kathleen Ryan, *Odd Man Out*
Dorothy McGuire, *Gentleman's
Agreement*
Wendy Hiller, *I Know Where I'm
Going*
Lilli Palmer, *Body and Soul, Beware
of Pity*

Charles Chaplin, *Monsieur Verdoux*
John Garfield, *Body and Soul,
Gentleman's Agreement*
Gregory Peck, *Duel in the Sun, The
Macomber Affair, Gentleman's
Agreement, The Yearling*
Joseph Cotten, *The Farmer's
Daughter, Duel in the Sun*
Robert Ryan, *Woman on the Beach,
Crossfire*

Martita Hunt, *Great Expectations*
Martha Raye, *Monsieur Verdoux*
Agnes Moorehead, *Dark Passage*
Judith Anderson, *Pursued*
Lillian Gish, *Duel in the Sun*

F. J. McCormick, *Odd Man Out*
Charles Bickford, *Woman on the
Beach, The Farmer's Daughter,
Duel in the Sun, Brute Force*
Richard Widmark, *Kiss of Death*
Walter Huston, *Duel in the Sun*

Francis L. Sullivan, *Great Expectations*

Paule Croset, *The Exile* (Ingenue)
Jean Simmons, *Great Expectations* (Ingenue)
Wanda Hendrix, *Ride the Pink Horse* (Ingenue)
Jane Greer, *Out of the Past* (Ingenue)

1948

Joan Fontaine, *Letter from an Unknown Woman*
Marlene Dietrich, *A Foreign Affair*
Jane Wyman, *Johnny Belinda*
Katharine Hepburn, *State of the Union*
Gail Russell, *Moonrise*

John Garfield, *Force of Evil*
Montgomery Clift, *Red River, The Search*
Laurence Olivier, *Hamlet*
John Wayne, *Fort Apache, Red River*
Ronald Colman, *A Double Life*

Shelley Winters, *A Double Life*
Joan Greenwood, *The Smugglers*
Claire Trevor, *Key Largo*
Betsy Blair, *Another Part of the Forest, A Double Life*
Hope Emerson, *Cry of the City*

Walter Huston, *The Treasure of the Sierra Madre*
Glenn Anders, *The Lady from Shanghai*
Everett Sloane, *The Lady from Shanghai*
Ward Bond, *Fort Apache*
Walter Brennan, *Red River*

Beatrice Pearson, *Force of Evil* (Ingenue)
Moira Shearer, *The Red Shoes* (Ingenue)

1949

Barbara Bel Geddes, *Caught*
Susan Hayward, *House of Strangers, My Foolish Heart*
Ingrid Bergman, *Under Capricorn*
Michele Morgan, *Fallen Idol*
Linda Darnell, *Letter to Three Wives*

James Cagney, *White Heat*
Ralph Richardson, *Fallen Idol*
John Wayne, *She Wore a Yellow Ribbon, Three Godfathers*
James Mason, *The Reckless Moment, Caught*
Gene Kelly, *On the Town*

Mary Astor, *Act of Violence*
Mercedes McCambridge, *All the King's Men*
Margaret Wycherly, *White Heat*
Mildred Natwick, *She Wore a Yellow Ribbon*
Thelma Ritter, *Letter to Three Wives*

Ward Bond, *Three Godfathers*
Denis O'Dea, *Fallen Idol*
Sydney Greenstreet, *Flamingo Road*
Millard Mitchell, *Thieves' Highway*
Curt Bois, *Caught*

Lola Albright, *Champion* (Ingenue)
Peggy Cummins, *Gun Crazy* (Ingenue)
Judy Holliday, *Adam's Rib* (Ingenue)
Jean Hagen, *Adam's Rib* (Ingenue)

INDEX OF FILMS

INDEX OF NAMES